The Gold Standard and Related Regimes
Collected Essays

This book contains a collection of Michael D. Bordo's essays, written singly and with colleagues, on the classical gold standard and related regimes based directly or indirectly on gold convertibility. The gold standard (and its variants) was the basis for both international and domestic monetary arrangements from the third quarter of the nineteenth century until 1971, when President Nixon closed the U.S. gold window, effectively ending the Bretton Woods International Monetary System. Although the gold standard and its variants are now history, it still has great appeal for policymakers and scholars. Several desirable features of the gold standard are relevant to the ongoing issue of international monetary reform. They include its record as a stable nominal anchor, its automaticity, and its role as a credible commitment mechanism. The essays in this collection are organized around several themes: gold and the international monetary system; the commodity theory of money; the gold standard as a rule; and variants of the gold standard including the interwar gold standard; and the Bretton Woods International Monetary System.

Michael D. Bordo has been a professor of economics at Rutgers University since 1989, where he is Director of the Center for Monetary and Financial History. Professor Bordo has also taught at the University of South Carolina and Carleton University, Canada, and has been a visiting professor at Princeton University, Carnegie Mellon University, UCLA, the Federal Reserve Bank of St. Louis, and the International Monetary Fund, and is a research associate of the National Bureau of Economic Research.

Professor Bordo has authored and edited a number of books on the gold standard and related topics, including: *Monetary Regimes in Transition* (with Forrest Capie, Cambridge University Press, 1993), *A Retrospective on the Bretton Woods International Monetary System: Lessons for International Monetary Reform* (with Barry Eichengreen, University of Chicago Press, 1993), *A Retrospective on the Classical Gold Standard, 1821–1931* (with Anna J. Schwartz, University of Chicago Press, 1984). He has published many articles in monetary economics and monetary history in such journals as *The Journal of Economic History, Journal of Monetary Economics, Journal of Political Economy, Explorations in Economic History, Journal of Money, Credit and Banking*, and *Economic Inquiry*. Professor Bordo also serves as series editor of Studies in Macroeconomic History for Cambridge University Press, embracing the formerly titled Studies in Monetary and Financial History (Forrest Capie, coeditor).

Studies in Macroeconomic History

SERIES EDITOR: Michael D. Bordo, *Rutgers University*

EDITORS: Forrest Capie, *City University Business School*
Barry Eichengreen, *University of California, Berkeley*
Nick Crafts, *London School of Economics*
Angela Redish, *University of British Columbia*

The titles in this series investigate themes of interest to economists and economic historians in the rapidly developing field of macroeconomic history. The four areas covered include the application of monetary and finance theory, international economics, and quantitative methods to historical problems; the historical application of growth and development theory and theories of business fluctuations; the history of domestic and international monetary, financial, and other macroeconomic institutions; and the history of international monetary and financial systems. The series amalgamates the former Cambridge University Press series *Studies in Monetary and Financial History* and *Studies in Quantitative Economic History*.

Other books in the series:

(continued after last page of Index)

The Gold Standard and Related Regimes

Collected Essays

p.5 an independent central bank, constrained by a rule to follow low inflation may be a good durable commitment mechanism w/o the defects of the gold standard.

Michael D. Bordo

Rutgers University

CAMBRIDGE
UNIVERSITY PRESS

CAMBRIDGE UNIVERSITY PRESS
Cambridge, New York, Melbourne, Madrid, Cape Town, Singapore, São Paulo

Cambridge University Press
The Edinburgh Building, Cambridge CB2 2RU, UK

Published in the United States of America by Cambridge University Press, New York

www.cambridge.org
Information on this title: www.cambridge.org/9780521550062

First published 1999
This digitally printed first paperback version 2005

A catalogue record for this publication is available from the British Library

Library of Congress Cataloguing in Publication data
Bordo, Michael D.
The gold standard and related regimes: collected essays / Michael D. Bordo.
p.   cm. – (Studies in monetary and financial history)
ISBN 0–521–55006–8
1. Gold standard.   2. International finance.   3. Monetary policy.
I. Title.   II. Series.
HG297.B55   1999
332.4′22 – dc21   98-39626   CIP

ISBN-13 978-0-521-55006-2 hardback
ISBN-10 0-521-55006-8 hardback

ISBN-13 978-0-521-02294-1 paperback
ISBN-10 0-521-02294-0 paperback

Contents

Foreword

Anna J. Schwartz

Gold has had a varied history in human experience. Its earliest use was as one of many commodities that served as a medium of exchange. In time, gold attained preeminence over other commodity monies. In the fourteenth and fifteenth centuries gold coins were used to settle large transactions in international trade, with less valued metallic coins used in domestic trade. In 1717, Sir Isaac Newton, then Master of the Mint, assigned a higher silver price for the English gold guinea than the international market price, and, as a result, silver coins were driven from circulation. England inadvertently became a gold standard adherent, pledging to redeem in gold other forms of money. Other countries at the time were on a silver or bimetallic standard and also pledged convertibility.

Convertibility, however, was suspended in wartime, when governments raised money to finance their expenditures by borrowing at home and abroad, by explicit taxation, by debasing the coinage, and by expanding non-gold forms of money and thereby imposing an inflation tax. The part gold played in the monetary system was thus intimately related to the government's budget needs. In the last two decades of the nineteenth century many countries quit the silver or bimetallic standard and adopted the gold standard.

Many of the chapters in this collection focus on how the classical gold standard that prevailed from 1880 to 1914 worked in theory and in practice. The issues traditional theory has emphasized have been supplemented by recent theoretical explanations that treat the gold standard as a commitment mechanism. The chapters investigate many aspects of gold standard practice. How did gold discoveries affect its operations? How did adherence to the gold standard benefit countries that were fiscally prudent? How did the experience of countries at the periphery differ from that of the core of advanced country adherents? What was the effect of suspensions of convertibility on the credibility of the behavior of governments? The evidence the chapters offer on these questions is quantitative as well as qualitative.

The classical gold standard has served as a paradigm against which to measure the performance of monetary regimes that succeeded it. In each regime, markets and institutions behaved in distinctive ways. Theory blends with practice in highlighting why capital markets were unregulated, why the foreign exchange markets were stable, why the sphere of operations of central banks was well-defined under the classical gold standard, and why each of these phenomena differed under the successor monetary regimes of the gold exchange standard, Bretton Woods, and the current fiat money regime, in which gold as money has no special significance. In addition, the chapters on the performance of monetary regimes reveal why those regimes eventually broke down.

The enhancement of the role of central banks in regimes that succeeded the classical gold standard accounts for the prominence given to them in recent theory. For the proper functioning of a monetary regime, the theory emphasizes the importance of rules rather than discretion in the behavior of central banks, of discretion as inflation-biased and a temptation for central banks to be time-inconsistent, of central bank independence from the fiscal needs of the public sector, and of the credibility of their commitment to observe the rules.

A notable feature of this collection of studies is the light they shed on the varied aspects of past gold-based monetary regimes and the guidance they offer in understanding the current non-gold-based one. Readers have a rich menu from which to choose.

CHAPTER 1

The gold standard and related regimes: Introduction to the collection

1.1   The gold standard: A subject of perennial interest

The classical gold standard ended in 1914 but it has been the focus of great interest by policymakers and scholars ever since. On four occasions in this century the gold standard rose to the forefront of discussion: after World War I, during World War II, in the mid-1960s, and in the early 1980s.

After World War I, in the face of high inflation and volatile exchange rates, the great powers pushed to return to the gold standard. The Cunliffe Committee report of 1918 urged a return to the prewar standard except that the system would be based upon gold bullion rather than gold coin. The Genoa conference of 1922 recommended restoration of a gold exchange standard as soon as feasible. By 1928 most of the world was part of a gold exchange standard that collapsed several years later during the Great Depression.

During World War II, American planners for the postwar international monetary order attached priority to a gold nominal anchor for the dollar and hence for other currencies pegged to the dollar. Adherence to limited gold convertibility, they believed, would ensure exchange rate stability and thereby encourage the growth of international trade. The resulting Articles of Agreement negotiated at Bretton Woods in 1944, although incorporating the gold parity (at least for the dollar) of the classical gold standard, eschewed many of its other features.

In the mid-1960s, French officials led the call for a renewed classical gold standard that would allow the balance of payments of adherents to adjust primarily through gold flows. They were dissatisfied with the way in which the Bretton Woods system had evolved into an asymmetric gold-dollar standard, under which the United States, as provider of the key reserve currency, did not have to adjust to its persistent balance of payments deficit (Bordo, White, and Simard, 1995). The French were unsuccessful in converting Bretton Woods into a gold standard but they

For helpful comments on an earlier draft I thank Forrest Capie, Barry Eichengreen, Angela Redish, and Anna J. Schwartz.

strongly influenced the movement to create paper gold – the Special Drawing Right (SDR). Bretton Woods collapsed between 1968 and 1971 in the face of speculative attacks triggered by the U.S. pursuit of an inflationary policy inconsistent with its role as the key currency.

Finally, in the early 1980s, after all formal links between gold and the international monetary system had been severed, a renewed call for a return to the gold standard culminated in the *U.S. Gold Commission Report* of 1982 (Schwartz 1982). Gold advocates believed that a cure for the high inflation rates exhibited by Organization for Economic Cooperation and Development (OECD) countries in the 1970s and early 1980s would be a return to the discipline of a gold nominal anchor. The report, however, recommended no change in the status of gold in U.S. and international monetary arrangements.

What are the desirable features of the classical gold standard that explain its perennial appeal? The first is notable economic performance. The classical gold standard era from 1880 to 1914 for most countries was characterized by low inflation, stable exchange rates, relatively rapid economic growth, and less real instability than in the interwar period (Bordo 1981, 1993a). It also was an era of rapidly expanding international trade in commodities, services, and factors of production.

Many attribute this favorable economic performance to adherence to the gold standard. It placed an effective limit on monetary expansion, since national money supplies were based on gold, a durable commodity with desirable monetary properties. Monetary standards based on government fiat, by contrast, can expand money without limits. Stable money under the gold standard produced price stability and exchange rate stability. Indeed, with each country defining its national currency in terms of a fixed weight of gold, all countries were linked together in a fixed exchange rate system. The environment of stable money and prices, in turn, may have been responsible for real economic stability, although there is considerable evidence that the real economy was less stable before 1914 than since World War II (Bordo 1981, 1993a). Stable exchange rates, many argue, were a key determinant of the rapid growth in international trade and investment that occurred before World War I (Eichengreen 1995).

A second admired feature of the gold standard was its operation as an automatic system with limited government involvement. According to classical economic theory, once the monetary authorities pegged the nominal price of gold, the world price level was automatically determined by the demand for and supply of monetary gold. Supply depended on gold production and the non-monetary demand for gold. The distribution of gold between nations and the balance of payments adjustment mechanism operated automatically via arbitrage in the gold market according to the classical price-specie-flow mechanism. Adjustment was speeded up by short-term capital movements reflecting arbitrage in securities markets. Central banks were part of the story. By using their discount rates and other policy tools, they were supposed to speed up adjustment to balance of payments disequilibrium, by following "the rules of the game."

A third admired feature of the classical gold standard era was that it both fostered and was maintained by cooperation between the monetary authorities of different nations. Some scholars argue that, because London housed the world's principal gold, commodities, and securities markets, and England was the world's leading commercial power, the gold standard was judiciously managed by the Bank of England (Sayers 1957; Scammel 1965). When the Bank altered the discount rate, other central banks automatically followed. Others argue that the system was more symmetric, inasmuch as the Bank of England shared governance with the Banque de France and the Reichsbank (Eichengreen 1992; Gallarotti 1995). Moreover, in periods of financial crisis, the two continental central banks had to come to the aid of the Bank of England. Such cooperation, however, was rare and may have been so because the core countries of the gold standard successfuly followed the contingency rule aspect of the gold standard, discussed below (Eichengreen 1995). The perception that cooperation was successful before 1914 might have had more to do with the relatively tranquil state of international affairs during that period than with the way the gold standard worked.

A fourth admired feature of the classical gold standard was that it represented a credible commitment regime. Before 1914 many nations attached supreme importance to adherence to gold convertibility at the fixed parity. To avoid jeopardizing convertibility, they were willing to forgo using expansionary monetary and fiscal policy in the face of negative shocks to the economy. Eichengreen (1992) argues that this was possible only because before World War I those harmed by declining activity and employment as a consequence of policies to preserve external balance had little political power. Because of the primacy attached to maintaining convertibility, stabilizing private capital flows would tend to smooth out temporary payments imbalances and only in extreme emergencies would central bank cooperation be required. The only exception to strict obedience to the gold standard rule was in the contingency of an extreme emergency such as a war, or possibly a financial crisis not of the monetary authorities' own making. In that case, temporary suspension of gold parity was permitted on the assumption that resumption at the previous parity would be achieved as soon as possible (Bordo and

Kydland 1996). The fact that the major economic powers – Britain, the United States, and France – followed this rule further enhanced its credibility.

Although there are many admirers of the four features of the gold standard, there are also detractors. They emphasize numerous discrepancies between the stylized facts and history. One key problem with the favorable gold standard story the detractors stress is the different experience of core and peripheral countries. Though the former generally experienced smooth adjustment, the latter, in the face of periodic supply shocks, experienced balance of payments crises and recessions. These countries often abandoned the gold standard rule and found it difficult to follow credible financial policies (DeCecco 1974; Eichengreen 1992).

Other problems with the gold standard include: the international transmission of the business cycle and financial crises through the fixed exchange rate gold standard; the high resource costs of basing the monetary system on gold; inadequate gold supplies to prevent long-run deflation; periodic swings in the world price level produced by shocks to the demand (new countries joining the gold standard) and supply (gold discoveries); violation of the rules of the game; and lack of cooperation. Indeed, prominent contemporary economists such as Jevons, Marshall, Fisher, and Wicksell, who were dissatisfied with drift in the price level and other adverse characteristics of the gold standard, made interesting proposals for its reform. These include the tabular standard, symmetalism, and the compensated dollar (Bordo 1984).

Different attributes of the gold standard have been touted in each of the twentieth-century gold standard renaissances. In the 1920s, these attributes were price stability, exchange rate stability, and international harmony. Exchange rate stability, it was hoped, would restore stabilizing capital flows. In the 1940s, exchange rate stability was expected to foster the growth of trade and harmony. In the 1960s, emphasis was placed on the automatic and symmetric features of the adjustment mechanism. In the 1980s, low inflation and the discipline provided by gold as the nominal anchor were the essential attractions of the gold standard.

What about today? Today there is no longer any formal connection between either domestic money supplies or the international monetary system and gold. The only holdover from earlier gold-based regimes is that most countries and the International Monetary Fund (IMF) still hold substantial gold reserves. Resonance for a return to the gold standard has vanished, and strong arguments against it prevail – its high resource cost, an inadequate gold supply, and the difficulty of choosing the correct price at which to peg it.

Yet the gold standard still has relevance today. Two aspects of the gold standard experience stand out: its role as a commitment mechanism, and the importance of central bank cooperation. The performance of the gold standard contingent rule as a credible commitment mechanism is relevant to the ongoing search for ideal monetary rules. A commitment mechanism can prevent the monetary authorities from following otherwise time-inconsistent policies. An independent central bank, constrained by a rule to follow low inflation, may be a good durable commitment mechanism without the defects of the gold standard.

For developing countries, the commitment mechanism of the gold standard experience had great value. For them, adherence to the gold standard served as a "Good Housekeeping seal of approval" or a signal that they were following sound financial policies, that is, that they were disciplined. The signal gave them access to the capital markets of the core countries of Europe (Bordo and Rockoff 1996). Similar signaling devices such as currency boards and dollar pegs are valued today. Finally, the fixed nominal price of gold, as a norm for stable money, that served under the classical gold standard as a guide for stabilization in the aftermath of episodes of high inflation, is similar to exchange rate–based stabilization policies today. Thus the history of earlier stabilization episodes – some successful and some unsuccessful – under the gold standard has relevance today for coping with high inflation.

Some observers regard cooperation and policy coordination as an essential element of a viable international monetary system. It is intertwined with credible commitment by the member nations to common norms. The prewar gold standard is held up as an example for schemes today to establish a renewed gold standard (or Bretton Woods system) based on target zones and policy coordination. It is also relevant to the current discussion of European Monetary Union (EMU), since the gold standard had many characteristics of a unified currency area in that all national currencies were basically units of gold. The less successful experience of the interwar gold exchange standard and of the Bretton Woods system provides cautionary tales. Also relevant to today's issues is historical evidence that cooperation before 1914 was episodic and not crucial to the operation of the system. Such cooperation as there was evolved from each country acting in its own self-interest to preserve convertibility, not from international agreement (Gallarotti 1995).

The remainder of this chapter accomplishes two tasks. First, I examine five key themes in the literature on the classical gold standard that are developed in the collection. Second, I discuss the organization of the collection.

1.2   Key themes in the gold standard literature

Five themes dominate the gold standard literature and are at the core of my work on gold: gold as a monetary standard; gold and the international monetary system; the commodity theory of money; the gold standard as a rule; and variants of the gold standard, including the interwar gold exchange standard and the Bretton Woods international monetary system. In a postscript I consider some of the implications of the gold standard experience for the current movement toward the European Monetary Union (EMU).

1.2.1   Gold as a monetary standard

Under a gold standard the money supply is determined by (and in some cases consists partially or entirely of) the monetary gold stock. A gold standard provides a natural constraint to monetary growth because new production is limited (by increasing costs) relative to the existing stock. Under a fiat or paper monetary standard, by contrast, there is no limit to money issue other than the good performance of the monetary authorities. Unlike a fiat standard, however, under a gold standard, monetary authorities have considerably less flexibility to deal with shocks.

Under a gold standard the monetary authority defines the weight of gold coins or, alternatively, fixes the price of gold in terms of national currency. By being willing to buy and sell gold freely at the mint price, the authority maintains the fixed price.[1] There are no restrictions to the ownership or use of gold.

The gold standard evolved from earlier commodity money systems. The use of precious metals (gold, silver, copper) as money can be traced back to ancient Lydia. These metals were adopted as money because of their desirable properties (durability, recognizability, storability, portability, divisibility, and easy standardization). Earlier commodity money systems were bimetallic – gold was used for high-value transactions, silver for low-value ones. The bimetallic ratio (the ratio of the mint price of gold relative to the mint price of silver) was set close to the market ratio to ensure that both metals circulated. Otherwise, the overvalued metal would drive the undervalued metal out of circulation, in accordance with Gresham's Law.

One problem that plagued early bimetallic systems was deterioration in the quality of silver coins. It was dealt with by debasement and altera-

---

[1] The monetary authority, it is assumed, either owns the mint or sells the license to a private mint that operates under the government's standards.

tion of the bimetallic ratio (Glassman and Redish 1988). England solved the problem of devising an efficient commodity money standard (Redish 1990) by shifting to a monometallic gold standard with token silver coins early in the nineteenth century – a transformation made possible by technical improvements in coin production.[2] Another problem facing commodity systems in the premodern era was the tendency of monarchs to debase the currency to obtain revenue in wartime. The development of efficient tax systems and the use of standardized coins ended the practice (Bordo 1986).

The world switched from bimetallism to gold monometallism in the decade of the 1870s. Debate continues to swirl over the motivation for the shift. Some argue that it was primarily political (Friedman 1990a; Gallarotti 1995; Eichengreen 1995) – nations wished to emulate the example of England, the world's leading commercial and industrial power. After Germany used the Franco–Prussian War indemnity to finance the creation of a gold standard, other prominent European nations followed.[3] Others argue that massive silver discoveries in the 1860s and 1870s as well as technical advances in coinage were the key determinants (Redish 1990). Regardless of the cause, recent research suggests that the shift was unnecessary, since France, the principal bimetallic nation, had large enough reserves of both metals to continue effectively to maintain the double standard (Oppers 1996). Remaining on a bimetallic standard, through the production and substitution effects earlier analyzed by Irving Fisher (1922/1965), would have provided greater price stability than did gold monometallism (Friedman 1990b).

The simplest variant of a gold standard was a pure gold coin standard. Such a system imposes high resource costs; consequently, in most countries, substitutes for gold coin developed. In the private sector, commercial banks issued notes and deposits convertible into gold coins, which in turn were held as reserves to meet conversion demands. In the public sector, prototypical central banks (banks of issue) were established to help governments finance their ever expanding fiscal needs. Their notes were also convertible, backed by gold reserves. In wartime, convertibility was suspended, but always on the promise of renewal upon termination of hostilities. Thus the gold standard evolved into a mixed coin and fiduciary system based on the principle of convertibility.

---

[2] England switched de facto to a gold standard in 1717 when Sir Isaac Newton, Master of the Mint, changed the bimetallic ratio to favor gold. De jure demonetization of silver occurred in 1816.

[3] Gallarotti (1995) describes the shift of political power in favor of the gold standard in Germany. See Friedman and Schwartz (1963) and Friedman (1990b) for a discussion of the switch de facto to gold in 1879 in the United States.

A key problem with the convertible system was the risk of conversion attacks – of internal drains when a distrustful public attempted to convert commercial bank liabilities into gold, and external drains when foreign demands on a central bank's gold reserves threatened its ability to maintain convertibility. In the face of this rising tension between substitution of fiduciary money for gold and the stability of the system, central banks learned to become lenders of last resort and to use the tools of monetary policy to protect their gold reserves (Redish 1993).

The gold standard, both the pure coin variety and the more common mixed standards, were domestic monetary standards that evolved in most countries through market-driven processes. By defining their unit of account as a fixed weight of gold or alternatively by fixing the price of gold, each monetary authority also fixed its exchange rate with other gold standard countries and became part of an international gold standard.

1.2.2   Gold and the international monetary system

The international gold standard evolved from domestic standards with the common fixing of a gold price by member nations. Unlike later arrangements, the classical gold standard was not the result of an international agreement but was driven largely by market forces. Under the classical gold standard fixed exchange rate system, the world's monetary gold stock was naturally distributed according to the member nations' demands for money and use of substitutes for gold. Disturbances to the balance of payments were automatically equilibrated by the Humean price-specie-flow mechanism. Under that mechanism, arbitrage in gold kept nations' price levels in line. Gold would flow from countries with balance of payments deficits (caused, e.g., by higher price levels) to those with surpluses (caused by lower price levels), in turn keeping their domestic money supplies and price levels in line. Some authors stressed the operation of the law of one price and commodity arbitrage in traded goods prices, others, the adjustment of the terms of trade, and still others, the adjustment of traded relative to nontraded goods prices (Bordo, 1984). Debate continues on the details of the adjustment mechanism; however, there is consensus that it worked smoothly for the "core" countries of the world although not necessarily for the "peripheral" countries (Ford, 1962; DeCecco, 1974; Fishlow, 1985). The gold standard also facilitated a massive transfer of long-term capital from Europe to the new world in the four decades before World War I in a manner that has yet to be replicated.

Although in theory exchange rates were supposed to be perfectly rigid, in practice the rate of exchange was bounded by upper and lower limits – the gold points – within which the exchange rate floated. The gold points were determined by transactions costs, risk, and other costs of shipping gold.[4] Recent research indicates that, although in the classical period exchange rates frequently departed from par, violations of the gold points were rare (Officer 1996), as were devaluations (Eichengreen 1985). Adjustment to balance of payments disturbances was greatly facilitated by short-term capital flows. Capital would quickly flow between countries to rectify interest rate differentials. By the end of the nineteenth century the world capital market was so efficient that gold flows accounted for only a small fraction of the adjustment mechanism.

Central banks also played an important role in the international gold standard. By varying their discount rates and using other tools of monetary policy, they were supposed to follow "the rules of the game" to speed up adjustment to balance of payments disequilibria. In actual fact, many central banks violated the rules (Bloomfield 1959) by not raising their discount rates or by using "gold devices," which artificially altered the price of gold when deficits occurred. But the violations were never sufficient to threaten convertibility (Schwartz 1984). They were in fact tolerated because market participants viewed them as temporary attempts by central banks to smooth interest rates and economic activity while not deviating from the overriding constraint of convertibility (Goodfriend 1988).

An alternative to the view that the gold standard was managed by central banks in a symmetrical fashion is that it was managed by the Bank of England. By manipulating its Bank rate, the Bank of England could attract whatever gold it needed; furthermore, other central banks adjusted their discount rates to London's. They did so because London was the center for the world's principal gold, commodities, and capital markets, outstanding sterling-denominated assets were huge, and sterling served an an international reserve currency (as a substitute for gold). Considerable evidence supports this view (Lindert 1999; Giovannini 1986; Eichengreen 1987). Other evidence suggests that the two other European core countries, France and Germany, had some control over discount rates within their respective economic spheres.

Although the gold standard operated smoothly for close to four decades, the episode was punctuated by periodic financial crises. In most cases, when faced with both an internal and an external drain, the Bank of England and other European central banks followed Bagehot's rule of lending freely but at a penalty rate. On several occasions (e.g., 1890 and

[4] For more detail on these costs, see Officer (1996).

1907) even the Bank of England's adherence to convertibility was put to the test and, according to Eichengreen (1992), cooperation with the Banque de France and other central banks was required to save its adherence. Whether this was the case is a moot point: The cooperation that did occur was episodic, ad hoc, and not an integral part of the operation of the gold standard. Of greater importance is that during periods of financial crisis, private capital flows aided the Bank of England. Such stabilizing capital movements likely reflected market participants' belief in the credibility of England's commitment to convertibility.

By the end of World War I the gold standard had evolved de facto into a gold exchange standard. In addition to substituting fiduciary national monies for gold to economize on scarce gold reserves, many countries held convertible foreign exchange (mainly deposits in London) as international reserves. Thus the system evolved into a massive pyramid of credit built upon a narrow base of gold. As pointed out by Triffin (1960), the possibility of a confidence crisis, triggering a collapse of the system, increased as the gold reserves of the center diminished. The advent of World War I triggered the collapse. The belligerents scrambled to convert their outstanding foreign liabilities into gold. Although the gold standard was reinstated in two variants later in the twentieth century, the world discovered that the standard was like Humpty Dumpty – it could never be put together again.

1.2.3   The commodity theory of money

The gold standard contained a self-regulating mechanism that ensured long-run monetary and price level stability, referred to as the commodity theory of money. This theory was most clearly analyzed by Irving Fisher (1922/1965) (although it was well understood by earlier writers). The price level of the world, treated as a closed system, was determined by the interaction of the money market and the commodity or bullion market. The real price (or purchasing power of gold) was determined by the commodity market, given the fixed nominal price of gold set by the monetary authorities, and the price level was determined by the demand for and supply of monetary gold. The demand for monetary gold was derived from the demand for money; the monetary gold stock was the residual between the total world gold stock and the non-monetary demand. Changes in the monetary gold stock reflected gold production and shifts between monetary and non-monetary uses of gold.

Under the self-equilibrating gold standard, shocks to the demand for or supply of monetary gold would change the price level. Demand and supply changes would be reversed as changes in the price level affected the real price of gold, which offset changes in gold production and led to shifts between monetary and nonmonetary uses of gold. This mechanism produced mean reversion in the price level and a tendency toward long-run price stability. In the shorter run, shocks to the gold market created price level instability. Empirical evidence suggests that the mechanism worked roughly according to the theory (Cagan 1965; Bordo 1981; Rockoff 1984); however, other factors were also important, including government policy toward gold mining and the level of economic activity (Eichengreen and McLean 1994).

This simple picture is complicated by a number of important considerations: technical progress in gold mining; the exhaustion of high-quality ores; and depletion of gold as a durable exhaustible reserve. With depletion, in the absence of offsetting technical change, countries on a gold standard inevitably face long-run deflation (Bordo and Ellson 1985). Although there is evidence that the gold standard was self-regulating, the lags involved were exceedingly long and variable (between 10 and 25 years) (Bordo 1981), so that many observers were unwilling to rely on the mechanism as a basis for world price stability. Prominent contemporary authorities advocated schemes to improve upon its performance. Others, for example, Keynes (1930/1971), doubted the operation of the self-regulating mechanism and attributed whatever success the gold standard had before 1914 to purely adventitious circumstances – timely gold discoveries in Australia and California in the 1850s, invention of the cyanide process in the 1880s, and gold discoveries in South Africa and Alaska in the 1890s.

1.2.4   The gold standard as a rule

One of the most important features of the gold standard was that it embodied a monetary rule or commitment mechanism that constrained the actions of the monetary authorities. To the classical economists, a system in which monetary authorities followed rules was superior to one in which monetary policy was subject to the discretion of well-meaning officials. Today a rule is viewed as a way of binding policy actions over time. This view of policy rules, in contrast to the earlier tradition that stressed both their impersonality and automaticity, stems from the recent literature on the time inconsistency of optimal government policy.

According to this approach, adherence to the basic convertibility rule served as a credible commitment mechanism (or a rule) for monetary and fiscal policies that otherwise would be time-inconsistent. A policy is said to be time-inconsistent when a policy plan, calculated as optimal based on the government's objectives and expected to hold indefinitely into the future, is subsequently revised. Discretion, in this context, means setting policy sequentially, leading to policies and outcomes very different from the optimal plan. Market agents would rationally incorporate government actions into their planning. For that reason, the government would benefit from having access to a commitment mechanism to keep it from changing planned future policy.

Adherence to the fixed price of gold served as a credible commitment mechanism to prevent governments from either pursuing the otherwise time-inconsistent policies of creating surprise fiduciary money issues in order to capture seigniorage revenue or defaulting on outstanding debt (Bordo and Kydland 1996; Giovannini 1993). On this basis, adherence to the gold standard rule before 1914 enabled many countries to avoid the problems of high inflation and stagflation that have marked the late twentieth century.

The gold standard rule in the century before World War I can be viewed as a contingent rule, or a rule with escape clauses (Grossman and Van Huyck 1988; DeKock and Grilli 1989; Flood and Isard 1989; Bordo and Kydland 1996). The monetary authority maintains the standard – keeps the price of the currency in terms of gold fixed – except in the event of a well-understood emergency such as a major war. In wartime it may suspend gold convertibility and issue paper money to finance its expenditures, and it can sell debt issues in terms of the nominal value of its currency, on the understanding that debt will eventually be paid off in gold. The rule is contingent in the sense that the public understands that the suspension will last only for the duration of the wartime emergency plus some period of adjustment, and that afterward the government will adopt the deflationary policies necessary to resume payments at the original parity.

Observing such a rule will allow the government to smooth its revenue from different sources of finance: taxation, borrowing, and seigniorage (Lucas and Stokey 1983; Mankiw, 1987). That is, in wartime when present taxes on labor effort would reduce it when it is most needed, relying on future taxes (borrowing) would be optimal. At the same time, positive collection costs may also make it optimal to use the inflation tax as a substitute for conventional taxes (Bordo and Vegh 1995). A temporary suspension of convertibility will then allow the government to use the optimal mix of the three taxes.

It is crucial that the rule be transparent and simple and that only a limited number of contingencies be included. Transparency and simplicity avoid the problems of moral hazard and incomplete information

(Canzoneri 1985; Obstfeld 1992); that is, they prevent the monetary authority from engaging in discretionary policy under the guise of following the contingent rule. In this respect, a second contingency – a temporary suspension in the face of a financial crisis, which in turn was not the result of the monetary authority's own actions – might also have been part of the rule. However, because of the greater difficulty of verifying the source of the contingency, as in the case of war, invoking the contingency under conditions of financial crisis or in the case of a shock to the terms of trade (a third possible contingency) would be more likely to create suspicion that discretion was the order of the day. The basic gold standard rule is a domestic rule, and it was enforced by the reputation of the gold standard itself, that is, by the historical evolution of gold as money. An alternative commitment mechanism was to guarantee gold convertibility in the constitution, as was done in Sweden before 1914 (Jonung 1984).

The gold standard contingent rule worked successfully for the "core" countries of the classical gold standard: Britain, France, and the United States (Bordo and Schwartz 1996). In all these countries the monetary authorities adhered faithfully to the fixed price of gold except during major wars. During the Napoleonic War and World War I for England, the Civil War for the United States, and the Franco–Prussian War for France, specie payments were suspended and paper money and debt were issued. But in each case, after the wartime emergency had passed, policies leading to resumption at the prewar parity were adopted. Indeed, successful adherence to the pre–World War I rule may have enabled the belligerents to obtain access to debt finance more easily in subsequent wars. In the case of Germany, the fourth "core" country, no occasions arose before 1914 for application of the contingent aspect of the rule before 1914. Otherwise its record of adherence to gold convertibility was similar to that of the other three countries. By contrast, a number of peripheral countries had difficulty in following the rule, and their experience was characterized by frequent suspensions of convertibility and devaluations.

One author argues that the commitment to gold convertibility by England and the other "core" countries was made possible by a favorable conjuncture of political economy factors. The groups who were harmed by the contractionary policies required to maintain convertibility, when faced with a balance of payments deficit, did not have political power before 1914. By contrast, in some "peripheral" countries, powerful political groups (e.g., Argentine ranchers and American silver miners) benefited from inflation and depreciation (Eichengreen 1992).

The gold standard rule originally evolved as a domestic commitment mechanism, but its enduring fame is as an international rule. As an international standard, the key rule was maintenance of gold convertibility at the established par. Maintenance of a fixed price of gold by its adherents in turn ensured fixed exchange rates. The fixed price of domestic currency in terms of gold provided a nominal anchor to the international monetary system.

According to the game-theoretic literature, for an international monetary arrangement to be effective both between countries and within them, a time-consistent credible commitment mechanism is required (Canzoneri and Henderson 1991). Adherence to the gold convertibility rule provided such a mechanism. Indeed, Giovannini (1993) finds the variation of both exchange rates and short-term interest rates within the limits set by the gold points in the 1899–1909 period consistent with market agents' expectations of a credible commitment by the "core" countries to the gold standard rule. In addition to the reputation of the domestic gold standard and constitutional provisions that ensured domestic commitment, adherence to the international gold standard rule may have been enforced by other mechanisms (see Bordo and Kydland, 1996): the operation of the rules of the game, the hegemonic power of England, central bank cooperation, and improved access to international capital markets.

Indeed, the key enforcement mechanism of the gold standard rule for "peripheral" countries was access to capital obtainable from the "core" countries. Viewing adherence to the gold standard as a signal of good behavior, like the "Good Housekeeping seal of approval," explains why countries that always adhered to gold convertibility paid lower interest rates on loans contracted in London than did other countries with less consistent performance (Bordo and Rockoff 1996).

1.2.5   Variants of the gold standard

The interwar gold exchange standard: The gold standard was reinstated after World War I as a gold exchange standard. Britain and other countries, alarmed by the postwar experience of inflation and exchange rate instability, were eager to return to the halcyon days of gold convertibility before the war. The system reestablished in 1925 was an attempt to restore the old regime but to economize on gold in the face of a perceived gold shortage. Based on principles developed at the Genoa conference in 1922, members were encouraged to adopt central bank statutes that substituted foreign exchange for gold reserves and discouraged gold holdings by the private sector. The new system lasted only six years, crumbling after Britain's departure from gold in September 1931. The system failed because of several fatal flaws in its structure and because it did not embody a credible commitment mechanism.

The fatal flaws included the adjustment problem (asymmetric adjustment between deficit countries such as Britain and surplus countries such as France and the United States); the failure by countries to follow the rules of the gold standard game; e.g., both the United States and France sterilized gold flows; the liquidity problem (inadequate gold supplies, the wholesale substitution of key currencies for gold as international reserves, leading to a convertibility crisis); and the confidence problem (leading to sudden shifts among key currencies and between key currencies and gold) (Bordo 1993a; Eichengreen 1990).

The commitment mechanism of the gold standard was much weaker than that of the classical gold standard. Because monetary policy was highly politicized in many countries, the commitment to convertibility was not believed and, hence, invoking the contingency clause and altering parity would have led to destabilizing capital flows. Moreover, central bank cooperation was ineffective. The system collapsed in the face of the shocks of the Great Depression.

Bretton Woods: The Bretton Woods system was the last convertible regime. It was a variant of the gold standard in the sense that the United States (the most important commercial power) defined its parity in terms of gold and all other members defined their parities in terms of dollars. The Articles of Agreement, signed at Bretton Woods, New Hampshire, in 1944, represented a compromise between American and British plans. It combined the flexibility and freedom for policymakers of a floating rate system, which the British team wanted, with the nominal stability of the gold standard rule, emphasized by the United States. The system established a pegged exchange rate but members could alter their parities in the face of a fundamental disequilibrium. Members were encouraged to use domestic stabilization policy to offset temporary disturbances, and they were protected from speculative attack by capital controls. The IMF was created to provide temporary liquidity assistance and to oversee the operation of the system.

Although based on the principle of convertibility, the Bretton Woods system differed from the classical gold standard in a number of fundamental ways. First, it was an arrangement mandated by an international agreement between governments, whereas the gold standard evolved informally from private arrangements. Second, domestic policy autonomy was encouraged even at the expense of convertibility – in sharp contrast to the gold standard, where convertibility was key.

Third, capital movements were suppressed by controls. It became an asymmetric system, with the United States rather than Britain as the central country.

The Bretton Woods system, in its convertible phase from 1959 to 1971, was characterized by exceptional macroeconomic performance of the advanced countries. It had the lowest and most stable inflation rate and the highest and most stable real growth rates of any modern regime (Bordo 1993a). However, it was short-lived. Moreover, it faced smaller demand and supply shocks than under the gold standard (Bordo 1993b). This suggests that the reason for its brief existence was not the external environment but, like the gold exchange standard, structural flaws in the regime and the lack of a credible commitment mechanism.

The flaws of the Bretton Woods system echoed those of the gold exchange standard. Adjustment was inadequate, prices were downwardly inflexible, and declining output was countered by expansionary financial policy. Under the rules, the pegged exchange rate could be altered, but in practice it rarely was because of the fear of speculative attack, reflecting market beliefs that governments would not pursue the policies necessary to maintain convertibility (Eichengreen 1995). Hence the system in its early years was propped up by capital controls and in its later years, by G-10 lending. The liquidity problem echoed that of the interwar gold exchange standard. As a substitute for scarce gold, the system relied increasingly on U.S. dollars generated by persistent U.S. payments deficits. The resultant asymmetry between the United States and the rest of the world was resented by the French. The Bretton Woods confidence problem was manifest in the risk of a run on U.S. gold reserves as outstanding dollar liabilities increased relative to gold reserves.

The Bretton Woods system collapsed between 1968 and 1971. The United States broke the implicit rules of the dollar standard by not maintaining price stability. The rest of the world did not want to absorb additional dollars that would lead to inflation. Surplus countries (especially Germany) were reluctant to revalue.

Another important source of strain on the system was the unworkability of the adjustable peg under increasing capital mobility. Speculation against a fixed parity could not be stopped by either traditional policies or international rescue packages. The Americans' hands were forced by British and French decisions in the summer of 1971 to convert dollars into gold. The impasse was ended when President Nixon closed the gold window on August 15, 1971.

The Bretton Woods system, like the gold standard, can be interpreted as a regime following a contingent rule. Unlike the example of Britain under the gold standard, however, the commitment to maintain gold convertibility by the United States, the center country, lost credibility by the mid-1960s. Also, the contingency aspect of the rule proved unworkable, besides being ill-defined. Devaluations were avoided because they were an admission of unsustainable policy and because they were accompanied by speculative attack even in the presence of capital controls. Once controls were removed, the system was held together only by G-10 cooperation, and once conflicts developed between the interests of the United States and other members, even cooperation became unworkable.

Under the Bretton Woods system, gold still served as a nominal anchor. This link to gold likely was important in constraining U.S. monetary policy (at least until the mid-1960s) and therefore that of the rest of the world. This may explain the low inflation rates and the low degree of inflation persistence observed in the 1950s and 1960s (Alogoskoufis and Smith 1991, Bordo 1993b). However, credibility was considerably weaker than under the gold standard, and it was not as effective a nominal anchor (Giovannini 1993). Moreover, when domestic interests clashed with convertibility, the anchor cable was stretched and then overthrown (Redish 1993). This was evident in the U.S. reduction and then removal of gold reserve requirements in 1965, the closing of the Gold Pool in 1968, and the closing of the gold window itself in 1971. The absolute termination of a role for gold in the international monetary system was proclaimed in the Second Amendment to the Articles of Agreement in 1976.

Large gold reserves are still held by the IMF and most nations. Presumably this is the case because the memory of their role as a commitment mechanism has not totally faded and because of fears that selling off the gold reserves (valued in many countries at less than market value and not earning interest) would be a signal of a lack of discipline. As the years with low inflation under a fiat money regime lengthen, no doubt the credibility role of the world monetary gold reserves will decline. Especially as the influence of the Bretton Woods generation wanes, gold reserves will be exchanged for interest-earning assets (Bordo and Eichengreen 1998).

1.3 Postscript: the gold standard and the European Monetary Union

The world has moved to a managed floating exchange rate system. Major countries are not interested in a return to a pegged exchange rate system such as Bretton Woods, although many such plans have been aired. The reason is that, based upon the Bretton Woods experience, major countries are unwilling to subordinate their domestic interests to the demands of a fixed exchange rate or to be subject to the constraints of an international exchange rate arrangement that they cannot control (Bordo 1995).

This is not the case at the regional level, where interests are more harmonious than they are between major countries. Indeed, Europe is rapidly moving toward creating a monetary union based on a new currency, the euro, with perfectly fixed exchange rates. This reflects the desire of fifteen countries for economic and political integration. To that end, the European Monetary System (EMS), established in 1979, was modeled after Bretton Woods (although not based no gold), with more flexibility and better financial resources (Bordo 1993b). It was successful for a few years in the late 1980s when member countries followed policies similar to those of Germany, the central country. It then broke down in 1992–93 in a manner similar to the collapse of Bretton Woods in 1968–71, and for similar reasons – because pegged exchange rates, capital mobility, and policy autonomy do not mix. It collapsed under massive speculative attack on countries following policies inconsistent with their pegs to Germany and also on countries that seemingly were following the rules but whose ultimate commitment to the peg was suspect in the face of rising unemployment.

The lesson from this experience is that the only real alternatives for the European countries are to go to monetary union, perfectly fixed exchange rates, and the complete loss of monetary independence, or else revert to floating. Halfway measures such as pegged exchange rate systems do not last. Schemes to reimpose capital controls (Eichengreen, Tobin, and Wyploz 1995) will be undermined and will only misallocate resources. The legacy of the experience of the gold standard and its variants for the EMU is the importance played by gold as the nominal anchor and adherence to a credible policy rule to maintain it. Cooperation and harmonization of policies under the gold standard was episodic and not by design – in contrast with Bretton Woods, the EMS, and the EMU. For the EMU plan to succeed, members must have the same credible commitment to their common goal as did the advanced nations to the gold standard rule a century ago.

1.4   The collection

The collection of chapters that follows develops many aspects of the five themes discussed above. Part I contains three chapters on the gold standard viewed through the lens of the history of economic thought.

Chapter 2, "The Gold Standard: Theory," contains a succinct overview of theories on the operation of the gold standard as a form of commodity money standard and as an international monetary arrangement.

Chapter 3, "The Gold Standard: The Traditional Approach," is an extensive survey of the history of major writers on the gold standard from the eighteenth century to the present. The survey examines the work of five schools of thought: the classical economists, the neoclassical economists, the Harvard neoclassical school, interwar critics, and post–World War II reinterpretations of the gold standard. Six themes are examined: gold as an ideal monetary standard, the price-specie-flow-mechanism, the law of one price, the role of capital flows, the role of central banks, and proposals for monetary reform.

Chapter 4, "John E. Cairnes on the Effects of the Australian Gold Discoveries, 1851—73: An Early Application of the Methodology of Positive Economics," reexamines the writings of John E. Cairnes, one of the principal members of the classical school, on the effects of the Australian gold discoveries on the classical price-specie-flow mechanism. Cairnes found that, as a precursor to the methodology of positive economics, the evidence on the pattern of price adjustment both within countries and between them behaved as the theory predicted.

Part II contains two chapters on the theory and operation of the gold standard as a commodity standard. Chapter 5, "The Classical Gold Standard: Some Lessons for Today," explains how the classical gold standard operated from 1880 to 1914. It provides evidence for the United States and Britain on how well the gold standard performed compared to other regimes in creating a stable price level and overall economic stability. Chapter 6, "A Model of the Classical Gold Standard with Depletion," written with Richard Wayne Ellson, develops a model of the classical gold standard as a form of commodity money standard that incorporates the durable nature of gold subject to depletion. Using numerical simulation techniques, we demonstrate an inescapable tendency to long-run deflation when account is taken of the resource constraint.

Part III contains three chapters on the theme of the gold standard as a contingent rule. Chapter 7, "The Gold Standard as a Commitment Mechanism," written with Finn E. Kydland, views the gold standard as a commitment mechanism to prevent the monetary authorities from following time-inconsistent policies. We show, for major countries during the classical gold standard period, that the rule was contingent in the sense that the fixed price of gold could be temporarily abandoned in the face of a well-understood, exogenously produced, emergency.

Chapter 8, "The Operation of the Specie Standard: Evidence for Core and Peripheral Countries, 1880–1990," written with Anna J. Schwartz, provides evidence for the theory developed in Chapter 7. The chapter surveys the history of the specie standard as a contingent rule for twenty-one countries divided into core and peripheral countries. Evidence on the stability of macro variables as well as measures of demand and supply shocks shed light on the determinants of successful and unsuccessful adherence to the rule.

Chapter 9, "The Gold Standard as a 'Good Housekeeping Seal of Approval,'" written with Hugh Rockoff, provides evidence based on the experience of a number of "peripheral" countries in the classical gold standard era on a key enforcement mechanism of the gold standard rule – access to capital markets. Our econometric results show that countries with poor adherence records paid substantial risk premiums compared to those with good records, enough to explain the determined effort by a number of capital-importing countries to maintain the gold standard.

Part IV complements the chapters in Part III by offering two detailed historical case studies of the operation of the gold standard as a contingent rule. Chapter 10, "A Tale of Two Currencies: British and French Finances During the Napoleonic Wars," written with Eugene N. White, is a case study of the gold standard contingent rule. Britain was able to suspend payments in 1797 and to finance much of its war effort by fiat money issue and bond sales because market agents believed, based on the past record of fiscal and monetary probity, that the gold standard would be restored once the emergency passed. By contrast, France's record of fiscal profligacy in the late eighteenth century prevented Napoleon from using bond finance and seigniorage to finance his wartime activities. Instead, restoration of the gold standard during wartime (when the flexibility of a fiat money regime is needed most) was required to restore credibility. Chapter 11, "Money, Deflation, and Seigniorage in the Fifteenth Century: A Review Essay," focuses on a commodity money precursor of the classical gold standard in an age when the monetary authorities did not always follow the rules of the fixed price of gold and used debasement to raise seigniorage revenue.

Finally, Part V focuses on the Bretton Woods international monetary system as a variant of the classical gold standard. Two chapters examine the Bretton Woods experience within the context of comparative regime performance. Chapter 12, "The Bretton Woods International Monetary System: A Historical Overview," presents an overview of the Bretton Woods experience. The Bretton Woods system was a derivative of the gold standard, since the United States defined the dollar in terms of gold and all other members pegged their currencies to the dollar. The chapter analyzes the Bretton Woods system's performance relative to earlier and subsequent regimes, and also its origins, operation, problems, and demise. Chapter 13, "Is There a Good Case for a New Bretton Woods International Monetary System?," considers the validity of the case for a renewal of a Bretton Woods–type arrangement. Based on an examination of the history of Bretton Woods, its macro performance, and its record as a credible commitment mechanism compared to that of other historical regimes, the case for a new Bretton Woods system is found to be dubious.

References

Alogoskoufis, G. S. and Smith, R. (1991). The Phillips Curve, the Persistence of Inflation and the Lucas Critique: Evidence From Exchange-Rate Regimes. *American Economic Review*, 81(2):1254–1273.

Bloomfield, A. (1959). *Monetary Policy Under the International Gold Standard, 1880–1914*. New York: Federal Reserve Bank of New York.

Bordo, Michael D. (1981). "The Classical Gold Standard: Some Lessons for Today." *Federal Reserve Bank of St. Louis Review*, 64(5):2–17.

Bordo, Michael D. (1984). "The Gold Standard: The Traditional Approach." In M. D. Bordo and A. J. Schwartz (eds.), *A Retrospective on the Classical Gold Standard, 1821–1931*. Chicago: University of Chicago Press.

Bordo, Michael D. (1986). "Money, Deflation and Seigniorage in the Fifteenth Century: A Review Essay." *Journal of Monetary Economics*, 18.

Bordo, Michael D. (1993a). "The Bretton Woods International Monetary System. An Historical Overview." In M. D. Bordo and B. Eichengreen (eds.), *A Retrospective on the Bretton Woods System: Lessons for International Monetary Reform*. Chicago: University of Chicago Press.

Bordo, Michael D. (1993b). "The Gold Standard, Bretton Woods and Other Monetary Regimes: An Historical Appraisal." In *Dimensions of Monetary Policy: Essays in Honor of Anatole B. Balbach. Federal Reserve Bank of St. Louis Review, Special Issue*. April–May.

Bordo, Michael D. (1995). "Is There a Good Case for a New Bretton Woods International Monetary System?" *American Economic Association Papers and Proceedings*, 85(2):317–322.

Bordo, Michael D. and Eichengreen, Barry (1998). "The Rise and Fall of a Barbarous Relic: The Role of Gold in the International Monetary System, Past, Present and Future," NBER Working Paper No. 6436, February.

Bordo, Michael D. and Ellson, R. E. (1985). "A Model of the Classical Gold Standard with Depletion." *Journal of Monetary Economics*, 16(1).

Bordo, Michael D. and Kydland, Finn (1996). "The Gold Standard as a Commitment Mechanism." In Tamin Bayoumi, Barry Eichengreen and Mark Taylor (eds.), *Economic Perspectives on the Classical Gold Standard*. Cambridge: Cambridge University Press.

Bordo, Michael D. and Rockoff, Hugh (1996). "The Gold Standard as a 'Good Housekeeping Seal of Approval.'" *Journal of Economic History*. Vol 56. No. 2 June, pp 389–428.

Bordo, Michael D. and Schwartz, Anna J. (1996). "The Operation of the Specie Standard: Evidence for Core and Peripheral Countries, 1880–1990." In Barry Eichengreen and Jorge Braga de Macedo (eds.), *Historical Perspectives on the Gold Standard: Portugal and the World*. London: Routledge, pp. 11–83.

Bordo, Michael D. and Vegh, Carlos (1995). "If Only Alexander Hamilton Had Been Argentinean: A Comparison of the Early Monetary Experiences of Argentina and the United States." Rutgers University. Mimeo.

Bordo, Michael D., White, Eugene N. and Simard, Dominique (1995). "France and the Bretton Woods International Monetary System 1960 to 1968." In Jaime Reis (ed.), *The History of International Monetary Arrangements*. London: Macmillan.

Cagan, Philip (1965). *Determinants and Effects of Changes in the Stock of Money 1875–1960*. New York: Columbia University Press.

Canzoneri, Matthew (1985). "Monetary Policy Games and the Role of Private Information." *American Economic Review*, 75:1056–1070.

Canzoneri, Matthew B. and Henderson, Dale W. (1991). *Monetary Policy in Interdependent Economies*. Cambridge: Massachusetts Institute of Technology Press.

DeCecco, Marcello (1974). *Money and Empire: The International Gold Standard*. London: Blackwell.

DeKock, Gabrielle and Grilli, Vittorio (1989). "Endogenous Exchange Rate Regime Switches." NBER Working Paper No. 3066, August.

Eichengreen, Barry (1985). "Editor's Introduction." In B. Eichengreen (ed.), *The Gold Standard in Theory and History*. London: Methuen.

Eichengreen, Barry (1987). "Conducting the International Orchestra: Bank of England Leadership Under the Classical Gold Standard." *Journal of International Money and Finance*, 6:5–29.

Eichengreen, Barry (1990). *Elusive Stability*. New York: Cambridge University Press.

Eichengreen, Barry (1992). *Golden Fetters: The Gold Standard and the Great Depression, 1919–1939*. New York: Oxford University Press.

Eichengreen, Barry (1995). "Central Bank Co-operation and Exchange Rate Commitments: The Classical and Interwar Gold Standards Compared." *Financial History Review*, 2:99–117.

Eichengreen, Barry (1996). *Globalizing Capital: A History of the International Monetary System*. Princeton: Princeton University Press.

Eichengreen, Barry and McLean, I. (1994). "The Supply of Gold Under the Pre-1914 Gold Standard." *Economic History Review*, Manuscript XL VIII, pp. 288–309.

Eichengreen, Barry, Tobin, James, and Wyploz, C. (1995). "Two Cases for Sand in the Wheels of International Finance." *Economic Journal*, 105, January pp. 162–172.

Fisher, Irving [1922] (1965). *The Purchasing Power of Money*. Augustus M. Kelly Report. New York.

Fishlow, Albert (1985). "Lessons from the Past: Capital Markets During the 19th Century and the Interwar Period." *International Organization*, 39:383–439.

Flood, Robert P. and Isard, Peter. (1989). "Simple Rules, Discretion and Monetary Policy." NBER Working Paper No. 2934.

Ford, A. G. (1962). *The Gold Standard 1880–1914: Britain and Argentina*. Oxford: Clarendon Press.

Friedman, Milton (1990a). "Bimetallism Revisited." *Journal of Economic Perspectives*, 4(4):85–104.

Friedman, Milton (1990b). "The Crime of 1873." *Journal of Political Economy*, 98:1159–1194.

Friedman, Milton and Schwartz, Anna J. (1963). *A Monetary History of the United States 1867 to 1960*. Princeton: Princeton University Press.

Gallarotti, Giulio M. (1995). *The Anatomy of an International Monetary Regime: The Classical Gold Standard 1880–1904*. New York: Oxford University Press.

Giovannini, A. (1986). "'Rules of the Game' during the International Gold Standard: England and Germany." *Journal of International Money and Finance*, 5:467–483.

Giovannini, Alberto (1993). "Bretton Woods and Its Precursors: Rules versus Discretion in the History of International Monetary Regimes." In M. D. Bordo and B. Eichengreen (eds.), *A Retrospective on the Bretton Woods System: Lessons for International Monetary Reform*. Chicago: University of Chicago Press.

Glassman, D. and Redish, Angela (1988). "Currency Depreciation in Early Modern England and France." *Explorations in Economic History*, 25. No. 1 January, pp 75–97.

Goodfriend, M. (1988). "Central Banking Under the Gold Standard." *Carnegie-Rochester Conference Series on Public Policy,* 19:85–124.

Grossman, Herschel J. and Van Huyck, John B. (1988). "Sovereign Debt as a Contingent Claim: Excusable Default, Repudiation, and Reputation." *American Economic Review*, 78:1088–1097.

Jonung, Lars (1984). "Swedish Experience Under the Classical Gold Standard, 1873–1914." In M. D. Bordo and A. J. Schwartz (eds.), *A Retrospective on the Classical Gold Standard, 1821–1931*. Chicago: University of Chicago Press.

Keynes, John Maynard [1930] (1971). *The Applied Theory of Money: A Treatise on Money*. Vol. 1. *The Collected Writings*. Cambridge: Cambridge University Press.

Lindert, Peter (1969). *Key Currencies and Gold, 1900–1913*. Princeton Studies in International Finance, No. 24. Princeton: Princeton University Press.

Lucas, Robert E., Jr. and Stokey, Nancy L. (1983). "Optimal Fiscal and Monetary Policy in an Economy without Capital." *Journal of Monetary Economics*, 12:55–93.

Mankiw, Gregory N. (1987). "The Optimal Collection of Seigniorage: Theory and Evidence." *Journal of Monetary Economics*, 20:327–342.

Obstfeld, Maurice (1992). "Destabilizing Effects of Exchange Rate Escape Clauses." NBER Working Paper No. 3606.

Officer, Lawrence (1996). Between the Dollar-Sterling Gold Points: Exchange Rates, Parity, and Market Behavior. Cambridge: Cambridge University Press.

Oppers, Stefan (1996). "Was the Worldwide Shift to Gold Inevitable? An Analysis of the End of Bimetallism." *Journal of Monetary Economics,* 37(1):143–162.

Redish, Angela (1990). "The Evolution of the Gold Standard in England." *Journal of Economic History*, 50(4):789–806.

Redish, Angela (1993). "Anchors Aweigh: The Transition From Commodity Money to Fiat Money in Western Economics." *Canadian Journal of Economics*, 26(4):777–795.

Rockoff, Hugh (1984). "Some Evidence on the Real Price of Gold, Its Cost of Production, and Commodity Prices." In M. D. Bordo and A. J. Schwartz (eds.), *A Retrospective on the Classical Gold Standard, 1821–1931*. Chicago: University of Chicago Press.

Sayers, R. S. (1957). *Central Banking After Bagehot*. Oxford: Clarendon Press.

Scammell, W. M. (1965). "The Working of the Gold Standard." Yorkshire Bulletin of Economic and Social Research, 12:32–45.

Schwartz, Anna J. (1982). "Reflections on the Gold Commission Report." *Journal of Money Credit and Banking*. Part I. 14(4):538–551.

Schwartz, Anna J. (1984). "Introduction." In M. D. Bordo and A. J. Schwartz (eds.), *A Retrospective on the Classical Gold Standard, 1821–1931*. Chicago: University of Chicago Press.

Triffin, Robert (1960). *Gold and the Dollar Crisis*. New Haven: Yale University Press.

United States (1982). *Report to the Congress of the Commission on the Role of Gold in the Domestic and International Monetary Systems*. Washington, D.C.

PART I

History of doctrine and the gold standard

The gold standard: Theory

The gold standard, a variant of a commodity money standard, was the prevalent monetary arrangement in the world from 1880 to 1914. England was the first country to adopt a gold standard (*de facto*) in 1717, the rest of the world followed over the next two centuries, and, by the 1870s, virtually all had abandoned bimetallism and opted for gold.

Commodity standards based on silver and gold bimetallism and silver and gold monometallism emerged as part of the evolution from barter to a money economy. Primitive monies were commodities. The precious metals because of their special properties – they were durable, easily recognizable, storable, portable, divisible, and easily standardized – ensured their universal adoption as monies. In addition to the properties of precious metals that made them desirable as a standard of value and medium of exchange, they were also viewed as a good store of value because new production was limited relative to the existing stock and because, via the operation of the classical commodity theory of money, the money supply would vary with the profitability of gold production, in turn ensuring long-run price stability. Indeed the classical economists admired the gold standard for its automatic qualities – the operation of the commodity theory of money providing long-run price stability for the gold standard world as a whole and the price-specie-flow mechanism preserving the uniformity of prices between countries on the standard. This performance was compared to inconvertible paper monetary standards which, in the absence of the checks of a "natural" market mechanism, they believed, would degenerate into rapid inflation.

The basic rule of the gold standard was for the monetary authority of each country to define the price of gold in terms of its currency and keep the price fixed. This involved defining a gold coin as a fixed weight of gold called, for example, one dollar. The dollar in 1879 (when the United States joined the gold standard) was defined as 23.22 fine grains of gold with 480 grains to the fine troy ounce. This was equivalent to $20.67 per

Reprinted from the *New Palgrave Dictionary of Money and France*. Edited by Peter Newman, Murray Milgate, and John Eatwell. London: Macmillan, 1992, pp. 267–271.

ounce. The monetary authority was then committed to keep the mint price of gold fixed by being willing to buy or sell gold in unlimited amounts (free coinage). The monetary authority was willing to convert into coin gold bullion brought to it by the public, charge a fee for the service – called brassage (although the United States did not charge a fee) – and also sell coins freely to the public in any amount and allow the public to convert it into bullion or export it. The government needed only to define a gold coin in terms of the unit of account. Private mints could then supply the demand for coin. In most countries, however, the mint was under government authority.

A number of variants of the gold standard exist in theory and history (Schwartz 1986). The simplest variant is a pure gold coin standard where only gold coins circulate as money. Before the invention, in the eighteenth century, of milling and other techniques to produce high quality coins, gold coins circulated by weight rather than tale. Under that system, in contrast to the pure gold coin standard, prices were not always expressed in terms of the national unit of account but expressed as weights of metal (Redish 1990).

The variant that prevailed during the heyday of the classical gold standard, 1880–1914, was a fractional reserve gold coin standard. Under that standard both government-issued notes and notes issued by commercial banks (also deposits) circulated alongside gold coins. These forms of currency – issued to economize on the scarce resources tied up in gold – were convertible on demand into gold. Gold reserves were held by the issuer as an earnest to maintain convertibility.

A third variant, proposed in 1816 by David Ricardo, was a gold bullion standard. To further economize on gold, coins would not circulate at all but fiduciary currency would be convertible into gold bullion. Such a standard prevailed in the twentieth century during the interwar period.

The gold standard can be viewed as both a domestic and an international standard. As a domestic standard, it pertains to the arrangements regulating the domestic money supply or, treating the world as a closed economy, the arrangements regulating the world money supply. As an international standard it pertains to the arrangements regulating the external value of a country's currency. By fixing the prices of their currencies in terms of gold, countries ensured fixed exchange rates.

2.1   The domestic gold standard

The Classical economists viewed the price level in a closed economy under the gold standard as determined by the marginal cost of producing gold. According to Nassau Senior (1840) the exchange value of gold in terms of all other commodities (the real price) would always equal the opportunity cost (in terms of forgone labor and other factors of production) of producing gold. According to Mill (1848) this would hold in the long run. In the short run, the price level was determined by the Quantity Theory of Money – by the interaction of the quantity of money supplied (money defined as gold coins and Bank of England notes) and the quantity demanded (in turn influenced by the money substitutes of commercial bank notes and deposits), given the volume of transactions.

The Neoclassical economists Marshall (1871) and Fisher (1911) viewed the price level as determined by the Quantity Theory in both the long and short run. They viewed the gold standard as a particular set of institutional arrangements determining the supply of money (Laidler 1991). For them the money supply under a fractional reserve gold standard depended on the monetary gold stock, which in turn was determined by the relationship between the real price of gold and gold production on the one hand, and the real price of gold and the non-monetary demand for gold on the other hand.

In the modern theory of the gold standard (Niehans 1978; Barro 1979; McCallum 1989) the price level is determined by the mutual interaction of the money market and the commodity market. Demand and supply conditions in the commodity market determine the real price of gold and, given the fixed (at the mint) nominal price of gold, the price level is determined by the demand and supply for the monetary stocks.

In more detail, in a fractional-reserve gold standard, the money supply is determined by the monetary gold stock, given the fixed price of gold and the ratio of the monetary gold stock to the total money supply (gold coin, fiduciary notes, and bank deposits). The latter depends upon the precautionary reserve-holding pattern of the commercial banks and the central bank, the preferences by the public for gold coins relative to other forms of money, and legal gold reserve ratios. Money demand (for gold coins, notes, and deposits) depends upon the community's wealth (or real income) and the opportunity cost of holding money relative to commodities – the expected rate of inflation.

Changes in the monetary gold stock derive from two sources: gold production and shifts between monetary and non-monetary holdings. Gold production (in a competitive, increasing cost industry) increases with the real price. Non-monetary gold is used in the arts and industry. Shifts from non-monetary to monetary uses of gold occur with rises in the real price. If the public has a target for its non-monetary gold holdings, then adjustment of the desired to the actual stock may take time.

The flow demand for non-monetary gold incorporates adjustment to both the desired stock and replacement demand, which is assumed to be proportional to the stock. Given its commitment to peg the price of gold, the monetary authority then serves as the residual buyer or seller of gold and changes in the monetary gold stock represent the difference between gold production and the flow demand for non-monetary gold. In the steady state, assuming no growth in the economy, gold production will equal replacement demand, the monetary gold stock will be constant, and the price level stable.

The gold standard has a self-equilibrating mechanism whereby shocks to the supply of or demand for monetary gold, which produce changes in the price level, are reversed via changes in gold production and shifts between monetary and non-monetary holdings of gold. An historical example of the operation of the commodity theory was the response to a technological advance in gold mining such as the invention of the cyanide process in the 1880s. The technical advance (assuming an initial equilibrium) – which permitted the extraction of gold from lower quality ores – reduced the marginal cost of gold production below the exchange value (real price) of gold. The new gold, in time, would add to the world's gold stock and to the monetary gold stock, in turn raising the price level. The rise in the price level, however, given the fixed nominal price of gold, would begin to reduce the real price, in turn reducing profits and production in the gold mining sector. At the same time the fall in the real price would encourage a shift of gold from monetary uses to non-monetary uses. Both factors ultimately would check the expansion in the monetary gold stock and reverse the initial inflationary surge. Similar results would follow a gold discovery.

Shocks to the demand for monetary gold such as increased productivity in the nongold sector of the economy, or an increase in the number of countries on the gold standard, would have deflationary effects. These would eventually be offset as the decline in the price level would raise the real price of gold, encouraging both gold production and shifts from non-monetary to monetary gold holding. Thus, under a gold standard one would expect to observe long-run price stability, although the price level might rise or fall for years at a time.

A number of important complications, based on historical reality, must be added to the stylized operation of the gold standard. First, in the face of steady growth in the real economy, technological advance in gold mining at the same pace as in the rest of the economy, or the discovery of new bodies of ore, would be required to prevent long-run deflation. The development of the cyanide process and South African and Alaskan gold discoveries in the 1880s and 1890s probably reflected a response to deflation but there also may have been an adventitious element involved (Rockoff 1984). Indeed the contemporary economists, Jevons, Marshall, Fisher, and Wicksell, advocated various proposals for reform including a tabular standard, indexation, and a broader commodity base (i.e. symmetallism) – to prevent the "vagaries of the gold standard" from producing a cycle of deflation and inflation (Bordo 1984). Second, the classical mechanism did not account for the fact that gold was a durable resource subject to depletion. According to Hotelling's rule (1931), the rent on unexploited reserves of such a resource should increase over time at the real rate of interest. This theorem predicts a continuously rising real price of gold and long-run deflation (Bordo and Ellson 1985). However, the pattern could be temporarily broken by technical break-throughs and discoveries that reduce the rate of increase in marginal cost below the growth of the real price (Levhari and Pindyck 1981). Third, the positive response of gold production to rises in the real price could be reversed in the face of the exhaustion of high quality ores – such as occurred in South Africa in the mid-twentieth century (Hirsch 1968). Finally, with rational expectations, the adjustment of the price level to gold discoveries and other shocks would be more rapid than the gradual adjustment postulated by the theory (Barro 1979).

2.2 The open economy gold standard

With more than one country defining the weight of their currencies in gold, the international gold standard was an example of a fixed exchange rate regime. The theory of the international gold standard is concerned with the interrelated issues of the distribution of the world's monetary gold stock, the balance of payments adjustment mechanism, and the "rules of the game."

According to the classical economists, Ricardo, Mill, and Cairnes, the world's monetary gold stock was naturally distributed (Bordo 1984). Each country's gold holding varied with the determinants of money demand, the nature of its banking system, and its share of world real income. Moreover, whether or not a country possessed gold mines, a balance of trade surplus would assure it of its required gold holdings.

Disturbances to the natural distribution would be automatically cor-rected by the price-specie-flow mechanism, first analyzed by Cantillon (1755) and given most prominence by Hume (1752). The basic idea was that arbitrage in gold kept monetary gold stocks and price levels in line among countries. Given the fixed nominal price of gold in each country, departures of the real price led to corrective gold flows. Gold flows, by changing the country's money supply, then also changed its level of prices.

An alternative way of viewing the same mechanism was to focus on the balance of trade. A rise in the domestic price level raised prices of domestic goods and exports relative to prices of imports, leading to a balance of trade deficit, a gold outflow, and a contraction of the money supply. Thus, the price-specie-flow mechanism was the means by which arbitrage in one commodity – gold – between nations and regions served to keep overall national price levels in line and to maintain balance of payments equilibrium.

Within this context, different authors stressed the problem of adjustment of particular classes of commodities, for example, the prices of tradable goods relative to those of domestic (nontradable) goods (Mill 1865). To the extent that gold prices between nations could differ, reflecting transportation and other costs of transferring gold (the difference between the upper and lower bounds referred to as the gold points), changes in exchange rates (the domestic relative to the foreign price of gold) also served to equilibrate the balance of payments without requiring a gold flow. An additional factor aiding adjustment was the role of real income – changes in the quantity of money consequent upon gold flows affected total expenditures and income in addition to, or in some cases instead of, affecting prices (Ford 1962).

The final element in the classical adjustment mechanism was the role of short-term capital flows as part of the equilibrating mechanism. A decline (rise) in the domestic money stock led to a rise (fall) in short-term interest rates and consequently attracted (repelled) funds from abroad. As the nineteenth century wore on and world capital markets became more integrated, emphasis on the role of capital mobility increased to the point where it was regarded as the dominant adjustment mechanism. Indeed, by the heyday of the classical gold standard, 1880–1914, the capital market was so efficient that the difference between interest rates of the core countries of Britain, France, Germany, and the United States, adjusted for changes in the exchange rate, was rarely large enough to violate the gold points (Officer, 1986).

The theory of the international gold standard also analyzed the transfer of resources associated with long-term lending by mature countries, such as England and France, to developing nations such as the United States, Canada, and Argentina. Capital flows from the Old to the New World were accompanied by gold flows, raising the price levels in the capital-importing country and lowering them in the exporting country. The resultant change in relative price levels produced a current account surplus in the capital exporting country and a deficit in the importing country. Thus the transfer of capital resulted in a transfer of real resources. The process could continue for many years, with developing (developed) countries running a persistent balance of payments deficit (surplus) on current account financed by long-term capital inflows (outflows).

An alternative analysis of adjustment is the monetary approach to the balance of payments. Based on evidence that national price levels, interest rates, and money supplies moved synchronously during the classical gold standard era, Triffin (1964), Whale (1937), Williamson (1964), and McCloskey and Zecher (1976) postulated a mechanism whereby balance of payment deficits or surpluses equilibrated the money market.

It is based on the "Law of One Price" – that arbitrage in individual traded commodities would ensure similar prices in a common currency for similar goods, taking account of transportation costs and trade impediments. Via substitution in production and consumption, domestic (nontraded) goods prices, determined primarily by domestic forces, would be forced into line with traded goods prices. Interest rate movements would also be synchronized through capital mobility. Given the price level and interest rates, a monetary disturbance such as a gold discovery would create an excess supply of money that would appear as a balance of payments deficit and a gold outflow. Similarly, technological advance at a more rapid pace in one country than another would create an excess demand for money, a balance of payments surplus and a gold inflow. An increase in the domestic fiduciary money stock would increase domestic prices only to the extent that the gold, thereby displaced, increased the world money stock and world price level.

The final theme in the theory of the international gold standard is the role of central banks and the "rules of the game." At the most basic level there is no need for central banks to manage the gold standard. All that is required is that some monetary authority be ready to maintain convertibility of national currency into gold. In a frictionless world the authority would not need to maintain a gold reserve. The authority would just sell bonds to the private market and buy gold to meet redemption demand. Private arbitrage would eliminate departures of the market price of gold from the fixed (at the mint) price (Goodfriend, 1988).

However, central banks emerged in Europe originally as government fiscal agents and then (naturally) evolved into both a banker's bank and a repository of the nation's gold reserves (Goodhart, 1985). Central banks became important during the classical gold standard era as a lender of last resort – to allay both internal demands for conversion of bank money into high-powered money and external demands for conversion of fiduciary money into gold. The gold standard came to be regarded as a managed standard – managed by central banks' use of changes in the discount rate and other policy tools to facilitate adjustment to both internal and external gold drains.

Central banks were supposed to follow the "rules of the game," that is, to use their policy tools to speed up the adjustment mechanism to an external shock. According to the rules, the central bank of a country experiencing a gold outflow (inflow) was supposed to contract (expand) the domestic money supply. Two channels promoted adjustment in the case of a gold outflow: an internal channel, whereby the contraction in the money supply, by raising interest rates, reduced domestic expenditure and the price level; and an external channel, whereby the rise in domestic interest rates attracted capital flows from abroad.

Evidence that most central banks did not abide by the rules – either by not varying their discount rates sufficiently or by offsetting gold outflows by expanding domestic credit – has led to reinterpretation of the rules. According to the monetary approach to the balance payments, the rules were not followed because they were inconsequential in a world characterized by perfect arbitrage in goods and capital markets. A central bank, even an important one such as the Bank of England, did not control the monetary base. It could only control the composition of the base between gold reserves and domestic credit (McCloskey and Zecher, 1976). Alternatively, according to the asset pricing approach in a world with rational expectations, central banks, by holding gold reserves (although not required) and allowing them to vary, did not violate the rules; rather they optimally pursued interest rate or price level smoothing policies (Goodfriend 1988).

A different version of the rules of the game is that the gold standard was managed by the Bank of England. By manipulating its Bank Rate it could attract whatever gold it needed and furthermore, other central banks adjusted their discount rate to hers. They did so because London was the center for the world's principal gold, commodities, and capital markets, outstanding sterling denominated assets were huge, and sterling served as an international reserve currency (as a substitute for gold).

The evidence suggests that the Bank did have some influence over other European central banks (Lindert 1969). According to Eichengreen (1987) the Bank of England was engaged in a leadership role in a Stackelberg strategic game with other central banks as followers. The other central banks accepted a passive role because of the benefits to them of using sterling as a reserve asset. The Bank of England's success in managing the gold standard may have resulted from belief in its commitment to the gold standard rule of convertibility – based on its return to gold after the Napoleonic wars and maintaining convertibility during financial crises (Bordo and Kydland 1992). The credibility of England's commitment encouraged stabilizing private capital inflows in times of threats to convertibility in 1890 and 1907 (Eichengreen 1989).

By the eve of World War I the gold standard had evolved *de facto* into a gold exchange standard, further institutionalized during the interwar (1925–1931) and Bretton Woods (1946–71) periods. In addition to substituting fiduciary national monies for gold to economize on scarce gold reserves, many countries also held convertible foreign exchange (before 1914, mainly deposits in London; during the interwar period, deposits in London and New York; and under Bretton Woods, dollar assets – referred to as the gold dollar standard). Thus the system evolved into a massive pyramid of credit built upon a tiny base of gold. As pointed out by Triffin (1960), the possibility of a confidence crisis triggering a collapse of the system increased as the gold reserves of the center (countries) diminished.

Indeed, use of a commodity reserve as a buffer to peg its price as under the gold standard opens up the possibility of a speculative attack. In a world with perfect foresight, a speculative attack on the gold standard will occur when the stock of gold reserves falls below some critical threshold. The timing of the attack will be determined by the process governing the growth of the fiduciary money supply. However, a stable monetary policy can prevent it (Flood and Garber 1984). By contrast, in a world characterized by stochastic shocks, a commodity price-fixing scheme such as the gold standard is bound to collapse as shocks to gold supply or demand breach the support price (Salant 1983).

2.3 The viability of the gold standard

The classical gold standard collapsed in 1914. It was reinstated as a gold exchange standard between 1925 and 1931, and as the gold dollar standard from 1959 to 1971. The gold standard, while highly successful for a time, lost credibility in its twentieth-century reincarnations and was ultimately abandoned in 1971.

Among the weaknesses that contributed to its abandonment were the cost of maintaining a full-bodied gold standard. Friedman (1953) estimated the cost for the United States in 1950 as $1\frac{1}{2}$ percent of real GNP. Shocks to the demand for and supply of gold that produced drift in the price level also weakened support for the gold standard, leading many economists to advocate schemes for reform (Cagan 1984). Finally, in a growing world, the gold standard, based on a durable exhaustible resource, posed the prospect of deflation.

The key benefits of the gold standard, in hindsight, were that it provided a relatively stable nominal anchor and a commitment mechanism to ensure that monetary authorities followed time-consistent policies. However, the gold standard rule of maintaining a fixed price of gold meant, for a closed economy, that full employment was not a viable policy objective and, for an open economy, that domestic policy considerations would be subsumed to those of maintaining external balance. In the twentieth century few countries have been willing to accept the gold standard's discipline.

MICHAEL D. BORDO

See also CROSS OF GOLD; GOLD EXCHANGE STANDARD; GOLD STANDARD; GOLD SUPPLY; MONETARY APPROACH TO THE BALANCE OF PAYMENTS; PRECIOUS METALS, DISTRIBUTION OF; RULES VERSUS DISCRETION; SPECIE-FLOW MECHANISM.

Bibliography

Barro, R. 1979. Money and the price level under the gold standard. *Economic Journal* 89: 13–33.

Bordo, M.D. 1984. The gold standard: the traditional approach. In *A Retrospective on the Classical Gold Standard; 1821–1931*, ed. M.D. Bordo and A.J. Schwartz, Chicago: University of Chicago Press.

Bordo, M.D. and Ellson, R.E. 1985. A model of the classical gold standard with depletion. *Journal of Monetary Economics* 16(1), July: 109–20.

Bordo, M.D. and Kydland, F.E. 1992. The gold standard as a rule. Federal Reserve Bank of Cleveland Working Paper 9205, March.

Cagan, P. 1984. On the Report of the Gold Commission (1982) and convertible monetary systems. *Carnegie Rochester Conference Series on Public Policy* 21, Autumn: 247–68.

Cantillon, R. 1755. *Essai sur la Nature du Commerce en Général*. London: Fletcher Iyles; translated, ed. H. Higgs, London: Macmillan, 1931; New York: Augustus M. Kelley, 1964.

Eichengreen, B. 1987. Conducting the international orchestra: Bank of England leadership under the classical gold standard. *Journal of International Money and Finance* 6: 5–29.

Eichengreen, B. 1989. The gold standard since Alec Ford. University of California (Mimeo).

Fisher, I. 1911. *The Purchasing Power of Money*. New York: Macmillan; reprinted, New York: Augustus M. Kelley, 1965.

Flood, R.P. and Garber, P.M. 1984. Gold monetization and gold discipline. *Journal of Political Economy* 92(1): 90–107.

Ford, A.G. 1962. *The Gold Standard, 1880–1914: Britain and Argentina.* Oxford: Clarendon Press.

Friedman, M. 1953. Commodity-reserve currency. In *Essays in Positive Economics*, Chicago: University of Chicago Press.

Goodfriend, M. 1988. Central banking under the gold standard. *Carnegie Rochester Conference Series on Public Policy* 29, Autumn: 85–124.

Goodhart, C.A.E. 1985. *The Evolution of Central Banks.* London: London School of Economics.

Hirsch, F. 1968. Influences on gold production. *International Monetary Fund Staff Papers* 15: 405–88.

Hotelling, H. 1931. The economics of exhaustible resources. *Journal of Political Economy* 39: 137–75.

Hume, D. 1752. Of the balance of trade. Reprinted in *Writings on Economics*, ed. E. Rotwein, Madison: University of Wisconsin Press; London: Nelson, 1955.

Laidler, D. 1991. *The Golden Age of the Quantity Theory.* Princeton: Princeton University Press.

Levhari, D. and Pindyck, R. 1981. The pricing of durable exhaustible resources. *Quarterly Journal of Economics* 76: 365–77.

Lindert, P.H. 1969. Key currencies and gold, 1900–1913. *Princeton Studies in International Finance*, no. 24, Princeton: Princeton University Press.

McCallum, B.T. 1989. *Monetary Economics: Theory and Policy.* New York: Macmillan.

McCloskey, D.N. and Zecher, J.R. 1976. How the Gold Standard Worked, 1880–1913. In *The Monetary Approach to the Balance of Payments*, ed. H.G. Johnson and J. Frenkel, Toronto: University of Toronto Press.

Marshall, A. 1871. Money. In *The Early Economic Writings of Alfred Marshall*, 2 vols., ed. J. Whitaker, London: Macmillan, 1975.

Mill, J.S. 1848. *Principles of Political Economy.* Reprinted, New York: Augustus M. Kelley, 1961.

Niehans, J. 1978. *The Theory of Money.* Baltimore: Johns Hopkins Press.

Officer, L.H. 1986. The efficiency of the dollar–sterling gold standard, 1890–1908. *Journal of Political Economy* 94, October: 1038–73.

Redish, A. 1990. The evolution of the gold standard in England. *Journal of Economic History* 50, December: 789–806.

Ricardo, D. 1816. Proposals for an economical and secure currency; with observations into profits of the Bank of England as they regard the properties of Bank stock. In *The Works and Correspondence of David Ricardo*, vol. IV, ed. P. Sraffa, Cambridge: Cambridge University Press, 1951.

Rockoff, H. 1984. Some evidence on the real price of gold, its cost of production and commodity prices. In *A Retrospective on the Classical Gold Standard, 1821–1931*, ed. M.D. Bordo and A.J. Schwartz, Chicago: University of Chicago Press.

Salant, S.W. 1983. The vulnerability of price stabilization schemes to speculative attack. *Journal of Political Economy* 91: 1–38.

Schwartz, A.J. 1986. Alternative monetary regimes: the gold standard. In *Alter-*

native Monetary Regimes, ed. C.D. Campbell and W.R. Dougan, Baltimore: Johns Hopkins Press.

Senior, N.W. 1840. *Three Lectures on the Value of Money*. Reprinted, London: London School of Economics and Political Science, *Scarce Tracts in Political Economy*, No. 4, 1931.

Triffin, R. 1960. *Gold and the Dollar Crisis*. New Haven: Yale University Press.

Triffin, R. 1964. The evolution of the international monetary system: historical reappraisal and future perspectives. *Princeton Studies in International Finance*, No. 12, Princeton: Princeton University Press.

Whale, P.B. 1937. The working of the pre-war gold standard. *Economica* 4, February: 18–32.

Williamson, J.G. 1964. *American Growth and the Balance of Payments, 1820– 1913*. Chapel Hill: University of North Carolina Press.

CHAPTER 3

The gold standard: The traditional approach

3.1   Introduction

What was the traditional approach to the gold standard? In this chapter, I try to provide an answer to the question by examining the works of major writers on the subject since the eighteenth century.[1] The choice of writers and works surveyed is based on my judgment that the works encompassed a significant share of the content of the traditional approach and that the writers played a significant role in the history of economic thought.

Six major themes formed the traditional approach, and five major schools of thought may be identified.

3.2   Major themes in the literature

The first theme, which runs from Cantillon to present-day writers, was that gold (the precious metals) was an ideal monetary standard, domestically and internationally, because of its unique qualities both as a standard of value and a medium of exchange. A stable price level in the long run that an automatically operated gold standard produced, in line with the commodity theory of money, was invariably contrasted to the evils of inconvertible fiduciary money. At the hands of even well-meaning policymakers the latter would inevitably lead to depreciation of the value of money. However, most writers, following Adam Smith, emphasized the social saving from using fiduciary money instead of a commodity money and hence were concerned with the properties of a convertible (or mixed) standard to ensure price stability.

This chapter originally appeared in Michael D. Bordo and Anna J. Schwartz (eds.), *A Retrospective on the Classical Gold Standard, 1821–1931*. Chicago: University of Chicago Press, 1984, pp. 23–113.

For helpful comments and suggestions the author would like to thank Michael Connolly, John McDermott, Peter Lindert, Anna Schwartz, and Larry White; he would also like to thank Fernando Santos and Glen Vogt for able research assistance.

[1] Some of the material covered is drawn from, and may overlap, earlier surveys by Viner (1937), Fetter (1965), and McCloskey and Zecher (1976).

The second theme was the price-specie-flow mechanism. The essence of the gold standard was the maintenance of a fixed mint price of national money in terms of gold (achieved by specifying the weight of a nation's coinage in terms of gold). That rule ensured uniformity of the price of gold across nations (and regions) through the process of arbitrage in gold.[2] Moreover, each country's price level was determined by its stock of monetary gold, which in turn was determined (naturally distributed) by the nation's real income and money-holding habits. Consequently, the price levels of all countries were linked together under the gold standard by the fixed definition of the monetary unit in terms of gold. Any disturbance away from the natural distribution of precious metals affecting one nation's (region's) price level, and hence the market price of gold, would inevitably lead to an equilibrating process through arbitrage in the gold market. Gold flows, by changing the nation's (region's) money supply, would then also change its level of prices.

For example, a gold discovery in one country would lead to an increase in its money supply, an increase in its price level, and a fall in the domestic market price of gold. The divergence between the domestic and world gold prices would quickly lead to a gold outflow, a contraction in the domestic money supply, and a fall of the domestic price level. An alternative way of viewing the same mechanism was to focus on the balance of trade – the rise in the domestic price level would raise prices of domestic goods and exports relative to prices of imports, leading to a balance-of-trade deficit, a gold outflow, and a contraction of the money supply.

Thus the price-specie-flow mechanism was the means by which arbitrage in one commodity – gold – between nations and regions served to keep overall national (regional) price levels in line and to maintain balance-of-payments equilibrium. Within this context, different authors stressed the pattern of adjustment of particular classes of commodities. Thus Mill focused on the behavior of the prices of tradable goods relative to those of domestic (nontradable) goods. Others focused on the secondary role of changes in the exchange rate. To the extent that gold prices between nations could differ, reflecting transportation and other costs of transferring gold (the difference between the upper and lower bounds referred to as the gold points), changes in exchange rates (the domestic relative to the foreign price of gold) would also serve to equilibrate the

---

[2] The meaning of the price of gold is its relative or real price or the purchasing power of gold. This meaning is not explicitly stated by all writers but presumably it is what they intended. It is the fixed mint price of gold in terms of national currency divided by some commodity price index.

balance of payments without requiring a gold flow. In addition, a number of writers focused on the role of real income in the adjustment mechanism – changes in the quantity of money consequent upon gold flows would affect total expenditure and income in addition to, or in some cases instead of, affecting prices.

The third theme, which is intimately connected to the second, was the "law of one price" – the notion that arbitrage in individual traded commodities would ensure similar prices in a common currency for similar goods, taking account of transportation costs and trade impediments. Along these lines, a distinction was made between domestic (nontraded) goods whose prices are determined primarily by domestic forces and traded goods whose prices are determined by the world market.

One question is how to reconcile the law of one price with the price-specie-flow mechanism, since the latter stressed primarily consequences of arbitrage in gold, while the former stressed arbitrage in all traded commodities. For the classical economists, it was assumed that arbitrage in gold was more effective than in other commodities because of gold's special properties; moreover, since gold served as the money supply (or as the monetary base), alterations in its quantity would impinge on all prices. Ultimately, which goods serve as vehicles for arbitrage is an empirical question. The answer depends on the total costs of arbitrage, including information costs. In the eighteenth and early nineteenth centuries, gold was the commodity with the lowest arbitrage costs; hence gold flows rapidly kept gold prices in line and other goods prices followed. Later in the nineteenth century, with improvements in communications technology and the development of international securities and commodity markets, arbitrage in securities and traded commodities reduced the role for gold flows in the adjustment mechanism.

The fourth theme was the role of capital flows in the gold standard balance-of-payments adjustment mechanism. The original conception of the price-specie-flow adjustment mechanism was that it operated through flows of goods and money, but by the middle of the nineteenth century, emphasis was also placed on the role of short-term capital flows as part of the equilibrating mechanism. According to the traditional approach, a decline (rise) in the domestic money stock led to a rise (fall) in short-term interest rates and consequently attracted funds from abroad. Thus in the example of a gold discovery, the increased money supply would reduce domestic interest rates relative to interest rates in other countries, producing both a short-term capital and gold outflow, thereby reducing the amount of adjustment required through changes in the domestic price level. As the nineteenth century wore on and world capital markets became more integrated, emphasis on the role of capital mobility increased to the point where it was regarded as the dominant adjustment mechanism.

In addition to short-term capital flows, the role of long-term capital flows was noted as a source of disturbance to the balance of payments. Thus one element of the traditional approach was the role of long-term lending by mature countries, such as England and France, to developing nations, such as the United States, Canada, and Argentina. Capital flows from the Old to the New World were also accompanied by gold flows, raising the price level in the capital-importing country and lowering it in the exporting country. The resultant change in relative price levels produced a current-account surplus in the capital-exporting country and a deficit in the importing country. Thus the transfer of capital resulted in a transfer of real resources.[3] The process could continue for many years, with developing (developed) countries running a persistent balance-of-payments deficit (surplus) on current account financed by long-term capital inflows (outflows).

The fifth theme, which focuses primarily on the performance of the Bank of England, was the role of central banks in helping or hindering the adjustment mechanism. This theme was a reflection of the British flavor of the gold standard literature and the key role played by the Bank of England in the analysis of the gold standard.

Several aspects of the central-bank theme may be noted. One was the debate over rules versus discretion. In the early part of the nineteenth century, emphasis was placed on the advantage of combining the automatic-monetary-rule aspect of the gold standard with the benefits of low-resource-cost fiduciary money. That approach culminated in the Bank Charter Act of 1844 and the separation of the Bank of England into the Issue Department, based on a gold standard rule, and the Banking Department, based on commercial-banking principles.

Second, several money-market crises and threats to convertibility in the succeeding quarter century led to attention in the literature to the Bank's disregard of domestic-money-market conditions in its operation as a private profit-maximizing institution following a gold standard rule. Thus the Bank, in keeping with its private role, would maintain as low a gold reserve as possible while using its Bank-rate weapon to protect its reserve from gold outflows. Bagehot's statement of the "responsibility doctrine" and a prescription for effective central-bank management, referred to as Bagehot's rule, emerged from the scrutiny of the Bank's behavior. A later development was the discussion of the inherent conflict

---

[3] For some writers changes in incomes rather than changes in relative price levels produced the adjustments.

between internal and external price stability under a fixed exchange rate such as the gold standard.

In addition, the gold standard came to be regarded as primarily managed by central banks' use of changes in the discount rate to facilitate adjustment to both internal and external gold drains. Among the issues stressed were: how Bank rate was made "effective," in the sense of inducing corresponding changes in market interest rates; the use of other policy tools to protect the gold reserves; the channels by which changes in Bank rate would affect the required adjustment in the balance of payments – by inducing short-term capital flows or by changing domestic price levels, economic activity, and the terms of trade.

Finally, discussion turned on the extent to which central banks followed the "rules of the game," that is, used their policy tools to speed up the adjustment mechanism to an external shock. According to the rules, the central bank of a country experiencing a gold outflow (inflow) should engage in policies to contract (expand) the domestic money supply.

The sixth and final theme in the traditional approach was the advocacy of a number of proposals for reform. Many writers suggested schemes for reform of the gold standard at both the national and international levels.

At the national level, a persistent theme ranging from Thornton ([1802] 1978) to Keynes ([1923] 1971) was the importance of managing the gold standard so as to reduce the conflict between external and internal stability, i.e., for the central bank to intervene and shield the domestic money supply from external shocks. Related to this theme were schemes to protect the monetary gold stock from internal currency drains, e.g., Ricardo's gold-bullion standard. Finally, schemes were designed to separate the medium-of-exchange function of gold from the store-of-value function. All these proposals attempted to rectify an important defect of the gold standard – basing a nation's money supply on one commodity subject to changing demand and supply conditions. Schemes along these lines included creation of a tabular standard, bimetallism, symmetallism, and Fisher's (1920) compensated dollar.

At the international level, proposals designed to provide world price stability included schemes such as bimetallism, symmetallism, and the basing of international money on a wide commodity basket; and also, to ensure international harmony of price-level movements, they favored the creation of some form of supranational central bank.

3.3   Schools of thought

On the basis of both common views and chronology, the five schools of thought on the gold standard are the classical school, the neoclassical school, the Harvard school, the interwar critics, and the post–World War II reinterpreters. A brief summary of the views of the leading exponents of each school follows. Detailed documentation of these views is provided in five appendixes, one for each school.

3.3.1 Classical school

Eight economists – Cantillon, Hume, Ricardo, Thornton, Mill, Cairnes, Goschen, and Bagehot – constituted the classical school. From the writings of these men we can distill the essence of the traditional approach. Cantillon developed the law of one price and aspects of the international adjustment mechanism. Hume is famous for the price-specie-flow mechanism. Ricardo developed the natural distribution of precious metals and made contributions to issues related to the monetary standard and monetary reform. Mill, perhaps the key writer of the school, covered virtually all the major themes of the traditional view, and Cairnes tested some of the theoretical implications. Finally, Goschen focused on the role of short-term capital flows, while Bagehot outlined the principles of central-bank management under the gold standard.

3.3.2 Neoclassical school

Marshall, Fisher, and Wicksell of the neoclassical school extended and perfected the mechanisms analyzed by the classical school. They, however, explored some of the detrimental effects, both for individual nations and for the world, of adhering to the gold standard, and consequently the need for reform.

3.3.3 Harvard school

F. W. Taussig and his students (Viner, Graham, White, Williams, and Beach) attempted to formulate and test a more comprehensive version of the traditional balance-of-payments adjustment mechanism to the external disturbance of long-term capital movements by incorporating gold flows, changes in relative price levels, short-term capital flows, and changes in discount rates.

The evidence for the United States, Great Britain, France, Canada, and Argentina produced by this massive research project was largely inconclusive, and in many respects cast doubt on the traditional emphasis on relative price-level changes as the heart of the adjustment mechanism.

J. W. Angell, a critic of Taussig, integrated the law of one price in the relative price-specie-flow adjustment mechanism. Despite its critical approach, his work is classified as part of the Harvard-school studies.

3.3.4   Interwar critics

After World War I, a number of writers considered the case for and against a return to the gold standard as it existed pre–World War I. Brown and Smit, accepting in the main the stylized facts of the gold standard as succinctly portrayed by the Cunliffe report (United Kingdom, Parliament [1918] 1979), assessed the gold standard as having been successful before World War I because it was a managed standard – managed by London – and then documented the special institutional characteristics of the sterling standard. Keynes and Viner discussed the inherent policy conflict between adherence to the gold standard and domestic economic activity, and addressed a plea for more international cooperation. Whale cast doubt on the stylized facts of how the gold standard worked, suggesting that perhaps the traditional approach was incorrect.

3.3.5   Post-World War II reinterpreters

In the post–World War II period, scholars reexamined the operation of the classical gold standard on the basis of new evidence and new theoretical and statistical tools. The issues they stressed included the balance-of-payments adjustment mechanism, capital flows, and rules of the game. The balance-of-payments adjustment mechanism under the gold standard was reexamined from a Keynesian perspective by Ford, from a modern quantity-theory perspective by Friedman and Schwartz, and from the perspective of the monetary approach to the balance of payments by Williamson, Triffin, and McCloskey and Zecher. The role of capital flows was reexamined by Morgenstern and Bloomfield. Finally the operation of central banks under the gold standard with respect to rules of the game was reconsidered by Sayers, Bloomfield, and Lindert.

3.4   A retrospective

The development of the literature on the traditional approach can be viewed from a number of perspectives. I briefly sketch out the elements of two of them: the first, that the interpretation of the gold standard by each school reflected the policy concerns of the time; the second, that the evolution of the interpretation of the gold standard has many of the characteristics of a Kuhnian scientific revolution.

According to the first perspective, the development of the traditional approach by the classical economists was strongly influenced by the concern over finding the ideal monetary standard consistent with the classical principles of free enterprise and free trade. This concern thus explains the emphasis on the automatic qualities of the gold standard both as a national and an international standard, the operation of the commodity theory of money that would ensure long-run world price stability (in a stationary world), and the price-specie-flow mechanism that would ensure the natural distribution of precious metals and uniformity of price structures across the world. Behind this smoothly functioning monetary veil, real resources would be efficiently allocated to their best uses by the forces of competition between individuals and enterprises across the world. The introduction of the real-world problems of friction in the balance-of-payments adjustment mechanism and the possible conflict, at least in the short run, between the constraint of the gold standard and internal economic stability led to the development of rules of proper central-bank management of the gold standard.

The neoclassical economists, writing at a time when the gold standard was the prevailing standard, accepted its rationale, but concerned themselves with removing one of its major shortcomings – specifically, the tendency for the world price level to exhibit alternating swings of deflation and inflation, reflecting major shocks to the demand for and supply of gold.

The Harvard economists, like the neoclassicists, writing about the heyday of the gold standard, sought a better understanding of the mechanism by which one of the most important structural changes in modern economic history took place – the transfer of real resources associated with massive lending by the mature countries of Western Europe to the developing countries of the New World.

The interwar critics, writing after the collapse of the gold standard, yet strongly influenced by its heritage, were concerned with the possibility of restoring the old system. Much of their work reflected skepticism on this score because for them "special circumstances" in the prewar period made the system work: the unique interrelationship between the London gold, securities, and commodities markets that created a "sterling standard"; the commitment by major participants to maintain convertibility as their key policy goal; and relatively free trade and factor mobility. These special circumstances no longer existed.

Other interwar critics focused on the negative aspects of the gold standard: the tendency for short-run price instability, the asymmetry between the adjustment mechanism of central and peripheral countries, the conflict between external and internal stability, and the tendency for economic fluctuations to be transmitted internationally by the gold standard. Hence these interwar critics doubted the wisdom of returning to the standard's iron discipline. However, in elaborating proposals for a better system, the consensus favored maintaining a fixed-exchange-rate system based on gold, with expanded national discretionary management and the establishment of a supranational central bank.

Finally, in the postwar period, operating in an institutional environment far enough removed from the events before 1914, scholars of the gold standard could objectively ask how the gold standard in its many aspects worked. Armed with new theoretical and statistical tools and new compilations of data, the consensus of this work has been that the international gold standard did function smoothly in the sense of ensuring international price harmony, in allowing the international transfer of resources, and in maintaining balance-of-payments equilibria for most countries over long periods of time, but that many elements of the story – particularly the operation of the price-specie-flow mechanism and the importance of the rules of the game – were subject to doubt.

According to the second perspective, the development of the gold standard literature reflected a Kuhnian scientific revolution (Kuhn 1970).

Along this line, we start with the development of the classical–gold standard paradigm by the classical economists, culminating in the magnum opus of J. S. Mill. The paradigm was further extended and perfected by the neoclassical economists, especially Irving Fisher. However, anomalies begin to appear by the end of the nineteenth century: the price-specie-flow mechanism emphasizing the adjustment of relative price levels could not explain the actual adjustment process to international lending in a number of countries; in some cases the mechanism could be detected, in others the adjustment of price levels between countries seemed to be too rapid for the theory; and it appeared that many countries did not follow the rules of the game but engaged in extensive sterilization activities. However, the reaction to these anomalies by Taussig and others was to incorporate them into the theory as special cases. The assault on the classical paradigm began in the interwar period with the grave doubts raised by Keynes, Williams, Cassel, and others, but it was probably the 1937 article by Whale, challenging the whole classical interpretation of how the gold standard worked, that started the revolution. The further revelation of evidence inconsistent with the classical story in the postwar period added ammunition to the case presented by Williamson, Triffin, and finally McCloskey and Zecher. The last authors completely upended the classical paradigm and argued passionately that all aspects of the gold standard could be explained by the newly developed monetary approach. The scientific revolution was complete.

In conclusion, we can ask: Is this the end of the gold standard story? McCloskey and Zecher, in tying together much of the unfavorable evidence against the traditional approach and then reinterpreting the facts to be consistent with the implications of the monetary approach to the balance of payments, make a strong case for a successful conclusion, except that the evidence they marshal in favor of their approach, based largely on correlation tests of commodity arbitrage, is neither extensive nor conclusive enough to end the story.

Appendix A   The classical economists

In this appendix the writings of eight key economists who first formulated the tenets of the traditional approach to the gold standard are summarized:[4] Cantillon, Hume, Ricardo, Thornton, Mill, Cairnes, Goschen, and Bagehot.

Richard Cantillon

Richard Cantillon ([1931] 1964), writing in 1755, was one of the first writers to analyze the working of a money economy. Operating within a crude quantity-theory-of-money framework,[5] Cantillon regarded the quantity of money as consisting entirely of specie – gold and silver coins. Gold and silver emerged as money commodities as a result of the evolution of natural market forces – they best satisfied the properties of money, viz., they are "of small volume, equal

---

[4] Some would argue that Adam Smith ([1776] 1976) should be included in this list. Smith subscribed to most of the views expressed by the other classical economists. He viewed the world specie stock and its exchange value in the long run as determined by the richness of gold and silver mines. He also stressed the social saving of using paper money for specie up to the point of convertibility. However, he did not discuss the price-specie-flow mechanism, and his belief in the real-bills doctrine (see Mints 1945) has resulted in the downgrading of his contribution to the traditional view. Recently, however, Girton and Roper (1978) and Laidler (1981) have argued that Smith may have been correct after all, if interpreted according to the recent monetary approach to the balance of payments. According to these authors, Smith viewed a country such as contemporary Scotland as a small open economy on a fixed exchange rate with an exogenously determined price level. Under such circumstances, the quantity of money would adjust to the demand for money – a result consistent with both the real-bills approach and the absence of any change in the terms of trade.

[5] This discussion draws heavily on Bordo (1983).

goodness, easily transported, divisible without loss, convenient to keep, beautiful and brilliant in the articles made of them and durable almost to eternity" (Cantillon [1931] 1964, p. 111). Moreover, the choice between gold and silver (as well as the desired ratio in a bimetallic system) is determined by market forces – on the demand side by tastes and income, on the supply side by relative scarcity (pp. 97 and 277). In the long run, the world's monetary specie stock as well as its exchange value is determined by the foregone cost in terms of the land and labor required to extract precious metals.[6] In the short run, the two key sources of a nation's money supply are its balance-of-payments surplus and the presence of domestic gold and silver mines (bk. 2, chaps. 6, 7).

Perhaps Cantillon's most important contribution was setting out a dynamic version of the quantity theory of money or what has often been referred to as monetary-disequilibrium theory. Cantillon carefully analyzed the dynamic process by which the quantity of money affected economic activity and the price level. An important element of his analysis was the international repercussions in the specie-standard world of fixed exchange rates of domestically induced monetary change:

If more money continues to be drawn from the Mines all prices will owing to this abundance rise to such a point that ... there will be a considerable profit in buying them [goods] from the foreigner who makes them much more cheaply. This will naturally induce several people to import many manufactured articles made in foreign countries, where they will be found very cheap: this will gradually ruin the Mechanics and Manufacturers of the State. (p. 165)

That is, domestic inflation, by raising the prices of domestically produced goods relative to foreign-produced goods (changing the terms of trade), will generate a balance-of-trade deficit. This deficit will induce a specie outflow, a reduction in the domestic money stock, and a reduction in domestic output and prices – the price-specie-flow mechanism.

In addition to the terms-of-trade effect, the balance of payments will adjust by a direct-expenditure effect. According to this mechanism, an excess supply of money will cause domestic expenditures to exceed income; some of this expenditure will be made directly on foreign-produced goods (whose prices are determined abroad), leading to a specie outflow:

It is usual in States which have acquired a considerable abundance of money to draw many things from neighbouring countries where money is rare and consequently everything is cheap: but as money must be sent for this the balance of trade will become smaller. (p. 169)

---

[6] Cantillon ([1931] 1964, bk. 2, chap. 16). Indeed the intrinsic value of the precious metals and hence long-run supply is determined by the cost of production of the least productive mine (p. 101), i.e., by marginal cost. Temporary variations of the exchange value of money from its intrinsic value can be caused by changes in the demand for precious metals (for nonmonetary uses), but in the long run exchange value will equal intrinsic value (p. 97).

Cantillon's final main contribution to the traditional view[7] was a clear statement of the law of one price – commodity arbitrage will ensure that the prices of similar traded goods will be the same across countries and across regions within countries, allowing for the influence of tariffs and transportation costs.

> The difference of prices in the Capital and in the Provinces must pay for the costs and risks of transport, otherwise cash will be sent to the Capital to pay the balance and this will go on till the prices in the Capital and the Provinces come to the level of these costs and risks. (p. 151)

Moreover, he clearly distinguished between traded and nontraded goods on the basis of trade impediments and transportation costs. Thus the prices of traded goods that are determined abroad will be largely unaffected by domestic monetary conditions, whereas the prices of nontraded goods will respond fully, viz.

> In England it is always permitted to bring in corn from foreign countries, but not cattle. For this reason however great the increase of hard money may be in England the price of corn can only be raised above the price in other countries where money is scarce by the costs and risks of importing corn from these foreign countries.

> It is not the same with the price of Cattle, which will necessarily be proportioned to the quantity of money offered for Meat in proportion to the quantity of Meat and the number of Cattle bred there. (p. 179)

This suggests that the distinction between the terms of trade and the direct-expenditure mechanisms rests on the distinction between traded- and nontraded-goods prices. The excess-money-induced expenditure falls on both traded and nontraded goods. To the extent the expenditure affects nontraded goods, their prices rise, inducing the substitution of traded goods. To the extent it affects traded goods whose prices are determined abroad, it leads to a direct specie outflow. Presumably, the effect on nontraded-goods prices will be short-lived – until substitution and the decline in the domestic money supply consequent upon the specie outflow have caused the relative prices of traded and nontraded goods to return to their initial equilibrium.

David Hume

In his essay, "Of the Balance of Trade" ([1752] 1955), Hume is generally believed to have originated the theory of the traditional balance-of-payments adjustment mechanism of an international specie standard (see Viner 1937, pp. 291–92).

---

[7] Other aspects of the traditional view mentioned in Cantillon's *Essai* include a discussion on capital mobility (pp. 191–93), the gold points (pp. 253, 255, 257, 261), the use of bills of exchange to settle international balances (pp. 229, 245, 247), and the operation of the forward exchange market (p. 259).

According to Hume, a domestic monetary disturbance such as a sudden decrease in the specie stock will lead to a proportional decline in all prices and wages, a consequent decline in the prices of exports relative to the prices of imports, a balance-of-payments surplus, a specie inflow, and an increase in the domestic stock of specie.

Suppose four-fifths of all the money in Great Britain to be annihilated in one night, ... what would be the consequence? Must not the price of all labour and commodities sink in proportion ... ? What nation could then dispute with us in any foreign market, or pretend to navigate or to sell manufactures at the same price, which to us would afford sufficient profit? In how little time, therefore, must this bring back the money which we had lost, and raise us to the level of all the neighboring nations? Where, after we have arrived, we immediately lose the advantage of the cheapness of labour and commodities; and the farther flowing in of money is stopped by our fulness and repletion. (Hume [1752] 1955, pp. 62–63).

Thus, the domestic specie stock in a country (or province within a country) under a specie standard will be automatically regulated by its balance of payments. Moreover, this mechanism will ensure that each nation's (province's) price level will be consistent with adherence to the specie standard.

In addition, variations in the exchange rate within the gold points will act as an additional factor to correct balance-of-payments disequilibria.

There is another cause, though more limited in its operation, which checks the wrong balance of trade, to every particular nation to which the kingdom trades. When we import more goods than we export, the exchange turns against us, and this becomes a new encouragement to export; as much as the charge of carriage and insurance of the money which becomes due would amount to. For the exchange can never rise but a little higher than that sum. (p. 64n).

Hume also discussed the law of one price, viz.

Any man who travels over Europe at this day, may see, by the prices of commodities, that money ... has brought itself nearly to a level; and that the difference between one kingdom and another is not greater in this respect, than it is often between different provinces of the same kingdom. ... The only circumstances which can obstruct the exactness of these proportions [between money and real economic activity] is the expense of transporting the commodities from one place to another. (p. 66)

Some writers have argued that there appeared to be an inconsistency between the law of one price, which suggests rapid adjustment of commodity prices through arbitrage, and the price-specie-flow mechanism, which suggests noticeable time lags.[8] However, as is made most clear by Ricardo, the price-specie-flow

---

[8] Viner (1937, pp. 316, 319) argued that the distinction between the law of one price as pertaining to the equality of prices stated in a common currency of identical traded goods, allowance being made for transport costs, and the price-specie-flow mechanism, which

mechanism is a reflection of arbitrage in the gold market, which, because of its special properties, is more rapid than arbitrage in other markets. Other prices are kept in line through the influence of changes in the quantity of gold as money. In accordance with this interpretation, Hume may have regarded the law of one price as a long-run equilibrium condition in all markets with the price-specie-flow mechanism as the means to achieve that result.

David Ricardo

GOLD AS THE STANDARD

Ricardo ([1811] 1951, [1816] 1951), in the classical tradition, viewed the world quantity of specie as determined in the long run by cost of production (Ricardo [1811] 1951, p. 52). The quantity of precious metals used as money in each country depended "first, on its value; – secondly, on the amount or value of the payments to be made; – and, thirdly, on the degree of economy practiced in effecting those payments" (Ricardo [1816] 1951, p. 55).

Each country's share of the world specie stock and hence the natural distribution of precious metals is determined by its share of world real income and factors determining velocity (or the demand for money).

The precious metals employed for circulating the commodities of the world, . . . have been divided into certain proportions among the different civilized nations of the earth, according to the state of their commerce and wealth, and therefore according to the number and frequency of the payments which they had to perform. While so divided they preserved everywhere the same value, and as each country had an equal necessity for the quantity actually in use, there could be no temptation offered to either for their importation or exportation. ([1811] 1951, p. 52)

The choice of gold and silver as monetary standard was "the comparative steadiness in the value of the precious metals, for periods of some duration" ([1816] 1951, p. 55). In the choice between gold and silver, gold has in its favor "its greater value under a smaller bulk" which "qualifies it for the standard in an opulent country," but coupled with the disadvantage that it is subject to "greater variations of value during periods of war or extensive commercial discredit." Silver he viewed as "much more steady in its value, in consequence of its demand and supply being more regular." The only objection to its use as a standard "is its bulk, which renders it unfit for the large payments required in a wealthy country" (p. 63).

involved changes in the relative prices of import and export goods (the terms of trade), was held by all the classical writers. Samuelson (1971) viewed the "inconsistency" as an error of interpretation by Viner and others. According to him, when prices in each country are measured relative to wages, the equality of identical-traded-goods prices will hold after a gold discovery initially affects the money supply and prices in one country.

However, using both precious metals as the standard has the disadvantage that prices expressed in terms of gold and silver will vary with changing demand and supply conditions for each commodity. To avoid this instability, Ricardo suggested the substitution of paper money and "by the judicious management of the quantity, a degree of uniformity . . . is secured" (pp. 57–58).[9] In addition, the substitution of bank notes for specie "enables us to turn the precious metals (which, though a very necessary part of our capital, yield no revenue) into a capital which will yield one" ([1811] 1951, p. 55). However, "the issuers of paper money should regulate their issues solely by the price of bullion" ([1816] 1951, p. 64). Indeed, for Ricardo, the key advantage of the gold standard was that adherence to the standard acted as a check against the overissue of paper money – it provided discipline (p. 78).

BALANCE-OF-PAYMENTS ADJUSTMENT MECHANISM

Beginning with the natural distribution of precious metals, Ricardo demonstrated how this distribution would be neutral with respect to monetary changes. Any movement away from the natural distribution would be corrected by the price-specie-flow mechanism. Thus if a gold mine were discovered in one country

the currency of that country would be lowered in value in consequence of the increased quantity of the precious metals brought into circulation, and would therefore no longer be of the same value as that of other countries. Gold and silver, whether in coin or in bullion, obeying the law which regulates all other commodities, would immediately become articles of exportation; they would leave the country where they were cheap, for those countries where they were dear, and would continue to do so, as long as the mine should prove productive, and till the proportion existing between capital and money in each country before the discovery of the mine were again established, and gold and silver restored everywhere to one value. In return for the gold exported, commodities would be imported; and though what is usually termed the Balance of Trade would be against the country exporting money or bullion, it would be evidence that she was carrying on a most advantageous trade, exporting that which was no way useful to her, for commodities which might be employed in the extension of her manufactures, and the increase of her wealth. (Ricardo [1811] 1951, p. 54)[10]

Thus gold as a commodity flows to the market with the highest price and thereby maintains price uniformity between nations.

As long as different countries (regions within countries) fixed the prices of their currencies in terms of gold (specified a gold weight of their coins),

---

[9] Also paper has the advantage that it is flexible and can be supplied quickly in periods of crisis (Ricardo [1816] 1951, p. 58).

[10] In addition the issue of bank notes will produce the same effect as a gold discovery (Ricardo [1811] 1951, p. 55).

then arbitrage allowing for transportation costs would always keep gold prices in line.[11] This principle, referred to as the law of one price, would hold for all traded commodities, and hence in logic there was no reason why commodity arbitrage would not occur for all commodities. However, for Ricardo and other classical economists, arbitrage took place primarily in gold because of its special properties as money and because it involved the lowest arbitrage costs. Consequently since all other commodity prices were set in terms of gold – the numeraire of the system – gold flows would then keep all prices in line for countries (regions) on a gold standard. However, some prices would react more quickly to the mechanism than others, specifically prices of tradable goods, and this quick reaction probably explains the later emphasis in the literature on the role of changes in sectional prices and the terms of trade (see appendix B on Marshall).

Ricardo clearly distinguished between the adjustment mechanism under the gold standard and under irredeemable paper money. An issue of convertible paper currency, e.g., Bank of England notes, will displace, through the balance of payments, a corresponding amount of specie (p. 67). However, as long as convertibility in terms of gold is maintained, the domestic price level will not be affected.[12] Once all specie is displaced and convertibility suspended, however, domestic prices will rise, and a depreciated exchange rate will be the indicator of overissue (pp. 58–59, 63–64, 72–78). In the *Bullion* report ([1810] 1978, pp. ccxvii–ccxxi), a distinction is made between the real exchange rate – determined by the ratio of the mint prices of gold between two gold standard countries – and the market exchange rate or the *computed par*. The market exchange rate includes both the influence of real factors causing a divergence from par within the gold points and the depreciation of the exchange rate (premium on the price of gold) due to a rise in the price level.

Thus for Ricardo, the increase in irredeemable paper following the suspension of payments in 1797 was responsible for both a rise in all commodity prices in England with no corresponding rise in prices abroad and the depreciation of the pound (pp. ccxiv–ccxv).

PROPOSALS FOR MONETARY REFORM

As mentioned above, Ricardo viewed a properly regulated convertible paper currency as superior to a precious-metals standard. However, he believed that convertibility into gold was necessary to avoid the temptation of overissue (Ricardo [1816] 1951, p. 69).

And in the *Bullion* report ([1810] 1978, p. ccxlvi) a strong case is made in favor of a gold standard rule and against discretionary monetary policy:

---

[11] Ricardo also described the force of arbitrage in maintaining equality between prices (the value of money) in the country and in London ([1811] 1951, p. 87).

[12] Because it was legal to export bullion, but illegal to export coin, the price of bullion would initially rise above the mint price. Eventually, however, people would evade the prohibition and melt coin into bullion (Ricardo [1811] 1951, p. 64n).

The most detailed knowledge of the actual trade of the country, combined with the profound science in all the principles of money and circulation, would not enable any man or set of men to adjust, and keep always adjusted, the right proportion of circulating medium in a country to the wants of trade. When the currency consists entirely of the precious metals, or of paper convertible at will into the precious metals, the natural process of commerce, by establishing exchanges among all the different countries of the world, adjusts, in every particular country, the proportion of circulating medium to its actual occasions, according to that supply of the precious metals which the mines furnish to the general market of the world. The proportion, which is thus adjusted and maintained by the natural operation of commerce, cannot be adjusted by any human wisdom or skill. If the natural system of currency and circulation be abandoned, and a discretionary issue of paper money substituted in its stead, it is vain to think that any rules can be devised for the exact exercise of such a discretion.

As a remedy for defects of a purely metallic standard with no discretion for central bankers, he proposed a convertible banknote issue backed by bullion (Ricardo [1816] 1951, p. 66).

Free export and import of bullion would be permissible. Under this scheme the costs of frequent conversions of coin into bullion would be eliminated, but the risks of attempted conversion of banknotes into specie in a money-market panic would not be.[13]

Henry Thornton

THE GOLD STANDARD

Like Ricardo, Thornton ([1802] 1978, p. 21a) viewed convertibility as a key feature of the gold standard.[14] Also, like Ricardo, he viewed the substitution of paper money for specie up to the point of convertibility as a social saving. However, he extended the analysis to consider the effects of a domestic issue of bank notes on the world price level.

First, since the issue of paper money would displace specie in the domestic circulation, specie would be exported abroad, leading to an increase in the world money stock and a rise in world prices. The country displacing specie would thereby raise its capital stock (Thornton [1802] 1978, pp. 269–70).

Second, to the extent the use of paper money reduced the demand for gold as money, and hence the price of bullion, this development would cause "those mines which have not yielded any rent, to be no longer worked; and the supply of gold . . . to be in consequence, somewhat reduced." The process would continue until

---

[13] According to Sayers (1953), Ricardo perceived that the essential condition of a gold standard is not gold coinage, but convertibility into gold for international transactions.

[14] Chronologically, Thornton preceded Ricardo by several years, but it is convenient to present his views following those of Ricardo.

all mines will be unable to defray the charge of extracting the ore, except those which now yield the very highest rent. At this point the fall will necessarily stop ... gold and silver must continue to bear that price, or nearly that price, ... at which they are now exchangeable for commodities. (p. 266)

BALANCE-OF-PAYMENTS ADJUSTMENT MECHANISM

Thornton clearly elucidated the price-specie-flow mechanism. The primary mechanism of adjustment following an increase in the domestic money supply (an increase in Bank of England note issue) is the effect on prices at home relative to those abroad.

It is obvious, that in proportion as goods are rendered dear in Great Britain, the foreigner becomes unwilling to buy them, the commodities of other countries which come into competition with our's obtaining a preference in the foreign market; and, therefore, that in consequence of a diminution of orders from abroad, our exports will be diminished.... But not only will our exports lessen ...; our imports also will increase; for the high British price of goods will tempt foreign commodities to come in nearly in the same degree in which it will discourage British articles from going out. (Thornton [1802] 1978, p. 198)

The resultant deficit in the balance of payments will, however, be offset to a certain extent by changes in the exchange rate within the gold points. However, to the extent an unfavorable balance persists and the exchange rate falls to the specie-export point, this will lead to a specie outflow until trade balance is restored (pp. 145–47).

Finally, Thornton discussed an alternative adjustment mechanism – the direct-expenditure-income mechanism:

There is in the mass of the people ... a disposition to adapt their individual expenditure to their income. Importations conducted with a view to the consumption of the country into which the articles are imported ... are limited by the ability of the individuals of that country to pay for them out of their income.... If, therefore, ... the value of the annual income of the inhabitants of a country is diminished, either new economy on the one hand, or new exertions of individual industry on the other, fail not, after a certain time, in some measure, to restore the balance. And this equality between private expenditures and private incomes tends ultimately to produce equality between the commercial exports and imports. (pp. 142–43)

LAW OF ONE PRICE

According to Thornton, different prices within Great Britain for identical goods cannot exist as long as country bank notes are convertible into Bank of England notes.

A very considerable advance in the price of commodities bought and sold in one quarter of this kingdom, while there was no such rise in any other, was not supposable; because the holders of the circulating medium current in the spot in which goods were ... rendered dear, would exchange it for the circulating medium of the part in which they were assumed to be cheap, and would then buy the commodities of the latter place, and transport them to the former, for the sake of the profit on the transaction.

Moreover, the law of one price can be extended from one kingdom to the whole world as long as currencies are convertible.

We may ... extend our views, and conceive of Europe, and even of the world, as forming one great kingdom, over the whole of which goods pass and repass ... nearly in the same manner in which they spread themselves through this single country.

However, prices can differ between countries within the limits of the gold points:

But British paper is not exchangeable for the circulating medium of the continent, unless a discount ... be allowed. Of this fluctuating discount ... the variations in the course of exchange are the measure. (Thornton [1802] 1978, pp. 260–61)

Finally, he argued that under a specie standard, one country alone can affect world (traded) goods prices only to the extent that it has monopoly power in their production. Great Britain may have this power in the short run, but in the long run the existence of substitutes will diminish the power.

POLICY CONSIDERATIONS

Thornton was one of the first to recognize the possibility of a conflict between external and internal policy goals. In the case of an unfavorable balance of trade caused by an exogenous event such as a harvest failure, the central bank could respond to the resulting gold outflow by reducing the money supply, but taking such a course of action might depress domestic activity. Hence, it would be prudent to maintain an adequate gold reserve to permit the bank to increase its loans while losing gold.[15]

John Stuart Mill

Perhaps the clearest statement of the traditional approach to the gold standard is in J. S. Mill's *Principles of Political Economy* ([1865] 1961). Much of the subsequent literature is either a refinement of Mill or attempts to verify his theory. In discussing Mill, I focus on three topics: (*a*) gold as a commodity money; (*b*) the natural distribution of precious metals and the adjustment mechanism; and (*c*) the distinction between real and nominal disturbances.

---

[15] The size of the gold reserve should be determined by the degree of confidence "between independent countries" and the "largeness of the balance between the independent places" (Thornton [1802] 1978, pp. 155–56).

Gold as a commodity money

Mill carefully analyzed the economics of commodity money, according to which market forces ensure a determinate money stock and price level.

In the long run, according to Mill, the exchange value of gold – what it will purchase in terms of other goods and services or the inverse of the price level – will be equal to its cost of production – "the cost in labor and expense, at the least productive sources of supply which the then existing demand makes it necessary to work" (Mill [1865] 1961, p. 502). The conformity will be maintained by deviations in gold output in response to variations in the exchange value of gold relative to its cost of production.

However, because the existing stock of gold is large relative to additions to the stock, it takes a long time for full adjustment to take place.

And hence the effect of all changes in the conditions of production of the precious metals are at first, and continue to be for many years, questions of quantity only, with little reference to cost of production. (p. 503)

Thus, in the short run, the price level is determined by the relationship between the demand for and supply of money, and only in the long run is it determined by cost of production.

Mill then compared a bimetallic standard to a single metallic standard – "There is an obvious convenience in making use of the more costly metal for larger payments and the cheaper one for smaller" (p. 507), but the arrangement works only if the ratio of the two metals is consistent with their relative costs of production. If relative values change, e.g., the value of gold rises relative to silver, this change will cause replacement of gold by silver coins and the melting of gold coins.

Mill therefore preferred a limping standard.

The advantage without the disadvantages of a double standard, seems to be best obtained by those nations with whom one only of the two metals is a legal tender, but the other is also coined (the more costly metal), and allowed to pass for whatever value the market assigns to it. (p. 509)

Finally, Mill, like his predecessors, viewed the substitution of paper money for specie up to the point of convertibility as "a national gain," but beyond that "a form of robbery" (p. 551). Moreover, the social saving from the issue of paper money is transmitted to the rest of the world. The specie displaced through the balance of payments will initially lead to a rise in the world price level, but ultimately to a reduction in gold output. The world price level will then return to normal.[16]

---

[16] There may, however, be distribution effects between gold mining and other countries since the reduction in the use of gold as money will reduce the price levels of mining countries relative to those of the rest of the world. In addition, there will be first-round effects depending on how the money is issued – by private bankers or the government. Money issued by bankers would lead to a fall in the interest rate, a capital outflow, and

NATURAL DISTRIBUTION OF PRECIOUS METALS AND BALANCE-OF-PAYMENTS
ADJUSTMENT MECHANISM

In the long run, each country in the world will have that quantity of money to
effect exchange consistent with keeping its value in terms of its cost of production, hence the natural distribution of precious metals across countries is determined by real forces.[17]

Mill then compared the international adjustment mechanism under a barter
system with that under a money system. Starting from a state of stable equilibrium where the value of exports equals the value of imports "the process by
which things are brought back to this state when they happen to deviate from it,
is, at least outwardly, not the same in a barter system and in a money system."
Under barter,

a country which wants more imports than its exports will pay for, must offer its
exports at a cheaper rate, as the sole means of creating a demand for them
sufficient to reestablish the equilibrium. When money is used, the country
. . . takes the additional imports at the same price as before, and as she exports no
equivalent, the balance of payments turn against her; the exchange becomes
unfavourable, and the difference has to be paid in money. This is in appearance
a very distinct operation from the former. (Mill [1865] 1961, pp. 619–20)

However, this difference is only apparent; in both cases prices must adjust to
restore equilibrium. In the case of a money economy:

When . . . the state of prices is such that the equation of international demand
cannot establish itself, the country requiring more imports than can be paid for
by exports; it is a sign that the country has more of the precious metals . . . than
can permanently circulate, and must necessarily part with some of them before
the balance can be restored. The currency is accordingly contracted: prices fall,
and among the rest, the prices of exportable articles; for which, accordingly,
there arises, in foreign countries, a greater demand: while imported commodities
have possibly risen in price, from the influx of money into foreign countries, and
at all events have not participated in the general fall. (pp. 620–21)

Thus, through the price-specie-flow mechanism the same results will be achieved
as under barter, with the only difference that relative prices adjust as a consequence of changes in the quantity of money induced by specie flows rather than
adjust directly. "In international, as in ordinary domestic interchanges, money is

a gold outflow, with no effect on the price level. If issued by government or by private
manufacturers, the initial effect would be on domestic prices, leading to a current-
account deficit and a gold outflow.

[17] Here Mill ([1865] 1961, p. 625) cited Ricardo (*Principles*, 3rd ed., p. 143). "Gold and
silver having been chosen for the general medium of circulation, they are, by the
competition of commerce, distributed in such proportions amongst the different countries of the world as to accommodate themselves to the natural traffic which would take
place if no such metals existed, and the trade between countries were purely a trade of
barter."

to commerce only what oil is to machinery, or railways to locomotion – a contrivance to diminish friction" (p. 622).

Mill made a clear distinction between temporary and permanent disturbances to the balance of payments. When a disturbance is temporary, most of the adjustment takes place through variations in the exchange rate, within the gold points. Thus the deficit will be "soon liquidated in commodities, and the account adjusted by means of bills, without the transmission of any bullion" (pp. 617–18). In the case of a permanent disturbance to the balance of payments, the adjustment must be made by "the subtraction of actual money from the circulation of one of the countries" (p. 618).

DISTINCTION BETWEEN REAL AND NOMINAL DISTURBANCES

Since the natural distribution of precious metals is determined by real forces, changes in that distribution will only follow from a change in real forces. Thus Mill made a clear distinction between the effects of a real disturbance, such as a remittance from one country to another, and a purely nominal disturbance, such as the discovery of a hoard of treasure.

In the first case, he starts from a state of equilibrium, after the first remittance is

made in money. This lowers prices in the remitting country, and raises them in the receiving. The natural effect is that more commodities are exported than before, and fewer imported, and that . . . a balance of money will be constantly due from the receiving to the paying country. When the debt thus annually due to the tributary country becomes equal to the annual tribute . . . no further transmission of money takes place; the equilibrium of exports and imports will no longer exist, but that of payments will; the exchange will be at par, the two debts will be set off against one another, and the tribute or remittance will be virtually paid in goods.

In addition, the terms of trade will turn against the paying country and in favor of the receiving country. "The paying country will give a higher price for all that it buys from the receiving country, while the latter . . . obtains the exportable produce of the tributary country at a lower price." (Mill [1865] 1961, pp. 627–28)

In contrast, a disturbance in the money market changes the world price level with no real effects. Thus the discovery of a hoard of treasure in a country with a purely metallic currency will raise prices there, check exports, and encourage imports, leading to a balance-of-payments deficit and diffusion of the new stock of money over the commercial world; consequently the country's price level will revert to its previous level.

John E. Cairnes

Cairnes in his essays on gold (first published in 1858–60, reprinted in 1873) used the monetary history of the Australian colonies following the gold discoveries of 1851 to test some of the principal conclusions of classical monetary and trade theory.[18] In particular, he tested the ability of the quantity theory of money to predict the comparative static effects of the gold discoveries on the money supplies and price levels of the major countries of the world, and the ability of the Hume-Ricardo-Thornton-Mill adjustment mechanism to predict the distribution of precious metals.[19]

Starting with the long-run cost-of-production theory of money, Cairnes argued that "the rate of gold earnings [is] . . . the circumstance which, in the final resort, regulates the value of the metal and sets the limit beyond which depreciation cannot permanently pass" (Cairnes [1873] 1965, p. 41); and since gold earnings in Australia increased by 50 percent, i.e., the cost of gold fell by one-half, he expected the price level in Australia to double. The inflation process would spread across the world until either prices doubled or the cost of producing gold rose. Finally, as prices in the rest of the world rose, gold would become a less profitable commodity to produce and export until, in the limit, when the price of Australian imports increased by the amount of the fall in the cost of gold, Australia would cease to have a comparative advantage in gold and would divert resources back to agriculture (p. 48).

In 1872, twelve years after writing his essays on gold, Cairnes found, as he had predicted, that (a) exhaustion of the mines and the resulting rising costs of production and (b) rises in the price of imports led to a considerable shift of resources out of gold production and back into agriculture.

Next Cairnes examined the factors that determine the pace of price adjustment across countries. He argued that the rise in prices would be most rapid in countries with the most advanced banking systems – the more developed the system of banking and credit, the smaller the amount of new gold required to effect a given rise in prices. Furthermore, since Australia and California conducted most of their trade with the United States and England, most of the new gold would tend to go first to these countries, and from there it would spread to the continent of Europe and to Asia (pp. 67–68).[20]

In general, Cairnes found the evidence agreeable to his predictions – prices

---

[18] This section is based on Bordo (1975). Note that Jevons ([1884] 1964) considered the same issue as Cairnes and in the course of his investigation constructed a price index to measure the extent of depreciation of the value of gold caused by the discoveries.

[19] Cairnes also tested Ricardo's theory of comparative advantage in predicting Australia's switch from being a net exporter to a net importer of agricultural products, and the Cantillon transmission mechanism to predict the dispersion of price changes between different commodity groupings.

[20] Cairnes argued that England and the United States, because of their efficient banking and credit systems, should gain relative to France and the rest of the Continent since they would require less gold to finance the necessary price rise. The gold flowing out of England into France would serve to displace silver, since France was on a silver standard. The displacement of silver would for a time act as a parachute preventing French prices from rising until gold completely replaced silver; at the same time the released silver would flow eastward and into the silver currencies of Asia, augmenting gold flowing there directly. At this point in an argument similar to that of Jevons ([1884] 1964), Cairnes pointed out that the "parachute effect" would not be as important as Chevalier (1859) maintained in preventing a rise in French prices, since gold and silver were substitutes, so that as gold currency substituted for silver, the price of silver would tend to fall along with the price of gold.

increased most in Australia, followed by price increases in descending order of magnitude in Great Britain and the United States, the Continent, and finally Asia. Moreover, in a postscript, Cairnes reported that (*a*) world gold production doubled by 1868 and (*b*) most of the gold ended up in France and India, although much of it passed through England (pp. 160–65).

George J. Goschen

The clearest statement of the classical position on short-term capital flows in the balance-of-payments adjustment mechanism is in Goschen ([1892] 1978).

Changes in interest rates and short-term capital flows facilitate the balance-of-payments adjustment mechanism since

money will be dear and scarce in the country which owes much to foreign creditors, and plentiful in that which has exported much; and, high interest will be attracting money to that quarter whence specie is flowing out in payment of foreign debts.

[An] adverse balance of trade will . . . render the bills on the country which is most in debt difficult of sale, and tend to compel it to export specie; whereas the high rate of interest, which is generally contemporaneous with a drain . . . of specie, will revive a demand for bills on this same country, and enhance their value in other quarters, for there will be a general desire to procure the means of remitting capital to that market where it commands the highest value. (Goschen [1892] 1978, p. 127)

Thus,

where a considerable efflux of specie is taking place, the rate of interest will rise in the natural course of things. The abstraction caused by the bullion shipments will of itself tend to raise that rate. (p. 132)

Moreover, a country can finance a temporary balance-of-payments deficit by borrowing abroad. Finally, arbitrage in the securities market will ensure that interest rates for a similar class of bills will be equal between financial centers, account being taken of transportation costs and exchange risks.

If at any time the rate of interest here falls below that which rules on the continent, it is inevitable that the whole mass of these bills will at once be sent to London, and be discounted there at the cheaper rate, so that the proceeds may be remitted in gold to the continent to be invested there in local securities at the supposed higher rate. (p. 138)

Walter Bagehot and the responsibility of the Bank of England

The pure gold standard in England – when the money supply consisted in large part of specie, and variations in its amount were determined mainly by the balance of payments – became a managed gold standard in the course of the nineteenth century – when the money supply consisted primarily of convertible notes and deposits, and variations in its amount were determined by operations of the Bank of England conforming to the external constraint of the gold standard. The evolution to a managed gold standard evoked considerable debate in the economics literature.[21]

In the decades after the restoration of convertibility in 1821, British monetary history was punctuated by a series of monetary crises in 1825, 1836, 1838, 1847, 1859, and 1866 (see Viner [1937] 1975, pp. 218–20). These crises occurred when the necessary contraction of the money stock consequent upon a specie outflow (an external drain) coincided with a demand by deposit and note holders for specie currency (an internal drain). In such a situation it was difficult for the Bank to maintain convertibility of its notes without resort to special measures. The Bank Charter Act of 1844 was an attempt to rectify the situation by dividing the Bank of England into an Issue Department and a Banking Department. The former was charged with the responsibility of maintaining the gold standard link by following the "currency principle": The note circulation should fluctuate one-for-one with changes in the Bank's holdings of gold.[22] The latter was to follow the principles of a profit-maximizing banking enterprise, accepting deposits and making discounts.

The arrangement was criticized on two grounds: (1) the currency principle ignored the role of deposits as an increasingly important component of the money stock;[23] and (2) the Banking Department in operating on a sound commercial-banking basis could not act responsibly as a central bank. In that role, it had to maintain a gold reserve large enough to protect the rest of the banking system from the effects of both internal and external specie drains.[24] This criticism culminated in the 1860s with the formulation by Walter Bagehot, the influential editor of the *Economist*, of the "responsibility doctrine" and the establishment of guidelines for a central bank under a gold standard.

In *Lombard Street* ([1873] 1969), Bagehot clearly set out the conflict between the private concern of the Banking Department to reduce the holding of specie reserves to minimize foregone interest costs and its public concern to hold larger reserves (p. 38).

Bagehot argued for the "responsibility doctrine" – that the Bank of England must fulfill its special obligations as a bankers' bank and as holder of the nation's specie reserves. In consequence, he established clear guidelines for central-bank behavior in times of crisis.

---

[21] See Viner (1937) and Fetter (1965) for a complete history of the debates.

[22] That was the recommendation of the currency school which argued that a mixed currency – one consisting of both specie and notes – should be made to operate as if it were a pure specie standard. See Fetter (1965, p. 130).

[23] This was the banking school's position. For them convertibility into gold and free competition in banking were sufficient to maintain an adequate money supply consistent with both internal and external balance. See Viner (1937, pp. 222–24).

[24] See Viner 1937, pp. 264–70, and White (1981), who has reformulated the currency–banking schools debate as turning on the question whether to centralize the right of note issue in a single institution or to allow competition ("free banking").

First, in the case of a purely external drain,

the Bank of England requires the steady use of an effectual instrument. That instrument is the elevation of the rate of interest. If the interest of money is raised, it is proved by experience that money does come to Lombard Street, and theory shows it ought to come. (p. 46)

The rise in Bank rate will initially lead to a short-term capital inflow and a gold inflow.

And there is also a slower mercantile operation. The rise in the rate of discount acts immediately on the trade of this country. Prices fall here; in consequence imports are diminished, exports are increased, and, therefore, there is more likelihood of a balance in bullion coming to this country after the rise in the rate than there was before. (p. 47)

Second,

the best way for the Bank ... to deal with a drain arising from internal discredit is to lend freely. ... A panic ... is a species of neuralgia, and according to the rules of science you must not starve it. The holders of the cash reserve must be ready not only to keep it for their own liabilities, but to advance it most freely for the liabilities of others. (pp. 48, 51)

In brief, the central bank has a responsibility to act as lender-of-last-resort.
Finally, in the case of both an internal and an external drain, the central bank should follow what has come to be known as Bagehot's rule.

We must look first to the foreign drain, and raise the rate of interest as high as may be necessary. Unless you can stop the foreign export, you cannot allay the domestic alarm. The Bank will get poorer and poorer, and its poverty will protect or renew the apprehension. And at the rate of interest so raised, the holders ... of the final Bank reserve must lend freely. Very large loans at very high rates are the best remedy for the worst malady of the money market when a foreign drain is added to a domestic drain. (p. 56)

Bagehot was aware of the limitations to the Bank's control mechanism. The Bank could only temporarily affect market interest rates. The initial effect of an increase in central-bank lending is to lower interest rates, but it also leads to an "increase of trade and increase of prices." The rise of prices and trade leads to an increase in the demand for loanable funds and also to an increase of imports and a decrease in exports. The resultant balance-of-trade deficit leads to a specie outflow and a reduction in reserves, and hence the rate of interest must be raised (pp. 12–14).

In conclusion, Bagehot proposed several remedies for reform. Of key importance, "there should be a clear understanding between the Bank and the public that, since the Bank holds our ultimate banking reserve, they will recognize and act on the obligations which this implies" (p. 70); and the

Bank should hold an adequate reserve to be determined by "experience" (p. 304).[25]

Following the publication of *Lombard Street*, the Bank of England's special position as both lender-of-last-resort and holder of the nation's reserve was recognized, but increasing stress was laid on the Bank's vulnerability in view of London's growing international liabilities (see Sayers, 1957). Though Bagehot and other writers urged the Bank to meet the problem by maintaining a larger specie reserve (an approach taken by other countries), the Bank's solution was to alter its discount rate whenever its international reserves were affected, thereby primarily influencing short-term capital movements. The Bank also supplemented the use of Bank rate with other tools of monetary policy, especially open-market operations, and in addition learned to protect its reserves by using special techniques referred to as "gold devices" (see Viner [1937] 1975, p. 277; Sayers 1936, chap. 3). Thus the ultimate answer to Bagehot's concern was the use "of a powerful bank rate weapon with a 'thin film of gold'" (Sayers 1951, p. 116).

Appendix B The neoclassical economists: Extension of the traditional approach

In this appendix, attention will center on the works of three neoclassical economists – Alfred Marshall, Irving Fisher, and Knut Wicksell – who wrote extensively on the gold standard and whose contribution can be viewed as a refinement or extension of the traditional approach.

Alfred Marshall

Marshall's contribution (1923, 1926) to the traditional approach can be classified under two headings: the monetary standard and proposals for reform and the balance-of-payments adjustment mechanism.

THE MONETARY STANDARD AND PROPOSALS FOR REFORM

For Marshall, the primary purpose of a monetary standard is to ensure price stability:

Violent fluctuations of prices are less distasteful to the heads of business enterprises than a gradual fall of prices. But I believe they are far more injurious both physically and morally to the community at large. (Marshall 1926, p. 20)

Nevertheless, a gold or silver standard may not be the best mechanism to ensure price stability, at least in the long run.

---

[25] In addition, Bagehot was in favor of publication of the accounts of the Banking Department of the Bank of England and employing more professionals and fewer amateurs in the government of the Bank ([1873]) 1969, pp. 302, 72).

Gold and silver, separately or conjointly, can set good standards of general purchasing power, in regard to obligations and business transactions, which do not range over more than a few years; but obligations which range over long periods, call for standards that are not dependent on the hazards of mining. (Marshall 1923, p. 52)

Marshall admitted that in past years, technical advances in mining precious metals had kept pace with technical advances elsewhere, so the real cost of producing the precious metals had remained constant over long periods of time, which was no accident; but he still believed that

as the arts of life progress . . . man must demand a constantly increasing precision from the instruments which he uses, and from money among others: and he is beginning to doubt whether either gold or silver, or even gold and silver combined, give him a sufficiently stable standard of value for the ever widening range of space and time over which his undertakings and contracts extend . . . [indeed] gold and silver have had a less stable value, during the history of the world, than has accrued to those staple grains, which have supplied the chief means of supporting life to the great mass of the people in every age. (pp. 53–54)

Over shorter periods of time, however, gold and silver represent good monetary standards because changes in the stock are small relative to the existing stock (1926, p. 177).

In addition, following the classical tradition, Marshall regarded gold as an inefficient form of money tying up scarce resources. Civilization had advanced sufficiently for an expanded role for convertible paper (p. 137).

Finally, following Mill, he opposed bimetallic schemes based on a fixed ratio of gold to silver on the ground that changes in relative costs of production would lead to continuous shifts towards the lower-cost metal, thus producing more instability than reliance on one metal alone (1923, p. 63).

To solve the shortcomings of reliance on precious metals as a monetary standard, Marshall proposed two alternative schemes – symmetallism and a tabular standard.

Under the symmetallic scheme, currency would be exchangeable for a combination of gold and silver bullion bars in fixed proportions.

A gold bar of 100 grammes, together with a silver bar, say, 20 times as heavy, would be exchangeable . . . for an amount of the currency which would be calculated and fixed once for all when the scheme was introduced. . . . Anyone who wanted to buy or sell gold or silver alone in exchange for currency could get what he wanted by exchanging gold for silver, or silver for gold, at the market rate. Government fixing its own rates from day to day, so as to keep its reserve of the two metals in about the right proportion, might safely undertake this exchange itself, and then anyone could buy or sell either gold or silver for currency in one operation. (1926, p. 29)

The scheme would provide a better monetary standard than Ricardo's gold-bullion-reserve scheme, because it causes the value of legal tender money to vary with the mean of the values of both of these metals . . . and because it would be convenient both to those countries which now chiefly use gold and to those which now chiefly use silver. (p. 28)

In contrast, the tabular scheme, similar to that of Fisher, would separate the standard of value from the medium of exchange. Under this scheme, long-term contracts would be tied to "an official index number, representing average movements of the prices of important commodities" (1923, p. 36). In addition, he proposed regulation of an inconvertible currency so that "the value of a unit of it is maintained at a fixed level," based on an index number (p. 50).

Finally, Marshall stressed the need for an international currency or else for the international harmonization of monetary policies:

There is a real, though very slow moving, tendency for national interests to overrule provincial interests, and international interests to overrule national, and I think the time will come at which it will be thought as unreasonable for any country to regulate its currency without reference to other countries as it will be to have signalling codes at sea which took no account of signalling codes at sea of other countries. (1926, p. 135)

BALANCE-OF-PAYMENTS ADJUSTMENT MECHANISM

Following Ricardo, Marshall argued that gold flows reflect arbitrage in a widely traded commodity (gold)

[so] as to bring gold prices at the seaboards of the two countries to equality, allowance being made for carriage. If they are higher in A than in B, there will be a small temporary bounty on exportation from B to A corresponding to this difference, which must always be small. Bills drawn in B on A will multiply, and, specie point being reached, gold will go from A to B till prices in B are as high as in A. (Marshall, 1926, p. 170)

However, he questioned why gold has to be the commodity used to settle payments imbalances. Thus in the case of a balance-of-payments deficit

the value of gold, as a means of purchasing foreign commodities by being exported in exchange for them, will rise so much that it will be profitably exported for the purpose: . . . But under these conditions merchants are likely to look around them, and see whether there is not some other thing which the country does not produce herself, and therefore does not habitually export; but which could under the circumstances be marketed profitably abroad. (1923, p. 153)

For example, the balance of payments could be settled by the exportation of lead once "lead point" has been reached. The choice of which commodity is used

depends partly on its portability and partly on the extent of the market which it finds in either country. The power of gold for this purpose is therefore of primary importance between two countries which have a gold currency, for gold has in each a practically unlimited market. (1926, p. 172)[26]

Marshall then discussed the internal adjustment mechanism to an external disturbance such as a gold outflow. The gold outflow would lower the Bank of England's reserves, the Bank would respond by raising its discount rate, and "the result would be a check to speculative investments, a diminished demand for commodities, and a fall of prices" (p. 158).[27] At the same time, the rise in the discount rate, if not matched by an equal rise in the discount rate abroad, would attract gold from abroad (p. 160).

Finally, he discussed the role of a force that would weaken the traditional adjustment mechanism – the international integration of markets for securities and commodities:

The growing tendency of intercommunication has shown itself in the discount market more than in any other; fluctuations in the price of wheat are being held in check by the growing internationality of the wheat market; but the discount market is becoming international more rapidly even than the wheat market. (pp. 127–28)

Thus in Marshall's view, more of the adjustment to balance-of-payments disequilibrium takes place through capital flows than through the arbitrage of traded goods, with less of the burden placed on gold flows.

Irving Fisher

I focus on three important aspects of Fisher's (1920, [1922] 1965) treatment of the gold standard: his exposition of the operation of a commodity money standard, his discussion of the international adjustment mechanism, and his criticism of the gold standard and advocacy of a "compensated dollar."[28]

---

[26] Also Marshall stated that "a person who had to bring home the returns of any sales in a country had to elect what commodity he would bring, and the question whether he should bring lead or tin was governed ... by exactly the same conditions as whether he should bring lead or gold. If after allowing for expenses of carriage you get a little more by bringing home the lead and selling it than by bringing home the tin, he would choose the lead; if he would get a little more by bringing home gold and selling it, he would bring home the gold" (1926, p. 121).

[27] However this is only a temporary effect; in the long run changes in gold have no effect on the rate of interest, which is determined by "the average profitableness of different business" (Marshall, 1926, p. 130).

[28] The views on the gold standard of Fisher's contemporary, J. Laurence Laughlin (1903), according to Girton and Roper (1978), anticipated the monetary approach to the balance of payments. A critic of the traditional approach, Laughlin disagreed with the Hume price-specie-flow mechanism which postulated lengthy lags until relative-price-level differences led to corrective gold flows. He argued (in a manner similar to Angell, see p. 66) that commodity arbitrage tended to keep price levels of gold standard countries always in line. In addition, in the tradition of Adam Smith, he reversed the causation of money and prices of the classical quantity theory. According to Laughlin, for an

THE COMMODITY THEORY OF MONEY

Fisher's exposition of the working of a commodity money standard is perhap the most lucid extension of Mill's theory. First Fisher demonstrated how, under a gold standard with unrestricted coining and melting, the price of gold bullion would conform to the price of coin, allowing for seigniorage. Thus, in the case of unrestricted coinage, if the price of gold bullion exceeds that of coin, gold users such as jewellers will melt coin into bullion; in the opposite situation, bullion owners will take bullion to the mint and have it coined. The effect of melting the coin will decrease the stock of gold coins relative to bullion, reducing the value of gold as bullion relative to gold as money, thus lowering the price level and restoring equality between bullion and money. In the opposite case, the effect of minting bullion into coin will restore equilibrium (Fisher [1922] 1965, p. 97).

Next Fisher demonstrated how the world gold stock and the world monetary gold stock are influenced by the production and consumption of gold:

As the stock of bullion and the stock of money influence each other, so the total stock of both is influenced by production and consumption. The production of gold consists of the output of the mines which constantly tends to add to the existing stocks both of bullion and coin. The consumption of gold consists of the use of bullion in the arts. (p. 99)

He then made the analogy to a reservoir, "production would be the inflow from the mines, and consumption the outflow to the arts, by destruction and loss" (p. 99). Gold production is regulated by the relationship between "the estimated marginal cost of production" and the purchasing power or exchange value of gold. He assumed that gold mining is an increasing-cost industry. Thus,

gold production will always tend toward an equilibrium in which the marginal cost of production will ... be equal to the value of the product. ... If [the] purchasing power of gold is above the cost of production in any particular mine, it will pay to work that mine. ... Thus the production of gold increases or decreases with an increase or decrease in the purchasing power of gold. (pp. 101–3)

And the purchasing power of gold in turn would vary inversely with the prices of other goods.

The consumption of gold "in the arts" – nonmonetary uses of gold – is related to "consumption for monetary purposes" – monetary uses of gold – by a comparison of the purchasing power of gold with the "marginal utility of what is consumed." Thus consumption of gold – the diversion of gold from monetary to nonmonetary uses – will be "stimulated by a fall in the value (purchasing power) of gold, while the production of gold is decreased" (p. 104).

The two forces of production and consumption, operating in opposing

open economy, the supply of money adjusted through the balance of payments to the demand for money, determined in turn by the "needs of trade." Thus gold did not flow to equilibrate price levels but to satisfy an excess demand for (supply of) money.

directions, regulate the monetary gold stock and hence the price level. In the case of increased gold production due to the discovery of new mines, the increase in production will lead to a filling up of "the currency reservoir," and "a decrease in the purchasing power of money. This process will be checked finally by the increase in consumption. And when production and consumption become equal, an equilibrium will be established" (pp. 108–9).

INTERNATIONAL ADJUSTMENT MECHANISM

Fisher effectively argued that for a small open economy that is part of an international gold standard, as is the case for one state within the United States, the money supply is not an independent variable, but is determined by the need for the domestic price level to conform to foreign price levels. However, he preserved the classical quantity-theory notion of causality between the quantity of money and the price level (see Girton and Roper 1978).

The price level in an outside community is an influence outside the equation of exchange of that community, and operates by affecting its money in circulation and not by directly affecting its price level. The price level outside of New York City, for instance, affects the price level in New York City only via changes in the money in New York City. Within New York City it is the money which influences the price level, and not the price level which influences the money. The price level is effect and not cause. (Fisher [1922] 1965, p. 172)

Following the tradition of Ricardo and Marshall, Fisher argued that the force of arbitrage would tend to produce equality in the prices of traded commodities, but to the extent that international (and interlocal) trade does not bring about uniformity of price levels,[29] "it will ... produce an adjustment of these levels toward uniformity by regulating ... the distribution of money" (p. 93).

Thus gold flows because it is the most efficient international medium of exchange and because it affects the prices of *all* commodities.

In ordinary intercourse between nations ... there will always be a large number of commodities thus acting as outlets and inlets. And since the quantity of money itself affects prices for all sorts of commodities, the regulative effect of international trade applies, not simply to the commodities which enter into that trade, but to all others as well. (p. 93)

CRITICISMS OF THE GOLD STANDARD AND PROPOSALS FOR REFORM

Like Marshall, Fisher criticized the basing of the monetary standard on a single commodity – gold or, for that matter, silver – because of instability in supply and demand conditions of the money metal.

---

[29] Fisher cites a number of reasons why prices may not be equal. "Distance, ignorance as to where the best markets are to be found, tariffs, and costs of transport help to maintain price differences. ... Practically, a commodity will not be exported at a price which would not at least be equal to the price in the country of origin, plus the freight" ([1922] 1965, p. 92).

The commercial world has become more and more committed to the gold standard through a series of historical events having little if any connection with the fitness of that or any other metal to serve as a *stable* standard . . . so far as the question of monetary stability is concerned, . . . we have hit upon the gold standard by accident. (Fisher [1922] 1965, p. 323)

Instead, in a comparison of the purchasing power of gold with that of a number of other commodities he concluded that "in terms of general purchasing power, gold is no more stable than eggs and considerably less stable than carpets" (Fisher 1920, p. 41).[30]

In addition, Fisher, a number of years later, criticized the gold standard because it allows price-level movements and business fluctuations to be transmitted from one country to another.[31]

As a remedy for the inherent instability in the purchasing power of money under the gold standard, Fisher offered his scheme for a compensated dollar: Issue gold certificates backed by gold bullion, but vary the weight of the gold backing per dollar so as to maintain a constant purchasing power of money by tying the weight to an index number – "to mark up or down the weight of the dollar (that is, to mark down or up the price of gold bullion) in exact proportion to the deviations above or below par of the index number of prices" ([1922] 1965, p. 498). This would allow us to "keep the metal gold for the good attributes it has – portability, durability, divisibility, salability – but correct its instability, so that one dollar of it will always buy approximately [a] composite basketful of goods." It would "retain gold as a good medium [of exchange] and yet . . . make it into a good standard" (1920, pp. 88–89).

Knut Wicksell

Wicksell's views ([1898] 1965) on the gold standard will be discussed under three headings: the commodity theory of money, the international adjustment mechanism, and proposals for reform.

---

[30] Fisher also considered the case of bimetallism and rejected it on grounds similar to those noted by other classical writers – it tends to degenerate into monometallism whenever the market ratio of gold to silver diverges from the official ratio ([1922] 1965, pp. 123, 325). He also argued against an irredeemable paper standard because of the inevitable tendency of governments to overissue (p. 131), against Marshall's symmetallism scheme because it bases the standard on too narrow a base of commodities (p. 328), and against a tabular standard: how to express money to conform to that standard was a problem (p. 335).

[31] On the basis of a statistical investigation in 1933 of price-level movements of twenty-seven countries. Fisher found that the price levels of gold standard countries tended to move together, those of silver standard countries moved together, and the average price level of each group varied with changes in the relative prices of gold and silver. Moreover, he found evidence for a short-run trade off between price-level changes and changes in trade and employment within countries. Finally, evidence that countries not on the gold standard during the Great Depression, e.g., Spain and China, avoided the deflation suffered by gold standard countries and the concomitant contraction in output and employment, convinced him that "depressions travel international . . . the infection is carried chiefly via the monetary standard" (1935, pp. 15–16).

In contrast to Fisher, for Wicksell the stabilizing features of the commodity theory were too slow to be of consequence for price-level movements except in the very long run. Either the underlying mechanism was weak or, by the end of the nineteenth century, institutional developments had neutralized or obscured it. Thus

the newly extracted *gold* – passes, for the most part, not into circulation, but into the stocks of cash of monetary institutions; and gold for industrial uses is mainly taken either out of these stocks or directly out of imported stocks of uncoined metal. In neither case can it be supposed that there is any *direct* effect on prices. (Wicksell [1898] 1965, p. 31)

The use of gold purely as a monetary base was utopian.

In such a system the value of money would be *directly* exposed to the effects of every fortuitous incident on the side of the production of the precious metal and every caprice on the side of its consumption. It would undergo the same violent fluctuations as do the values of most other commodities. (p. 35)

INTERNATIONAL ADJUSTMENT MECHANISM

Wicksell was skeptical of the Hume price-specie-flow mechanism – disturbances affecting one country's price level relative to another's would affect the terms of trade, and the balance of payments would then be corrected by gold flows. Although the explanation was fundamentally correct, he expressed reservations:

It is . . . clear that international equilibrium of prices is usually reached far more rapidly and far more directly. The increase in the supply of foreign goods and the diminution in the demand for exports must themselves exert, directly and indirectly, a pressure on domestic prices which is quite independent of any simultaneous movement of precious metals. (Wicksell [1898] 1965, pp. 157–58)

For Wicksell, changes in real income must be brought into the adjustment mechanism.

PROPOSALS FOR REFORM

Like Fisher, Wicksell was concerned with price stabilization, both nationally and internationally. He favored the use of gold certificates backed by a reserve of gold bullion, with each central bank maintaining convertibility and agreeing to accept other central banks' notes and clearing them through an international clearing house (Wicksell [1898] 1965, pp. 186–87). In addition, the central bank of each nation would stabilize its internal price level by keeping the market rate of interest in line with the "natural rate of interest" following simple criteria:[32]

So long as prices remain unaltered the bank's rate of interest is to remain unaltered. If prices rise, the rate of interest is to be raised; and if prices fall, the rate of interest is to be lowered; and the rate of interest is henceforth to be maintained at its new level until a further movement of prices calls for a further change in one direction or the other.

To achieve international price stability, central banks would need to manipulate their gold stocks cooperatively to keep interest rates in line between nations (p. 192).

Appendix C   The Harvard neoclassical school

F. W. Taussig of Harvard and his students – Jacob Viner, F. D. Graham, J. H. Williams, and H. D. White – and W. A. Beach (a student of Allyn Young and J. H. Williams) formulated and tested some of the main tenets of the classical Ricardo-Mill theory of the international adjustment mechanism. Taussig's reformulation of the theory and the evidence for Great Britain, the United States, France, Canada, and Argentina in the pre–World War I era are summarized here. In addition the writings of J. W. Angell, a contemporary critic of the Harvard School and a precursor of the modern monetary approach to the balance of payments, are examined.

F. W. Taussig

In an article (1917) and a book ([1927] 1966), Taussig clearly reformulated the traditional approach in a manner suitable for empirical verification and then summarized some of the evidence.

For Taussig, international borrowing was the most important disturbance to the pre–World War I international economy. He analyzed the effects of the transfer of capital on the balance of payments, money supplies, and price

---

[32] See Jonung (1979) for a discussion of Wicksell's theory of price-level movements. Basically Wicksell argued that price levels will rise cumulatively if the market rate of interest, determined in the loan market, diverged from the natural rate of interest, determined by the forces of thrift and productivity. If the market rate were below the natural rate, prices would rise cumulatively, the price rise being arrested only by a gold outflow that would reduce the banking system's reserves, causing banks to raise their loan rate. When the market rate of interest was above the natural rate, a cumulative deflation would occur. Wicksell explained periods of secular inflation and deflation in the nineteenth century using this approach. In contrast to Wicksell, the Swedish economist Cassel applied classical doctrine, explaining episodes of world inflation and deflation by the growth of the world's gold supply relative to the growth in demand for gold, the former influenced primarily by the production of new gold, the latter by the growth of real income.

levels of both lender and borrower. Several of his studies of British and U.S. experience, beginning with the earliest period he covered, will be reviewed here.

In an examination of the British balance of payments in the period 1853 to 1879, Taussig found that the adjustment of the merchandise balance of trade to changes in invisibles – both payments and shipping earnings – and to capital exports was much more rapid and smooth than classical theory would lead one to expect:

No signs of disturbance are to be observed such as the theoretic analysis previses; and some recurring phenomena are of a kind not contemplated by theory at all. Most noticeable . . . is the circumstance that periods of active lending have been characterized by rising prices rather than by falling prices, and that the export of goods apparently has taken place, not in connection with a cheapening of goods in the lending country, but in spite of the fact that its goods have seemed to be dearer at times of great capital export. (Taussig [1927] 1966, p. 239)

In addition, he found specie movements to be small relative to merchandise movements, a fact to be explained by the sensitivity of the British money supply. Moreover, he found it difficult to separate specie flows consistent with the theory from the more steady series of gold flows into Britain following the gold discoveries in the 1840s and 1850s.

The general lack of conclusive evidence sympathetic to the classical mechanism for the period 1853–79 is reversed for the period 1880–1914. That period is conveniently divided into two parts: 1880–1900 and 1901–1914. The first period was characterized by a deficit on merchandise account financed by shipping earnings and income from abroad with no unusual capital exports. The second was dominated by massive capital exports, which were quickly reflected in a decline in the merchandise deficit.

According to Taussig, the change in circumstances offered a good test of the theory. Had the trends before 1900 continued, Britain would have continued to enjoy an improvement in her terms of trade, but the terms of trade turned around after 1900. That phenomenon, he believed, was consistent with classical theory:

That the gross barter terms of trade should vary as they do, becoming more favorable until 1900, thereafter less favorable, is indeed easily in accord with theory. They will naturally fluctuate in the same direction as the balance of payments. . . . More significant . . . is the fact that the net barter terms of trade move in the same direction, . . . [w]e have argued that when a country has payments to receive for other items than merchandise, the direct and simple exchange of goods for goods is also affected, and is affected to the country's greater advantage. (p. 256)[33]

---

[33] Several years later A. G. Silverman (1931) tested the classical theory that capital exports, ceteris paribus, would lead to a rise in the price of imports relative to the price of exports. Using British data over the period 1880–1913, he compared "year to year percentage changes . . . for the ratio of import to export prices . . . with year to year absolute differences for Hobson's indirect estimates of capital exports . . . expressed in terms of its

The improvement in the terms of trade raises domestic real income because money incomes rise, while the price of imported commodities falls. Taussig found the evidence that money wages rose until 1900, after which they turned down, consistent with his theory.[34]

However, a continuing puzzle for Taussig was how to separate the influence of equilibrating gold flows from the effects of the steady inflow of gold into Britain, the world's principal gold market. Moreover, the puzzle was complicated by the fact that commodity exports and imports

[respond] with surprising promptness to the balance of international payments as a whole. The promptness is surprising because each constituent transaction . . . is purely in terms of money. . . . Yet the recorded transactions between countries show surprisingly little transfer of the only "money" that moves from one to the other – gold. It is the goods that move, and they seem to move at once; almost as if there were an automatic connection between these financial operations and the commodity exports or imports. That the flow of goods should ensue in time, perhaps even at an early date, is of course to be expected. . . . What is puzzling is the rapidity, almost simultaneity, of the commodity movements. The presumable intermediate stage of gold flow and price changes is hard to discern, and certainly is extremely short. (p. 261)

He also examined a case under the gold standard of U.S. borrowing long-term capital from Great Britain.[35] To the extent that not all of the proceeds of the loan are spent on British goods

the increase in remittances from London to New York will cause a demand for New York exchange in London. New York exchange will rise in London, sterling exchange will fall in New York. . . . The fluctuations in foreign exchange will necessarily be confined within the gold points. (Taussig, 1917, p. 394)

The next step is a gold flow from London to New York once the specie-export point is reached. Elsewhere, Taussig argued that in the case of temporary disturbances, gold rarely flows. Much of the adjustment is taken up by movements in the exchange rate within the gold points that speculators promoted. In addition, in the prewar era, sterling bills acted as a substitute for gold in important money-

---

average deviation" and found that over the whole period "an annual increase or decrease in capital exports is more often than not accompanied by an opposite change in the ratio of import to export prices." Thus he concluded that "the orthodox analysis . . . does not seem to be borne out. For most of the period under consideration 'net barter terms of trade' in their yearly variations become more favorable with an increase in capital exports, and vice versa" (p. 124). His explanation for this result was that "an increase in British demand for foreign securities was apparently offset by an increased foreign demand for English goods" (p. 124).

[34] In Canada, the primary recipient of the new capital, the opposite took place after 1900 – an improvement in the terms of trade and rising money wages. See the discussion on Viner, pp. 60–61.

[35] According to the theory, if the proceeds of the loan were spent in the lending country then the price-specie-flow mechanism would not operate (Taussig [1927] 1966, p. 230).

market centers and were transferred in lieu of gold flows. Finally short-term capital movements acted as a substitute for gold flows.[36] "In the last resort, when all expedients for adjusting and equalizing the payments between nations have been utilized and exhausted, specie will flow in payment of balances" ([1927] 1966, pp. 220–21).

The gold inflow into the United States and the gold outflow from Great Britain then raises and lowers the money supplies of the two countries respectively (1917, p. 394). However, the effects of gold flows on domestic money supplies depend on institutional arrangements in each country.[37] In the pre–World War I era of fractional reserve banking and convertible fiduciary money

the inflow or outflow of specie ... primarily affects the discount policy of the banks. Their discount policy in turn affects the volume of accommodation which they offer to the borrowing public, and this in turn affects the volume of notes and deposits. ([1927] 1966, p. 201)

The next step is a "train of consequences familiar to the reader of Ricardo and Mill. Prices will fall in Great Britain and will rise in the United States" (1917, p. 394). Within the United States, prices of domestic goods and exports rise relative to prices of imports, and opposite movements of sectional prices occur in Great Britain.[38] Finally, because the terms of trade have turned in favor of the United States, her citizens are better off: "Their money incomes have risen, the prices of imported commodities have fallen; as buyers of imported commodities they gain" (p. 395).

---

[36] "Still another equalizing factor is the movement of securities that have an international market. They are sold between the great financial centers in a way that replaces or lessens the transmission of gold. ... In any given financial center, a tight money market and a high discount rate tend to lower the prices of ... international securities among them. ... An inflow of gold, which might be expected to take place toward the country of tight money, is replaced by an outward movement of securities" (Taussig [1927] 1966, pp. 218–19).

[37] In a description of the monetary system of Great Britain, the United States, Canada, and France, Taussig demonstrated how different the response mechanism to gold flows can be, ranging from the sluggish response of the French system with its high specie-money ratio to the rapid response of the British monetary system with its low gold-reserve ratio and loaned-up banking system. The Canadian system, with gold reserves held abroad in New York and London, gave the impression that deposits and notes increased before the gold inflow (Taussig [1927] 1966, pp. 201–7). Thus "in all countries using deposits and checks freely, the looseness of the connection between bank reserves and bank deposits leads ... to a chronological order different from that assumed in the Ricardian reasoning. An inflow of specie may follow, not precede, an enlargement of the circulating medium and a rise in prices. So it may be, at least for a short time, even for a period of many months. Indeed, if there be further forces at work than those merely monetary, it may remain so for years" (pp. 207–8).

[38] In his analysis of the massive capital inflows to Canada, Taussig stated, "If the world level of prices had remained unchanged, we should have expected in Canada a fall in the prices of imported goods, and a rise in the prices of domestic goods. Exported goods in the long run would have shown a movement similar to that of the domestic, but with a lag which would for some time keep their prices either on the same low level as the imported, or in a position intermediate between that of the imported and the domestic articles" ([1927] 1966, p. 228).

The opposite takes place in Great Britain. In the case of the United States after 1879 when it was a net importer of British capital and from 1900 to 1914 when it financed a merchandise surplus with immigrant remittances and other invisibles, Taussig expected to observe gold movements and terms-of-trade effects opposite to those he had observed in the British case.

As in the British case, Taussig ([1927] 1966, p. 299) found it difficult to separate the effects of equilibrating gold flows from primarily domestic gold production and consumption. However, unlike the British case, the terms of trade did not behave according to theory. It was difficult to discern a marked trend, though the net barter terms of trade were slightly less favorable before 1900 than afterwards. This, he stated

is an unexpected result. . . . On general principles we should look for terms of trade more unfavorable in the second stage. The excess in the money volume of exports meant . . . that the United States, in meeting the diverse additional charges for immigrants' remittances . . . sent out goods having a greater money value than the goods she bought. . . . The case shows an outcome different from that in Great Britain and Canada during the same period. For these countries, the actual course of events proves to be in accord with theoretical prevision. For the United States it does not. (p. 303)

Taussig attempted to account for the poor results for the United States compared to those for Great Britain and Canada by reference to disturbing causes not present in the other countries. Among these were the tariff that made the terms of trade more favorable than otherwise and an exogenous increase in demand by foreigners for U.S. manufactured goods.

Taussig then analyzed effects of a capital transfer under flexible exchange rates, the example relevant for the period 1862–78 when the United States had inconvertible paper money and Great Britain was on the gold standard (1917, p. 386).

The initial effect of U.S. borrowing in London is to reduce the specie premium in New York (i.e., the U.S.-dollar price of gold falls). This reduction leads to a fall in the paper prices of U.S. exports (as well as domestic goods) and a rise in the paper prices of U.S. imports. As a consequence, export industries in the United States are discouraged, imports are encouraged. The opposite effects take place in Great Britain. Thus the total volume of commodities bought and sold in the United States increases, as exports are shifted to domestic consumption.

Moreover, real income rises in the United States because holding the money supply constant, nominal income remains unchanged but prices have fallen. U.S. residents gain not only as purchasers of imports (they do under a gold standard as well), but also as purchasers of domestic commodities. In contrast to the gold standard case, the U.S. terms of trade improve not because U.S. residents have larger money incomes and lower prices, but because they have the same money incomes and lower prices. The opposite results occur in Great Britain.

Taussig's analysis may be contrasted with that in Friedman and Schwartz (1963, pp. 84–85), of the effect on the gold premium of U.S. Treasury gold purchases abroad before resumption.

THE EVIDENCE

Taussig's students presented evidence for the classical adjustment mechanism based on detailed examination of the monetary history of a number of countries under the gold standard and under inconvertible paper money. Initially the case studies for Great Britain, the United States, Canada, and France under the gold standard and then for the United States and Argentina under inconvertible paper will be reported.

W. Beach

In contrast to Taussig, Beach (1935) presented evidence for Great Britain for the period 1881–1913 unfavorable to the classical price-specie-flow model. Beach argued that if differences in the levels of commodity prices were to dominate the adjustment mechanism, then gold would be expected to flow

because the price levels of one country do not rise or fall in accordance with the levels in other countries. The movement of gold forces all countries to keep the same pace through the various phases of the business cycle. (Beach 1935, p. 170)

Thus one would expect gold to flow out of a country in the upswing of the business cycle. Also, according to the classical model, one would expect capital exports to move procyclically so that other things equal, an upswing in a creditor country would induce a capital flow to a debtor country, accompanied by a gold outflow, unless offset by increased purchases of the creditor's exports. Yet Beach found that there was a tendency for gold imports to increase during the prosperity stages of business cycles and for exports to grow during depression, in both Great Britain and the United States.

Beach's explanation of this anomaly relied on several pieces of evidence. First, he observed a high correlation between business conditions and (long-term) capital exports from Great Britain. The volume of new loans, he suggested, was determined primarily by business conditions (pp. 171–73). Second, in the upswing of the business cycle in Great Britain (and the United States), there was an increased internal demand for gold currency. Third, short-term balances (loans) were sensitive to changes in discount rates, more so than domestic business and prices. Hence in the business-cycle upswing, the internal currency drain put pressure on the reserves of the banking system and the Bank of England, which led to a rise in the discount rate, a short-term capital inflow, and, ceteris paribus, a gold inflow.[39]

Thus

cyclical fluctuations in the movement of specie might easily be controlled by the movements of these balances. This explanation for the cyclical movements of

---

[39] Beach, 1935, p. 180. In an appendix, he presented evidence for the United States, supportive of this explanation, that agrees with an earlier study by A. P. Andrew (1907).

gold found for England and the United States seems more adequate than the explanation based upon price level differences. (p. 180)

Jacob Viner

Viner (1924) tested the classical balance-of-payments adjustment mechanism for Canada during the period 1900–1913.[40] During that period, the great disturbing factor was the inflow of foreign capital into Canada. The adjustment to be explained was the "process whereby the Canadian borrowings, negotiated in terms of money, entered Canada in the form of goods and not in gold" (Viner 1924, p. 145).

The mechanism to be tested was that of J. S. Mill. The capital inflow initially would raise the price of foreign exchange to the gold export point. This would then be followed by a gold flow from the lending to the borrowing country. Prices would rise in the borrowing country and fall in the lending country, leading to a change in imports and exports, with the borrowing country experiencing an unfavorable balance of trade and the lending country, a favorable balance. Once the unfavorable balance of the borrowing country equaled the rate of borrowing, the exchanges would return to parity, gold movements would cease, and relative prices in the two countries would stabilize at their new levels.

First, examining the effects of changes in the exchange rate within the gold points, Viner argued that since transportation and insurance costs were very low between Montreal and New York, the gold points were so narrow that changes in the exchange rate were not likely to have much effect on the balance of trade (p. 155).

Second, Viner found evidence that gold flows were highest in the years when Canadian borrowing was most in excess of Canadian loans to others (p. 160). At this point, Viner digressed on the role of gold in the Canadian financial system. Before World War I, gold did not circulate as hand-to-hand currency but did act as a reserve asset for the chartered banks. (Canada did not have a central bank in this period.)[41] The Canadian monetary base consisted of a fixed issue of government fiduciary notes – Dominion notes and gold reserves, largely maintained as "outside reserves" on call in New York or London, or as balances with commercial banks in those centers. According to Viner, changes in outside reserves in New York acted in a manner similar to gold flows in the classical balance-of-payments adjustment mechanism. Thus the transfer of foreign capital from London to Canada usually passed through the New York money market, raising outside reserves of Canadian banks. Then on the basis of the increased outside reserves, Canadian banks would increase their deposits (pp. 177–79).

---

[40] Viner's contribution is summarized in Taussig ([1927] 1966, chap. 19). For the literature critical of Viner, see Meier (1953) and Dick (1981).

[41] Until 1935, although the largest commercial bank, the Bank of Montreal, performed many of the functions of a central bank. See Rich (1978).

Third, the increase in the Canadian money supply would produce a rise in the Canadian price level (relative to the rest of the world) in accordance with the classical theory[42] and a rise in sectional price levels. The initial effect would be on the prices of domestic goods and not on the prices of imports, which for a small open economy such as Canada are determined abroad. Some substitution away from domestic goods toward imports would follow as would also a rise in the price of exports (to the extent Canada had monopoly power in their production), leading to a reduction in exports.[43]

The evidence generally confirms these predictions: between 1900 and 1913 indexes of the prices of imports increased least, followed by the prices of exports, while domestic prices increased the most. Moreover, a beginning-of-period weighted index of the price of exports declined relative to an unweighted index, suggesting that commodities shifted from the export to either the domestic or import category. In addition, the ratio of domestic-goods prices to the wholesale price index increased more in Canada than in the United States.[44] Finally a decline in exports and a rise in imports completed the case for Viner in favor of the classical adjustment mechanism.[45]

This theory has been verified inductively for Canada during the period 1900 to 1913. [Moreover,] a corollary of this reasoning [is] that during a period of international borrowings the terms of international exchange shift in favor of the borrowing country and against the lending country. . . . Adequate inductive verification of this proposition is supplied by the demonstration already made that export prices rose relative to import prices. (p. 295)

Harry D. White

White (1933) examined the French evidence for the classical price-specie-flow explanation of the effects of capital exports. Like Britain, France in the four

---

[42] Viner disputed Laughlin's view that all price levels are tied together via arbitrage, citing large differences in the price of gold among countries (Viner 1924, p. 206). He distinguished between traded goods, whose prices are closely linked internationally, and domestic goods, whose prices are affected only indirectly.

[43] However, prices of most Canadian exports were determined internationally, hence the rise in the price of international goods produced in Canada by the increased price of domestic goods and services would cause a decrease in exports.

[44] Also an index of the price of services rose relative to the overall price index, as did an index of money wages relative to those in the United States and Great Britain, confirming the relative price adjustment mechanism (Viner 1924, pp. 241, 248).

[45] Much of the reduced exports came from the diversion of raw materials to domestic use, while a large share of the increased imports consisted of capital goods, largely from the United States – both forces conducive to economic development. The fact that most of the proceeds of the loan were not spent in the lending country, Great Britain, is given as further verification of the classical mechanism, which otherwise would not come into play. See Taussig ([1927] 1966, pp. 230 and 259), where he states, "It was to be expected that Canada, getting a growing excess of imports over exports in terms of money, should also get more imported commodities in proportion to her commodities exported. But for the verification of theory it is particularly significant that the net barter terms also

decades before World War I lent large sums abroad, and as in the British case, for contemporary economists, the income from foreign investment permitted a persistent merchandise-trade deficit. In a careful reconstruction of the French balance-of-payments accounts, White demonstrated that the income from foreign investment over the 1880–1913 period was no greater than the total export of capital for the same period. Moreover he found, contrary to the official figures, that in twelve out of the thirty-four years surveyed, France had a surplus on merchandise account; and the years when the French accounts showed a deficit on merchandise trade it was paid for not by revenue from French foreign investment but by foreign-tourist expenditures in France (White 1933, p. 301).

White then attempted to determine, as Taussig did for Great Britain, the adjustment mechanism by which the net capital export affected the balance of trade:

Tho the totals of capital exports and net revenue from foreign investment over the period as a whole were not far apart, for any one year during most of the period they differed considerably, thereby raising the question of the mechanism for adjustment of the disequilibrium caused by changes in the volume of capital exports. (p. 302)

First, he found that in France's trade with gold standard countries, exchange-rate movements had a negligible effect on merchandise movements, but in the case of a number of countries not on the gold standard, from which France obtained one quarter of her imports, fluctuations in the exchange rate made a significant difference to French importers.

Second, he concluded that in the French case, only a small portion of the sums loaned abroad were spent on French exports.

Third, the movements of sectional price changes and of the volume of merchandise trade revealed a relationship in accordance with the classical sequence. Relative increases in import prices were accompanied by a decline in physical quantities and vice versa. The changes continued until there was a rough approximation between changes in the values of merchandise balances and capital exports.[46]

Fourth, he could find no evidence of the linkage of gold flows to the reserves of the Bank of France and thence to the domestic money supply. According to

become more favorable. The Canadians not only got more of physical goods in proportion to the goods they sent out, but they got, on better terms, those imported goods which may be regarded as coming in payment for their own exported goods, and which had no relation to the borrowings."

[46] White (1933, p. 303). Nevertheless, he concluded that "the influence of sectional price changes as a force in the adjustment does not in the case of France appear to have played so prominent a role as is presupposed by the neo-classical doctrine.... Shifts in demand schedules were doubtless a more effective medium. No substantiation of this view could be found in the French trade statistics, but actual substantiation would in any case be impossible because fluctuations in prices as a causal factor in merchandise movements could not be excluded; it would be impossible to determine what proportion of the changes in the volume of merchandise imports and exports was due to changes in demand schedules and what proportion to changes in sectional prices."

White, the Bank of France would raise the discount rate only to offset a large gold outflow, but not to influence domestic economic activity. Moreover France's large gold reserves relative to other major gold standard countries enabled it to follow such a passive discount-rate policy.

Fifth, White argued that it was possible that there existed a direct link between gold flows and price-level movements because such a large fraction of the French money supply consisted of gold currency, but

no clear evidence on . . . the relationship of the quantity of money in circulation to prices is revealed by the comparison between the fluctuations in the quantity of specie and notes outside the Bank of France and the movement of prices. Moreover, even if such a relationship were revealed, the absence of correlation between the annual movements of capital and specie renders dubious the interpretation that changes in sectional price levels were induced by capital movements. (p. 304)

Finally, the mixed evidence led him to conclude that

the specie-flow-specie mechanism is doubtless one of the forces, but there seems to be no justification for assuming that it is the sole or even the dominant means of adjustment. . . . The neoclassical theory is not the complete explanation. The theory fails in that it explains what happens only under certain given conditions seldom found. It expounds a sequence of changes which undisturbed would in time bring about adjustment, but which seldom, if ever, operates unchecked by the frictions and rapid changes characteristic of modern economic conditions. By ignoring some of these forces and minimizing others, the neoclassical exposition exaggerates the effectiveness of gold flows and sectional price changes as a means for establishing equilibrium in international accounts. (p. 306)

Frank D. Graham

Graham tested Taussig's (1917) theory of the adjustment mechanism under depreciated paper. In the period 1862–1878, when the United States was on an inconvertible paper standard – the greenback standard – while her principal trading partner, Great Britain, was on a gold standard, the premium on gold was a close proxy for the dollar–pound exchange rate.[47] Graham analyzed the effects of British capital flows – the major source of disturbance during this period to the balance of payments, and hence the exchange rate.

The period can conveniently be divided into two episodes: 1863–1873, a period of heavy and continuous borrowing from London, and 1874–1878, a period when the borrowing dropped off.

According to Taussig's theory, one would expect the period of heavy borrowing to be associated with a deficit in the balance of trade and the period of cessation with a reversal in the balance of trade. Graham's evidence showed a

[47] See Kindahl (1961) and Friedman and Schwartz (1963) for further discussion.

large annual excess of commodity imports over exports in the period of heavy borrowing, the opposite in the period of cessation (Graham, 1922, pp. 231–34).

Also, according to Taussig's theory, one would expect, ceteris paribus, the period of heavy borrowing to be associated with a decline in the exchange rate (the premium on gold), and the period of cessation to be associated with a rise in the exchange rate. Graham found the evidence corroborated this prediction. In comparing the price of gold with an index number of general commodity prices, he found the quarterly average price of gold to be lower than the general price level from April 1865 through June 1876, while from July 1876 to the end of the period it was higher, with the price of gold rising relative to the overall price level after 1874.

Next, according to Taussig, one would observe the following effects on sectional prices: in the first period, low paper prices of exports, gradually declining paper prices of imports, and relatively high paper prices of domestic commodities; in the second period, a gradual reversal toward higher paper prices of exports, gradually rising paper prices of imports, and relatively low prices of domestic goods. A comparison of the arithmetic means of the three different groups of commodities between the two periods provided evidence consistent with the theory.

Finally, one would observe different effects on money wages (as a measure of relative prosperity) in the two periods: in the first period declining wages in the export industries relative to the domestic-goods industry, as resources are diverted from it in the face of falling prices; and the opposite movement in the second period. Again, using Mitchell's wage data and classifying U.S. industries into domestic and export industries, Graham found the evidence consistent with the theory (pp. 267–70).

At the same time as these effects occurred in the United States, opposite ones would occur in Great Britain, although the fluctuations in the U.S. dollar would have only limited effects on British prices since Great Britain was on a gold basis and movements of the dollar would affect only a portion of her trade.[48] Again Graham found the evidence consistent with the theory.

John H. Williams

Williams (1920) tested for Argentina Taussig's theory of the adjustment mechanism under depreciated paper but unlike Graham found the evidence too incon-

---

[48] According to Graham, in the first period, exporters to the United States will obtain for a time practically the same paper prices as before the lending, and these translated into gold will be higher than before. At the same time, import prices in Great Britain will rise because the gold obtained by American sellers for their products when translated into paper yields less than before the depreciation of gold. Unless the British buyers can import from some other country, the U.S. sellers will gradually be able to raise their prices. The ultimate effect will be a rise in the British price level which will appear as a relative increase in the price of domestic goods. The opposite forces will occur in the second period (Graham 1922, pp. 259–60).

clusive to be of more than limited support to the theory. First, according to Taussig's theory, a rising premium on gold would stimulate exports. "It does so by virtue of the fact that export prices rise more rapidly than costs, creating an extra profit or bounty for the producing and exporting classes" (Williams 1920, p. 233). Williams presented evidence indicating a rise in the price of exports concomitant with a rising premium on gold in the period 1885–1891. However, according to the theory, the value of exports ought to rise – but it did not. This result Williams attributed to the presence of other forces such as "the character of the Argentine exports . . . agricultural and grazing products . . . [which are] extremely susceptible to vagaries of climate" and the fact that "though [the] quantity of exports increased, the greater quantity was sold for a lower gold price per unit" (p. 234).

Second, according to Taussig's theory, a rising gold premium should reduce the value of imports, which the evidence confirmed.

We find first of all that the diminution of value of imports asserted by theory . . . did occur: that, in fact, the diminution was very marked. . . . On comparing the course of imports with the gold premium, . . . there was in every year an inverse relation between imports and the premium on gold. (p. 253)

In sum, the evidence marshalled by the Harvard school in favor of the classical adjustment mechanism is mixed. Overall price levels adjust in accordance with the theory, but sectional price adjustment in accordance with the thory is limited. Little support was found for the role of gold flows, the money supply, and discount rates in the mechanism. A common finding was that the commodity trade balance adjusted rapidly to the external disturbance of capital flows, more rapidly than would be expected by a theory postulating links from price-level differences to gold flows, to changes in money supplies, to changes in sectional price levels, and then adjustment of the commodity trade balance. Explanations given by the school for the rapidity of adjustment – with no supporting evidence – included the growing integration of goods and securities markets, the role of income effects, and the sensitivity of the money-supply process.

J. W. Angell

Angell ([1925] 1965), a student of Taussig's, had a distinctly different interpretation of the international adjustment mechanism under the pre–World War I gold standard. Angell focused on the relationship between individual commodity prices and national price levels.

First, he argued that the classical division of the overall price level into export, import, and domestic-goods prices was "extremely misleading and may lead to erroneous conclusions." The distinction he preferred was between international or traded commodities and domestic or nontraded commodities, with the dividing line between the two types of commodities to be determined empirically:

Any movable article whatsoever may enter international trade. . . . The first requisite for movement is that the money prices receivable, translated through a common measure, shall be higher in one country than in the other; the second, that the difference shall at least cover costs of transportation of all sorts, including tariff[s] (Angell [1925] 1965, pp. 375–76)

He cited evidence for equality in the world prices of traded goods (staple commodities) at one extreme, and at the other extreme, no international competition and hence no reason for price equalization of nontraded goods, with an in-between third category – partially traded goods. Arbitrage would ensure equality for traded-goods prices but arbitrage may not take place for many commodities because of: (a) "lack of accurate information, in each market," (b) "lack of sufficient initiative and enterprise, on the part of the manufacturers and dealers to take advantage of the discrepancy," (c) "selling in a new market requires the prior erection of trade connections," and (d) monopoly power (pp. 379–80).

Second, Angell discussed evidence showing long-run similarity of national price-level movements between countries on the same metallic standard. He defined national price structures as

a series of solar systems, which maintain a fairly constant relationship in their movements through space. But the component parts of the system – individual prices – are in a state of ceaseless change relative to the elements in both their own and other systems. (p. 390)

However, he argued that the similarity of movement of national price levels coupled with the tendency to price equalization of internationally traded goods suggests that domestic (nontraded-goods) prices conform to the pattern set by traded-goods prices. Further, since the process of substitution between domestic and traded goods is a relatively weak one, the key mechanism that keeps price levels in line is the

classical price specie flow analysis. . . . No other type of explanation can adequately account for the known facts. Prices in different countries do not move together, over long periods of time, by sheer accident. There must evidently be some connecting link between them. But the influence exerted by international prices alone, on the various national price structures, is not great enough to provide this link. It is necessary to discover some condition or element that is capable of affecting the totality of prices indiscriminately, and fairly rapidly. This element is found in the mechanism by which the balance of international payments is kept in equilibrium. (p. 393)

Angell offered his own version of the price-specie-flow mechanism. He downplayed the role of actual gold flows in the mechanism, arguing that

neither the magnitudes nor the directions of the international flow of gold are adequate to explain those close and comparatively rapid adjustments of payment disequilibria, and of price relationships, which were witnessed before the war. (p. 400)

Moreover,

the character of modern banking [will not] permit the assumption of any very high degree of intimacy to the connection between a country's metallic stock and its price level. Finally, gold is among the least sensitive of the media of international payments, one of the slowest to move. (pp. 400–401)

His own version of the mechanism relies on the importance of foreign bills of exchange which act as a substitute for gold. Temporary disequilibria will be offset by movements in the exchange rate. If that proves inadequate, gold will flow, prompting a change in discount rates. Finally, if the disturbance is more than temporary, then

an alteration will take place in the underlying conditions that govern the general course of international exchange itself. The volume of purchasing power in circulation in the creditor country will be built up, in consequence of the increase in the banks' holdings of bills. In the other country it will be reduced, through the decline there in bill holdings. These changes, in turn, will operate upon the corresponding general price levels. The latter effect is often, though not always, strengthened by alterations in the discount rates. The movements in prices will then influence the commodity balance of trade . . . and will continue to do so until the change in the commodity trade has become great enough to offset and correct the original disturbance in the balance of international payments. (p. 413)

Appendix D   Interwar critics

With the outbreak of war in 1914 and Britain's suspension of convertibility, the classical gold standard expired. The gold exchange standard existed briefly from 1925 to 1931, after which the problem of international monetary reform and the creation of a more viable international monetary system took center stage.

The traditional approach to the gold standard was subjected to extensive reinterpretation and criticism, much of it derived from concern over the monetary instability of the interwar period. The reinterpretation of the gold standard began with the Cunliffe report ([1918] 1979), which succinctly restated the stylized facts of the operation of the pre-1914 gold standard and appealed for a return to the old order. Another view (Brown, Smit) of the prewar gold standard stressed that it was successful because it was a managed standard – managed by London. Followers of this institutional approach then documented all the many respects in which the structure of the British money, gold and commodity markets – "pax Britannica" – and the astute management of the Bank of England made the system work. The key implication of the approach was that a successful gold standard could be restored if a similar institutional milieu could be re-created. A related approach (Cassel) argued that the gold standard worked well for England, and possibly for several other major countries, but not for the rest of the world. Moreover, the fact that it worked so well for England was largely an accident of history (Viner).

A recurrent theme in the interwar literature was the inherent policy conflict between internal and external stability under the gold standard fixed-exchange-rate system. According to this view (Keynes), the prewar gold standard worked because nations were willing to subsume domestic economic objectives to the maintenance of gold convertibility; but in the postwar period, a return to the harsh discipline of the prewar gold standard would be disastrous. This approach proposed the creation of a supernational monetary agency or similar means to ensure international harmonization of economic policy.

The final theme in the literature was the expression of doubt about the stylized facts of how the gold standard worked. Returning to the anomalies between fact and theory discussed by the Harvard school, the critics (Whale) argued that perhaps the traditional approach itself was incorrect.

The views of writers identified with each of the foregoing themes are summarized below.

THE STYLIZED FACTS

In the interwar period, a persistent thread in the literature was a view of the prewar gold standard as the ideal monetary standard. A classic statement of this view appeared in the Cunliffe report, but it was repeated by others including R. G. Hawtrey, T. E. Gregory, and the *Interim Report of the Gold Delegation of the Financial Committee* of the League of Nations ([1931] 1979).

The Cunliffe report ([1918] 1979) to Parliament succinctly presented what seemed to be the salient features of the operation of the prewar gold standard in Great Britain and a series of proposals for a quick return to gold.[49]

As the report documented, the money-supply process before the war was based on the Bank Charter Act of 1844. Apart from a fixed fiduciary issue, hand-to-hand currency consisted entirely of gold and subsidiary coins or of gold certificates. Gold was freely coined and there were no restrictions on the import or export of gold, so changes in the monetary base, aside from movements of gold to and from the arts, were determined by inflows from abroad and outflows. In addition, upon this base of a fixed fiduciary issue and gold and gold-backed currency rested an extensive system of checkable bank deposits, so that pre–World War I British money supply consisted mainly of deposits.

Second, the report described the operation of the balance-of-payments adjustment mechanism. A disturbance to the balance of payments led to a gold flow and a corresponding change in the money supply. Thus, e.g., when the balance of

---

[49] According to Nurkse [(1944) 1978), the general picture of the adjustment process and the role of central-bank policy presented in the Cunliffe report "was one which during much of that [interwar] period dominated men's ideas both as to the actual working of the gold standard before 1914 and as to the way the gold standard should be made to work after its restoration" (p. 67). Thus the prewar gold standard was portrayed in similar terms in both the *Interim Report of the Gold Delegation of the Financial Committee* (League of Nations [1931] 1979) and the Macmillan report (1931).

trade was unfavorable and the exchanges adverse, it became profitable to export gold, and the would-be exporter bought the gold from the Bank of England. The Banking Department in turn obtained gold from the Issue Department in exchange for notes from its reserve, with the result that liabilities to depositors and the reserve were reduced by an equal amount, and the ratio of reserves to liabilities declined.[50] The next step was a rise in the discount rate:

If the process was repeated sufficiently often to reduce the ratio in a degree considered dangerous, the Bank raised its rate of discount. The raising of the discount rate had the immediate effect of retaining money here which would otherwise have been remitted abroad and of attracting remittances from abroad to take advantage of the higher rate, thus checking the outflow of gold and even reversing the stream. (Cunliffe report [1918] 1979, par. 4)

Thus raising Bank rate by inducing a short-term capital inflow would be sufficient to stem a temporary balance-of-payments deficit. However, in the case of a permanent disturbance, the discount-rate rise would additionally reduce domestic credit.

This description of the operation of Bank rate to facilitate the adjustment mechanism has often been referred to as the rules of the game.[51] According to Nurkse:

Whenever gold flowed in, the central bank was expected to increase the national currency supply not only through the purchase of that gold but also through the acquisition of additional domestic assets; and, similarly, when gold flowed out, the central bank was supposed to contract its domestic assets also.... The chief methods to be used for changing the volume of domestic central bank assets in accordance with this principle were changes in the discount rate, designed to make borrowing from the central bank either more or less attractive, and purchases or sales of securities in the open market on the central bank's own initiative. (Nurkse [1944] 1978, pp. 66–67)

Moreover, the gold standard also provided an automatic mechanism to offset an internal disturbance:

When ... credit at home threatened to become duly expanded, the old currency system tended to restrain the expansion and to prevent the consequent rise in domestic prices which ultimately causes such a drain. The expansion of credit, by forcing up prices, involves an increased demand for legal tender currency both from the banks in order to maintain their normal proportion of cash to liabilities and from the general public for the payment of wages and for retail

---

[50] The report ignored the role of fluctuations in the exchange rate within the gold points and the temporary sterilization of gold flows.

[51] The rules were never formally spelled out. According to the Macmillan report (1931), "the management of an international standard is an art and not a science, and no one would suggest that it is possible to draw up a formal code of action admitting of no exceptions and qualifications, and adherence to which is obligatory, on peril of wrecking the whole structure" (par. 47).

transactions. In this case also the demand for such currency fell upon the reserve of the Bank of England, and the Bank was thereupon obliged to raise its rate of discount in order to prevent the fall in the proportion of that reserve to its liabilities. The same chain of consequences . . . described [above] followed and speculative trade activity was similarly restrained. (Cunliffe report [1918] 1979, par. 6)

Thus

there was therefore an automatic machinery by which the volume of purchasing power in this country was continuously adjusted to world prices of commodities in general. . . . Under these arrangements . . . [the] country was provided with a complete and effective gold standard. The essence of such a standard is that notes must always stand at absolute parity with gold coins of equivalent face value, and that both notes and gold coins stand at absolute parity with gold bullion. When these conditions are fulfilled, the foreign exchange rates with all countries possessing an effective gold standard are maintained at or within the gold specie points. (pars. 6–7)

The committee recommended a restoration of the gold standard "without delay" (par. 15), to be achieved by the cessation of government borrowings and the reduction of Bank of England note issue. In addition, the committee recommended allowing the free external movement of gold and the use of Bank rate to check outflows and inflows. However, following Ricardo's "Proposal for a Secure Currency," it recommended against the use of gold coins for domestic circulation and in favor of use of all the nation's gold to be held by the Bank of England as backing for the nation's monetary base – a gold-bullion standard. Most of the proposals were adopted when Britain returned to gold in 1925.

Hawtrey (1935) summarized and expanded upon the stylized facts of the Cunliffe report. He documented the domestic aspects of a gold standard. A gold-coin standard with free coinage and free export and import serves as a device to provide a limit on the supply of money, but the authorities must maintain the quality of the coin. Thus,

the essence of the gold standard is that the price of gold, the value of gold in monetary units, is fixed by law and this determines the wealth value of the monetary unit itself. The use of gold coin . . . provides a fairly close approximation to this ideal. (Hawtrey 1935, p. 20)

A central bank acting as a bankers' bank by holding a pool of gold reserves can reduce the foregone interest cost on commercial banks' holdings of gold coins to maintain convertibility of their liabilities. However, since commercial banks keep their reserves with a central bank, it must accept the responsibility of acting as a lender-of-last-resort.

For the banks and the public do not trouble themselves about the interchangeability of gold and credit. That is the affair of the Central Bank alone. Anyone can sell the Central Bank as much gold as he likes and can procure from it as much gold as he chooses to pay for. The Central Bank is in the gold market as both buyer and seller in unlimited quantities at a fixed price. (p. 24)

The central bank has the power to control the domestic money supply by using its principal tool – its discount rate. By raising the rate, the central bank can check lending by "improvident banks" and by lowering the rate it can stimulate lending.

Hawtrey then described the mechanism by which a change in Bank rate operates.

The power of the central bank over the wealth value of the monetary unit ultimately depends on the deterrent effect of a high Bank rate upon the borrowing operations of the customers of the banks. Bank rate is essentially a short term rate of interest. . . . It is the borrowing of money for the *purchase of goods* that is likely to respond most promptly to a restriction or relaxation of credit, because a trader who wishes to reduce his indebtedness in respect of goods held in stock can readily do so by postponing or reducing his purchases. When traders are tending generally to do this, the effect is immediately felt by the *producers* of the goods in decreased order. . . .

. . . The installation of capital is usually financed by the raising of funds from the long-term investment market, but short-term borrowing is often resorted to in anticipation of the raising of funds from that source or for the purchase and holding of securities. If Bank rate is raised, the holding of capital assets with money temporarily borrowed is discouraged. But the effect on productive activity will be relatively slow, for the installation of capital is a prolonged process, and any such project is likely to be preceded by a long preliminary period of preparation. (pp. 25–26)

Thus, changes in Bank rate have their primary impact on the holding of inventories.

Hawtrey also discussed international aspects of a gold standard. The commitment by a number of countries to fix the prices of their currencies in terms of gold establishes a fixed-exchange-rate system. The prices in any one currency of gold in different places cannot differ by more than the cost of transporting gold between the different places – arbitrage in the gold market will ensure that outcome. To maintain convertibility of the currency – the primary responsibility of a central bank – an adequate gold reserve is essential. The threat of a loss of gold is more serious than a possible gain, since in the former case the country may be forced to leave the gold standard before the necessary adjustment can take place; in the latter case, although the central bank may temporarily lose control of the market, the stimulus to lending will eventually lead to a reversal of a gold inflow.

Finally, Hawtrey, like Keynes, saw an analogy between the operation of a clearing system between banks within one country and a clearing system of central banks under the gold standard.

In his analysis of the balance-of-payments adjustment mechanism following a monetary disturbance, Hawtrey incorporated elements of both the classical adjustment mechanism and the role of income changes. An increase in bank lending in an open economy by stimulating demand will ultimately lead to an increase in production and real income, assuming less than full employment, but will initially lead to an increase in sales and reduction in inventories. Merchants and dealers will therefore seek to replenish their stocks. Those dealing in home-produced goods will do so partly by ordering fresh supplies from producers and partly by diverting to the home market goods that might have been sold abroad, while those dealing in foreign-produced goods will order fresh supplies from abroad. The diversion of production from exports and the increase in imports will create an adverse balance of payments and a gold outflow. The process continues until a new higher equilibrium level of income is reached with a lower than initial balance-of-payments deficit.

Once full employment is reached, the increased spending will affect prices. However, the prices of traded goods cannot be fully raised.

These, which may conveniently be called "foreign trade products", comprise not only actual imports and exports but all importable and exportable goods. The prices of foreign trade products are governed by prices in world markets and are fixed in gold. The demand for them will expand as the consumers' income expands, and as the demand expands the loss of gold grows greater and greater. (Hawtrey 1935, p. 41)

In addition, some of the increased income will be diverted to the purchase of foreign securities which will worsen the current-account balance. The process can be arrested and the deficit reduced by an increase in the discount rate – quickly offsetting the capital inflow and ultimately reducing the rise in income. However, "the contraction of the consumers' income is the only substantial corrective" to the balance-of-payments deficit (p. 43).

For Gregory ([1932] 1979), like Hawtrey, the essence of the gold standard is convertibility of national currency into a fixed weight of gold. One of the great advantages of the gold standard therefore is

that ... *it eliminates fluctuating rates of exchange* ... [that] international trade and investment can be conducted without any fear that the sums risked in a particular trade or investment transaction will not be recovered ... owing to changes in the relative exchange values of different moneys at the date of payment. (Gregory [1932] 1979, p. 9)[52]

In addition, he related the development of the international gold standard in the second half of the nineteenth century to the growth of international trade and investment in that period, and stressed the role

played by gold movements in the establishment of the conditions necessary to secure equilibrium in the international balance of payments of the various countries upon the gold standard. ...

---

[52] Moreover Gregory doubted the ability of forward exchange markets to cover exchange risk because he felt that "just when the relative values of currencies are most uncertain and when, therefore, the advantages to be derived from the organization of a forward exchange market would be greatest, the difficulties of organizing it ... are greatest also" ([1932] 1979, p. 10).

What the international gold standard does . . . is to force prices and incomes in different trading areas into such a relationship that the balance of payments can be adjusted without gold flows in either direction. . . . The international gold standard creates, *not a common price level but an integrated price-and-income structure.* (pp. 11, 14–15)

The gold standard can operate successfully in the context of modern banking systems and central banks (provided sterilization activity is not undertaken) and of tariffs, capital flows, and transfers.

The role of London

An important theme in the literature of the gold standard, developed in the interwar period, was that the gold standard was successful primarily because it was a sterling standard.[53] Perhaps the most succinct statement of the position is in Smit (1934), although a similar viewpoint is expressed in Brown (1940).

Accoridng to Smit, by 1914,

all the leading money and trade centers in the world were interconnected in a triangular fashion through London, although smaller patterns, directly centered around Paris, Berlin and New York, were woven into the main pattern of the picture. (Smit 1934, p. 53)

In the prewar world, sterling balances instead of gold were increasingly used by foreign financial institutions to settle international payments:

The most important key to the world's foreign exchange markets lay in the sterling balances of foreign bankers kept in London. . . . London acted as one bank for a customer-neighborhood of bankers that comprised not only the small British island but the whole world. . . . The pound, which was internationally wanted for settling commercial and capital indebtedness with the British Isles, became more and more, as a consequence of the world-wide demand that it commanded, a conventional credit counter for settling indebtedness among all countries. (p. 54)

The primary financial interconnection between countries centered on the London discount market because much of the world's foreign trade was financed by sterling bills.[54]

---

[53] This theme also appeared in the prewar literature in Keynes ([1913] 1971). See the discussion below. It has played an important role in the postwar explanation of the classical gold standard's success. See, e.g., Triffin (1964), Lindert (1969), D. Williams (1968), and Palyi (1972).

[54] Behind this elaborate network of financial flows was the real process of the transfer of capital to developing countries from the developed countries and the real flow of goods through the current account. According to Williams (1947, p. 155), "England's creditor position in the nineteenth century had developed gradually, along with the development of a world economy involving the division of productive effort between the older

The Bank of England by its discount rate and open-market operations was able to exercise considerable influence over this market. Thus

the extraordinary effectiveness of the English official bank rate in influencing foreign exchange rates and international gold movements before the war cannot be explained unless one sees the integration that had taken place in the world credit structure. (p. 55)

In addition, the spread of the gold standard and integration of the international credit system were closely intertwined as "the legal guarantees of the gold standard limited the risk factor of foreign exchange fluctuations and inspired confidence" and "London possessed the world's central gold market. . . . The possession of sterling balances was the surest means of getting gold when wanted" (p. 56).

Finally, Smit argued that at the same time as the world moved towards a sterling standard, there was growing internationalization of commodity prices centered in British commodity exchanges. A key consequence of international integration of both commodity and money markets was that the traditional explanation of how the prewar gold standard operated placed too much emphasis on "the existence of different national monetary systems, and the quantitative relations between the separate national money and credit systems and domestic price levels" (p. 55).

Even before World War I, Keynes ([1913] 1971) had noted the unique role of London in the operation of the gold standard. By World War I, England had developed a sound currency and, aided by the effective use of Bank rate, required only a small gold reserve to maintain convertibility in the face of external shocks. However, according to Keynes, most other countries were not as successful in staying on the gold standard. One key difference between Britain and other countries was that she was a net creditor in the international short-loan market, whereas most other countries were debtors.

In the former case, which is that of Great Britain, it is a question of reducing the amount lent; in the latter case, it is a question of increasing the amount borrowed. A machinery which is adapted for action of the first kind may be ill-suited for action of the second. Partly as a consequence of this, partly as a consequence of the peculiar organization of the London money market, the "bank rate" policy for regulating the outflow of gold has been admirably successful in this country, and yet cannot stand elsewhere unaided by other devices. (Keynes [1913] 1971, p. 13)

Most other countries in adopting the gold standard used gold as a medium of exchange but were unable to use the discount rate as an effective method to preserve the standard because, in addition to not being net international lenders,

industrialized areas and the younger agricultural areas and the flow of accumulated savings from the former to the latter. The same circumstances which assigned to England the leading role in capital export made London the international money market and the Bank of England the administrator of the gold standard."

they had not established the elaborate financial network of the London money market.

Consequently other countries used other mechanisms to supplement their inadequacies: they held large gold reserves "so that a substantial drain . . . may be faced with equanimity"; they partially suspended payment in gold; and they kept "foreign credits and bills . . . which can be drawn upon when necessary" (p. 14).

Most countries (especially less-developed ones) tended to rely on the last method because it economized on the foregone interest cost of holding gold reserves.[55] Thus the gold-exchange standard evolved

out of the discovery that, so long as gold is available for payments of *international* indebtedness at an approximately constant rate in terms of the national currency, it is a matter of comparative indifference whether it actually *forms* the national currency. . . . The gold exchange standard may be said to exist when gold does not circulate in a country to an appreciable extent, when the local currency is not necessarily redeemable in gold, but when the government or central bank makes arrangements for the provision of foreign remittances in gold at a fixed maximum rate in terms of the local currency, the reserves necessary to provide those remittances being kept to a considerable extent abroad. (p. 21)

Cassel (1935) went even further than Keynes, arguing that the gold standard was an international standard in neither the pre – nor the post–World War I periods. It was only a British standard. He argued that the automatic balance-of-payments adjustment mechanism of price levels adjusting to gold flows never in fact worked that way – that central banks for the sake of security maintained larger reserves than legally required, and therefore exports and imports of gold did not necessarily influence the domestic money supply or the price level.

The gold supply of a country exercised such an influence only via the policy of the central bank and its regulation of the market by means of its rate of discount and its open market operations. Thus the currency necessarily became a "managed currency" whose value depended entirely on the policy of the central bank. (Cassel 1935, p. 3)

In addition, capital flows hindered the automatic functioning of the international gold standard:

A country normally exporting capital could compensate for a loss of gold simply by a reduction of its lending; and a country normally importing capital could compensate for a loss of gold by borrowing more. Thus it was possible to prevent gold imports or exports from having any influence on the price level of the country. (pp. 3–4)

---

[55] Important pre-1914 European examples were Austria-Hungary and Russia. In Asia, India and the Philippines represented the classic successful examples of the operation of the gold-exchange standard.

Finally, the international gold standard did not guarantee a natural distribution of gold:

Creditor countries were in a position to accumulate, if they chose to do so, disproportionate gold stocks without using them for any other purpose than for exercising political influence or merely for satisfying a national pride in the possession of gold. Debtor countries could provide gold reserves by increasing their foreign indebtedness.... The size of these reserves had very little to do with the balance of trade of the country. Nor did gold imports and exports have any distinct relation to changes in the balance of trade. (p. 4)

That the international gold standard functioned so well before World War I

can only be explained by the basic position that the pound sterling held in this system. Indeed, the pre-war gold standard system may not inadequately be described as a sterling bloc held together by London's position as the world's financial clearing center and by the service of the pound sterling as a generally recognized means for international payments. (pp. 4–5).

Next, in Cassell's view, the international gold standard was fundamentally defective because it was based on the tacit assumption that the purchasing power of gold would be stable and hence that maintenance of a fixed gold parity guaranteed stability in the purchasing power of a country's currency. According to Cassel:

the gold standard ... [suffered] from an inherent and irreparable instability. This instability results partly from the instability of the value of gold itself, and partly from the insecurity of the redemption in gold of gold-standard currencies (p. 6)

On the first score, he presented evidence of considerable variability in the value of gold for the period 1850–1910, based on the Sauerbeck wholesale price index. This evidence he explained by "deviations of the actual gold supply from the normal gold supply"[56] and "variations in the monetary demand for gold."[57]

On the second score, he alleged that only Britain had a completely convertible currency in the prewar period; other countries usually put barriers in the way of the large gold exports and "eagerly watched their gold reserves." Indeed, he

---

[56] Calculated on the basis of the underlying trend growth rate of real income. See Cassell in the *Interim Report ... of the Financial Committee* (League of Nations [1931] 1979).

[57] Among the key sources of variation in monetary demand in the pre–World War I era were "the large accumulation of gold in the United States in preparation for the introduction of the gold standard" in 1879 (Cassell, 1935, p. 11), and the competition by central banks to strengthen their gold reserves: "the orthodox use of gold reserves for ironing out temporary deficits in the balance of trade fell into the background and often lost all importance in comparison with the gold movements caused by competition for gold and ultimately traceable to the artificial position given to gold in the world's monetary system" (p. 13).

argued that by the end of the period most countries kept large gold reserves as a matter of national pride and consequently the key aim of policy was to protect the gold reserve rather than use the gold reserve to protect convertibility. Thus when World War I broke out, the redeemability of currency was immediately suspended in order to safeguard the gold reserve.

Like Cassel, Viner (1932) argued that the prewar gold standard

would ... have been found impracticable and would have been generally abandoned ... [if not for] the development of a deliberate and centralized mechanism of control of gold movements, using central bank discount policy and credit control as its chief instruments. (Viner 1932, p. 9)

Moreover, the Bank of England pioneered in the development of the technique of central-bank control. England became the manager of the international gold standard.

However, the evolution of the Bank of England's effective management of the gold standard emerged as a by-product of the Bank's learning by a process of trial and error to protect its slim gold reserves. The Bank of England in the nineteenth century was primarily a profit-seeking institution and hence tried to minimize its non-interest-bearing gold holdings. However, by the close of the century, the Bank gradually began to accept responsibility for maintenance of an English gold standard:[58]

The Bank of England, at first as the sole issuer of paper money and the most important deposit bank, later under pressure of public opinion and in self-defense against the irresponsibility of the other English banks, partially accepted the role of a central bank with some degree of special responsibility for the mode of operation of the English gold standard and especially for the protection of the convertibility of the English paper currency. (pp. 12–13)

As a consequence, the Bank learned to makes its discount rate effective to protect its gold reserve in the face of an external drain and to hold adequate reserves to meet the exigencies of both external and internal drains.[59]

Moreover, according to Viner, in the nineteenth century fluctuations in the exchange rates within the gold points and short-term capital flows aided the adjustment mechanism and reduced the size of gold flows necessary to offset a disturbance to the balance of payments. Finally, Viner made a case for the continuation of the gold standard, despite the fact that it did not produce a stable price level, because a system of inconvertible paper currencies linked by flexible exchange rates would be far worse.[60]

---

[58] Viner (1937) described how the conflict between private and public interests of the Bank was resolved in the period 1844–1870. Also see the discussion above on Bagehot (p. 46).

[59] Not, however, without courting disaster on numerous occasions (Viner 1932, p. 16); also, Viner (1937, pp. 259–74).

[60] Viner's (1937) chronicle of the history of nineteenth-century debates over the monetary standard centered on the role of discretionary management under a gold standard rule. "Although most present day writers seem to believe either that the non-automatic character of the modern gold standard is a discovery of the postwar period or that it was

We know too little . . . of the possibilities of stabilization to take immediately any major steps in that direction. The hostility of central bankers and the menace of political control are genuine and important factors in the situation. The gold standard is a wretched standard, but it may conceivably be the best available to us. Its past record, bad as it is, is not necessarily conclusive in this respect, as the only alternatives which have actually been tried have, on the whole, had an incomparably worse record. (p. 37)

The conflict between internal and external goals

A major theme of the interwar period was the potential conflict between internal price stability and a fixed exchange rate under the gold standard. By fixing the price of gold in terms of domestic currency, movements in internal price levels (and real income) would be determined by external-price-level (and real-income) movements. The prewar gold standard period, characterized by both price stability (in a long-run sense) and fixed exchange rates, was an accident of history never to be repeated. At the same time, flexible exchange rates and abandonment of the gold standard rule were not embraced because of the risk of unstable exchange rates and the fear of the consequences of discretionary policy. That theme is echoed in the works of Keynes, Cassel, Viner, Nurkse, and others. To remedy the conflict between external and internal goals, various schemes were proposed to promote international harmonization of price-level movements under a managed gold standard. The views of major writers of the interwar period are surveyed briefly below.

For Keynes ([1923] 1971) the policy options facing Great Britain in the immediate postwar period were to go back to the gold standard at the prewar parity, which would involve deflation, or else to fix parity after devaluing the pound. The choice between devaluation and deflation was part of a more general dilemma – the choice between price stability and exchange-rate stability. Keynes then asked, "In the light of our answers to the first two questions, is a gold standard, however imperfect in theory, the best available method for attaining our ends in practice?" ([1923] 1971, p. 117).

Because of its adverse effects on income distribution, Keynes rejected deflation. When internal and external price stabilities were incompatible, he chose

only in the postwar period that the gold standard lost its automatic character, currency controversy during the entire nineteenth century concerned itself largely with the problems resulting from the discretionary or management elements in the prevailing currency systems. The bullion controversy . . . turned largely on the difference in the mode of operation in the international mechanism of a managed paper standard currency, on the one hand, and of a convertible paper currency, on the other, with the latter treated generally, but not universally, as if it were automatic. Later, the adherents of both the currency and the banking schools distinguished carefully between the way in which a supposedly automatic 'purely metallic' currency (which, in addition to specie, included bank deposits but not bank notes) would operate and the way in which the Bank of England was actually operating a 'mixed' currency (which, in addition to specie and bank deposits, included bank notes)" (pp. 388–89).

internal price stability. Under the prewar gold standard, the choice was made in favor of fixed exchange rates and the subservience of the internal price level to external considerations. "We submitted, partly because we did not dare trust ourselves to a less automatic . . . policy, and partly because the price fluctuations experienced were in fact moderate" (p. 126). But the circumstances of the pre-1914 era were partly accidental, and it should not be presumed they would ever be repeated.

The special conditions Keynes cited for the past good performance of the gold standard were first,

that progress in the discovery of gold mines roughly kept pace with progress in other directions – a correspondence which was not altogether a matter of chance, because the progress of that period, since it was characterized by the gradual opening up and exploitation of the world's surface, not unnaturally brought to light *pari passu* the remoter deposits of gold. But this stage of history is now almost at an end. A quarter of a century has passed by since the discovery of an important deposit. Material progress is more dependent now on the growth of scientific and technical knowledge, of which the application to gold mining may be intermittent. (p. 133)

Second, the independent influences coming from the demand for gold in the arts and for hoarding purposes in Asia had a steadying influence. Third, central banks allowed their gold reserves to vary slightly, absorbing much of the additional gold produced after major discoveries and reducing some of their accumulated gold when it was relatively scarce. They thus minimized the effects on price levels.

Given the special circumstances that made the gold standard successful before World War I, Keynes argued that the standard would be unlikely to work as well in the postwar period. Even if all countries adopted the gold standard – an important condition for it to be successful – the prewar system of balance-of-payments adjustment was "too slow and insensitive in its mode of operation" to handle the "large [and] sudden divergences between the price levels of different countries as have occurred lately" (pp. 128–29). Moreover, though short-term capital flows in response to interest-rate differentials helped speed up the adjustment mechanism in the prewar period, especially when the disturbance was temporary, in the case of permanent disturbances, the adjustment "might obscure the real seriousness of the situation, and enable a country to live beyond its resources for a considerable time at the risk of ultimate default" (p. 130). This problem would be more serious in the postwar period.

The case for flexible exchange rates and managed fiduciary money was that balance-of-payments adjustment to external shocks would be much more rapid under flexible than under fixed rates despite the risk of instability.[61] Thus Keynes

---

[61] "This means that relative prices can be knocked about by the most fleeting influence of politics and of sentiment, and by the periodic pressure of seasonal trades. But it also means that the postwar method [of flexible exchange rates] is a most rapid and powerful corrective of real disequilibria in the balance of international payments arising from whatever causes, and a wonderful preventive in the way of countries which are inclined to spend abroad beyond their resources" (Keynes [1923] 1971, p. 130).

came out strongly against restoration of the classical gold standard by the United Kingdom.

In truth, the gold standard is already a barbarous relic. All of us, from the Governor of the Bank of England downwards, are now primarily interested in preserving the stability of business, prices, and employment, and are not likely, when the choice is forced on us, deliberately to sacrifice these to outworn dogma, which had its value once, of £3 17s. 10½ d. per ounce. Advocates of the ancient standard do not observe how remote it now is from the spirit and the requirements of the age. A regulated nonmetallic standard has slipped in unnoticed. *It exists.* (p. 138)

In contrast to his earlier focus on the policy dilemma facing one country alone, Keynes ([1930] 1971) concentrated on the international monetary system as a whole. The interrelationship between central banks in an international fixed-exchange-rate system such as the gold standard was analogous, he noted, to the relationship between commercial banks and the central bank within a national economy.[62]

Under the pre–World War I gold standard, commercial banks operated in step within one country and central banks operated in step internationally except that reserve ratios did adapt somewhat to relative scarcity or abundance of gold. Behavior of the long-run price level depended on whether new gold available for reserves was increasing faster or slower than trade of the gold standard countries, which in turn depended on the rate of discoveries and technological improvements in gold mines, the use of gold as currency, the number of countries joining the gold standard, and the growth of real per capita income.

Some important differences in the relationship between central banks under the gold standard and between member banks and the central bank in a national economy, however, Keynes observed, were that central banks tended to have more variable reserve ratios;[63] that more of their own money returns to the central bank than is the case for commercial bank's; that there is a higher degree of competition for short-term capital between central banks through varying discount rates than is the case between commercial banks.[64]

Thus in an international system, a central bank can pursue an independent policy – oriented primarily to domestic considerations – only within narrow limits and for short periods, with the degree of independence determined by its relative size. Thus, under a fully operative gold standard, "credit cycles have an interna-

---

[62] The analogy holds perfectly if we assume that each central bank has a rigid gold-reserve ratio so that the aggregate quantity of central-bank money is determined by the aggregate gold reserves of the central banks; that no gold is used as currency; and hence that variations in the world monetary gold stock are determined by the difference between the amount of new gold mined and the amount consumed in the arts (Keynes [1930] 1971, p. 250).

[63] This reflects two factors: a central bank cannot turn to a "lender of last resort" if its reserves are deficient; a central bank does not maximize profits and thus may keep higher reserves than otherwise (Keynes [1930] 1971, p. 252).

[64] In the British banking system there is little interest-rate competition (Keynes [1930] 1971, p. 254).

tional character" because member central banks must follow the average behavior. This implies a "real divergence of interest; and we must not expect of central banks a degree of international disinterestedness far in advance of national sentiment and of the behaviour of other organs of national government" ([1930], 1971, p. 237).

The dilemma between internal-balance and external-balance considerations for one country on the gold standard is thus apparent.[65] Keynes argued that in a world of perfect capital mobility, the domestic interest rate must correspond to world interest rates:

If any country tried to maintain a higher rate than its neighbours, gold would flow towards it until either it gave way or the international system broke down by its having absorbed all the gold in the world. And if it tried to maintain a lower rate, gold would flow out until either it gave way or had to leave the international system through having lost all its gold. Thus the degree of its power of independent action would have no relation to its local needs. (p. 271)

The problem arises for a country

if its foreign balance is inelastic, and if, at the same time, it is unable to absorb the whole of its savings in new investment at the world rate of interest. It will also tend to happen even where the foreign balance is elastic, if its money costs of production are sticky. ... This, then, is the dilemma of an international monetary system – to preserve the advantages of the stability of the local currencies of the various members of the system in terms of the international standard, and to preserve at the same time an adequate local autonomy for each member over its domestic rate of interest and its volume of foreign lending. (pp. 271–72)[66]

As a solution to the problem, Keynes advocated a number of policies to increase the discretion of national monetary authorities while still remaining on a gold standard. One set of policies to protect a country's domestic stability in the face of "inconvenient fluctuations in the rate of foreign lending" is to maintain a large enough level of reserves: either in gold reserves at home or by holding "liquid balances in foreign centers," by arranging overdraft facilities with other central banks or by "borrowing and lending arrangements between central banks

---

[65] J. H. Williams, "Monetary Stability and the Gold Standard" (1932) in Williams (1947) covered much the same ground.

[66] Keynes argued that this dilemma did not present itself to Great Britain before 1914 because "the influence of London on credit conditions throughout the world was so predominant that the Bank of England could almost have claimed to be the conductor of the international orchestra. By modifying the terms on which she was prepared to lend, aided by her own readiness to vary the volume of her gold reserves and the unreadiness of other central banks to vary the volume of theirs, she could to a large extent determine the credit conditions prevailing elsewhere" (Keynes [1930] 1971, p. 274). However, since World War I, the decline of Great Britain's influence on world credit conditions meant that she now faced the dilemma.

and a supernational bank" (p. 278). A second policy is to manipulate the gold points – to create an artificial spread between the official buying and selling price of gold. This can be done by direct authority or by the central bank manipulating the forward rate of exchange.[67] Finally, he suggested direct controls over capital movements. Keynes's ideal solution to the problem of combining an ideal international standard and internal equilibrium was a gold standard managed by a supernational bank.[68]

The objectives of a supernational monetary agency would be to ensure long-run stability and to smooth short-run cycles around the long-run trend. One way to achieve long-run price stability would be to adopt a commodity standard based on an international aggregate of commodities. "The long-period trend in the value of gold should be so managed as to conform to a somewhat crude international tabular standard" (p. 351). To solve the problem of short-run disturbances within individual countries, Keynes advocated giving individual central banks more discretion within the fixed-exchange-rate system.

The supernational bank would be established by all the world's central banks and would act as a lender-of-last-resort to them alone. It would hold as assets gold, securities, and advances to central banks, and its liabilities would be deposits by the central banks. These deposits, called supernational bank money (S.B.M.), would be fully convertible into gold and would serve along with gold as reserves for the member banks. The supernational central bank would then use the normal tools of monetary policy – bank rate and open-market operations – to "maintain . . . the stability of the value of gold (or S.B.M.) in terms of a tabular standard based on the principal articles of international commerce" and to avoid "general profit inflations and deflations of an international character" (p. 360).

The interwar criticism of the traditional approach to the gold standard culminated in a provocative and path-breaking article by Whale (1937). He challenged both the price-specie-flow adjustment mechanism and the operation of the rules of the game.

Whale referred to four pieces of puzzling evidence: (1) Taussig's finding that the adjustment of national price levels to disturbances occurred much

[67] See Sayers (1936) for a discussion of how this was frequently done on a de facto basis by the Bank of England in the 1890–1914 period.

[68] As in the *Tract*, Keynes considered the case for a managed money standard with flexible rates but ultimately rejected it because the uncertainty associated with exchange-rate fluctuations would impede long-term capital mobility. "If we . . . desire that there should be a high degree of mobility for international lending, both for long and for short periods, then this is, admittedly, a strong argument for a fixed rate of exchange and a rigid international standard" ([1930] 1971, p. 299). Also, see Williams (1947), who recommended maintenance of the gold standard as a restraint, setting the "limits to which monetary variation can be carried" but widening the role of discretionary monetary policy (pp. 187–88). Ultimately "the logical end of the evolution of credit management, and the only real hope of solution of the conflict between external and internal stability, would be closer cooperation of central banks looking toward some form or degree of supernational management" (p. 190).

more rapidly than the theory postulated; (2) Beach's finding that gold flows to Great Britain moved procyclically contrary to the classical prediction, and that they were more closely related to interest rate differentials than to price-level differences; (3) the finding that many prewar central banks did not follow the rules of the game, e.g., the central banks of France and Belgium rarely changed their discount rates yet remained on the gold standard; (4) the finding that price levels between regions with varying levels of economic activity moved synchronously, suggesting a linkage through arbitrage rather than adjustment with a lag to specie flows, as in the traditional theory.[69] Might not the national price level be similarly determined by the world system of prices?" (Whale 1937, p. 22).

On the basis of this evidence, Whale suggested an alternative hypothesis to the classical mechanism: Rather than the demand for money in an open economy with a fixed exchange rate adjusting to the supply of money (and specie flows) as the classical theory predicts, specie flows and the money supply are determined by the demand for money, which in turn is determined by real income and the price level.

Thus, according to Whale, an increase in real economic activity, for a given price level (determined by the world price level), would increase the demand for money, causing a balance-of-payments surplus and a gold inflow. Similarly an increase in the domestic money supply would lead to a balance-of-payments deficit, a gold outflow, and a decline in the reserves of the banking system. If the markets of the country are closely linked with foreign markets, the decline of bank reserves should lead to "an almost immediate correction" of the money supply (p. 27).

Interest rates also play a different yet still important role in the alternative mechanism:

What is contended is that . . . the raising of interest rates did not have the effect of producing a *relative* reduction of prices in certain countries. High rates in London led rather to a world fall in prices, partly because of the sympathetic movement of rates elsewhere, partly because of the effect on British entrepot trade and British long-term foreign investment. (p. 27)

Two important implications follow. First, the classical transfer mechanism of Mill and Taussig must be reinterpreted. According to Whale, a transfer of capital involves a redistribution of spending power. However, rather than this process involving a change in the direction of demand and in the terms of trade, "the redistribution of spending power itself, . . . apart from any change in the direction of demand and the terms of trade, may require a redistribution of money . . . effected by a movement of gold" (pp. 28–29). Second, "since gold movements . . . and discount rate adjustments are displaced from their central position in the process of international price adjustment, the question of 'observing the rules of the game' . . . loses much of its importance" (p. 31).

---

[69] Whale cited evidence of rapid price adjustment between Lancashire and the rest of England, and between England and Scotland.

Appendix E   Post–World War II reinterpreters of the gold standard

In the period since World War II, economists have reexamined and reinterpreted the operation of the classical gold standard on the basis of new evidence and new theoretical and statistical tools. The principal areas of research are the adjustment mechanism, the role of capital flows, the managed gold standard, and the rules of the game.

In the reconsideration of the international adjustment mechanism, several approaches can be distinguished. The Keynesian open-economy-multiplier approach (Ford) explains most of the adjustment to the transfer of capital before World War I in terms of changes in economic activity rather than relative price levels. Extension of the classical price-specie-flow mechanism (Friedman and Schwartz) focuses on relative price levels and interest rates in the adjustment process. The monetary approach to the balance of payments (Triffin, Williamson, and McCloskey and Zecher) integrates elements of both Keynesian and classical mechanisms and views gold flows by themselves, rather than the effects they have on price levels, incomes, and interest rates, as the equilibrating mechanism in the adjustment of the balance of payments.

A major reexamination of the role of capital flows in the transmission mechanism (Morgenstern) raised serious doubts about the classical theory, though the analysis in turn was criticized (Borts). Evidence favorable to the traditional approach was also presented (Bloomfield).

Evidence on the managed gold standard amplified the view that London managed the prewar gold standard (Lindert, Sayers, Goodhart). Other studies showed that the rules of the game were largely violated before 1914 (Bloomfield) and that they were inconsequential (McCloskey and Zecher).

The adjustment mechanism

Ford (1962) downplayed the role of price-level and monetary change in the explanation of the adjustment of the balance of payments under the prewar gold standard. He stressed three themes: (1) the key element in the adjustment mechanism for Great Britain was the change in real income, working through an open-economy-multiplier process; (2) the important link between Great Britain and periphery nations via lending and exports worked primarily through changes in income; (3) there was an asymmetry between the gold standard experience of Great Britain and Argentina (an example of a periphery country). For Great Britain the gold standard mitigated the adjustment to external disturbances, for Argentina the gold standard aggravated it. These divergent experiences reflected the operation of fundamentally different gold standard financial institutions and the presence and absence of "other favorable circumstances." Ford was highly critical of the stylized facts of the traditional approach summarized in the Cunliffe report. His objections were that the report omitted the crucial role of income effects; placed weight on a link between changes in interest rates and economic activity that he believed to be tenuous; treated relative prices as the primary mechanism of adjustment in the balance of trade, based on the doubtful assumption of elastic demands for imports and exports; inappropriately ignored the feedback effects of changes in income of the major trading nation – Great Britain – on other countries; and made no mention of the important role of foreign lending.

Instead, Ford emphasized the key role of changes in income in the balance-of-payments adjustment mechanism.[70] A disturbance to the balance of payments such as the exogenous decline in exports would reduce much of the initial balance-of-payments deficit by a decline in real income, working via the multiplier, and would reduce the demand for imports without any change in price levels.[71] The extent to which the balance of payments was equilibrated, without requiring a gold outflow and changes in the money supply, depended on the relative sizes of the marginal propensities to import and to save.[72] In addition, feedback effects of changes in other countries' income due to the fall in British demand for their products would (depending on the size of the other country) also facilitate the adjustment.

The second adjustment mechanism was change in the money supply. To the extent the balance of payments was not equilibrated by income change, the resultant gold outflow would reduce the domestic money supply, which would raise interest rates and lower domestic economic activity, imports, and the balance-of-payments deficit. The rise in interest rates would also induce a short-term capital inflow, providing a temporary cushion for the balance of payments. A rise in the central bank's discount rate would further stimulate the reduction in domestic activity and encourage a short-term capital inflow. However, Ford did not regard the Bank of England's playing by the rules of the game as the key element in the process, and he downplayed the accommodating role of central-bank policy in other countries.[73]

Finally, Ford presented evidence he regarded as consistent with the key role of income in the adjustment process for Great Britain. Comparing deviations from a nine-year moving average of exports, imports, and income from 1870 to 1914, he found that

[70] Ford argued that accounting for real-income changes would also explain Taussig's puzzle, "that periods of active lending have been characterized by rising prices rather than falling prices and that the export of goods apparently has taken place, not in conjunction with a cheapening of goods in the lending country, but in spite of the fact that its goods have seemed dearer at times of great capital export" (Taussig [1927] 1966, p. 219).

[71] Ford does not entirely dismiss the role of price changes, but doubts that the elasticities are high enough or prices flexible enough to carry the full burden (1962, p. 12; 1977, p. 17).

[72] Ford estimated the marginal propensity to import at about 0.3 and the marginal propensity to save at 0.1 to 0.2. This produces an open-economy multiplier of 2 to 2.5, which is not sufficient to equilibrate the balance of payments (1962, p. 54).

[73] Following Keynes ([1923] 1971) and Bloomfield (1959), Ford argued that the rules of the game were followed only by creditor countries, and not even by all of them (1962, p. 16). Britain's playing by the rules was facilitated by the location in London of the world's principal capital and gold markets (pp. 11–12).

the parallelism between movements of deviations from nine year moving averages of exports, imports and national income is marked, with some slight tendency for imports to lag behind exports, . . . these movements provide powerful evidence both for the exports-income-import automatic adjustment mechanism and for the view that in *most* British booms and slumps variations in export values were a vital factor. (Ford 1962, p. 61)[74]

According to Ford, British loans to developing nations such as Argentina, Australia, and Canada were primarily transferred through changes in real income, in contrast to the classical approach, which emphasized changes in sectoral prices. A British loan to a country such as Argentina would lead to an increase in imports from Britain and an increase in debt service. When the investment projects in the borrowing country matured, production of exportables would increase, some of which would be imported by Britain. The resultant rise in Argentine incomes would then generate the revenues necessary to service the foreign debt as well as increase demand for British goods.

The arrangement worked well in the long run, but in the short run problems could arise for the borrowing country. If the amount lent abroad temporarily exceeded Britain's current-account surplus, a gold outflow from Britain would occur, and the Bank of England would raise the Bank rate. As a result, the borrowing country would experience a gold outflow. Important investment projects might be halted before completion, leading to a balance-of-payments crisis if the borrower were unable to meet the debt-service obligations.

Ford examined in detail the cyclical adjustment mechanism in Argentina under the gold standard (and under inconvertible paper). The typical cycle can be described as follows: A rise in the price of Argentina's primary staple exports, generated by an increase in foreign demand, would produce a current-account surplus, a rise in economic activity, and a gold inflow. The gold inflow would lead to a rise in the domestic money supply. Some of the increased expenditure would go to the production of additional exports, some to the purchase of imports, and some into the nontraded sector – primarily for the purchase of land. A land boom would develop, followed by further foreign investment and further expansion. Ultimately, the boom would be choked off, either by a reduction in foreign economic activity that reduced the demand for Argentinian exports, or by a rise in the discount rate by the Bank of England to offset a gold outflow. Furthermore, were speculation in land to get out of hand, there would ultimately be a collapse in land prices and a domestic liquidity crisis associated with bank failures. Foreign lending would be discouraged. If the internal drain were accompanied by an external drain, then domestic gold reserves would be insufficient to withstand the onslaught and the country would suspend convertibility. This was the sequence of events in 1885 and 1913.

Ford argued that the gold standard experience of periphery countries such as Argentina was considerably less favorable than that of center countries such as

---

[74] This evidence is contrasted to Ford's finding, unfavorable to the classical relative-price mechanism, that "the cyclical behavior of the net barter terms of trade shows no such consistent pattern" (1962, p. 76).

Britain. For two reasons the cycle in British economic activity was dampened by the gold standard whereas the cycle in Argentina was aggravated. First, Britain's position as the center of the world's money market meant that in the face of an external drain, a rise in Bank rate would draw on short-term capital and sterling balances in London without loss of gold, while Argentina lacked the cushioning financial institutions.[75] Second, it was easier for a creditor nation to obtain immediate relief from external pressure by reduced foreign lending, "whereas ... in a period of stringency it was difficult or even impossible for a debtor country (with a past history of depreciation) to offset gold exports by increasing its borrowing abroad" (p. 182).

In their monumental study of U.S. monetary history, Friedman and Schwartz (1963) treated the gold standard in a traditional way in their analysis of the role of monetary forces and of the price-specie-flow mechanism to explain balance-of-payments adjustment under the gold standard; in their application of the commodity theory of money to explain secular price movements; and finally, in their discussion of the role of central-bank management under the gold standard.

They described the role of the money supply under an international specie standard that the United States adhered to from 1879 to 1933, as follows:

The amount of money in any one country must be whatever is necessary to maintain international balance with other countries on the same standard, and the amount of high-powered money will alter through imports and exports of specie in order to produce this result ... the amount of high-powered money is a dependent rather than an independent variable, and is not subject to governmental determination. (Friedman and Schwartz 1963, pp. 51–52)

Moreover,

for a country which is an economically minor part of the gold standard ... the major channel of influence is from fixed rates of exchange with other currencies through the balance of payments to the stock of money, thence to the level of internal prices that is consistent with these exchange rates.... [However] the links have much play in them, so that domestic policies can produce sizable short-term deviations in the stock of money from the level dictated by external influences. (pp. 89–90)

Under a flexible-exchange-rate regime, by contrast, such as the greenback period from 1862 to 1879, "the amount of high-powered money is determined by governmental action" (p. 51).

Adjustment to both external and internal disturbances was facilitated by the classical relative-price-level adjustment mechanism and capital flows. The events of the period 1879–82 are analyzed in these terms. Good harvests in 1880–81 led to an increase in U.S. exports. The resulting increase in demand for dollars

---

[75] Favorable circumstances for Britain other than the institutional environment stressed by Ford were: confidence in the convertibility of sterling, the alternating pattern of trends in home and foreign investment, and the sensitivity of British exports to British overseas lending (1962, p. 190).

implied a relatively higher U.S. price level consistent with balance-of-payments equilibrium.[76] Pending the rise in prices, a gold inflow ensued that led to a rise in the money stock and the price level. At the same time, a gold outflow from Great Britain led to a monetary contraction and a decline in the price level. As a consequence the Bank of England raised the Bank rate, reversing the gold flow to the United States.

The gold inflow was a passive reaction which temporarily filled the gap in payments. In its absence, there would have had to be an appreciation of the dollar relative to other currencies – a solution ruled out by the fixed exchange rate under the specie standard – or a more rapid rise in internal U.S. prices. At the same time, the gold inflow provided the basis and stimulus for an expansion in the stock of money and thereby a rise in internal prices at home and downward pressure on the stock of money and prices abroad sufficient to bring an end to the necessity for large gold inflows. It would be hard to find a much neater example in history of the classical gold standard mechanism in operation. (p. 99)

Other episodes are treated similarly: prices and incomes, aided by capital flows, adjust to maintain external balance.[77] The brunt of the adjustment was sustained in some cases by changes in the money stock, in others by changes in velocity or real output.

Economically, these were the channels whereby a necessary adjustment was worked out. They were not the forces determining what adjustment was necessary. . . . The discipline of the balance of payments under the gold standard enforced that adjustment and determined its size. (p. 101)[78]

Friedman and Schwartz applied the classical commodity theory of money to explain secular price-level movements:

Under a specie standard confined to a single country, or for the world as a whole under an international standard, the existing amount of specie is determined by

---

[76] "The price level in the U.S. relative to that in Britain rose from 89.1 to 91.1" (Friedman and Schwartz, 1963, p. 98).

[77] However, one conspicuous example, discussed by Friedman and Schwartz, when the classical approach could not fully explain the adjustment mechanism, was the period 1896–1901.

[78] A study by Macesich (1960), using a similar approach, demonstrated that the monetary instability in the period 1834–45 was not caused primarily by the Bank war and Jacksonian policy, as traditionally believed, but rather was produced by external events. Given that the United States was part of the international specie standard, the author argued, internal prices had to adjust to external prices, and how they did so did not matter. Macesich isolated the different determinants of monetary change and found that changes in the ratio of the public's holdings of deposits-plus-notes to specie and the ratio of the bank's liabilities to specie explained most of the change in the money supply reflecting uncertainty engendered by the Bank war. The approach of Temin (1969), based on different data sources, was similar to Macesich's, but attached greater importance to changes in high-powered money, and less to the ratios, in explaining monetary movements.

the available physical stock plus the relative demand for monetary and other uses; and changes in the amount of specie, by relative costs of production of specie and other goods and services. (p. 52)

They explained the secular deflationary episode of 1879–96 by

[a] combination of events, including a slowing of the rate of increase of the world's stock of gold, the adoption of the gold standard by a widening circle of countries, and a rapid increase in aggregate economic output, . . . despite the rapid extension of commercial banking and of other devices for erecting an ever larger stock of money on a given gold base. (p. 91)

The subsequent turnaround in prices and secular-inflation episode is explained by

fresh discoveries of gold in South Africa, Alaska, and Colorado combined with the development of improved methods of mining and refining, especially the introduction of the cyanide process. These occurred during a period when there were few further important extensions of the gold standard yet a continued development of devices for "economizing" gold. (p. 91)

Moreover, the period of secular deflation "was an important factor in stimulating the search for gold and for economical techniques for extracting gold from low-grade ore" (p. 188).

Finally, in their discussion of the sterilization of gold inflows in the 1920s by the Federal Reserve system, Friedman and Schwartz explain how violations of the rules of the game weakened the adjustment mechanism of the gold standard.

The sterilization of gold could be justified as a means of insulating internal monetary conditions from external changes. Its international effect, however, was to render the maintenance of the international gold standard more difficult. Suppose all countries linked by a gold standard were to sterilize gold flows. Gold flows would then set in train no forces tending to bring them to a halt or to reverse them. The system could last only as long as the flows resulted from purely temporary imbalances of sufficiently small magnitude to right themselves before draining the countries losing gold of their reserves. The effect would be to insulate the countries from minor adjustments at the cost of letting them accumulate into major ones. (p. 283)

Friedman and Schwartz attributed the Federal Reserve system's failure to stem the banking crisis of 1931 to its failure to follow the classical medicine prescribed by Bagehot for central-bank operations in the face of both an external and an internal drain – to lend freely but at a high discount rate (p. 395).

Emphasis on the "stylized facts" of the gold standard on intercountry adjustment via specie flows that produced relative price-level adjustments, aided by capital flows and by central banks following the rules of the game, failed, according to Triffin (1964), "to bring out the broader forces influencing the *overall pace* of monetary expansion on which individual countries were forced to align themselves" (p. 2).

Evidence damaging to the traditional story included: "enormous degree of parallelism – rather than divergent movements – between export and import fluctuations *for any one country*, and in the general trend of foreign-trade movements *for the various trading countries* . . . from 1880 to 1960" (p. 3); and "overall parallelism – rather than divergence – of price movements, expressed in the same unit of measurement, between the various trading countries maintaining a minimum degree of freedom of trade and exchange in their international transactions" (p. 4); downward wage rigidity among countries that maintained exchange stability; Bloomfield's (1959) evidence of the failure of most central banks to play by the rules of the game; the ineffectiveness of changes in discount rates in many countries to stem capital flows or change relative prices; and the important role of long-term capital flows in maintaining enduring balance-of-payments disequilibrium without relative price adjustment. Triffin accordingly painted a different picture of how the gold standard worked.

The most important aspect of the gold standard was exchange-rate stability maintained by "pressures for international harmonization of the pace of monetary and credit expansion [between central banks] similar . . . to those which . . . limit divergent rates of expansion among private banks within each national monetary area" (p. 11), enforced by the constraint of convertibility into gold of fiduciary money.[79] Given stable exchange rates, then

national *export* prices remained strongly bound together among all competing countries, by the mere existence of an international market not broken down by any large or frequent changes in trade or exchange restrictions. . . . National price and wage levels also remained closely together internationally, even in the face of divergent rates of monetary and credit expansion, as import and export competition constituted a powerful brake on the emergence of any large disparity between internal and external price and cost levels. (p. 10)

As a consequence, monetary expansion generating

inflationary pressures could not be contained within the domestic market, but spilled out *directly* . . . into balance of payments deficits rather than into uncontrolled rises of internal prices, costs, and wage levels. These deficits led, in turn, to corresponding monetary transfers from the domestic banking system to foreign banks, weakening the cash position of domestic banks and their ability to pursue expansionary credit policies. (pp. 10–11)

[79] Following Keynes ([1923] 1971, [1930] 1971) and Cassel (1935), Triffin doubted the strength of the long-term equilibrating forces of the commodity theory of money and termed the gold discoveries of the nineteenth century favorable accidents temporarily reversing a tendency to secular deflation. Instead, "the reconciliation of high rates of economic growth with exchange-rate and gold-price stability was made possible by the rapid growth and proper management of bank money, and could hardly have been achieved under the purely, or predominantly, metallic systems of money creation characteristic of the *previous* centuries" (Triffin 1964, p. 15). Triffin (1960) foresaw that a gold-exchange standard based on key currencies, such as that which dominated the interwar and the post–World War II periods, would ultimately fail because of a growing threat to the convertibility of the key currencies as their use as international reserves increased.

Central banks could only temporarily slow down the adjustment process by engaging in offsetting open-market operations or using other tools of monetary policy, because ultimately their international reserve ratios would decline. Thus, in the gold standard world of fixed exchange rates, price levels were closely linked together and the balance-of-payments deficit (surplus) reflected both money-market disequilibrium and the method by which it was eliminated.

In an approach similar to that of Triffin, Williamson (1961, 1963) reinterpreted U.S. experience under the gold standard. He urged analysis of the balance of payments in a general-equilibrium context, with the long-swing cycle in the growth of real output determining specie and capital flows.[80] Increased real growth would lead to both an excess demand for goods (a balance-of-trade deficit), an excess supply of bonds (a capital inflow), and an excess demand for real balances. The excess demand for money would be satisfied by a specie inflow, with little change in the price level, accompanied by a long swing in capital inflows (Williamson 1961, p. 379). The external balance was both a cause as well as a reflection of the long swing, since in the 1830s it was British demand for U.S. cotton that was the key source of the long swing in output, which in turn induced British investment in railroads and canals.[81]

In an important article applying the recently developed monetary approach to the balance of payments to the operation of the classical gold standard from 1880 to 1914, McCloskey and Zecher (1976) extended the challenge to the traditional approach intimated by Marshall in the 1880s, endorsed by Whale in the 1930s, and repeated by Triffin and Williamson.

The monetary approach states that for an open economy with fixed exchange rates, the national stock of money, rather than prices, adjusts to changes in the public's demand for money (see Frenkel 1971; Johnson 1976; Mundell 1971). Contrary to the Hume price-specie-flow mechanism – which postulates significant lags in the adjustment of price – because of instant arbitrage, according to the monetary theory, no lags are observed in the adjustment of world prices. In the most rigid version of the theory, an increase in the demand for money cannot reduce prices because prices of internationally traded goods are determined in world markets and kept comparable in different countries by international arbitrage, and prices of domestic goods and services are kept in line with prices of internationally traded goods by domestic arbitrage. The reduction in the public's demand for goods and securities leads to reduced imports and expanded exports on the goods side and to higher interest rates and capital imports on the securities side. The current account or the capital account or both move into surplus. To prevent appreciation of the currency, the monetary authority buys foreign exchange from its nationals, paying out newly created high-powered money. The increase in high-powered money leads to a multiple expansion of the domestic quantity of money which continues until the public's demand is satisfied.

[80] See similar approaches by Abramovitz (1973) and Thomas (1973).
[81] In the postbellum period it was the foreign demand for wheat that was the key source of the long swing. Williamson's interpretation of the 1830s differs markedly from that of Macesich and Temin (n. 78), who each stressed the role of external monetary forces as the key disturbing factor.

In open economies on a fixed exchange rate, a once-for-all increase in the quantity of money in one country and a decrease in another would produce a balance-of-payments deficit in the first and surplus in the second and lead to a flow of money to the second until equilibrium was reestablished. If a monetary authority in one country alone increased high-powered money, that would be equivalent to an increase in the world money supply. That country would experience a temporary balance-of-payments deficit until the world money supply was redistributed in proportion to the size of the country of issue, and the world price level would rise accordingly. In the long run, domestic monetary policy in a small country has a negligible influence on international prices, although in the short run the monetary authority can affect its price and income level by open-market sales (purchases) equal to its balance-of-payments surplus (deficit) that will maintain the national money stock below (above) its equilibrium value. The closer the links among world commodity markets, the higher the degree of capital mobility, the less scope for independent monetary policy in the short run. The greater the elasticity of substitution between traded and nontraded goods, the less successful will such policy be. In the long run, however, independent monetary policy is inconsistent with fixed exchange rates.

McCloskey and Zecher tested the key assumptions of commodity arbitrage by examining correlations among price changes between countries and between regions within countries. For traded goods such as wheat, they found synchronous correlations equally high between regions as between nations, unlike the case of nontraded goods such as labor services and bricks. For overall price indexes, they found a significant correlation between the U.S. and U.K. wholesale price indexes, less so for GNP deflators, and even less for consumer price indexes. The higher correlation for the wholesale price than for the other index undoubtedly reflects the larger share of traded goods in the former.[82]

They conclude:

What has been established here is that there is a reasonable case . . . for the postulate of integrated commodity markets between the British and American economies in the late nineteenth century, vindicating the monetary theory. There appears to be little reason to treat these two countries on the gold standard differently in their monetary transactions from any two regions within each country. (McCloskey and Zecher 1976, pp. 379–80)

They also cite less conclusive evidence in favor of capital-market arbitrage. They tested their model by comparing gold flows – predicted by a simple demand for money function less the money supply produced by domestic credit expansion – with actual gold flows and found a close relationship. In their view,

we have established at least a prima facie case for viewing the world of the nineteenth century gold standard as a world of unified markets, in which flows of gold represented the routine satisfaction of demands for money. (p. 385)

---

[82] However, the evidence to date on commodity arbitrage, based on more recent evidence, is far from conclusive, with the majority of studies casting doubt on its effectiveness for other than internationally traded commodities (see Kravis and Lipsey 1978).

Capital movements

Both short-term and long-term capital movements play an important role in the traditional approach to the gold standard. Short-term capital flows were to act as an equilibrating mechanism, to economize on gold flows and to reduce the burden of adjustment by changes in relative price levels. Private short-term capital movements, assumed to be highly responsive to interest-rate differentials (induced by changes in the discount rate), would act to equate interest rates (adjusted for exchange risk) in different money markets. Morgenstern examined the evidence in favor of the "solidarity hypothesis," that arbitrage would ensure uniformity of interest-rate differentials to exchange risk (measured by the difference of the exchange rate from the gold points), and found it to be inconsistent with the principles of the gold standard. Borts, in criticizing both his methodology and data, put Morgenstern's conclusions into serious doubt. Bloomfield found evidence that private short-term capital flows responded to interest differentials and expected exchange-rate changes as predicted.

Long-term capital flows, a key disturbing force in the traditional approach, were believed to have been well accommodated by the gold standard balance-of-payments adjustment mechanism. They allowed both developing debtor nations and mature creditor nations to run persistent balance-of-payments disequilibria without requiring adjustment in the balance of trade. Bloomfield's study supported the integral role of long-term capital flows in the development of the "Atlantic economy."

Morgenstern (1959) examined short-term-interest-rate data of different maturities, exchange rates, and the gold points for four key gold standard countries: Great Britain, France, Germany, and the United States in the periods 1870–1914 and 1925–38, subjecting the "assumption of international solidarity of money markets" to three tests.[83]

The first test compared derived exchange rates, based on cross rates in third markets, with the actual exchange-rate series. If arbitrage were effective, differentials between the series would vanish. Morgenstern found evidence of differentials persisting in both periods, but more so after World War I, with the greatest deviations occurring in periods of crisis or disturbance such as the 1890 Baring crisis.

The second test identified deviations of exchange rates beyond the median gold import and export points. Violations persisted for long periods, with greater

---

[83] "When two (or more) countries are on the gold standard then there exist definite limits for the absolute differences between their short-term interest rates. The actual differences at a given moment depend on the absolute stand of the exchange rates at the same moment, which in turn can vary only between the gold points of the currencies. ... When the interest rates of two countries conform, then we say that their money markets are in a state of *solidarity*; when the differentials do not conform with the respective absolute positions of the exchange rates, i.e., when they exceed the respective "permissible limits," then we say that they *violate* that solidarity ... the principles of the gold standard" (Morgenstern 1959, pp. 166–68).

frequency of deviations beyond the gold export point than beyond the gold import point.

The third test compared market-interest-rate differentials with the "absolute maximum permissible" differential determined by the distance between the gold points. Violation of the principle occurred in both prewar and postwar periods.

Morgenstern concluded that we ought to view

the period of the classical gold standard as inadequately described by the typical mechanism at least in one respect: the interaction between two and more money markets via exchange rates and interest rates is not nearly as precise and rigid as postulated. (Morgenstern 1959, p. 569)

He explained these results by "friction" and central-bank intervention, suggesting the replacement of the interpretation of the gold standard as a mechanism by the notion that central banks and other market participants engage in game strategy in a struggle for gold. Borts (1964) criticized both Morgenstern's methodology and his data. Borts attributed the results of the first test comparing cross with own exchange rates to the methods of making exchange quotations. Morgenstern's data were either exchange quotations in the form of single prices at which brokers cleared the market or the average of bid-ask spreads. For Borts the bid-ask spreads were likely measures of transactions cost; hence "what appears to be an opportunity for arbitrage profit could be the difference between the clearing price and the prevailing practice of giving quotations" (Borts 1964, p. 225).

Borts found the results of the second test comparing the spot exchange rate with the gold points ambiguous. In deriving the gold points, Morgenstern assumed circumstances favoring his results since he took into account neither different methods of covering exchange risk nor frequent operations by the monetary authorities on the gold points. These ambiguities could be sorted out, according to Borts, by directly examining gold movements "in an effort to confirm the position of the exchanges with regard to the gold points" (p. 227).[84]

Finally, Morgenstern's third test comparing interest differentials to the maximum exchange risk on uncovered funds was faulty, in Borts's view, because (1) "[he converted] the percent movement in the exchange rate into a percent difference on one-year paper. The exchange risk . . . has no time dimension and exists no matter what the maturity of the paper held" (p. 227); (2) he did not account for possible forward cover.[85]

---

[84] Morgenstern explicitly rejected the available data on gold movements because his study (1955) found them to be unreliable. In that study, using official data of imports and exports of gold coin and bullion for the United States, Great Britain, Germany, France, and Canada and a sample of four years, 1900, 1907, 1928, and 1935, official gold exports from one country did not square with gold imports for another.

[85] "Without examining the future exchange prices, the author cannot make a case that the maximum permissible interest rate differentials were in fact violated. For the market will respond to the best opportunity. If New York interest went to a 1% premium over

Bloomfield examined the role of both short-term (1963) and long-term (1968) capital flows under the pre-1914 gold standard. He suggested that private short-term capital movements served to equilibrate the balance of payments in the short run by tending to reduce the size of gold flows or acting as substitutes for changes in official exchange holdings (Bloomfield, 1963, p. 44). To test the latter hypothesis, he compared the signs of the first differences of annual changes in the stock of net foreign short-term assets of commercial banks with annual changes in the stock of central-bank gold and foreign-exchange reserves of the Scandinavian countries and found the postulated negative relationship (p. 58).[86]

Long-term capital flows in the classical gold standard period in the form of portfolio investment came mainly from Britain and France, followed by Germany; the bulk of the funds went to the developing countries of the new world to finance the development of infrastructure and production and exportation of primary products. Following the work of Williamson (1964), Cairncross (1953), O'Leary and Lewis (1955), Thomas (1973), Bloomfield (1968, pp. 18–34) found evidence of a long-swing cycle in long-term capital movements. Consistent with their theories, he found for debtor countries positive correlations between capital imports and indicators of domestic investment such as domestic building, and between capital imports and net immigration; for creditor countries a negative correlation between capital exports and domestic investment, and a positive one between capital exports and net emigration.[87] These results, plus the evidence that similar long-swing movements in the United States and Canada in turning points were inversely related to swings in British building and economic activity in general, gave support to Thomas's (1973) thesis of an Atlantic economy. Finally, contrary to theory, interest rates did not explain movements in annual data of British capital exports and U.S. capital imports. In the multiple regressions that Bloomfield estimated, domestic and foreign investment activity were the significant regressors.

The managed gold standard

The mainstream view of the classical gold standard that emerged from the interwar period (appendix D) was that it evolved into a sterling standard. The concentration of world capital, commodity, and gold markets in London made the pound sterling an attractive reserve asset in addition to gold and made it easier for the Bank of England to control its gold-reserve ratio by altering Bank

London, Morgenstern would say the market was not operating perfectly. Yet with a premium on spot exchange, it would be perfectly consistent with the operations of a competitive market. The question of interest differentials which exceed the maximum exchange risk then involves the interest parities of forward exchange rates. Morgenstern did not examine this at all" (Borts 1964, p. 227).

[86] However, a similar test for Canada revealed no correlation (Bloomfield 1963, p. 65).

[87] For Canada and Sweden, merchandise exports in real terms also showed long swings that tended to lead those in other variables.

rate, in the process affecting the policies of other central banks and influencing economic conditions both at home and abroad.[88]

In the post–World War II period, the degree of management of the prewar standard was further explored. Key currencies other than sterling were shown to have been important in the pre–World War I period, though sterling's role was still predominant, and the Bank of England's use of the Bank-rate weapon was deemed to be less effective than traditionally believed (Lindert 1969). The ways in which the Bank of England managed the gold standard were described (Sayers 1936, 1957; Goodhart 1972).

Following Bloomfield (1963), Lindert (1969, pp. 13–27) found that holdings of several major currencies – the pound, the franc, and the mark – represented an important and growing fraction of the international reserves held by many countries in the period 1900–1913.[89] As expected, London was the primary reserve center for the world but francs and marks were popular on the Continent.

According to Lindert, key currencies were held for the interest income they earned; they involved lower transaction and transportation costs than gold, and maintenance of balances in a foreign currency such as sterling often gave easier access to credit in the London money market. Perhaps the key reason these currencies were held was that their good brand name guaranteed with certainty that they could be converted into gold on demand. In the case of the pound, the location in London of the international money market and the world's gold market likely enhanced its brand name.

Because their currencies were widely held, the central-reserve countries could run larger balance-of-payments deficits than otherwise and could maintain them longer. However, each central bank was sensitive to its gold-reserve ratio and when it declined the bank would react by raising its discount rate.[90] Lindert found that when Great Britain raised the Bank rate, other central banks on the Continent would respond, but London had stronger "pulling" power and could always attract short-term funds from the Continent.[91] A flow of short-term funds proceeded from peripheral European nations, running balance-of-payments sur-

---

[88] Scammel (1965) echoed this view by stating "it is, in the writer's view, arguable that the gold standard was in fact quasi-organizational, being operated by a team of central bankers cooperating under the leadership of the Bank of England on behalf of the world business community" (p. 34).

[89] Foreign-exchange reserves accounted for 19 percent of total world reserves in 1913. Japan, Russia, and India held the largest fraction of their reserves in sterling.

[90] Of four effects of a rise in discount rate to correct the balance of payments, Lindert ruled out the effect on aggregate demand as involving too lengthy a lag to account "for the remarkable smoothness and rapidity with which exchange rates, international gold flows, and gold reserves of central banks seem to have been altered." Moreover he found the lag between changes in Bank rate and import prices also to be too long to be relevant, and the evidence on the effect on new issues of long-term foreign securities to be unclear. Hence only the effect on short-term funds operated as the key channel of influence of Bank rate (1969, pp. 43–47).

[91] As a test of the relative "pulling" power of the different currencies, Lindert (1969, p. 50) regressed each exchange rate on the other two exchange rates, on its own discount rate, and the second center's rate. He found a hierarchy of dominance running from London to Paris to Berlin.

pluses to Paris and Berlin, and then to London. The asymmetry in discount-rate drawing power may be explained by the fact that for the center countries, short-term foreign assets tended to be less liquid than short-term liabilities; "since tighter monetary policy tends to stimulate shifts toward liquid assets, banks would react by seeking greater key-currency balances at the expense of bills on lesser centers" (Lindert 1969, p. 78).

Thus, the indisputable position of London as the dominant financial center during the prewar years meant that "other countries, had, therefore, to adjust their conditions to hers."[92]

After the publication of *Lombard Street* (Bagehot [1873]1969), the Bank of England began to take seriously its responsibilities for both maintaining convertibility and preventing domestic monetary instability, doing so not by increasing its gold reserves, as Bagehot suggested, but by altering its discount rate whenever its gold reserves were threatened (Sayers 1951, pp. 109–10).

Sayers described the prewar techniques used to make Bank rate "effective" in the sense of linking it tightly to short-term market rates. The methods included open-market operations, eligibility requirements, and the switch to a penalty rate in 1878.[93] In addition, under special circumstances, when it feared the internal repercussions of raising the Bank rate, the Bank would protect its gold reserve by using "gold devices" – direct operations in the gold market. It is generally agreed, however, that the Bank achieved full control over its reserves after 1890 (Presnell 1968).

According to the traditional approach, a rise in Bank rate would equilibrate the balance of payments via two principal channels: by inducing a short-term capital inflow (reducing an outflow) and by checking domestic economic activity, the domestic price level, and the price of imports. Lindert (1969, pp. 43–44), Bloomfield (1959, p. 42), and Goodhart (1972, chap. 15) evaluated the evidence for the domestic channel as indicating at best a weak and protracted adjustment with the case for the link via capital flows sacrosanct. The case made against the domestic channel was twofold: the limited response of the domestic money supply to changes in the Bank of England's gold reserve, and the limited response of domestic economic activity to changes in the interest rate.

With respect to the money supply, Goodhart (1972, p. 208) was unable to detect any close, positive association between the cash base (reserves) of the

---

[92] Quotation from the Macmillan report (1931, p. 125) in Lindert (1969, p. 49). The fact that London and the other centers could maintain "deficits without tears" in the pre–World War I period ultimately led to a weakening of the balance-of-payments adjustment mechanism because the longer the process continued, the more difficult it became "to undertake the contractionary measures that would have been required to restore payments 'equilibrium'" (Lindert 1969, p. 79). Also see Triffin (1960).

[93] Additional methods used were the outright sale or purchase of securities, selling consols spot and buying for the account, borrowing in the market, borrowing from clearing banks, borrowing from special depositors, and moral suasion.

After 1878, the Bank lent to its own customers at the market rate of interest, while at the same time it charged discount houses a penalty rate above the market rate. "The position of the penal rate was *ordinarily* a matter of daily concern and therefore influential over the market rate itself" (Sayers 1951, p. 115).

commercial banks, represented by bankers' balances at the Bank of England, and the Bank's gold reserves.

According to him, the direction of causation was the reverse of the traditional one. An increase in economic activity would lead to an increase in commercial-bank lending and deposits, and the increase in bank reserves required to maintain stable reserve ratios would be supplied by the Bank of England at the expense of its other discounts, thus producing both a lower gold-reserve ratio at the Bank of England (the proportion) and a higher discount rate. The rise in the discount rate would then lead to a gold inflow restoring the Bank's proportion.[94]

Goodhart concluded (1972, p. 219):

Indeed, on this view, the great years of the gold standard (1890–1914) were remarkable, *not* because the system enforced discipline and fundamental international equilibrium on this country by causing variations in the money supply, but because the system allowed for the development of such large-scale, stabilising and equilibrating, short-term, international capital flows, that autonomous domestic expansion was rarely disrupted by monetary or balance of payments disturbances.

With respect to domestic economic activity, Tinbergen (1950, p. 133) found that

the influence of interest rates on the course of investment activity – which is the chief influence interest rates exert, according to our results – is only moderate. A rise in interest rates depresses investment activity, but only to a modest extent . . .

and Pesmazoglu (1951, p. 61) that

variations . . . in the long-term rate of interest did not have an important influence on fluctuations of British home investment between 1870 and 1913.[95]

The rules of the game

According to the traditional approach, the key objective of monetary policy was to maintain convertibility into gold and to use monetary policy, specifically the discount rate, to facilitate internal adjustment to external disequilibria. However, Bloomfield (1959, pp. 25–26) found that while central banks were primarily

---

[94] Goodhart's analysis follows closely that of Whale (1937). Both Goodhart's and Whale's results can be reinterpreted as consistent with the monetary approach to the balance of payments. According to that approach, a rise in economic activity in an open economy such as Great Britain would generate an excess demand for money that would be satisfied in part by a gold inflow. Indeed Mills and Wood (1978), applying the Granger-Sims causality test to the pre–World War I U.K. money supply and national-income data, found that income caused money, evidence that they considered sympathetic to the monetary approach.

[95] Also see A. G. Ford (1977, p. 42), who cites similar evidence on investment activity.

concerned with maintaining convertibility, their policy actions were discretionary, not automatic:

Not only did central banking authorities . . . *not* consistently follow any simple or single rule or criterion of policy, or focus exclusively on considerations of convertibility, but they were constantly called upon to exercise, and did exercise, their judgment on such matters as whether or not to act in any given situation and, if so, at what point of time to act, the kind and extent of action to take, and the instrument or instruments of policy to use. . . . It does indicate that discretionary judgment and action were an integral part of central banking before 1914, even if monetary management was not oriented toward stability of economic activity and prices in the broader modern sense.

In a test of the extent to which central banks under the pre-1914 gold standard played by the rules of the game, Bloomfield interpreted the rules as meaning "that central banks were supposed to *reinforce* the effect of these flows [gold flows] on commercial bank reserves, not merely not to neutralize them. This implied . . . that central banks were supposed to lower their discount rates in the face of persisting gains of gold . . . and to raise them when there were persisting losses." Such a policy would have the effect of "increasing central bank holdings of domestic earning assets when holdings of external reserves rose, and of reducing domestic assets when reserves fell" (Bloomfield 1959, p. 47).

Following Nurkse's approach in his examination of central-bank behavior in the 1929–38 period, Bloomfield compared year-to-year changes in international and domestic assets for twelve central banks in the 1880–1914 period and found that, in the case of every central bank, the changes in the two classes of assets were more often than not in the opposite direction (with the Bank of England coming close to being the exception to the rule).

Thus,

Far from responding invariably in a mechanical way, and in accord with some simple or unique rule, to movements of gold . . . , central banks were constantly called upon to exercise, and did exercise, discretion and judgment in a wide variety of ways. Clearly the pre-1914 gold standard system was a managed and not a quasi-automatic one from the viewpoint of the leading individual countries. (Bloomfield 1959, p. 60)

Based on their reinterpretation of the classical gold standard according to the monetary approach to the balance of payments, McCloskey and Zecher (1976) denied that the Bank of England could have "acted as conductor of the international orchestra" as in Keynes's ([1930] 1971) description, but "was no more than the second violinist, not to say the triangle player, in the world's orchestra" (McCloskey and Zecher 1976, pp. 358–59).

The monetary theory holds that the world's economy is unified by arbitrage and that the world's price level is determined by the world's money supply. Then the Bank of England's

potential influence on prices (and perhaps through prices on interest rates) depended simply on its power to accumulate or disburse gold and other reserves available to support the world's supply of money.... Only by decreasing the securities and increasing the gold it held ... could the Bank exert a net effect on the world reserves.... Had the Bank in 1913 sold off all the securities held in its banking department it would have decreased world reserves by only 0.6 percent; had it sold off all the gold in its issue department, it would have increased world reserves by only 0.5 percent. (McCloskey and Zecher 1976, p. 359)

Finally, according to McCloskey and Zecher, the central banks of the world ignored the rules of the game – stipulating that a deficit in the balance of payments be accompanied by contractionary monetary policy, a surplus by expansionary policy – because the rules were "inconsequential." According to the monetary theory "neither gold flows nor domestic deflation have effects on prevailing prices, interest rates, and incomes" (p. 361) since the central bank of a country adhering to the gold standard could control the composition of the monetary base only as between international reserves and domestic credit, not its total amount.

References

Abramovitz, Moses. 1973. The monetary side of long swings in U.S. economic growth. Memorandum no. 146, Stanford University Center for Research on Economic Growth. Mimeo.

Andrew, A. P. 1907. The Treasury and the banks under Secretary Shaw. *Quarterly Journal of Economics* 21 (Aug.): 519–68.

Angell, J. W. [1925] 1965. *The theory of international prices.* Reprint. New York: Augustus M. Kelley.

Bagehot, W. [1873] 1969. *Lombard Street.* Reprint of the 1915 edition. New York: Arno Press.

Beach, W. 1935. *British international gold movements and banking policy, 1881–1913.* Cambridge: Harvard University Press.

Bloomfield, Arthur I. 1959. *Monetary policy under the international gold standard.* New York: Federal Reserve Bank of New York.

  1963. *Short-term capital movements under the pre-1914 gold standard.* Princeton Studies in International Finance, no. 11. Princeton: Princeton University Press.

  1968. *Patterns of fluctuation in international investment before 1914.* Princeton Studies in International Finance, no. 21. Princeton: Princeton University Press.

Bordo, M. D. 1975. John E. Cairnes on the effects of the Australian gold discoveries, 1851–73: An early application of the methodology of positive economics. *History of Political Economy* 7 (no. 3): 337–59.

  1983. Some aspects of the monetary economics of Richard Cantillon. *Journal of Monetary Economics* 12 (Aug.): 235–58.

Borts, G. H. 1964. Review of *International financial transactions and business cycles*, by O. Morgenstern. *Journal of the American Statistical Association* 59 (Mar.): 223–28.

Brown, William A. 1940. *The international gold standard reinterpreted, 1914–1934.* New York: National Bureau of Economic Research.

Bullion report. 1810. See *Report . . . on the high price of bullion* [1810] 1978.

Cairncross, Alec K. 1953. *Home and foreign investment, 1870–1913.* Cambridge: Cambridge University Press.

Cairnes, J. E. [1873] 1965. *Essays in political economy: Theoretical and applied.* Reprint. New York: Augustus M. Kelley.

Cantillon, R. [1931] 1964. *Essai sur la nature du commerce en général.* Ed. H. Higgs. Reprint. New York: Augustus M. Kelley. (First published 1755.)

Cassel, Gustav. 1935. *The downfall of the gold standard.* Oxford: Clarendon Press.

Chevalier, M. 1859. *On the probable fall in the value of gold! The commercial and social consequences which may ensue, and the measures which it invites.* Translated from the French by Richard Cobden. 3d ed. Manchester: A. Ireland.

Cunliffe report. [1918] 1979. *See* United Kingdom, Parliament [1918] 1979.

Dick, Trevor. 1981. Canadian balance of payments, 1896–1913: Mechanisms of adjustment. Mimeo.

Fetter, Frank W. 1965. *The development of British monetary orthodoxy, 1717–1875.* Cambridge: Harvard University Press.

1953. The Bullion Report re-examined. In *Papers in English monetary history*, ed. T. S. Ashton and R. S. Sayers. Oxford: Clarendon Press.

Fisher, I. 1920. *Stabilizing the dollar.* New York: Macmillan.

[1922] 1965. *The purchasing power of money.* Reprint. New York: Augustus M. Kelley.

1935. Are booms and depressions transmitted internationally through monetary standards? *Bulletin of the International Statistical Institute* 28 (no. 1): 1–29.

Ford, A. G. 1962. *The gold standard, 1880–1914: Britain and Argentina.* Oxford: Clarendon Press.

1977. International financial policy and the gold standard, 1870–1914. Mimeo.

Frenkel, J. 1971. A theory of money, trade, and the balance of payments in a model of accumulation. *Journal of International Economics* (May): 159–87.

Friedman, M., and A. J. Schwartz. 1963. *A monetary history of the United States, 1867–1960.* Princeton: Princeton University Press.

Girton, L., and D. Roper. 1978. J. Laurence Laughlin and the quantity theory of money. *Journal of Political Economy* 86 (Aug.): 599–625.

Goodhart, C. A. E. 1972. *The business of banking, 1891–1914.* London: Weidenfield and Nicolson.

Goschen, G. J. [1892] 1978. *The theory of the foreign exchanges.* Reprint. New York: Arno Press.

Graham, F. D. 1922. International trade under depreciated paper: The United States, 1862–79. *Quarterly Journal of Economics* 36 (Feb.): 220–73.

Gregory, T. E. [1932] 1979. *The gold standard and its future.* Reprint. New York: Arno Press.

Hawtrey, R. G. 1935. *The gold standard in theory and practice.* 5th ed. London: Longmans Green.

Hume, D. [1752] 1955. Of the balance of trade. Reprint. In *Writings on economics,* ed. E. Rotwein. Madison: University of Wisconsin Press.

Jevons, W. S. [1884] 1964. *Investigations in currency and finance.* Reprint. New York: Augustus M. Kelley.

Johnson, H. G. 1976. The monetary approach to balance of payments theory. In *The monetary approach to the balance of payments,* ed. J. Frenkel and H. G. Johnson. Toronto: University of Toronto Press.

Jonung, Lars. 1979. Knut Wicksell and Gustav Cassel on secular movements in prices. *Journal of Money, Credit, and Banking* (May): 165–81.

Keynes, J. M. [1913] 1971. *Indian currency and finance.* Vol. 1 of *The collected writings of John Maynard Keynes.* Reprint. London: Macmillan and New York: Cambridge University Press for the Royal Economic Society.

[1923] 1971. *A tract on monetary reform.* Vol. 4 of *The collected writings. See* Keynes [1913] 1971.

[1930] 1971. *The applied theory of money: A treatise on money.* Vol. 6 of *The collected writings. See* Keynes [1913] 1971.

Kindahl, J. K. 1961. Economic factors in specie resumption. *Journal of Political Economy* 69 (Feb.): 30–48.

Kravis, Irving B., and Robert E. Lipsey. 1978. Price behavior in the light of balance of payments theories. *Journal of International Economics* 8 (May): 193–246.

Kuhn, T. 1970. *The structure of scientific revolutions.* 2d ed. Chicago: University of Chicago Press.

Laidler, D. 1981. Adam Smith as a monetary economist. *Canadian Journal of Economics* 14 (May): 185–200.

Laughlin, J. L. 1903. *The principles of money.* New York: Scribner's.

League of Nations. [1931] 1979. *Reports of the gold delegation: Interim report of the gold delegation of the financial committee.* Reprint. New York: Arno Press.

Lindert, Peter H. 1969. *Key currencies and gold, 1900–1913.* Princeton Studies in International Finance, no. 24. Princeton: Princeton University Press.

Macesich, G. 1960. Sources of monetary disturbances in the U.S., 1834–45. *Journal of Economic History* 20 (Sept.): 407–34.

Macmillan report. 1931. *See* United Kingdom, Parliament 1931.

Marshall, Alfred. 1923. *Money, credit, and commerce.* London: Macmillan.

1926. *Official papers.* London: Macmillan.

McCloskey, D. N., and J. R. Zecher. 1976. How the gold standard worked, 1880–1913. In *The monetary approach to the balance of payments. See* Johnson 1976.

Meier, Gerald M. 1953. Economic development and the transfer mechanism: Canada, 1895–1913. *Canadian Journal of Economics and Political Science* 19 (Feb.): 1–19.

Mill, J. S. [1865] 1961. *Principles of political economy.* Reprint. New York: Augustus M. Kelley.

Mills, T. C., and C. E. Wood. 1978. Money-income relationships and the exchange rate regime. *Federal Reserve Bank of St. Louis Review* 60 (Aug.): 22–27.

Mints, L. 1945. *A history of banking theory in Great Britain and the United States.* Chicago: University of Chicago Press.

Morgenstern, Oskar. 1955. *The validity of international gold movement statistics.* Special Papers in International Economics, no. 2. Princeton: Princeton University Press.

   1959. *International financial transactions and business cycles.* Princeton. Princeton University Press.

Mundell, R. 1971. *Monetary theory.* Pacific Palisades, Calif.: Goodyear.

Nurkse, R. [1944] 1978. *International currency experience.* Reprint. New York: Arno Press. (First published by the League of Nations.)

O'Leary, P. J., and W. Arthur Lewis. 1955. Secular swings in production and trade, 1870–1914. *The Manchester School* 23 (May): 118–25.

Palyi, Malchior. 1972. *The twilight of gold, 1914–1936: Myths and realities.* Chicago: Henry Regnery.

Pesmazoglu, J. S. 1951. A note on the cyclical fluctuations of British home investment, 1870–1913. *Oxford Economic Papers* 3 (Feb.): 39–61.

Presnell, L. S. 1968. Gold reserves, banking reserves, and the Baring crisis of 1890. In *Essays in money and banking in honour of R. S. Sayers,* ed. C. R. Whittlesey and J. S. C. Wilson. Oxford: Clarendon Press. *Report from the select committee on the high price of bullion.* [1810] 1978. New York: Arno Press.

Ricardo, D. [1811] 1951. High price of bullion: A proof of the depreciation of bank notes. In *The works and correspondence of David Ricardo,* ed. Piero Sraffa, 3. Cambridge: Cambridge University Press.

   [1816]. 1951. Proposals for an economical and secure currency; with observations on the profits of the Bank of England as they regard the public and the proprietors of Bank stock. In *The works and correspondence of David Ricardo. See* Ricardo [1811] 1951.

Rich, G. 1978. The cross of gold: Money and the Canadian business cycle. 1867–1913. Mimeo.

Samuelson, P. 1971. An exact Hume-Ricardo-Marshall model of international trade. *Journal of International Economics* 1 (Feb.): 1–11.

Sayers, R. S. 1936. *Bank of England operations, 1890–1914.* London: P. S. King and Son.

   1957. *Central banking after Bagehot.* Oxford: Clarendon Press.

   1951. The development of central banking after Bagehot. *Economic History Review,* 2d ser., 4 (no. 1): 109–16.

   1953. Ricardo's views on monetary questions. In *Papers in English monetary history. See* Fetter 1953.

Scammel, W. M. 1965. The working of the gold standard. *Yorkshire Bulletin of Economic and Social Research* 17 (May): 32–45.

Silverman, A. G. 1931. Some international trade factors for Great Britain, 1880–1913. *Review of Economics and Statistics* 13 (Aug.): 114–24.

Smit, J. C. 1934. The pre-war gold standard. *Proceedings of Academy of Political Science* 13 (Apr.): 53–61.

Smith, A. [1776] 1976. *An inquiry into the nature and causes of the wealth of nations.* Reprint. Chicago: University of Chicago Press.

Taussig, F. W. 1917. International trade under depreciated paper, a contribution to theory. *Quarterly Journal of Economics* 21 (May): 380–403.

Taussig, F. W. [1927] 1966. *International trade.* New York: Augustus M. Kelley.

Temin, P. 1969. *The Jacksonian economy.* New York: W. W. Norton.

Thomas, B. 1973. *Migration and economic growth.* 2d ed. Cambridge: Cambridge University Press.

Thornton, H. [1802] 1978. *An inquiry into the nature and effects of the paper credit of Great Britain.* Fairfield, N.J.: Augustus M. Kelley.

Tinbergen, J. 1950. *Business cycles in the United Kingdom, 1870–1914.* 2d ed. Amsterdam: North-Holland.

Triffin, Robert. 1960. *Gold and the dollar crisis.* New Haven: Yale University Press.

1964. *The evolution of the international monetary system: Historical reappraisal and future perspectives.* Princeton Studies in International Finance, no. 12. Princeton: Princeton University Press.

United Kingdom. Parliament. [1918] 1979. *First interim report of the committee on currency and foreign exchanges after the war.* Cmnd. 9182. Reprint. New York: Arno Press.

1931. *Report of the committee on finance and industry.* (Macmillan report). Cmnd. 3897. London: HSMO.

Viner, Jacob. 1924. *Canada's balance of international indebtedness, 1900–1913.* Cambridge: Harvard University Press.

[1937] 1975. *Studies in the theory of international trade.* Reprint. New York: Augustus M. Kelley.

1932. International aspects of the gold standard. In *Gold and monetary stabilization*, ed. Q. Wright. Chicago: University of Chicago Press.

Whale, P. Barrett. 1937. The working of the pre-war gold standard. *Economica* 4 (Feb.): 18–32.

White, H. D. 1933. *The French international accounts, 1880–1913.* Cambridge: Harvard University Press.

White, L. H. 1981. Free banking in Britain: Theory, experience, and debate, 1900–1945. Ph.D. diss., University of California at Los Angeles.

Wicksell, Knut. [1898] 1965. *Interest and prices.* Reprint. New York: Augustus M. Kelley.

Williams, D. 1968. The evolution of the sterling system. In *Essays in money and banking in honour of R. S. Sayers. See* Presnell 1968.

Williams, John. 1920. *Argentine international trade under inconvertible paper money, 1800–1913.* Cambridge: Harvard University Press.

1947. Gold and monetary stabilization. In *Postwar monetary plans and other essays.* New York: Knopf.

Williamson, Jeffrey G. 1964. *American growth and the balance of payments, 1820–1913.* Chapel Hill: University of North Carolina Press.

1961. International trade and U.S. economic development 1827–1843. *Journal of Economic History* 21 (Sept.): 372–83.

1963. Real growth, monetary disturbances, and the transfer process: The U.S., 1879–1900. *Southern Economic Journal* 29 (Jan.): 167–80.

CHAPTER 4

John E. Cairnes on the effects of the Australian gold discoveries, 1851–73: An early application of the methodology of positive economics

4.1   Introduction

John E. Cairnes (1823–75) is considered to be the last important economist of the British Classical tradition, a close follower of John Stuart Mill
and "the most eminent of the English Economists of this period who
undertook to mend the structure [of J. S. Mill]."[1] Cairnes was most highly
regarded by his contemporaries; indeed Mill expressed his admiration
for him in the preface to the sixth edition of his *Principles*, calling him
"one of the most scientific of living political economists."[2]

Cairnes is best remembered today for his contributions to the methodology of economic science and for the theory of noncompeting groups.
In addition, his popular writings on slavery and on the effects of the
Californian and Australian gold discoveries gave him an audience far
wider than the ranks of political economists.

The present chapter will examine Cairnes' writings on the effects of
the gold discoveries as a case study of the methodology of positive
economics – that the test of a good theory lies in its ability to predict
rather than the realism of its assumptions.[3] The chapter will be based
mainly on Cairnes' principal published work on the gold discoveries – his
"Essays Towards a Solution of the Gold Question (1858–60)."[4] As well,

This chapter is reprinted from Michael D. Bordo (1975), *History of Political Economy*,
7(3):337–359.

I would like to thank the following for their helpful suggestions: George Stigler, E. G.
West, Thomas K. Rymes, John McManus, Anna J. Schwartz, Mark Blaug, Samuel Hol-
lander, and two referees from *History of Political Economy*. I, of course, accept full
responsibility for any errors. In addition, I am grateful to Mr. Eli Weinberg for permitting
me to examine the research of his late wife, Adelaide Weinberg, on Cairnes' unpublished
"Lectures on Money" (1864/65).

[1] J. Schumpeter, *History of Economic Analysis* (New York, 1966), p. 533.

[2] J. S. Mill, *Principles of Political Economy*, 6th ed. (London, 1865).

[3] See M. Friedman, "The Methodology of Positive Economics," in *Essays in Positive
Economics* (Chicago, 1954).

[4] These essays appear in John E. Cairnes, *Essays in Political Economy: Theoretical and
Applied* (1873; New York, 1965).

however, we will examine some of his other writings – his articles in the *Economist* and the *Report of the British Association for the Advancement of Science*,[5] his unpublished Manuscripts on Gold,[6] and his unpublished "Lectures on Money"[7] given at Galway 1864/65. Though Cairnes' work on the gold discoveries has long been recognized as a contribution to positive economics,[8] this study hopes to shed new light on the subject.

In addition, we will briefly examine Cairnes' important writings on methodology – *The Character and Logical Method of Political Economy* (1857) and *Some Leading Principles in Political Economy Newly Expounded* (1874) – in order to compare his prescriptions on the proper methods to be applied by the economist to his own empirical studies of the gold question. It will be argued that Cairnes' empirical work does not differ markedly from his prescriptions on methodology.

Finally, since an important motivation for much of Cairnes' empirical research was to provide ammunition for his attack on the poor theorizing of some of his contemporaries, we will examine the work of William Newmarch and others on the gold question.

4.2   Cairnes' Essays on Gold as a case study of positive economics

Cairnes used the monetary history of the Australian colonies following the gold discoveries of 1851 to test some of the principal conclusions of classical monetary and trade theory. Specifically, in the course of the "Essays" and elsewhere Cairnes tested the ability of the quantity theory of money to predict the comparative static effects of the gold discoveries on the money supplies and price levels of the major countries of the world, the ability of Ricardo's theory of comparative advantage to predict Australia's switch from being a net exporter to a net importer of agricultural products, the ability of the Humean international adjustment mechanism to predict the distribution of precious metals, and the ability of his version of the Cantillon transmission mechanism to

---

[5] Cairnes. "On Some of the Principal Effects of the New Gold, as an Instrument of Purchase, in the Production and Distribution of Real Wealth." *Report of the British Association for the Advancement of Science* 27 (1857), transactions pp. 156–58. Idem, "Have the Discoveries of Gold in Australia and California Lowered the Value of Gold?" *Economist*, 30 May 1863. Idem, "The Consequences of the Gold Discoveries," *Economist*, 27 June 1863.

[6] Cairnes, unpublished Manuscripts on Gold, National Library of Ireland. MS 8984.

[7] Cairnes, unpublished "Lectures on Money" given at Galway 1864/65. National Library of Ireland, MS 8981, transcribed by A. Weinberg.

[8] See William D. McDonnell, "Prediction as a Test in Political Economy," *Economic Review* 4 (Oct. 1894): 477–89; and J. N. Keynes, *The Scope and Method of Political Economy* (London, 1917), p. 271.

predict the dispersion of price changes between different commodity groupings. Twelve years after writing the *Essays*, Cairnes compared his predictions with the evidence and found them, for the most part, to be substantiated.

Cairnes' purpose in writings the *Essays* was to demonstrate conclusively to his contemporaries that increases in the quantity of money caused by the gold discoveries of 1848 and 1851 explain the subsequent fall in the value of money. Furthermore he wished to lay bare the fallacy that "a depreciation of money could only show itself in a uniform action upon all prices."[9] by tracing out explicitly the course of depreciation.

4.2.1   *Cairnes's monetary theory*

By the quantity theory of money Cairnes meant the relationship between the quantity of money and its value or its purchasing power.[10] By money he meant gold and silver coins as well as Bank of England notes. Like Mill he distinguishes between credit (which includes commercial bank notes, bank deposits, and bills of exchange) and the circulating medium or money, but he acknowledges that credit also has an important influence on prices.[11]

Like Mill and Senior[12] he distinguishes between the short-run quantity theory and the long-run. In the short run the value of money is determined by the interaction of the quantity of money supplied and the quantity demanded, given the volume of transactions, or to put it another way, by the ratio of money times its velocity (rapidity of circulation) to the volume of transactions. In the long run, the volume of money (in the cases of both a full-bodied currency and a convertible mixed circulation) depends upon the cost of obtaining precious metals:

"with all other factors being equal"

[9] Cairnes, *Essays* (supra n. 4), p. 9.

[10] Cairnes never explicitly used the phrase "quantity theory of money." In his "Lectures on Money" (supra n. 7), Lectures on Currency II, he called it the "First elementary law of money – that, ceteris parbus, its value varies inversely as its quantity."

[11] "Now credit, whatever be the form which it assumes, so long as it is credit, will operate on purchases and affect prices in exactly the same way as if it were actually the coin which it represents." *Essays* (supra n. 4), p. 95. In his Lectures on Currency II, he has an extended discussion on the proper definition of money. The basic distinction between money and credit is whether prices are affected permanently or temporarily. He argues that credit will affect prices only temporarily because its ability to do so depends on the public's belief in the solvency of the issuer, while only currency possessing intrinsic value or convertible notes given artificial value by law can permanently affect prices.

[12] Mill (supra n. 2). N. Senior, *Three Lectures on the Cost of Obtaining Money, and on Some Effects of Private and Government Paper Money* (1830; London, 1931).

The value of a circulating medium, convertible on demand into gold, of course, depends in the long-run on the cost of obtaining gold; but its value at any given time and the fluctuations in its value, are determined by the quantity which happens to be in circulation, compared with the functions which it has to perform, and its efficiency in performing them: – that is to say, the value of a circulating medium depends on three conditions; the quantity of it in circulation; the number of exchanges which it has to accomplish; and its efficiency, or as it is called in technical language, "the rapidity of circulation." . . . The number of exchanges to be performed depends upon the state of commerce in the country; the rapidity of the circulation depends on the commercial facilities at the disposal of the public, the state of public confidence, etc.[13]

Note that unlike Ricardo, but like Mill, Cairnes does not postulate a strict proportional relationship between the quantity of money and the price level, since he explicitly considers velocity to be an economic variable.[14] Also he emphasizes the short-run effects on real income and employment of changes in the quantity of money.[15] In short, for Cairnes the neutrality of money is a comparative static proposition which holds only in the long run.[16]

---

[13] J. E. Cairnes, *An Examination into the Principles of Currency Involved in the Bank Charter Act of 1844* (New York, 1966), p. 18. Also for a clear elucidation of the long-run theory of money see Cairnes, "Consequences" (supra n. 5), p. 705: "It follows that wages and profits in gold mining afford a constant and accurate measure of the cost of gold; and since these afford the standard to which wages and profits in other departments of industry in the same country conform, the general rate of wages and profits in gold countries (measured in gold) obviously afford the criteria of which we are in search. Every advance in these denotes a corresponding decline in the cost of gold, every decline a corresponding advance."

[14] See Cairnes (supra n. 7), Lectures on Currency II, for a comprehensive discussion of the determinants of velocity.

[15] See Cairnes, *Report* (supra n. 5), p. 157, where he discusses two possible ways in which increases in the quantity of money can have real effects: "first, by practicing some illusions on the understanding, so as to induce men to undergo a greater sacrifice for a given reward than formerly; or secondly, by causing such a change in the distribution of wealth, as might, at the expense of the idle or less actively producing classes and nations, operate as a premium on its production."

[16] Cairnes was well aware of the distinction between nominal and real magnitudes which has led to so much confusion in modern-day monetary theory. In his *Essays* he repeatedly refers to the gold discoveries as causing a fall in real income. A gold discovery either at home or abroad involves the use of real resources – labor and capital, which, if full employment is assumed, would be better employed elsewhere. The extraction of nominal gold involves a once-and-for-all resource loss in terms of real income forgone in other sectors of the economy. This resource loss if it occurs abroad is transferred around the world by the gold-producing country trading its new gold for real products. See *Essays* (supra n. 4), pp. 44–46. Furthermore, he applies this argument in favor of fiduciary note issues to save on the resource cost of using a full-bodied currency: "Where a country does not itself yield gold or silver" – in a footnote he says even if it does, the labor and capital used in obtaining it could be better employed elsewhere – "every increase of its metallic circulation must be obtained – can only be obtained – by parting with certain elements of real wealth. It is in enabling a nation to reduce within the

The Classical writers distinguished two mechanisms by which changes in the quantity of money affect economic activity (nominal income): the direct and the indirect. According to the direct mechanism, individuals (on average) hold a desired quantity of real cash balances (a given number of weeks' income in the form of cash), and if there is an unexpected increase in the quantity of money, distributed equiproportionately, people will attempt to spend their excess cash balances. Since one man's expenditure is another's receipt, this process will lead to an increase in the level of nominal income and, assuming full employment, to an increase in prices, until the real value of cash balances is restored to its original level. This mechanism is to be distinguished from the indirect mechanism generally attributed to Thornton[17] in which it is assumed that excess cash balances are spent in the securities market, an increase in the quantity of money leading to an excess demand for securities, a rise in their prices, and hence a fall in the rate of interest. This fall in the rate of interest will stimulate investment expenditures and will lead to a rise in nominal income.

In the *Essays* as well as his other works Cairnes places his main emphasis on the direct mechanism. However, in his "Lectures on Money," Lecture IV, the Rate of Interest, he argues that new money will affect the rate of interest to the extent it affects the demand for and supply of loanable funds:[18]

The rate of interest, we know, does not depend on the quantity of money in a given country or in the world, but on the quantity of money disposable on loan as compared with the number and needs of borrowers . . . an increase in currency may either produce one effect or the other, according to the circumstances. What circumstances? According to the way in which the new money is employed. If it

---

narrowest limits this unproductive portion of its stock, that the chief advantage of a good banking system consists; and if the augmentation of the metallic currency of a country be not an evil, then it is difficult to see in what way the institution of banks is a good." However, in his Lectures on Currency II (supra n. 7), Cairnes argues strongly against eliminating the use of coin altogether because coin is required to give confidence to a currency, and "by confidence in the stability of values is meant . . . confidence in the substantial stability in the value of that commodity by which we are in the habit of estimating others, at all events, over periods which affect the great mass of commodity transactions."

[17] H. Thornton, *An Enquiry into the Nature and Effect of the Paper Credit of Great Britain* (1802; New York, 1965).

[18] Note the similarity between Cairnes' views on interest theory and that expressed by H. G. Johnson. "Monetary Theory and Policy," *Essays in Monetary Economics* (Cambridge, Mass., 1967), p. 45, in his summary of the issues involved in the liquidity preference versus loanable funds controversy of the 1950s. Much of the discussion in the "Lectures on Money" on capital theory and the rate of interest is derived from J. Cairnes, "Capital and Currency," *North British Review* 28, no. 55 (Feb.–May 1858): 191–230.

comes into the hands of persons who prefer lending to spending it, the increase of money will depress the rate of interest. If, on the other hand, the new additions come into the hands of persons who prefer spending it to lending it, their effect will be to raise the rate of interest. It does this by raising prices and thus increasing the needs of the borrowers. The latter was what happened in the gold countries. The new gold came in the first instance into the hands of miners, who either spent it unproductively or employed it in carrying on mining operations; in either case the effect was to raise prices, and thus to increase the needs of borrowers without increasing the loan fund.

Probably Cairnes' most important theoretical contribution was his extension of Cantillon's analysis of the dynamic effects following a change in the quantity of money in his *Essays on the Effects of the Gold Discoveries*. According to Cairnes the dynamic effects on prices and real output of a change in money depend upon "the first round," i.e., the way in which new money is introduced into the economic system. Thus the adjustment mechanism within any country depends upon who receives the new cash, what it is spent on, and the relative elasticities of demand and supply in the different sectors of the economy. The adjustment mechanism between countries depends upon the importance of international trade to each country and the degree of development of the banking systems. As we shall see, Cairnes predicted (with considerable accuracy) the course of depreciation in the exchange value of gold both within the gold-producing countries and across the world.

Finally, Cairnes' analysis of the international monetary adjustment mechanism is derived mainly from Hume and Mill. In the *Essays* he demonstrated how Californian and Australian gold is carried across the world through the initial export of new gold to England and the eastern United States in exchange for real goods and services, and then how the new gold raises the price level in these countries and is transmitted through a deficit in the balance of trade to the rest of the world. In the *Essays* the adjustment mechanism is strictly Humean – the increased circulation raises domestic prices, leading to a rise in the prices of exports relative to imports, a balance-of-trade deficit, and a gold outflow, with no explicit reference to the additional influence on the adjustment process of changes in the interest rate and capital flows. However, this secondary mechanism is mentioned in the *Currency Principles* (supra n. 13, p. 35), as well as the influence of changes in real income.

4.2.2   Cairnes' application of theory

In the first essay on gold, "The Australian Episode" (1859), Cairnes examined the effects of the gold discovery on prices and output in the

Australian economy. Initially, he argued, the gold discoveries of 1851 led to a substantial increase in the wages of gold miners with the decline in the amount of labor required to obtain a given amount of gold. This increase in gold wages was then quickly transmitted to the rest of the economy and reflected in a rise in all domestic prices. However, before prices and wages could rise, he argued, the new gold had first to appear as additions to the existing currency. Indeed, in the first few months after the discovery, he pointed out, the value of gold bullion fell relative to coin because of the absence of a mint in Australia; i.e., prices did not rise as much as would be expected from the increased supplies of gold, and it was only with the arrivals of new gold sovereigns from England that prices rose at the expected rate.[19] The rise in the prices of all domestic commodities rapidly changed Australia's comparative advantage from a producer of pastoral products to gold production and converted her from a net exporter to a net importer of food.[20] The resource loss caused by the diversion of real resources from agriculture to gold mining was then transmitted abroad as Australia traded new gold for foreign agricultural and manufactured products.[21]

Cairnes argued further that "the rate of gold earnings ... is ... the circumstance which in the first resort, regulates the value of the metal and sets the limit beyond which depreciation cannot permanently pass,"[22] and since gold earnings increased by 50 percent, i.e., the cost of gold fell by one-half, he expected that the price level in Australia would double. The inflation process would continue across the world until either prices doubled or else the cost of producing gold rose:

Whether that value will ever be lowered in the same proportion, whether gold will ever fall throughout the world at large as it has fallen in Australia and California depends upon whether the conditions which have lowered its value in them can be generally satisfied – that is to say, depends upon whether the

[19] Lectures on Currency II (supra n. 7).

[20] In his *Some Leading Principles of Political Economy Newly Expounded* (New York, 1900), p. 215, Cairnes says "I have always regarded the commercial results of the Australian and Californian discoveries (for things in California followed a very similar course) as one of the most striking experimental verifications which a purely abstract doctrine [Ricardo's theory of comparative cost] has ever received."

[21] Cairnes, *Essays* (supra n. 4), pp. 37–40.

[22] Ibid., p. 41. In the *Essays*, Cairnes uses earnings and wages interchangeably; however, in the *Economist*, 27 June 1863, p. 705, he argues that though "wages and profits measured in gold, afford a constant criterion of the cost of gold ... the element of profit forms but a small proportion of the whole return to the industry ... [and] variations in profits seldom amount to more than a very small fraction of the whole. With a view therefore to practical purposes we shall not go seriously wrong if we simply omit profits altogether. We thus reach the conclusion ... that the rate of gold wages ... forms an approximately correct criterion of the cost of obtaining gold."

increased supply which such a fall would render necessary can be obtained at the present cost.[23]

Finally, he argued, as prices in the rest of the world rise, gold would become a less profitable commodity to produce and export, until, in the limit when the price of Australian imports increased by the amount of the fall in the cost of gold, Australia would cease to have a comparative advantage in gold and would divert resources back to agriculture.[24]

In keeping with his positivist methodology, Cairnes examined the evidence on Australian commodity trade twelve years later and found, as predicted, that both (a) exhaustion of the mines leading to rising costs of production[25] and (b) rises in the price of imports led to a considerable shift of resources out of gold production and back into agriculture. This was reflected, comparing 1870 to 1856, in a decline in annual gold production in Victoria from £12 million to £6 million, an increase in non-gold exports from £3.5 million to £6.3 million, a decline in total commodity trade from £15.5 million to £12.5 million, and a doubled population.[26]

In the second essay, "The Course of Depreciation" (1858), Cairnes examined the factors influencing the transmission process within Australia following the gold discoveries, as well as the factors influencing its international distribution. In this essay he demonstrated that a non-uniform advance in prices is consistent with the quantity theory of money.

Cairnes distinguished two processes by which an increase in the quantity of money raises prices: a direct process whereby the increased gold operates "through the medium of an enlarged money demand," and an indirect process operating "through a contraction of supply."[27]

In the direct process, an increase in the cash balances of the miners is quickly spent in an attempt to restore their real cash balances to their

[23] *Essays*, p. 42.

[24] Ibid., p. 48. Also see McDonnell (supra n. 8), p. 487: "I have claimed for Ricardo the credit of having, in substance, predicted the immediate results of the gold discoveries. To Cairnes is due the honour of having, not in substance merely, but in the most minute detail, predicted their remote consequences."

[25] It is important to note that Cairnes fails to distinguish clearly between technical exhaustion of the gold mines – a depletion in the stock of gold – and economic exhaustion representing a rising marginal cost curve in gold production. Thus, on p. 50 of the *Essays* he refers to "failing gold mines," on p. 51 to "diminishing returns of her gold mines." Again, on p. 49 he states "until through the exhaustion of the present gold fields, gold can no longer be produced at its present cost."

[26] *Essays*, pp. 50–51.

[27] Ibid., p. 56.

original level.[28] This increased expenditure leads to increased prices of the commodities purchased; the increased prices then induce producers to increase output, tending to reduce prices again; but in order to increase production, firms must demand more labor, and once full employment is reached, this will lead to a rise in wages. Finally, in order to maintain profits, all firms must then increase their prices.[29]

In the indirect process, a rise in wages in industries directly affected by the new gold expenditure will lead to a rise in wages in other industries (assuming perfect labor mobility); this will lower profits in these industries and tend to discourage production; the resultant decline in supply will raise prices until "that point which will place the producers on the same footing of advantage as those in other walks of industry."[30]

At this stage, Cairnes argued, the sectoral distribution of price advance depends, first, on "the direction of the new expenditure; secondly [on] the facilities for extending the supply of different kinds of commodities; and thirdly, [on] the facilities for contracting it" – in modern terms, upon the short-run elasticities of demand and supply and the pattern of shifts in the various demand and supply curves.[31]

The direction of new expenditure, he stated, is determined by "the habits and tastes of the people who first receive the new money." These, he argues, would be mainly low-income people, indicating that goods with low-income elasticities would be first affected.[32]

The facilities for extending supply depend on two circumstances; "(1) the extent to which machinery is employed in production; (2) on the degree in which the process of production is independent of natural agencies which require time for accomplishing their ends."[33] Thus, he distinguished between crude and manufactured products, and within crude products, between animal and vegetable products.

Cairnes predicted that prices of crude products would rise more rapidly than those of manufactured goods, while within crude products, animal-product prices would rise faster than vegetable-product prices because of the greater difficulty involved in increasing output.[34]

The facilities for contraction of supply in the indirect case depend on

---

[28] In the *Essays*, Cairnes did not clearly distinguish between a once-and-for-all change in the quantity of money and a continuous increase; nor did he mention whether the increased cash is anticipated or not, thus omitting any discussion of the effects of the gold discoveries on velocity. However, in his Lectures on Currency II (supra n. 7), he states that the gold discoveries by raising "the state of commercial confidence" raised velocity.

[29] *Essays*, p. 58.

[30] Ibid., p. 59.

[31] Ibid., p. 58.

[32] Ibid., p. 59.

[33] Ibid., p. 60.   [34] Ibid.

the amount of fixed capital employed. Thus he predicted that the production most difficult to contract would be that of manufactured products: "manufactured articles can never be very long in advance of the general movement of prices, [but] they may, of all commodities, be the largest in arrear of it."[35]

Next, Cairnes examined the factors which determine the rapidity of price adjustment across countries. He argued that the rise in prices would be most rapid in the countries which have the most advanced banking systems, that "the quantity of metallic money necessary to support any required advance of prices throughout a given range of business will vary with the character of the currency into which it is received; that the quantity received will be greater in proportion as the metallic element of the currency is greater; and on the other hand, less in proportion as the credit element prevails."[36]

He argued that the more developed the system of banking and credit, the less will be the amount of new gold required to effect a given rise in prices. On this basis he expected that "a given addition to the metallic stock of Great Britain or the United States, in whose monetary systems credit is very efficacious, will cause a greater expansion of the total circulation, and therefore will support a greater advance in general prices, than the same addition to the currency of countries like France, in which credit is less active, . . . still less in India and China whose currencies are almost purely metallic."[37] Furthermore he argued that since Australia and California conduct most of their trade with the United States and England, one would expect that most of the new gold would go first to these countries and from them it would spread to the continent of Europe and to Asia.[38]

To test his predictions on the rate of price dispersion both within countries and between countries, Cairnes compared the prices of commodities in the three broad groupings of manufactures, animal, and vegetable products, for every year from 1848 to 1858, for each of Australia, the United States, Great Britain, the Continent, and Asia. In his experiment he accounted for two distorting influences: the normal tendency for the prices of manufactured goods to decline with the rapid technological progress of the 1850s; and the additional inflationary im-

---

[35] Ibid., p. 64. One difficulty that arises here is Cairnes' asymmetric treatment of the capital stock in the direct and indirect cases. In the direct case an increase in demand leads to an increase in output with no mention of a change in the stock of capital, while in the indirect case the contraction of output does require a change in the stock of capital. It would appear that the direct case refers to the short run, while the indirect case refers to the long run.
[36] Ibid., p. 66.
[37] Ibid.   [38] Ibid., pp. 67–69.

pact of increases in credit, which he attempted to minimize by ending his comparison with the postpanic year of 1858. In general he found the evidence agreeable to his predictions. Across countries, prices increased most in Australia, then Great Britain and the United States, then the Continent, and finally Asia. Within countries, prices of manufactured goods increased least, followed by the prices of vegetable and mineral raw materials and then by the prices of wool, meat, and tallow. Finally, reexamining the evidence twelve years later in 1872, he found both the price dispersion within countries and the movement of prices between countries to be generally in accord with his predictions. The only major exception to his predictions was the United States in the period 1858–68, which experienced a much greater inflation as a result of the Civil War–induced issues of paper money.[39]

Neither the third essay, "International Results" (1860), nor the fourth, "Summary of the Movement: M. Chevalier's View" (1860), contains very much that was not discussed in the first two essays. In the third essay, Cairnes stressed the advantage to each country of rapidly expanding its money supply and price level by the same amount as the fall in the cost of producing gold, to avoid the resource loss from trading real goods and services for gold:[40]

As has been already stated, the local value of gold in Australia and California has fallen to one half, – the prices of their production having risen in a two fold proportion; and prices in other parts of the world having undergone no corresponding change. . . . The world has thus, through the gold discoveries, been placed in its dealings with California and Australia at a commercial disadvantage; and from this disadvantage it can only escape (always supposing the present conditions of producing gold to continue) by raising the prices of its production

[39] Ibid., pp. 74–76, 347–59. Furthermore, in the *Economist*, 30 May 1863, p. 592. Cairnes is encouraged by the fact that Jevons in independent research reaches the same results. "This absolute coincidence . . . in the results of two independent inquiries affords, I submit, solid grounds for confidence in the soundness of the common conclusions to which they have conducted; but, to give due weight to this corroboration, it should be added, that these conclusions have been reached, not merely by independent investigators, but by investigators pursuing perfectly distinct paths. The view advanced in the latter of the two extracts [Cairnes's] was based exclusively upon economic, as distinguished from statistical grounds and was indeed distinctly put forward as an economic speculation; whereas it is from statistical data above that Mr. Jevons' conclusions are derived." Also, for further discussions on Jevons' investigations, see J. Cairnes' letter to the editor, "The Alleged Depreciation of Gold," *Times*, 9 Sept. 1863.

[40] In an important sense the third essay has a modern ring. Proponents of the recently developed monetary theory of the balance of payments – see H. G. Johnson, "The Monetary Approach to Balance of Payments Theory," in *International Economics: The Geneva Essays*, ed. M. Conally and A. Swoboda (London, 1973) – have recently (1971) urged surplus countries such as West Germany to increase the domestic credit component of the monetary base to capture the seigniorage which would normally accrue to the issuers of modern day gold, the U.S. government.

in a corresponding degree. Every country, therefore, is interested in raising as rapidly as possible the prices of its productions. . . . The sooner this is effected, the sooner will the country be returning to its natural commercial footing in relation to Australia and California; while in relation to countries where prices do not rise with the same rapidity, it will possess the same kind of advantage which is now enjoyed by the gold countries.[41]

It is also in this essay that Carirnes stated his preference for a fiduciary currency, condemned the augmentation of monetary gold as an evil, and discussed the influence of credit on prices.

In both essays, he expanded upon his earlier discussion of the transmission of precious metals around the world. He argued that England and the United States because of their efficient banking and credit systems should gain relative to France and the rest of the Continent, since they would require less gold to finance the necessary price rise. The gold flowing out of England and into France would serve to displace silver, since France was on a silver standard. This displacement of silver would for a time act as a parachute preventing French prices from rising until gold completely replaced silver,[42] at the same time that the released silver would flow eastward into the silver currencies of Asia, augmenting gold flowing there directly. At this point, in an argument similar to that of Jevons,[43] Cairnes pointed out that the "parachute effect" would not be as important as Chevalier maintained in preventing a rise in French prices, since gold and silver can be considered as substitutes, so that as gold currency is substituted for silver, the price of silver will tend to fall along with the price of gold.

The final result of the movement would be that "while the metallic systems of England and the United States are receiving but small permanent accession, those of India and China are absorbing enormous supplies."[44] Thus India and China will in the long run become the permanent victims of the monetary disturbances."[45]

In a postscript to the fourth essay, Cairnes reported that (a) world gold production doubled by 1868 and (b) most of the gold ended up in France and India, although much of it passed through England.[46]

---

[41] *Essays*, pp. 84–85.

[42] The "parachute effect" is first attributed to M. Chevalier. *On the Probable Fall in the Value of Gold* (1857), p. 142.

[43] W. S. Jevons, "A Serious Fall in the Value of Gold Ascertained," in *Investigations in Currency and Finance* (London, 1909). Also see Cairnes, "Consequences" (supra n. 5), p. 704, his Manuscripts on Gold (supra n. 6), and his letter to the *Times*, 9 Sept. 1863.

[44] Cairnes, *Essays*, p. 95.

[45] Ibid., p. 99.

[46] Ibid., pp. 160–65. It is important to note that J. S. Mill did not completely agree with Cairnes on the mechanism by which the new gold is transmitted around the world. In a letter to Cairnes dated 26 Dec. 1863, he states: "Shortly before the gold discoveries, there had begun to take place, and has been taking place ever since, a great increase of

To conclude our discussion of the *Essays* I should like to ask the question: How do Cairnes' predictions on the long-run effects of the gold discoveries compare with better evidence than he had available to him? To answer this question, Table 4.1 compares for both the United States and Great Britain the average annual percentage change in the monetary gold stock, the price level, real output, and the money supply (for the United States only) between 1849 and 1858, and between 1849 and 1868, the years Cairnes used as benchmarks.

Since reliable British monetary data are unavailable, and I am not convinced of the accuracy of Cairnes' gold stock estimates,[47] more emphasis should be placed on the U.S. data. In general the evidence substantiates Cairnes' predictions. In the first period, in both countries, prices did not rise as much as did the gold stock (and the money supply in the United States), and the difference, as Cairnes explained, is largely accounted for by substantial increases in real output. In the second period, the relationship between gold, prices, and output remains the same in England but not in the United States, since in the 1860s the country was on a flexible exchange rate and virtually all of the increases in money were caused by government issues of irredeemable paper currency.

4.3   Cairnes' views on methodology

In *The Character and Logical Method of Political Economy* (1st ed. 1857), Cairnes sets forth the Classical View on the methodology of

facilities of communication and a great enfranchisement of trade; having for their necessary effect to bring the price of many commodities in different parts of the world, far nearer to equality than they had ever been before. Had there been no gold discoveries, this equalization would have taken place, partly indeed by a rise of prices in the more remote and poorer regions of the earth, but partly also, and perhaps still more, by a fall of prices in the great manufacturing countries. The influx of gold had first to make this phenomenon disappear, before its effect would be apparent at all in a rise of English prices. During the interval it would be steadily rising prices in the distant countries and in those which export raw produce. In those countries the gold would co-operate with other causes tending to a rise; in England it would be acting in opposition to causes tending to a fall; *consequently there would be little or no rise of prices in England until there had been a rise in the distant markets sufficient to bring about that nearer approximation of prices in the two regions, which corresponds to the increased facilities of trade* [emphasis mine]. This . . . would account for the rise of general prices in England being in a considerably less ratio than that of the increased quantity of gold in the world." F. E. Mineka and D. N. Lindley, eds., *Collected Works of John Stuart Mill: The Later Letters, 1849–73*, vol. 15 (Toronto, 1972), p. 976.

[47] An alternative and more recent source of reference on the British monetary gold stock, the National Monetary Commission, *Statistics for Great Britain, Germany, and France, 1867–1909* (Washington, 1910), Table 5, p. 75, uses the same data for the 1840s and 1850s as did Cairnes, i.e., Newmarch's estimates; but for 1868 it uses Jevons' estimate of £80 million, which produces only a 56 percent increase in gold from 1846 to 1868.

Table 4.1. *Average annual percentage changes in gold and prices after 1848*

	1849–1858	1849–1868[a]
England		
Monetary gold stock (1)	4.4%	3.7%
Prices (2)	2.4	1 5
(3)	2.0	1.0
Real output (4)	3.2	3.1
United States		
Monetary gold stock (5)	8.2	0
Money supply (6)	6.8	8.8
Prices (7)	4.0	3.4
Real output (8)	5.4	n.a.

[a] For the United States the second comparison is between 1849 and 1869 because of the lack of available money, gold, and real-output estimates for 1860–68.
Sources by row: (1) Cairnes, *Essays* (supra n. 4), pp. 101, 163. (2) Sauerbeck-Statist Wholesale Price Index, in Mitchell and Deane, *Abstract of British Historical Statistics* (Cambridge, 1962), p. 474. (3) W. S. Jevons (supra n. 43), p. 145. (4) Hoffman index of industrial production, in Mitchell and Deane (1962), p. 272. (5) M. Friedman and A. Schwartz, *Monetary Statistics of the United States* (New York, 1970), Table 13. (6) Friedman and Schwartz (1970), Table 13. (7) Warren and Pearson, Wholesale Price Index, in *Historical Statistics of the United States* (U.S. Department of Commerce, 1961), p. 101. (8) R. Gallman, unpublished real GNP series available at the National Bureau of Economic Research. Because of difficulties in reconciling the base year of Gallman's implicit price deflaters, before and after the Civil War, I do not repeat any entry for the second period.

economic science. This comprehensive treatise on methodology, which shows similarity to the views of both Mill and Senior,[48] had a strong influence on J. N. Keynes in his classic work *The Scope and Method of Political Economy* (1917; see supra n. 8). Perhaps the most memorable contribution made by Cairnes in this work was the distinction between "positive economics which is concerned with 'what is' and normative economics which is concerned with 'what ought to be.'"

Cairnes argued that political economy was an abstract science – abstract because "it has to leave out of account many circumstances which are of importance in individual cases but unimportant when instances are taken in the mass."[49]

[48] Although, as M. Bowley, *Nassau Senior and Classical Economics* (New York, 1949), points out, there are some notable dissimilarities.
[49] J. N. Keynes (supra n. 8), p. 14.

Economic laws are based on two crucial premises: the basic desire for human wealth, derived from introspection; and the physical constraint of nature.[50] Furthermore these premises represent "positive fact" like those of the premises of physics,[51] i.e. they are above testing.

Cairnes' belief in the inviolability of the basic premises of economics differs from the views of Friedman – that assumptions do not have to be real to be important to a theory[52] – but is similar to the extent that it implies that the testability of the assumptions of economic theory is not important.

Next, on the basis of these premises, as well as "secondary influences which influence human conduct in the pursuit of wealth"[53] such as political and social institutions, we can derive "hypothetical conclusions" – conclusions which "when applied to facts can only be said to be true in the absence of disturbing causes; which is, in other words, to say that they are true on the hypothesis that the premises include all the causes affecting the results."[54]

Furthermore, Cairnes argues that political economy like physical science has reached the deductive stage:

> Its premises are not arbitrary figments of the mind, formed without reference to concrete existences, like those of Mathematics; nor are its conclusions mere generalized statements of observed facts, like those of the purely inductive natural sciences. But like Mechanics or Astronomy, its premises represent positive facts; while its conclusions, like the conclusions of these sciences, may or may not correspond to the realities of external nature, and therefore must be considered as representing only hypothetical truth.[55]

Induction is not suitable for economics because of the difficulty of conducting an experiment in the rigorously scientific sense of the word – in view of the complexity of human interactions in preventing the establishment of a perfectly controlled environment.[56] However, he argues, in the absence of direct experimentation the economist can use hypothetical cases as an inferior substitute. Thus

although precluded from actually producing the conditions suited to his purpose, there is nothing to prevent the economist from bringing such conditions before

---

[50] J. E. Cairnes, *The Character and Logical Method of Political Economy*, 2d ed. (1875; New York, 1965), p. 52.

[51] Ibid., p. 62.

[52] See Friedman (supra n. 3), p. 14: "Truly important and significant hypotheses will be found to have 'assumptions' that are wildly inaccurate descriptive representations of reality, and in general, the more significant the theory, the more unrealistic the assumptions (in this sense)."

[53] Cairnes, *Character*, p. 57.

[54] Ibid., p. 61.

[55] Ibid., p. 62.   [56] Ibid., p. 77.

his mental vision, and from reasoning as if these only were present, while some agency comes into operation – whether it be a human feeling, a material object, or a political institution – the economic character of which he desires to examine.[57]

Finally, since it is possible in using hypothetical experiments to overlook an important condition or for there to be a flaw in "the reasoning by which the action of the particular cause under consideration is established," the economist should supplement the "process in question" with "such sorts of verification as economical inquiry admits of."[58] If possible, he should compare his hypothesis to a real-world case which approximates it and then he should "observe how far the results realized in the actual case correspond with his hypothetical conclusions; and in case, as would usually happen, the correspondence was not complete, he would have to consider how far the discrepancy admitted of being explained by reference to the presence of *known disturbing causes*" (emphasis mine).[59]

Thus, for Cairnes, empirical evidence should be used both as a test of the theory and as a way of determining whether we have left out an important parameter. This differs from the view that the only test of a theory is how well it predicts.[60]

However, in a later work, *Some Leading Principles of Political Economy Newly Expounded* (1874), Cairnes makes a statement which is closer in meaning to that of the positive methodology if we take the view that explanation and prediction are one and the same: "the only test by which a theory is justified . . . [is that of] explaining facts, and if it be a new theory, . . . explaining facts not explicable, or not so simply explicable, by received theories."[61]

And finally in his "Lectures on Money" he states that "though we cannot prove an economic law from statistics: we may use statistics to

---

[57] Ibid., p. 90.   [58] Ibid., p. 92.

[59] Ibid. Compare this statement to that of J. S. Mill. "We cannot too carefully endeavour to verify our theory, by comparing . . . the results which it would have led us to predict, with the most trustworthy accounts we can obtain of those which have been actually realized. . . . The discrepancy between our anticipations and the actual fact is often the only circumstance which would have drawn our attention to some important disturbing cause which we had overlooked." *Essays on Some Unsettled Questions of Political Economy* (1844; London, 1948), p. 154.

[60] See M. Blaug, "The Empirical Content of Ricardian Economics," *Journal of Political Economy* 64 (1956): 47: "The Classical economists were agreed . . . that economics was a deductive science based on simple premises derived from experience and conscious introspection. Methodological disputes took the form of disagreement over the relative significance and sufficiency of the underlying assumptions on which the whole deductive structure was built. Whether the structure itself was empirically meaningful was a question which was never squarely considered."

[61] Cairnes, *Some Leading Principles* (supra n. 20), p. 20.

verify a law; i.e. we may show that the facts are such as fall in fairly with the course of things the law would lead us to expect."[62]

In sum, Cairnes' writings on methodology do not place him squarely in the Friedman camp – though his discussion of the basic premises of economics being "positive fact" can be interpreted as being close to Friedman's views on assumptions, and though he discusses both the importance of being able to test hypotheses and the use of predictability as a test – since he still believes that an important function of empirical evidence is to search for disturbing causes, i.e., to make the assumptions as complete as possible.

To assess Cairnes' contribution to positive economics we must rely on his empirical work; and as we have seen, there he certainly placed great weight on the systematic use of evidence to illustrate theory and to assess the predictions of theory. Indeed his return to the data twelve years after publishing the *Essays* is a unique and by modern standards a very useful research strategy. Whether Cairnes would have been willing to discard a theory whose predictions were not consistent with the evidence is an interesting question. On the one hand, in his "Lectures on Money," in seeking ways to reduce the discrepancies between his own theoretical expectations and the evidence, he resorts to the search for disturbing causes;[63] while on the other hand, he was not above using the evidence to reject somebody else's theory.[64]

4.4   Cairnes and his contemporaries

The rationale for much of Cairnes' and later W. S. Jevons'[65] writings on the effects of the gold discoveries is to defend the quantity theory of money from the criticism of contemporary economists and commercial writers.[66] Because of the lack of accurate price indexes, and because the substantial increase in the world's money supply in the 1850s was also accompanied by rapid growth in real income in most countries, many

---

[62] Cairnes (supra n. 7), Lectures on Currency II.

[63] The tendency to seek out disturbing causes to explain deviations from theoretical expectations is a practice commonly used by modern empirical economists. Indeed, why should one give up a "good" theory because of a single contrary piece of evidence unless there is reason to believe both that the evidence has been adequately constructed and that the paradox it suggests can be explained by an alternative theory that is more adequate in this narrow sense and is also potentially more fruitful as a research program?

[64] See Section 4.4., on William Newmarch.

[65] "A Serious Fall" (supra n. 43).

[66] See R. Sayers, "The Question of the Standard in the Eighteen Fifties," *Economic History*, Jan. 1993; and C. D. W. Goodwin, "British Economists and Australian Gold," *Journal of Economic History*, vol. 30 (1970).

writers felt that the classical link between the quantity of money and the price level was broken.

Chief among Cairnes' antagonists and the person who is criticized most in his work is William Newmarch, a well-known commercial writer and co-author with Thomas Tooke of volume 6 of the *History of Prices*. In a series of articles in the *Report of the British Association for the Advancement of Sciences* and in the *History of Prices*,[67] Newmarch examined exactly the same phenomena as did Cairnes: the gold discoveries in Australia and their effects on prices and incomes there; and the transmission of new gold around the world. He arrived at vastly different conclusions.

Basically Newmarch argues that the main effect of the new gold was not to raise the price level but to increase real income:

It is not true that even an increase by one third of the quantity of metallic money has led to a corresponding increase of general prices; nor in the case of large groups of commodities, to any increase of price whatsoever; but, on the contrary, that prices have rather sunk to a lower, than risen to a higher level.[68]

And

the real and vital changes which have taken place, are additions to the Real Wealth of the World, by means of greater Production and more active Enterprise; and that the elements of Circulation and Price have so far not been ultimate results, but inferior and ultimate agencies employed.[69]

Finally, he says:

To increase, therefore, the Stock of Money is almost the same thing as to impart to production that impulse which would be communicated by the conversion of a common Turnpike into a Railway; . . . And to increase the Stock of Money year by year, is very much the same thing as to construct, year by year, a new and additional Network of Railways, . . . it follows that, an addition to the quantity of money is the same thing as an addition to the Fixed Capital of the Country.[70]

In both the *History of Prices* and his articles, Newmarch argues that the new supplies of gold led to increased ("Trebled and Quadrupled") incomes of both workers and capitalists in the gold-mining industry, that the spending of this new gold acted to directly stimulate industry and

---

[67] W. Newmarch, "Facts and Statements Connected with the Question, Whether, in Consequence of the Discoveries Within the Last Six Years, the Exchangeable Value of Gold in This Country Has Fallen Below Its Former Level," *Report of the British Association for the Advancement of Science* 24 (1854); T. Tooke and W. Newmarch, *A History of Prices*, vol. 6 (London, 1857).

[68] Tooke and Newmarch, p. 194; and for a similar statement see Newmarch, *Report*, p. 143.

[69] Tooke and Newmarch, p. 193.   [70] Ibid., p. 216.

employment in other sectors,[71] that it also led to a fall in the rate of interest which further stimulated demand,[72] and that it was then distributed throughout the world "in proportion to the skill and resources of each country in the production of Exportable Goods in demand in the Gold Regions."[73] Within England, the increased income generated by exports to the gold countries directly stimulated spending and raised production.[74] Finally, over time, prices would rise, tending to neutralize the real effects of the increased money supply.[75]

Later in a detailed analysis of the events in Victoria, Australia, in 1851, Newmarch argues that immediately after the discoveries the price of bullion fell by 20 percent below its current value and that despite a shortage of coin, prices rose because the increased bullion, acting as an increase in capital in the hands of the workers, was quickly spent. He then argues that high prices were the cause for an increase in coin and bank notes in 1853 and 1854.[76]

Cairnes, in both his "Lectures on Money" and in the *Essays*, takes Newmarch to task on three counts: bad theorizing, neglecting important disturbing causes, and misreading the evidence.

First, he criticizes Newmarch's analogy of increases in the stock of money to the conversion of a common turnpike into a railway as a failure to distinguish between nominal and real magnitudes – it would hold only "if the value of money were fixed."[77]

Second, he attacks Newmarch's interpretation of the Victorian inflation of 1851 as not being caused by increases in the quantity of money, for neglecting to consider other important conditions, viz., "the quantity of business transacted during this time representing the functions of money; the employment of credit; and the rapidity of circulation."

Cairnes notes that immediately following the discoveries, there was a general disorganization of industry as people left for the gold fields, that this led to a fall in the volume of trade, tending to raise prices; as well as that the Bullion Act of 1852 in South Australia permitted the banks to issue notes against bullion, thus acting to increase the quantity of money there and subsequently in neighboring states; and finally that velocity increased with the optimism engendered by the discoveries.[78]

---

[71] Ibid., p. 189.   [72] Ibid.   [73] Ibid., p. 210.
[74] Ibid., p. 213, and *Report* (supra n. 67), p. 110.
[75] Tooke and Newmarch, p. 217.
[76] Ibid., pp. 30, 808.
[77] Cairnes (supra n. 7), Lecture II. The Cost of the Precious Metals Regulating Their Values.
[78] In the same lecture he criticizes R. Torrens' interpretation of the events of 1851. Torrens (R. Torrens, *Sir Robert Peel's Act Explained and Defended*, 3d ed., p. 386) had argued that the quantity theory does not hold because according to it, the gold discoveries

Finally, as we have seen in Section 4.2, Cairnes, through a systematic analysis of the data in the *Essays on Gold*, demonstrates that there was indeed a substantial worldwide increase in prices, i.e., that Newmarch misread the empirical evidence.

The key difference between Newmarch and Cairnes appears to be one of methodology. While Cairnes systematically used the quantity theory of money to explain the facts of the gold discoveries, Newmarch started from the facts and then tried to construct a plausible theoretical explanation. As a result, Newmarch never put forward a coherent competing theory of money. For Cairnes, economic theory was paramount, and the real world of commercial affairs served as a valuable source of evidence to illustrate and test theory; for Newmarch, the real world of commercial affairs was paramount, and economic theory was used occasionally to impart some order into his explanation of current events.

Throughout his work, Cairnes systematically attacked the writings of commercial writers in the *Times*, the *Examiner*, and other journals for their inability to use economic theory to separate the important from the unimportant causes of events. Perhaps his most stinging attack is on the writers who subscribe to the "absorption principle."

In *The Character and Logical Method*[79] he attacks a writer in the *Examiner* (13 Dec. 1856) who

> maintains that not only has gold not fallen in value in consequence of the recent discoveries, but that it has never fallen in consequence of former discoveries; . . . that the additional supply of the precious metals has stimulated the industry of the world, and in fact produced an amount of wealth, in representing which they have been themselves, as it were absorbed.

Says Cairnes

> It is to be regretted that the writer did not favour us with his notion of the manner in which the alleged "stimulus" to industry operates, and the supposed absorption is effected. The stimulus, it seems is not felt, according to the popular view, in a rise of price; for this, he asserts, the new gold has no tendency to produce: nor does it take place through an increase of demand, for this could only manifest itself through a rise of price; nor does it operate through a fall in the rate of interest, for it is notorious that during recent years the rate of interest has been high; while with the modus operandi of "absorption," we are equally left in ignorance.

"Such attempts," he argues,

> should have led to a fall in the value of money; instead they led to a rise. Besides criticizing Torrens for getting his facts on the direction of change in the value of money wrong, Cairnes criticizes him for neglecting the fact that initially the quantity of sovereigns in circulation was limited because of the lack of a mint in Australia.

[79] Cairnes (supra n. 50), pp. 137–38.

at an explanation of economic phenomena remind us of some of the physical speculations of the Schoolmen . . . [e.g.,] a doctrine maintained by these philosophers that a vessel full of ashes would contain as much water as an empty vessel. The mysterious capacity of "absorption" which in this case was attributed to the ashes, is by the political economist of the Examiner attributed to wealth and population.

In sum, Cairnes' systematic use of theory to explain economic events and his ability to systematically marshal evidence to test theory certainly gave him a decided edge over most of his contemporaries.

4.5 Conclusions

Cairnes' contribution to positive economics stems mainly from his careful and interesting application of the positive methodology in his *Essays Toward a Solution of the Gold Question*. The idea of tracing out the effects of new gold on the economic system was not original; it can be traced back to Jean Bodin in the sixteenth century,[80] but Cairnes' use of his theory to predict the course of depreciation and the distribution of the new gold, and then his subsequent examination of the evidence twelve years later, are novel and would be considered today a very useful strategy.

Cairnes' views on methodology differ from those of Friedman over the question of the realism of assumptions, but are similar in the placing of emphasis on prediction as a test of theory. Moreover, Cairnes' invocation of disturbing causes to explain deviations from expected theoretical results is consistent with modern practice.

Despite differences in substance, Cairnes' distinction between positive and normative economics and his discussion on the verification of the conclusions of economic theory influenced J. N. Keynes and ultimately helped spawn Friedman's explicit elucidation of a methodology of positive economics.

---

[80] Jean Bodin, "Response au paradoxe de Malestroit touchant l'enchérissement de toutes choses." English version in *Early Economic Thought*, ed. A. E. Monroe (Cambridge, Mass., 1924), pp. 123–41.

PART II

The gold standard as a commodity standard

CHAPTER 5

The classical gold standard: Some lessons for today

The widespread dissatisfaction with almost two decades of worldwide inflation has prompted interest in a return to some form of a gold standard.[1] Some crucial questions must be answered, however, before such interest can be taken seriously. Two questions immediately come to mind: How did the actual gold standard operate? What was its record for providing stable prices and overall economic stability?

This chapter attempts to answer these two questions. It focuses primarily on what is commonly referred to as the "Classical Gold Standard," which prevailed in its most pristine form between 1880 and 1914.[2]

The first section discusses some fundamentals of the gold standard. This is followed by a discussion of the "Managed Gold Standard," which characterized much of the pre–World War I period. Following that is a brief narration of the history of the gold standard. Next, some empirical evidence is presented on the performance of the economies of the United States and the United Kingdom under the gold standard. Finally, the case for a return to the gold standard is examined.

The evidence presented in this chapter suggests that, in several respects, economic performance in the United States and the United Kingdom was superior under the classical gold standard to that of the subsequent period of managed fiduciary money.[3] In particular, both the

This chapter is reprinted from the May 1981 *Federal Reserve Bank of St. Louis Review*, 63(5):2–17.

[1] Indeed, the recently appointed federal Gold Commission has been established to consider the case for a greater role for gold in the U.S. monetary system. For a recent discourse on the case for a return by the United States to some form of the gold standard, see Robert M. Bleiberg and James Grant, "For Real Money: The Dollar Should be as Good as Gold," editorial commentary, *Barron's*, June 15, 1981.

[2] However, aspects of the gold standard persisted in various forms until the 1971 breakdown of the Bretton Woods System.

[3] "Managed fiduciary money" means a monetary standard under which the government is not committed to maintain a fixed price of gold. The United States had such a standard from 1861 to 1878, and has been on one since 1971. Under such a standard, monetary authorities have complete control over the domestic money supply. An alternative situation, often characterized as "managed" money, occurs when monetary authorities, though committed to maintaining a fixed price of gold, engage in a systematic policy of

price level and real economic activity were more stable in the pre–World War I gold standard era than in the subsequent six-and-one-half decades. Much of the relatively poor performance of the post–World War I period, however, occurred in the interwar period, a period characterized by deflation, real output instability, and high unemployment.

5.1   What was the gold standard?

The gold standard essentially was a commitment by participating countries to fix the prices of their domestic currencies in terms of a specified amount of gold. The countries maintained these fixed prices by being willing to buy or sell gold to anyone at that price. Thus, for example, from 1821 to 1914, Great Britain maintained a fixed price of gold at £3, 17s, 10 1/2d; the United States, over the 1834–1933 period, maintained the price of gold at $20.67 per ounce (with the exception of the Greenback era from 1861 to 1878).

5.1.1   Why gold?

Gold has the desirable properties of money that early writers in economics have stressed. It is durable, easily recognizable, storable, portable, divisible, and easily standardized. Especially important, changes in its stock are limited, at least in the short run, by high costs of production, making it costly for governments to manipulate.[4] Because of these physical attributes, it emerged as one of the earliest forms of money.

More important, gold was a *commodity* money, and a commodity money standard, regardless of the commodity involved, has a very desirable property: it ensures through the operation of the competitive market a tendency toward *long-run* price stability.[5] Under a commodity money standard, the purchasing power of a unit of commodity money, or

---

sterilizing (or neutralizing) the influence of gold flows on the domestic money supply by using offsetting open market operations. Although the United States was still on the gold standard, the period from 1914 to 1933 in U.S. monetary history can thus be viewed as a period of "managed" money because of the frequent sterilizing activity of the Federal Reserve System. See Milton Friedman and Anna Jacobson Schwartz, *A Monetary History of the United States 1867–1960* (Princeton University Press, 1963).

[4] Of course, in earlier times, governments have manipulated gold by debasement. clipping, etc. Such practices, however, were the exception. See Anna J. Schwartz, "Secular Price Change in Historical Perspective," *Journal of Money, Credit and Banking* (February 1973, Part 2), pp. 243–69.

[5] For a lucid discussion of the theory of commodity money, see Milton Friedman, "Commodity-Reserve Currency" in Milton Friedman, *Essays in Positive Economics* (University of Chicago Press, 1953).

what it will buy in terms of all other goods and services, will always tend toward equality with its long-run cost of production.

5.1.2 The gold standard and a closed economy

Consider first the example of a closed economy – one that does not trade with any other country – that produces gold and uses only gold coins as money. In this country, the government is commited to purchase gold from the public on demand at a fixed price and to convert it into gold coin. Similarly, the government will sell gold to the public at the fixed price.[6] The price level (the average of the prices of all goods and services produced in the country) will be determined by the equality of the quantity of gold coins demanded and supplied.

The supply of gold coins is determined by the supply of gold in the economy and by the amount of gold used for nonmonetary purposes. The supply of gold in the long run is determined by the opportunity cost of producing gold – the cost in terms of forgone labor, capital, and other factors engaged in producing an additional unit of gold. The fraction of gold devoted to nonmonetary uses is determined by the purchasing power of gold in terms of all other commodities. The demand for gold coins is determined by the community's wealth, tastes, and the opportunity cost of holding money relative to other assets (the interest rate).

In the long run, competition in the gold-producing industry ensures that the purchasing power of gold money in terms of all other goods will equal the opportunity cost of producing an additional unit of gold money.

To see how this works, consider what happens when a technological advance improves productivity in the non-gold-producing sectors of the economy. This improvement leads to a rise in real economic activity, an increase in the demand for money (gold coins) and, with an initially given stock of money, a fall in the price level (a rise in the purchasing power of gold money). The fall in the price level means that gold producers will be earning economic profits. These profits will encourage existing owners to increase production and new entrepreneurs to enter the industry, resulting in an increase in gold production.[7] At the same time, people will take gold previously used for non-monetary purposes and convert it

---

[6] In actuality the buying and selling prices will differ, reflecting the cost of certifying and minting coins. This difference is referred to as brassage.

[7] In addition, exploration for new sources of gold and attempts to more efficiently mine existing sources will result.

to monetary uses (e.g., they will sell gold jewelry to the government and have it coined). These forces will increase the gold coin supply, reversing the initial decline in the price level.[8]

In a similar manner, increases in the price level, caused, for example, by a gold discovery that increases the stock of gold and the supply of gold coins, will, by reducing the purchasing power of gold money, cause the community to shift gold from monetary to non-monetary uses, and will eventually reduce production in the gold-producing industries. Both factors will tend to reduce the gold money supply and reverse the initial rise in the price level. Thus, under a gold standard, one would expect to observe long-run price level stability, though it may take several years for a declining or rising price level to be reversed.[9]

5.1.3   The gold standard and open economies

If, instead of a closed economy, we have a world in which a number of countries are on a gold coin standard, a mechanism is introduced that ensures uniform price movements across these countries.

Consider, for example, two countries that were on the gold standard, the United States and the United Kingdom. As mentioned above, each country fixed the price of its currency in terms of gold – the United States fixed the price of one ounce of gold at \$20.67, while the United Kingdom set it at £3, 17s, 10 1/2d. Thus, the dollar/pound exchange rate was perfectly determined. The fixed exchange rate of \$4.867 per pound was referred to as the *par* exchange rate.[10]

---

[8] Also, rising prices will be accompanied by rising wages and other costs, making gold mining a less profitable activity. This analysis assumes constant costs; with increasing costs the purchasing power of gold will be higher and the price level lower.

[9] This analysis is static. In a dynamic context, growing real output will produce a tendency towards secular deflation unless gold output expands at the same rate as real economic activity. This will happen if the rate of technological advance is the same in the gold-producing sectors of the economy as in the rest of the economy or if the opening of new mines proceeds apace with real growth. In a world characterized by purely stochastic events such as major gold discoveries, the price level will diverge from its long-run trend for a very long time, giving the appearance of long-run price instability. However, to the extent that gold discoveries are not random events but occur in response to rises in the purchasing power of gold, these extended periods of inflation and deflation are part of the equilibrating process of a commodity standard.

[10] The U.K. definition of an ounce of gold was 11/12 of the U.S. definition. Actually, under the gold standard, the exchange rate was never exactly fixed. It varied within a range bounded by the gold points – the costs of transporting gold between the United States and the United Kingdom. Thus, if Americans reduced their demand for British goods and hence for pounds to pay for them, the dollar price of the pound would decline. When the dollar price of the pound declined to, say, \$4.80, it would pay to melt down English gold sovereigns into bullion, ship the bullion to the United States, and convert it into U.S. gold coins.

Under the gold standard fixed exchange rate system, disturbances in the price level in one country would be wholly or in part offset by an automatic balance-of-payments adjustment mechanism called the *price-specie-flow* mechanism. Consider again the example where a technical advance in the United States lowers the U.S. price level. The fall in U.S. prices will result in lower prices of U.S. exports, which will decline relative to the prices of imports, determined largely by prices in the rest of the world. This change in terms of trade (the ratio of export prices to import prices) will cause foreigners to demand more U.S. exports, and U.S. residents to demand fewer imports. A U.S. balance-of-payments surplus will be created, causing gold to flow into the United States from the United Kingdom.[11] The gold inflow will increase the U.S. money supply, reversing the initial fall in prices. At the same time, in the United Kingdom, the gold outflow will reduce the U.K. money supply, thus reducing its price level. In final equilibrium, price levels in both countries will be somewhat lower than they were prior to the technical advance in the United States. Thus, the operation of the price-specie-flow mechanism served to keep prices in line across the world.[12]

In sum, the gold standard as a commodity money standard provided a mechanism to ensure long-run price level stability for both individual countries and groups of countries. Each country had only to maintain a fixed price of gold.

5.2　The managed gold standard

The simple model of the gold standard just described was seldom followed in practice. The pure gold coin standard had two features that

---

[11] In this simple example, the increased British demand for U.S. goods lowers the pound to the gold export point. As a consequence, British importers convert pounds into bullion and ship them to the United States, converting them to U.S. gold dollars to pay for the American goods.

[12] An alternative to the balance-of-payments adjustment mechanism described above is called the Monetary Approach to the Balance of Payments. See Harry G. Johnson, "The Monetary Approach to Balance of Payments Theory" in Jacob A. Frenkel and Harry G. Johnson, eds., *The Monetary Approach to the Balance of Payments* (Allen and Unwin, 1976). According to this approach, through the process of arbitrage – the buying and selling of similar commodities in different markets – the prices of all internationally traded goods, exports, imports, and close substitutes will be the same around the world expressed in similar currency units. Moreover, the prices of domestic goods and services (non-traded goods) will be kept in line with prices of internationally traded goods by domestic arbitrage. Hence, instead of U.S. prices falling first in response to an excess demand for money, and the terms of trade subsequently changing, the excess demand for money will be satisfied directly by the import of gold (through a balance-of-payments surplus) with no change in the terms of trade.

caused most countries to modify its operation: (1) very high resource costs were required to maintain a full commodity money standard and (2) strict adherence to the "iron discipline" of the gold standard required each country to subsume its internal balance (domestic price and real output stability) to its external balance (balance-of-payments equilibrium). Thus, if a country was running a balance-of-payments deficit, the "rules of the game" required it to deflate the economy until "purchasing power parity" was restored at the par exchange rate.[13] Such deflation leads to a reduction in real output and employment. Consequently, a meaningful discussion of how the gold standard actually operated before World War I requires a discussion of the ways in which nations modified the gold standard to economize on gold and to shield domestic economic activity from external disturbances.

5.2.1   The use of fiduciary money

As mentioned above, high resource costs are required to maintain a full commodity money standard. Discovering, mining, and minting gold are costly activities.[14] Consequently, as nations developed, they evolved substitutes for pure commodity money. These substitutes encompassed both government-provided paper money (referred to as fiat money) and privately produced fiduciary money (bank notes and bank deposits). As long as governments maintained a fixed ratio of their notes to gold, and commercial banks kept a fixed ratio of their liabilities to gold (or to government notes and gold), a gold standard could still be sustained. This type of standard prevailed throughout the world before World War I.

One aspect of this "mixed" gold standard system was that one unit of a country's gold reserves could support a multiple number of units of domestic money (e.g., the U.S. ratio of money to the monetary gold stock was 8.5 in the 1880–1913 period). This meant that in the short run gold flows had powerful effects on the domestic money supply, spending, and prices.[15]

---

[13] Purchasing power parity is the ratio of the domestic country's price level (value of money) to that of its principal trading partners.

[14] Friedman estimated the cost of maintaining a full gold coin standard for the United States in 1960 to be more than $2\frac{1}{2}$ percent of GNP. See Milton Friedman, *A Program for Monetary Stability* (Fordham University Press, 1959).

[15] It also meant that changes in the composition of the money supply between high-powered money (gold coins and government paper) and bank-provided money (notes and deposits) could be a source of monetary instability.

5.2.2   International capital flows

So far, the discussion abstracts from the role of capital flows between countries. In the pre–World War I gold standard era, most international trade was financed by credit, the issuing of short-term claims in the London money market.[16] In addition, economic projects in the less-developed economies were generally financed by long-term loans from investors in England, France, and other advanced countries.[17] The influence of these capital flows significantly reduced the burden of gold flows in the adjustment mechanism.

Consider the example of a gold discovery in a particular country. The discovery would lead to a rise in the domestic money supply, which both raises domestic price levels and reduces domestic interest rates in the short run.[18] The reduction in domestic interest rates relative to interest rates in other countries would induce investors to shift their funds to foreign money markets. This produces a gold outflow, thereby reducing the amount of adjustment required through changes in the terms of trade. Also, to the extent that short-term capital serves as a substitute for gold as an international reserve asset, and domestic financial intermediaries hold balances with correspondents abroad, smaller gold flows would be required to settle international payments imbalances.

Finally, consider the role of long-term capital movements. In the pre–World War I era, the real rate of return on capital was higher in developing countries such as the United States, Canada, and Australia than in European countries such as the United Kingdom and France. As a consequence, British investors, for example, invested heavily in American industries and utilities by purchasing long-term securities. The demand by British investors for American securities (other things equal) created an excess demand for dollars at the par exchange rate (or equivalently an excess supply of pounds). The resulting gold inflow into the United States raised the U.S. money supply, leading to a rise in the U.S. price level. The resultant rise in export prices relative to import prices led to an increased demand by U.S. residents for im-

---

[16] See Arthur I. Bloomfield, *Short-Term Capital Movements Under the Pre-1914 Gold Standard*, Princeton Studies in International Finance No. 11 (Princeton University, 1963).

[17] See Arthur I. Bloomfield, *Patterns of Fluctuation in International Investment before 1914*, Princeton Studies in International Finance No. 21 (Princeton University, 1968).

[18] This is the so-called liquidity effect. To induce the community to hold a larger fraction of its wealth in the form of money rather than interest-bearing securities, the price of securities must rise (the interest rate must fall).

ports (primarily manufactured goods from the United Kingdom). Thus, the transfer of capital resulted in a transfer of real resources from the United Kingdom to the United States. Indeed, in the pre–World War I era, it was normal for a developing country such as the United States to run a persistent balance-of-payments deficit on current account (imports of goods and services exceeding exports of goods and services), financed primarily by long-term capital inflows.

5.2.3   The role of central banks in the gold standard

Under a strict gold standard, there is no need for a central bank. What is required is a governmental authority to maintain the fixed domestic currency price of gold by buying and selling gold freely.[19] Indeed, many countries on the gold standard prior to World War I (e.g., the United States and Canada) did not have central banks. Most European countries, on the other hand, have had central banks that predated the gold standard. These institutions, in most cases, had evolved from large commercial banks that served as bankers to the government (e.g., the Bank of England, founded in 1697) into institutions serving as lenders of last resort to the banking community.

Under the classical gold standard, central banks were supposed to follow the rules of the game – to speed up the adjustment of the domestic money supply and price level to external gold flows. The classical model of central bank behavior was the Bank of England, which played by the rules over much of the 1870–1914 period.[20] Whenever Great Britain faced a balance-of-payments deficit and the Bank of England saw its gold reserves declining, it raised "bank rate," the rate of interest at which it was willing to discount money market paper. By causing other interest rates to rise, the rise in bank rate was supposed to produce a reduction in holdings of inventories and a curtailment of other investment expenditures. The reduction in investment expenditures would then lead to a reduction in overall domestic spending and a fall in the price level. At the same time, the rise in bank rate would stem any short-term capital outflow and attract short-term funds from abroad.

For most other countries on the gold standard, there is evidence that interest rates were never allowed to rise enough to contract the

---

[19] However, a substantial gold reserve is required to do this effectively.

[20] However, most other central banks apparently did not. See Arthur I. Bloomfield. *Monetary Policy under the International Gold Standard: 1880–1914* (Federal Reserve Bank of New York, 1959).

domestic price level – that these countries did not follow the rules of the game.[21] Also, many countries frequently followed policies of sterilizing gold flows – attempting to neutralize the effects of gold flows on the domestic money supply by open market purchases or sales of domestic securities.[22]

5.2.4   Reserve currencies and the role of sterling

An important addition to the gold standard story is the role of key currencies.[23] Many countries under the pre–World War I gold standard held their international reserves in gold and in the currencies of several major countries. The center of the international payments mechanism was England, with the Bank of England maintaining its international reserves primarily in gold. Most other countries kept reserves in the form of gold and sterling assets. Between 1900 and 1914, two other major European capitals also served as reserve centers – Paris and Berlin, each of which held reserves in gold, sterling, and the other country's currency. Finally, a number of smaller European countries held reserves in the form of francs and marks.

In addition, an elaborate network of short-term financial arrangements developed between private financial institutions centered in the London money market. This network of reserve currencies and short-term international finance had two important results. First, England (the Bank of England) could act as an umpire (or manager) of the world gold standard system without having to hold excessive gold reserves.[24] By

---

[21] Noted examples are France and Belgium. See P. B. Whale, "The Working of the Pre-War Gold Standard," *Economica* (February, 1937), pp. 18–32, and Bloomfield, *Monetary Policy under the International Gold Standard*.

[22] Usually, gold outflows were offset by open market purchases of domestic securities. For the U.S. experience, see Friedman and Schwartz, *A Monetary History of the United States*. For other countries see Bloomfield, *Monetary Policy under the International Gold Standard*. Such behavior could not persist, however, if a country wished to maintain its link with gold, because if the disequilibrium producing the gold flow were permanent (e.g., the domestic price level were higher than world prices), then gold outflows would continue until all of the country gold reserves were exhausted. (In the case of an inflow, it would continue until the monetary base consisted entirely of gold.)

[23] Much of this discussion derives from Peter H. Lindert, *Key Currencies and Gold, 1900–1913*, Princeton Studies in International Finance No. 24 (Princeton University, 1969).

[24] Indeed, England's total gold reserves in 1913 accounted for only 9.5 percent of the world's monetary gold stock while the Bank of England's holdings accounted for 3.6 percent. See John Maynard Keynes, *A Treatise on Money: 2, The Applied Theory of Money*, in Elizabeth Johnson and Donald Moggridge, eds., *The Collected Writings of John Maynard Keynes*, vol. VI (Macmillan, 1971).

altering its bank rate, the Bank of England caused repercussions around the world.[25]

Second, much of the balance-of-payments adjustment mechanism in the pre–World War I period did not require actual gold flows. Instead, the adjustment consisted primarily of transfers of sterling and other currency balances in the London, Paris, Berlin, and New York money markets.[26] In addition, short-term capital flows accommodated the balance-of-payments adjustment mechanism in this period.[27] Indeed, the pre–World War I gold standard has often been described as a sterling standard.[28]

In sum, the gold standard that emerged before World War I was very different from the pure gold coin standard outlined earlier. Unlike the pure gold coin standard, countries economized on the use of gold both in their domestic money supplies and as a means of settling international payments imbalances. In addition, to avoid the iron discipline of the gold standard, central banks in some countries did not follow the rules of the game, and some countries even abandoned the gold standard periodically.[29] The final modification to the pure gold standard was the key role played by the Bank of England as umpire to the system. The result was a "managed gold standard," not the pure gold coin standard often extolled as the best example of a commodity money system.

5.3   Chronology of the gold standard: 1821–1971

This section briefly sketches the chronology of the gold standard from the end of the Napoleonic Wars to the collapse of Bretton Woods.

5.3.1   *The classical gold standard: 1821–1914*

In the 18th century, England and most other countries were on a bimetallic standard based primarily on silver.[30] When Great Britain restored

---

[25] It likely caused monetary crises in the United States in the 1838–43 period and 1873. See Peter Temin, The *Jacksoman Economy* (W. W. Norton, 1969), and Friedman and Schwartz, *A Monetary History of the United States.*

[26] Also in the period after 1900, instead of gold actually being transported between centers, the practice of "earmarking" gold holdings in major centers gained importance.

[27] See Bloomfield, *Short-Term Capital Movements.*

[28] See Melchior Palyi, *The Twilight of Gold, 1914 to 1936: Myths and Realities* (Henry Regnery Co., 1972), and David Williams, "The Evolution of the Sterling System," in C. R. Whittlesey and J. S. G. Wilson, eds., *Essays in Money and Banking in Honour of R. S. Sayers* (Clarendon Press, 1968).

[29] Argentina and other Latin American countries, for example. See Alec George Ford, *The Gold Standard, 1880–1914, Britain and Argentina* (Clarendon Press, 1962).

[30] Under a bimetallic standard, each of two precious metals, gold and silver, serves as legal tender, and the two metals are kept by the mint in a fixed proportion to each other. The

specie payments in 1821 after the Napoleonic War inflation episode, the gold standard was restored. From 1821 to 1880, the gold standard steadily expanded as more and more countries ceased using silver.[31] By 1880, the majority of countries in the world were on some form of a gold standard.

The period from 1880 to 1914, known as the heyday of the gold standard, was a remarkable period in world economic history. It was characterized by rapid economic growth, the free flow of labor and capital across political borders, virtually free trade, and, in general, world peace. These external conditions, coupled with the elaborate financial network centered in London and the role of the Bank of England as umpire to the system, are believed to be the *sine qua non* of the effective operation of the gold standard.[32]

5.3.2   The gold exchange standard: 1925–31

The gold standard broke down during World War I,[33] was succeeded by a period of "managed fiduciary money," and was briefly reinstated from 1925 to 1931 as the Gold Exchange Standard. Under the Gold Exchange Standard, countries could hold both gold and dollars or pounds as reserves, except for the United States and the United Kingdom, which held reserves only in gold. In addition, most countries engaged in active sterilization policies to protect their domestic money supplies from gold flows.

The Gold Exchange Standard broke down in 1931 following Britain's departure from gold in the face of massive gold and capital flows and was again succeeded by managed fiduciary money.

5.3.3   The Bretton Woods System: 1946–71

The Bretton Woods System was an attempt to return to a modified gold standard using the U.S. dollar as the world's key reserve currency. All

---

relationship between the official exchange rate of gold for silver and the market rate will determine whether either one or both metals is used as money. For example in 1834, the United States raised the mint ratio of silver to gold from 15:1 to 16:1, hence valuing silver slightly lower relative to gold than the world market. As a result, little silver was offered for coinage and the United States was in effect on the gold standard. See Leland B. Yeager, *International Monetary Relations: Theory, History and Policy*, 2nd ed. (Harper and Row, 1976), p. 296.

[31] The switch from silver to gold reflected both changes in the relative supplies of the two precious metals resulting from the gold discoveries of the 1840s and '50s and a growing preference for the more precious metal as world real income rose.

[32] See Palyi, *The Twilight of Gold*, and Yeager, *International Monetary Relations*.

[33] The United States alone remained on the gold standard, except for a brief embargo on gold exports from 1917 to 1919.

other countries – except for the sterling bloc – settled their international balances in dollars. The United States fixed the price of gold at $35.00 per ounce, maintained substantial gold reserves, and settled external accounts with gold bullion payments and receipts.

In the post–World War II period, persistent U.S. balance-of-payments deficits helped finance the recovery of world trade from the aftermath of depression and war. However, the steady growth in the use of U.S. dollars as international reserves and persistent U.S. deficits steadily reduced U.S. gold reserves and the gold reserve ratio, reducing public confidence in the ultimate ability of the United States to redeem its currency in gold.[34] This "confidence problem" coupled with many nations' aversion to paying both seigniorage and an "inflation tax" to the United States in the post-1965 period, led to the ultimate breakdown of the Bretton Woods System in 1971.[35] The U.S. decision in 1971 to abandon pegging the price of gold was the final demise of the gold standard.

5.4　The record of the gold standard

This section briefly examines the stability of the price level and real output for the United Kingdom and the United States under both the gold and managed fiduciary money standards. Figures 5.1 and 5.2 portray the behavior of the wholesale price index from 1800 to 1979 for both countries.

From 1797 to 1821, during and immediately following the Napoleonic Wars, the United Kingdom was on a fiat (or paper) standard; it officially joined the gold standard in 1821, maintaining a fixed price of gold until 1914. There is little change in the U.K. price level comparing the first year of the gold standard, 1821, to the last, but over the whole period there was a slight downward trend in prices, declining on average by 0.4 percent per year. Within the approximate 100-year span, however, periods of declining prices alternated with periods of rising prices, a pattern consistent with the commodity theory of money. Prices fell until the mid-1840s, reflecting the pressure of rising real incomes on the limited stock of gold. Following the California and Australian gold discoveries of the late 1840s and early 1850s, prices turned around and kept rising until the late 1860s. This was followed by a 25-year period of declining prices,

---

[34] See H. G. Johnson, "Theoretical Problems of the International Monetary System," in R. N. Cooper, ed., *International Finance* (Penguin Books, 1971), pp. 304–34.

[35] Seigniorage here refers to the return earned by the U.S. monetary authorities on the issue of outstanding paper money liabilities. It is measured by the interest forgone by foreign holders of U.S. money balances. The "inflation tax" refers to the depreciation in real purchasing power of outstanding money balances.

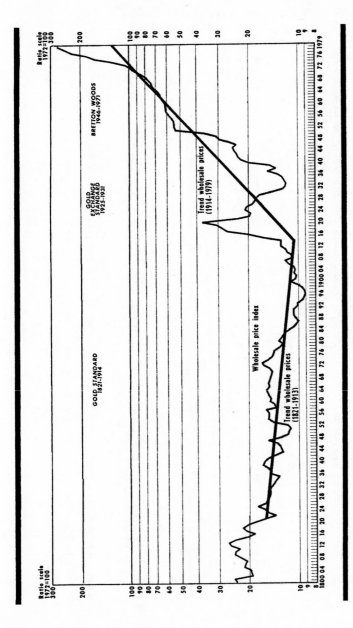

Figure 5.1. Wholesale Price Index, United Kingdom.

161

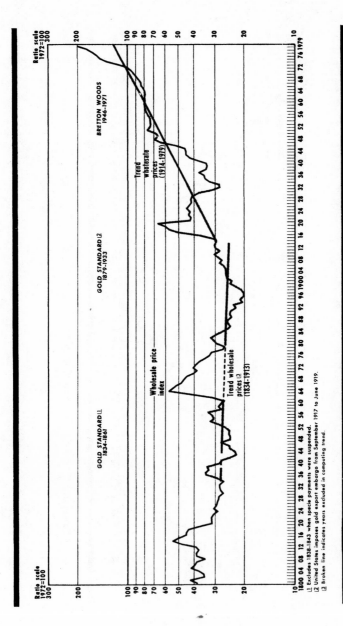

Figure 5.2. Wholesale Price Index, United States.

again reflecting both rising real income and expansion of the number of countries on the gold standard. This deflation ended after technical advances in gold processing and major gold discoveries in the late 1880s and 1890s increased world gold supplies.

The United States followed a pattern similar to the United Kingdom, experiencing a slight downward trend in the price level with prices declining on average by 0.14 percent per year from 1834 to 1913. The country adopted the gold standard in 1834 (it had been on silver for the preceding 35 years) and remained on it at the same price of gold until World War I, with the exception of the Greenback episode from 1861 to 1878.[36] During that period, the country abandoned the gold standard and prices increased rapidly until 1866. To restore convertibility to gold, prices had to fall sufficiently to restore the prewar purchasing power parity. This occurred in the rapid deflation from 1869 to 1879.

The period since World War I has not been characterized by price stability except for the 1920s under the Gold Exchange Standard, and the 1950s and early 1960s under the Bretton Woods System. Indeed, since the end of the gold standard, price levels in both countries have on average been rising. The U.K. price level increased at an average annual rate of 3.81 percent from 1914 to 1979, while the U.S. price level increased by an average annual rate of 2.2 percent.

Figures 5.3 and 5.4 present further evidence on the operation of a commodity money standard and on the long-run price stabilizing character of the gold standard.

Figure 5.3 compares the purchasing power of gold for the world (measured by the ratio of an index of the price of gold to the wholesale price index for the United Kingdom) in relation to its trend with the world monetary gold stock in relation to its trend over the period 1821–1914.[37]

The purchasing power of gold index presented here varies inversely with the wholesale price index presented in Figure 5.1. This inverse association is a reflection of the fixed price of gold over this period.[38] The trends of both series were rising over the whole period. The upward trend in the purchasing power of gold series reflects a more rapid growth

---

[36] Also to be excluded from the gold standard are the turbulent years 1838–1843, during which specie payments were generally suspended.

[37] The United Kingdom was chosen to represent the pre-1914 world because it was a large open economy with few trade restrictions. Hence the wholesale price index would be dominated by internationally traded goods.

[38] Indeed, this inverse relationship prevailed virtually until the late 1960s. Since the freeing of the price of gold in 1968, the purchasing power of gold has varied directly with the wholesale price index. This primarily reflects rising demand for gold as a hedge against inflation, and increasing world political and monetary instability.

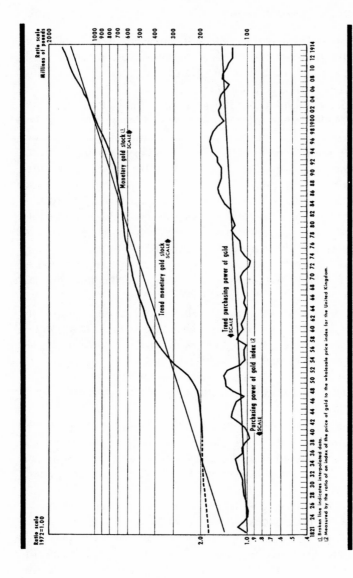

Figure 5.3. Monetary gold stock and purchasing power of gold index, world.

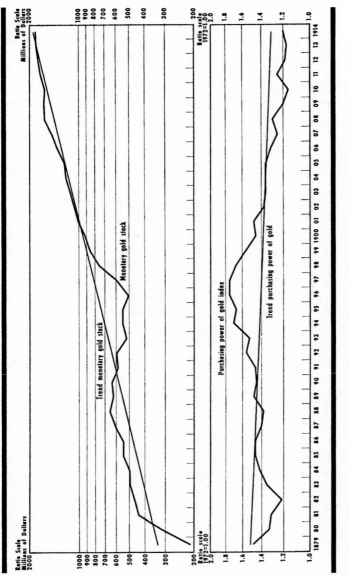

Figure 5.4. Monetary gold stock and purchasing power of gold index, Unites States.

165

of world real output and, hence, in the demand for monetary gold than could be accommodated by growth in the world's monetary gold stock.

In comparing deviations from trend in the purchasing power of gold to that in the world monetary gold stock, one would expect that deviations from trend in the monetary gold stock would produce corresponding changes in the price level and, for a given nominal price of gold, would inversely affect the purchasing power of gold. A comparison reveals this negative association, with deviations from trend in the world monetary gold stock leading deviations from trend in the purchasing power of gold.[39]

In addition, according to the operation of a commodity money standard, movements in the purchasing power of gold would be expected to precede movements in the monetary gold stock – a rising purchasing power of gold would induce both a shift from nonmonetary to monetary uses of gold and increased gold production. Such a positive association between deviations from trend of the two series is observed.[40] Thus the 1820s and '30s were largely characterized by the purchasing power of gold exceeding its long-run trend. This was followed by a rapid increase in the world monetary gold stock after 1848 as the output of the new California and Australian mines was added to the world's stock. Subsequently, the purchasing power of gold declined from its peak above trend in the mid-1850s and was succeeded by a marked deceleration in the monetary gold stock after 1860. The same pattern can be observed comparing the rise in the purchasing power of gold in the 1870s and '80s with the subsequent increase in the monetary gold stock in the mid 1890s.

Figure 5.4 compares the U.S. purchasing power of gold in relation to its trend with the U.S. monetary gold stock in relation to its trend over the 1879–1914 gold standard period.[41]

In this period, the trends of the two series moved in opposite directions. The declining trend in the purchasing power of gold series, reflect-

---

[39] The highest statistically significant negative correlation in the 1821–1914 period occurred with deviations from trend in the monetary gold stock leading deviations from trend in the purchasing power of gold by two years. The correlation coefficient, −0.644, was statistically significant at the 1 percent level.

[40] The highest statistically significant positive correlation in the 1821–1914 period occurred with deviations from trend in the purchasing power of gold leading deviations from trend in the world monetary gold stock by 25 years. The correlation was 0.436, statistically significant at the 1 percent level.

[41] An important difference in comparing the behavior of the U.S. monetary gold stock with that of the world is that short-run movements in the U.S. series would reflect, in addition to changes in gold production and shifts between monetary and nonmonetary uses of gold, gold movements between the United States and other countries.

ing more rapid growth in the U.S. monetary gold stock than in real output, was a consequence of two developments: the accumulation of monetary gold from the rest of the world early in the period following the resumption of specie payments, and the effects of gold discoveries in the 1890s.

As in Figure 5.3, a negative association between deviations from trend in the monetary gold stock and the purchasing power of gold is observed.[42] Also, similar to the evidence in Figure 5.3, deviations in trend in the purchasing power of gold preceded deviations from trend in the monetary gold stock with a lead.[43] Thus, declines in the purchasing power of gold from 1879 to 1882 preceded declines in the monetary gold stock below trend in the late 1880s and early 1890s, while rises in the purchasing power of gold after 1882 can be associated with a rising monetary gold stock after 1896. Finally, a declining purchasing power of gold in the mid-1890s can be associated with a falling monetary gold stock after 1903.

One important implication of the tendency for price levels to revert toward a long-run stable value under the gold standard was that it ensured a measure of predictability with respect to the value of money: though prices would rise or fall for a few years, inflation or deflation would not persist.[44] Such belief in long-run price stability would

[42] The highest statistically significant negative correlation in the 1879–1914 period occurred with a contemporaneous relationship between deviations from trend in the monetary gold stock and deviations from trend in the purchasing power of gold. The correlation coefficient, -0.656, was statistically significant at the 1 percent level.

[43] The highest statistically significant positive correlation in the 1879–1914 period occurred with deviations from trend in the purchasing power of gold leading deviations from trend in the monetary gold stock by 14 years. The correlation coefficient was 0.793, which was statistically significant at the 1 percent level.

The highest statistically significant positive correlation in the 1879–1914 period occurred with deviations from trend in the *world* purchasing power of gold leading deviations from trend in the *world* monetary gold stock by 16 years. The correlation coefficient was 0.863, which was statistically significant at the 1 percent level. The considerably longer lead observed over the 1821–1914 period in footnote 40 above likely reflects a longer adjustment period in the early part of the 19th century.

[44] See Benjamin Klein, "Our New Monetary Standard: The Measurement and Effects of Price Uncertainty, 1880–1973," *Economic Inquiry* (December 1975), pp. 461–84, for evidence of long-run price stability for the United States under the gold standard. His evidence that positive (negative) autocorrelations of the price level are succeeded by negative (positive) autocorrelations is consistent with the hypothesis that the price level reverted back to its mean level. A consequence of this mean reversion phenomenon was that year-to-year changes in the price level were substantial for each country. However, the standard deviations of year-to-year changes in the Wholesale price index were still considerably lower in the pre–World War I gold standard era compared with the post–World War I managed fiduciary money era. For the United Kingdom, the standard deviations were: 1821–1913, 6.20; 1919–79 (excluding 1939–45), 12.00. For the United States, the standard deviations were: 1834–1913 (excluding 1838–43 and 1861–78), 6.29; 1919–79 (excluding 1941–45), 9.28.

encourage economic agents to engage in contracts with the expectation that, should prices of commodities or factors of production change, the change would reflect real forces rather than changes in the value of money.

Belief in long-term price level stability has apparently disappeared in recent years, as people now realize that the long-run constraint of the gold standard has vanished.[45] As a consequence, it is more difficult for people to distinguish between changes in relative prices and changes in the price level. Such absolute vs. relative price confusion has increased the possibility of major economic losses as people fail to respond to market signals.[46]

Finally, evidence on real output stability for the United Kingdom and the United States is presented. It is frequently argued that under the gold standard, when countries had to subordinate internal balance considerations to the gold standard's iron discipline, real output would be less stable than under a regime of managed fiduciary money. Figures 5.5 and 5.6 show the deviations of real per capita income from its long-run trend over the period 1870–1979.

For the United Kingdom, Figure 5.5 shows both a single trend line for the 1870–1979 period and separate trend lines for each of the pre– and post–World War I subperiods. The U.K. data were split into two subperiods because the trend line for the entire period results in real output after 1919 being virtually always below trend. This suggests that World War I permanently altered the trend growth rate of real per capita income in the United Kingdom, and hence the two periods should be handled separately. Examining the deviations from trend (using the subperiod trends) suggests that real per capita income was less variable in the pre–World War I period than subsequently. The mean absolute value of the percentage deviations of real per capita income from trend was 2.14 percent from 1870 to 1913 and 3.75 percent from 1919 to 1979 (excluding 1939 to 1945).

As in the U.K. case, U.S. real per capita income was more stable under the gold standard from 1879 to 1913 compared with the entire

---

[45] Indeed, evidence presented by Klein, "Our New Monetary Standard," shows a marked decline since 1960 in long-term price level predictability, the belief about long-term price behavior (measured by a moving standard deviation of changes in the price level). At the same time, short-term price level predictability, the belief about price level behavior in the near future, has improved in the post-war period.

[46] See Friedrich August von Hayek, *A Tiger by the Tail*, Hobart Papers (Institute of Economic Affairs, 1972); Milton Friedman, "Nobel Lecture: Inflation and Unemployment," *Journal of Political Economy* (June 1977), pp. 451–72; and Axel Leijonhuvud, "Costs and Consequences of Inflation," in Axel Leijonhuvud, *Information and Co-ordination: Essays in Macro Economic Theory* (Oxford University Press, 1981).

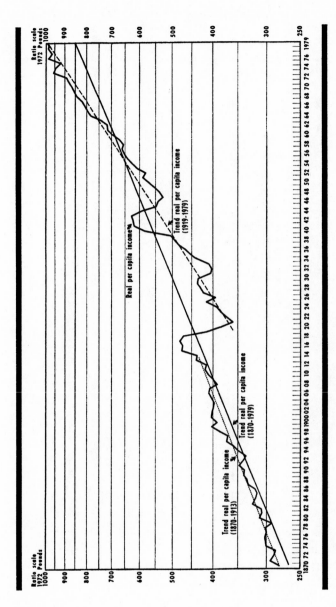

Figure 5.5. Real per capita income, United Kingdom.

169

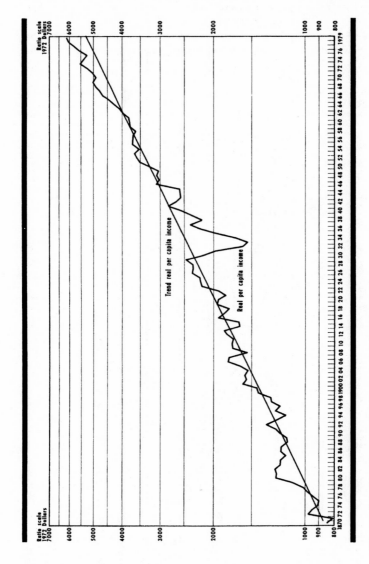

Figure 5.6. Real per capita income, United States.

170

post–World War I period. The mean absolute values of the percentage deviations of real per capita income from trend were: 6.64 percent from 1879 to 1913 and 8.97 percent from 1919 to 1979 (excluding 1941 to 1945).

Moreover, unemployment was on average lower in the pre-1914 period in both countries than in the post–World War I period. For the United Kingdom, the average unemployment rate over the 1888–1913 period was 4.30 percent, while over the period 1919–1979 (excluding 1939–1945) it was 6.52 percent. For the United States, average unemployment rates by subperiod were: 1890–1913, 6.78 percent, and 1919–1979 (excluding 1941–1945), 7.46 percent.

Thus, the evidence suggests that the managed fiduciary money system superceding the gold standard generally has been associated with less real economic stability.

5.5 The case for a return to gold

The pre–World War I gold standard was the closest thing to a worldwide commodity money standard. Hence, an examination of the record for that period is crucial in determining what we might expect should we return to some form of commodity standard.

One dominant feature of that period was long-run price stability. This contrasts favorably with the behavior of the price level under the managed fiduciary money standard for much of the period since World War I. Also, though real output varied considerably from year to year under the gold standard, it did not vary discernibly more than it has in the entire period since World War I.[47]

One problem with comparing the pre–World War I gold standard to the managed fiduciary money standard after World War I is that the latter period includes the turbulent interwar years, a period that may bias the case against managed fiduciary money. To account for this, Table 5.1 compares several measures of performance of the price level, real output, and money growth for three time periods: the pre–World War I gold standard period, the interwar period, and the post–World War II period.[48]

---

[47] The standard deviations of year-to-year percentage changes in real per capita income for the United States were: 1879–1913; 5.79: 1919–79 (excluding 1941–45), 6.34. For the United Kingdom: 1870–1913, 2.62: 1919–79 (excluding 1939–45), 3.24.

[48] In this comparison, both World Wars are omitted. This was done for two reasons. First, both wars were accompanied by rapid inflation in both countries, and in each case wartime government expenditures were largely financed by the issue of government fiat money. Hence, a comparison of the price-stabilizing characteristics of the two monetary

Table 5.1. *A comparison of the behavior of price level, real output, and money growth in the United Kingdom and the United States*

	The gold standard[1]		The interwar period		Post–World War II	
	U.K.	U.S.	U.K.	U.S.	U.K.	U.S.
	1870–1913 (1821–1913)	1879–1913 (1834–1913)	1919–38	1919–40	1946–79	1946–79
(1) The average annual percentage change in the price level	-0.7% (-0.4)	0.1% (-0.1)	-4.6%	-2.5%	5.6%	2.8%
(2) The coefficient of variation of annual percentage changes in the price level (ratio)	-14.9 (-16.3)	17.0 (6.5)	-3.8	-5.2	1.2	1.3
(3) The coefficient of variation of annual percentage changes in real per capita income (ratio)	2.5	3.5	4.9	5.5	1.4	1.6
(4) The average level of the unemployment rate	4.3%[2]	6.8%[3]	13.3%	11.3%	2.5%	5.0%
(5) The average annual percentage change in the money supply	1.5%	6.1%	0.9%	1.5%	5.9%	5.7%
(6) The coefficient of variation of annual percentage changes in the money supply (ratio)	1.6	0.8	3.6	2.4	1.0	0.5

Notes: Rows 1 and 5 calculated as the time coefficient from a regression of the log of the variable on a time trend. Rows 2, 3, and 6 calculated as the ratio of the standard deviation of annual percentage changes to their mean.
[1] Data for the longer periods (in parentheses) were available only for the price level. Years 1838–43 and 1861–78 were excluded for the United States.
[2] 1888–1913.
[3] 1890–1913.

Data sources: See data appendix.

First, row 1 presents evidence on long-run price level stability as measured by the average annual rate of change in the price level over the period. As can be observed, the interwar period of both countries was characterized by substantial deflation in both the United States and the United Kingdom, while the post–World War II period has been characterized by inflation. This performance is in marked contrast to the near price stability of the gold standard period. However, price variability, measured in row 2 by the coefficient of variation of percentage year-to-year changes in the price level, reveals a slightly different picture. Prices were more variable under the gold standard than in both post-gold-standard periods, with the least variability occurring in the post–World War II period.

Second, row 3 presents evidence on real output stability as measured by the coefficient of variation of year-to-year percentage changes in real per capita output. Real output was considerably less stable in both countries in the interwar period than in either the gold standard or the post–World War II period, with the latter period having the best record. In addition, the evidence on average unemployment rates in row 4 agrees with the evidence on real output stability: unemployment was by far the highest in the interwar period and by far the lowest in the post–World War II period in both countries.[49]

Finally, a comparison is made across periods in the average annual rate of monetary growth in row 5, and in the variability in monetary growth measured by the coefficient of variation of percentage year-to-year changes in the money supply in row 6. According to monetary theory, a reduction in monetary growth below the long-run trend of real output growth will produce deflation, while a rise in monetary growth above the long-run trend of real output growth will lead to inflation. In the transition between different rates of monetary growth, both the levels and growth rates of real output will deviate considerably from long-run trend. Thus monetary variability will lead to real output variability.[50]

The rate of monetary growth was lower in both countries in the interwar period than in both the post–World War II and the gold standard periods. In the case of the United Kingdom, the post–World War II

standards – including two major wars in the case of the managed fiduciary money standard and none in the gold standard – would bias the case against the former. Second, measured real output would tend to be higher than otherwise in wartime to the extent that resources (both employed and otherwise unemployed) are devoted to (nonproductive) wartime use. Hence, including wartime real output would bias the case in favor of managed fiduciary money.

[49] A comparison between the two unemployment rates and the measures of real output stability reveals an interesting difference. Real output was less stable in the United

period exhibits more rapid monetary growth than under the gold standard, while for the United States, monetary growth rates are similar in both the post-war and gold standard periods.

Finally, monetary growth was more variable in both countries in the interwar period than in the other two periods, with the post–World War II period displaying the least variability in monetary growth.

The poor economic performance of the interwar period compared with either the preceding gold standard period or the post–World War II period has been attributed to the failure of monetary policy. Indeed, the attempt by the Bank of England to restore convertibility to gold at the pre-war parity has often been characterized as the reason for British deflation and unemployment in the 1920s.[51] Likewise, the failure of the Federal Reserve System to prevent the drastic decline that occurred in the U.S. money supply from 1929 to 1933 has been blamed for the severity of the Great Depression in the United States.[52] On could well argue that the greatly improved performance of monetary policy and economic stability in the two countries in the post–World War II period reflects learning from past mistakes. This suggests that in considering the case for a return to the gold standard, a meaningful comparison should really by made between the post–World War II period and the gold standard. In such a comparison, the gold standard provided us with greater *long-run* price stability, but at the expense of both *short-run* real output and price stability. The higher rates of inflation and lower variability of real output (and lower unemployment) in the two countries in the recent period likely reflects changing policy preferences away from long-run price stability and toward full employment. Indeed, the strong commitment to full employment in both countries likely explains the worsening of inflation in the post-war period.[53]

In assessing the case for a U.S. return to a gold standard, the benefits of such a policy must be weighed against the costs. The key benefit of a

States, but unemployment was higher in the United Kingdom. One explanation offered for the high and persistent unemployment in the United Kingdom in the interwar period is that it was caused by significant increases in the ratio of unemployment benefits to wages. See Daniel K. Benjamin and Levis A. Kochin, "Searching for an Explanation of Unemployment in Interwar Britain," *Journal of Political Economy* (June 1979), pp. 441–78.

[50] See Milton Friedman, *A Theoretical Framework for Monetary Analysis*, Occasional Paper No. 112 (National Bureau of Economic Research, 1971).

[51] See John Maynard Keynes, "The Economic Consequences of Mr. Churchill," in Johnson and Moggridge, eds., *Collected Works of John Maynard Keynes*, vol. IX (1972).

[52] See Friedman and Schwartz, *A Monetary History of the United States*.

[53] Friedman forcefully argued this point in his 1968 presidential address to the American Economic Association. See Milton Friedman, "The Role of Monetary Policy," *The American Economic Review* (March 1968), pp. 1–17.

return to a gold standard would be long-run price stability. The costs, however, are not inconsiderable. A commodity money standard such as the gold standard involves significant economic costs: (1) the resource costs of maintaining the standard and (2) the short-run instability of both the price level and real output that would accompany the adjustment of the commodity to changing supply and demand conditions.

Moreover, the history of the pre–World War I gold standard suggests that it worked because it was a "managed" international standard. In addition, the concentration of world capital and money markets in London and the use of sterling as a key currency enabled the system to function smoothly with limited gold reserves and to withstand a number of severe external shocks. Perhaps of paramount importance for the successful operation of the managed gold standard was the tacit cooperation of the major participants in (ultimately) maintaining the gold standard link and its corollary, long-run price stability, as the primary goal of economic policy.[54] This suggests that one country alone on the gold standard would likely find its monetary gold stock and hence its money supply subject to persistent shocks from factors beyond its control.

A fiduciary money standard based on a monetary rule of a steady and known rate of monetary growth could provide both greater price level and real output stability than a return to the gold standard. The key problem with a fiduciary system, however, is to ensure that such a rule is maintained and that a commitment be made to the goal of long-run price stability.

Data Appendix

Figure 5.1

UNITED KINGDOM

1. **Wholesale Prices 1800–1979.** (1972 = 100). Data for 1800–1938 and 1946–1975 from Roy W. Jastram, *The Golden Constant* (John Wiley and Sons, New York, 1977), Table 2, pp. 32–33; 1939–1945 from B. R. Mitchell, *Euro-*

pean Historical Statistics 1750–1970 (Columbia University Press, New York, 1975), Table I1, p. 739; 1976–78 Central Statistical Office, *Economic Trends Annual Supplement 1980 Edition* (Her Majesty's Stationery Office, London, 1979), p. 112, series: Wholesale Prices for All Manufactured Products, 1976 figure used was an average of the CSO 1976 value and Jastram's

---

[54] Other conditions amenable to the successful operation of the gold standard were the free mobility of labor and capital, the absence of exchange controls and the absence of any major wars.

1976 value; 1979 from CSO, *Monthly Digest of Statistics* (Her Majesty's Stationery Office, London, Nov. 1980), p. 159, series: same as 1976–1978.

Figure 5.2

UNITED STATES

1. **Wholesale Prices 1800–1979.** (1972 = 100). Data for 1800–1975 from Roy W. Jastram, *The Golden Constant* (John Wiley & Sons, New York, 1977), Table 7, pp. 145–46; 1976 from U.S. Dept. of Labor, Bureau of Labor Statistics, *Wholesale Prices and Indexes Supplement 1977* (1977), Table 4, series: All Commodities; 1977 from Dept. of Labor, BLS, *Monthly Labor Review* (April 1978), Table 26, series: All Commodities; 1978 from *Monthly Labor Review* (April 1979), Table 27, series: All Commodities; 1979 from Dept. of Labor, BLS, *Supplement to Producer Price and Price Indexes Data for 1979* (1980), Table 4, series: All Commodities.

Figure 5.3

WORLD

1. **United Kingdom Purchasing Power of Gold 1821–1914.** (1972 = 1.00). 1821–1914 from Roy W. Jastram, *The Golden Constant* (John Wiley & Sons, New York, 1977), Table 3, pp. 36–37.
2. **World Monetary Gold Stock 1821–1914.** Data for 1821–1838 represent interpolation between

values for 1807, 1833 and 1839. These values, along with the 1839–1914 values, from League of Nations, *Interim Report of the Gold Delegation and Report of the Gold Delegation* (Arno Press, New York, 1978), Table B, col. (1), series: Monetary Stock of Gold, end of year, millions of pounds at 84s 11$\frac{1}{2}$ per fine oz.

Figure 5.4

UNITED STATES

1. **Purchasing Power of Gold 1879–1914.** (1972 = 1.00). Data for 1879–1914 from Roy W. Jastram. *The Golden Constant* (John Wiley & Sons, New York, 1977), Table 8, pp. 147–48.
2. **Monetary Gold Stock 1879–1914.** Data for 1879–1914 from Phillip Cagan, *Determinants and Effects of Changes in the Stock of Money 1875–1960* (Columbia University Press, New York, 1965), Appendix F, Table F-7, col. (1), current par value = $20.67 per oz. Cagan's sources include the following: 1879–1907, *Annual Report*, Mint, 1907; 1908–1913, *Circulation Statement of United States Money*; 1914, *Banking and Monetary Statistics*, FRB, 1941.

Figure 5.5

UNITED KINGDOM

1. **Real per Capita Income** 1870–1979. (1972 pounds).
   (a) *Nominal Income* 1870–1979. Data for 1870–1975 from Milton Friedman and Anna J.

Schwartz, forthcoming *Monetary Trends in the United States and the United Kingdom: Their Relation to Income, Prices, and Interest Rates 1867–1975*, National Bureau of Economic Research, Chapter 4, Table 4-A-2, col. (2). Nominal income for 1976–1979 computed as GNP at factor cost less consumption of fixed capital. 1976–1978 GNP at factor cost from CSO, *Economic Trends Annual Supplement 1980 Edition*, Table 36, col. (2); 1979 GNP at factor cost from CSO, *Monthly Digest of Statistics* (Jan. 1981), Table 1.2, col. (2). 1976–1979 Consumption of fixed capital from OECD, *National Accounts of OECD Countries* (Paris, 1981), Vol. 1, p. 70, series #36: Consumption of the Fixed Capital.

(b) *Implicit Price Deflator* 1870–1979. (1972 = 100). Data for 1870–1975 from Friedman and Schwartz, *Monetary Trends*, Chapter 4, Table 4-A-2, col. (4); 1976–1979 from International Monetary Fund, *International Financial Statistics* (Jan. 1981), p. 404; deflator calculated as P = 100 × (nominal GDP/real GDP), real and nominal GDP appearing in *IFS*.

(c) *Population* 1870–1979. Data for 1870–1965 from C. Feinstein, *National Income, Expenditure and Output of the United Kingdom, 1855–1965*, Table 44, col. (1); 1966–75 from CSO, *Annual*

Statistical Abstract; 1976–1979 from CSO, *Monthly Digest of Statistics* (Nov. 1980), p. 16.

Figure 5.4

UNITED STATES

1. Real Per Capita Income 1870–1979. (1972 dollars). This series is the result of splicing together two series, the earlier based upon data from Friedman and Schwartz, *Monetary Trends*, and the later based upon data from U.S. Dept. of Commerce, *Survey of Current Business*.

For 1870–1949, a real per capita income series was computed using the following data: nominal income, Friedman and Schwartz, *Monetary Trends*, Chapter 4, Table 4-A-1, col. (2); implicit price deflator, 1972 = 100, Chapter 4, Table 4-A-1, col. (1); population, U.S. Department of Commerce, *Historical Statistics* (1960). This series was then adjusted in the following way:

$$[Y/(P \times N)]_t = \exp[\ln(FS_t) + (\ln(SCB_{1950}) - \ln(FS_{1950}))],$$
$$t = 1870, \dots, 1949$$

Where FS_t = Friedman-Schwartz value of real per capita income in time t and SCB_t = *Survey of Current Business* value in time t. The adjusted series was then joined to the 1950–1979 series computed from the following data in the *Survey of Current Business*: nominal NNP, average of quarterly figures, seasonally adjusted and NNP implicit price deflator, average of quarterly figures, 1972 = 100; population data (resident population less armed forces, average of monthly figures) from U.S. Dept. of Commerce, Bureau of the Census.

Other data used

1. **U.S. Unemployment Rates 1890–1979.** Data for 1890–1900 from Stanley Lebergott, "Changes in Unemployment 1800–1960," in Robert W. Fogel and Stanley L. Engerman, eds., *The Reinterpretation of American Economic History* (Harper & Row, New York, 1971). p. 80, Table 1; 1901–1957 from Dept. of Commerce, Bureau of the Census, *Historical Statistics of the United States* (1960), series D-47; 1958 from Dept. of Labor. BLS, *Monthly Labor Review Statistical Supplement* (1959), Table I-1; 1959–1962 from *MLR Statistical Supplement* (1962), Table I-1, p. 1; 1963 from *MLR Statistical Supplement* (1963), Table I-1; 1964–1979 from Dept. of Labor, BLS, *Monthly Labor Review* (Jan. 1981), Table 1.

2. **Great Britain Unemployment Rates 1888–1979.** Data for 1888–1966 from B. R. Mitchell, *European Historical Statistics 1750–1970* (Columbia University Press, 1975), Table C2, series: UK:GB; 1967–72 from CSO, *Monthly Digest of Statistics* (March 1973), Table 21, series: Percent unemployed of total employees for Great Britain; 1973–1977 from same publication as for 1967–1972 (Oct. 1978), Table 3.9, series: same as that for 1967–1972; 1978–1979 from same publication as 1967–1972 (Nov. 1980), Table 3.10, series: same as that for 1967–1972.

3. **U.S. Money Supply 1879–1979.** Data for 1879–1975 from Friedman and Schwartz, *Monetary Trends*, Chapter 4, Table 4-A-1, col. (1); 1976–1979 from Board of Governors of the Federal Reserve System. Statistical Release: Money Stock Measures, H.6, series M2, annual average of monthly figures, seasonally adjusted.

4. **U.K. Money Supply 1870–1979.** Data for 1870–1975 from Friedman and Schwartz, *Monetary Trends*, Chapter 4, Table 4-A-2, col. (1); 1976–1979 from CSO, *Financial Statistics* (Her Majesty's Stationery Office, London, Nov. 1980), p. 144, series M3, not seasonally adjusted, end of second quarter.

CHAPTER 6

A model of the classical gold standard with depletion

Written with Richard Wayne Ellson

The operation and properties of the classical gold standard are well recognized. However, one aspect that has not been dealt with is that gold has the characteristics of a durable, but depletable resource. In this chapter, we compare the simple classical model of the gold standard with a model of the gold standard that incorporates the durable, depletable nature of gold. Using numerical simulation techniques, we demonstrate an inescapable tendency to long-run deflation when account is taken of the resource constraint. These results are consistent, with and without technological progress and variable real rates of return.

6.1   Introduction

Recent dissatisfaction with high rates of inflation and real economic instability in the U.S. and elsewhere has led to criticism of the operation of the present fiat-based monetary system. Some economists have advocated a return to the classical gold standard, based on a government maintained fixed price of gold in terms of the national currency, on the grounds that the gold standard would provide greater price stability than under current arrangement.[1] Indeed, such interest led to the establishment of the U.S. Congressional Gold Commission in 1981.[2]

A second desirable attribute of the gold standard stressed by its advocates is that the monetary gold stock and hence the money supply is determined by competitive market forces according to the classical commodity theory of money largely independent of government policy. The classical tradition of Thornton (1802), Mill (1865), Fisher (1922), and Friedman (1953) viewed the monetary gold stock and hence the money

This chapter is reprinted from the July 1985 *Journal of Monetary Economics*, 16(1):109–120.

The first author is also affiliated with the National Bureau of Economic Research, Cambridge, MA 02138. For helpful comments annd suggestions, we would like to thank the following: John Chilton, Mike Connolly, Stephen Ferris, Milton Friedman, Levis Kochin, John McDermott, Blaine Roberts, Charlie Stuart, Anna Schwartz, and an anonymous referee.

[1] For some historical evidence on the record of price level and real output stability of the gold standard for the U.S. and the U.K., see Bordo (1981).

[2] For a discussion of the deliberations and conclusions of the Gold Commission, see Schwartz (1982).

supply and the price level under the gold standard as determined by two offsetting sets of equilibrating forces producing a tendency to long-run price stability: the response of gold production to changes in the real price of gold, and shifts between monetary and non-monetary uses of gold by households and firms in response to changes in the real price of gold.[3]

In a recent article, Barro (1979) has provided a lucid formal exposition of the operation of the classical gold standard. One important aspect of the operation of a commodity standard such as the gold standard not treated by Barro or elsewhere in the literature is that of gold as a durable, but depletable resource. This view takes above ground gold as a commodity that depreciates at a very slow rate and incorporates the potential exhaustion of gold mines. In the literature on exhaustible resources following Hotelling (1931), the long-run growth rate of the real price of a resource, determined in a competitive market, and assuming zero marginal costs, should equal the real rate of interest.[4] Indeed, the long-run behavior of the monetary gold stock and the price level when depletion of below ground stocks of gold is accounted for will differ from that suggested by the classical model. In this chapter we combine the treatment of gold as a durable depletable resource, following the recent approach taken by Levhari and Pindyck (1981), with that of the gold standard by Barro (1979).

The key differences we find between the simple classical model of the gold standard and a model of the gold standard accounting for the durable depletable resource aspect of gold are: an inescapable tendency to long-run deflation when account is taken of the resource constraint, and a tendency for the equilibrating mechanism of the classical gold standard to be muted by the operation of the resource constraint.

Our approach in Section 6.2 is to construct a simple model of a closed economy gold standard accounting for the resource constraint. In addition we incorporate technological progress and a variable real rate of return into the model. In Section 6.3 the model is then parameterized and simulated to generate hypothetical paths for its key endogenous variables: gold production, the growth of non-monetary gold demand, the monetary gold stock, the money supply, and the price level. Comparisons are then made between the performance of the model under

---

[3] For a discussion of the traditional approach to the Gold Standard, see Bordo (1984).

[4] In the presence of rising costs and/or monopoly, the growth rate of net rent should equal the real interest rate. This holds for a non-durable resource with constant demand. In the presence of durability and growing demand the price path may differ from Hotelling's rule. See Pindyck (1978) and Stewart (1980), for example.

both classical gold standard and resource model assumptions. Section 6.4 contains a brief conclusion.

6.2 The model

6.2.1 The classical model

We start with Barro's treatment of the classical model for a closed economy, adapting it slightly to account for a variable real rate of interest and to allow for technological progress. Equations (6.1) to (6.6) represent the money market. Equation (6.1) represents the money supply:

$$M^s = \mu P_G G_M, \tag{6.1}$$

where M^s equals the money supply expressed in terms of dollars, μ the money multiplier – the ratio of the sum of currency and deposits to the value of the monetary gold stock (it is the product of both the ratio of the money supply to the monetary base and the monetary base to the value of the monetary gold stock), P_G the fixed nominal price per ounce of gold, and G_M the monetary gold stock in ounces. Equation (6.2) represents the income velocity of circulation. We assume it is a logarithmic function of the nominal interest rate:[5]

$$V = \overline{V} i^a. \tag{6.2}$$

Following Fisher (1930) we define the nominal interest rate as

$$i = r + \pi, \tag{6.3}$$

where r represents the real rate of interest and π the expected rate of change in the price level. Following Mundell (1970), we assume the real rate of interest to be a negative function of the expected rate of price change:

$$r = \overline{r} - a\pi. \tag{6.4}$$

Finally, we assume perfect foresight, so that

$$\pi = (P_t - P_{t-1})/P_{t-1}.^6 \tag{6.5}$$

---

[5] We depart from Barro, who, in the text of his paper, assumes a constant real rate of return and makes the demand for money a function of the expected rate of change in the price level. But following Barro, eq. (6.2) assumes the real income and price elasticities of real money demand to be one.

[6] We also tried an adaptive expectations scheme. As expected, the adjustment path of the model differed under the two schemes of generating expectations, but the long-run equilibrium values of the endogenous variables were not affected.

Equilibrium in the money market requires that

$$P = \mu V P_G G_M / y, \tag{6.6}$$

given μ, P_G, the assumption of perfect foresight, and assuming a constant level of real output, y, the price level is determined by the monetary gold stock.

Equations (6.7) to (6.9) represent the "real" conditions of the gold market. These equations in combination with (6.1) to (6.6) determine a unique equilibrium money supply and price level. We assume that gold production is characterized by increasing costs and that the supply function for new gold is simply

$$g = \bar{g} P_g^\beta e^{\gamma t}, \tag{6.7}$$

where g equals production, P_g the real price of gold, P_G/P, and t is a time trend to allow for exogenous technological progress.[7] The demand for non-monetary gold is assumed to be a flow function of the form

$$\dot{G}_N = (\varepsilon + \delta)\left(G_N^* - G_N\right), \tag{6.8}$$

where $\dot{G}_N$ equals the net change in the non-monetary gold stock, and G_N^* is the target or desired stock of non-monetary gold. G_N^* is defined as

$$G_N^* = \bar{G}_N P_g^{-\theta} y^\eta i^{-\Phi}.$$

The parameter ε is a partial adjustment factor, δ is the depreciation rate or normal replacement flow, and G_N represents the actual stock of non-monetary gold.

Finally, on the assumption that the monetary authorities are committed to maintaining a fixed price of gold, the change in the monetary gold stock is simply the residual,

$$\dot{G}_M = g - \dot{G}_N, \tag{6.9}$$

where $\dot{G}_M$ equals the net change in the monetary gold stock.

Assuming y, P_G, and μ are fixed, taking logs, and solving eqs. (6.1) to (6.9) simultaneously, the steady-state solutions for the model are $\dot{P} = \dot{G}_M = \dot{G}_N = 0$ (in terms of growth rates). This also implies that $g = \delta G_N^*$ – that gold production at any point in time is equal to the depreciation rate multiplied by the desired non-monetary gold stock.

[7] Barro does not explicitly account for technological progress in his model but discusses the implications of accounting for it. We assume technological progress is exogenous to simplify the discussions. However, there is evidence that major technological changes in the gold industry were both induced and exogenous [Rockoff (1984)].

6.2.2 The resource model

The real sector of the classical gold model described above assumes that gold production, g, is a function of the real price of gold and exogenous technical change. However, if we treat gold as a durable finite resource, then gold production would be affected not only by the real price of gold but also by the cost characteristics of production.

The simple Hotelling rule (1931) states that the (real) price of an exhaustible resource should rise at the rate r (the real interest rate), under conditions of certainty and zero marginal costs. As Levhari and Pindyck (1981) point out, the Hotelling rule properly defined implies that the resource rent (price minus marginal cost) increases by r, assuming perfect competition and certainty. This is an important distinction. In the classical model gold production is directly related to the real price of gold, whereas in the exhaustible resource literature, gold production can increase as the real price falls as long as marginal costs decline more rapidly, thus resulting in an increase in resource rents.

Our price and production equations are taken from Levhari and Pindyck. With respect to the former,

$$\dot{P}_g = (r + \delta)P_{g,t-1} - f(Q)e^{\lambda t}, \tag{6.10}$$

where $f(Q)e^{\lambda t}$ is the marginal value of services from a stock of resource, Q, and $e^{\lambda t}$ is the growth of real output. In our model, $f(Q) = (G_N/G_M)^{-a}$, where G_N and G_M represent non-monetary and monetary stocks, respectively.

We have assumed a Cobb–Douglas specification for total costs accounting for both production and depletion of the resource:

$$C = Ag^p X^{-v},$$

where C is total cost, X equals the remaining stock, and neutral technological progress enters through A. Because of depletion, our production equation differs slightly from Levhari and Pindyck and also includes the effect of depletion on marginal costs:

$$\dot{g} = \frac{1}{C_{gg}}[(\delta P_g) + rC_g - f(Q)e^{rt} - C_{gX}g], \tag{6.11}$$

with C_g marginal cost, C_{gg} the derivative with respect to output, and C_{gX} the cross-effect. Although one would expect the latter to be positive, there is substantial evidence that the discontinuities of gold deposits could have a negative effect. Thus, we have taken the term to be zero in our simulations.

Equations (6.10) and (6.11) can then be solved simultaneously to determine the equilibrium real price and output paths for gold. The resource model can then be integrated with the monetary sector. This integrated model consists of five simultaneous equations from the resource sector including eqs. (6.8), (6.10), and (6.11) plus equations for C_g and C_{gg}. This is combined with the monetary sector described by eqs. (6.1) through (6.6), and accordingly, $\dot{G}_M$ and G_M are also determined.

6.3   Parameters of the models and comparisons

6.3.1   Parameters

The initial values of the parameters in the model are given in panel A of Table 6.1. The depreciation of gold, δ, is assumed to be 1.0 percent and the adjustment parameter, ε, in the $\dot{G}_N$ equation is 0.5. We further assume that the money multiplier, μ, has a constant value of 10 over the simulation period, and that the rate of economic growth and the rate of technological progress are exogenous and equal to 3.0 percent per time period. Finally, we assume the autonomous growth rate in desired demand for the resource to equal the real rate of interest. Thus, producers have no incentive to withhold or expand production based on a differential here. The remaining parameters are basically consistent with estimates found in the literature and were selected to correspond to the start values for the endogenous variables that are listed in panel B of Table 6.1.

Both the classical model and the integrated model were simulated over twenty-five time periods using the parameters discussed above and the start values. The initial values of the gold variables are hypothetical and were chosen for analytical convenience. However, they reasonably correspond to estimates for the world in the late 1920s.[8]

6.3.2   Comparison of the models

We now compare the performance of the classical model relative to the integrated model for the key endogenous variables. Table 6.2 represents the values at five period intervals as well as the overall period mean of: gold production, the net change in the non-monetary demand for gold, the monetary gold stock, and the money supply and the price level. Four experiments are reported:

---

[8] See the Statistical Compendium to the *Report to the Congress of the Commission on the Role of Gold in the Domestic and International Monetary Systems*, Vol. 1 (1982).

Table 6.1. *Parameters and initial values of the model*

___

(A) *Parameters*

$\bar{V}$ = 1.1

α = 0.5

a = 0.1

$\bar{g}$ = 1.6

β = 0.6

$\bar{G}_N$ = 0.03

Θ = 1.2

η = 1.0

Φ = 0.1

$\bar{r}$ = 0.03

σ = 1.3

ρ = 1.75

ν = 0.02

(B) *Initial values*

P_G = 20; fixed nominal price of gold, dollars per ounce

P_g = 20; real price of gold, dollars per ounce

P = 100; price index

y = 270; real output; $billions

M^s = 90; money supply, $billions

G_n = 550; non-monetary gold stock, millions of ounces

G_m = 450; monetary gold stock, millions of ounces

g = 30; gold production first period, millions of ounces

X = 1000; remaining stock, millions of ounces

r = 0.03; real interest rate

V = 3; velocity

i = 0.03; nominal interest rate

___

(A) the two models assuming constant real interest rates, no expected change in the price level, and the absence of technological change – the benchmark case (and the closest comparison with Barro's model);

(B) the two models assuming constant real interest rates, no expected change in the price level, with technical change at 3 percent per period;

(C) the two models assuming variable real interest rates, expected change in the price level, and no technical change; and

(D) the two models with variable real interest rates, expected change in the price level, and technical change at 3 percent.

Table 6.2. *Comparisons of (a) the classical model with (b) the integrated resource model*

	(1) g		(2) G_n		(3) G_M		(4) M^s		(5) P	
	(a)	(b)	(a)	(b)	(a)	(b)	(a)	(b)	(a)	(b)
(A) Assuming a constant real rate of interest, no expected change in the price level, no technical change										
1	30.0	30.0	16.5	16.5	463.5	463.5	92.7	92.7	100	100
5	30.3	29.8	18.4	22.9	511.9	499.2	102.4	99.8	98.1	95.7
10	31.0	29.7	19.2	27.4	571.1	519.3	114.2	103.9	94.4	85.9
15	32.0	30.2	20.1	30.5	630.2	522.3	126.0	104.5	89.9	74.5
20	33.1	31.5	21.2	32.8	689.6	517.3	137.9	103.5	84.9	63.6
25	34.4	33.7	22.4	34.6	749.6	511.6	149.9	102.3	79.6	54.3
Mean	31.8	30.7	19.8	28.2	606.6	510.2	121.3	102.0	91.1	78.6
(B) Assuming a constant real rate of interest, no expected change in the price level, and exogenous technological change										
1	30.9	30.1	16.8	16.5	464.0	463.6	92.7	92.7	100	100
5	35.0	30.5	20.8	23.0	519.0	500.9	103.8	100.2	99.5	96.0
10	40.9	32.0	24.6	27.9	595.9	527.5	119.2	105.5	98.5	87.2
15	47.7	34.9	29.0	32.2	684.5	542.9	136.9	108.6	97.6	77.4
20	55.8	39.1	34.2	36.5	786.4	555.6	157.3	110.1	96.8	68.3
25	65.1	45.0	40.4	41.3	903.5	571.6	180.7	114.3	95.9	60.7
Mean	46.0	35.0	27.8	30.2	660.7	530.8	132.1	106.2	98.0	81.2

(C) Assuming a variable real rate of interest, expected change in the price level, no technical change

1	30.0	30.0	16.5	16.5	463.5	463.5	92.7	92.7	100	100
5	30.4	30.0	18.4	22.3	501.1	512.5	102.5	100.2	98.0	95.5
10	31.1	30.2	19.2	26.2	527.8	572.2	114.4	105.6	94.3	86.4
15	32.0	30.9	20.1	29.2	540.1	631.7	126.3	108.0	89.7	76.2
20	33.2	32.4	21.1	31.8	544.7	691.6	138.3	108.9	84.6	66.2
25	34.5	34.6	22.3	34.1	547.2	752.1	150.4	109.4	79.4	57.4
Mean	31.8	31.2	19.8	27.3	525.5	608.1	121.6	105.1	90.9	79.9

(D) Assuming a variable real rate of interest, expected change in the price level, and exogenous technical change

1	30.9	30.1	16.9	16.5	463.6	463.9	92.8	92.7	100.2	100
5	35.0	30.7	20.8	22.4	502.6	519.1	103.8	108.5	99.4	95.8
10	40.9	32.5	24.6	26.9	535.3	596.2	119.2	107.1	98.5	87.7
15	47.7	35.7	29.0	31.3	559.3	684.8	137.0	111.9	97.6	79.0
20	55.8	46.4	34.2	36.0	581.0	786.7	157.4	116.2	96.7	70.8
25	65.1	46.9	40.4	41.6	605.2	903.9	180.8	121.1	95.9	63.7
Mean	46.0	35.8	27.8	29.6	545.0	661.0	132.2	109.0	98.0	82.4

Column 1 shows the pattern of gold production, g. In the benchmark case A gold production rises over the whole period in the classical model. This reflects the influence of the assumed real growth of 3 percent per period creating an excess demand for money, which in turn produces deflation, raising the real price of gold and encouraging production. By contrast in the integrated model, production initially declines slightly because of increasing costs and declining resource rents. Introducing technological change in case B virtually doubles gold production in the classical model, whereas by contrast, in the resource model production increases by a much smaller amount reflecting the effects of depletion of the resource. Introducing a variable real rate of return and expected deflation produces virtually no change in the classical model,[9] but in the resource model production is increased relative to the benchmark case because of the additional, expected deflation which raises the real interest rate, and hence via Hotelling's rule raises production.

Column 2 shows $\dot{G}_N$, the net change in non-monetary demand for gold. In both models it is a function of real output and the real price of gold. We would expect $\dot{G}_N$ to rise reflecting the direct effect of real growth but to decline reflecting the indirect effect of deflation producing substitution of monetary for non-monetary gold stocks. In the benchmark case A, $\dot{G}_N$ rises above its corresponding values in the classical model because of the greater rise in the real price, which in turn reflects the decline in production in that model as real rents decline. Technological change, case B, raises $\dot{G}_N$ in both models via increased gold production raising the monetary gold stock, the money supply, and the price level, and lowering the real price of gold, in turn encouraging substitution of monetary for non-monetary gold. This effect is considerably weaker in the integrated model because of the greater deflationary effect associated with the resource constraint. Finally, the assumptions of a variable real rate of interest and expected deflation have virtually no effect in the classical model, but in the resource model they slightly reduce $\dot{G}_N$. This reflects the effects of a higher real interest rate in raising the real price of gold.

Column 3 displays G_M, the monetary gold stock, which in the benchmark case A rises at a much slower rate in the integrated model than in the classical model reflecting the forces described above. In addition, technological change produces a smaller rise in G_M in the integrated model than in the classical model. Introducing a variable real rate and

---

[9] This result reflects the effect of our assumed interest elasticity of velocity (0.5), interest elasticity of nonmonetary gold demand (-0.1) and a low rate of deflation.

expected deflation has virtually no effect on G_M in the classical model, while it raises G_M in the integrated model, reflecting the effect of a rising real interest rate on gold production.

Column 4 shows M^s, the money supply, whose movement is governed by and reflects the behavior of G_M.

Finally, column 5 portrays movements in the price level. In the benchmark case, deflation prevails over the entire period in both models. However, deflation is much greater in the integrated model because of the decrease in gold production over the period. Thus, the offsetting influences to deflation of the classical model through the substitution between monetary and non-monetary gold holding and the effects of a rising real price of gold on production are completely swamped when we account for the resource effects.

Furthermore, introducing technological progress at the same rate as the underlying growth rate of the economy (case B) almost fully offsets the deflation in the classical model – restoring price stability. However, this is definitely not the case in the resource model, where deflation prevails. Moreover, while accounting for a variable real rate of interest and expected deflation (case C) does offset some of the deflationary pressure in the integrated model, it does not negate it.

The qualitative results above are not materially changed when the key parameters of the models (σ, ρ, v, α, a, ε, and Φ) are varied. Particularly important are α, a, and Φ, for which ranges are suggested by the literature.[10] In addition, raising the rate of technological change from 3 percent to 5 percent per period reduces the rate of deflation in the resource model by a relatively small amount.

6.4   Conclusion

When account is taken of the durable, depletable resource property of gold, the operation of the classical gold standard is modified in two significant ways. First, in the presence of real growth there is an inescapable tendency towards long-run deflation, a tendency that is not overcome by technological change or by a variable real rate of interest and expected deflation. Second, the equilibrating mechanism of the classical model towards the long-run equilibrium price path is muted by the operation of the resource constraint.

---

[10] Model C was simulated over the following ranges of parameters: σ, 1.3 to 1.4; ρ, 1.75 to 1.8; v, 0.02 to 0.025; α, 0.1 to 0.5 to 0.6; a, 0.1 to 0.5 to 1.0; Φ, 0.1 to 0.5 to 0.85; ε, 0.25 to 0.75. The results of the sensitivity analysis are available upon request from the authors.

These conclusions have important implications. The greater tendency towards long-run deflation suggests that the likelihood of gold discoveries and technological advances in gold production being sufficient to offset the tendency towards deflation are even more remote than would be suggested by the classical model in the presence of real growth. On the other hand, the rate of deflation that satisfies Hotelling's rule would, if perfectly anticipated, also satisfy Friedman's (1969) optimum quantity of money rule – giving the community the satisfaction level of real cash balances.[11]

References

Barro, R., 1979, Money and the price level under the gold standard, Economic Journal 89, 13–33.

Bordo, M. D., 1981, The classical gold standard: Some lessons for today, Federal Reserve Bank of St. Louis Review 63, 2–17.

Bordo, M. D., 1984, The gold standard: The traditional approach, in: M. D. Bordo and A. J. Schwartz, eds., A retrospective on the classical gold standard 1821–1931 (University of Chicago Press, Chicago, IL).

Fisher, I., 1965, The purchasing power of money, 2nd ed. (Augustus M. Kelly, New York).

Friedman, M., 1953, Commodity reserve currency, in: Essays in positive economics (University of Chicago Press, Chicago, IL).

Friedman, M., 1969, The optimum quantity of money, in: Optimum quantity of money and other essays (Aldine, Chicago, IL).

Hotelling, H., 1931, The economics of exhaustible resources, Journal of Political Economy 39, 137–175.

Levhari, D. and R. Pindyck, 1981, The pricing of durable exhaustible resources, Quarterly Journal of Economics 96, 365–377.

Mill, J. S., 1962, Principles of political economy (1865) (Augustus M. Kelly, New York).

Pindyck, R. S., 1978, The optimal exploration and production of nonrenewable resources, Journal of Political Economy 86, 841–861.

Report to the Congress of the Commission on the Role of Gold in the Domestic and International Monetary Systems, Vol. 1 (1982).

Rockoff, H., 1984, Some evidence on the real price of gold, its costs of production, and commodity prices, in: M. D. Bordo and A. J. Schwartz, eds., A retrospective on the classical gold standard 1821–1931 (University of Chicago Press, Chicago, IL).

Schwartz, A. J., 1982, Reflections on the Gold Commission report, Journal of Money Credit and Banking 4, 538–551.

[11] See, e.g., Rockoff (1984, pp. 619–620).

Stewart, M. B., 1980, Monopoly and the international production of a durable extractable resource, Quarterly Journal of Economics 95, 99–111.

Thornton, H., 1978, An inquiry into the nature and effects of the paper credit of Great Britain (1802) (Augustus M. Kelly, New York).

PART III

The gold standard as a contingent rule

CHAPTER 7

The gold standard as a commitment mechanism

Written with Finn E. Kydland

7.1   Introduction

The gold standard has been a subject of perennial interest to both econo-mists and economic historians. Attention has focused on three aspects of the gold standard's performance: as an international exchange rate ar-rangement; as a provider of macroeconomic stability; and as a constraint on government policy actions.

The balance of payments adjustment mechanism, or the link between the money supplies, price levels, and real outputs of different countries under fixed exchange rates, has long been studied as the key aspect of the international exchange rate arrangement of the gold standard.[1] The durability of fixed exchange rates, the absence of exchange market crises, and the smooth adjustment to the massive transfers of capital in the decades before 1914 have been features stressed in monetary reform proposals ever since.

The gold standard has often been viewed as ensuring long-run, though not necessarily short-run, price stability via the operation of the classical commodity theory of money. Recent comparisons between the classical gold standard and subsequent managed fiduciary monetary regimes sug-gest, however, that the record is mixed with respect to both price level and real output performance.[2]

Finally, the gold standard has also been viewed as a form of constraint over monetary policy actions – as a form of monetary rule. The Currency

This chapter is reprinted from Tamin Bayoumi, Barry Eichengreen, and Mark Taylor (eds.), *Economic Perspectives on the Classical Gold Standard*. Cambridge: Cambridge University Press, 1996, pp. 55–100.

For helpful comments and suggestions on earlier drafts of this chapter we would like to thank Charles Calomiris, Barry Eichengreen, Marvin Goodfriend, Lars Jonung, Leslie Presnell, Hugh Rockoff, Anna Schwartz, Guido Tabellini, Warren Weber, and participants at seminars at Carnegie–Mellon University, the Federal Reserve Bank of Richmond, Columbia University, Queens University, Carleton University, the NBER Macroeconomic History Conference (June 1989), and the NBER Summer Institute (1991). For valuable research assistance we thank Mary Ann Pastuch and Bernard Eschweiler.
[1] For surveys of this literature, see Bordo (1984) and Eichengreen (1985, 1992a).
[2] See Bordo (1981), Cooper (1982), and Meltzer and Robinson (1989).

School in England in the early 19th century made the case for the Bank of England's fiduciary note issue to vary automatically with the level of the Bank's gold reserve ("the currency principle"). Following such a rule was viewed as preferable (for providing price level stability) to allowing the note issue to be altered at the discretion of the well meaning and possibly well informed directors of the Bank (the position taken by the opposing Banking School).[3]

In this chapter, we focus on the third aspect of the gold standard's performance – on the gold standard as a rule. However, our meaning of the concept of a "rule" differs radically from what used to be the traditional one. In our view, a rule can be regarded as a way of binding policy actions over time. This view of policy rules, in contrast to the earlier tradition that stressed both impersonality and automaticity, stems from the recent literature on the time inconsistency of optimal government policy. Suppose the government calculates today an optimal plan, according to its objectives, for current and future policy choices. Now suppose that, some time in the future, the remainder of the plan is re-evaluated by calculating the optimal plan from then on. Assuming the objectives have not changed, is this plan simply the continuation of the original one? The answer generally is "no." This is what it means for government policy to be time inconsistent. Discretion, in this context, means setting policy sequentially, which then could lead to policies and outcomes that are very different from the optimal plan. The literature on time inconsistency has demonstrated that, in almost all intertemporal policy situations, the government would benefit from having access to a commitment mechanism preventing it from changing planned future policy. In this chapter, we use that literature as a framework for understanding the historical operation of the gold standard.

For the period from 1880 to 1914, the gold standard is often viewed as a monolithic regime where all countries religiously followed the dictates of the rule of a fixed price of gold. Before 1880, most countries were on a form of specie standard: either bimetallism or silver or gold monometallism. As we point out below, however, from our perspective the bimetallic standards that many countries followed were a variant of the gold standard rule. This is contrasted to the period since 1914, when central banks and governments to a great extent have geared their policies to satisfy more immediate objectives without considering intertemporal consequences in terms of lack of commitment to a long-run rule governing policy. In this chapter, we show that the rule followed by a number of key countries – England, the United States, and France – before 1914

---

[3] For a discussion of the Currency Banking School debate, see Viner (1937), Fetter (1965), and Schwartz (1987).

was consistent with such a commitment. The experiences of these major countries suggest that the gold standard was intended as a contingent rule. By that, we mean that the authorities could temporarily abandon the fixed price of gold during an emergency (such as a war) on the understanding that convertibility at the original price would be restored when the emergency passed.

The next section presents a framework for discussing the benefits of being able to commit to future government policy. Moreover, it interprets the institutions of the gold standard era in light of this framework. We then survey the historical record on the adherence to the gold standard rule by three core countries: England, the United States, and France, and by a country that is generally believed not to have adhered to the rule: Italy. The final section attempts to draw some lessons from history.

7.2   The gold standard as a contingent rule

7.2.1   The value of commitment

A long-standing question in public finance is how to finance varying quantities of government expenditures in such a way as to minimize deadweight loss to society. In the last decade, this question, which dates back to the pioneering work by Ramsey (1927), has shifted more and more from static to dynamic environments. We shall argue that the intertemporal framework presented in this literature is the appropriate one for evaluating the operation of the gold standard.

The focus of this literature initially centered around the incentives (in the absence of a commitment mechanism to prevent the government from changing its policy rule in the future) for excessive taxation of capital income. Clearly, however, similar arguments can be made with respect to the taxation of (or default on) government debt. We discuss the source of time inconsistency of optimal policy in both contexts. We start with the former because capital income, at least in this century, probably would be a main source of emergency financing, for example during a war, for a government without the credibility to issue much debt. Then, we introduce government debt policy, which we contend is the major reason why the gold standard was adhered to in some countries for long periods of time.

Consider the following prototype model of optimal taxation.[4] The

---

[4] The following framework is essentially identical to that in Kydland and Prescott (1980a). Also in the main example of Kydland and Prescott (1977) time inconsistency is the result of the effects of tax policy on the incentives for capital accumulation.

economy is inhabited by a large number of consumers who, for simplicity, are treated as identical. Each consumer maximizes infinite-horizon discounted utility,

$$E\sum_{t=0}^{\infty}\beta^t u(c_t, n_t, g_t, \sigma_t),$$

where c_t is consumption, n_t is hours of work, g_t is *per capita* government purchases, and β is the subjective discount factor. The parameter σ_t is stochastic and may indicate, for instance, how the value of defense expenditures varies over time depending on the political situation. There is little loss of generality, however, in simply assuming that the g_t process itself is exogenous. Thus, the typical consumer is assumed to maximize

$$E\sum_{t=0}^{\infty}\beta^t u(c_t, n_t, g_t) \tag{7.1}$$

subject to

$$k_{t+1} + c_t \leq k_t + (1 - \theta_t)r_t k_t + (1 - \tau_t)w_t n_t$$

and non-negativity constraints. Here, w_t is the real wage rate, and θ_t and τ_t are the tax rates for capital and labor income, respectively. One can think of k_t as including various forms of capital, with r_t being the rental income from owning the capital stock. With little modification, one could also include human capital, which in practice can be taxed more heavily, for example, by increasing the progressivity of the income tax schedule.

In this economy, consumers choose sequences of c_t, n_t, and k_{t+1}, while the government decides on sequences θ_t and τ_t. Interpreting aggregate quantities as measured in *per capita* terms, a formulation of the optimal taxation problem is: choose a sequence

$$\pi_0 = \{\theta_t, \tau_t\}_{t=0}^{\infty}$$

so as to maximize the typical consumer's utility function (1) subject to the government budget constraint

$$g_t \leq \theta_t r_t k_t + \tau_t w_t n_t$$

and the constraints implied by equilibrium aggregate behavior of the atomistic private agents. Their decisions can be written as sequences

$$x_0(\pi_0) = \{c_t(c_t(\pi_0), \quad n_t(\pi_0), \quad k_{t+1}(\pi_0)\}_{t=0}^{\infty};$$

in other words, the equilibrium aggregate private decisions at any time t depend on the entire sequence of government policy. The solution, π_0^*, to this optimal taxation problem, together with the associated equilibrium, $x_0(\pi_0^*)$, is sometimes called a Ramsey allocation.

The heart of the time consistency issue is as follows. Suppose π_0^* is the plan that solves the optimal taxation problem as of time zero. Imagine now that the analogous problem is contemplated as of time $s > 0$. The optimal taxation problem then has a solution π_s^*, which generally is different from the part of π_0^* that specifies the plan for periods $t = s, s + 1, \ldots$ In other words, the original plan, π_0^*, is inconsistent with the passage of time. The reason is that π_0^* takes into account the effects of government policy planned for dates on or after period s on private behavior at dates before s. At time s, however, when π_s^* is computed, private behavior at earlier dates, of course, can no longer be affected.

This prototype model highlights two points. One is that the source of time inconsistency is not that the objective function of the government has a different form than the individuals' utility functions. Secondly, time inconsistency arises in spite of an unchanging objective function over time. Instead, the key factor is that decisions are made sequentially over time in environments in which future government policy affects current private behavior.

In the optimal plan, when an increase in g_t occurs, the effects on labor input of raising τ_t are weighed against the effects on savings behavior from changing θ_t. Once the capital stock is in place, however, the optimal plan from then on, taking history up to that point as given, is to tax that capital more heavily, as it will be supplied inelastically, and to reduce future capital taxation. Of course, such an action by the government is likely to create the belief among the public that a similar change of plans will take place again some time in the future, government announcements to the contrary notwithstanding.

This framework assumes that the government balances its budget in every period. If the changes in government expenditures at times are large, for example during wars, the required changes in tax rates would severely reduce the incentives for economic activity just when the need for such activity is the greatest. Borrowing from the public gives the government the flexibility to smooth tax rates over time. The benefits of tax smoothing, not only during wars, but also under normal circumstances, are discussed in Barro (1979) and in Kydland and Prescott (1980b).

Introducing debt affects neither consumers' objectives nor those of the government. The key difference is in the budget constraints. To illustrate, we use notation that follows closely that of Chari and Kehoe (1989), who build upon the characterization of Ramsey policies with debt in Lucas and Stokey (1983). Consider the government budget constraint,

$$g_t + (1 - \delta_t)q_t \cdot b_t \leq a_t + q_t \cdot b_{t+1}.$$

Here, a_t stands for tax revenue (the sum of revenue from capital and labor taxation and other sources, such as customs duties), δ_t is the rate of default on the government debt (usually because of inflation), and b_t is government debt of different maturities, treated as discount bonds, with prices q_t. We think of high-powered money (for example, greenbacks during the Civil War) as a form of debt and include it in b. Let $_sb_t$ be the amount of debt maturing in period s that is outstanding at the beginning of period t, and let $_sq_t$ be its corresponding price. Define the notation

$$q_t \cdot b_t = \sum_{s=t+1}^{\infty} {}_s q_{ts} b_t.$$

In practice, the quantities $_sb_t$ will usually equal zero if s is large enough. In the case of a one-period bond, for example, the price $_{t+1}q_t$ of new debt issue is determined by

$$_{t+1}q_t = (1-\delta_{t-1})/(1 + r_t),$$

where r_t is the interest rate between periods t and $t + 1$, and δ_{t-1} is the default rate expected to prevail in period $t + 1$.

The time consistency problem is that in the absence of a commitment mechanism, the government in period $t + 1$ would like to default to a greater extent than the original plan specifies. Such default reduces the need for distortionary taxes, but also affects expectations of future defaults and therefore the price q at which the public is willing to hold government debt. In Prescott (1977), for example, the government can finance a given stream of expenditures either through taxes on labor income (abstracting from capital) or by selling debt. For that model, Prescott finds that if the government has no commitment mechanism for future actions, the government will always default on outstanding debt to avoid levying distorting taxes. As a consequence, the equilibrium implies that government debt is zero and that the government always runs a balanced budget. This policy and the implied allocation are, of course, inferior to the Ramsey allocation for that model.

Some more recent papers investigate circumstances under which Ramsey policies are sustainable in the sense of being an equilibrium arising endogenously within the environment considered. Chari and Kehoe (1989, 1990) have studied this issue for situations in which time consistency problems can arise either because of capital taxation or because of the presence of government debt. An expository introduction is in Chari (1988). The typical finding is that a Ramsey allocation will not occur in equilibrium when the horizon is finite. When the horizon is infinite, on the other hand, the Ramsey allocation may be one among a large, usually infinite, number of equilibriums. The conditions that have been used to achieve this result restrict the applicability severely. What supports Ramsey policies as equilibriums in those cases is the belief by consumers that as long as the government has chosen Ramsey policies in the past, it will continue to do so.[5]

To overcome the shortcomings associated with the lack of an endogenous commitment mechanism, society may attempt to design such mechanisms, for example in the form of laws that are hard to change. Such is the case with patent protection. The law may ensure sufficient incentives for inventive activity by allowing firms the exclusive use of new inventions for a period of time without fear that the government will remove the patent right and allow the price of the product to be driven toward the competitive price. Our thesis is that, although the gold standard is easier to change than, for example, the patent law, this institutional arrangement has the potential for working as an explicit, transparent, well understood rule.

In an uncertain world, the Ramsey plan generally would be a contingent plan or rule. Strictly speaking, in a realistic environment the Ramsey plan would include many contingencies, some of which may make little difference to society's welfare. In the patent case, one can imagine that an optimal arrangement occasionally, under special circumstances, would permit nonexclusive use. Drawbacks of including many contingencies, however, are lack of transparency and possible uncertainty among the public regarding the will to obey the original plan. Thus, a practical rule may include only the contingency that is considered most important. In this sense, the rule does not quite reach the maximum of the social welfare function, but the sacrifice is small. By discretion, then, we mean any purposeful deviation, under whatever guise, from such a rule. The excuse for such a deviation could be a "bad outcome," in the language of Grossman and van Huyck (1988), that is not included as a contingency in the original plan. Deviations are tempting because of their immediate benefits (perhaps accompanied by promises not to repeat the breach of the rule). Because of the effect on future beliefs, however, these benefits are outweighed by the long-run implications of having given up on the original, nearly optimal, rule.

---

[5] The idea that reputation may support optimal policy has been studied in a different context by Barro and Gordon (1983).

7.2.2   *The gold standard*

The essence of the gold standard rule is that each country would define the price of gold in terms of its currency and keep the price fixed. This involves defining a gold coin as a fixed weight of gold called, for example, one dollar. The dollar in 1792 was defined as 24.75 grains of gold with 480 grains to the ounce, equivalent to \$19.39 per ounce. The monetary authority was then committed to keep the mint price of gold fixed through the purchase and sale of gold in unlimited amounts. The monetary authority was willing to convert into coin gold bullion brought to it by the public, to charge a certain fee for the service – called brassage – and also to sell coins freely to the public in any amount and allow the public to convert them into bullion or export them.[6]

This rule applies to a pure gold coin standard. In fact, the standard that prevailed in the 19th century was a mixed standard containing both fiduciary money and gold coins. Under the mixed standard, the gold standard rule required that fiduciary money (issued either by private banks or by the government) be freely convertible into gold at the fixed price.

Most countries, until the third quarter of the 19th century, maintained bimetallic systems using both gold and silver at a fixed ratio. Defining the weight of both gold and silver coins, freely buying and selling them, and maintaining the ratio fixed can be viewed as a variant of the basic gold standard rule, since it is a fixed value of the unit of account that is the essence of the rule.[7]

A variant of the gold standard rule that we believe is particularly pertinent applies to the case of a war. Assume for the moment that a country finds the gold standard rule to have good operating characteristics if the gold standard is maintained under all circumstances except for a war. Let z_t equal one if the country is on the gold standard at time t and zero otherwise. Let h_i represent the start of war i and e_i its end. A reasonable rule could be to choose $z_t = 0$ if $t \in [h_i, e_i + d]$ for all i and $z_t = 1$ otherwise; in other words, it is understood that in order to finance

[6] Strictly speaking, the government need define a gold coin only in terms of the unit of account. Private mints could then supply the demand for coin. Indeed, this was the case shortly after the California gold discoveries (Bancroft, 1890, p. 165). In most countries, however, the mint was under government authority.

[7] Viewed, however, as a rule in the traditional sense – as an automatic mechanism to ensure price stability – bimetallism may have had greater scope for automaticity than the gold standard because of the additional cushion of a switch from one metal to the other. See Friedman (1990b). Garber (1986) regards bimetallism as a gold standard with an option.

the war, the gold standard will be suspended for the duration of the war plus a delay period d, which is the same in every war. Such a policy, if implemented as planned, is consistent with a gold standard rule. It is clear that when people foresee a war in the near future, this rule will result in different prices q_t for the issue of new debt than under the unconditional $z_t = 1$ rule. These effects would be regarded as negative, although they presumably would be outweighed by the benefits of being better able to finance the war.

This description is consistent with the results of Lucas and Stokey (1983), in which financing of wars is a contingency rule that is optimal in one of their environments. In their example, where the occurrence and duration of the war are uncertain, the optimal plan is for the debt not to be serviced during a war. Under this policy, people realize when they purchase the debt that effectively it will be defaulted on in the event that the war continues. Under the rule, the sovereign maintains the standard – keeps fixed the price of its currency in terms of gold – except in the event of a major war, in which circumstances it can suspend specie payments and issue paper money to finance its expenditures, and it can sell debt issues in terms of the nominal value of its currency on the understanding that the debt will eventually be paid off in gold. The rule is contingent in the sense that the public understands that the suspension will last only for the duration of the wartime emergency plus some period of adjustment; it assumes that, afterward, the government will follow the deflationary policies necessary to resume payments.

In this situation, an example of discretion is, after war i has ended, to decide at time $e_i + d$ to delay further the resumption of the gold standard, perhaps as a result of the perceived current situation in terms of the fraction of the war that has been paid for and the undesirable effects of alternative means of financing, such as by raising taxes. This change is all the more tempting if the public had accepted the debt at a reasonably high price q in the expectation that the gold standard would be resumed as scheduled. If the government breaks the rule by effectively choosing a high default rate δ in the future, it is obvious that, should there be another war within memory of the previous one, then people's behavior would be quite different from that in the previous war, even if the situation is otherwise similar and the government claims to subscribe to the same fixed delay rule.

Finally, a second contingency aspect of the rule could arise during financial crises. Temporary restrictions on convertibility of bank liabilities could be used to reduce the extent of a banking panic.

7.2.3   Commitment mechanisms

How was the gold standard rule enforced? One possible explanation focuses on reputational considerations within each country. Long-run adherence to the rule was based on the historical evolution of the gold standard itself. Gold was accepted as money because of its intrinsic value and desirable properties such as durability, storability, divisibility, portability, and uniformity. Paper claims, developed to economize on the scarce resources tied up in commodity money, became acceptable only because they were convertible into gold.[8]

In turn, the reputation of the gold standard would constrain the monetary authorities from breaching convertibility, except under well understood contingencies. Thus, when an emergency occurred, the abandonment of the standard would be viewed by all to be a temporary event since, from their experience, only gold or gold-backed claims truly served as money.

An alternative commitment mechanism was to guarantee gold convertibility in the constitution. This was the case in Sweden before 1914, where laws pertaining to the gold standard could be changed only by two identical parliamentary decisions with an election in between (Jonung, 1984, p. 368).

With respect to outright suspension of convertibility, it is difficult to distinguish between a suspension as part of the operation of a contingent rule as mentioned above, or as evidence of a change in regime. As we discuss below, statments by the monetary authorities, debates in Parliament, frequency of suspension, and changes in expectations as reflected in people's decisions all can be used to distinguish between the two.

7.2.4   Technical adjustments, or opportunity for discretion?

There are some aspects of the operation of a gold standard that are not so clear-cut. In designing its details (for example, the gold/silver ratio under bimetallism – a variant of the gold standard), it can be difficult to anticipate exactly what the optimal ratio is. New knowledge may be gained over time that would have been helpful when the standard was designed. When the new information is revealed, a potentially difficult question is what happens if the government goes ahead and makes the

---

[8] Goodfriend (1989) describes how the evolution of contractual arrangements in the financial system in 18th- and 19th-century England had to overcome the problem of fraud. Private markets developed an elaborate system of monitoring financial arrangements, but ultimately convertibility into gold lay behind them.

technical adjustment in the standard. If most people accept the claim that new information is the reason for the change, then the associated private behavior should be approximately the same as if this had been the standard from the very beginning. On the other hand, the greater the suspicion among the public that the change is partly a form of discretion, for which the government certainly has a strong incentive, the greater will be the change in private behavior reflecting the adjustment in the public's beliefs about likely future discretionary actions by the government. The same argument can be made regarding the choice of a different price when the gold standard is resumed after a temporary abandonment.[9]

7.2.5 An international rule

The gold standard rule also has an international dimension. Under the rule, there would be no restriction on the nationality of individuals who presented bullion to the mint to be coined, or who exported coin or bullion to foreign countries. Moreover, because every country following the rule fixed the price of its currency in gold, this created a system of fixed exchange rates linking all countries on the same standard. The international aspect of the gold standard may have been particularly important to the countries that were relatively less developed and therefore depended on access to international debt markets. The thesis of this chapter, however, is that the essence of the gold standard rule was as a domestic commitment mechanism. To the extent that the commitment was honored in relation to other countries, this served to strengthen the credibility of the domestic commitment.[10]

An aspect of the international gold standard given considerable attention in the literature is the operation of the "rules of the game." According to the traditional story, central banks or the monetary authorities were supposed to use their monetary policy to speed up the adjustment mechanism to a change in external balance. To the extent that the "rules" were followed, this presumably would strengthen the commitment to convertibility.

The enforcement of the international gold standard seems to have taken a particular form that was conducive to making it credible. A key

[9] An additional source of discretion was government policies to regulate gold production, such as taxation, the enforcement and relaxation of environmental regulations, and subsidies to encourage gold production in periods of depression. For examples of the use of such policies, see Rockoff (1984, pp. 632–9).

[10] The role of spillover effects on reputation through multiple relationships is discussed in Cole and Kehoe (1991).

factor may have been the role of England – the leading financial and commercial center of the gold standard era. The financial institutions of London provided the world with a well defined and universally accepted means, based on gold, of executing bilateral trades and obtaining credit. As we shall argue later, the gold standard provided England with the necessary benefits to enforce it and for many other countries to follow England's lead. Exchange in both goods and capital was facilitated if countries adhered to a standard based on a rule anchored by the same commitment mechanism. This arrangement may also have contributed to making the commitment mechanism a transparent one, a condition that we think is important for its likely success.

7.3   History of the gold standard as a rule

In this section, we discuss the history of the gold standard, viewed first as a domestic rule binding the monetary authorities. In this context, we survey in some detail the operation of the gold standard as a contingent rule in four countries: England and the United States – two key nations under the standard; and France and Italy – the former a "core" country of the classical gold standard, the latter an important peripheral country.[11] We also summarize briefly the gold standard experience of other countries. Then, we survey the record of the gold standard as an international rule governing the interrelationships between nations.

Our survey extends primarily from the early 19th century to 1933, with the main focus on the classical period ending in 1914. Although the United States continued to maintain gold backing for the dollar until 1971 and although the Bretton Woods system from 1945 to 1971 was based in part on gold, we view the period after World War II as far enough removed from the gold standard rule to be omitted from this survey.[12]

7.3.1   *The gold standard as a domestic rule*

England, 1717–1931: England can be viewed as the most important country to follow the gold standard rule. The gold standard in England,

---

[11] We do not include Germany, the fourth "core" country of the classical gold standard, in the survey because its history as a unified nation on the gold standard – from 1871 to 1914 – did not include a period of contingent suspension of payments (McGouldrick, 1984).

[12] See Bordo (1993). McKinnon (1993), however, views the Bretton Woods system as a dollar standard with a set of rules that incorporated many of the features of the classical gold standard.

as in other Western European countries, evolved from the use of a commodity as money. Standardization of coins of specific weight evolved by the early 18th century from a rudimentary bimetallic specie standard where coins frequently circulated by weight, not tale (face value).[13] England adopted a *de facto* gold standard in 1717, after having been on a *de facto* silver standard at least back to the 13th century. Over the 500-year period on silver, the price of silver and the bimetallic ratio were rarely changed – the principal exception being the Great Debasement of the 16th century. According to Glassman and Redish (1988), this episode represented an attempt to gain seigniorage – to follow discretionary policy – rather than a technical adjustment in the coinage.[14]

The early standard was plagued by the problems of deterioration in quality and counterfeiting. This was especially serious for small-denomination silver coins and may explain periodic recoinage and occasional debasement in the early modern era (Glassman and Redish, 1988). The emergence of the standard in its modern guise reflects the development of milling and other techniques of producing high-quality coin. The gold standard emerged in England *de facto* by the unintended overvaluation of gold at the mint from 1717 by the Master of the Mint, Sir Isaac Newton. It became *de jure* in 1816.[15]

The gold standard prevailed, with the price of gold fixed at £3.85 per ounce, from 1717 to 1931, with two major departures: 1797–1821 and 1914–1925. The first departure, referred to as the "Suspension Period" or the "Paper Pound" during the Napoleonic Wars, is generally viewed as an example of the operation of a contingent rule (Barro, 1987). The suspension of payments on February 26, 1797, whereby the Bank of England received permission from the government not to have to redeem its notes in terms of gold, followed a run on the country banks and the depletion of the Bank of England's gold reserve with the threat of a

---

[13] Even under the pre-1914 gold standard, however, weight mattered for sovereigns. Bankers had tiny scales for weighing sovereigns, which might be credited at less than 20 shillings. Loss on light gold was clearly a consideration for George Rae, himself a leading banker at the time (*The Country Banker*, 1885, Letter XIX). (Our thanks to Leslie Presnell for bringing this to our attention.)

[14] By contrast to England, monetary authorities in medieval France and Burgundy would often change arbitrarily the face value of silver coins to raise revenue – a discretionary breach of the rule, a policy that would succeed until the public caught on, raising prices in proportion to the change in unit of account.

[15] One interpretation of England's early abandonment of bimetallism was based on the continuous difficulties encountered in providing a fractional silver coinage (Redish, 1990). Alternatively, Lord Liverpool's decision to adopt gold may have been strongly influenced by Ricardo's ([1819] 1952) belief that technical change in silver mining would lead to a massive increase in its supply. See Friedman (1990b).

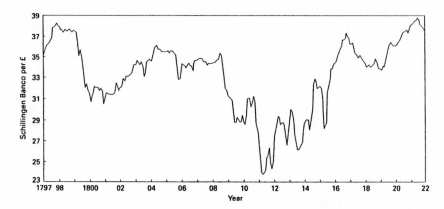

Figure 7.1. London exchange rate on Hamburg Schillingen Banco, 1797–1822, monthly. *Source*: Gayer, Rostow, and Schwartz (1983).

French invasion.[16] Figure 7.1 portrays monthly movements in the price of the pound in terms of the Hamburg Schillingen Banco, the only exchange rate series continuously available over the entire period. (The par of exchange before suspension was approximately 35.)[17]

The suspension was universally viewed as a temporary event, initially expected to last for a period of months.[18] As the French wars dragged on, however, and the Bank of England freely discounted government securities to finance military expenditures, the pound depreciated on the foreign exchange market. Consequently, the Bank repeatedly requested an extension of the suspension. Concern about the depreciation of the paper pound led to the *Bullion Report* of 1810, which attributed the depreciation to the Bank of England's note issue.

The *Bullion Report* recommended that immediate steps be taken to resume payments in two years from the date of the report at the presuspension parity.[19] The debate that ensued in Parliament and in the

[16] Though the Bank of England was a private institution until 1946, we treat its policies as not independent of the wishes of the government. The government had two powerful checks over the Bank: periodic renewal of its charter, and its role as the government's banker. For a contrary view, see Gallarotti (1991).

[17] In interpreting this exchange rate, adjustments must be made to allow for the Hamburg currency being on silver and sterling being effectively on gold, as well as the interest charge implicit in the prices of bills of exchange used to derive the series. As Ricardo pointed out, when these factors are taken into account, the Hamburg exchange rate understated the depreciation of the Bank of England note in terms of gold (Fetter, 1965, p. 28).

[18] The Order in Council of February 26, suspending the specie convertibility of Bank of England notes, recommended resumption by June 24, 1797.

[19] The report's exact words were:

press revolved around the themes of the extent, if any, of depreciation, and responsibility for the depreciation – the Bank of England blaming it on external real factors.[20] There was little discussion of the possibility of not resuming payments or of resuming at a depreciated level of the pound in the ensuing ten years.

Despite the government's opposition to resumption during wartime conditions, there exists considerable evidence that the government wished to confirm its commitment to a return to the gold standard once hostilities ceased (Bordo and White, 1991).[21] Several attempts were made to pick a date for resumption (1816, 1818), but as each occasion approached, the Bank requested a postponement on the grounds that the exchanges were unfavorable. It is important to note that this occurred after the wartime emergency ended in 1815.[22] Finally, Parliament agreed on July 2, 1819 (Peel's Act), on resumption in stages from February 1, 1820 to full redemption on demand on May 1, 1823,[23] and it was agreed that the government would retire its outstanding securities held by the Bank and the Bank would reduce its note issue to achieve the aim. During the year preceding resumption, considerable opposition to the plan emerged in Parliament by interests (especially agriculture and the Birmingham industrial area) hurt by deflation. They advocated return to parity at a depreciated pound. This opposition was not sufficient,

Your Committee would suggest, that the restriction on cash payments cannot safely be removed at an earlier period than two years from the present time; but your Committee is of the opinion, that early provision ought to be made by parliament for terminating, by the end of the period, the operation of the several statutes which have imposed and continued that restriction. (*Report from the Select Committee on the High Price of Bullion; Bullion Report* [1810] 1978, p. cclxi)

It went on to stress that, even if peace came in less than two years, two years should be allowed for resumption because of the increase likely, both in mercantile activity on the coming of peace, and in demands on the Bank for discount. But, "even if the war should be prolonged, cash payments should be resumed by the end of that period [of two years from the date of the Report]."

[20] The "Bullionist debate" pitted the Bullionists, who blamed the depreciation of the pound on the excessive issue of Bank of England notes, against the anti-Bullionists, who attributed the depreciation to extraordinary wartime foreign remittances and other real factors. See Laidler (1987) and Viner (1937).

[21] The government's failure to confront the *Bullion Report's* criticism directly can be understood in this light. The government felt unable to argue that continued suspension was justified by wartime fiscal needs because it was concerned that this position would weaken both internal and external confidence in the paper pound. Instead, the government took the much maligned position of both disputing the facts of depreciation and presenting a list of non-monetary causes (O'Brien, 1967, chapter 6).

[22] According to Neal (1991), the Bank was opposed to resumption after hostilities ceased because it feared the loss of its gold reserves as capital was repatriated to the continent.

[23] Initially, resumption would be at £4. 15s. 0d. on gold bars. The price would then be reduced in stages and the terms extended finally to include coin at mint par of £3. 17s. 10½ d. (Clapham, 1944, p. 71).

however, to prevent resumption from being achieved (Feavearyear, 1963, pp. 224–5; Fetter, 1965, pp. 73–6; Laidler, 1987).

We interpret the repeated requests for postponement, especially after the end of hostilities in 1815, as the use of discretionary policy.[24] Moreover, each postponement gave a negative signal to the public of the government's intention of ever resuming. Nevertheless, the fact that resumption was achieved suggests that observing the rule was paramount.

Evidence for the credibility of the commitment to the gold standard in the Napoleonic War is provided in Bordo and White (1991). There it is shown that although the British government pursued a policy of tax smoothing (setting tax rates over time so as to minimize deadweight losses), it did not follow a policy of revenue smoothing (smoothing revenue from both taxes and seigniorage). These results suggest that, although specie payments were suspended, the commitment to resume prevented the government from acting as it would have done under a pure fiat regime.

The Bank Charter Act of 1844 and the separation of the Bank of England, into the Issue department to regulate the currency and the Banking department to follow sound commercial banking principles, further demonstrated England's commitment to the gold standard rule. The Issue department, by varying directly its fiduciary issue (over and above a statutory limit of £14 million) with the level of gold reserves ("the currency principle"), was designed to make the long-run maintenance of the (mixed) gold standard more credible.[25]

A second contingency aspect of the rule developed with experience of financial crises. Restrictions on convertibility of bank liabilities for gold were used to reduce the extent of a banking panic. The Bank was authorized to expand its unbacked note issue in the face of a depletion of its reserves without suspending convertibility of its notes into gold.

From 1821 to 1914, the gold standard rule was continuously honored. However, on three occasions – the crises of 1847, 1857, and 1866 – the second contingent aspect of the rule came into play. The policy was

---

[24] Although one could argue that the war did not really end until reparations were paid and the Allies ended their occupation of France in 1818. See White (1991).

[25] The Bank Charter Act was criticized on two grounds: (1) the currency principle ignored the role of deposits as an increasingly important component of the money stock; and (2) the Banking department, in operating on a sound commercial banking basis, could not act responsibly as a central bank. The latter criticism was at the heart of the traditional case for "discretion." This criticism culminated in the 1860s with the formulation by Walter Bagehot, the influential editor of *The Economist*, of the "responsibility doctrine" and the establishment of guidelines for a central bank under a gold standard (Bordo, 1984, pp. 45–6).

successful in alleviating the pressure, and the Bank retired the excess issue shortly thereafter.[26]

The Overend Gurney crisis of 1866 was the last real financial crisis (that is, banking panic) in British financial history (Schwartz, 1986). After that point, the Bank of England learned to follow Bagehot's rule – in the face of both an external and an internal drain "to lend freely but at a penalty rate." Although Bagehot intended the Bank to use its discretion (in the traditional sense) to avert a financial crisis, it can be argued that the successful performance of the Bank as lender of last resort actually served to strengthen the credibility of the Bank's commitment to the gold standard rule, because a key threat to the maintenance of convertibility was removed. Evidence of the credibility of England's commitment to the gold standard rule is provided by private short-term capital inflows during the incipient crises of 1890 and 1907 (Eichengreen, 1992).

The 1914–1925 episode was similar in many respects to the earlier suspension period, although the extent of the inflation and the depreciation of the pound were considerably greater. Indeed, it appears that the successful resumption of 1821 may have been a factor enabling the British to finance an even larger share of the World War I expenditures by debt finance and the issue of fiat money (see Table 7.1).[27]

Figure 7.2 shows monthly movements in the dollar/sterling exchange rate from 1914 to 1925. Note that from the beginning of hostilities in August 1914 until March 1919, the country was still formally on the gold standard, but the monetary authorities prevented conversion and pegged the pound close to the old parity (Crabbe, 1989).

After hostilities ended, the official view in the *Cunliffe Report* (1918) and other documents was for an immediate resumption at the old parity of $4.867. Consequently, the Bank of England began following a deflationary policy in early 1920. The exchange rate was close to parity by December 1922, but resumption was delayed because of unfavorable events on the continent (the Germans' refusal to pay reparations and the Belgian–French occupation of the Ruhr in 1923). By the end of 1924, the pound was again close to parity and resumption was announced by Winston Churchill in the Budget Speech of April 28, 1925.

Though the official view from 1920 to 1925 was in favor of resumption,

---

[26] On all three occasions, the Treasury issued a letter allowing the Bank to expand its fiduciary issue, but only in 1857 did it actually do so. On the other two occasions, the announcement alone was sufficient to allay the panic (Clapham, 1944, vol. II, pp. 208–9).

[27] The contribution of high-powered money to the finance of wartime expenditure is a lower bound estimate of the contribution of money to wartime finance, since in both episodes the banking system participated in the operation.

Table 7.1. *The financing of wartime expenditures in the French wars and World War I*

	French wars 1793–1815 (Great Britain)	World War I 1914–1918 (United Kingdom)[a]
Percentage of total wartime expenditures financed by:		
Taxes[1]	58.0	31.8
Bonds[2]	40.5	64.4
High-powered money[3]	1.5	3.8

Note:
[a]Wartime expenditures are calculated as total government expenditures *less* 1903–1913 annual average of total government expenditures.
Source:
1. 1793–1815: O'Brien (1967, Table 4); 1914–1918: Mitchell and Deane (1962, pp. 392–5, 396–8).
2. 1793–1815: O'Brien (1967, Table 4): 1914–1918: Mitchell and Deane (1962, pp. 392–5, 396–8).
3. 1793–1815: Mitchell and Deane (1962, pp. 441–3); 1914–1918: Capie and Webber (1985, Table 1(1), pp. 52–9).

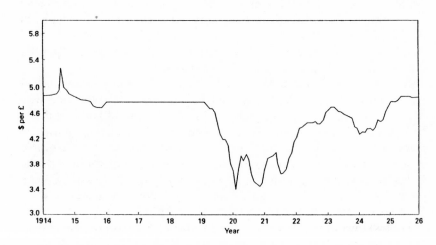

Figure 7.2. Dollar/sterling exchange rate, 1914–1926, monthly. *Source*: Board of Governors of the Federal Reserve System (1944).

and a key argument made was the maintenance of credibility by returning to gold at the old par,[28] vociferous opposition to it was voiced by J. M. Keynes ([1925] 1972) and other academics, by labor (not the official Labour Party), and by industry groups. Most of the opposition, however, with the principal exception of Keynes, was opposed not to resumption at the old parity *per se* but to the deflationary policies used to attain it.[29] The successful resumption in 1925 and the painful deflation that accompanied it can be viewed as evidence of the British commitment to the gold standard rule.[30]

The United States, 1792–1933: The U.S. Constitution (Section 8) gave Congress power over the currency – "to coin money and regulate the value thereof." The Coinage Act of 1792 defined U.S. coinage as both gold and silver. Thus, the original monetary standard was a bimetallic standard. One dollar was defined as 371.25 grains of silver or 24.75 grains of gold. This yields a bimetallic ratio of the value of gold to silver of 15:1. Soon after instituting the 15:1 ratio, the market ratio increased to $15\frac{1}{2}$:1. Consequently, silver became overvalued at the mint, gold became undervalued, and, via the operation of Gresham's Law, the United States after a few years was on a *de facto* silver standard.

The situation was altered by a new Coinage Act in 1834 and another in 1837, which changed the bimetallic ratio to 16:1, presumably in an attempt to restore bimetallism. As it turned out, gold became overvalued at the mint, silver became undervalued, and the United States switched to a *de facto* gold standard. If we interpret periodic adjustment of the bimetallic mint ratio to the market ratio as an example of a contingent rule, and if the public expects such adjustments, then the question arises whether the switch from 15:1 to 16:1 rather than to $15\frac{1}{2}$:1 was a mistake or a deliberate use of discretionary policy. Indeed, O'Leary (1937) viewed this episode as a deliberate attempt by the Jacksonians to discredit the Second Bank of the United States. The resultant flood of gold coins would obviate the necessity for its notes. The 1834 Act was also passed at the urging of the gold producing states of South Carolina, North Carolina, and Georgia (Friedman, 1990a).

---

[28] According to Moggridge (1969), the key reason cited was the maintenance of London's prominent position in international finance.

[29] See Pollard (1970, editor's Introduction), and especially Brown (1929), Sayers (1960), and Hume (1963).

[30] Smith and Smith (1990) view resumption in 1925 as an example of a stochastic process switch. Their numerical estimates suggest that, contrary to some contemporary views, the appreciation of sterling prior to April 1925 appears to have been due to fundamentals, such as restrictive monetary policy, rather than to the expectation of a change in regime.

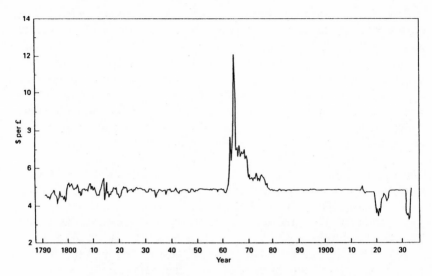

Figure 7.3. Dollar/pound exchange rate, 1792–1925, quarterly. *Source*: Friedman and Schwartz (1982); Officer (1883, 1985).

Figure 7.3 shows the dollar/pound exchange rate on an annual basis from 1792 to 1925. The market exchange rate is defined in terms of gold, so that during the period when the United States was on a bimetallic standard it varied, reflecting changes in the market bimetallic ratio, changes in the official ratio, and other forces in the market for foreign exchange.[31] As can be seen in Figure 7.3, the exchange rate in the bimetallic era before the Civil War was much less stable than during the pure gold standard period, from 1879 to 1913.

The fixed price of $20.67 per ounce prevailed from 1837 to 1933 with one significant departure – the greenback episode in 1862–1879. Figure 7.4 plots the greenback price of gold over that period. It can be viewed in conjunction with the exchange rate in Figure 7.3.

The greenback episode, at least at the outset, can be interpreted as the operation of a contingent rule. The federal government originally intended to finance its expenditures through borrowing and taxation, but within a year resorted to the issue of paper notes. Under the Legal Tender Acts, these notes were issued on the presumption that they would be convertible, but the date and provisions for convertibility were not specified.

---

[31] See Officer (1983, 1985) for a valuable discussion on measuring both the par of exchange and the market exchange rate.

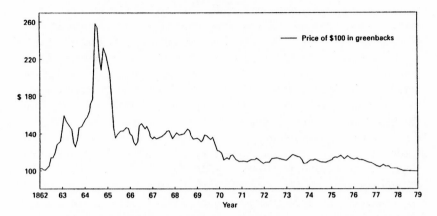

Figure 7.4. Price of gold in greenbacks, 1862–1879, monthly. *Sources*: Mitchell (1908); Friedman and Schwartz (1963).

Shortly after the war, the government made its intentions clear to resume payments at the prewar parity in the Contraction Act of April 12, 1866, which provided for the limited withdrawal of U.S. notes. Declining prices from 1866 to 1868 led to a public outcry and to repeal of the Act in February 1868. Over the next seven years a fierce debate raged between the hard money forces – advocates of rapid resumption – and the soft money forces, some of whom were opposed to restoring the gold standard, others who wanted to restore it at a devalued parity, and yet others who just wanted to prevent any undue deflation and allow the economy to grow up to its money supply (Unger, 1964; Sharkey, 1959). Alternating victories by the conflicting forces were manifest in legislation, alternately contracting and expanding the issue of greenbacks (the Public Credit Act 1869 contracting it, the reissue of $26 million of retired greenbacks in 1873 expanding it) and, in Supreme Court decisions, initially declaring the Legal Tender Acts unconstitutional (*Hepburn* v. *Griswold*, February 1870), and then reversing the decision (*Knox* v. *Lee*, May 1871). Finally, the decision to resume payments on January 1, 1879 was made in the Resumption Act of 1875, which the lame-duck Republican Congress passed by a majority of one. Despite the announcement of resumption, however, and of steps taken by the Treasury to accumulate a gold reserve and to retire greenbacks, the bitter election of 1876 was fought between Cooper (the greenback candidate, who was opposed to resumption), Tilden (a soft money Democrat), and Hayes (a hard-money Republican). Hayes won by one electoral vote. Yet, had Tilden won, according to one authority, resumption would not have been prevented; only the date may have been changed (Unger, 1964, pp. 310–1).

Though the ferocity of the reversals in policy suggest to us that many features of the post–Civil War period can be interpreted as incorporating elements of a discretionary regime, other evidence argues in favor of the contingent gold standard rule. As Calomiris (1988) points out, credibility in the restoration of the gold standard rule was probably established in 1869 by the actual redemption of bond principal in gold by the Act of March 18, 1869, guaranteeing payment in gold, and the Supreme Court decision in *Venzie Bank* v. *Fenno*, which supported the constitutionality of gold clauses (Calomiris, 1988, p. 208fn).[32]

Moreover, both Roll (1972) and Calomiris (1988) present evidence of expected appreciation of the greenback based on a negative interest differential between bonds that were paid in greenbacks and those paid in gold. Calomiris (see Table 7.2) calculates the appreciation forecast error on a semi-annual basis from January 1869 to December 1878, defined as the difference between his calculation of expected appreciation and actual appreciation. The errors are close to zero for most of the periods, with two exceptions: January–June 1869, when the error is 1.53, and January–June 1876, when it is −1.49. The former positive exchange rate surprise reflects the credibility of the government's commitment to the redemption of bond principal in gold; the latter negative surprise reflects the temporary threat to resumption by the election of 1876.

In the ensuing seventeen years, though the United States was back on a gold basis, the battle between hard and soft money forces continued over the issue of free coinage of silver. Silver advocates can be classified into several groups. There were those who believed that, had silver not been demonetized by the "Crime of '73" (the Coinage Act of February 1873), then bimetallism at 16:1 would have yielded less deflation than actually occurred from 1873 to 1896, as relatively more abundant silver was substituted for increasingly scarce gold. Such a position is consistent with maintenance of a rule. Other silver advocates (such as the Populist party), however, viewed the issue of silver certificates as a potential engine of inflation to stimulate the economy, as well as to reverse the redistribution of income from debtors to creditors. In this sense, the pressure in favor of discretion did not disappear.

The free-silver forces succeeded in passing two pieces of legislation

---

[32] According to Calomiris (1988), following Mitchell (1903) and Roll (1972), the pace and timing of resumption depended solely on fiscal news – legislation and policy announcements affecting the government's budget. Rolnick and Wallace (1984) also view interpretation of this episode as dependent only on overall government fiscal expectations.

Table 7.2. *Expected and actual appreciation of the greenback dollar, 1869–1878*

		Average differential between gold and greenbacks' yield[a] (1)	Expected appreciation (current differential *less* differential for July–December 1878) (2)	Average actual rate of greenbacks' appreciation to 1881[b] (3)	Appreciation forecast error [(2)–(3)] (4)
January–June	1869	1.33	3.53	2.00	1.53
July–December	1869	0.49	2.69	1.85	0.84
January–June	1870	−0.52	1.68	0.93	0.75
July–December	1870	−0.42	1.78	0.93	0.85
January–June	1871	−1.01	1.19	1.09	0.10
July–December	1871	−0.95	1.25	1.10	0.15
January–June	1872	−0.02	2.18	1.26	0.92
July–December	1872	0.01	2.21	1.40	0.81
January–June	1873	−0.09	2.11	1.90	0.21
July–December	1873	−0.26	1.94	1.39	0.55
January–June	1874	−0.65	1.55	1.60	−0.05
July–December	1874	−0.45	1.75	1.50	0.25
January–June	1875	0.07	2.27	2.36	−0.09
July–December	1875	0.09	2.29	2.30	−0.01
January–June	1876	−1.19	1.01	2.50	−1.49
July–December	1876	−1.07	1.13	1.76	−0.63
January–June	1877	−1.22	0.98	1.36	−0.38
July–December	1877	−1.21	0.99	0.84	0.15
January–June	1878	−1.32	0.88	0.40	0.48
July–December	1878	−2.20	0.00	0.10	−0.10

Notes:

[a] $\frac{1}{6}\sum_{j=1}^{6}[i_{ap}(j) - i_{gr}(j)] = d.$

[b] The average of monthly exchange rate closings for the period was used to measure current gold price of greenbacks. The 6s of 1881 were redeemable June 1, 1881.

Source: Calomiris (1988, Table 5).

that increased the outstanding stock of silver coins: the Bland–Allison Act of 1878 and the Sherman Silver Purchase Act of 1890. The latter increased the stock of high-powered money sufficiently to threaten convertibility into gold (Friedman and Schwartz, 1963). As Grilli (1989, Figure 3) shows, however, the probability of a speculative attack on the gold dollar at the height of the agitation over silver in 1893 (before the repeal of the Sherman Silver Purchase Act) was not much greater than 6 percent.[33]

A second departure from the gold standard, an embargo during World War I (1917–1919) on gold exports, did not affect internal convertibility of gold. Hence, we believe it should be viewed as merely a temporary adjustment in the standard.[34]

Financial crises characterized by banking panics were frequent in U.S. monetary history until the establishment of the Federal Reserve System. Before 1914, pressure on the banking system's reserves was often relieved by a restriction on convertibility of bank notes and deposits into high-powered money. The restrictions in 1837–1838, 1839, and 1857 did involve suspensions of convertibility into gold. It could be argued, however, that such temporary departures were viewed as a contingent aspect of the rule. The restrictions of 1873, 1893, and 1907–1908 did not involve suspension of convertibility into gold and hence cannot be viewed as breaking the gold standard rule.

Franklin Roosevelt's decision to devalue the dollar in 1933 (in order to raise the price level) represents a clear departure from the gold standard rule and a clear case of discretion. Though the price of gold was again fixed, at $35 per ounce, gold ownership by U.S. residents was prohibited, and the standard that reemerged has been described as "a discretionary fiduciary standard" with gold just a commodity whose price was fixed by an official support program (Friedman and Schwartz, 1963).

---

[33] Garber and Grilli (1986) present estimates of silver risk in the yields of dollar-denominated assets in this period. Also see Garber (1986) for estimates of the value of the silver option on bimetallic bonds.

[34] The United States, unlike the British example comparing World War I to the French wars, did not finance a larger fraction of its expenditures in World War I by debt and fiat money issue than in the Civil War. The fractions are:

	Civil War 1861–1865 Percentage of wartime expenditure financed by:	World War I 1917–1918 Percentage of wartime expenditure financed by:
Taxes[1]	21	25
Bonds[2]	61	61
High-powered money[3]	18	14

Sources: 1.–3. 1861–1865: Friedman (1952).
1.–3. 1917–1918: Walton and Rockoff (1989, p. 443).

France: France followed a bimetallic standard from the Middle Ages until 1878. From the 13th to the 15th century, the rule was honored in the breach more than the observance, with frequent debasements, devaluations, and revaluations. This reflects internal political instability, frequent wars, and the lack of an adequate tax base (Bordo, 1986). By the 16th century, France had developed a stable bimetallic system, although the ancient regime was punctuated by several devaluations and revaluations (Murphy, 1987), and the infamous system of John Law – a paper-money-induced inflation – from 1716 to 1720 (Bordo, 1987a).

The French revolution spawned the assignat hyperinflation from 1789 to 1795 – the aftermath of which led to the establishment of official bimetallism with the fixing of the ratio of silver to gold at $15\frac{1}{2}:1$ in 1803, a rule that was successful for 75 years (Bordo and White, 1991). Until the late 1840s, abundant supplies of silver threatened to displace gold, but with gold discoveries in California and Australia the process was reversed until the 1860s, when major silver discoveries again threatened the bimetallic standard. In 1865, France formed the Latin Monetary Union with Belgium, Switzerland, and Italy (later joined by the Papal States, Greece, and Romania). By agreeing to mint silver coins of the same fineness, these countries expanded the size of the bimetallic currency area. The Latin Monetary Union continued the free coinage of silver until, swamped by massive supplies of new silver from discoveries in the Americas and by the abandonment of the silver standard in Germany and other European countries emulating the gold standard example of Britain, the leading commercial power (Friedman, 1990b), it limited silver coinage in 1874 and fully demonetized silver in 1878 (Bordo, 1987b).

France followed the gold standard rule (albeit in its bimetallic form until 1878) until World War I. Figure 7.5 shows the pound/franc exchange rate from 1821 to 1938. As can be seen, the rate was very stable until 1914, rarely departing more than one percentage in gold points from the parity of 25.22 francs to the pound. France, like the other two countries in this period, suspended specie convertibility in times of national emergency. On two occasions, the Bank of France announced *Cours Forcé* – the first from March 15, 1848, to August 6, 1850, following the February 1848 revolution, and the second during and after the Franco–Prussian war from August 12, 1870, to January 1, 1878. It is interesting to note that during these periods, the exchange rate varied close to parity. On both occasions, the Bank of France limited its note issue, acting as if it were constrained by the gold standard rule (Lacroix and Dupieux, 1973).

Like other belligerents in World War I, France switched to fiat-money

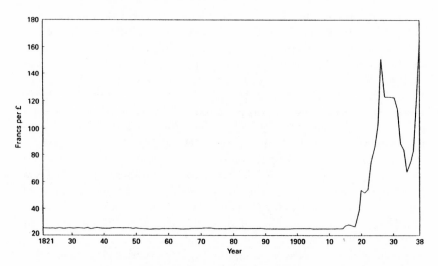

Figure 7.5. Pound/franc exchange rate, 1821–1938, annually. *Sources*: Gayer, Rostow, and Schwartz (1953); British Parliamentary Papers (1888); St. Marc (1983).

issue to finance the war, intending to resume payments after hostilities ended. Unlike the British case, the aftermath of the war was a period of rapid inflation and depreciation of the franc. The forces of discretion carried the day even with the ultimate return of the franc to gold convertibility at a vastly depreciated level in 1928.[35] France stayed on the gold standard until 1936.

Italy: In contrast to England, France, and the United States, Italy departed from the gold standard rule more than it followed it. The newly unified Italian state adopted a gold standard in 1865 but abandoned it in May 1866 and did not return to convertibility until March 1883. According to Fratianni and Spinelli (1984), inconvertibility was a consequence of both financing the war against Austria in 1866 and conducting the government's subsequent liberal fiscal policy. According to Fratianni and Spinelli, "Politicians had no difficulties in throwing off the straitjacket of the gold standard when it stood in the way of large budget deficits" (p. 419). A return to sound fiscal policy permitted

---

[35] According to Eichengreen (1992b), following Alesina and Drazen (1991), the rapid inflation in the early 1920s and the *de facto* stabilization of the franc at an undervalued rate in 1926 reflected a compromise outcome from a war of attrition between debtors and creditors. By contrast, Britain's return to the old parity represented a victory by the creditor class.

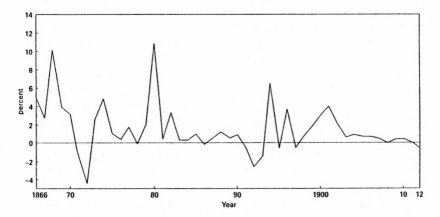

Figure 7.6. Risk premium, lira/franc exchange rate, 1866–1912, Italian government bond yield *minus* French 3 percent *rentes*. *Source*: Fratianni and Spinelli (1984).

restoration of gold payments from 1883 to February 1894, after which the Italian currency remained inconvertible until December 1927, when gold convertibility was resumed at a depreciated value of the lira.[36] During the pre–World War I period, however, the monetary authorities acted as if they were on the gold standard. The exchange rate with France returned close to parity in 1903 and remained there until the outbreak of war. Money growth was low, and the budget was often in surplus (Tonniolo, 1990, p. 188). This episode suggests that commitment to the gold standard rule was of considerable importance to the Italian monetary authorities.

Evidence for the credibility of the commitment to the gold standard can be seen in the risk premium on Italian government long-term securities relative to their French counterparts over the period 1866 to 1912, shown in Figure 7.6.[37] In the first period of inconvertibility (1866–1883),

[36] This did not occur until after wartime inflation was in large part reversed by Mussolini's contractionary policies. See Kindleberger (1984, 383).

[37] Following Fratianni and Spinelli (1984), we calculate the country risk premium as

$$D_t = \ell\mathrm{n}(1 + i_{I,t}) - \ell\mathrm{n}(1 + i_{F,t}) - \ell\mathrm{n}E_{t+1}^t + \ell\mathrm{n}E_t,$$

where $i_{I,t}$ is the yield on Italian bonds at time t; $i_{F,t}$ is the yield on French bonds, E_{t+1}^t is the lira/franc exchange rate for $t + 1$ expected at t, and E_t is the exchange rate at t. Their calculation holds constant transactions costs and assumes perfect foresight in the exchange market, that is, $\ell\mathrm{n}E_{t+1}^t = \ell\mathrm{n}E_{t+1}$. We also calculated the risk premium using an alternative measure of the expected change in the exchange rate, $\ell\mathrm{n}E_t - \ell\mathrm{n}E_{t-1}$, and the picture was virtually the same.

the risk premium averaged more than 2 percent per year; in the gold standard period (1884–1894), it averaged close to zero; and in the second inconvertibility period (1894–1912), it declined from 2 percent in the first half of the period to 0.5 percent after 1902.

A number of other countries followed the gold standard rule until 1914 as strictly as the three core countries just discussed.[38] These include Germany (the fourth "core" country), the Scandinavian countries, and the British Dominions. The latter two sets of countries, like England, returned to gold at the original parity in the mid-1920s. A number of countries that were not formally on the gold standard acted as if they were, by maintaining price levels as stable as the gold standard countries. These include Spain and the Austro–Hungarian empire before 1892. Finally, a number of countries, most notably Argentina, followed the example of Italy by alternately following and then abandoning gold convertibility during the period of falling prices, 1880–1900, and of rising prices, 1900–1913 (Ford, 1962).[39]

7.3.2   Some evidence for the credibility of the gold standard rule

We have described the gold standard experience of four important countries: three "core" countries (England, the United States, and France) that followed the gold standard rule, and Italy, a country that, though officially on the gold standard, suspended convertibility more than half the time. One way to summarize this experience is to present evidence on the persistence of inflation.

Barsky (1987) presents evidence for the United Kingdom and the United States that inflation under the gold standard was very nearly a white noise process. This is compared to the post–World War II period, when the inflation rate exhibited considerable persistence. Evidence for the absence of inflation persistence does not prove that countries followed the gold standard rule. It is, however, not inconsistent with the suggestion that market agents expect that the monetary authorities will not continuously follow an inflationary policy – an expectation that is also consistent with belief in following a convertibility rule.

To develop this further, following Barsky's approach, we examine in Table 7.3 the autocorrelations of inflation using annual wholesale price indices for the four countries for different periods covering the entire gold standard experience. The results in Table 7.3 confirm those of

---

[38] See Bordo and Kydland (1990) for a more detailed discussion.

[39] Other Latin American countries also had experiences of alternating adherence to gold convertibility. See Fishlow (1987).

Table 7.3. *Autocorrelations of inflation (wholesale prices, annual data)*

Sample period	Regime	Ljung–Box Q-test 5% critical value (standard error)	Lags	Autocorrelations			
United Kingdom							
1730–	*de facto*	Q(18) = 16.79	1–4	−0.02	−0.59	−0.13	−0.32
1796	Gold	C(18) = 28.87	5–8	0.11	−0.05	0.02	0.09
		(0.12)	9–12	0.04	−0.04	0.12	0.02
1797–	Paper	Q(12) = 15.21	1–4	0.26	−0.37	−0.41	0.11
1821	pound	C(12) = 21.03	5–8	0.37	−0.03	−0.12	0.03
		(0.20)	9–12	0.12	−0.10	−0.19	0.08
1822–	Gold	Q(24) = 25.50	1–4	0.04	−0.01	−0.14	−0.22
1913	standard	C(24) = 36.42	5–8	−0.20	0.01	0.13	0.14
		(0.10)	9–12	0.17	0.04	−0.07	−0.10
1914–	Paper and	Q(6) = 3.71	1–3	0.32	0.09	0.03	
1931	gold exchange	C(6) = 14.07	4–6	−0.05	−0.10	−0.29	
		(0.24)					
1730–	Mixed	Q(24) = 44.50	1–4	0.12	−0.15	−0.24	−0.15
1913		C(24) = 36.42	5–8	0.10	0.08	0.04	0.09
		(0.07)	9–12	0.07	−0.05	−0.02	0.02
1730–	Mixed	Q(24) = 35.69	1–4	0.20	−0.05	−0.11	−0.10
1931		C(24) = 36.42	5–8	0.05	20.05	0.00	0.10
		(0.07)	9–12	0.09	−0.02	−0.07	−0.03
United States							
1793–	Bimetallic	Q(24) = 34.69	1–4	0.16	−0.10	−0.13	0.12
1861		C(24) = 36.42	5–8	−0.04	−0.20	−0.34	0.13
		(0.24)	9–12	0.14	0.09	0.05	−0.15
1862–	Greenback	Q(6) = 5.53	1–3	0.51	0.17	−0.07	
1878		C(6) = 14.07	4–6	−0.04	−0.05	−0.17	
		(0.24)					
1879–	Gold	Q(12) = 3.75	1–4	0.05	0.18	0.04	−0.16
1913	standard	C(12) = 21.03	5–8	0.01	−0.07	0.16	−0.02
		(0.17)	9–12	0.02	0.09	0.02	−0.06
1914–	Gold	Q(6) = 3.76	1–3	0.23	0.05	0.02	
1933	exchange	C(6) = 14.07	4–6	−0.33	−0.15	0.02	
		(0.22)					
1793–	Mixed	Q(24) = 55.97	1–4	0.26	−0.01	−0.12	−0.02
1913		C(24) = 36.42	5–8	−0.06	−0.23	−0.17	0.13
		(0.09)	9–12	0.18	0.15	−0.07	−0.08
1793–	Mixed	Q(24) = 50.12	1–4	0.25	0.01	0.07	−0.11
1933		C(24) = 36.42	5–8	−0.08	−0.15	−0.10	0.11
		(0.09)	9–12	0.13	0.18	−0.03	−0.11
France							
1803–	Bimetallic	Q(18) = 10.98	1–4	0.11	0.04	−0.04	−0.09
1869		C(18) = 28.87	5–8	0.06	−0.12	0.11	−0.02
		(0.12)	9–12	−0.03	−0.01	−0.19	−0.10

Table 7.3. *(cont.)*

Sample period	Regime	Ljung–Box Q-test 5% critical value (standard error)	Lags	Autocorrelations			
1870–1878	Suspension	$Q(3) = 1.34$ $C(3) = 7.82$ (0.33)	1–3	0.18	−0.26	−0.22	
1879–1913	Gold standard	$Q(12) = 9.49$ $C(12) = 21.03$ (0.17)	1–4 5–8 9–12	0.35 −0.06 0.00	0.01 −0.04 0.20	−0.07 0.21 0.20	−0.11 0.09 0.15
1914–1938	Paper and gold exchange	$Q(8) = 4.68$ $C(8) = 15.51$ (0.20)	1–4 5–8	0.27 −0.15	0.18 −0.07	0.14 −0.10	−0.14 0.08
1803–1913	Specie	$Q(24) = 17.28$ $C(24) = 36.42$ (0.10)	1–4 5–8 9–12	0.15 0.05 −0.00	0.02 −0.11 0.03	−0.05 0.12 −0.14	−0.07 −0.00 −0.07
1803–1938	Mixed	$Q(34) = 33.25$ $C(24) = 36.42$ (0.09)	1–4 5–8 9–12	0.29 −0.03 0.08	0.16 −0.02 0.06	0.11 −0.01 0.02	−0.07 0.11 −0.04
Italy 1861–1913	Mixed	$Q(18) = 16.38$ $C(18) = 28.87$ (0.14)	1–4 5–8 9–12	0.06 0.21 0.02	−0.26 0.09 −0.12	−0.17 −0.13 0.03	0.01 −0.06 0.19

Sources:
United Kingdom: Mitchell and Deane (1962).
United States: Jastram (1977).
France: Mitchell (1975).
Italy: Mitchell (1975).

Barsky: inflation in all four countries was very nearly white noise, as seen in the low autocorrelations. These results hold for different subperiods when the countries concerned followed the bimetallic variant of the rule and for subperiods when they departed from convertibility following the contingent aspect of the rule. As did Klein (1975) and Barsky (1987), we observe negative serial correlation at a number of lags in all the subperiods.[40] This is consistent with the commodity money adjustment mechanism of the gold standard discussed by Rockoff (1984) and Barsky and Summers (1988). The Q-statistics, which test the joint hypothesis

[40] Klein (1975) also presents evidence for mean reversion of the price level under the gold standard.

that the first n autocorrelations are all zero for specified n, do not reject the white noise hypothesis for any of the subperiods. Over the entire period 1730–1938 for the United Kingdom and the entire periods 1793–1913 and 1793–1933 for the United States, however, the hypothesis is rejected at the 5 percent significance level. These periods represent conglomerates of different regimes that had different mean rates of inflation. Aggregation then may induce serial correlation.

We also tested for a unit root in the inflation series using the Dickey–Fuller test. In only one episode – the United States, 1862–1878 – could one be detected at the 10 percent significance level.

In sum, we interpret this evidence as consistent with agents' beliefs in the credibility of the commitment to the gold standard convertibility rule. Because the power of the tests is admittedly low, however, this evidence is only suggestive.

7.3.3   The gold standard as an international rule

The classical gold standard emerged as a true international standard by 1880 following the switch by the majority of countries from bimetallism, silver monometallism, and paper to gold as the basis of their currencies.[41] As an international standard, the key rule was maintenance of gold convertibility at the established par. Maintenance of a fixed price of gold by its adherents in turn ensured fixed exchange rates. Recent evidence suggests that, indeed, exchange rates throughout the 1880–1914 period were characterized by a high degree of fixity in the principal countries. Although exchange rates frequently deviated from par, violations of the gold points were rare (Officer, 1986), as were devaluations (Eichengreen, 1985).[42]

The international gold standard was a successful example of a fixed exchange rate system, although gold convertibility is not required to operate a fixed exchange rate system successfully [as is evident from the case of the European Monetary System (EMS) in the late 1980s; see Giavazzi and Giovannini, 1989]. The gold standard rule was primarily a domestic rule with an important international dimension. This dimension in turn may have served to make the domestic gold standard rule more credible in a number of significant ways. In addition to the reputation of the domestic gold standard and constitutional provisions, adher-

---

[41] See Eichengreen (1985, p. 5) for a chronology of countries adopting gold.

[42] Giovannini (1993) views the facts that both exchange rates and short-term interest rates varied within the limits set by the gold points in the 1899–1909 period as consistent with market agents' expectations of a credible commitment by the four "core" countries to the gold standard rule in the sense of this chapter.

ence to the international gold standard rule may have been enforced by other mechanisms. These include improved access to international capital markets, the operation of the "rules of the game," and the hegemonic power of England.

Many countries viewed maintenance of gold convertibility as important in obtaining access at favorable terms to the international capital markets of the "core" countries, especially England and France. It was believed that creditors would view gold convertibility as a signal of sound government finance and the future ability to service debt. This was the case both for developing countries wishing to have access to long-term capital, such as Austria–Hungary (Yeager, 1984) and Latin America (Fishlow, 1989), and for countries wishing to finance war expenditures, such as Japan, which financed the Russo–Japanese war of 1905–1906 with foreign loans seven years after joining the gold standard (Hayashi, 1989). Once on the gold standard, such countries feared the consequences of departure.[43] The fact that England, the most successful country of the 19th century, as well as other "progressive" countries were on the gold standard was probably a powerful argument for joining (Gallarotti, 1991; Friedman, 1990b).

The operation of the "rules of the game," whereby the monetary authorities were supposed to alter the discount rate to speed up the adjustment to a change in external balance, may also have been an important part of the commitment mechanism to the international gold standard rule. Thus, for example, when a country was running a balance of payments deficit and there was a gold outflow, the monetary authority, observing a decline in its gold reserves, was supposed to raise its discount rate in order to reduce domestic credit. The resultant drop in the money supply would reduce the price level. The adjustment process would be aided by higher short-term domestic interest rates attracting capital from abroad. To the extent the "rules" would be followed and adjustment facilitated, this would strengthen the commitment to convertibility, as conditions conducive to abandonment would be lessened.

There exists considerable evidence on the operation of the "rules of the game." Bloomfield (1959), in a classic study, showed that, with the principal exception of England, the rules were frequently violated in the sense that discount rates were not always changed in the required direction (or by sufficient amounts) and in the sense that changes in domestic credit were often negatively correlated with changes in gold reserves.[44] In

---

[43] See Eichengreen (1992a, 60) and Fishlow (1987, 1989).

[44] According to Giovannini (1986), however, the Bank of England did not follow the "rules," while the Reichsbank did.

addition, a number of countries used gold devices – practices to prevent gold from leaving.[45] According to Goodfriend (1988), central banks operating under the gold standard did so to achieve "interest rate smoothing" through the use of gold stockpiling. Such practices, in our approach, could be viewed as a form of discretion, because following them could lead the public to believe that ultimately convertibility would be abandoned.

For the major countries, however, at least before 1914, such policies were not used extensively enough to threaten the convertibility into gold – evidence for commitment to the rule (Schwartz, 1984). Moreover, as McKinnon (1993) argues, to the extent that monetary authorities followed Bagehot's rule and prevented a financial crisis while seemingly violating the "rules of the game," the commitment to the gold standard in the long run may have been strengthened.

An additional enforcement mechanism for the international gold standard rule may have been the hegemonic power of England, the most important gold standard country (Eichengreen, 1989). A persistent theme in the literature on the international gold standard is that the Classical gold standard of 1880–1914 was a British-managed standard (Bordo, 1984). Because London was the center for the world's principal gold, commodities, and capital markets, because of the extensive outstanding sterling-denominated assets, and because many countries used sterling as an international reserve currency (as a substitute for gold), it is argued that the Bank of England, by manipulating its bank rate, could attract whatever gold it needed and, furthermore, that other central banks would adjust their discount rates accordingly. Thus, the Bank of England could exert powerful influences on the money supplies and price levels of other gold standard countries.

The evidence suggests that the Bank did have some influence on other European central banks (Lindert, 1969). Eichengreen (1987) views the Bank of England as engaged in a leadership role in a Stackelberg strategic game with other central banks as followers. The other central banks accepted a passive role because of the benefits to them of using sterling as a reserve asset. According to this interpretation, the gold standard rule may have been enforced by the Bank of England.[46] Thus, the monetary authorities of many countries may have been constrained from

---

[45] Alternatively, the gold devices could be interpreted as an effort to strain every nerve to *avoid* abandoning convertibility.

[46] According to Eichengreen (1992a), the Bank of England's ability to ensure convertibility was aided by cooperation with other central banks. In addition, as mentioned previously, belief based on past performance that England attached highest priority to convertibility encouraged stabilizing private capital movements in times of threat to convertibility, such as in 1890 and 1907.

following independent discretionary policies that would have threatened the adherence to the gold standard rule.[47]

The benefits to England as leader of the gold standard – from seigniorage earned on foreign-held sterling balances, from returns to activities generated by its central position in the gold standard, and from access to international capital markets in wartime – were substantial enough to make the costs of not following the rule extremely high.

7.4   The lessons from history

The history of the gold standard suggests that the gold convertibility rule was followed continuously by only a few key countries – the best example being England from 1821 to 1914. Most major countries, however, did follow the rule during the heyday of the Classical gold standard, 1880–1914. Peripheral countries and several fairly important nations – Italy and Argentina – alternately followed and then departed from the rule, but even they were constrained in a looser sense.

The gold standard rule also proved to be successful as a commitment mechanism for England, the United States, and France in preventing default on debt and ensuring that paper-money issues were not permanent. It may have been successful as a commitment device because it had the virtues of being simple and transparent.

We have suggested a number of reasons why the gold standard rule was so successful as a commitment mechanism before 1914. First, as a contingent rule it permitted nations to have access to revenue in times of wartime emergency. The commitment to return to gold parity after the war would enable the authorities to issue debt and to collect seigniorage at more favorable terms than otherwise.[48]

---

[47] According to Giovannini's (1989) regressions, the French and German central banks adapted their domestic policies to external conditions, whereas the British did not. This can be interpreted as evidence for British management.

[48] Grossman's (1990) interpretation of the historical record, though emphasizing different factors, accepts this view. Thus, according to him, the ratio of government debt to GNP increased during major wartime episodes in Britain and the United States from the mid-18th century until after World War I, reflecting intertemporal substitution. Such borrowing represented a temporary effort to shift resources from the future to the present. Following each war, the ratio of debt to income would then be reduced by contractionary fiscal policy accompanied by deflationary monetary policies that maintained the real rate of return on outstanding bonds. According to Grossman, such a policy was an investment in the credibility capital of the sovereign borrower – a reputation for responsible repayment of the principal and for preservation of the real value of interest payments that enhanced the probability of being able to borrow heavily again at favorable rates in the event of a future war.

Second, in England and possibly in other countries, gold emerged early on as a way of certifying contracts. This certifying characteristic of gold carried forward to the relationship between the private and public sectors. Abandoning gold convertibility was viewed as a serious breach of contract. The gold standard emerged in the stable political environment of England after the 17th century, where the rule of law sanctified private contracts.[49] Only a few countries had comparable stability. Countries fraught with more unstable internal politics found it more difficult to refrain from running budget deficits, ultimately financed by paper-money issue (for example, Italy and Argentina), although the benefits of convertibility placed some constraints on their behavior.[50]

The gold standard was also successful as an international rule: by pegging their currencies to gold, countries became part of a fixed exchange rate system. The international aspect of the gold standard may have reinforced the domestic commitment mechanism because of the perceived advantages of more favorable access to international capital markets, by the operation of the "rules of the game," and by the importance of England as a hegemonic power.

The advantages accruing to England as the center of the gold standard world – the use of sterling as a reserve asset and the location in London of the world's key asset and commodity markets – made the costs of not following the gold standard rule (except in wartime emergency) extremely high. Furthermore, because England was the most important country in the gold standard era and access to the London capital market was considered to be of great benefit to developing countries, it is likely that many countries adhered to the gold standard that otherwise would not have, given the high resource costs of maintaining gold reserves. Also, because of the Bank of England's leadership role, other central banks may have been prevented from using discretionary policies, threatening adherence to the rule.

---

[49] According to North and Weingast (1989), this process was complete by the Glorious Revolution of 1688. After that date, capital markets developed in an environment free of the risk of sovereign appropriation of capital.

[50] An alternative and complementary explanation to that offered in this chapter relates to political economy considerations and the distribution of income. The configuration of political interest groups in the 19th century was favorable to the hard money, pro-gold standard rule position. This may have been related to the more limited development of democracy and less-than-universal suffrage. Thus, a comparison of the debates over resumption in England from 1797 to 1821 and in the United States from 1865 to 1878 suggests that the more limited suffrage in England in the early period served as a brake on the soft money forces favoring permanent depreciation. In the United States, the soft money forces favoring redistribution of income to debtors and other groups (such as Midwestern manufacturers) almost carried the day.

A comparison of the pre-1914 period with the subsequent period is of great interest. The gold exchange standard, which prevailed for only a few years from the mid-1920s to the Great Depression, was an attempt to restore the essential features of the Classical gold standard while allowing a greater role for domestic stabilization policy. It also attempted to economize on gold reserves by restricting its use to central banks and by encouraging the use of foreign exchange as a substitute. As is well known, the gold exchange standard suffered from a number of fatal flaws (Kindleberger, 1973; Eichengreen, 1992; Temin, 1989). These include the use of two reserve currencies, the absence of leadership by a hegemonic power, the failure of cooperation between the key members, and the unwillingness of its two strongest members, the United States and France, to follow the "rules of the game," instead exerting deflationary pressure on the rest of the world by persistent sterilization of balance of payment surpluses. The gold exchange standard collapsed, but according to Friedman and Schwartz (1963), Temin (1989), and Eichengreen (1992b), not before transmitting deflation and depression across the world.

While the gold standard rule was widely upheld before 1914, it has not been since, although to a lesser extent both the short-lived gold exchange standard and the Bretton Woods system incorporated a number of its features. Today, one could characterize most nations as following a discretionary standard, although rhetoric over the importance of rules abounds. This may seem surprising, since the benefits of having a commitment mechanism seem more relevant today than 100 years ago. On the other hand, there may have been the perception that government debt was, and is, less important as an emergency source of funds than it was in the gold standard era. For example, the stocks of physical and human capital have risen substantially. The time inconsistency literature has taught us that the incomes therefrom have broadened the scope for policymakers to use discretionary policy. For example, marginal tax rates for people with above-average human capital rose dramatically during World War II. In the absence of a commitment mechanism, these rates were not returned to prewar levels.

The gold standard rule was simple, transparent, and, for close to a century, successful. Even though it was characterized by some defects from the perspective of macroeconomic performance, a better commitment mechanism has not been adopted. Despite its appeal, many of the conditions that made the gold standard so successful vanished in 1914, and the importance that nations attach to immediate objectives casts doubt on its eventual restoration.

References

Alesina, A. and A. Drazen (1991). "Why Are Stabilizations Delayed?," *American Economic Review* 81(8), 1170–1188.

Bancroft, H. H. (1890). *History of California*, VII, San Francisco: The History Company.

Barro, R. J. (1979). "On the Determination of the Public Debt," *Journal of Political Economy* 87, 940–971.

   (1987). "Government Spending, Interest Rates, Prices, and Budget Deficits in the United Kingdom, 1701–1918," *Journal of Monetary Economics* 20, 221–248.

Barro, R. J. and D. B. Gordon (1983). "Rules, Discretion and Reputation in a Model of Monetary Policy," *Journal of Monetary Economics* 12, 101–121.

Barsky, R. B. (1987). "The Fisher Hypothesis and the Forecastability and Persistence of Inflation," *Journal of Monetary Economics* 19(1) (January), 3–24.

Barsky, R. B. and L. H. Summers (1988). "Gibson's Paradox and the Gold Standard," *Journal of Political Economy* 96(3) (June), 528–550.

Bloomfield, A. (1959). *Monetary Policy Under the International Gold Standard, 1880–1914*, New York: Federal Reserve Bank of New York.

Board of Governors of the Federal Reserve System (1994). *Banking and Monetary Statistics*, New York.

Bordo, M. D. (1981). "The Classical Gold Standard: Some Lessons for Today," *Federal Reserve Bank of St. Louis Review* 64(5) (May), 2–17.

   (1984). "The Gold Standard: The Traditional Approach," in M. D. Bordo and A. J. Schwartz (eds.), *A Retrospective on the Classical Gold Standard, 1821–1931*, Chicago: University of Chicago Press for NBER, 23–199.

   (1986). "Money, Deflation and Seigniorage: A Review Essay," *Journal of Monetary Economics* 18(3), 337–346.

   (1987a). "John Law," in P. Newman, M. Milgate and J. Eatwell (eds.), *The New Palgrave Dictionary of Economics*, London: Macmillan.

   (1987b). "Bimetallism," in R. Newman, M. Milgate and J. Eatwell (eds.), *The New Palgrave Dictionary of Economics*, London: Macmillan.

   (1993). "The Bretton Woods International Monetary System: An Historical Overview," in M. D. Bordo and B. Eichengreen (eds.), *A Restrospective on the Bretton Woods System: Lessons for International Monetary Reform*, Chicago: University of Chicago Press for NBER.

Bordo, M. D. and F. E. Kydland (1990). "The Gold Standard as a Rule," NBER, *Working Paper* 3367 (May).

Bordo, M. D. and E. N. White (1991). "A Tale of Two Currencies: British and French Finance During the Napoleonic Wars," *Journal of Economic History* (June), 303–316.

   (1993). "British and French Finance During the Napoleonic Wars," in M. D. Bordo and F. Capie (eds.), *Monetary Regimes in Transition*, Cambridge: Cambridge University Press.

British Parliamentary Papers (1888). "Second and Final Reports From the Royal Commission on the Recent Changes in the Relative Values of Precious Metals with Minutes of Evidence, Appendices, and Index," Shannon, Ireland: Irish University Press.

Brown, W. A. (1929). *England and the New Gold Standard, 1919–1926*, New Haven: Yale University Press.

Bullion Report ([1810] 1978) *Report from the Select Committee on the High Price of Bullion*, New York: Arno Press.

Calomiris, C. W. (1988). "Price and Exchange Rate Determination During the Greenback Suspension," *Oxford Economic Papers* (December).

Capie, F. and A. Webber (1985). *A Monetary History of the United Kingdom, 1870–1982*, vol. 1, *Data, Sources, Methods*, London: George Allen & Unwin.

Chari, V. V. (1988). "Time Consistency and Optimal Policy Design," *Quarterly Review*, Federal Reserve Bank of Minneapolis (Fall).

Chari, V. V. and P. J. Kehoe (1989). "Sustainable Plans and Debt," Federal Reserve Bank of Minneapolis, *Staff Report* 125.

  (1990). "Sustainable Plans," *Journal of Political Economy* 98, 783–802.

Clapham, J. (1944). *The Bank of England: A History*, vols. I and II, Cambridge: Cambridge University Press.

Cole, H. L. and P. J. Kehoe (1991). "Reputation With Multiple Relationships: Reviving Reputation Models of Debt," Federal Reserve Bank of Minneapolis, *Staff Report* 137.

Cooper, R. (1982). "The Gold Standard: Historical Facts and Future Prospects," *Brookings Papers on Economic Activity* 1, 1–45.

Crabbe, L. (1989). "The International Gold Standard and Monetary Policy in the United States from the First World War to the New Deal," Board of Governors of the Federal Reserve System, mimeo.

Cukierman, A. (1988). "Rapid Inflation – Deliberate Policy or Miscalculation?," *Carnegie–Rochester Conference Series on Public Policy* 29, 11–76.

Cunliffe Report (1918). *First Interim Report of the Committee on Currency and Foreign Exchanges After the War*, Cmnd. 9182, reprint, New York: Arno Press.

Eichengreen, B. (1985). "Editor's Introduction," in B. Eichengreen, *The Gold Standard in Theory and History*, London: Methuen.

  (1987). "Conducting the International Orchestra: Bank of England Leadership Under the Classical Gold Standard," *Journal of International Money and Finance* 6, 5–29.

  (1989). "Hegemonic Stability Theories of the International Monetary Systems," in R. Bryant (ed.), *Can Nations Agree: Aspects of International Cooperation?*, Washington: Brookings Institution.

  (1992a). "The Gold Standard Since Alec Ford," in S. M Broadberry and N. F. R. Crafts (eds.), *Britain in the International Economy, 1870–1939*, Cambridge: Cambridge University Press.

  (1992b). *Golden Fetters: The Gold Standard and the Great Depression, 1919–1939*, New York: Oxford University Press.

Feavearyear, A. (1963). *The Pound Sterling*, Oxford: Clarendon Press.

Fetter, F. (1965). *Development of British Monetary Orthodoxy, 1797–1875*, Cambridge, MA: Harvard University Press.

Fischer, S. (1980). "Dynamic Inconsistency. Cooperation, and the Benevolent Dissembling Government," *Journal of Economic Dynamics and Control* 2, 93–108.

Fishlow, A. (1987). "Market Forces or Group Interests: Inconvertible Currency in Pre-1914 Latin America," University of California at Berkeley, mimeo.

(1989). "Conditionality and Willingness to Pay: Some Parallels from the 1890s," in B. Eichengreen and P. Lindert (eds.), *The International Debt Crisis in Historical Perspective*, Cambridge, MA: MIT Press.

Ford, A. G. (1962). The Gold Standard, 1880–1914: Britain and Argentina, Oxford: Clarendon Press.

Fratianni, M. and F. Spinelli (1984). "Italy in the Gold Standard Period, 1861–1914," in M. D. Bordo and A. J. Schwartz (eds.), *A Retrospective on the Classical Gold Standard, 1821–1931*, Chicago: University of Chicago Press for NBER.

Friedman, M. (1952). "Price, Income and Monetary Changes in Three Wartime Periods," *American Economic Review* (May), 612–625.

(1990a). "The Crime of 1873," *Journal of Political Economy* 98 (December), 1159–1194.

(1990b). "Bimetallism Revisited," *Journal of Economic Perspectives* 4(4), 85–104.

Friedman, M. and A. J. Schwartz (1963). *A Monetary History of the United States, 1867–1960*, Princeton: Princeton University Press for NBER.

(1982). *Monetary Trends in the United States and in the United Kingdom 1870–1970*, Chicago: University of Chicago Press for NBER.

Gallarotti, G. M. (1991). "Centralized versus Decentralized International Monetary Systems: The Lessons of the Classical Gold Standard," in J. Dorn (ed.), *Alternatives to Government Fiat Money*, Dordrecht: Kluwer.

Garber, P. (1986). "Nominal Contracts in a Bimetallic Standard," *American Economic Review* 76, 1012–1030.

Garber, P. and V. Grilli (1986). "The Belmont–Morgan Syndicate as an Optimal Investment Banking Contract," *European Economic Review* 30, 641–677.

Gayer, A. D., W. W. Rostow and A. J. Schwartz (1953). *The Growth and Fluctuations of the British Economy, 1790–1850*, Oxford: Clarendon Press.

Giavazzi, F. and A. Giovannini (1989). *Limiting Exchange Rate Flexibility*, Cambridge, MA: MIT Press.

Giovannini, A. (1986). "'Rules of the Game' during the International Gold Standard: England and Germany," *Journal of International Money and Finance* 5, 467–483.

(1989). "How Do Fixed Exchange-Rate Regimes Work: The Evidence From the Gold Standard, Bretton Woods and the EMS," in M. Miller, B. Eichengreen and R. Portes (eds.), *Blueprints for Exchange Rate Management*, London: CEPR, 13–46.

(1993). "Bretton Woods and Its Precursors: Rules versus Discretion in the History of International Monetary Regimes," in M. D. Bordo and B.

Eichengreen (eds.), *A Retrospective on the Bretton Woods System: Lessons for International Monetary Reform*, Chicago: University of Chicago Press for NBER, 109–154.

Glassman, D. and Redish, A. (1988). "Currency Depreciation in Early Modern England and France," *Explorations in Economic History* 25.

Goodfriend, M. (1988). "Central Banking Under the Gold Standard," *Carnegie–Rochester Conference Series on Public Policy* 19, 85–124.

(1989). "Money, Credit, Banking and Payments System Policy," in D. B. Humphrey (ed.), *The US Payments System: Efficiency, Risk, and the Role of the Federal Reserve*, Boston: Kluwer Academic.

Grilli, V. (1989). "Managing Exchange Rate Crises: Evidence from the 1890s," NBER, *Working Paper* 3068 (August).

Grossman, H. (1990). "The Political Economy of War Debts and Inflation," in W. S. Haraf and P. Cagan (eds.), *Monetary Policy for a Changing Financial Environment*, Washington, DC: American Enterprise Institute.

Grossman, H. I. and J. B. Huyck (1988). "Sovereign Debt as a Contingent Claim: Excusable Default, Repudiation, and Reputation," *American Economic Review* 78, 1088–1097.

Hayashi, F. (1989). "Japan's Saving Rate: New Data and Reflections," NBER, *Working Paper* 3205.

Hume, L. J. (1963). "The Gold Standard and Deflation: Issues and Attitudes in the Nineteen Twenties," *Economica* 30, 225–242.

Jastram, R. (1977). *The Golden Constant: The English and American Experience, 1560–1976*, New York: John Wiley.

Jonung, L. (1984). "Swedish Experience Under the Classical Gold Standard, 1873–1914," in M. D. Bordo and A. J. Schwartz (eds.), *A Retrospective on the Classical Gold Standard, 1821–1931*, Chicago: University of Chicago Press for NBER.

Keynes, J. M. ([1913] 1971). *Indian Currency and Finance, The Collected Writings of John Maynard Keynes*, vol. I, reprinted in London: Macmillan and New York: Cambridge University Press for the Royal Economic Society.

([1925] 1972). "The Economic Consequences of Mr. Churchill," in *The Collected Writings of John Maynard Keynes*, vol. IX, *Essays in Persuasion*, London: Macmillan.

Kindleberger, C. P. (1973). *The World in Depression, 1929–1939*, Berkeley, CA: University of California Press.

(1984). *A Financial History of Western Europe*, London: George Allen & Unwin.

Klein, B. (1975). "Our New Monetary Standard: Measurement and Effects of Price Uncertainty, 1880–1973," *Economic Inquiry* 13, 461–484.

Kydland, F. E. and E. C. Prescott (1977). "Rules Rather than Discretion: The Inconsistency of Optimal Plans," *Journal of Political Economy* 85 (June), 473–492.

(1980a). "Dynamic Optimal Taxation, Rational Expectations and Optimal Control," *Journal of Economic Dynamics and Control* 2, 79–91.

(1980b). "A Competitive Theory of Fluctuations and the Feasibility and Desirability of Stabilization Policy," in S. Fischer (ed.), *Rational Expectations and Economic Policy*, Chicago: University of Chicago Press for the NBER.

Lacroix, A. and P. Dupieux (1973). *Le Napoleon ou les drames de la monnaie française depuis deux mille ans*, Paris: Les Presses de L'Imprimerie, Tardy-Quevey-Auvergne.

Laidler, D. E. W. (1987). "The Bullionist Controversy," in P. Newman, M. Milgate, and J. Eatwell (eds.), *New Palgrave Dictionary of Economics*, London: Macmillan.

Lindert, P. (1969). *Key Currencies and Gold, 1900–1913, Princeton Studies in International Finance* 24, Princeton: Princeton University Press.

Lucas, R. E. Jr. and N. L. Stokey (1983). "Optimal Fiscal and Monetary Policy in an Economy Without Capital," *Journal of Monetary Economics* 12, 55–93.

McCullum, B. (1989). *Monetary Economics: Theory and Policy*, New York: St. Martin's Press.

McGouldrick, R. (1984). "Operations of the German Central Bank and the Rules of the Game, 1879–1913," in M. D. Bordo and A. J. Schwartz (eds.), *A Retrospective on the Classical Gold Standard, 1821–1931*, Chicago: University of Chicago Press for NBER.

McKinnon, R. (1993). "Alternative International Monetary Systems: The Rules of the Game Reconsidered," *Journal of Economic Literature* 31, 1–44.

Meltzer, A. H. and S. Robinson (1989). "Stability Under the Gold Standard in Practice," in M. D. Bordo (ed.), *Money, History and International Finance: Essays in Honor of Anna J. Schwartz*. Chicago: University of Chicago Press.

Mitchell, B. R. (1975). *European Historical Statistics, 1750–1970*, London: Macmillan.

Mitchell, B. R. and P. Deane (1962). *Abstract of British Historical Statistics*, Cambridge: Cambridge University Press.

Mitchell, W. C. (1903). *A History of the Greenbacks*, Chicago: University of Chicago Press.

(1908). *Gold, Prices and Wages Under the Greenbacks Standard*, Berkeley, CA: University of California Press.

Moggridge, D. (1969). *The Return to Gold, 1925: The Formulations of Economic Policy and Its Critics*, London: Cambridge University Press.

Murphy, A. (1987). *Richard Cantillon: Entrepreneur and Economist*, Oxford: Clarendon Press.

Neal, L. (1991). "A Tale of Two Revolutions: The Effects of Capital Flows 1789–1815," *Bulletin of Economic Research* 43(1) (January), 57–92.

North, D. and B. Weingast (1989). "Constitution and Commitment: Evolution of Institutions Governing Public Choice," *Journal of Economic History*, 69(4) (December), 803–837.

O'Brien, P. (1967). "Government Revenue 1793–1815: A Study in Fiscal and Financial Policy in the Wars Against France," Oxford University, unpublished D. Phil. thesis.

O'Leary, P. M. (1937). "The Coinage Legislation of 1834," *Journal of Political Economy* 45, 80–94.

Officer, L. (1983). "Dollar–Sterling Mint Parity and Exchange Rates, 1791–1834," *Journal of Economic History*, 43(3) (September), 579–616.

(1985). "Integration in the American Foreign Exchange Market, 1791–1900," *Journal of Economic History*, 45(3) (September), 557–586.

(1986). "The Efficiency of the Dollar–Sterling Gold Standard, 1890–1908," *Journal of Political Economy* 94 (October), 1038–1073.

Pollard, S. (ed.) (1970). *The Gold Standard and Employment Policies Between the Wars*, London: Methuen.

Prescott, E. (1977). "Should Control Theory Be Used for Economic Stabilization?," *Carnegie–Rochester Conference Series on Public Policy* 7, 13–38.

Presnell, L. S. (1956). *Country Banking in the Industrial Revolution*, Oxford: Clarendon Press.

(1982). "The Sterling System and Financial Crises Before 1914," in C. P. Kindleberger and J. P. Laffargue (eds.), *Financial Crises: Theory, History and Policy*, New York: Cambridge University Press.

Rae, G. (1885). *The Country Banker*, London.

Ramsey, F. (1927). "A Contribution to the Theory of Taxation," *Economic Journal* 37, 47–61.

Redish, A. (1990). "The Evolution of the Gold Standard in England," *Journal of Economic History* (December), 789–806.

Ricardo, D. ([1819] 1952). "Minutes of Evidence Taken Before the Secret Committee on the Expediency of the Bank Resuming Cash Payments" (March 4, 1819), reprinted in P. Sraffa (ed.), *The Works and Correspondence of David Ricardo*, vol. 5, *Speeches, Evidence*, Cambridge: Cambridge University Press.

Rockoff, H. (1984). "Some Evidence on the Real Price of Gold, Its Cost of Production, and Commodity Prices," in M. D. Bordo and A. J. Schwartz (eds.), *A Retrospective on the Classical Gold Standard, 1821–1931*, Chicago: University of Chicago Press for NBER.

Roll, R. (1972). "Interest Rates and Price Expectations During the Civil War," *Journal of Economic History* 32.

Rolnick, A. J. and N. Wallace (1984). "Suspension and the Financing of the Civil War: A Critique of Newcomb and Mitchell," Federal Reserve Bank of Minneapolis, *Working Paper* 265.

St. Marc, M. (1983). *Histoire monétaire de la France, 1800–1980*, Paris: Presses Universitaires de France.

Sayers, R. S. (1960). "The Return to Gold, 1925," in L. S. Presnell (ed.), *Studies in the Industrial Revolution*, London.

Schwartz, A. J. (1984). "Introduction," in M. D. Bordo and A. J. Schwartz (eds.), *A Retrospective on the Classical Gold Standard, 1821–1931*, Chicago: University of Chicago Press for NBER.

(1986). "Real and Pseudo Financial Crises," in F. Capie and G. E. Wood (eds.), *Financial Crises and the World Banking System*, London: Macmillan.

(1987). "Banking School, Currency School, Free Banking School," in P.

Newman, M. Milgate, and J. Eatwell (eds.), *New Palgrave Dictionary of Economics*, London: Macmillan.

Sharkey, R. D. (1959). *Money, Class, and Party*, Baltimore: Johns Hopkins University Press.

Smith, W. S. and R. T. Smith (1990). "Stochastic Process Switching and the Return to Gold 1925," *Economic Journal* 100 (March), 164–175.

Temin, P. (1989). *Lessons from the Great Depression*, Cambridge, MA: MIT Press.

Tonniolo, G. (1990). *An Economic History of Liberal Italy: 1850–1918*, New York: Routledge.

Unger, I. (1964). *The Greenback Era: A Social and Political History of American Finance, 1865–1879*, Princeton: Princeton University Press.

Viner, J. (1937). *Studies in the Theory of International Trade*, Chicago: University of Chicago Press.

Walton, G. and H. Rockoff (1989). *History of the American Economy*, 6th edn., New York: Harcourt, Brace & Jovanovich.

White, E. (1991). "French Reparations after the Napoleonic Wars," Rutgers University (July), mimeo.

Yeager, L. (1976). *International Monetary Relations*, 2nd edn., New York: Harper & Row.

(1984). "The Image of the Gold Standard," in M. D. Bordo and A. J. Schwartz (eds.), *A Retrospective on the Classical Gold Standard, 1821–1931*, Chicago: University of Chicago Press.

CHAPTER 8

The operation of the specie standard: Evidence for core and peripheral countries, 1880–1990

Written with Anna J. Schwartz

8.1 Introduction

The classical gold standard era from 1880 to 1914, when most countries of the world defined their currencies in terms of a fixed weight (which is equivalent to a fixed price) of gold and hence adhered to a fixed exchange rate standard, has been regarded by many observers as a most admirable monetary regime. They find that its benefits include long-run price level stability and predictability, stable and low long-run interest rates, stable exchange rates (McKinnon, 1988), and hence that it facilitated a massive flow of capital from the advanced countries of Europe to the world's developing countries.

Others have taken a less favorable view of the gold standard's performance. Some criticize the record of relatively high real output and short-term price variability (Bordo, 1981; Cooper, 1982; Meltzer and Robinson, 1989), and some have faulted it for subordinating domestic stability to the maintenance of external convertibility (Keynes, 1930).

A persistent critique of the gold standard is that it provided a favorable experience for the core countries (France, Germany, the United Kingdom, and the United States), but a less favorable experience for the peripheral countries of the developing world (DeCecco, 1974). For the core countries the balance of payments adjustment mechanism was stable, so few crises occurred; the peripheral countries, by contrast, were subject to shocks imported under fixed exchange rates from abroad and frequently suffered exchange rate crises and a destabilized growth pattern.

This chapter is reprinted from Barry Eichengreen and Jorge Braga de Macedo (eds.), *Historical Perspectives on the Gold Standard: Portugal and the World.* London: Routledge, 1996, pp. 11–83.

For able research assistance we would like to thank Alexandre Hohmann. For supplying us with data and valuable information we are indebted to the following: Pablo Martin-Aceña, Lance Davis, Marc Flandreau, Lars Jonung, Sophie Lazaretou, Augustin Llona Rodriguez, Gerardo della Paollera, David Pope, Angela Redish, Jaime Reis, Georg Rich, and Fernando Santos. The usual disclaimer holds.

An alternative approach to these issues of gold standard history posits that adherence to the fixed price of specie, which characterized all convertible metallic regimes including the gold standard, served as a credible commitment mechanism to monetary and fiscal policies that otherwise would be time inconsistent (Bordo and Kydland, 1996; Giovannini, 1993). On this basis, adherence to the specie standard rule enabled many countries to avoid the problems of high inflation and stagflation that have troubled the late twentieth century. The specie standard that prevailed before 1914 was a contingent rule, or a rule with escape clauses. Under the rule, specie convertibility could be suspended in the event of a well understood, exogenously produced emergency, such as a war, on the understanding that after the emergency had safely passed, convertibility would be restored at the original parity. Market agents would regard successful adherence as evidence of a credible commitment and would allow the authorities access to seigniorage and bond finance at favorable terms.

On this view, the core countries were good players of the classical gold standard game – they adhered strictly to the rule, whereas many peripheral countries were not. Some never adhered to the rule. Others joined it when conditions were favorable to them, ostensibly to obtain access to capital from the core countries, but they quickly abandoned it when economic conditions deteriorated.

The interwar gold standard can be regarded as an extension of the pre-1914 system because it was based on gold convertibility. However, it was less successful because the commitment to convertibility was often subordinated to other politically induced objectives. The Bretton Woods international monetary system can be regarded as a distant relative of the classical gold standard in that the center country, the United States, maintained gold convertibility. It was also based on a rule with an escape clause – parities could be changed in the event of a fundamental disequilibrium. However, it differed from the basic specie standard rule in that a credible commitment to the fixed parity was not of such primary importance.

This chapter surveys the history of the specie standard as a contingent rule from the early nineteenth century, when most countries were still on a bimetallic or silver standard, until the gold standard's final collapse in the late 1930s. As a comparison we also briefly consider the Bretton Woods system and the recent managed floating regime. We then present some evidence on the economic performance of the core and a number of peripheral countries under the various regimes.

This chapter first defines the contingent specie standard rule and discusses how the commitment to convertibility was maintained. It then presents and discusses a chronology of adherence to the rule by 21 countries under variants of the specie standard prevailing before World War II. A similar chronology is included for the Bretton Woods system. There is then offered some graphical evidence on capital flows from 1865 to 1914 from the United Kingdom to two countries of recent settlement – Argentina and the United States – during episodes of both suspension and adherence to convertibility. It suggests that adherence to the rule may have had some influence on the decision by British investors to invest abroad.

Evidence is then presented on economic performance for 21 countries (both core and peripheral) across several regimes. Such evidence may shed light on whether differing economic performance can explain why some countries successfully adhered to the rule and others did not, or whether adherence/non-adherence may have influenced performance. We examine the stability of both nominal and real macro variables across four regimes (pre-1914 gold standard; interwar gold standard; Bretton Woods; the subsequent managed exchange rate float). We then present measures of both demand shocks (reflecting policy actions specific to the regime) and supply shocks (reflecting shocks to the environment independent of the regime). These measures allow us to determine whether adherents to the rule consistently pursued different policy actions from non-adherents, and whether persistent adverse shocks to the environment may, for some countries, have precluded adherence to the rule. The chapter concludes with answers to the questions: How successful was the specie standard rule as a contingent rule? Why was it successful when it was? Why did some countries adhere while others did not?

8.2   The specie standard as a contingent rule

8.2.1   The domestic specie standard

A specie standard has been traditionally viewed as a form of monetary rule or constraint over monetary policy actions. Following a rule, such as adherence to the specie standard, that would cause the money supply to vary automatically with the balance of payments was viewed as superior to entrusting policy to the discretion of well-meaning and possibly well-informed monetary authorities (Simons, 1951).[1] In contrast to the

---

[1] The Currency School in England in the early nineteenth century made the case for the Bank of England's fiduciary note issue to vary automatically with the level of the Bank's gold reserve (the currency principle). Following such a rule was viewed as preferable (for providing price-level stability) to allowing the note issue to be altered at the discretion of the well-meaning and possibly well-informed directors of the Bank (the position taken by

traditional view, which stresses both impersonality and automaticity, the recent literature on the time inconsistency of optimal government policy regards a rule as a credible commitment mechanism binding policy actions over time.

The absence of a credible commitment mechanism leads governments, in pursuing stabilization policies, to produce an inflationary outcome (Kydland and Prescott, 1977; Barro and Gordon, 1983). In a closed economy environment, once the monetary authority has announced a given rate of monetary growth, which the public expects it to validate, the authority then has an incentive to create a monetary surprise to either reduce unemployment or capture seigniorage revenue. The public, with rational expectations, will come to anticipate the authorities' perfidy, leading to an inflationary equilibrium. A credible commitment mechanism, by preventing the government from cheating, can preserve long-run price stability.

Following a rule also allows a government to use debt to smooth distortionary taxes over time. In addition to choosing optimal taxes the government can also choose an optimal default rate on its outstanding debt. In a commitment regime the government can force itself to honor its outstanding debt and not default via inflation or suspension of payments. If the government cannot follow a binding commitment – in other words, if it follows a discretionary regime – rational bond-holders would expect the government to have an incentive to default on its outstanding debt. Hence, in a discretionary equilibrium, bond-holders will be averse to purchasing government debt.

Under the specie standard, the pledge to fix the price of a country's currency in terms of gold, silver, or both represents the basic rule. This involved, for instance in the case of a monometallic gold standard, defining a gold coin as a fixed weight of gold, called, for example, one dollar. The monetary authority was then committed to keep the mint price of gold fixed through the purchase and sale of gold in unlimited amounts. Under the bimetallic system that prevailed in most countries until the third quarter of the nineteenth century, the monetary authorities would define the weight of both gold and silver coins, freely buying and selling them. Maintaining a fixed bimetallic ratio is a variant of the basic convertibility rule, since it is the fixed value of the unit of account that is the essence of the rule.[2]

the opposing Banking School). For a discussion of the Currency Banking School debate, see Viner (1937), Fetter (1965), and Schwartz (1987).

[2] Viewed, however, as a rule in the traditional sense – as an automatic mechanism to ensure price stability – bimetallism may have had greater scope for automaticity than the gold standard, because of the additional cushion of a switch from one metal to the other. See Friedman (1990).

The specie standard rule followed in the century before World War 1 can be viewed as a form of contingent rule or rule with escape clauses (Grossman and Van Huyck, 1988; DeKock and Grilli, 1989; Flood and Isard, 1989; Bordo and Kydland, 1996). The monetary authority maintains the standard – keeping the price of the currency in terms of specie fixed – except in the event of a well understood emergency such as a major war. In wartime it may suspend gold convertibility and issue paper money to finance its expenditures, and it can sell debt issues in terms of the nominal value of its currency, on the understanding that debt will eventually be paid off in specie. The rule is contingent in the sense that the public understands that the suspension will last only for the duration of the wartime emergency plus some period of adjustment. It assumes that afterwards the government will follow the deflationary policies necessary to resume payments at the original parity.[3] Following such a rule will allow the government to smooth its revenue from different sources of finance: taxation, borrowing, and seigniorage (Lucas and Stokey, 1983; Mankiw, 1987).[4]

As we document later in this chapter, the gold standard contingent rule worked successfully for three core countries of the classical gold standard: Britain, France, and the United States. In all these countries the monetary authorities adhered faithfully to the fixed price of gold except during major wars. During the Napoleonic War and World War I for England, the Civil War for the United States, and the Franco-Prussian War for France, specie payments were suspended and paper money and debt were issued. But in each case, after the wartime emergency had passed, policies leading to resumption were adopted.[5] Indeed,

---

[3] This description is consistent with a result from a model of Lucas and Stokey (1983), in which financing of wars is a contingency rule that is optimal. In their example, where the occurrence and duration of the war are uncertain, the optimal plan for the debt is not to service it during the war. Under this policy, people realize when they purchase the debt that effectively it will be defaulted on in the event the war continues.

[4] A case study comparing British and French finances during the Napoleonic Wars shows that Britain was able to finance its wartime expenditures by a combination of taxes, debt, and paper money issue – to smooth revenue; whereas France had to rely primarily on taxation. France had to rely on a less efficient mix of finance than Britain because she had used up her credibility by defaulting on outstanding debt at the end of the American Revolutionary War and by hyperinflating during the Revolution. Napoleon ultimately returned France to the bimetallic standard in 1803 as part of a policy to restore fiscal probity, but because of the previous loss of reputation, France was unable to take advantage of the contingent aspect of the bimetallic standard rule. See Bordo and White (1993).

[5] The behavior of asset prices (exchange rates and interest rates) during suspension periods suggests that market agents viewed the commitment to gold as credible. For the United States see Roll (1972) and Calomiris (1988), who present evidence of expected appreciation of the greenback during the American Civil War based on a negative interest differential between bonds that were paid in greenbacks and those paid in gold.

successful adherence to the rule may have enabled the belligerents to obtain access to debt finance more easily in subsequent wars.[6]

Examples of discretion – breaches of the rule – include postponement of resumption after the war and reasonable delay period have passed, and pegging to specie at a devalued parity. Under both situations, should there be another war within memory of the previous one, then the public's willingness to absorb government debt would be quite different from that in the previous war, even if the situation were otherwise similar and the government claimed to subscribe to a reasonable delay rule.

It is crucial that the rule be transparent and simple and that only a limited number of contingencies be included. Transparency and simplicity would avoid the problems of moral hazard and incomplete information (Canzoneri, 1985; Obstfeld, 1992), i.e., prevent monetary authorities from engaging in discretionary policy under the guise of following the contingent rule. In this respect a second contingency – a temporary suspension in the face of a financial crisis, which in turn was not the result of the monetary authorities' own actions, may also have been part of the rule. However, because of the greater difficulty of verifying the source of the contingency than in the case of war – invoking the escape clause under conditions of financial crisis, or in the case of a shock to the terms of trade (a third possible contingency) would be more likely to create suspicion that discretion was being followed.

The specie standard rule may have been enforced by reputational considerations. Long-run adherence to the rule was based on the historical evolution of the standard itself; thus, for example, gold was accepted as money became of its intrinsic value and desirable properties. Paper claims, developed to economize on the scarce resources tied up in a commodity money, became acceptable only because they were convertible into gold.

In turn, the reputation of the specie standard would constrain the monetary authorities from breaching convertibility, except under well-understood contingencies. Thus, when an emergency occurred, the abandonment of the standard would be viewed by all to be a temporary event since, from their experience, only specie or specie-backed claims truly served as money. An alternative commitment mechanism was to guaran-

---

Also, see Smith and Smith (1993), who demonstrate that movements in the premium on gold from the Resumption Act of 1875 until resumption was established in 1878 were driven by a credible belief that resumption would occur. For the case of Britain's return to gold in 1925, see Smith and Smith (1990), Miller and Sutherland (1992) and (1994). An application of the stochastic process switching literature suggests that the increasing likelihood that resumption would occur at the original parity gradually altered the path of the dollar–sterling exchange rate towards the new ceiling, several months in advance.

[6] For suggestive evidence see Bordo and Kydland (1996).

tee gold convertibility in the constitution. This was the case, for example, in Sweden before 1914, when laws pertaining to the gold standard could be changed only by two identical parliamentary decisions with an election in between (Jonung, 1984, p. 368). Convertibility was also enshrined in the laws of a number of gold standard central banks (Giovannini, 1993).

8.2.2   *The international gold standard*

The specie standard rule originally evolved as a domestic commitment mechanism but its enduring fame is as an international rule. The classical gold standard emerged as a true international standard by 1880 following the switch by the majority of countries from bimetallism, silver monometallism, and paper to gold as the basis of their currencies (Eichengreen, 1985). As an international standard, the key rule was maintenance of gold convertibility at the established par. Maintenance of a fixed price of gold by its adherents in turn ensured fixed exchange rates. The fixed price of domestic currency in terms of gold provided a nominal anchor to the international monetary system.

Recent evidence suggests that, indeed, exchange rates throughout the 1880 to 1914 period were characterized by a high degree of fixity in the principal countries. Although exchange rates frequently deviated from par, violations of the gold points were rare (Officer, 1986), as were devaluations (Eichengreen, 1985).

According to the game theoretic literature, for an international monetary arrangement to be effective both between countries and within them, a time consistent credible commitment mechanism is required (Canzoneri and Henderson, 1991). Adherence to the gold convertibility rule provided such a mechanism. Indeed, Giovannini (1993) finds the variation of both exchange rates and short-term interest rates within the limits set by the gold points in the 1899–1909 period consistent with market agents' expectations of a credible commitment by the "core" countries to the gold-standard rule in the sense of this chapter.[7] In addition to the reputation of the domestic gold standard and constitutional provisions which ensured domestic commitment, adherence to the international gold-standard rule may have been enforced by other mechanisms. These include: improved access to international capital

---

[7] Also see Officer (1993). His calculations of speculative bands (bands within which uncovered interest arbitrage prevails consistent with gold point arbitrage efficiency) for the interwar dollar–sterling exchange rate show serious violations only in 1931, at the very end of the gold exchange standard.

markets; the operation of the rules of the game; the hegemonic power of the United Kingdom; and central bank cooperation.

Support for the international gold standard likely grew because it provided improved access to the international capital markets of the core countries. Countries were eager to adhere to the standard because they believed that gold convertibility would be a signal to creditors of sound government finance and the future ability to service debt.[8]

This was the case both for developing countries seeking access to long-term capital, such as Austria-Hungary (Yeager, 1984) and Latin America (Fishlow, 1989), and for countries seeking short-term loans, such as Japan, which financed the Russo–Japanese war of 1905–06 with foreign loans seven years after joining the gold standard (Hayashi, 1989). Once on the gold standard, these countries feared the consequences of suspension (Eichengreen, 1992a, p. 19; Fishlow 1987, 1989). The fact that England, the most successful country of the nineteenth century, was on the gold standard, as well as other, "progressive" countries, was probably a powerful argument for joining (Friedman, 1990; Gallarotti, 1993).

The operation of the "rules of the game," whereby the monetary authorities were supposed to alter the discount rate to speed up the adjustment to a change in external balance, may also have been an important part the commitment mechanism played under the international gold-standard rule. To the extent the "rules" were followed and adjustment facilitated, the commitment to convertibility was strengthened and conditions conducive to abandonment were lessened.

Evidence on the operation of the "rules of the game" questions their validity. Bloomfield (1959), in a classic study, showed that, with the principal exception of the United Kingdom, the rules were frequently violated, in the sense that discount rates were not always changed in the required direction (or by sufficient amounts) and in the sense that changes in domestic credit were often negatively correlated with changes in gold reserves. In addition, a number of countries used gold devices – practices to prevent gold outflows.

One can reconcile the violation of the "rules of the game" and the use of gold devices, with maintenance of credibility in the commitment to gold, by viewing the gold points as a form of target zone (Eichengreen, 1994). Belief that intervention would occur at the upper and lower gold

---

[8] A case study of Canada during the Great Depression provides evidence for the importance of the credible commitment mechanism of adherence to gold. Canada suspended the gold standard in 1929 but did not allow the Canadian dollar to depreciate nor the price level to rise for two years. Canada did not take advantage of the suspension to emerge from the depression, because of concern for its credibility with foreign lenders. See Bordo and Redish (1990).

points created a honeymoon effect whereby stabilizing capital flows caused the market exchange rate to revert towards parity before reaching the gold points (Krugman, 1991). Within the zone, the monetary authorities could alter discount rates to effect domestic objectives such as stabilizing real activity and smoothing interest rates (Svennson, 1994).[9] Moreover, for the major countries, at least before 1914, such policies were not used extensively enough to threaten the convertibility into gold (Schwartz, 1984).

An additional enforcement mechanism for the international gold-standard rule may have been the hegemonic power of England, the most important gold-standard country (Eichengreen, 1989). A persistent theme in the literature on the international gold standard is that the classical gold standard of 1880 to 1914 was a British-managed standard (Bordo, 1984). Because London was the center for the world's principal gold, commodities, and capital markets, because of the extensive outstanding sterling-denominated assets, and because many countries used sterling as an international reserve currency (as a substitute for gold), it is argued that the Bank of England, by manipulating its bank rate, could attract whatever gold it needed and, furthermore, that other central banks would adjust their discount rates accordingly. Thus, the Bank of England could exert a powerful influence on the money supplies and price levels of other gold-standard countries.

The evidence suggests that the Bank did have some influence on other European central banks (Lindert, 1969). Eichengreen (1987) treats the Bank of England as engaged in a leadership role in a Stackelberg strategic game with other central banks as followers. The other central banks accepted a passive role because of the benefits to them of using sterling as a reserve asset. According to this interpretation, the gold-standard rule may have been enforced by the Bank of England. Thus, the monetary authorities of many countries may have been constrained from following independent discretionary policies that would have threatened adherence to the gold-standard rule.

Indeed, according to Giovannini (1989), the gold standard was an asymmetric system. England was the center country. It used its monetary policy (bank rate) to maintain gold convertibility. Other countries accepted the dictates of fixed parities and allowed their money supplies to passively respond. His regressions support this view – the French and

---

[9] Eschweiler and Bordo (1993) provide evidence for this interpretation for Germany over the period 1883–1913 based on an estimation of the Reichsbank's reaction function. They find that the central bank's pursuit of an interest rate smoothing policy (an obvious violation of "the rules of the game") was subordinate to its commitment to keep the exchange rate within the gold points.

German central banks adapted their domestic policies to external conditions, whereas the British did not.

The benefits to England as leader of the gold standard – from seigniorage earned on foreign-held sterling balances, from returns to financial institutions generated by its central position in the gold standard, and from access to international capital markets in wartime – were substantial enough to make the costs of not following the rule extremely high.

Finally, Eichengreen (1992b) argues that episodic central bank cooperation may have also strengthened the credibility of the gold standard. Lines of credit arranged between the Banque de France, other central banks, and the Bank of England during incipient financial crises such as those of 1890 and 1907 may in turn have encouraged private stabilizing capital movements to offset threats to convertibility.

8.2.3 *The classical gold standard, the gold exchange standard, and Bretton Woods*

Eichengreen (1994) posits three prerequisites for a successful international monetary arrangement: the capacity to undertake relative price adjustment; adherence to robust monetary rules; and ability to contain market pressures. According to him the classical gold standard contingent rule satisfied these criteria for the core countries because the credible commitment to maintain convertibility above all else allowed the escape clause to accommodate major shocks, and because central bank cooperation eased market pressures in the face of speculative attacks. By contrast, for peripheral countries, the credibility of commitment to the gold standard was considerably weaker, reflecting strong domestic political pressures to alter exchange rates (Frieden, 1993).

Though gold convertibility was restored by 1926 by most countries, the interwar gold exchange standard was a much less successful application of the specie standard rule. The escape clause could not be invoked (lest it lead to destabilizing capital outflows), absent a credible commitment to maintain gold parity in the face of a politicized money supply process and, according to Eichengreen (1992b), the failure of cooperation.

The Bretton Woods international monetary system can also be viewed within the context of the specie standard rule, although it is a distant variant of the original specie standard. Under the rules of Bretton Woods, only the United States, as central reserve country and provider of the nominal anchor, was required to peg its currency to gold; the other members were required to peg their currencies to the dollar (McKinnon, 1993). They also were encouraged to use domestic stabilization policy to offset temporary disturbances. The Bretton Woods system had an escape clause for its members – a change in parity was allowed in the face of a fundamental disequilibrium, which could encompass the contingencies under the specie standard rule – but it was not the same as under the specie standard because it did not require restoration of the original parity.[10] The rule for members (other than the United States) was enforced, as under the gold standard, by access to U.S. capital and to the IMF's resources. For the United States, there was no explicit enforcement mechanism other than reputation and the commitment to gold convertibility. Capital controls were viewed as a method to contain market pressures.

The system was successful as long as the United States maintained its commitment to convertibility (i.e. maintained price stability). But the escape clause mechanism quickly proved defective since the fundamental disequilibrium contingency was never spelled out and hence parity changes would be accompanied by speculative attacks which became more serious as capital controls became increasingly ineffective. Ultimately, by following highly expansionary monetary and fiscal policies beginning in the mid-1960s, the United States attached greater importance to domestic concerns than to its role as the center of the international monetary system, and the system collapsed.

Thus, although the Bretton Woods system can be interpreted as one based on rules, the system did not provide a credible commitment mechanism.[11] The United States was unwilling to subsume domestic considerations to the responsibility of maintaining a nominal anchor. At the same time other Group of Seven (G-7) countries became increasingly unwilling to follow the dictates of the U.S.-imposed world inflation rate.

8.3   Chronology of adherence to and suspension of specie rules, pre– and post–Bretton Woods

8.3.1   Conforming to specie rules

Tables 8.1 and 8.2 give a snapshot record of the conformity of 21 countries to specie rules – commitment to a fixed parity with an escape clause. Table 8.1 refers to the extended period from the nineteenth century

---

[10] The United States could change the dollar price of gold if a majority of members (and every member with 10 percent or more of the total quotas) agreed.
[11] Indeed, Giovannini's (1993) calculations show that during the Bretton Woods convertible period credibility bounds on interest rates for the major currencies, in contrast to the classical gold standard, were frequently violated.

Table 8.1. *Pre–Bretton Woods specie convertibility and suspensions*

Country	Dates of bimetallic or silver convertibility	Dates of suspensions	Reasons for suspensions	Dates of gold convertibility	Dates of suspensions	Reasons for suspensions	Change in parity?
Part 1: Core countries							
France	1803	1848–1850	Gov. Overthrown	1878	1914	War	Yes
	1850	1870–78	War	1928	1936	Depression	Yes
Germany				12/1871	1914	War	Yes
				1924	1931	Depression	Yes
United Kingdom	1694	1797–1821	War	1816–1821	1847[a]	Panic	No
					1857[a]	Panic	No
					1866[a]	Panic	No
					1914	War	No
				1925	1931	Crisis	Yes
United States	1792	1834[b]		1875/1879	1893	Panic[c]	No
	1834	1837[c]	Panic	1893	1907	Panic[c]	No
	1838	1857[c]	Panic	1908	1933	Depression	Yes
	1858	1862	War				
		1873[c]	Panic				
Part 2: New Anglo-Saxon settlement countries							
Australia	1829			1852	1915	War	No
				04/1925	12/1929	Crisis	Yes
				03/1930			

Table 8.1. (cont.)

Country	Dates of bimetallic or silver convertibility	Dates of suspensions	Reasons for suspensions	Dates of gold convertibility	Dates of suspensions	Reasons for suspensions	Change in parity?
Canada	1821	1837	Crisis	1853	1914	War	No
	1839			06/1926	09/1931	Crisis	No
							Yes
Part 3: Latin America							
Argentina	1822	1825	War	1863	05/1876	Conv. Failed	No
				1881		Lax Fisc	
				1883	01/1885	Conv. Failed	No
				1899	1914	War	Yes
				08/1927	1929	Crisis	Yes
Brazil		1833	Lax Fisc	1846	1857	Crisis	
				1888	1889	Gov. Overthrown	Yes
				1906	1914	War	Yes
				1927	1930	Crisis	Yes
Chile	1818	1851		1887		Conv. Failed	Yes
	1851	1866		1895	1898	War Threat	Yes
	1870	1878	Crisis	1925	1931	Crisis	Yes

Part 4: Southern Europe

				01/1885	08/1885	Conv. Failed	
Greece	02/1833	04/1848	Panic	04/1910	12/1914	War	No
	01/1849	12/1868	War	05/1928	04/1932	Lax Fisc	Yes
Italy	08/1870	05/1877	War	1884	1894	Depression	Yes
	1862	1866	Lax Fisc; War	12/1927	10/1936	Crisis	Yes
Portugal	1846			1854	1891	Crisis	Yes
				07/1931	09/1931		Yes

Part 5: Scandinavian countries

				01/1885	08/1885	Conv. Failed	
Denmark				12/1872	12/1914	War	No
				01/1927	09/1931	Crisis	Yes
Finland				1877	1914	War	Yes
				01/1926	10/1931	Crisis	Yes
Norway				1875	1914	War	No
				05/1928	09/1931	Crisis	Yes
Sweden	1803	1809	War	1873	1914		No
	1834	1873		1922/1924	1931		Yes

Part 6: Western Europe

				01/1885	08/1885	Conv. Failed	
Belgium	1832	1848	Crisis	1878	1914	War	Yes
				10/1926	03/1935	Crisis	Yes
Netherlands	1847			1875	1914	War	No
				04/1925	10/1936		Yes

252

Table 8.1. *(cont.)*

Country	Dates of bimetallic or silver convertibility	Dates of suspensions	Reasons for suspensions	Dates of gold convertibility	Dates of suspensions	Reasons for suspensions	Change in parity?
CanaSwitzerland	1850			1878	1914		Yes
				1929	1936		Yes
Part 7: Japan							
Japan	1885	1897		1897	1917	Crisis	No
				12/1930	12/1931	Crisis	Yes

Notes:

[a] Suspension of Banking Act of 1844.

[b] Change in mint ratio.

[c] Restriction of payments by banks.

Sources: Bernanke and James (1991); Bordo and Kydland (1996); Butlin (1986); Cortés-Condé (1989); Eichengreen (1992b); Fratianni and Spinelli (1984); Fritsch and Franco (1992); Haavisto (1992); Jonung (1984); Lazaretou (1984); Llona-Rodriguez (1993); Martin-Aceña (1993); Pelaez and Suzigan (1976); Reis (1991); Shearer and Clark (1984); Shinjo (1962).

Table 8.2. *Bretton Woods, 1946–1971, par values, suspensions, and par changes*

Country	Dates of par value declared to IMF	Date of par value suspended	Dates of change of par value	Reasons for suspensions/par changes
Part 1: Core countries				
France	12/18/1946	01/26/1948	09/20/1949	Inflation
		08/11/1957	12/29/1958	Inflation
		11/1968	08/10/1969	Crisis
Germany	06/20/1948 (Undeclared) 01/30/1953		09/19/1949	
			03/06/1961	B. of P. surplus
			10/26/1969	
		05/09/1971		
		08/23/1971[a]	12/21/1971	
United Kingdom	07/15/1947 12/18/1948	08/20/1947	09/18/1949	
			11/18/1967	B. of P. imbalance
		08/1971		
United States	1946	8/15/1971	05/08/1972	
Part 2: New Anglo-Saxon settlement countries				
Australia	1947		09/1949	
			02/14/1966[b]	
		8/1971		
Canada	12/18/1946		09/19/1949	
		9/30/1950	05/02/1962	
		5/31/1970		
Part 3: Latin America				
Argentina			1955[c]	
	1957		1959	
			1962	
			1970	
Brazil	1948	[c]	1967[c]	
Chile	12/18/1946	[c]	10/1953[c]	
			07/1962	
Part 4: Southern Europe				
Greece	1961			
Italy	3/30/1960	08/1971	12/20/1971	
Portugal	1962	08/1971		
Spain	1959		11/1967	
Part 5: Scandinavian countries				
Denmark	12/18/1946		06/09/1957	
			11/1967	
		08/1971	12/1971	

Table 8.2. *(cont.)*

Country	Dates of par value declared to IMF	Date of par value suspended	Dates of change of par value	Reasons for suspensions/par changes
Finland	1951		09/05/1957	
			12/1971	
Norway	12/18/1946		09/1949	
		08/1971	12/1971	
Sweden	11/05/1951	08/1971	12/21/1971	
Part 6: Western Europe				
Belgium	1946	08/1971	09/21/1949	
			12/21/1971	
Netherlands	1946		09/22/1949	
			03/07/1961	
		05/09/1971	12/21/1971	
Switzerland	Not a member			
Part 7: Japan				
Japan	04/24/1949	08/1971	12/21/1971	

Notes:
[a] Dual exchange rates.
[b] Change from Australian pound to Australian dollar.
[c] Multiple exchange rates.
Sources: Bordo (1993a); DeVries (1976); Horsefield (1969).

through the post–World War I interwar years, when specie rules were acknowledged, whether or not observed; Table 8.2 refers to the Bretton Woods era, when specie rules were no longer acknowledged or observed (to a limited extent the United States was an exception) but countries submitted to the rule that only in the case of fundamental disequilibrium was a change in parity permissible. Countries did not lightly change the par values of their currencies.

The countries are divided into two main groupings: four core countries and 17 peripheral countries. Over the extended period covered by Table 8.1, core countries were faithful to specie rules under the classical gold standard from 1880 to 1914, but not invariably so in the decades before and after. The peripheral countries, which are classified in the main according to geographical location, were intermittently faithful over the extended period.

Table 8.1 separates experience under a bimetallic or silver standard, which prevailed before the last quarter of the nineteenth century, from experience under the gold standard that followed. For each standard and each country the table shows dates when a commitment was made to convert the national currency into specie, dates of suspension of the commitment, and the reasons for suspension. For the gold standard an additional column indicates whether a change in parity was made on resumption of convertibility after suspension. The column is omitted for bimetallic or silver experience because in these cases we have not established the dates of devaluations or revaluations after resumptions. Table 8.2, dealing with Bretton Woods, gives the dates each country (except for Switzerland, which was not a member) declared its par value to the IMF; dates of suspension, if any; dates of change of par value; and reasons for suspension or par change.

8.3.2 Evaluating pre–Bretton Woods adherence to specie rules

Core countries: The four countries that we designate as the core include France, Germany, the United Kingdom, and the United States. We discuss first the record for these countries before they adopted the gold standard. For the bimetallic/silver standard period, there are no entries for Germany, which was not unified until 1871. The individual German states, however, were on a bimetallic standard, as also were the other three core countries.

The year 1803 is the entry in the table for the date of convertibility of the French franc into gold or silver. A bimetallic system nevertheless predated that entry by centuries, but before 1803, France had endured devaluations, revaluations, John Law's inflationary inconvertible paper money experiment of 1716–20, and the revolutionary war assignat hyperinflation of 1789–95. So 1803 marks the beginning of a stable system, with only two interruptions until 1878, when France switched to gold. The two interruptions were suspensions in 1848–50, following the overthrow of the July monarchy, and 1870–78, following the Franco–Prussian war. Both of these interruptions qualify as consistent with adherence to specie rules, since the suspensions were valid exercises of the escape clauses.

Although the table shows 1694, the year the Bank of England was founded, as the date for convertibility of the British pound into silver, Britain was on a silver standard as far back as the thirteenth century. *De facto* the country was on a gold standard from 1717 on, owing to the overvaluation of gold by Sir Isaac Newton, the Master of the Mint; *de jure* the country adopted the gold standard in 1816, while suspension of convertibility was still in effect. There had been banking crises in 1763, 1772, and 1783, but no suspensions until the war with France ended convertibility from 1797 to 1821. This again we regard not as a breach of the rule but proper invocation of the escape clause not only for the duration of the war but for a period of adjustment thereafter. Resumption at the pre-war parity also respects the rule (Bordo and Kydland, 1996).

Whether the United States is eligible for inclusion among core countries in the nineteenth century is the subject of debate. We discuss the issue when we examine the status of the United States under the classical gold standard. Having concluded for the later period that the United States belongs among core countries, we also do not exclude it from the core group when it was on a bimetallic standard.

The U.S. Coinage Act of 1792 defined the bimetallic standard at a mint ratio of 15 to 1. In 1834 and again in 1837 the mint ratio was altered, remaining unchanged thereafter at 16 to 1. Banking panics in 1837 and 1857 led to temporary restriction of payments by banks, but no suspension of convertibility. The Civil War, however, occasioned suspension from 1862 to 1878. In 1873 there was a banking panic, like the earlier ones, in which the banks restricted payments of high-powered paper money. Despite contentious political opposition to deflation that resumption enforced, on January 1, 1879, resumption was achieved at the pre-war parity, in line with the declaration of the Resumption Act of 1875. Under the classical gold standard, both France and Germany observed specie rules until the outbreak of World War I. Each then suspended convertibility, and both devalued before resuming in the 1920s. Convertibility by France lasted for eight years, by Germany for seven years, and then both devalued after suspending in 1931. The public probably regarded suspension *per se* because of war and financial crisis as permissible under the escape clause. The change in parity, however, diluted the credibility of the countries' attachment to specie rules.

The United Kingdom's record before World War I is the epitome of proper conduct under the gold standard. As the country at the center of the system, operating with a small gold reserve, it nevertheless managed to serve both its domestic and international interests while maintaining convertibility. Three banking panics in 1847, 1857, and 1866 led to suspension of the Banking Act of 1844, which limited the Bank of England's fiduciary issue, but did no damage to the convertibility commitment. Thereafter the Bank acted to defuse panics before they emerged, as in 1890 and 1907. Convertibility was abandoned by the Bank in World War I (*de facto* in 1914 and *de jure* in 1919), taking advantage of the escape clause, and the return to the gold standard at the prewar parity was delayed until 1925, also consonant with the provisions of the escape clause. The convertibility commitment, however, lasted only for six years, and devaluation followed.

The view, alluded to above, that would exclude the United States as a member of the group of core countries, would shift it to the peripheral country group that includes Australia and Canada. That view takes its cue in part from the silver agitation and legislation of 1878 and 1890 that threatened the convertibility of U.S. dollars into gold (Eichengreen, 1992b, 1994; Giovanini, 1993; Grilli, 1990). If lasting damage to U.S. commitment credibility as a result of the threat had resulted, we would concur. Since the threat was a temporary one, and convertibility was never suspended, we conclude that the United States, by the end of the nineteenth century a colossus on the world stage, belongs with the core.

Another reason advanced for excluding the United States from the core is that before 1914 it was a net capital importer, and hence more like Australia and Canada than the core countries that provided the capital. This is a narrow dimension by which to judge the United States' relative economic importance. It was wealthier and more populous than the United Kingdom under the classical gold standard, and certainly more so than France and Germany. The United States was a capital exporter as well as an importer in the nineteenth century, and by 1914 it was a net capital exporter. These considerations reinforce our conclusion that it is properly a core country.

Apart from the silver threat, convertibility from 1879 to 1914 in the United States was never in doubt. It was preserved even during two banking panics in 1893 and 1907, when banks restricted payments. In World War I the United States embargoed gold exports, 1917–19, but did not otherwise attenuate the gold standard. Specie rules were, however, flouted by the devaluation of the dollar in 1933. The changed parity legislated in 1934 remained in effect until 1971.

The record of commitment by the core countries to specie rules is unblemished under the pre–World War I gold standard. Neither France nor Germany played by those rules during the interwar period, having resumed convertibility with devalued gold content of their currencies. The United Kingdom reverted to its prewar parity when it resumed convertibility in 1925 but by 1931 devalued and abandoned rules for discretion. The United States followed the United Kingdom in devaluing in 1933 and adopted a gold standard in 1934 that diverged in fundamental ways from the pre–World War I standard.

Australia and Canada: Australia and Canada, countries that were settled by the United Kingdom and were part of the British Empire, initially used the British currency system. Silver was the metallic medium in Australia before it adopted the gold standard, but it is not clear that a silver standard prevailed. Convertibility at a fixed Australian price of gold dated from 1852. Despite severe banking problems in the 1890s, Australia did not suspend convertibility until July 1915 during World War I. It resumed, along with the United Kingdom in 1925, at its prewar parity, and suspended at the end of 1929, when the world depression began. It devalued in March 1930 (Butlin, 1986).

In Canada the first bank charters in 1821 required convertibility of bank notes into silver. A financial crisis and political instability in 1837 led to suspension. Resumption occurred in 1839. Canada adopted the gold standard in 1853 and, although it experienced a sharp cyclical downturn in 1907–08, it did not suspend convertibility until 1914. However, no change was made in the statutory price of gold, and the gold reserve requirement for Dominion notes was not suspended, hence expansionary domestic monetary policy was subject to gold limits. Since export of gold was embargoed, exchange rates were at a discount from prewar parities. Canada restored legal convertibility at the prewar parity in July 1926, making the monetary adjustments to return to parity without a central bank. The *de facto* date of Canada's suspension of gold convertibility was 1929 (Shearer and Clark, 1984, p. 300). Canadian banks could not ship gold abroad, but foreign holders of Canadian currency obligations could redeem them in gold. *De jure* suspension occurred in September 1931 when both internal and external gold convertibility ended.

Both Australia and Canada were as faithful as the core countries in adhering to the gold standard before 1914, but devalued in the post–World War I period.

Latin America: The record of the three Latin American countries, Argentina, Brazil, and Chile, does not match that of Australia and Canada.

Before it adopted the gold standard, from 1822 to 1825 Argentina had a brief spell of convertibility of bank notes. The metallic medium was silver and gold. Convertibility ended at a time of large government expenditures related to a war with Brazil. For the following 35 years, a period of continuing fiscal improvidence, there was no convertibility. Between 1862 and 1865 contractionary monetary policy was in force.

Gold convertibility in Argentina began in February 1867 after a failed attempt in 1863. Convertibility was suspended in May 1876 after several years of political unrest and rising government deficits. Although the exchange rate reached parity by 1881, resumption that year failed. Convertibility was restored in 1883 but lasted only until January 1885, at a time of financial crisis in Europe and following a period of expansionary fiscal policy. Again inconvertibility thereafter until 1899 was associated with lax fiscal policy leading to debt default in 1890. In 1899 convertibility was restored at the original parity of 5 gold pesos to the pound with the return to fiscal orthodoxy in 1896 and the establishment of a form of currency board. However, paper pesos that had been circulating since 1885 at a large discount relative to gold were frozen at 2.27 per gold peso, in effect a substantial devaluation. Argentina suspended convertibility in 1914 on the outbreak of World War I. It resumed in August 1927 at a changed parity, and suspended again in 1929. Inconvertibility prevailed during the balance of the interwar period.

From 1808 onwards Brazil followed a bimetallic standard at the colonial ratio of 16:1. From then until 1846 when it was altered to favor gold, the ratio was changed three times. Gold convertibility was suspended in November 1857 in the wake of a banking crisis, and resumed in 1858. It was subsequently abandoned on several succeeding occasions (notably during the war with Paraguay) (Pelaez and Suzigan, 1976). It lasted for slightly more than a year in 1888–89. (1888 was the year slavery was abolished.) In 1888–89 capital inflows were extraordinarily large. A republican revolution in November 1889 coincided with the ending of convertibility (Fritsch and Franco, 1992). The gold standard was identified with the deposed monarchy, and the new government introduced a system of regional banks to increase the money supply. The real exchange rate depreciated, and convertibility was suspended. As a condition for a large funding loan from London bankers, Brazil was required to shift to contractionary fiscal and monetary policies around the turn of the century.

In 1906 Brazil restored convertibility to prevent continued appreciation of the milreis exchange rate that was harmful to coffee and rubber exporters. In addition it created a Conversion Office with a limit set to its issue of convertible notes at a newly established parity. Brazil's external position deteriorated in 1913, owing to falling coffee and rubber prices and shrinking international capital flows following the Balkan wars. A cyclical decline lasted until the outbreak of World War I, when convertibility ended to preserve the gold holdings of the Conversion Office.

As was the case in 1906, resumption in 1926 was sought to prevent appreciation of the exchange rate. It followed a program in 1925–26 to achieve monetary and fiscal discipline. As in the earlier case, a Stabilization Office, modeled on the Conversion Office, was created to issue notes at the new parity. The collapse of coffee prices in 1929 and the contraction in capital inflows led in late 1930 to an almost complete loss of gold reserves by the Stabilization Office. Convertibility was then abandoned for the duration of the remaining interwar years.

Chile was on a bimetallic standard from 1818 to 1851; it then made a technical change in the mint ratio, continuing on the bimetallic standard until 1866, when it suspended. It resumed in 1870, but by the end of 1874, with the fall in the price of silver, it was on a *de facto* silver standard. Bad crops during the next three years, and accompanying balance of payments deficits, were followed by bank runs in 1878. The authorities made bank notes inconvertible on July 23, 1878 (Llona-Rodriguez, 1993).

For the next 17 years, Chile remained on a paper standard. In 1879 the War of the Pacific began, with Chile opposing Bolivia and Peru, and ended in 1883 with Chile the victor. The war was financed by government note issues. Thanks to its seizure of provinces in the losing countries, Chile became the world's monopoly producer of nitrate. However, declining prices of nitrate and copper in world markets led to depreciation of the Chilean peso from 1883 to 1893, with the domestic inflation rate lower than exchange rate depreciation.

The first attempt to return to a metallic standard was made in 1887, but it failed. To appreciate the exchange rate, the government was required to retire its peso note issues and burn them, until the total issue had been reduced from 25 to 18 million pesos. It was also required to establish a silver fund for the eventual redemption of the outstanding amount. Bank issues were to be reduced from 150 percent to 100 percent of net worth, but neither margin was a real restraint. Bank notes rose and so did government notes.

An eight-month civil war from January to August 1891 resulted in further monetary expansion and exchange rate depreciation. A second conversion law in November 1892 was strictly implemented and the exchange rate appreciated, but again the government responded to political discontent by issuing notes. The exchange rate thereupon depreciated. A new conversion law of February 11, 1895, set June 1 as the day for redemption of government notes, devalued the gold content of the peso, and authorized loans and sales of nitrate fields to accumulate a gold reserve. Bank notes, with limits on the authorized total, had to be backed by gold or bonds to be acceptable for taxes. As a result, the banks contracted and the money supply shrank.

Following rumors of war with Argentina and a run on the banks in July 1898, the legislature ended convertibility and, to deal with the panic, bank notes were declared government obligations. Chile did not resume until 1925, when it again devalued, and in 1931 it abandoned the gold standard.

Common elements in the experiences of the Latin American ABC countries that made their adherence to the gold standard chancy were war and threats of war and fiscal and monetary policies incompatible with fixed exchange rates.

It is difficult, however, to isolate policy from the balance of payments problems that were their lot as exporters of primary products whose prices were set in world markets. Whereas for core countries war was a contingency that justified abandonment of the standard, it was a temporary abandonment with the commitment to return to it; for the Latin American peripheral countries, not only the aftermath of war but deflation generally were reasons for absence of commitment to convertibility.

Southern Europe: Except for Greece and Portugal, the record of adherence to specie rules is mainly blank for the Southern European countries included in Tables 8.1 and 8.2.

For 42 out of the 52 years between 1833 and 1885, when it adopted the gold standard, Greece was on a bimetallic standard. Until 1828 it had no national currency; Turkish coins were the medium of exchange. A commercial bank, established in 1842, operated *de facto* as a central bank (Lazaretou, 1994). Convertibility prevailed from February 1833 to March 1848, when suspension was declared for the balance of the year in response to panic worldwide. Resumption in January 1849 lasted through to December 1868. Although Greece signed on as a member of the Latin Monetary union in April 1867, it did not formally participate until November 1882, when it defined 1 drachma as equivalent to 1 French franc.

Greece suspended for a year and a half until July 1870 because of revolution in Crete, which remained under Turkish occupation until 1899. It resumed in August 1870 until May 1877, which marked the end of its bimetallic experience. From June 1877 through to December 1884, suspension was associated with the Russian–Turkish War of 1877–78. After the war ended, Greece made several attempts to resume, cutting back on monetary growth, while the government increased indirect taxes to raise revenues. From 1879 to 1884 it borrowed 360 million gold French francs. In 1882, it devalued the drachma.

Despite gold outflows because of high interest payments and a trade crisis at the end of 1884, Greece adopted the gold standard at that time. Convertibility, however, failed as gold outflows persisted, and by September 1885 Greece reverted to a paper money standard and floating exchange rates.

Continued borrowing from France until 1891 and low tax revenues led to debt default in December 1893. The defeat of Greece in 1897 in the war with Turkey, which saddled it with a huge war indemnity payable in funds convertible into gold, was the spur for the appointment in 1898 of an International Committee for Greek debt management. The Committee imposed fiscal prudence on the government, and a loan of 150 million gold French francs was arranged to enable Greece to pay the war indemnity to Turkey.

These measures restored confidence in Greek monetary and fiscal policies. A law of March 1910 required note circulation above a statutory ceiling to be backed by gold or foreign exchange. Bank notes were to be convertible into French francs at parity, and official reserves of the National Bank of Greece were stipulated as mainly interest-bearing deposits denominated in foreign currencies. In April 1910 Greece resumed convertibility on the gold exchange standard.

The new standard was successful until December 1914. Money creation then financed wartime spending. Exchange rate parity was maintained until reserves were depleted in August 1919. Exchange rates floated until May 1928, when Greece returned to the gold exchange standard. It instituted foreign exchange controls in September 1931 and devalued in April 1932, when convertibility ended.

Italy, unlike Greece, adhered to a specie standard for only 14 years during the 52 years before World War I but operated a paper standard during most of the rest of the period as if subject to specie constraints. In 1862 it adopted the bimetallic standard, although *de facto* the standard was gold. In 1865 Italy joined the Latin Monetary union. Fiscal improvidence and war against Austria in 1866, however, ended convertibility (Fratianni and Spinelli, 1984).

Fiscal and monetary discipline was achieved by 1874, and exchange rate parity was restored. The government announced on March 1, 1883, that it would restore convertibility on April 12, 1884, but convertibility took place only in silver because silver was overvalued at the mint. Public finances then deteriorated and unlawful bank issues indicated an absence of monetary discipline. By 1894 Italy was back on a paper standard, and floating exchange rates. Inconvertibility lasted until 1913. After periods of laxity, the government embraced fiscal and monetary rectitude as if it were on a gold standard.

Italy did not return to the gold standard until December 1927. It resorted to foreign exchange controls in May 1934, and devalued in October 1936.

Portugal was runner-up to Greece in the number of years it adhered to specie rules (Reis, 1992). It had been on a bimetallic standard since the 1680s with *de facto* gold predominance alternating with de facto silver predominance. In 1846 it was a weak country facing a civil war, and in no position to mint its own coin to any great extent. Instead, Portugal legalized silver coinage from other countries and set a new gold parity for the milreis at 4.5 to the pound sterling that effectively ensured that British money would mainly be the foreign inflow. England was Portugal's chief trading partner and creditor, to whom it shipped British coin to settle its accounts. Furthermore, the mint ratio that the law established favored gold.

The decision to shift to a gold standard in 1854 was made by the government as the most convenient for Portugal, since gold circulation was ample, and Bank of Lisbon paper that had been circulating at a discount was virtually back to par. The parity with the pound was unchanged from 1854 until 1891, during which period there were no convertibility crises. Gold coins circulated, notes and deposits constituting a minor proportion of the money supply. Yet Portugal's balance of trade, except for one year, was in deficit, and it was a net capital importer. Moreover, the government budget was typically short of revenue, but until 1890 Portugal succeeded in borrowing long-term funds at home or abroad to cover the shortfall.

In addition to borrowings, Portugal offset the negative elements in its balance of payments by remittances from Brazil and by earnings on Portuguese foreign investments. Thus Portugal, a debtor nation, was a regular importer of gold, unlike other peripheral nations. All this came to a halt in 1891, however, after which it was no longer able to raise foreign loans. An increase in the ratio of its debt service payments to revenues, and government support of failing Portuguese enterprises clouded its reputation as a creditworthy nation. The finance minister in office at this juncture was a soft-money silver supporter, which did not help Portugal's credit standing. Portugal's suspension of convertibility in 1891 lasted until after World War I.

It returned to gold in July 1931 at a devalued parity and suspended two months later with England.

Although Spain adopted a bimetallic regime in April 1848, it was not until the currency reform of 1868 that established the peseta as the monetary unit that the regime was fully operative (Martin-Aceña, 1993). In 1868 the gold–silver ratio was set at 15.5:1, as in the Latin Monetary union (which Spain did not join), whereas the 16:1 ratio set in 1848 was followed by six reductions in the intervening years. The Bank of Spain in 1874 became the monopoly issuer of bank notes that were freely convertible into both gold and silver.

With the fall in the market price of silver in the 1870s, the 15.5:1 ratio undervalued gold. Gold was driven out of circulation, and the gold reserves of the Bank of Spain declined, but until mid-1883 trade surpluses and capital imports sustained convertibility. Because foreign holders of Spanish bonds refused to accept the terms of a conversion the Treasury was engaged in at the time, there was a capital outflow and a fall in inflows. In addition, the trade balance declined sharply from 1881 to 1883. To avoid deflation, Spain ended convertibility.

Between 1888 and 1900 the peseta exchange rate depreciated, a budget deficit arose in every year but three from 1884 to 1899, the war with Cuba in 1898–99 was financed largely by money creation, and Spanish prices until 1905 fell much less than world prices – all factors hostile to resumption. These factors mainly after 1900 turned favorable to resumption, but it did not take place. Efforts by finance ministers to restore convertibility and adopt the gold standard before World War I foundered on the opposition of the Bank of Spain. Unlike other countries, Spain did not even briefly during the interwar period turn to gold convertibility. It adopted foreign exchange controls in May 1931.

Scandinavia: The Scandinavian countries were as faithful adherents to the classical gold standard as the core countries. Sweden and Denmark were independent countries throughout the period. Of the group, only Sweden has a monetary history available to us for the early nineteenth century, and its record of respect for specie rules during that period is not inferior to that of the core.

Sweden had a silver standard from 1803 to 1809. Large budget deficits to finance a war with Russia in 1808 bloated the money supply. In 1809 convertibility was suspended and a silver standard was not restored until 1834. This lasted until 1873, when Sweden adopted gold. The four Scandinavian countries show a common pattern of adoption of the gold standard between 1872 and 1877 and adherence to the standard until 1914.

Even during the period when the four countries adopted the gold standard, Finland and Norway were not independent. The former was an autonomous grand duchy of the Russian empire until 1917, the latter part of Sweden until 1905.

The Swedish constitution guaranteed the convertibility of the central bank's notes into gold, as noted earlier. For a change in gold standard arrangements to be adopted Parliament had to give its assent at two different dates with an election intervening. The central bank's decision in 1914 to make the notes inconvertible was unconstitutional, since the bank disregarded the provision for Parliamentary approval.

Only Finland devalued on resumption in 1926. The others resumed at their prewar parities. Sweden returned to gold *de jure* in March 1924, but *de facto* the prewar par rate of the krona in gold was restored in 1922.

What delayed the *de jure* return was the authorities' opposition to the krona being the sole convertible European currency. All the Scandinavian countries suspended in 1931 and devalued. In June 1933 the Swedish krona was fixed to the British pound, and the exchange rate was unchanged until after the start of World War II.

Western Europe: The three Western European countries listed in Part 6 of the table, Belgium, the Netherlands, and Switzerland, adopted the gold standard in the second half of the 1870s and adhered to it until World War I.

A note-issuing bank was established in Belgium in 1822 before the country became independent in 1832, when it was a bimetallic adherent. It suspended convertibility in 1848 in the face of French political and financial problems. The Netherlands was on a bimetallic standard in 1847, Switzerland in 1850.

All three countries suspended convertibility in 1914. Belgium lost the right of note issue following the German occupation. Switzerland declared bank notes legal tender in 1914. The Netherlands prohibited gold export in 1914. Belgium devalued when it returned to gold in October 1926, and devalued again in March 1935. The Netherlands returned to gold at the prewar parity in April 1925 and devalued in October 1936. Switzerland devalued in 1929 when it returned to gold and when it left the gold standard in 1936.

Japan: Convertibility was not firmly established in Japan until 1885, when it was on a silver standard (Shinjo, 1962). In 1868 Japan introduced a new monetary unit, the yen, defined as the same weight and fineness as the Mexican silver dollar. In an act of 1871 Japan prescribed a gold yen, but silver still remained the preferred metal for foreign trade. Bimetallism was in effect as judged by the government's metallic reserve. The government issued notes beginning in 1868 that were redeemable in silver, with an 1880 expiration date of redemption. In addition, government-issued currency notes were inconvertible.[12]

New national banks were created late in 1872 to issue bank notes against specie reserves of not less than two-thirds the amount emitted. The notes, however, quickly returned to the banks for redemption in silver. The petition in 1875 of four existing national banks to change from silver to government currency note convertibility was granted the

---

[12] In 1869 institutions to supply capital to new firms and industries by issuing notes convertible into government notes were established in eight commercial cities; only the one that issued notes convertible into silver coin found public acceptance.

following year. National banks multiplied and their issues sharply increased.[13]

From 1868 until 1878 the paper currency depreciated against both silver and gold. The government issue ceased in 1879. It was recognized that a budget surplus was essential to decrease the outstanding note issue and to accumulate specie. By 1881, after keeping government expenditure constant for three years, the government budget was in surplus, and this was used partly to destroy existing notes and the rest as specie reserve.

In October 1882 the Bank of Japan was founded, but it did not issue convertible notes, payable in silver on demand, until 1885. These notes, initially limited in amount, replaced government currency notes. In 1888 the bank was authorized to issue a substantial fiduciary circulation backed by government and commercial paper, any amounts in excess to be backed by gold and silver. National banks lost the right of issue after the expiration of their charters. Deposit banks replaced them.

The premium on silver disappeared once convertibility was established but, since the price of silver against gold was declining, the exchange rate against gold standard countries was unstable. By 1893 Japan recognized that it was desirable to adopt the gold standard, but the reform was not introduced until the indemnity China paid in gold for losing the Sino-Japanese war of 1894–95 enabled the government to acquire an adequate reserve.

The Coinage Act of 1897 established the gold standard. The act governing the Bank of Japan was revised to require convertibility of its notes into gold instead of silver. The government contributed the gold indemnity to the bank's reserve. Silver was limited to one-fourth of the specie reserve.

Japan adhered to the gold standard until September 1917, without interruption despite runs on banks in 1901 and 1907–08, war with Russia in 1904–05, extraordinary government expenditures financed by foreign loans, and an unfavorable balance of payments during most of the period. The decrease in the specie reserve prompted flotation of foreign bonds in London and Paris in every year from 1906 to 1915. Foreign capital maintained Japan's gold standard.

Japan was a beneficiary of the demand for its goods and services by

---

[13] Despite the monetary disarray, the Meiji government succeeded in floating two foreign loans in London in 1871 and 1873, the first for £1 million at 9 percent, for construction of a railroad between Tokyo and Yokohama, the second for £3.4 million pounds at 7 percent, to pay pensions to feudal lords and soldiers, the feudal clans having been abolished in 1870 by the new national government. During the same years, England, France, and Russia sold their bonds in Japan, paid for by gold exports from Japan.

World War I belligerents. It used the surplus in its balance of payments to increase the Bank of Japan's and the government's gold reserves, to replenish its foreign exchange balances abroad, to pay back foreign loans, and to increase its foreign investments. Japan became a creditor country.

In September 1917 Japan followed the United States in embargoing gold and silver export. Bank of Japan notes became inconvertible. Wartime prosperity ended in 1920, with failures of firms and runs on banks. A deflationary policy in 1921–22 provoked further runs on banks, and the policy was discontinued. An earthquake in September 1923 led to increased government expenditures. Again there was a move to deflation and a readiness to follow England's return to gold in April 1925. Financial panic in 1926 halted that step. A new government in 1929 adopted a program of lifting the gold embargo and returning to gold at the prewar parity, as it did in January 1930.

Speculative transactions to sell yen and buy dollars once the gold standard was restored reflected the market's belief that the yen would have to be devalued. The suspension of the gold standard in December 1931 came after huge gold losses by Japan. In March 1932 Japan began a series of devaluations of the gold content of the yen as the exchange rate of the yen declined. Foreign exchange controls were introduced in May 1933. The limit on the Bank of Japan's fiduciary note issue was repeatedly expended, and ultimately eliminated.

8.3.3   Evaluating adherence to rules during Bretton Woods

Core countries: Under Bretton Woods, the rule for countries other than the United States was that a change in par value was permissible to correct fundamental disequilibrium. Though undefined, the term was intended to refer to disturbances other than government policies that justified a change in par. Examples of such disturbances were a change in the terms of trade and in productivity trends, and other contingencies similar to those the gold standard escape clauses encompassed. Obtaining the advance agreement of the IMF to a change in par was a way of ensuring that such were the disturbances that prompted the action (Eichengreen, 1994).

As is well known, the Bretton Woods arrangements required countries other than the United States to peg their currencies to the dollar, and the United States to peg the dollar to gold. The system became fully operative in 1959 and broke down in 1971. The rules for the center and the other countries were unsuccessful (Bordo, 1993a; Giovannini, 1993).

Problems raised by the rule for countries other than the United States were apparent from the start of the system. We review the problems as evidenced by core country performance. When France devalued in January 1948, it did not seek IMF authorization. By creating multiple exchange rates, it took a discretionary action, contrary to the rule. It then restored unified exchange rates in the devaluation of 1949. The United Kingdom announced convertibility for current account transactions in July 1947, but suspended the next month, making sterling subject to exchange controls. It declared a par value in 1948, but devalued in September 1949 by a larger percentage than it had indicated to the IMF.

After the general realignment of September 1949, in which Germany joined, changes in par of the core countries were rare, possibly due to reluctance to alter their parities after the experience of the speculative attacks that occurred after the 1949 changes. Keynesian full-employment policies that many countries adopted conflicted with Bretton Woods obligations to maintain fixed exchange rates. In consequence, exchange rate crises erupted as market participants anticipated policy-induced pressures to devalue or revalue. The countries whose currencies the market targeted for attack resisted changing par values in the belief that domestic concerns should not yield to external concerns. They tried to buy time by imposing capital controls and deploying international reserves to preserve existing par values, but in the end failed. The meaning of fundamental disequilibrium, however, was altered to refer to government monetary and fiscal policies that were inconsistent with those par values. As events unfolded, it was difficult to distinguish the original correct use from this incorrect use of the escape clause.

The core country par values that changed reflected this shift in the meaning of fundamental disequilibrium. Two examples are France, under inflationary conditions, which devalued in 1957 and 1958, and the United Kingdom. Chronic United Kingdom balance of payments deficits during the 1960s led to devaluation of sterling in November 1967, despite rescue packages. France suspended the par value of the franc in November 1968 because of speculative attacks on its currency at a time of social unrest and inflation. Capital controls and massive international loans were not effective in preventing devaluation in August 1969. In contrast, Germany revalued in 1961, in response to a persistent balance of payments surplus reflecting higher productivity than her partners. In 1968 it resorted to border taxes and restricted capital inflows, but ultimately revalued again in September 1969.

During 1969–71 a persistent outflow of funds from the United States overwhelmed foreign exchange markets. In May 1971 Germany suspended dealings in Deutschmarks and allowed its currency to float, since it could not maintain exchange rates within the established margins. France introduced dual exchange rates in August 1971, and the United Kingdom suspended the sterling par value that month, and allowed sterling to float in June 1972.

If countries other than the United States did not observe the Bretton Woods rule on par value change as it was conceived, neither did the United States, the center country, comply with the gold convertibility rule. Faced with balance of payments deficits after 1957 that increased dollar liabilities while the monetary gold stock was shrinking, the United States had the problem of preserving convertibility. Many stratagems were devised to induce holders of dollars to refrain from cashing them in for gold. In addition, the elimination of the gold reserve requirement against Federal Reserve notes in 1968 betokened a weakening of the commitment mechanism to maintain stable money – an obligation of the reserve country. Moreover, by engaging in expansionary monetary policy after the mid-1960s, the United States exacerbated the convertibility problem, since the incentive to hold dollars declined as inflation rose. The closing of the gold window in August 1971 marked the end of the convertibility rule, and the readjustment of currency parities at the Smithsonian meeting in December 1971 marked the first dollar devaluation since 1934.

Peripheral countries: Like the core countries, peripheral countries under the Bretton Woods system differed in the extent to which they adopted expansionary monetary and fiscal policies. High-inflation countries repeatedly devalued; low-inflation countries did not.

Australia, at the start of the Bretton Woods era, was part of the sterling area. Along with the United Kingdom it declared the par value of its pound in 1947 and devalued in 1949. In 1966 it changed its currency unit to the Australian dollar, as it converted its currency to the decimal system. No appreciation or depreciation of the exchange rate accompanied the new monetary unit. Australia did not devalue with the United Kingdom in 1967. It suspended its par value in August 1971, but did not change it, so its currency appreciated relative to the U.S. dollar from the par value that existed before the closing of the U.S. gold window.

Canada declared its par value at the end of 1946 and devalued with the United Kingdom in 1949. It acquired a special status under Bretton Woods when the IMF did not actively oppose its decision to float its dollar in September 1950. Capital inflows from the United States were increasing Canada's reserves, with expansionary consequences for its money supply. Under fixed exchange rates Canada found it difficult to resist the inflationary results. It did not revert to fixed exchange rates until May 1962. In May 1970 Canada again decided to float for the same reason as it had two decades earlier. Its foreign exchange reserves were accelerating, and the situation that was created thereby was deemed unmanageable under fixed rates. Canada continued to float until the collapse of Bretton Woods.

The Latin American countries all had high inflation experiences during the Bretton Woods era. Before Argentina declared its par value in 1957 it had in 1955 introduced multiple exchange rates. It devalued in 1959, 1962, and 1970. Brazil was plagued by inflation from World War II on, and especially after 1958. It devalued in 1967, and in August 1968 introduced a flexible exchange rate policy which involved devaluation of the currency by small amounts at frequent irregular intervals. Similarly, Chile, which declared its par value in 1946, introduced multiple exchange rates in 1953 and devalued in 1962.

Of the four Southern European countries, only Spain devalued before 1971. It did so in November 1967. The IMF regarded the devaluation as a correction of a previously existing fundamental disequilibrium. In 1971 Spain maintained its par value unchanged, but widened the margin to up to $2\frac{1}{4}$ percent.

Of the Scandinavian countries, only Sweden did not devalue between 1951, the date of par declaration, and 1971. Denmark devalued in 1949 and 1967. Finland devalued in 1957 and 1967. Norway devalued in 1949.

In Western Europe Belgium and the Netherlands realigned with Germany in 1949 and the latter revalued with Germany in 1961.

Japan did not devalue between 1949, when it declared its par value, and 1971.

8.3.4   Conclusion

The chronology of adherence to rules before and after Bretton Woods reveals a decay of respect for rules over the century Tables 8.1 and 8.2 cover. Rules were not universally honored even during the classical gold standard era. A core group of countries was usually faithful to specie rules, but countries in Western Europe, the new Anglo-Saxon settlement countries, and the Scandinavian countries also conducted their financial affairs so that the fixed price of gold that defined their currencies was unchanged for extended periods. Monetary and fiscal policies in the remaining countries in the tables were such that suspensions of the specie rule were not exceptional, and they were followed by changes in the former parity. Only extraordinary events such as wars occasioned departures from the standard among the core and their cohorts, and until World War I resumption took place at the prewar parity.

In the interwar period a return to the gold standard was sometimes at the earlier parity, but often at a devalued rate. During most of the period floating exchange rates were common. The attempt under Bretton Woods to impose a rule that the par value of its currency with the dollar that each country member declared would be changed only under extraordinary circumstances, as under the classical gold standard, failed. Domestic economic objectives proved to be paramount to international obligations.

8.4 Capital flows and specie standard adherence: Argentina and the United States, 1865–1914

One of the enforcement mechanisms of the specie standard rule for peripheral countries was presumably access to the capital needed for their economic development from the core countries. Adherence to the convertibility rule would be viewed by lenders as evidence of financial probity – i.e. membership in the international gold standard would be like a "Good Housekeeping" seal of approval. It would signal that a country followed prudent fiscal and monetary policies and would only temporarily run large fiscal deficits in well understood emergencies. Moreover, the monetary authorities would be willing to go to considerable lengths to avoid defaulting on externally held debt. It would also presumably be a signal to the lenders in London and other metropolitan areas that the groups in power observed similar standards of financial rectitude.

This suggests that adherence to the specie standard rule, *ceteris paribus*, would make a difference in the volume of capital a country attracted from abroad. Presumably loans would be made only with gold clauses (or be sterling denominated), so that currency risk would not matter. But there still would be a risk of abrogation of the gold clauses or of total default on the debt. That eventuality would be reflected in a risk premium on the loan. In that case it would be attractive to a potential borrower to adhere to the specie standard rule as a signal of financial responsibility, to induce the lender to lower the risk premium.[14] But a more fundamental problem could arise in a world of asymmetric information with the possibility of a "lemons premium" (Akerlof, 1970; Stiglitz and Weiss, 1981). In that case, charging a high interest rate might

[14] Although Chile's experience of borrowing funds in sterling at prevailing rates in a period when the currency was inconvertible does not seem to support this statement (see Llona-Rodriguez, 1993, n. 9).

attract borrowers willing to engage in unduly risky projects. Lenders faced with imperfect information on borrowers' likely actions would then be reluctant to lend at any price. A credible commitment to the specie standard rule, as evidenced by the holding of substantial gold reserves, would provide a signal to lenders of the costs borrowers would be willing to bear to avoid default, and hence would circumvent the aversion to lending imposed by asymmetric information.

As a tentative step in the direction of examining the connection between capital flows and adherence to the specie standard rule, we briefly focus on the experience of two major borrowers of British capital in the late nineteenth century, each of which had a record of suspension and of specie standard adherence over the period 1865–1914 – Argentina and the United States. In that fifty-year period, Argentina was off gold in three episodes of suspension totalling twenty-four years (excluding the general breakdown of the international gold standard in 1914). The United States was off gold for seventeen years and the gold standard subsequently was under threat of suspension for another seven years.

In Figures 8.1 and 8.2 we present annual data on capital calls on new issues of securities – a measure of access to new capital in London for the two countries. The data, kindly supplied by Lance Davis, underlying Davis and Huttenback's (1986) study of the economics of British imperialism,[15] are expressed in millions of current U.S. dollars.[16] The periods of suspension (and for the United States the episode of silver threat to the gold standard) are marked off in the figures by shaded areas.

An ideal analysis of the influence of adherence to the specie standard rule would be based on a model of the determinants of capital flows, including such variables as: the expected real rates of return in both countries, the levels of real activity, the terms of trade, and the phase of the business cycle (see Ford, 1962; Abramowitz, 1973; Edelstein, 1982). One could then test for the marginal influence of adherence/non-adherence to the rule. Here our aims are much more modest – to simply compare the annual capital calls on new issues of securities with a

---

[15] Use of capital calls on the new securities issued is superior to the new foreign lending series used in earlier studies (e.g. Edelstein, 1982). This is because the capital calls give the amount of funds actually available to send to the receiving countries, whereas the new foreign lending series represents the face value of the bonds. The amounts actually available were only a fraction of the total issue which the investors committed themselves to provide over a period of years during which calls were made (see Davis and Huttenback, 1986, ch. 1).

[16] A real series deflated by the British Sauerbeck-Statist wholesale price index is very similar to the current dollar series presented here.

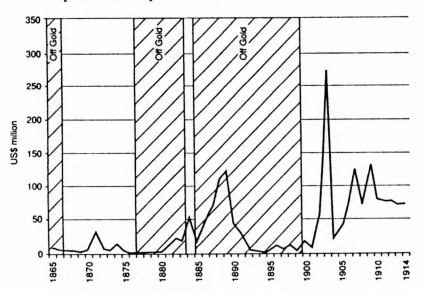

Figure 8.1. Capital calls on new issues of Argentine securities in London, 1865–1914 (current dollars).

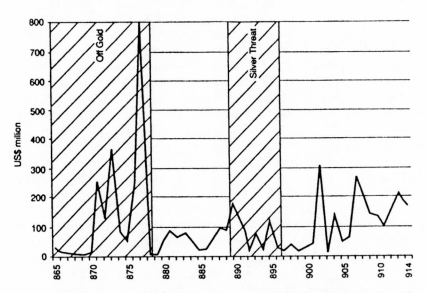

Figure 8.2. Capital calls on new issues of U.S. securities in London, 1865–1914 (current dollars).

chronology of events related to adherence to the rule. Any connection revealed should be treated merely as highly suggestive.

Bertalomé Mitre became president of Argentina in 1862 and succeeded in unifying the country after five decades of intermittent civil strife, external wars, and highly unstable monetary and fiscal policies (Cortés Condé, 1989). Under Mitre, contractionary monetary and fiscal policies were successful in achieving specie convertibility in 1867 (following a failed attempt in 1863). Argentina then began five decades of extraordinary economic growth, with rapid development in agriculture, transportation, and commerce. It also was the start of a wave of immigration from Europe and of the massive inflow of capital (Cortés Condé, 1989). The pattern for Argentina in Figure 8.1 reveals little change in capital flows from a low and stable level when the country joined the gold standard in 1867 until 1876. The period 1870–75 is characterized by a mild boom in capital calls, ending just before suspension of convertibility in 1876. It would be difficult to disentangle the effect of establishing convertibility in 1867 from that of restoring political stability as the key determinants of the beginning of capital flows from Europe.

Increasing civil strife in 1873–76, rising government deficits, and a downturn in the world business cycle account for the suspension of convertibility in 1876. It was followed by several years of negligible capital inflows. Thanks to contractionary fiscal policy in the late 1870s, the exchange rate reached parity in 1881 but it took until 1883 to restore convertibility (Cortés Condé, 1989). The commitment to restore convertibility may have led to the observed resumption of capital inflows. Convertibility was short-lived, however. Expansionary fiscal policy in 1884 led to a crisis and suspension on January 1, 1885. Again suspension is associated with a decline in capital flows, but the significant rebound from 1886 to 1889 under inconvertible money suggests that British investors placed more weight on the long-run economic prosperity of the Argentine economy than currency stability. The boom ended with a crash in 1890, following several years of exceedingly loose fiscal policy and the creation in 1887 of a free banking system that produced a plethora of bank money (Eichengreen, 1992b). A revolution in that year, followed by default on external debt, precipitated the Barings crisis in London. Capital inflows then plummeted until the authorities again instituted monetary and fiscal austerity. It took four years for convertibility to be restored in 1899. Restoration of convertibility along with the creation of a quasi currency board (the Caja de Conversion), which in essence tied the hands of the monetary authorities, succeeded in creating a climate conducive to the resumption of significant capital movements until World War I.

Table 8.3. *Descriptive statistics of new issues of securities in London (current and real values): 1865–1914*

	Nominal (US$ millions)		Real (US$ millions)	
Period	Mean	Stand. dev.	Mean	Stand. dev.
Argentina				
1865–66 Off Gold	6	1	5	1
1867–76	8	9	7	7
1877–83 Off Gold	6	9	6	8
1884	53	0	54	0
1885–99 Off Gold	32	37	37	42
1900–14	79	62	88	75
1865–1914	37	50	41	58
United States				
1865–78 Off Gold	145	174	119	174
1879–89	59	29	60	31
1890–96 Silver Threat	74	46	87	52
1897–1914	113	86	125	96
1879–1914	89	71	98	79
1865–1914	104	129	104	114

Source: Davis and Huttenback (1986).

This narrative suggests that adherence to the rule by Argentina may have had some marginal influence on capital calls on new issues of securities in London before 1890 (see Table 8.3, which suggests that the mean of capital calls in current and real dollars was higher during periods of adherence than of suspension), but that the key determinant was the opening up of the country's vast resources to economic development once unification and a modicum of political stability were achieved. The 1890 crisis was a major shock to investor confidence and it took years of austerity, the restoration of convertibility, and the establishment of a currency board before British investors' confidence was restored.

The U.S. experience under suspension has been well studied by others (Sharkey, 1959; Unger, 1964; Friedman and Schwartz, 1963; Roll, 1972; Calomiris, 1988). As can be seen in Figure 8.2 capital calls on new issues were low in the first five years after the Civil War. The debate over resumption in these years seems to have had little impact on the decision by investors to purchase securities in London destined for the United States, but then purchases picked up significantly in 1870 and 1871. This phenomenon may be explained by the Public Credit Act of 1869, which guaranteed that the principal on U.S. government bonds would be payable in gold (Calomiris, 1988). The subsequent decline may reflect adverse news of the likelihood of resumption with the reversal in 1871 of an earlier Supreme Court decision declaring the issue of greenbacks unconstitutional, as well as the Treasury's expansionary fiscal policy (Calomiris, 1993). Capital calls increase until they are reversed by the Panic of 1873, a decline in economic activity, and two years of soft money victories (the reissue of retired greenbacks in 1873 and the Inflation Bill of 1874). The Resumption Act of 1875 is then followed in the next two years by the largest increase in capital inflows over the whole fifty-year span. Resumption of specie payments on January 1, 1879, is followed by a rising but variable trend in capital calls on new issues but the volume is well below the average of the suspension period (see Table 8.3).

The period 1890–96 is important in the history of U.S. adherence to the rule. Passage of the Sherman Silver Purchase Act in 1890 led to a six-year period of uncertainty surrounding the nation's ability to remain on the gold standard (Friedman and Schwartz, 1963; Calomiris, 1993; Grilli, 1990). This episode is reflected in the capital calls on new issue series in Figure 8.2. They peak in 1890 and though they may have rallied following the repeal of the silver purchase part of the Sherman Silver Act in 1893, and the Belmont Morgan syndicate replenishment of the Treasury's gold reserves in 1895, they rebound significantly only after the 1900 Gold Standard Act.

In sum, for the United States as for Argentina, events suggesting the restoration of convertibility during suspension and threats to convertibility during adherence seem to be associated with increases and declines in capital calls on new issues of securities in London. More systematic research is required to distinguish these influences from the fundamental determinants of capital flows.

8.5   The economic performance of core and peripheral countries under alternative monetary regimes

In this section we present some evidence based on annual data over the past 110 years on the macroeconomic performance of the four core countries and seventeen peripheral countries during the classical gold standard (1880–1914) and three successive monetary regimes: the interwar period (1919–39); the Bretton Woods international monetary system (1946–70); and the recent managed float (1974–90). The Bretton Woods system, as a variant of the contingent specie standard rule, is directly comparable to the classical gold standard. The recent managed float, a regime not based on the rule, and the interwar period, which comprises episodes of free floating, adherence to the gold standard, and managed floating, are presented as contrasts to the two rule-based regimes.[17] The data are organized in the seven groupings shown in Tables 8.1 and 8.2, as well as broader aggregates.

Such evidence for the classical gold standard regime and for Bretton Woods may shed light on whether differing economic performance can explain why some countries successfully adhered to the convertibility rule and others did not, or whether adherence/non-adherence to the rule may have influenced performance. By contrast, under the recent floating regime we seek to determine whether the observed differences between countries' performance under convertible regimes persist in the absence of rules.

8.5.1 Stability and convergence

Tables 8.4 through 8.6 present descriptive statistics on three macro variables for each country pertinent to the issue of adherence to convertibility rules, the data for each variable converted to a continuous annual series from 1880 to 1989. The three variables are: the rate of inflation (GNP deflators), money growth, and the ratio of government expenditure less government revenues to GNP.[18] The definition of the variable used, e.g., M1 versus M2, was dictated by the availability of data over the entire period. For each variable and each country we present two summary statistics: the mean and standard deviation. For each of the seven country groupings from Table 8.1, and four aggregate groupings [all countries, all except the four core countries; the G-10 countries plus Switzerland (G-11); and all except the G-11], we show as a summary statistic: the grand mean. We comment on the statistical results for each variable.

Inflation (Table 8.4): The classical gold standard had the lowest rate of inflation of any monetary regime for all twenty-one countries, and the interwar period displayed mild deflation for all except Latin America (see Figure 8.3). Within the classical gold standard regime, the inflation rate was lowest in countries identified in Table 8.1 as following the convertibility rule: the four core countries; some of the different European groupings; and the Anglo-Saxon countries of new settlement (see

---

[17] For earlier applications of similar regime comparisons in a different context see Bordo (1993a,b), and Bordo and Jonung (1996).

[18] In Bordo and Schwartz (1994) we also present data for real per capita growth, and the absolute rates of change of nominal and real exchange rates.

Table 8.4. Descriptive statistics of selected open economy variables, 21 countries, 1881–1990: inflation. Annual data: means and standard deviation[a]

	Gold standard (1881–1913)		Interwar (1919–38)		Bretton Woods (1946–70)		Floating exchange (1974–90)	
(a) Core countries								
United States	0.3	3.1	−1.8	7.6	2.4	2.6	5.6	2.4
United Kingdom	0.3	3.1	−1.5	7.8	3.7	2.2	9.4	6.1
Germany	0.6	2.6	−2.1	4.7	2.7	4.0	3.3	1.2
France	0.0	4.9	2.2	9.1	5.6	4.1	8.8	3.2
mean	0.3	3.4	−0.8	7.3	3.6	3.2	6.8	3.2
(b) Anglo-Saxon countries of new settlement								
Australia	0.5	3.9	0.3	5.7	5.1	4.9	10.0	3.0
Canada	0.4	1.4	−1.9	6.1	2.7	3.0	7.3	2.6
mean	0.4	2.6	−0.8	5.9	3.9	4.0	8.6	2.8
(c) Latin America								
Argentina	2.6	14.2	−1.7	6.3	22.9	14.7	122.9	77.0
Brazil	4.3	17.5	3.0	6.3	24.3	14.8	94.5	87.0
Chile	5.2	9.1	5.5	7.3	27.7	13.0	30.9	41.2
mean	4.0	13.6	2.3	6.6	25.0	14.2	82.8	68.4
(d) Southern Europe								
Greece	na	na	1.8	5.4	7.8	9.7	15.9	3.2
Italy	0.6	3.2	−1.1	11.7	3.8	11.5	12.9	4.6

Portugal	0.6	3.5	7.9	15.4	2.2	3.2	17.4	3.6
Spain	−0.2	1.2	−0.7	7.3	8.6	5.8	12.6	4.5
mean	0.3	2.6	2.0	10.0	5.6	7.5	14.7	4.0
(e) Scandinavia								
Denmark	−0.3	3.1	−1.6	7.6	3.5	5.4	7.4	3.1
Finland	0.8	3.4	4.6	10.8	9.1	10.2	9.0	3.8
Norway	0.7	3.1	−3.1	9.7	3.7	3.9	7.6	3.6
Sweden	0.4	3.1	−2.3	6.1	3.9	4.0	8.4	3.0
mean	0.4	3.2	−0.6	8.5	5.0	5.9	8.1	3.4
(f) Other Western Europe								
Belgium	0.2	4.9	3.8	4.4	2.4	3.2	4.9	2.5
Netherlands	1.0	2.2	−3.1	5.6	4.1	3.1	3.6	2.9
Switzerland	na	na	−2.2	4.3	2.8	1.9	3.5	1.8
mean	0.6	3.6	−0.5	4.8	3.1	2.7	4.0	2.4
(g) Japan	4.6	5.5	−1.7	7.3	4.5	4.6	2.6	2.4
(h) All countries	1.2	4.9	0.2	7.4	7.3	6.2	19.0	12.5
(i) All except 4 core countries	1.4	5.3	0.4	7.5	8.2	6.9	21.9	14.7
(j) G-10 + Switzerland	0.8	3.4	−1.1	6.8	3.5	4.0	6.4	3.0
(k) All except G-10 + Switzerland	1.6	6.3	1.4	8.2	11.2	8.4	32.6	22.9

[a]Mean growth rate calculated as the time coefficient from a regression of the natural logarithm of the variable on a constant and a time trend.
Data sources: See Data Appendix.

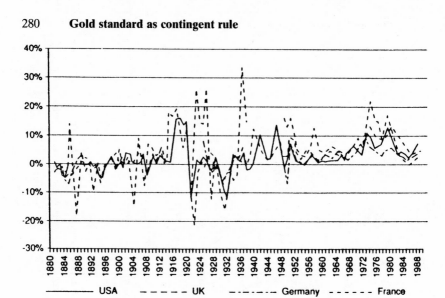

a. Core countries

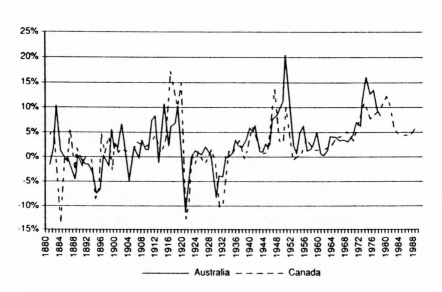

b. Anglo-Saxon countries of new settlement

Figure 8.3. Inflation rate, 1881–1990.

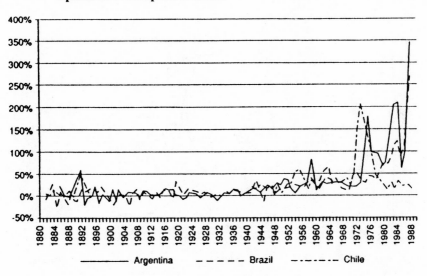

c. Latin America

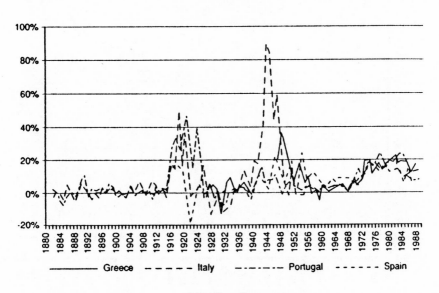

d. Southern Europe

Figure 8.3. *(cont.)*

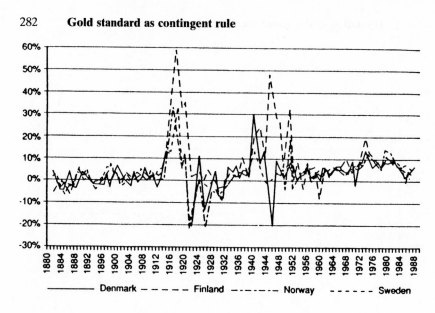

e. Scandinavia

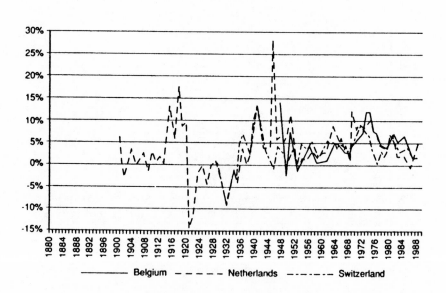

f. Other Western European countries

Figure 8.3. *(cont.)*

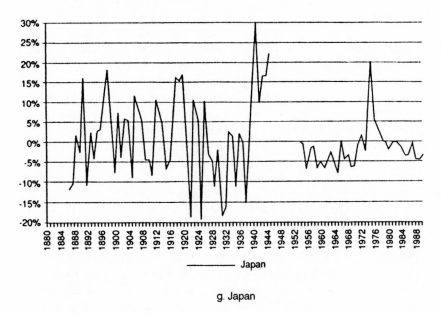

g. Japan

Figure 8.3. *(cont.)*

Figure 8.3).[19] It was considerably higher in Latin America and Japan. This pattern can also be seen in a comparison of the G-10 plus Switzerland aggregate (an expanded core group) with the other peripheral countries. The former grouping contains nine countries that followed the rules; the latter only three.

Under Bretton Woods, like the gold standard, a distinct difference can be observed between the core countries and a number of other groupings (Anglo-Saxon new settlement, other Western Europe, Japan), which had low inflation; and a set of countries with higher inflation (Latin America, to a lesser extent countries in Southern Europe and Scandinavia). This observed difference between country groupings also is found under the recent float. The evidence on inflation suggests that if the specie standard rule or its variant did provide a credible commitment mechanism for low inflation, it was strongest in the gold standard period followed by Bretton Woods. Within these regimes observance of the rule clearly demarcates inflation performance between countries.

The gold standard period had the most stable inflation rate of any regime (across all countries) judged by the standard deviation. This was

---

[19] The data sources for Figure 8.3 and all subsequent figures are listed in the Data Appendix.

followed by Bretton Woods, the interwar, and then the float. For the G-11 countries, the recent float is the most stable period. Within the gold standard regime, core countries and countries following the specie standard rule exhibited greater price stability than the others. For Bretton Woods a similar difference between country groupings is observed, with Japan joining the stable inflation group, and Southern Europe the unstable inflation group. These differences persist into the recent float.

The evidence of a high degree of price stability under the gold standard (and to a lesser extent under Bretton Woods) and of greater price stability during those periods in countries following the rules compared to those that did not is consistent with the traditional view that commodity-money-based regimes provide a stable nominal anchor; however, the price stability observed may also reflect the absence of major shocks.

Money growth (M_2) (Table 8.5): Money growth was considerably more rapid across all countries post–World War II than before the war (see Figure 8.4). For the core countries and most of the G-11 countries there is not much difference between Bretton Woods and the subsequent floating regime. Southern Europe, Latin America, and Japan exhibited considerably higher money growth under Bretton Woods than the others. For the Latin American countries money growth rates accelerated over the entire postwar period, reaching their highest levels under the float. By contrast with postwar, the gold standard exhibited lower money growth in both core and peripheral countries alike with the principal exception of Japan; however, it was still higher in core than in peripheral countries. The observation of lower money growth in both core and peripheral countries may be a reflection of the omnipresence of the specie standard rule.

Across all countries, money growth was least variable in the interwar and most variable in the recent float. However, for the core and G-11 countries it was least variable under the gold standard. Under that regime money growth variability was higher in the periphery than in the core. Under Bretton Woods and the recent float the difference between core and periphery money growth variability is less obvious, again with the principal exception of Latin America, which exhibits considerably greater money growth variability than all other countries. For these countries the increase in money growth variability reflects the breakdown of any linkage to a commitment regime.

Government deficit (Table 8.6): For the underlying data see Figure 8.5. For all twenty-one countries the average ratio of the government deficit to GNP is lowest during the Bretton Woods period, followed by the gold

Table 8.5. *Descriptive statistics of selected open economy variables, 21 countries, 1881–1990: money growth.*
Annual data: means and standard deviation

	Gold standard (1881–1913)		Interwar (1919–38)		Bretton Woods (1946–70)		Floating exchange (1974–90)	
(a) Core countries								
United States	6.1	4.1	0.6	8.6	6.3	5.8	8.6	2.4
United Kingdom	2.1	1.7	0.8	4.7	3.2	3.2	13.5	5.5
Germany	5.7	4.7	1.3	10.1	12.8	5.9	5.7	4.5
France	2.1	4.7	6.4	8.5	11.5	7.5	8.8	3.4
mean	4.0	3.8	2.3	8.0	8.5	5.6	9.2	4.0
(b) Anglo-Saxon countries of new settlement								
Australia	3.5	5.8	1.3	6.5	5.6	6.7	9.7	4.0
Canada	7.4	5.3	1.1	4.7	6.0	4.0	10.6	3.9
mean	5.4	5.5	1.2	5.6	5.8	5.3	10.2	4.0
(c) Latin America								
Argentina	6.7	12.1	1.8	8.9	22.2	10.1	124.6	82.6
Brazil	6.9	25.8	9.2	12.4	32.6	21.5	91.5	79.8
Chile	-3.7	9.7	5.1	15.1	29.7	12.8	32.2	39.3
mean	3.3	15.9	5.4	12.1	28.2	14.8	82.8	67.2
(d) Southern Europe								
Greece	4.4	4.4	na	na	12.1	4.6	17.0	2.3
Italy	3.2	3.1	3.6	6.2	13.3	7.8	13.4	4.9
Portugal	0.7	2.8	14.2	13.1	5.8	5.9	14.6	6.7

Table 8.5. (cont.)

	Gold standard (1881–1913)		Interwar (1919–38)		Bretton Woods (1946–70)		Floating exchange (1974–90)	
Spain	1.6	6.5	2.0	4.4	11.9	4.7	13.4	4.8
mean	2.5	6.7	6.6	7.9	10.8	5.7	14.6	4.7
(e) Scandinavia								
Denmark	4.7	4.2	−0.4	4.8	6.1	4.1	11.8	5.5
Finland	6.8	6.0	6.3	7.0	11.8	5.2	13.3	4.0
Norway	4.9	2.9	−1.6	5.6	5.8	3.6	12.1	3.4
Sweden	5.9	3.7	−0.8	4.9	7.1	3.5	8.6	4.8
mean	5.6	4.2	0.9	5.6	7.7	4.1	11.4	4.4
(f) Other Western Europe								
Belgium	na	na	6.3	9.8	4.5	3.2	4.4	3.7
Netherlands	4.2	3.5	−1.0	8.1	5.5	4.9	6.6	4.6
Switzerland	na	na	8.1	7.9	5.8	4.2	3.4	7.0
mean	4.2	3.5	4.5	8.6	5.3	4.1	4.8	5.1
(g) Japan	7.2	14.5	0.5	9.7	16.2	16.2	5.8	6.3
(h) All countries	4.2	7.1	3.2	8.1	11.2	6.9	20.5	13.5
(i) All except 4 core countries	4.3	8.0	3.5	8.1	11.9	7.2	23.1	15.7
(j) G-10 + Switzerland	4.9	5.0	2.4	7.6	8.4	6.0	8.1	4.6
(k) All except G-10 + Switzerland	3.5	7.9	4.2	8.6	14.3	7.9	34.0	23.2

Notes and sources: See Table 8.3.

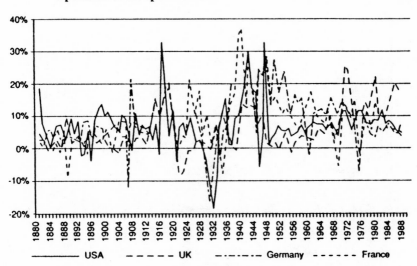

a. Core countries

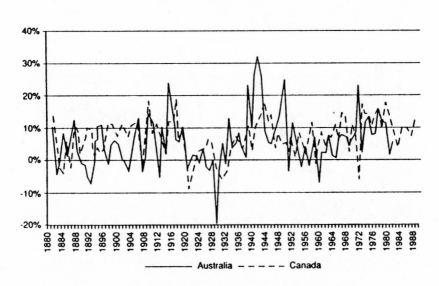

b. Anglo-Saxon countries of new settlement

Figure 8.4. Money growth rate, 1881–1990.

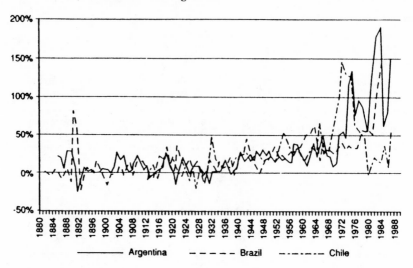

c. Latin America

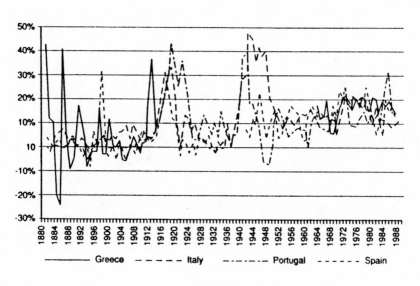

d. Southern Europe

Figure 8.4. *(cont.)*

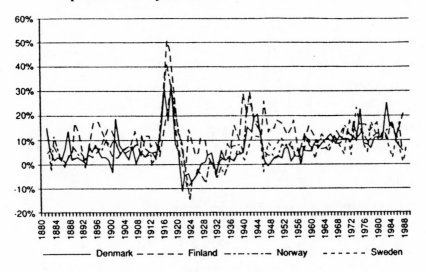

e. Scandinavia

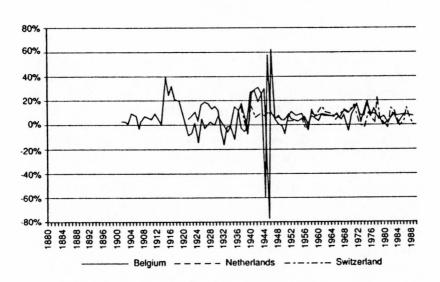

f. Other Western European countries

Figure 8.4. *(cont.)*

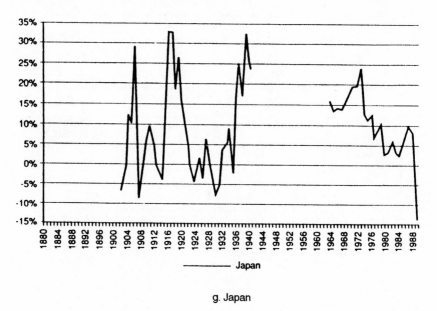

g. Japan

Figure 8.4. *(cont.)*

standard. The highest ratio is for the recent float. In all regimes, average deficit ratios are higher in peripheral than in core countries. (This also holds comparing the G-11 with the rest.) Under the gold standard, the highest average ratios were in the Anglo-Saxon countries of new settlement and Latin America; under Bretton Woods they occurred in Latin America and under the float in Latin America and Southern Europe. The standard deviations in fiscal policy followed a pattern similar to the means – they are generally lower in core than in peripheral countries. Thus, adherence to convertibility rules may have constrained fiscal policy in the same way as it did monetary policy. On the other hand, more limited fiscal needs during these regimes may have made it easier to adhere to the convertibility rule.

One group of countries stands out in the cross-country comparison. For the Latin American countries the fiscal deficit as a share of GNP increases dramatically between the pre–World War II and post–World War II regimes. In the postwar period it increases between regimes, reaching a peak with the float. Indeed a closer correlation between the fiscal deficit, money growth, and inflation can be observed across regimes for these countries than is the case for most countries in the G-11. Such a correlation may be evidence of lack of credibility in the commitment of the monetary regime.

Table 8.6. *Descriptive statistics of selected open economy variables, 21 countries, 1881–1990: government deficit as a percentage of GNP. Annual data: means and standard deviation*

	Gold standard (1881–1913)		Interwar (1919–38)		Bretton Woods (1946–70)		Floating exchange (1974–90)	
(a) Core countries								
United States	−0.3	0.6	1.9	4.4	−0.1	2.1	3.0	1.5
United Kingdom	0.1	0.8	−0.7	1.7	−2.3	2.8	2.2	1.6
Germany	2.8	1.0	1.4	1.1	0.1	1.8	1.5	0.8
France	0.6	1.1	3.8	3.8	2.2	2.3	1.5	1.3
mean	0.8	0.9	1.6	2.8	0.0	2.3	2.1	1.3
(b) Anglo-Saxon countries of new settlement								
Australia	15.1	2.1	12.6	2.2	5.0	2.4	1.4	0.3
Canada	0.5	1.1	1.5	2.5	−1.1	1.7	2.9	2.0
mean	7.8	1.6	7.1	2.4	2.0	2.1	2.2	1.2
(c) Latin America								
Argentina	2.5	2.4	1.7	1.8	6.0	3.7	9.3	6.8
Brazil	2.0	2.4	1.9	1.6	1.5	1.3	5.5	5.8
Chile	2.4	4.4	1.8	1.7	1.9	1.6	1.1	2.9
mean	2.3	3.1	1.8	1.7	3.1	2.2	5.3	5.2
(d) Southern Europe								
Greece	na	na	2.5	5.9	2.1	1.9	6.0	1.2
Italy	0.9	1.1	8.6	9.7	3.2	4.0	9.5	2.2
Portugal	1.2	0.7	2.5	3.6	1.8	1.2	12.7	3.8

Table 8.6. (cont.)

	Gold standard (1881–1913)		Interwar (1919–38)		Bretton Woods (1946–70)		Floating exchange (1974–90)	
Spain	-0.2	0.4	1.0	1.8	0.9	0.8	1.2	1.1
mean	0.6	0.7	3.7	5.3	2.0	2.0	7.4	2.1
(e) Scandinavia								
Denmark	0.5	1.2	0.1	0.8	-1.6	1.3	13.3	6.8
Finland	0.1	0.1	0.2	0.2	0.5	0.2	0.7	0.5
Norway	0.6	0.7	1.7	1.5	0.6	2.1	9.4	4.8
Sweden	0.0	0.6	1.6	1.2	-0.2	2.6	1.1	3.8
mean	0.3	0.7	0.9	0.9	-0.2	1.6	6.1	4.0
(f) Other Western Europe								
Belgium	na	na	3.9	1.2	4.8	4.8	7.3	2.7
Netherlands	2.1	0.3	5.6	3.2	0.6	2.6	3.8	2.4
Switzerland	na	na	0.0	0.5	-0.2	1.1	0.1	0.7
mean	2.1	0.3	3.2	1.6	1.7	2.8	3.7	1.9
(g) Japan	-3.1	3.3	-5.1	3.3	-0.1	3.2	4.5	1.9
(h) All countries	1.5	1.4	2.3	2.6	1.2	2.2	4.7	2.6
(i) All except 4 core countries	1.8	1.5	2.5	2.5	1.5	2.1	5.3	2.9
(j) G-10 + Switzerland	0.4	1.1	2.0	3.0	0.6	2.6	3.4	1.9
(k) All except G-10 + Switzerland	2.7	1.6	2.6	2.1	1.9	1.7	6.1	3.4

Notes and sources: See Table 8.3.

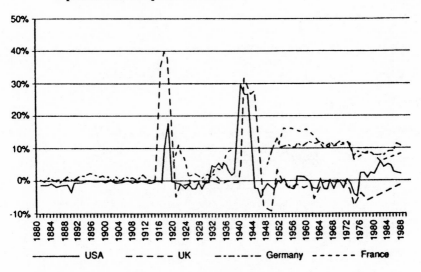

a. Core countries

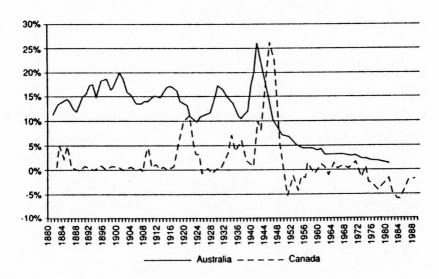

b. Anglo-Saxon countries of new settlement

Figure 8.5. Government deficit as a percentage of nominal GNP, 1881–1990.

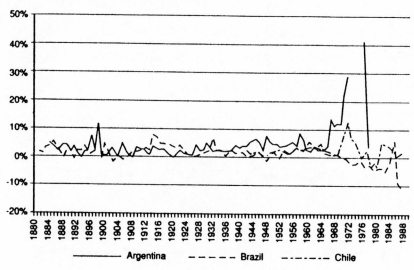

c. Latin America

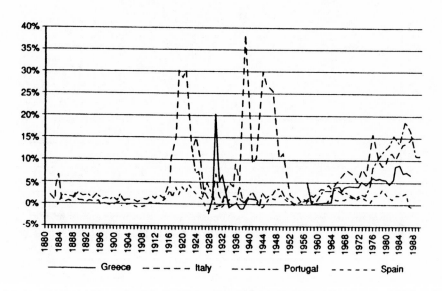

d. Southern Europe

Figure 8.5. *(cont.)*

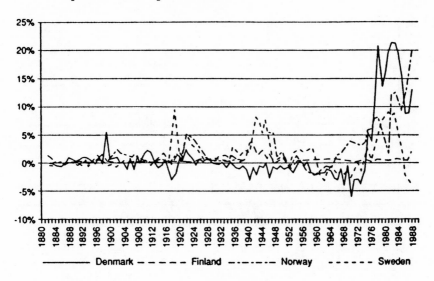

e. Scandinavia

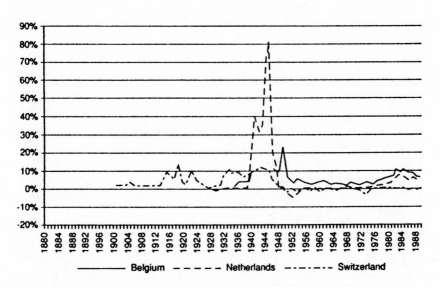

f. Other Western European countries

Figure 8.5. *(cont.)*

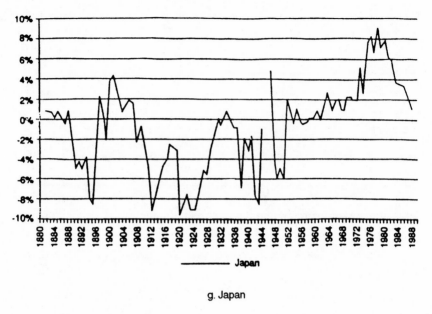

g. Japan

Figure 8.5. *(cont.)*

Summary: In summary, the gold standard regime had the lowest and least variable inflation performance for all countries. However, within that regime peripheral countries performed worse than the core (and expanded core). Bretton Woods exhibited a similar pattern with somewhat higher overall inflation. By contrast the recent float displayed both higher and more variable inflation than both regimes. This evidence may reflect a favorable influence of regime adherence on performance, but on the other hand adherence may have been possible because of greater stability.

Money growth was generally lowest and most stable under the gold standard across all countries, followed by Bretton Woods. Core countries within each regime followed more prudent and stable monetary policies than the periphery. By contrast, under the float, money growth was considerably higher, less stable across all countries. Lower and more stable money growth by core countries under the gold standard compared to the periphery may reflect better adherence to the commitment mechanism, or alternatively that there was less pressure to gear monetary policy for domestic purposes (Eichengreen, 1992b). The fact that peripheral countries' money growth was still relatively low and stable compared to later regimes may reflect their intention to adhere to the rule, when conditions were favorable. A similar but more muted pattern is observed in comparing Bretton Woods to the subsequent float.

Finally, the fiscal deficit, like monetary policy, is lowest and most stable under the gold standard, followed by Bretton Woods and in sharp contrast to the recent float. Within these regimes, however, weaker performance is observed for peripheral countries. Again like monetary policy, intended adherence to the regime, *ceteris paribus*, may have restrained policymakers during these periods compared to the recent float.

Thus, this statistical evidence reveals substantial differences in economic performance across regimes as well as differences between countries' and groupings of countries' performances within regimes. It is not clear, however, how much the different performance reflects adherence or non-adherence to rules and vice versa. Analysis of the shocks facing different countries may shed more light on this issue.

8.5.2 Demand and supply disturbances

An important issue is the extent to which the performance of alternative monetary regimes, as revealed by the data in the preceding tables, reflects the operation of the monetary regime in constraining policy actions or the presence or absence of shocks to the underlying environment. One way to shed light on this issue, following earlier work by Bayoumi and Eichengreen (1992, 1993, 1994a, 1994b), is to identify underlying shocks to aggregate supply and demand. According to them, aggregate supply shocks reflect shocks to the environment and are independent of the regime, but aggregate demand shocks likely reflect policy actions and are specific to the regime.

The approach used to calculate aggregate supply and demand shocks is an extension of the bivariate structural vector autoregression (VAR) methodology developed by Blanchard and Quah (1989). Following Bayoumi and Eichengreen (1994a), we estimated a two-variable VAR in the rate of change of the price level and output.[20] Restrictions on the VAR identify an aggregate demand disturbance, which is assumed to have only a temporary impact on output and a permanent impact on the price level, and an aggregate supply disturbance, which is assumed to have a permanent impact on both prices and output.[21] Overidentifying

---

[20] Both variables were rendered stationary by first differencing.

[21] Specifically, four restrictions are placed on the matrix of the shocks: two are simple normalizations, which define the variances of the shocks to aggregate demand and aggregate supply; the third assumes that demand and supply shocks are orthogonal; the

restrictions, namely, that demand shocks are positively correlated and supply shocks are negatively correlated with prices, can be tested by examining the impulse response functions to the shocks.

The methodology has important limitations that suggest that the results should be viewed with caution. The key limitation is that one can easily imagine frameworks in which demand shocks have permanent effects on output while supply shocks have only temporary effects.[22]

We estimated supply (permanent) and demand (temporary) shocks, using annual data for each of the 21 countries, over alternative regimes in the period 1880–1989. The VARs are based on data for three separate regime periods (to the extent available): 1880–1913, 1919–39, and 1946–89, omitting the war years because complete data on them were available for only a few of the countries. The VARs have two lags. We also did the estimation for aggregated price and output data for the seven country groupings and for the four broader aggregates of countries.

Table 8.7 presents the standard deviations of supply and demand shocks for the twenty-one countries by regimes. We also present aggregate shocks for the seven country groupings and for the four broad aggregates of countries. In addition we show, following Bayoumi and Eichengreen (1994a,b), the weighted average of the individual country shocks. Figure 8.6 shows the shocks for the seven country groupings and aggregate shocks for the four broad aggregates of countries.[23]

Table 8.7 shows for the seven country groupings, with the principal exception of Latin America, that the recent float regime was the most tranquil, with the lowest demand and supply shocks. The interwar period, again with the exception of Latin America, was the most volatile.[24] Bretton Woods experienced relatively high demand shocks in most of the country groupings with the exception of Japan. This likely reflects the widespread use of Keynesian demand management policies in this period. By contrast supply shocks were quite low across all groupings, not much different from the float. The gold standard in general exhibited fairly sizeable supply shocks. Indeed, for the core countries, the Anglo-

---

fourth is that demand shocks have only temporary effects on output, i.e., that the cumulative effect of demand shocks on the rate of change in output must be zero.

[22] See Keating and Nye (1991).

[23] Figures of the shocks for each of the twenty-one countries are available upon request.

[24] The results for most country groupings in the interwar period figures are similar to those reported for the United States by Cecchetti and Karras (1992), who estimated a three-variable VAR with monthly data. The late 1920s and early 1930s reveal a major negative demand shock consistent with Friedman and Schwartz's (1963) attribution of the onset of the Great Depression to monetary forces. After 1931, negative supply shocks predominate, consistent with Bernanke's (1983) and Bernanke and James' (1991) explanation for the severity of the Great Depression that stresses the collapse of the financial system.

Table 8.7. *Supply (permanent) and demand (temporary) shocks: 21 countries, 1881–1990. Annual data: standard deviations of shocks (percent)*

	Gold standard (1881–1913)		Interwar (1919–38)		Bretton Woods (1946–70)		Floating exchange (1974–90)	
1. Core countries								
United States	2.03	3.81	4.46	6.74	2.33	1.54	1.72	1.94
United Kingdom	2.66	2.16	1.93	3.52	2.62	1.95	3.57	4.31
Germany	2.36	2.32	4.47	3.13	2.88	2.65	1.66	1.39
France	4.58	3.75	7.17	5.19	3.50	1.75	1.93	1.52
Group aggregate[a]	2.37	2.92	4.07	4.46	2.38	1.79	2.02	1.85
Group aggregate[b]	2.07	3.12	4.75	4.57	2.32	1.57	1.89	1.93
Weights: United States 69%; United Kingdom 8%; Germany 10%; France 13%.								
2. Anglo-Saxon countries of new settlement								
Australia	3.92	3.97	3.37	4.02	3.73	2.48	1.15	1.16
Canada	0.93	2.75	4.01	8.61	2.42	2.60	2.66	2.10
Group aggregate[a]	2.54	3.61	3.92	6.50	3.17	2.24	1.85	1.43
Group aggregate[b]	2.24	3.27	4.08	6.71	3.01	2.65	1.89	1.57
Weights: Australia 30%; Canada 70%.								
3. Latin America								
Argentina	9.62	6.77	5.48	3.67	17.10	4.58	98.32	8.42
Brazil	15.91	6.69	5.76	6.15	16.67	5.54	18.16	7.50

Table 8.7. *(cont.)*

	Gold standard (1881–1913)		Interwar (1919–38)		Bretton Woods (1946–70)		Floating exchange (1974–90)	
Chile	8.55	6.90	9.98	9.41	12.73	5.62	27.00	8.06
Group aggregate[a]	11.32	5.19	5.93	5.98	14.50	5.87	37.83	8.99
Group aggregate[b]	9.32	5.81	4.86	4.72	15.20	5.25	40.01	8.68
Weights: Argentina 34%; Brazil 56%; Chile 10%.								
4. Southern Europe								
Greece	na	na	2.27	2.75	4.02	3.84	2.37	1.48
Italy	3.16	3.12	7.40	4.14	2.76	1.75	3.58	1.91
Portugal	4.81	3.77	5.02	6.46	2.30	2.20	2.70	2.26
Spain	1.09	1.33	2.22	2.05	4.42	2.76	2.07	3.29
Group aggregate[a]	2.89	2.47	4.07	3.56	3.57	2.36	2.81	2.52
Group aggregate[b]	3.10	2.91	4.72	3.98	3.24	2.23	2.85	2.35
Weights: Greece 6%; Italy 67%; Portugal 4%; Spain 23%.								
5. Scandinavia								
Denmark	2.69	2.89	4.94	1.88	1.61	2.41	1.89	1.79
Finland	2.31	2.26	3.53	2.91	7.89	2.21	1.14	1.18
Norway	2.54	1.43	7.50	3.94	4.33	1.22	3.40	1.88
Sweden	2.57	3.03	3.08	5.10	3.89	2.96	2.32	2.40
Group aggregate[a]	2.75	2.25	4.62	3.57	4.64	2.02	2.71	1.21
Group aggregate[b]	2.52	2.50	4.36	3.74	4.27	2.28	2.53	1.95

Weights: Denmark 22%; Finland 15%; Norway 17%; Sweden 46%.

6. Other Western Europe

Belgium	na	na	5.82	3.37	2.14	1.67	1.55	1.99
Netherlands	0.81	0.81	2.79	3.42	2.97	2.67	1.94	1.85
Switzerland	na	na	3.54	2.08	2.50	1.72	2.24	1.44
Group aggregate[a]	0.81	0.81	4.26	3.02	2.65	2.20	1.99	1.87
Group aggregate[b]	0.81	0.81	4.15	3.11	2.72	2.37	1.81	1.79

Weights: Belgium 32%; Netherlands 41%; Switzerland 27%.

G-10 + Switzerland[a]	2.71	2.97	4.36	4.16	2.48	2.30	2.23	2.24
G-10 + Switzerland[b]	2.46	3.42	4.57	5.37	2.49	2.05	2.11	2.26

Weights: Belgium 1%; Canada 4%; France 7%; Germany 9%; Italy 5%; Japan 11%; Netherlands 2%; Sweden 2%; Switzerland 1%; United Kingdom 6%; United States 52%.

All except G-11[a]	5.27	4.17	5.10	4.23	7.84	3.92	15.28	3.07
All except G-11[b]	6.73	4.04	4.65	4.60	8.85	3.25	17.69	4.71

Weights: Argentina 12%; Australia 18%; Brazil 21%; Chile 4%; Denmark 8%; Finland 5%; Greece 5%; Norway 6%; Porougal 3%; Spain 18%.

7. Japan

7. Japan	4.85	3.39	6.28	5.36	3.18	2.56	2.39	2.50

8. Aggregates

All countries[a]	4.23	3.51	4.92	4.61	5.12	2.80	8.87	2.81
All countries[b]	2.97	3.46	4.90	5.63	3.34	2.13	3.44	2.32

Table 8.7. (cont.)

	Gold standard (1881–1913)	Interwar (1919–38)	Bretton Woods (1946–70)	Floating exchange (1974–90)
Weights: Argentina 1%; Australia 2%; Belgium 1%; Brazil 2%; Canada 4%; Chile 0%; Denmark 1%; Finland 0%; France 7%; Germany 8%; Greece 0%; Italy 5%; Japan 9%; Netherlands 2%; Norway 1%; Portugal 0%; Spain 2%; Sweden 2%; Switzerland 1%; United Kingdom 6%; United States 46%.				
All except core countries[a]	4.41	5.20	5.77	10.41
	3.49	4.68	2.74	3.24
All except core countries[b]	3.67	5.42	4.52	6.47
	3.11	5.08	2.67	2.80
Weights: Argentina 3%; Australia 5%; Belgium 4%; Brazil 5%; Canada 12%; Chile 1%; Denmark 2%; Finland 2%; Greece 1%; Italy 15%; Japan 29%; Netherlannds 5%; Norway 2%; Portugal 1%; Spain 5%; Sweden 5%; Switzerland 3%.				

Notes:

[a] Aggregate data.

[b] Weighted average of individual country shocks. The weights are calculated as the share of each country's national income in the total income in the group of countries in 1970, where the GNP data are converted to dollars using the actual exchange rate.

Data sources: See Data Appendix.

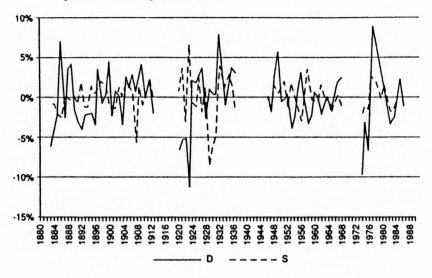

a. Core countries

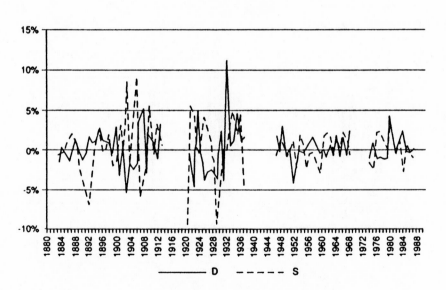

b. Anglo-Saxon countries of new settlement

Figure 8.6. Supply and demand shocks: country groups, 1881–1990.

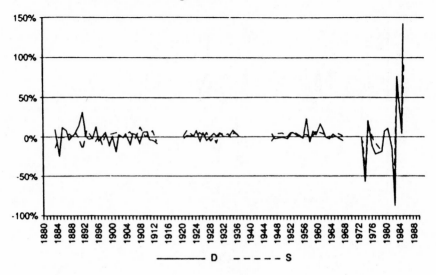

c. Latin America

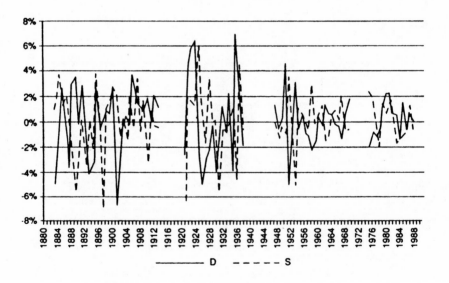

d. Southern Europe

Figure 8.6. *(cont.)*

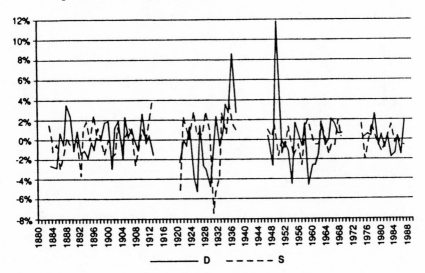

e. Scandinavia

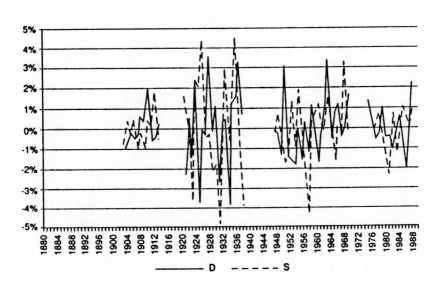

f. Other Western European countries

Figure 8.6. *(cont.)*

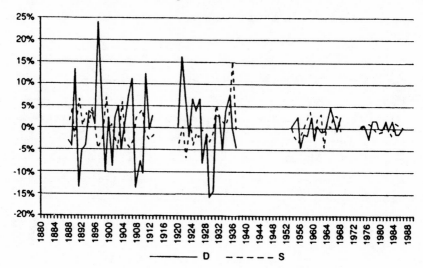

g. Japan

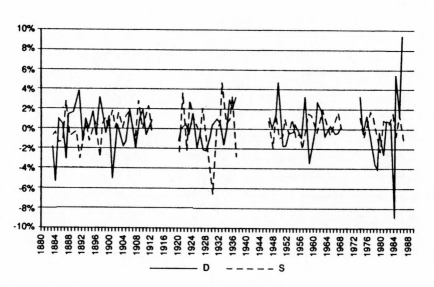

h. All countries

Figure 8.6. *(cont.)*

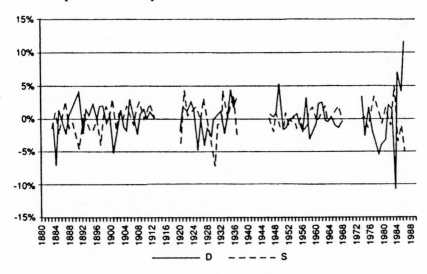

i. All except four core countries

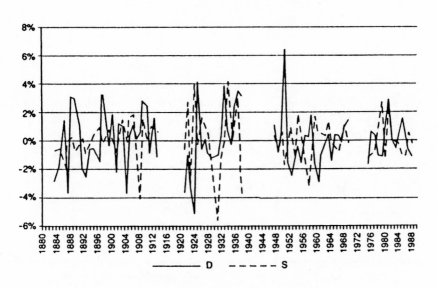

j. G-10 countries plus Switzerland

Figure 8.6. *(cont.)*

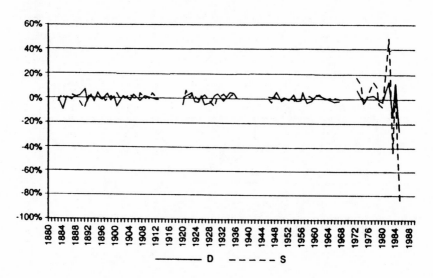

k. All except G-10 countries plus Switzerland

Figure 8.6. *(cont.)*

Saxon countries and Japan, they were more than twice as high as in the post–World War II period.[25] In Latin America demand shocks exceeded supply shocks in all regimes except the interwar. In the post–World War II period, for these countries, demand shocks considerably exceeded supply shocks, especially under the float. For these countries the constraints of the convertible regime appear to be much weaker than for the others, although one could argue that the much greater instances of supply shocks in these countries may in part account for the greater use of discretionary policy.

Across country groupings, the difference between the "expanded core" of countries and the periphery observed in Tables 8.4 to 8.6 is also apparent. Under the gold standard regime most of these countries had substantially lower supply and demand shocks than the others. This can be seen in the comparison between the G-11 aggregate and the aggregate of all countries except the G-11. The pattern also holds up in both post–World War II regimes.

[25] The rankings by regime for the weighted average of individual country shocks are similar to the group aggregates.

In sum, the evidence on demand and supply shocks complements the preceding evidence in Tables 8.4 to 8.6. For the 'expanded core' countries, represented roughly by the G-11, the gold standard was characterized by higher demand and especially higher supply shocks than in the post–World War II regimes, and within the post-war period both the Bretton Woods regime and the float were relatively stable.[26] This evidence suggests that, for these countries, it is unlikely that the convertible regimes prevailed because of the absence of supply shocks, since the size of demand and supply shocks was quite similar across both types of regimes. The durability or fragility of past convertible regimes likely had more to do with regime design (Bordo, 1993b).

By contrast, for the peripheral countries, especially Latin America and Southern Europe, demand shocks exceeded supply shocks across all regimes, and especially under the postwar float. The constraints of the convertible regime appear to be much weaker than for the G-11, although one could argue that the much greater incidence of supply shocks in peripheral countries may in part account for the greater use of discretionary policy.

8.6   Conclusion

In conclusion, we suggest answers to three questions. First, what is the evidence for the specie standard as a contingent rule? Second, why was the rule successful when it was? Third, why did some countries successfully adhere while others did not?

Our historical survey reveals that the contingent rule over the entire period was strictly followed by a relatively small number of countries – the core countries (with the exception of France and Germany after World War I); the Anglo-Saxon countries of new settlement, most of the Scandinavian and smaller Western European countries, and Japan. For the rest it was violated. If we focus only on the classical gold standard period, the basic convertibility rule was followed by a larger group of countries. For Bretton Woods, the rule was much less clearly defined, hence it is difficult to distinguish adherence and non-adherence. For that regime clearly, as statistical evidence of superior performance measured by nominal variables compared to other regimes shows, convertibility was important.

Second, the rule prevailed when it did for a number of possible reasons. The classical gold standard era was one of stable economic growth,

---

[26] These results are very similar to those presented for the G-7 in Bordo (1993b) and by Bayoumi and Eichengreen (1994a,b).

with few impediments to the free allocation of labor, capital, and goods both within and across countries. It was also a period characterized by relative political stability and, for many of the "expanded core" countries by the absence of populist pressure for demand management (Eichengreen, 1992a). In addition, it was an era characterized by the coincidence of beliefs in free trade and exchange rate stability by the dominant industrial commercial groups in different countries (Gallarotti, 1993). The dominance of England as a commercial power also was important. England's clear commitment to the rule and the benefits of access to her finance markets was a key determinant of other countries' adherence.

Third, the different experience of adherence to the rule by the expanded core countries and the peripheral countries may, we suggest, be explained by their different stages of economic development. By the beginning of the classical gold standard era the "expanded core" countries were industrialized, had experienced decades of rising per capita income, had stable polities, and were dominated by groups who perceived the benefits to them of monetary stability. In addition, as maturing diversified economies they were less subject to the disruptions of massive swings in the prices of primary products. These conditions were absent in the peripheral countries. Faced with frequent supply shocks, for them adherence to the rule was more difficult.

Data appendix

For the G-10 countries plus Switzerland, see data appendix in Bordo and Jonung (1996) and data appendix in Bordo (1993a) except for the following countries:

Australia

(1) Money 1880–1990, provided by David Pope, Australian National University. (2) Real GDP 1880–1990, David Pope. (3) GDP deflator 1880–1990, David Pope. (4) Exchange rate 1880–1990, David Pope. (5) Government expenditures and revenues 1880–1990, David Pope.

Denmark

(1) Money 1880–1990, provided by Lars Jonung. (2) Real GDP 1880–1990, Lars Jonung. (3) GDP deflator 1880–1988, B. R. Mitchell (1992). (4) Exchange rate 1880–1990, Lars Jonung. (5) Government expenditures and revenues 1880–1988, B. R. Mitchell (1992).

Finland

(1) Money 1880–1990, Lars Jonung. (2) Real GDP 1880–1990, Lars Jonung. (3) GDP deflator 1880–1988, B. R. Mitchell (1992). (4) Exchange rate 1880–1990, Lars Jonung. (5) Government expenditures and revenues 1880–1988, B. R. Mitchell (1992).

Greece

(1) Money 1880–1914, Sophia Lazaretou; 1962–90, International Financial Statistics (1992). (2) Real GDP 1927–88, B. R. Mitchell (1992). (3) GDP deflator 1927–88, B. R. Mitchell (1992). (4) Exchange rate 1880–1914, Sophia Lazaretou; 1962–90, International Financial Statistics (1992). (5) Government expenditures and revenues 1880–1936, Sophia Lazaretou; 1937–39, B. R. Mitchell (1992); 1956–86, B. R. Mitchell (1992).

Norway

(1) Money 1880–1990, Lars Jonung. (2) Real GDP 1880–1990, Lars Jonung. (3) GDP deflator 1880–1988, B. R. Mitchell (1992). (4) Exchange rate 1880–1990, Lars Jonung. (5) Government expenditures and revenues 1880–1988, B. R. Mitchell (1992).

Portugal

(1) Money 1880–1990, provided by Fernando Santos, Universidade do Porto. (2) Real GDP 1880–1990, Lars Jonung. (3) GDP deflator 1880–1988, B. R. Mitchell (1992). (4) Exchange rate 1890–1990, Fernando Santos. (5) Government expenditures and revenues 1880–1988, B. R. Mitchell (1992).

Spain

(1) Money 1880–1990, Estadisticas Historicas de Espana; 1981–88, B. R. Mitchell (1992). (2) Real GDP 1901–53, Estadisticas Historicas de Espana; 1954–88, B. R. Mitchell (1992). (3) GDP deflator, 1901–53, B. R. Mitchell (1992). (4) Exchange rate 1880–1980. Estadisticas Historicas de Espana; 1981–90, IFS (1992). Government expenditures and revenues 1880–1988, B. R. Mitchell (1992).

References

Abramowitz, Moses. 1973. The Monetary Side of Long Swings in U.S. Economic Growth. Stanford University Center for Research on Economic Growth. Memorandum No. 146 (mimeo).

Barro, Robert J. and David B. Gordon. 1983. Rules, Discretion and Reputation in a Model of Monetary Policy. *Journal of Monetary Economics* 12: 101–21.

Bayoumi, Tamin and Barry Eichengreen. 1992b. Is There a Conflict Between EC Enlargement and European Monetary Unification? NBER Working Paper No. 3950. January. *Greek Economic Review* (forthcoming).

Bayoumi, Tamin and Barry Eichengreen. 1993. Shocking Aspects of European Monetary Unification. In Francesco Torres and Francesco Giavazzi (eds) *Adjustment and Growth in European Monetary Union*. Cambridge: Cambridge University Press.

Bayoumi, Tamin and Barry Eichengreen. 1994a. Economic Performance Under Alternative Exchange Rate Regimes: Some Historical Evidence. In Peter B. Kenen, Francesco Papodia and Fabrizio Saccomani (eds) *The International Monetary System*. Cambridge: Cambridge University Press.

Bayoumi, Tamin and Barry Eichengreen. 1994b. Monetary and Exchange Rate Arrangements for NAFTA. *Journal of Development Economics* 43: 125–65.

Bernanke, Benjamin. 1983. Nonmonetary Effects of the Financial Crisis in the Propagation of the Great Depression. *American Economic Review* 73: 259–76.

Bernanke, Benjamin and Harold James. 1991. The Gold Standard, Deflation and Financial Crisis in the Great Depression: An International Comparison. In R. Glenn Hubbard (ed) *Financial Markets and Financial Crisis*. Chicago: University of Chicago Press: 33–68.

Blanchard, Olivier and Danny Quah. 1989. The Dynamic Effects of Aggregate Demand and Aggregate Supply Disturbances. *American Economic Review* (September): 655–73.

Bloomfield, Arthur. 1959. *Monetary Policy Under the International Gold Standard, 1800–1914*. New York: Federal Reserve Bank of New York.

Bordo, Michael D. 1981. The Classical Gold Standard: Some Lessons for Today. *Federal Reserve Bank of St. Louis Review* 63 (May): 2–17.

Bordo, Michael D. 1984. The Gold Standard: The Traditional Approach. In Michael D. Bordo and Anna J. Schwartz (eds) *A Retrospective on the Classical Gold Standard, 1821–1931*. Chicago: University of Chicago Press.

Bordo, Michael D. 1993a. The Bretton Woods International Monetary System: An Historical Overview. In Michael D. Bordo and Barry Eichengreen (eds) *A Retrospective on the Bretton Woods System: Lessons for International Monetary Reform*. Chicago: University of Chicago Press.

Bordo, Michael D. 1993b. The Gold Standard, Bretton Woods and Other Monetary Regimes: A Historical Appraisal. *Federal Reserve Bank of St. Louis Review* 75–2 (March/April): 123–91.

Bordo, Michael D. and Lars Jonung. 1996. Monetary Regimes, Inflation and Monetary Reform. In D. F. Vaz and K. Vellupillai (eds) *Inflation, Institutions and Information*. Essays in Honor of Axel Leijonhufvud. London: Macmillan.

Bordo, Michael D. and Finn E. Kydland. 1996. The Gold Standard As a Commitment Mechanism. In Tamin Bayoumi, Barry Eichengreen, and Mark Taylor (eds) *Modern Perspectives on the Gold Standard*. Cambridge: Cambridge University Press.

Bordo, Michael D. and Angela Redish. 1990. Credible Commitment and Exchange Rate Stability: Canada's Interwar Experience. *Canadian Journal of Economics* 23(2) 357–80.

Bordo, Michael D. and Anna J. Schwartz. 1994. The Specie Standard As a Contingent Rule: Some Evidence for Core and Peripheral Countries, 1880–1990. Rutgers University Working Paper No. 94–11.

Bordo, Michael D. and Eugene N. White. 1993. British and French Finance During the Napoleonic Wars. In Michael D. Bordo and Forrest Capie (eds) *Monetary Regimes in Transition*. Cambridge: Cambridge University Press.

Butlin, S. J. 1986. *The Australian Monetary System 1851–1914*. Sydney Australian Reserve Bank.

Calomiris, Charles W. 1988. Price and Exchange Rate Determination During the Greenback Suspension. *Oxford Economic Papers* December.

Calomiris, Charles. 1993. Greenback Resumption and Silver Risk: The Economics and Politics of Monetary Regime Change in the United States, 1862–1900. In Michael D. Bordo and Forrest Capie (eds) *Monetary Regimes in Transition* Cambridge: Cambridge University Press.

Canzoneri, Matthew. 1985. Monetary Policy Games and the Role of Private Information. *American Economic Review* 75: 1056–70.

Canzoneri, Matthew B. and Dale W. Henderson. 1991. *Monetary Policy in Interdependent Economies*. Cambridge: Massachusetts Institute of Technology Press.

Cecchetti, Stephen G. and Georgios Karras. 1992. Sources of Output Fluctuations During the Interwar Period: Further Evidence on the Causes of the Great Depression. NBER Working Paper No. 4049 April.

Cooper, Richard. 1982. The Gold Standard: Historical Facts and Future Prospects. *Brooking Papers on Economic Activity* 1: 1–45.

Cortés Condé, Roberto. 1989. *Dinero, Deuda y Crisis: Evolución Fiscal y Monetaria en la Argentina*. Editorial Sudamericana, Instituto Torcuato Di Tella: Buenos Aires.

Davis, Lance E. and Robert A. Huttenback. 1986. *Mammon and the Pursuit of Empire: The Political Economy of British Imperialism, 1860–1912*. Cambridge: Cambridge University Press.

DeCecco, Marcello. 1974. *Money and Empire: The International Gold Standard, 1890–1914*. New Jersey: Rowman and Littlefield.

DeKock, Gabriel and Vittorio Grilli. 1989. Endogenous Exchange Rate Regime Switches. NBER Working Paper No. 3066 August.

DeVries, Margaret G. 1976. *The International Monetary Fund 1966–1971: The System Under Stress, Vol. 1: Narrative*. Washington, DC: International Monetary Fund.

Edelstein, Michael. 1982. *Overseas Investment in the Age of High Imperialism: The United Kingdom, 1850–1914*. New York: Columbia University Press.

Eichengreen, Barry. 1985. Editor's Introduction. In Barry Eichengreen (ed.) *The Gold Standard in Theory and History*. London: Methuen.

Eichengreen, Barry. 1987. Conducting the International Orchestra: Bank of England Leadership Under the Classical Gold Standard. *Journal of International Money and Finance* (6): 5–29.

Eichengreen, Barry. 1989. Hegemonic Stability Theories. In Richard Cooper *et al.* (eds) *Can Nations Agree?* Washington, DC: Brookings Institution.

Eichengreen, Barry. 1992a. The Gold Standard Since Alec Ford. In S. N. Broadberry and N. F. R. Crafts (eds) *Britain in the International Economy: 1870–1939* Cambridge: Cambridge University Press.

Eichengreen, Barry. 1992b. *Golden Fetters: The Gold Standard and the Great Depression, 1919–1939.* Oxford University.

Eichengreen, Barry. 1993. Three Perspectives on the Bretton Woods System. In Michael D. Bordo and Barry Eichengreen (eds) *A Retrospective on the Bretton Woods System.* Chicago: University of Chicago Press and NBER.

Eichengreen, Barry. 1994. *International Monetary Arrangements for the 21st Century.* Washington, DC: Brookings Institution.

Eschweiler, Bernhard and Michael D. Bordo. 1993. Rules, Discretion and Central Bank Independence: The German Experience 1880–1989. NBER Working Paper No. 4547.

Fetter, F. 1965. *Development of British Monetary Orthodoxy, 1797–1875.* Cambridge: Harvard University Press.

Fishlow, Albert. 1987. Market Forces or Group Interests: Inconvertible Currency in Pre-1914 Latin America. University of California at Berkeley (mimeo).

Fishlow, Albert. 1989. Conditionality and Willingness to Pay: Some Parallels from the 1989s. In Barry Eichengreen and Peter Lindert (eds) *The International Debt Crisis in Historical Perspective.* Cambridge: Massachusetts Institute of Technology Press.

Flood, Robert P. and Peter Isard. 1989. Simple Rules, Discretion and Monetary Policy. NBER Working Paper No. 2934.

Ford, A.G. 1962. *The Gold Standard 1880–1914: Britain and Argentina.* Oxford: Clarendon Press.

Fratianni, M. and Spinelli, F. 1984. Italy in the Gold Standard Period 1861–1914. In Michael D. Bordo and Anna J. Schwartz (eds) *A Retrospective on the Classical Gold Standard, 1921–1931.* Chicago: University of Chicago Press.

Frieden, Jeffrey A. 1993. The Dynamics of International Monetary Systems: International and Domestic Factors in the Rise, Reign, and Demise of the Classical Gold Standard. In Jack Snyder and Robert Jervis (eds) *Coping with Complexity in the International System.* Colorado: Westview Press.

Friedman, Milton. 1990. Bimetallism Revisited. *Journal of Economic Perspectives* 4(4): 85–104.

Friedman, Milton and Schwartz, Anna J. 1963. *A Monetary History of the United States, 1867–1960.* Princeton: Princeton University Press.

Fritsch, Winston and Gustavo H. B. Franco. 1992. Aspects of the Brazilian Experience Under the Gold Standard. PUC Rio de Janeiro (mimeo).

Gallarotti, Giulio, M. 1993. The Scramble for Gold: Monetary Regime Transformation in the 1870s. In Michael D. Bordo and Forrest Capie (eds) *Monetary Regimes in Transition*, Cambridge: Cambridge University Press.

Giovannini, Alberto. 1989. How Do Fixed Exchange-Rate Regimes Work: The Evidence From the Gold Standard, Bretton Woods and the EMS. In Marvin Miller, Barry Eichengreen and Richard Portes (eds) *Blueprints for Exchange Rate Management*. London: Centre for Economic Policy Research: 13–46.

Giovannini, Alberto. 1993. Bretton Woods and Its Precursors: Rules Versus Discretion in the History of International Monetary Regimes. In Michael D. Bordo and Barry Eichengreen (eds) *A Retrospective on the Bretton Woods System*. Chicago: University of Chicago Press.

Grilli, Vittorio. 1990. Managing Exchange Rate Crises: Evidence from the 1890's. *Journal of International Money and Finance* 9: 258–275.

Grossman, Herschel J. and John B. Van Huyck. 1988. Sovereign Debt as a Contingent Claim: Excusable Default, Repudiation, and Reputation. *American Economic Review* 78: 1088–97.

Haavisto, Tarmo. 1992. *Money and Economic Activity in Finland 1866–1985*. Lund, Sweden. Lund Economic Studies.

Hayashi, Fumio. 1989. Japan's Saving Rate: New Data and Reflections. NBER Working Paper No. 3205.

Horsefield, Keith. 1969. *The International Monetary Fund, 1945–1965: Twenty Years of International Monetary Co-operation, Vol. 1. Chronicle*. Washington, DC: International Monetary Fund.

Jonung, Lars. 1984. Swedish Experience Under the Classical Gold Standard, 1873–1914. In Michael D. Bordo and Anna J. Schwartz (eds) *A Retrospective on the Classical Gold Standard, 1821–1931*. Chicago: University of Chicago Press.

Keating, John W. and John V. Nye. 1991. Permanent and Transitory Shocks in Real Output: Estimates from Nineteenth Century and Postwar Economies. St. Louis: Washington University Working Paper No. 160.

Keynes, John Maynard. [1930] 1971. *The Applied Theory of Money: A Treatise on Money*, Vol. 6 of *The Collected Writings of John Maynard Keynes*. Reprint London: Macmillan and New York: Cambridge University Press for the Royal Economic Society.

Krugman, Paul. 1991. Target Zones and Exchange Rate Dynamics. *Quarterly Journal of Economics* 56: 669–82.

Kydland, Finn E. and Prescott, Edward. 1977. Rules Rather than Discretion: The Inconsistency of Optimal Plans. *Journal of Political Economy* 85: 473–91.

Lazaretou, Sophia. 1994. Government Spending, Monetary Policies and Exchange Rate Regime Switches: The Drachma in the Gold Standard Period. *Explorations in Economic History*, October.

Lindert, Peter. 1969. *Key Currencies and Gold, 1900–1913*. Princeton Studies in International Finance, No. 24. Princeton: Princeton University Press.

Llona-Rodriguez, Augustine. 1993. Chile During the Gold Standard: A Successful Paper Money Experience. Instituto Torcuato Di Tella (mimeo).

Lucas, Robert E. Jr. and Nancy L. Stokey. 1983. Optimal Fiscal and Monetary Policy in an Economy Without Capital. *Journal of Monetary Economics* 12(1): (1)55–93.

McKinnon, Ronald I. 1988. An International Gold Standard Without Gold. *Cato Journal* 8 (Fall): 351–73.

McKinnon, Ronald I. 1993. International Money in Historical Perspective. *Journal of Economic Literature* 31(1): 1–44.

Mankiw, Gregory. 1987. The Optimal Collection of Seigniorage – Theory and Evidence. *Journal of Monetary Economics* 20: (2)327–41.

Martin-Aceña, Pablo. 1993. Spain During the Classical Gold Standard Years, 1880–1914. In Michael D. Bordo and Forrest Capie (eds) *Monetary Regimes in Transition*. Cambridge: Cambridge University Press.

Meltzer, Allan H. and Saranna Robinson. 1989. Stability Under the Gold Standard in Practice. In Michael D. Bordo (ed) *Monetary, History and International Finance: Essays in Honor of Anna J. Schwartz*. Chicago: University of Chicago Press: 163–95.

Miller, Marcus and Alan Sutherland. 1992. Britain's Return to Gold and Entry into the ERM. In Paul Krugman and Marcus Miller (eds) *Exchange Rate Targets and Currency Banks*. Cambridge: Cambridge University Press.

Miller, Marcus and Alan Sutherland. 1994. Speculative Anticipations of Sterling's Return to Gold: Was Keynes Wrong? *Economic Journal*. July.

Mitchell, Brian R. 1992. *International Historical Statistics: Europe 1750–1988*. New York: Stockton Press.

Obstfeld, Maurice. 1992. Destabilizing Effects of Exchange Rate Escape Clauses. NBER Working Paper No. 3606.

Officer, Lawrence. 1986. The Efficiency of the Dollar-Sterling Gold Standard, 1980–1908. *Journal of Political Economy* 94 (October): 1038–73.

Officer, Lawrence. 1993. Gold-Point Arbitrage and Uncovered Interest Arbitrage Under the 1925–1931 Dollar–Sterling Gold Standard. *Explorations in Economic History* 30(1): 98–127.

Pelaez, Carlos M. and Wilson Suzigan. 1976. *Historia Monetaria do Brazil*. Editoria Universidade de Brazilia.

Reis, Jaime. 1992. The Gold Standard in Portugal, 1854–1891. Universidale Nova de Lisbon (mimeo).

Roll, Richard. 1972. Interest Rates and Price Expectations During the Civil War. *Journal of Economic History* 32 (June): 476–98.

Schwartz, Anna J. 1984. Introduction. In Michael D. Bordo and Anna J. Schwartz (eds) *A Retrospective on the Classical Gold Standard, 1821–1931*. Chicago: University of Chicago Press.

Schwartz, Anna J 1987. 'Banking School, Currency School, Free Banking School.' In *New Palgrave Dictionary of Economics*. London: Macmillan

Sharkey, R. D. 1959. *Money, Class, and Party*. Baltimore: Johns Hopkins Press.

Shearer, Ronald A. and Carolyn Clark. 1984. Canada and the Interwar Gold Standard, 1920–1935: Monetary Policy Without a Central Bank. In Michael D. Bordo and Anna J. Schwartz (eds) *A Retrospective on the Classical Gold Standard 1821–1931*. Chicago: University of Chicago Press.

Shinjo, Hiroshi. 1962. *History of the Yen*. Research Institute for Economics and Business Administration. Japan: Kobe University.

Simons, Henry C. 1951. Rules Versus Authorities in Monetary Policy. In Richard D. Irwin (ed.) *Readings in Monetary Theory*. Homewood, Illinois.

Smith, Gregor and Todd Smith. 1993. Wesley Mitchell and Irving Fisher and the Greenback Gold Reforms 1865–1879. Queens University (mimeo).

Smith, W. S. and Smith, R. T. 1990. Stochastic Process Switching and the Return to Gold. *Economic Journal* 100 (March): 164–75.

Stiglitz, Joseph and Andrew Weiss. 1981. Credit Rationing in Markets with Imperfect Information. *American Economic Review* 71(6): 393–410.

Svennson, Lars E. O. 1994. Why Exchange Rate Bands? Monetary Independence in Spite of Fixed Exchange Rates. *Journal of Monetary Economics* 33(1): 157–99.

Unger, I. 1964. *The Greenback Era: A Social and Political History of American Finance. 1865–1879*. New Jersey: Princeton University Press.

Viner, Jacob. 1937. *Studies in Theory of International Trade*. Chicago: University of Chicago Press.

Yeager, Leland B. 1984. The Image of the Gold Standard. In Michael D. Bordo and Anna J. Schwartz (eds) *A Retrospective on the Classical Gold Standard, 1821–1931*. Chicago: University of Chicago Press.

CHAPTER 9

The gold standard as a "Good Housekeeping seal of approval"

Written with Hugh Rockoff

In this chapter we argue that during the period from 1870 to 1914 adherence to the gold standard was a signal of financial rectitude, a "Good Housekeeping seal of approval," that facilitated access by peripheral countries to capital from the core countries of western Europe. Examination of data from nine widely different capital-importing countries, using a model inspired by the Capital Asset Pricing Model, reveals that countries with poor records of adherence were charged considerably more than those with good records, enough to explain the determined effort to stay on gold made by a number of capital-importing countries.

The global economy in its present form emerged in the half century before World War I. That "golden age" was characterized by massive interregional flows of capital, labor, and goods. It was also an era when most nations adhered to (or attempted to adhere to) the gold standard rule of convertibility of national currencies into a fixed weight of gold. Common adherence to gold convertibility in turn linked the world together through fixed exchange rates. In this article we argue that adherence to the gold standard also served as "a Good Housekeeping seal of approval" that facilitated access by peripheral countries to capital vital to their development from the core countries of Western Europe.

We view the gold standard as a contingent rule or a rule with escape clauses. Members were expected to adhere to convertibility except in the

This chapter is reprinted from the June 1996 *Journal of Economic History*, 56(2):389–428. © The Economic History Association. All rights reserved. ISSN 0022-0507.

Hugh Rockoff is Professor of Economics at the Center for Monetary and Financial History at Rutgers University, P.O. Box 5055, New Brunswick, NJ 08903-5055.

We owe an immense debt to our research assistant Zhongjian Xia, who went beyond the usual duties to make valuable contributions to the analysis in the paper. For helpful suggestions we would like to thank Ehsan Choudhri, Michael Edelstein, Richard Grossman, Peter Kenen, Bruce Mizrach, Lawrence Officer, Gerardo Della Paolera, Angela Redish, Anna Schwartz, Hiroki Tsurumi, and participants at the International Economics Seminar at Princeton University. For providing us with data we are also indebted to Eliana Cordoso, Rudiger Dornbusch, Jaime Reis, Fernando Santos, and Franco Spinelli.

event of a well-understood emergency such as a war, a financial crisis, or a shock to the terms of trade. Under these circumstances, temporary departures from the rule would be tolerated on the assumption that once the emergency passed, convertibility at the original parity would resume.[1]

It is well known that a number of core countries (England, France, and Germany as well as several other developed Western European countries) adhered to this rule before 1914. Even a number of developing peripheral countries also did so (Canada, Australia, and the United States), or attempted to do so (Argentina, Brazil, and Chile), or "shadowed" the performance of the gold standard (Italy, Spain, and Portugal).[2] One possible reason for faithful adherence to the rule is that adherence provided improved access to capital vital to development.[3] This point, we believe, has been strangely neglected.[4] It explains why countries were so determined to adhere to gold even when doing so involved substantial costs: faithful adherence significantly lowered the cost of loans from metropolitan Europe. Thus, "the Good Housekeeping seal" provides an alternative to traditional explanations for the popularity of the gold standard that turn on internal differences between creditors and debtors or even on irrational prejudices in favor of gold. If adherence to the rule was evidence of financial rectitude – such as "the Good Housekeeping seal of approval" – it would signal that a country followed prudent fiscal and monetary policies and would only tempo-

---

[1] Bordo and Kydland, "Gold Standard."

[2] Eichengreen, *Golden Fetters*; Giovannini, "Bretton Woods"; Grilli, "Managing Exchange Rate Crises"; Bordo and Schwartz, "Operation"; and Morgenstern, *International Financial Transactions*.

[3] There is a debate about whether the United States should be treated as a core or peripheral country. Those who view it as a peripheral country do so for two reasons: first, because it was a net capital importer and hence more like Australia and Canada than the core countries that provided the capital; second, because the silver agitation and legislation of 1878 and 1890 threatened the convertibility of U.S. currency into gold. See Eichengreen, *Golden Fetters*; Giovanni, "Bretton Woods"; and Grilli, "Managing Exchange Rate Crises." The view that the United States was a core country stresses three reasons: first, the United States was wealthier and more populous than the United Kingdom and certainly than France or Germany; second, the United States was a capital exporter as well as an importer in the late nineteenth century, and by 1914 it was a net capital exporter; and third, the silver threat was temporary, and convertibility was never suspended. Therefore, the United States by the end of the nineteenth century, a colossus on the world stage, belongs in the core. See Bordo and Schwartz, "Operation"; and Morgenstern, *International Financial Transactions*. For purposes of this article, because we are focusing on the determinants of capital flows from the mature economies of Western Europe to countries of new settlement (as well as other developing countries), we include the United States with the other peripheral countries. Nevertheless, in terms of its role as a player in the international monetary system, we view it as part of the core.

[4] With the exception of Gallarotti, *Anatomy*, p. 39.

rarily run large fiscal deficits in well-understood emergencies. Monetary authorities then could be depended on to avoid defaulting on externally held debt.

In many cases loans were made with gold clauses or were sterling denominated, to minimize currency risk. But there still would be risk of abrogation of the gold clauses or of total default on the debt, which would be reflected in a country risk premium on the loan.[5] Moreover, in a world of asymmetric information, a credible commitment to the gold-standard rule would provide a signal to lenders of the costs borrowers would be willing to bear to avoid default and hence would circumvent the aversion to lending imposed by asymmetric information.[6]

In this article, we first define the concept of the gold standard as a contingent rule and as a credible commitment mechanism to serve as "the Good Housekeeping seal of approval." Then we survey the historical background of gold-standard adherence in the period from 1870 to 1914 by nine important peripheral countries. We next discuss the data and methodology for a test of "the Good Housekeeping seal of approval" hypothesis. We then present the results for the nine countries. The evidence suggests that in most cases successful adherence to gold significantly improved the terms at which peripheral countries could borrow from the core countries. Finally, we conclude with some lessons from history.

9.1   The gold standard as a commitment mechanism

Traditionally, a monetary rule such as the gold standard (or other specie standards such as silver or bimetallism) by causing a nation's money supply to vary automatically with the balance of payments, was deemed to be superior to entrusting policy to the discretion of well-meaning monetary authorities.[7] In contrast to this view, which stresses both im-

---

[5] Frankel, *On Exchange Rates*, pp. 41–69; and Frankel and Okungwu, "Liberalized Portfolio," decompose interest differentials between emerging and developed countries into a country-risk premium and a currency-risk premium. In our empirical work, in the absence of data suitable to measure expectations of change in exchange rates and hence to account for the currency-risk premium, we use, to the extent available to us, gold denominated securities to account for the country-risk premium.

[6] Stiglitz and Weiss, "Credit Rationing."

[7] Simons, "Rules." The Currency School in England in the early nineteenth century made the case for the Bank of England's fiduciary note issue to vary automatically with the level of the Bank's gold reserve ("The currency principle"). Such a rule was preferable (for providing price-level stability) to allowing the note issue to be altered at the discretion of the directors of the Bank (the position taken by the opposing Banking School). For a discussion of the Currency Banking School debate, see Viner, *Studies*; Fetter, *Development*; and Schwartz, "Banking School."

personality and automaticity, we adopt the approach to rules in the recent literature on the time inconsistency of monetary and fiscal policy.[8] A rule then serves as a credible commitment mechanism binding policy actions over time.

In the simplest sense, government policy is said to be time inconsistent when a policy plan, calculated as optimal based on the government's objectives and expected to hold indefinitely into the future, is subsequently revised. Discretion, in this context, means setting policy sequentially. This could then lead to policies and outcomes that are very different from the optimal plan as market agents rationally incorporate government actions into their planning. For that reason, society would benefit from the government having access to a commitment mechanism to keep it from changing planned future policy.

According to this approach, adherence to the fixed price of gold served as a credible commitment mechanism to prevent governments from following the otherwise time-inconsistent policies of creating surprise fiduciary money issues in order to capture seigniorage revenue or defaulting on outstanding debt.[9] On this basis, adherence to the gold-standard rule before 1914 enabled many countries to avoid the problems of high inflation and stagflation that troubled the late twentieth century.

The simplest example of how a commitment mechanism operates is in a modern closed economy where monetary authorities attempt to maintain full employment and zero inflation. Assume the monetary authority has announced at the beginning of the year a rate of monetary growth consistent with zero inflation. Assume further that the public believes the announcement, and it is incorporated into wage bargaining and other contracts that are binding over the year. In this circumstance, the authorities, in the absence of precommitment, have an incentive to create a monetary surprise (follow an expansionary monetary policy), to reduce unemployment (stimulate the economy), or to capture seigniorage revenue. However, the public, with rational expectations, will incorporate the government's actions into their behavior and in the next year, when new contracts are formed, will demand higher wages and prices. This will in turn lead to higher inflation and a return to the original level of employment and economic activity. In addition, desired real cash balances will decline, reducing the tax base for seigniorage. A credible precommitment mechanism, such as a rule that prevents the authorities from altering monetary growth from its preannounced path,

---

[8] Kydland and Prescott, "Rules."
[9] Bordo and Kydland, "Gold Standard"; and Giovannini, "Bretton Woods."

by preventing the government from cheating, can preserve long-run price stability.[10]

A second example is in the use of fiscal policy. Governments use debt finance to smooth tax revenues over time. When faced with unusual government expenditures such as in wartime, it is more efficient to sell bonds than to impose higher taxes that can reduce work effort. The debt is issued on the assumption that taxes will be raised once the emergency is passed in order to service and reduce the debt. In this context, a time-inconsistent fiscal policy would be to impose a capital levy or to default on the debt, once the public has purchased it. Following such a policy would capture additional resources for the government in the *present* but in the event of a *future* emergency would make it very difficult for the government to sell its bonds at favorable prices. A credible commitment mechanism can force the government to honor its outstanding debt.

The pledge to fix the price of a country's currency in terms of gold was just such a rule or commitment mechanism to prevent governments from following the previously mentioned practices. The rule defined a gold coin as a fixed weight of gold called, for example, one dollar. The monetary authority was then committed to keep the mint price of gold fixed through the purchase and sale of gold in unlimited amounts. Under the bimetallic system based on gold and silver that prevailed in most countries until the third quarter of the nineteenth century, the monetary authorities would define the weight of both gold and silver coins. Maintaining the bimetallic ratio fixed is a variant of the basic convertibility rule, since it is the fixed value of the unit of account that is the essence of the rule.[11] The gold-standard rule in the century before World War I can be viewed as a contingent rule, or a rule with escape clauses.[12] The monetary authority maintains the standard – keeps the price of the currency in terms of gold fixed – except in the event of a well-understood emergency such as a major war. In wartime it may suspend gold convertibility and issue paper money to finance its expenditures, and it can sell debt issues in terms of the nominal value of its currency on the understanding that debt will eventually be paid off in gold. The rule is contingent in the sense that the public understands that the suspension will last only for the duration of the wartime emergency plus some

---

[10] Barro and Gordon, "Rules."

[11] As a rule in the traditional sense – as an automatic mechanism to ensure price stability – bimetallism may have had greater scope for automaticity than the gold standard because of the possibility of a switch from one metal to the other. See Friedman, "Bimetallism."

[12] Grossman and Van Huyck, "Sovereign Debt"; DeKock and Grilli, "Endogenous Exchange"; Flood and Isard, "Simple Rules"; and Bordo and Kydland, "Gold Standard."

period of adjustment and that afterwards the government will adopt the deflationary policies necessary to resume payments at the original parity.[13] Observing such a rule will allow the government to smooth its revenue from different sources of finance: taxation, borrowing, and seigniorage.[14]

Examples of discretion – breaches of the rule – include postponement of resumption after the war and reasonable delay period had passed and pegging to specie at a devalued parity. As a result, in the event of another war within memory of the previous one, the public would be less willing to absorb government debt, even if the situation were otherwise similar, and the government proposed a reasonable delay.

It is crucial that the rule be transparent and simple and that only a limited number of contingencies be included. Transparency and simplicity avoided the problems of moral hazard and incomplete information, which prevented the monetary authority from engaging in discretionary policy under the guise of following the contingent rule.[15] In this respect a second contingency – a temporary suspension in the face of a financial crisis, which in turn was not the result of the monetary authority's own actions – might also have been part of the rule. However, because of the greater difficulty of verifying the source of the contingency than in the case of war, invoking the escape clause under conditions of financial crisis (or in the case of a shock to the terms of trade, a third possible contingency) would be more likely to create suspicion that discretion was the order of the day.

The gold-standard contingent rule worked successfully for three core countries (in the traditional sense) of the classical gold standard: Britain, France, and the United States.[16] In all these countries the monetary

[13] This description is consistent with a result from a model of Lucas and Stokey, "Optimal Fiscal and Monetary Policy," in which financing of wars is an optimal contingency rule. In their example, where the occurrence and duration of the war are uncertain, the optimal plan for the debt is not to service it during the war. Under this policy, people realize when they purchase the debt that it will be defaulted on in the event the war continues longer than expected.

[14] See Lucas and Stokey, "Optimal Fiscal and Monetary Policy"; and Mankiw, "Optimal Collection." A case study comparing British and French finances during the Napoleonic Wars shows that Britain was able to finance its wartime expenditures by a combination of taxes, debt, and paper money issue to smooth revenue; whereas France relied primarily on taxation. France relied on a less efficient mix of finance than Britain because it had used up its credibility by defaulting on outstanding debt at the end of the American War of Independence and by hyperinflating during the French Revolution. Napoleon ultimately returned France to the bimetallic standard in 1803 as part of a policy to restore fiscal probity, but because of the previous loss of reputation France was unable to take advantage of the contingent aspect of the bimetallic standard rule. See Bordo and White, "British and French Finances."

[15] Canzoneri, "Monetary Policy Games"; and Obstfeld, "Destabilizing Effects."

[16] Bordo and Schwartz, "Operation."

authorities adhered faithfully to the fixed price of gold except during major wars. During the Napoleonic War and World War I for England, the Civil War for the United States, and the Franco–Prussian War for France, specie payments were suspended and paper money and debt were issued. But in each case, after the wartime emergency had passed, policies leading to resumption at the prewar parity were adopted.[17] Indeed, successful adherence to the pre–World War I rule may have enabled the belligerents to obtain access to debt finance more easily in subsequent wars. In the case of Germany, the fourth core country, no occasions arose for application of the contingent aspect of the rule before 1914. Otherwise, its record of adherence to gold convertibility was similar to that of the other three countries.

A number of other countries also followed the rule. These included the British Dominions of Canada and Australia; the Western European countries of Sweden, the Netherlands, and Switzerland; and Japan. In marked contrast to this group are the countries of Southern Europe and Latin America (see Table 9.1 for a chronology of adherence). For the Southern European countries, adherence to the gold standard was an important objective but, for most of them, difficult to achieve. Their experience of low money growth, of low fiscal deficits (with the principal exception of Italy), and of exchange rates that never drifted far from parity suggests that the rule was important. The Latin American countries suspended convertibility in wartime and also in the face of financial crises and terms-of-trade shocks. They usually returned to gold at a depreciated parity. Their experience was characterized by higher money growth rates, higher fiscal deficits, and higher inflation rates than the other countries. For them gold convertibility was the exception rather than the rule.[18]

The gold-standard rule originally evolved as a domestic commitment

---

[17] The behavior of asset prices (exchange rates and interest rates) during suspension periods suggests that market agents regarded the commitment to gold as credible. For the United States, see Roll, "Interest Rates"; and Calomiris, "Price," who present evidence of expected appreciation of the greenback during the American Civil War based on a negative interest differential between bonds that were paid in greenbacks and those paid in gold. Also, see Smith and Smith, "Wesley Mitchell," who demonstrate that movements in the premium on gold from the Resumption Act of 1875 until resumption was established in 1879 were driven by a credible belief that resumption would occur. For the case of Britain's return to gold in 1925, see Smith and Smith, "Stochastic Process Switching"; and Miller and Sutherland, "Britain's Return" and "Speculative Anticipations." An application of the literature on stochastic process switching suggests that the increasing likelihood that resumption would occur at the original parity gradually altered the path of the dollar-pound exchange rate towards the new ceiling, several months in advance of resumption.

[18] Bordo and Schwartz, "Operation."

mechanism, but its enduring fame is as an international rule. The classical gold standard emerged as a true international standard by 1880 following the switch by the majority of countries from bimetallism, silver monometallism, and paper to gold as the basis of their currencies.[19] As an international standard, the key rule was maintenance of gold convertibility at the established par. Maintenance of a fixed price of gold by its adherents in turn ensured fixed exchange rates. The fixed price of domestic currency in terms of gold provided a nominal anchor to the international monetary system.

Recent evidence suggests that, indeed, exchange rates throughout the 1880 to 1914 period exhibited a high degree of fixity in the principal countries. Although exchange rates frequently deviated from par, violations of the gold points were rare, as were devaluations.[20]

According to the game theoretic literature, for an international monetary arrangement to be effective, both between countries and within them, a time-consistent credible-commitment mechanism is required. In other words each member must adhere to a credible rule.[21] Adherence to the gold convertibility rule provided such a mechanism. Indeed, Giovannini finds the variation of both exchange rates and short-term interest rates within the limits set by the gold points in the period from 1899 to 1909 consistent with market agents' expectations of a credible commitment by the core countries to the gold-standard rule in the sense of this chapter.[22] In addition to the reputation of the domestic gold standard and constitutional provisions that ensured domestic commitment, adherence to the international gold-standard rule may have been enforced by other mechanisms.[23] These include the operation of the rules of the game, the hegemonic power of England, central-bank cooperation, and improved access to international capital markets, the subject of this article.

One of the enforcement mechanisms of the gold-standard rule for peripheral countries was presumably access to capital obtainable from the core countries.[24] To the extent that adherence to the gold standard

[19] Eichengreen, "Editor's Introduction."
[20] Officer, "Efficiency"; and Eichengreen, "Editor's Introduction."
[21] Canzoneri and Henderson, *Monetary Policy*.
[22] Giovannini, "Bretton Woods." Also see Officer, "Gold-Point Arbitrage." His calculations of speculative bands (bands within which uncovered interest arbitrage prevails consistent with gold-point arbitrage efficiency) for the interwar dollar-sterling exchange rate show serious violations only in 1931, at the very end of the gold-exchange standard.
[23] Bordo and Kydland, "Gold Standard."
[24] In addition to developing countries seeking long-term capital, countries also sought short-term loans, such as Japan, which financed the Russo–Japanese War of 1905 to 1906 with foreign loans seven years after adopting the gold standard. See Hayashi, "Japan's Saving Rate."

served as a signal of good behavior we would expect to see countries that always adhered to gold convertibility to pay lower interest rates on loans contracted in London and other metropolitan centers than others with less consistent performance.

Our approach suggests that adherence to gold would affect the volume of capital attracted as well as the terms. However, we have been unable to assemble enough high-quality data to tell us how much more capital flowed to good adherents because of their reputation for financial rectitude relative to others.[25] An extensive earlier literature on capital flows focused on the determinants of long-term capital flows.[26] Those scholars attempted to ascertain whether "pull factors" (higher expected rates of return) in the periphery or "push factors" (poor investment prospects and higher savings rates) in the core predominated. Our approach builds upon this earlier literature to the extent that we grant that the key determinants of capital flows are the traditional variables they utilized: the expected real rates of return in both countries, the levels of real activity, the terms of trade, and the phase of the business cycle. But in addition we posit that adherence to the gold-standard rule would have an incremental and significant impact.

9.2   The record of adherence to the gold standard

To assess evidence for the "Good Housekeeping seal of approval" we examine the behavior of long-term bond yields for nine peripheral countries in the classical gold-standard period from 1870 to 1914. Our choice of countries was dictated partly by availability of the data and to give us a diverse sample reflecting four groups of countries. The groups include countries that always adhered to gold (Canada and Australia); countries that followed the contingent rule and temporarily suspended payments but returned to gold at the original parity (the United States and Italy for part of the period); countries that, for the period with data available to us, did not adhere to gold but may have shadowed it (Portugal, Spain,

---

[25] Virtually all of the available data on long-term capital flows for the countries we consider (if it exists) is calculated as the difference between the current account and changes in international reserves. Little attempt is made to distinguish between invisible items, errors, and omissions or to adequately separate short-term from long-term capital movements. An alternative measure is capital calls on new issues in London; see Davis and Cull, *International Capital Markets*. Preliminary investigation for a subset of our sample of the connection between capital calls, on the one hand, and a number of fundamental determinants and gold standard adherence, on the other, however, did not yield meaningful results.

[26] Ford, *Gold Standard*; Bloomfield, *Patterns*; Abramovitz, "Monetary Side"; Davis and Cull, *International Capital Markets*; and Edelstein, *Overseas Investment*.

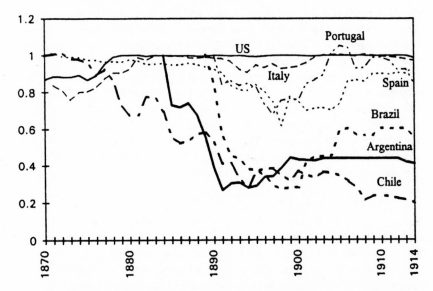

Figure 9.1. Normalized exchange rates for seven countries. *Note*: Australia and Canada are omitted because their currencies remained at par during the period. *Sources*: See the exchange rates (EXRT) for each country in the Appendix.

and Italy for part of the period); and countries that broke the gold-standard rule by intermittently suspending payments and devaluing their currencies (Argentina, Brazil, and Chile).

The chronology in Table 9.1 summarizes the adherence record until 1914 for each of the countries mentioned. In addition it shows the reasons for a change in monetary standard and an indication as to whether a country changed its parity when it returned to gold. A brief convertibility history of the nine countries follows. Also, Figure 9.1 shows each country's exchange rate in terms of sterling relative to gold parity at the beginning of the period (with the exception of Australia and Canada, which never depart from parity).

Canada adopted the gold standard in 1853. Although it experienced a sharp cyclical downturn in the years 1907 to 1908, Canada did not suspend convertibility until 1914.

Australia adopted the gold standard in 1852. Despite severe banking problems in the 1890s, Australia did not suspend convertibility until July 1915 during World War I.

The United States Coinage Act of 1792 defined a bimetallic standard at a mint ratio of 15 to 1. In 1834 and again in 1837 the mint ratio was altered, remaining unchanged thereafter at 16 to 1. This ratio overvalued gold at the mint so that by 1849 the United States was on a defacto gold standard. The Civil War led to suspension of specie payments from 1862 through 1878. Despite contentious political opposition to deflation that resumption enforced, resumption to gold was achieved at the prewar parity on January 1, 1879, in line with the declaration of the Resumption Act of 1875. Apart from the silver threat to gold convertibility in the mid 1890s stemming from Populist agitation, convertibility in the United States was never in doubt from 1879 to 1914. It was preserved even during two banking panics in 1893 and 1907 when banks restricted payments.

In 1862 Italy adopted the bimetallic standard, although in fact the standard was gold. In 1865 Italy joined the Latin Monetary Union. Fiscal improvidence and war against Austria in 1866, however, ended convertibility.[27] Fiscal and monetary discipline was achieved by 1874, and exchange-rate parity was restored. The government announced on March 1, 1883, that it would restore convertibility on April 12, 1884, but convertibility took place only in silver because silver was overvalued at the mint. Public finances then deteriorated, and unlawful bank issues indicated an absence of monetary discipline. By 1894 Italy was back on a paper standard. Inconvertibility lasted until 1913. After a period of laxity ending by 1903, the government embraced fiscal and monetary rectitude as if it were on a gold standard but did not formally resume (see Figure 9.1).[28]

Although Spain adopted a bimetallic regime in April 1848, with a ratio of 16 to 1, only after the currency reform of 1868 that established the peseta as the monetary unit was the regime fully operative. In 1868, following six reductions in the ratio, it was set at 15.5 to 1, as in the Latin Monetary Union (which Spain, however, did not join). With the fall in the market price of silver in the 1870s, the 15.5 to 1 ratio undervalued gold. Gold was driven out of circulation, and the gold reserves of the Bank of Spain declined. A declining trade balance and capital outflows from 1881 to 1883 led Spain to end convertibility to avoid deflation. Between 1888 and 1900 the peseta exchange rate depreciated, a budget deficit arose in every year but three from 1884 to 1899, money creation largely financed the war with Cuba in 1898 and 1899, and Spanish prices until 1905 fell much less than world prices. All of these factors proved hostile to resumption. After 1900 these factors mainly turned favorable

---

[27] Frantianni and Spinelli, "Italy."   [28] Tonniolo, *Economic History.*

to resumption, but it did not take place. Efforts by finance ministers to restore convertibility and adopt the gold standard before World War I foundered on the opposition of the Bank of Spain. Nevertheless, the behavior of the exchange rate and of both monetary and fiscal variables in this period suggest that Spain shadowed the gold parity rule (Figure 9.1).[29]

Portugal had been on a bimetallic standard since the 1680s with de facto gold predominance alternating with de facto silver predominance. The decision to shift to a gold standard in 1854 was made because gold circulation was ample.[30] The parity with the pound was unchanged from 1854 until 1891, a period during which there were no convertibility crises. Furthermore, the mint ratio the law established favored gold. All this came to a halt after an increase in the ratio of debt service payments to revenues, and government support of failing domestic enterprises clouded Portugal's reputation as a creditworthy nation. Suspension of convertibility in 1891 lasted until after World War I. However, from 1895 to 1914 Portugal pursued conservative fiscal and monetary policies as if it were shadowing the gold standard (see Figure 9.1).[31]

Gold convertibility in Argentina began in February 1867 after a failed attempt in 1863.[32] Convertibility was suspended in May 1876 after several years of political unrest and rising government deficits. Although the exchange rate reached parity by 1881, resumption that year failed. Convertibility was restored in 1883 but lasted only until January 1885, at a time of financial crisis in Europe and following a period of expansionary fiscal policy. Inconvertibility thereafter until 1899 was associated with a lax fiscal policy leading to debt default in 1890 in the infamous Baring crisis.[33] In 1899 convertibility was restored at the original parity of 5 gold pesos to the pound with the return to fiscal orthodoxy in 1896 and the establishment of a currency board. However, paper pesos that had been circulating since 1885 at a large discount relative to gold were frozen at 2.27 per gold peso, giving the effect of a substantial devaluation (see Figure 9.1). Argentina suspended convertibility in 1914 on the outbreak of war.

---

[29] Acena, "Spain."   [30] Reis, "Gold Standard."
[31] Macedo, "Convertibility."
[32] Cortés Condé, *Dinero*.
[33] Full service on the Argentine external national debt was postponed for three years by a moratorium arranged by a consortium of London creditor banks. Marichal, *Century*, p. 160. The provincial bonds were in default until 1898. We thank Gerardo Della Paolera for pointing this out.

From 1808 onwards Brazil was on a bimetallic standard at the colonial ratio of 16 to 1. From then until 1846, when it was altered to favor gold, the ratio was changed three times. Gold convertibility was suspended in November 1857 in the wake of a banking crisis and resumed in 1858. It was subsequently abandoned on several succeeding occasions, notably during the war with Paraguay.[34] Suspension lasted for slightly more than a year in 1888 and 1889, A republican revolution in November 1889 coincided with the ending of convertibility.[35] In 1906 Brazil restored convertibility to prevent continued appreciation of the milreis exchange rate that was harmful to coffee and rubber exporters. In addition it created a Conversion Office with a limit set to its issue of convertible notes at a newly established parity. Convertibility ended at the outbreak of World War I.

Chile was on a bimetallic standard from 1818 to 1851; it then made a technical change in the mint ratio but maintained the bimetallic standard until 1866. Although it resumed in 1870, by the end of 1874 with the fall in the price of silver, it was on a de facto silver standard. After bank runs in 1878 the authorities made bank notes inconvertible.[36] For the next 17 years, Chile remained on a paper standard. The War of the Pacific (1879 to 1883) was financed by government note issues. The first attempt to return to a metallic standard was made in 1887, but it failed. An eight-month civil war from January to August 1891 resulted in further monetary expansion and exchange-rate depreciation. A second conversion law in November 1892 was strictly implemented, and the exchange rate appreciated, but again the government responded to political discontent by issuing notes. The exchange rate thereupon depreciated. A new conversion law of February 11, 1895, set June 1 as the day for redemption of government notes, devalued the gold content of the peso, and authorized loans and sales of nitrate fields to accumulate a gold reserve. Following rumors of war with Argentina and a run on the banks in July 1898, the legislature ended convertibility and, to deal with the panic, bank notes were declared government obligations.

Thus our survey suggests a wide variance in adherence to the gold standard rule by peripheral countries. If the "Good Housekeeping seal of approval" hypothesis has validity we would expect, other things equal, that the country-risk premium on long-term bond yields would be lowest for Canada and Australia, followed by the United States and Italy, then

---

[34] Pelaez and Suzigan, *Historia.*
[35] Fritsch and Franco, "Aspects."
[36] Llona-Rodriguez, "Chile."

by Spain and Portugal, and then by Argentina, Brazil, and Chile. The next section considers the evidence.

9.3   Data, models, and econometric methodology

9.3.1   Data

Our data consist of annual interest rate observations (typically government bond rates) and related variables, including exchange rates, real income, fiscal deficits, and the money supply for nine countries during the classical gold-standard era.[37] The nine countries, as noted above, were chosen with one eye on the availability of the data and the other on the variety of experiences with the gold standard. The sample is divided into four groups of countries. The first group includes two countries that were always on gold, Australia and Canada. The second group includes the United States and Italy, two countries that observed the gold-standard contingent rule in the sense that they abandoned convertibility in the face of an emergency such as a war but returned to the original parity afterwards. However, unlike the U.S. experience, Italy, after its second suspension in 1894, did not restore convertibility at the original parity, but its exchange rate shadowed it (see Figure 9.1). The countries also differed on the reasons for departure (see Table 9.1). For the United States it was a wartime emergency; for Italy it was lax fiscal policy. The third group consists of Spain and Portugal, which in the period before our data begin adhered to convertibility but during our sample period did not do so. However, the performance of their exchange rates (see Figure 9.1), and their inflation, money growth rates, and fiscal deficits suggest that their policies shadowed gold.[38] The final group includes Argentina, Brazil, and Chile, which intermittently adhered to gold convertibility but at altered parities. The Appendix gives full descriptions of the data and sources.

The interest rates are plotted in Figures 9.2 through 9.7. The panels in each figure show the rate of return on representative long-term bonds for a particular country (or, to save space, two comparable countries)

---

[37] All the series used except for the United States were yields on national or federal government debt. For the United States we used a long-term corporate bond rate. Here we follow Friedman and Schwartz, *Monetary Trends*, p. 120, who prefer this series because some U.S. long-term governments bore the circulation privilege and because none were outstanding in some years.

[38] Bordo and Schwartz, "Operation."

Table 9.1. *A chronology of adherence to the gold standard for nine countries: circa, 1870–1914*

Country	Period	Standard	Reason for change	Change in parity?
Canada	1853–1914	Gold	War	No
Australia	1852–1915	Gold	War	No
United States	1792–1861	Bimetallic (de facto gold after 1834)		No
	1862–1878	Paper (greenbacks)	War	
	1879–1917[a]	Gold	War	No
Italy	1862–1866	Bimetallic	Lax fiscal policy, war	No
	1866–1884	Paper		
	1884–1894	Gold	Lax fiscal policy	Yes
	1894–1914	Paper		
Spain	1868–1883	Silver	Crisis	Yes
	1883–1914	Paper		
Portugal	1854–1891	Gold	Crisis	Yes
	1891–1914	Paper		
Argentina	1867–1876	Gold		No
	1876–1883[b]	Paper	Lax fiscal policy	
	1883–1885	Gold		Yes
	1885–1899	Paper	Lax fiscal policy	
	1899–1914	Gold	War	Yes
Brazil	1857–1888	Paper		
	1888–1889	Gold		Yes
	1889–1906	Paper	Revolution	
	1906–1914	Gold	War	Yes
Chile	1870–1878	Bimetallic	Crisis	Yes
	1878–1895[c]	Paper		
	1895–1898	Gold	War threat	Yes
	1898–1925	Paper		

[a] Gold Embargo 1917–1919, Standard not suspended.
[b] Failed attempt to restore convertibility in 1881.
[c] Failed attempt to restore convertibility in 1887.
Source: Bordo and Schwartz, "Operation."

and, for comparison, the return on British consols. The periods when a country was on the gold standard are indicated by boxes within the figures.

Interest rates for Canada and Australia, the only countries that stayed on the gold standard throughout the period from 1870 to 1914, were generally quite close to the consol rate, especially after 1900, when a

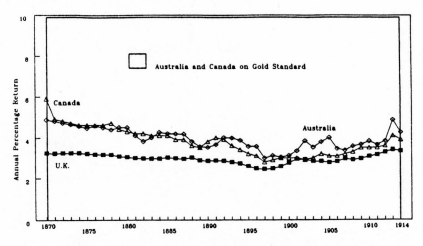

Figure 9.2. Long-term rates for Australia and Canada. *Sources*: See LTIR.UK, LTIR.AUS, and LTIR.CAN in the Appendix.

general convergence of foreign rates with the consol rate took place (Figure 9.2).[39]

Of the two interest rates for the United States over the period 1870 to 1914, the higher rate from 1870 to 1878 is for gold bonds (bonds that promised interest and principal in gold before the United States returned to gold), and the lower rate is for bonds that promised interest and principal in paper, the famous greenbacks (Figure 9.3).[40] At first glance it may seem strange that the gold rate is above the paper rate during a time of flexible exchange rates. The explanation is that gold was the depreciating currency. At the end of the Civil War the price of gold dollars in terms of greenback dollars was well above one, but this price was expected to fall, as it in fact did, until resumption of convertibility in 1879 at the rate of one greenback dollar per one gold dollar. The gold interest

[39] One possible explanation for the similarity between the U.K. consol rate and the Australian and Canadian rates, in addition to our maintained hypothesis, is that after 1893 Dominion government securities were endowed with the status of "trustee investments" by the British government. This could be construed as a strong signal of their quality. See Havinden and Meredith, *Colonialism*, pp. 88–90. We thank Shizuyu Nishimura for bringing this to our attention.

[40] The attempt to estimate gold rates and paper rates for the United States has a long history, going back at least to Fisher, *Theory of Interest*, pp. 401–3. Here we use recent estimates by Calomiris, "Historical Perspectives," pp. 137–43, although we also tried the estimates computed by Macaulay, *Movements*, Table 19, pp. 217–18, in our regressions to see if it made a difference.

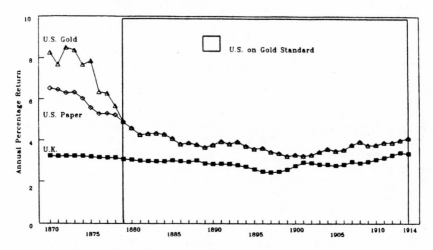

Figure 9.3. Long-term rates for the United States. *Sources*: See LTIR.UK, LTIR.US, and LR.USGC in the Appendix.

rate, in other words, had to be higher before redemption to compensate for the expected future loss on the conversion of gold into greenbacks. As can clearly be seen in Figure 9.3 both the gold and paper rates lay well above the U.K. consol rate before resumption and converged quite markedly thereafter.

Two rates for Italy, a gold rate and a paper rate, were somewhat higher than the rates for Australia, Canada, and the United States (Figure 9.4).[41] Also note that there is no decisive downward movement during the brief period in which Italy was officially on the gold standard. If anything, there is an upward trend during this interval.

Paper rates for Spain (beginning in 1883) and Portugal (beginning in 1891), after both countries had abandoned convertibility, appear to have been declining (Figure 9.5). The Spanish rate, in particular, closes in on the consol rate after 1900 in much the same way as the Australian, Canadian, Italian, and U.S. rates.

The gold rate for Argentina (beginning in 1885) peaks with the 1890 Baring crisis. Brazil's rate begins in 1892. Both rates fell after 1900 as both countries returned to the gold standard (Figure 9.6). But it is difficult to determine whether it was the result of adherence to gold or of some other factor that produced the general convergence of rates after 1900.

---

[41] The gold rate for Italy is the rate for long-term government bonds quoted in Paris. The rates for other countries in our sample were quoted in London.

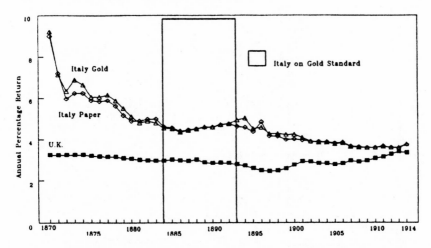

Figure 9.4. Long-term rates for Italy. *Sources*: See LTIR.UK, LTIR.IT, and LTIR.ITG in the Appendix.

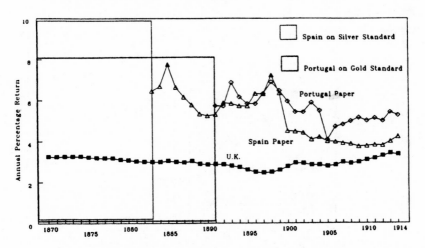

Figure 9.5. Long-term rates for Portugal and Spain. *Sources*: See LTIR.UK, LTIR.POR, and LTIR.SP in the Appendix.

For Chile, (Figure 9.7), the relationship between the London rate payable in gold and a domestic rate payable in paper differs from the U.S. case. The paper rate is well above the gold rate, confirming our intuition that paper rates are higher because of the risk of a fall in the gold value of the currency. More telling is that the gold rate, although

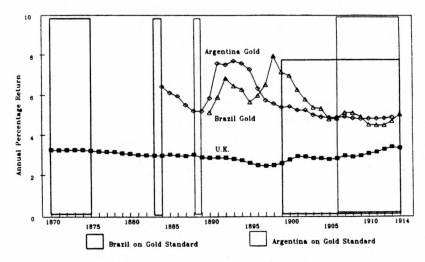

Figure 9.6. Long-term rates for Argentina and Brazil. *Sources*: See LTIR.UK, LTIR.ARG, and LTIR.BRZ in the Appendix.

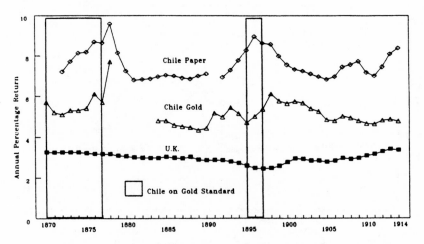

Figure 9.7. Long-term rates for Chile. *Sources*: See LTIR.UK and LTIR.CH in the Appendix.

lower than the paper rate, is substantially higher than are the Australian, Canadian, U.S., and Italian gold rates. Simply promising to pay in gold was not enough to achieve the lowest international rates; country risk mattered even for gold bonds.

One phenomenon apparent in all the figures is convergence after 1900 of the long-term yields with the U.K. consol yield. One explanation is growing confidence in the safety of international investments (a decline in the market price of risk), produced in part by the general acceptance of the gold standard.[42] But there may also have been other factors at work such as factor-price equalization reflecting the high degree of mobility of capital as well as labor during the "golden age" before 1914.[43] Thus, a preliminary inspection of the long-term yields suggests that long-term commitment to the gold standard mattered, even when bonds were denominated in gold. Countries that remained on gold throughout the Classical era were charged lower rates than countries that had a mixed record of adherence. The evidence on the effect of short-term attachments to or departures from the gold standard, however, is less clear.

9.3.2 The model

To explore these issues further we estimated regressions of the following form:

$$R_{it} - R_{\text{UK}t} = a_i + b_{i1}(\overline{R}_t - R_{\text{UK}t}) + b_{i2}dum_{it} + b_{i3}M_{i,t-1}$$
$$+ b_{i4}D_{i,t-1} + \varepsilon_{it} \tag{9.1}$$

$$\varepsilon_{it} = \rho_i\varepsilon_{it-1} + \mu_{it}, \qquad i = 1, 2, \ldots 9$$

where R_{it} equals the interest rate of country i in year t; $R_{\text{UK}t}$ equals the interest rate of the United Kingdom in year t; $\overline{R}_t$ equals the average of all rates in the sample at time t; dum_{it} equals a dummy variable that takes the value 1 if country i is on the gold standard in year t; $M_{i,t-1}$ equals the rate of growth of money less the rate of growth of real GNP in country i between $t-2$ and $t-1$ (Monetary Policy); and $D_{i,t-1}$ equals the level of government expenditures less taxes divided by nominal GNP in country i in year $t-1$ (Fiscal Policy).[44]

We use the average spread $(\overline{R}_t - R_{\text{UK}t})$ as our benchmark because our preliminary inspection of the data suggested that some sort of benchmark was needed to account for marketwide rate fluctuations. One possible rationale for this benchmark is the Capital Assets Pricing Model

---

[42] Friedman and Schwartz, *Monetary Trends*, pp. 515–16, concluded that the decline in the difference between short-term interest rates in the United States and the United Kingdom after 1896 was the result of the resolution of concerns about the free-silver movement in the United States.

[43] O'Rourke and Williamson, "Were Hechsher and Ohlin Right?"

[44] Durbin-Watson tests on OLS regressions for eq. (9.1) always show significant positive autocorrelation in error terms. We assume that the error terms follow an AR(1) process.

(CAPM).[45] On this analogy, $\overline{R}_t$ is a proxy for the return on the efficient market portfolio (although, obviously, it is far removed from the variable prescribed by the theory) and R_{UK_t} is a proxy for the risk-free rate (perhaps not a bad proxy given the reputation of British consols). Thus, b_{i1} can be viewed as an analogue of beta, the measure of systematic risk in CAPM. Below we report results for an unweighted average $\overline{R}_t$ and for an average weighted by a country's share of debt in the total issued by the sample countries and held by Britain in 1914.[46] We also experimented with a GNP weighted average, but the results were unsatisfactory because the average was completely dominated by the United States.

To test directly whether adherence to gold influences rates paid we include a dummy variable that takes the value one when a country is on the gold standard and zero when it is off. An on–off dummy is the simplest way to estimate the effects of adherence to gold, but it may miss subtler, long-run effects. For a country on the gold standard, but subject to political and economic upheaval, long-term interest rates might not be unusually low. For a country off the gold standard because of a war but expected shortly to resume, long-term interest rates might not be unusually high. In both cases a country's beta (b_{i1}) may yield as much or more information as the gold dummy because the beta reflects, we conjecture, long-term commitment.

The model also includes monetary and fiscal policy variables to test whether investors looked beyond adherence to gold to fundamentals that would determine the probability that a country would be unable to pay its debts or could do so only in a depreciated currency. Rapid growth of the stock of money relative to output, we presumed, would raise the probability of a devaluation and raise interest rates (although alternatively, in the short run, it would lower interest rates via the liquidity effect). A large government deficit relative to national income, we conjectured, would raise interest. (Alternatively, a country charged a low

---

[45] The CAPM was first developed in classic papers by Sharpe, "Capital Asset Prices"; and Lintner, "Valuation." Since then an enormous literature has grown up describing limitations, variants, and alternatives. Brennan, "Capital Asset Pricing Model," is an accessible recent survey.

[46] The weights in percentages were Canada 22.8, Australia 18.5, the United States 33.5, Italy 0.6, Spain 0.8, Portugal 0.4, Argentina 14.2, Brazil 6.6, and Chile 2.7; Feis, *Europe*, p. 23. Feis's estimates have been subject to considerable criticism. It is not clear, however, that there are superior alternatives for our purposes. Moreover, although London was the principal capital market during the era of the classical gold standard, Paris was not far behind. In our sample the three Southern European countries borrowed more in Paris than in London so the weights we use understate their role as borrowers in the world capital market.

interest rate might be encouraged to borrow more, creating a negative correlation.)[47]

9.3.2   Econometrics methods

We first estimated separate regressions for each bond in our sample using only the data for the country that issued the bond. These results are reported below. However, there are two problems with estimating separate equations for each country. First, the gold dummy cannot be included for those countries that were always on gold (Australia and Canada) or that were always off during our sample period (Portugal and Spain). With no change in the country's status, the effects of being on or off gold cannot be separated from the constant term in eq. (9.1). Second, innovations in interest rates may be correlated across countries. Although estimates of eq. (9.1) are consistent, even when each country is treated separately, a seemingly unrelated-regressions (SUR) model that pools data for a number of countries increases the efficiency of our procedure.

We use a restricted SUR model that allows for autocorrelation and unequal numbers of observations. Our assumptions for the innovations are as follows:

$$\varepsilon_{it} = \rho_i \varepsilon_{it-1} + \mu_{it}, \mu_{it} \sim \left(0, \sigma_i^2\right), \qquad \text{for } i = 1, 2, \ldots 9 \qquad (9.2)$$

$$E\left(\mu_{it}, \mu_{jt^*}\right) = \sigma_{ij}, \qquad \text{if } t = t^*$$

$$E\left(\mu_{it}, \mu_{jt^*}\right) = 0, \qquad \text{if } t \neq t^*$$

That is, innovations in country i's interest rate are first-order autocorrelated, and the innovations in the interest rates of country i and j are also correlated, provided there is an observation for both countries in that year.

We applied the SUR model separately to a sample including only gold bonds (seven countries) and only paper bonds (five countries) because we expected them to react differently to a country's commitment to gold. We checked this division of the sample by applying the SUR model to two pooled samples that combined gold and paper bonds. One included one rate from each country, choosing the gold rate when it was available (seven gold rates and two paper rates); the other was a

---

[47] The level of national debt, a variable we did not have, might have been a better measure of the creditworthiness of a country. But the interest payments on a burdensome debt should be reflected eventually in the fiscal deficit.

paper-weighted sample that included four gold rates and five paper rates. The results for these pooled regressions were similar to those reported below.

The coefficients on the gold dummy are restricted to be the same across countries. This allows information for those countries that are always on or off gold to be used. The coefficients on the fundamentals are also restricted to be the same across countries.

We used the following procedure to estimate the model. We ran ordinary least squares (OLS) regressions for the nine countries. The original data were transformed using the Cochrane-Orcutt method.[48] We ran OLS regressions on the transformed data and used the residuals to estimate the contemporaneous covariance, σ_{ij}. The transformed data were then used in an SUR model to produce final estimates of the coefficients of eq. (9.1). We created an R^2 that is analogous to the one used with OLS regressions, but the statistical properties of our analogue are unknown.

9.4   The results

Tables 9.2 and 9.3 show individual country regressions with the sample divided into gold bonds and paper bonds.[49] For each country we show two regressions: a pure CAPM regression and a CAPM-plus-policy-variables regression. In most cases the improvement in the equations from adding the policy variables was marginal at best.

The results for the gold dummy for the gold bonds (Table 9.2) offer some support for our story. The coefficient is negative for four of the five countries and statistically significant in the case of Chile and the case of Italy when the CAPM-plus-policy-variables model is used. The gold dummy is marginally significant in the case of the United States. These bonds, we should note, were payable in gold even when the ordinary currency of the country was not convertible into gold at a fixed rate. The higher price of gold bonds when the domestic currency was convertible presumably reflected the lower probability of some kind of national bankruptcy.

A stronger confirmation is provided by the beta coefficients. Almost all of the betas are highly statistically significant, except for one regression each in the cases of Brazil and Chile. The betas are substantially less than one for Canada and Australia, two countries that demonstrated

---

[48] The first observations were dropped because alternative procedures became extremely complicated.

[49] We include Australia and Canada with the countries issuing gold bonds because their currencies were convertible throughout the period.

Table 9.2. *Individual country regressions dependent variables: yields on gold bonds*

Country	Intercept	Beta	On gold?	Monetary policy	Fiscal policy	AR(1)	Adj R^2	DW	N
Canada	−0.17	0.63***	—	—	—	0.79***	0.91	1.08	44
	(0.91)	(4.84)				(11.0)			
	−0.03	0.57***	—	−0.19	0.46	0.93***	0.94	1.62	42
	(0.12)	(5.02)		(−1.07)	(0.29)	(14.9)			
Australia	0.21	0.53***	—	—	—	0.53***	0.60	1.89	44
	(1.05)	(3.99)				(3.82)			
	−0.58	0.72***	—	−0.40	3.83	0.70***	0.56	1.95	42
	(1.22)	(3.70)		(1.08)	(1.53)	(5.41)			
United States	0.047	1.00***	−0.42	—	—	0.90***	0.96	2.24	44
	(0.08)	(4.01)	(1.46)			(17.2)			
	0.34	0.72**	−0.41	−0.48	2.20	0.83***	0.96	2.62	42
	(0.71)	(3.10)	(1.60)	(0.95)	(0.18)	(18.6)			
Italy	0.12	1.04***	−0.17	—	—	0.61***	0.91	1.27	44
	(0.40)	(4.56)	(0.92)			(6.99)			
	−0.51	0.39*	−0.34**	0.37	−0.74	0.97***	0.94	1.77	42
	(0.16)	(1.90)	(2.04)	(0.91)	(0.37)	(20.5)			
Argentina	0.13	2.06***	0.004	—	—	0.81***	0.91	1.81	29
	(0.23)	(5.04)	(0.02)			(5.47)			
	−0.29	2.57***	−0.19	−0.53	0.50	0.47***	0.90	1.63	27
	(0.43)	(5.86)	(0.62)	(0.80)	(0.10)	(1.96)			
Brazil	0.87	1.67**	−0.11	—	—	0.82***	0.80	1.45	24
	(0.74)	(2.17)	(0.19)			(5.97)			
	1.19	1.41	−0.08	0.18	−3.21	0.86***	0.79	1.20	24
	(0.88)	(1.63)	(0.13)	(0.39)	(0.96)	(6.15)			
Chile	2.35	0.44	−0.99***	—	—	0.93***	0.38	2.05	38
	(38.3)	(1.22)	(4.67)			(7.54)			
	1.40***	0.89**	−0.89***	0.04	1.59	0.76***	0.30	2.00	36
	(10.3)	(2.28)	(3.62)	(0.11)	(0.68)	(5.35)			

* means significant at the 10 percent level.
** means significant at the 5 percent level.
*** means significant at the 1 percent level.
Notes: The coefficients in each row were estimated from the data for the country named on the left by ordinary least squares with an adjustment for first order autocorrelation. The "On gold?" dummy was omitted for countries that were at par throughout the period. The Monetary and Fiscal variables were excluded in the top regression for each country. Absolute values of *t*-statistics are in parentheses.

considerable commitment to gold. For the United States, also a strong gold adherent, the beta equaled one in the simple CAPM regression and was less than one in the augmented regression. At the other extreme, two countries with poor records of adherence, Argentina and Brazil, had very high betas as expected. In the case of Italy, which for a few years followed the gold standard contingent rule and for a longer period shadowed gold, the beta in the simple regression was close to that of the United States. However, when the policy variables were added the beta was somewhat lower than we would have expected. This was also the

Table 9.3. *Individual country regressions dependent variables: yields on paper bonds*

Country	Intercept	Beta	On gold?	Monetary policy	Fiscal policy	AR(1)	Adj R^2	DW	N
United	0.35	0.42***	−0.11	—	—	0.91***	0.97	1.77	44
States	(1.08)	(3.50)	(0.78)			(25.2)			
	0.26	0.49***	−0.07	−0.45*	−11.3*	0.88***	0.97	1.78	42
	(1.02)	(4.16)	(0.53)	(1.83)	(1.87)	(21.2)			
Italy	0.41	0.75***	−0.09	—	—	0.64***	0.89	1.38	44
	(1.29)	(3.16)	(0.51)			(8.15)			
	−0.30	0.36*	−0.27	0.14	0.23	0.97***	0.92	2.18	42
	(0.10)	(1.75)	(1.58)	(0.34)	(0.11)	(17.8)			
Spain	0.32	1.22***	—	—	—	0.86***	0.83	1.79	31
	(0.31)	(2.12)				(9.09)			
	0.16	0.49	—	−0.04	19.3	0.84***	0.72	1.61	11
	(0.25)	(0.88)		(0.04)	(1.51)	(5.53)			
Portugal	0.56	1.81***	—	—	—	0.60***	0.68	1.95	23
	(0.74)	(2.87)				(3.44)			
	−0.33	2.30***	—	1.30	24.2	0.53***	0.69	1.75	22
	(0.35)	(3.43)		(0.66)	(0.81)	(3.10)			
Chile	3.59***	0.79**	0.23	—	—	0.62***	0.11	1.29	42
	(20.0)	(2.33)	(0.84)			(5.43)			
	3.62***	0.78**	0.29	0.23	−1.31	0.58***	0.09	1.27	42
	(18.5)	(2.26)	(1.02)	(0.52)	(0.51)	(4.84)			

* means significant at the 10 percent level.
** means significant at the 5 percent level.
*** means significant at the 1 percent level.
Notes: The coefficients in each row were estimated from the data for the country named on the left by ordinary least squares with an adjustment for first-order autocorrelation. The "On gold?" dummy was omitted for countries that were at par throughout the period. The Monetary and Fiscal variables were excluded in the top regression for each country. Absolute values of *t*-statistics are in parentheses.

case for Chile, although these equations were the least well estimated in the gold sample.[50]

For the paper bonds (Table 9.3) none of the coefficients on the gold dummy are statistically significant at conventional levels. Again, however, the betas confirm the importance of long-term commitment. In this subsample the U.S. beta is well below one, a result consistent with its relatively high commitment. Italy, Spain, and Portugal, which shadowed gold, in general had higher betas, although the results were not uniform across specifications and countries. In the case of Chile, as with the gold bonds, the beta was somewhat lower than expected.

In general the OLS results are consistent with the "Good Housekeeping" hypothesis, although there are some anomalies. Part of the problem

[50] This may reflect missing observations in a number of crisis periods.

may be the inefficiency of the OLS approach, and there is some evidence for this in the insignificant coefficients and low R^2 in some of the regressions. The pooled, seemingly unrelated, regressions presented in Tables 9.4 and 9.5, we believe, address these issues.

Turning to the results for the unweighted gold-bond sample, the gold dummy is negative and highly significant in both regressions. Moreover, the betas line up for the most part as expected. And most supportive of our hypothesis is that the betas for the three countries with poor adherence records were considerably higher than the others. The results for the sample in which the average rate was weighted by the shares in British overseas investment were quite similar to the regressions that use unweighted averages. The main exceptions are that the monetary policy variable is significant and the U.S. beta is somewhat higher than expected. The latter result may reflect the heavy weight of the United States in the weighted average.

Table 9.5 shows the pooled, seemingly unrelated, regressions for the paper-bond sample. The gold dummy is insignificant in the regressions that use the unweighted average interest rate and significant in the regressions that use an average interest rate weighted by the shares of British overseas investment. However, the coefficients are half the size of those in the gold-bond sample.

One explanation is that the paper sample includes more temporary departures and returns to the gold standard that the market ignored, whereas the gold sample includes more cases of long-term commitment. It is also possible that paper and gold bonds appealed to different classes of investors and that the more risk-averse investors who insisted on gold bonds were more sensitive to whether a country was currently adhering to gold. Alternatively, the explanation may be that borrowers could effectively price discriminate between domestic and foreign lenders.[51]

As in the case of the gold-bond sample the betas in both unweighted cases lined up as expected. The only anomaly is Spain in the British-overseas-investment weighted-policy-variables regression where the beta is unusually low and insignificant.[52]

In sum the pooled results provide strong support for the "Good Housekeeping seal." In both the pooled-gold and pooled-paper samples we find a similar correspondence between gold standard adherence

---

[51] Calomiris, "Motives," shows that the United States tailored its debt in the nineteenth century on the assumption that the long-term bond market was more sensitive to default risk.

[52] This may reflect the small number of observations for Spain.

Table 9.4. *Pooled regressions dependent variables: yields on gold bonds*

:	Average interest differential unweighted		Average interest differential: weighted by share in British overseas investment	
	(1)	(2)	(3)	(4)
Intercept	0.15	0.30**	0.41***	0.37***
	(1.30)	(2.24)	(4.44)	(4.01)
Canada	0.47***	0.37***	0.53***	0.62***
	(5.67)	(4.41)	(5.65)	(6.03)
Australia	0.54***	0.49***	0.73***	0.66***
	(6.96)	(5.66)	(7.19)	(7.15)
United States	0.42***	0.49***	0.90***	0.80***
	(2.79)	(5.10)	(4.61)	(5.76)
Italy	0.72***	0.50***	0.79***	0.60**
	(8.07)	(4.08)	(5.89)	(2.62)
Argentina	1.49***	1.42***	1.99***	1.95***
	(14.2)	(11.1)	(14.2)	(13.0)
Brazil	1.49***	1.43***	2.06***	2.06***
	(13.0)	(13.6)	(7.58)	(8.34)
Chile	1.26***	1.22***	1.16***	1.43***
	(9.05)	(8.34)	(3.08)	(4.45)
On gold?	−0.34***	−0.38***	−0.41***	−0.41***
	(4.15)	(4.70)	(5.51)	(6.02)
Monetary policy	—	−0.08	—	−0.22***
		(0.74)		(3.10)
Fiscal policy	—	−0.17	—	0.88*
Simulated R^2	0.57	0.24		(1.72)
		(0.63)	0.70	0.66
DW	1.87	1.98	1.81	1.87
N	267	255	267	255

*means significant at the 10 percent level.
**means significant at the 5 percent level.
***means significant at the 1 percent level.

Notes: The coefficients in each column were estimated from the pooled sample of gold bonds by seemingly unrelated regression with adjustments for autocorrelation and the unequal number of observations for each country. The coefficient for each country is its "beta," the relationship between its interest rate differential with London and an average differential. Absolute values of *t*-statistics are in parentheses.

Table 9.5. *Pooled regressions dependent variables: yields on paper bonds*

	Average interest differential: unweighted		Average interest differential: weighted by share in British overseas investment	
	(1)	(2)	(3)	(4)
Intercept	0.09	0.28**	0.78***	0.88***
	(0.68)	(2.02)	(3.80)	(4.48)
United States	0.39***	0.36***	0.44***	0.31**
	(5.21)	(5.54)	(3.39)	(2.36)
Italy	0.64***	0.42***	0.45***	0.38**
	(7.57)	(3.24)	(2.88)	(2.12)
Spain	1.35***	0.55***	1.17***	0.18
	(5.44)	(4.40)	(2.87)	(0.85)
Portugal	1.41***	1.38***	1.66***	1.64***
	(16.7)	(15.6)	(6.73)	(6.36)
Chile	2.10***	2.13***	2.34***	2.50***
	(10.6)	(14.4)	(7.40)	(9.24)
On gold?	0.06	−0.01	−0.24**	−0.18**
	(0.71)	(0.16)	(2.27)	(2.05)
Monetary policy	—	−0.19	—	−0.08
		(1.31)	(0.49)	
Fiscal policy	—	−0.42	—	−0.78
		(0.38)	(0.62)	
Simulated R^2	0.74	0.81	0.66	0.76
DW	1.61	1.44	1.60	1.54
N	184	159	184	159

*means significant at the 10 percent level.
**means significant at the 5 percent level.
***means significant at the 1 percent level.
Notes: The coefficients in each column were estimated from the pooled sample of paper bonds by seemingly unrelated regression with adjustments for autocorrelation and the unequal number of observations for each country. The coefficient for each country is its "beta," the relationship between its interest rate differential with London and an average differential. Absolute values of *t*-statistics are in parentheses.

(including shadowing) and low country risk as measured by the betas. In addition, the gold-adherence dummy that may capture the impact of adherence not accounted for by the betas was negative and significant as predicted. Indeed, if we were to single out one number to represent our findings with respect to the significance of the gold-adherence dummy it would be 40 basis points, approximately the coefficient of the gold dummy in the British-overseas-investment weighted regression (or in the current parlance the "haircut" charged for not being on gold). In other words, all other things equal, the rate on a gold bond would be 40 basis points lower if the country were on the gold standard. Other factors, perhaps related to regional preferences, undoubtedly also played a role in determining the country-risk premia. But our analysis suggests that a willingness to commit to the discipline of the gold standard was an important determinant of the risk premia established in the London capital market.

9.4.1   The bottom line

Was it worthwhile for a country to adopt the gold standard to gain the seal of good (financial) housekeeping? Figures 9.8 and 9.9 illustrate the benefits. On the left in each figure, for comparison, is the average British consol rate over the years 1870 to 1914, our proxy for the risk-free rate. Next to it are predicted rates for each country measured in percentage. The countries are ranked from left to right in descending order according to their adherence to gold. Figure 9.8 shows the gold bonds, which were especially important because they were a major vehicle for the transmission of capital from the core to the periphery, and Figure 9.9 shows the paper bonds. In each case we computed the predicted rate from the betas and gold dummy that we estimated and the average price of risk (the average return for the sample less the average consol rate) for the entire period. In this way we were able to compare countries even when the underlying interest series were not available for the same periods.

It is clear from Figure 9.8 that the benefits of committing to gold were significant in economic as well as statistical terms. Where commitment was high, rates were low; where commitment was low, rates were high. Over the whole period the risk-free rate averaged about 3 percent. Canada, Australia, and the United States, countries with strong commitments, paid about one percentage point more. Italy, which had a decidedly worse formal adherence record, paid only a fraction more. Presumably the markets attached nearly as much weight to close shadowing the gold standard as actual adherence. Argentina, Brazil, and Chile, which adhered intermittently at altered parities, paid two to three percentage points more.[53] Figure 9.9 for the paper bonds tells a similar story. In this sample the United States and Italy paid a little more than

---

[53] Although Chile had a worse gold standard–adherence record than Argentina and its exchange rate depreciated more, the fact that Argentina defaulted on its gold debt in 1890 while Chile did not may explain why its projected interest rate was more than 100 basis points lower.

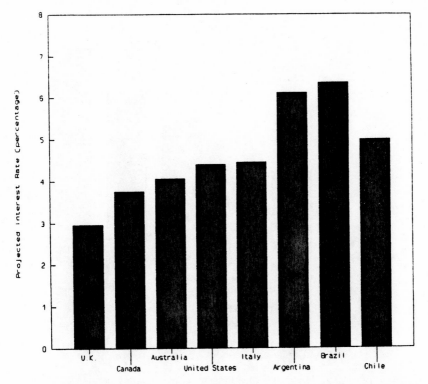

Figure 9.8. The value of adhering to gold: gold bonds, 1870–1914. *Note*: Data were computed by using the coefficients of regression 3 in Table 9.4.

one percentage point above the U.K. rate (125 and 140 basis points respectively). The Chilean rate, on the other hand, was more than four percentage points higher. The Spanish and Portuguese rates lie between these extremes.

Both figures underscore the point that the difference in rates was substantial for countries that were attempting to raise large amounts of capital on international markets. Or to put it somewhat differently, the numbers make it easy to see why there were strong economic pressures on countries that were off the gold standard to resume and strong pressures on countries that were on the gold standard to stay on.

9.5 Conclusions

Our principal findings are that the interest rates charged on long-term bonds in core capital markets during the era of the classical gold standard

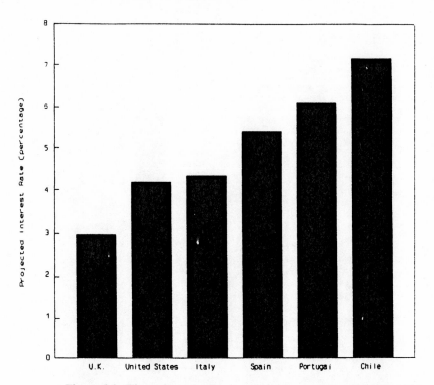

Figure 9.9. The value of adhering to gold: paper bonds, 1870–1914.
Note: Data were computed by using the coefficients of regression 3 in
Table 9.5.

differed substantially from country to country and that these differences
were correlated with a country's long-term commitment to the gold
standard. Countries that adhered faithfully to the standard were charged
rates only slightly above the British consol rate; countries that made only
sporadic attempts to maintain convertibility and that altered their parities were charged much higher rates. Countries that did not formally
adhere but that followed policies that shadowed gold fell in between. We
interpret these findings to mean that adhering to gold was like the "Good
Housekeeping seal of approval."

It should be emphasized that adherence to the gold standard rule,
although a simple and transparent test, implied a far more complex
set of institutions and economic policies. Indeed, those countries that
adhered to the gold standard rule generally had lower fiscal deficits,
more stable money growth, and lower inflation rates than those that did

not.[54] But those countries that adhered to gold also paid a price for doing so because they gave up the flexibility to react to adverse supply shocks by following expansionary financial policies and altering the exchange rate. Those countries that did not adhere to the rule in fact faced greater supply shocks than those that did.[55] In responding to those shocks, and thereby sacrificing the rule, this group of countries, through the substantial risk premia they had to pay, may have reduced their long-run growth prospects. However, countries may have abandoned the rule not in response to adverse supply shocks but in response to other (possible political economy) factors. Whether in particular cases sacrificing the rule was worth it or not is an empirical question and a subject for future research.

Although the world today is very different from the world before 1914, the same issues are at stake. Many emerging countries have tried to re-create the "Good Housekeeping seals" by pegging their currency to a stronger one or by establishing currency boards. However, whether a "Good Housekeeping seal" as transparent and durable as the gold standard can be recreated today is an open question.

Appendix: Data description

In this study we use annual data for nine countries: Argentina, Australia, Brazil, Canada, Italy, Portugal, Spain, the United Kingdom, and the United States. Our goal was to include data for each country for the entire era of the classical gold standard, 1870 to 1914, but in a number of cases we were able to find data for only part of the period. The series are arranged by country. In each case we give our variable name, the definition of the variable, and a parenthetical reference. In some cases we include notes that describe special features of the series.

Cross-country studies of this sort are inevitably a community effort. In a number of cases variables were supplied to us by scholars from their personal files, for which we are very grateful. These series may not be available in published sources. Users of this data set should consult these scholars directly for permission to use their data.

Argentina

CCAL.ARG($m): Total Capital Calls of Argentina, 1865–1914. *Sources*: Figures provided by Lance Davis, California Institute of Technology and Robert Gallman, University of North Carolina, Chapel Hill.

---

[54] Bordo and Schwartz, "Operation."
[55] Bordo and Jonung, "Monetary Regimes"; Bordo and Schwartz, "Operation."

FB.ARG($M): Foreign Borrowing of Argentina, 1884–1900. *Source*: Ford, *Gold Standard*, Table 14, p. 139.

CUK.ARG($M): U.K. Issues for Argentina, 1881–1914. *Source*: Ford, *Gold Standard*, Table 25, p. 195.

LNCI.ARG($M): Net Capital Inflow of Argentina, 1884–1914. *Source*: Ford, *Gold Standard*, derived from Table 25, p. 195.

DFT.ARG: GDP Deflator of Argentina, 1884–1914. 1913 = 1. *Source*: Paolera, "How the Argentine Economy Performed During the International Gold Standard: A Re Examination," Phd Thesis, University of Chicago, 1988," Table 37, p. 186.

EXRT.ARG(Arg/$): Exchange Rate of Argentina (5 gold pesos = 1 pound), 1884–1914. *Source*: Paolera, "How the Argentine Economy Performed," Table 37, p. 186.

GDP.ARG: (millions of paper pesos) Nominal GDP of Argentina, 1884–1914. *Source*: Paolera, "How the Argentine Economy Performed," Table 37, p. 186.

RGDP.ARG (millions of paper pesos): Real GDP of Argentina, 1884–1914. *Source*: Paolera, "How the Argentine Economy Performed," Table 37, p. 186.

G.ARG (millions of paper pesos): Government Expenditure of Argentina, 1883–1914. *Source*: Paolera, "How the Argentine Economy Performed," Table 36, p. 183.

T.ARG (millions of paper pesos): Government Revenue of Argentina, 1883–1914. *Source*: Paolera, "How the Argentine Economy Performed," Table 36, p. 183.

LTIR.ARG: Argentina Average Annual Yield on External Bond, 1884–1913. *Source*: Paolera, "How the Argentine Economy Performed," Table 33, p. 178.

M.ARG (millions of paper pesos): Argentina Money Supply, 1883–1913. *Source*: Paolera, "How the Argentine Economy Performed," Table 37, p. 186.

POP.ARG (millions): Argentina Population. *Source*: Mitchell, *International Historical Statistics: The Americas*.

TOT.ARG: Argentina Terms of Trade, 1884–1913. 1913 = 100. *Source*: Paolera, "How the Argentine Economy Performed," Table 37, p. 186.

Australia

CCAL.AUS(U.S. $m): Total Capital Calls of Australia in millions of U.S. dollars, 1865–1914. *Source*: Figures provided by Lance Davis, California Institute of Technology and Robert Gallman, University of North Carolina, Chapel Hill.

LNCI.AUS($M): Net Apparent Capital Inflow of Australia. *Source*: Pope, "Australia's Payments," Appendix 2, pp. 231–32.

CPI.AUS: Consumer Price Index of Australia, 1913 = 100. *Source*: Pope, "Australia's Payments," Appendix 2, pp. 231–32.

DFT.AUS: GDP Deflator of Australia. 1913 = 1. *Source*: Pope, "Australia's Payments," Appendix 2, pp. 231–32.

EXRT.AUS($A/U.S. $): Exchange Rates of Australia. *Source*: Pope, "Australia's Payments," Appendix 2, pp. 231–32.

G.AUS($m): Government Expenditures of Australia. (1870–1971 as 1870). *Source*: Pope, "Australia's Payments," Appendix 2, pp. 231–32.

GDP.AUS($m): Nominal GDP of Australia, 1861–1900. *Source*: Pope, "Australia's Payments," Appendix 2, pp. 231–32. The original was in £m; we converted to $m. Figures after 1900 are from Butlin, "Our 200 Years," pp. 229–30.

RGDP.AUS($m): Real GDP of Australia. RGDP.AUS = GDP.AUS/(GDP Deflator).

LTIR.AUS: Long-term Interest Rates of Australia. Government bonds. *Source*: Vamplew, *Australians*, p. 2.

STIR.AUS Short-term Interest Rates of Australia. Savings bank deposit rates. *Source*: Vamplew, *Australians*, p. 2. PF1, p. 240.

M2.AUS($m): Australian Money Stock. M2. M2.AUS = M1.AUS + public's saving banks deposits, where M1.AUS is currency held by the public + trading banks current deposits. *Source*: Vamplew, *Australians*, p. 247, PF 57–63, column 61 (original in calendar years), and p. 248, PF 64–71, column 69 (converted to calendar years).

POP.AUS (millions): Population of Australia. *Source*: Mitchell, *International Historical Statistics: The Americas.*

T.AUS($m): Government Revenue of Australia. *Source*: Pope, "Australia's Payments," Appendix 2, pp. 231–32.

TOT.AUS: Australian Terms of Trade. TOT.AUS = (Export price index)/(Import price index). *Source*: Pope, "Australia's Payments," Appendix 2, pp. 231–32. The base year is 1913. The 1914 figure was obtained by averaging the 1913 estimate (1.163) and the 1914 to 1915 estimate (1.210).

Brazil

DFT.BRZ: GDP Deflator of Brazil, 1880–1914. *Source*: Bordo and Jonung, "Monetary Regimes," Data Appendix.

EXRT.BRZ (cruzeiros/$): Exchange Rate of Brazil, 1889–1914. *Source*: Bordo and Jonung, "Monetary Regimes," Data Appendix.

GDP.BRZ (millions of cruzeiros): Nominal GDP of Brazil, 1880–1914. *Source*: Bordo and Jonung, "Monetary Regimes," Data Appendix.

RGDP.BRZ (millions of cruzeiros): Real GDP of Brazil. The base year is 1913. *Source*: Bordo and Jonung, "Monetary Regimes," Data Appendix.

G.BRZ (millions of cruzeiros): Government Expenditure of Brazil, 1880–1914. *Source*: Bordo and Jonung, "Monetary Regimes," Data Appendix.

T.BRZ (millions of cruzeiros): Government Tax Revenue of Brazil, 1880–1914. *Source*: Bordo and Jonung, "Monetary Regimes," Data Appendix.

LTIR.BRZ: Long-Term Interest Rates of Brazil, 1890–1914. *Source*: Figures provided by Eliana A. Cardoso, World Bank, and Rudiger Dornbusch, Massachusetts Institute of Technology; and *Commercial and Financial Chronicle*. A graph of the price of the bonds is presented in Cardoso and Dornbusch, "Brazilian Debt Crises." We use the current yield: the coupon divided by the price of the bond. We also calculated yields to maturity because there were deep discounts on Brazilian bonds, the case in which current yields and yields to maturity will differ the most. But the yield to maturity produced almost identical results in the regressions. In our results we report only regressions on current yields to maintain comparability with the other series.

M.BRZ (millions of cruzeiros): Money Supply of Brazil, 1880–1914. *Source*: Bordo and Jonung, "Monetary Regimes," Data Appendix.

POP.BRZ: Population of Brazil, 1880–1914. *Source*: Bordo and Jonung, "Monetary Regimes," Data Appendix.

TOT.BRZ: Terms of Trade of Brazil, 1870–1914. *Estatisticas historicas do Brasil*, p. 597.

Canada

CCAL.CAN(U.S. $million): Total capital Calls of Canada, 1865–1914. *Source*: Figures provided by Lance Davis, California Institute of Technology and Robert Gallman, University of North Carolina, Chapel Hill.

LNCI.CAN: Long-Term Net Capital Inflow, 1871–1913. *Source*: Dick and Floyd, *Canada*, Table B1, pp. 190–91.

CPI.CAN: Consumer Price Index of Canada, 1870–1914. 1913 = 100. *Source*: Maddison, *Dynamic Forces*, Table E2, pp. 296–97.

DFT.CAN: Price Deflator of Canada. 1913 = 1. *Source*: Urquhart, "New Estimates," pp. 30–31.

EXRT.CAN: Exchange Rate of Canada, 1870–1914. *Source*: Bordo and Jonung, "Monetary Regimes," Data Appendix.

G.CAN (in millions of $): Government Expenditure of Canada, 1870–1914. *Source*: Mitchell, *International Historical Statistics: The Americas*, pp. 654–56.

T.CAN (in millions of $): Government Revenue of Canada, 1870–1914. *Source*: Mitchell, *International Historical Statistics: The Americas*.

LTIR.CAN: Long-term Interest Rates of Canada. *Source*: Bordo and Jonung, *Long-Run Behavior*, p. 160; and Neufeld, *Financial System*, Table 15.

M.CAN: Money Supply of Canada. (M2). *Source*: Bordo and Jonung, *Long-Run Behavior*, p. 160.

GNP.CAN($mm): Nominal GNP of Canada, 1870–1914. *Source*: Urquhart, "New Estimates of GNP," pp. 31–31.

RGNP.CAN($mm): Real GNP of Canada, 1870–1914. *Source*: Urquhart, "New Estimates of GNP," pp. 30–31.

TOT.CAN: Terms of Trade of Canada. 1913 = 1. *Source*: Social Science Federation of Canada, *Historical Statistics*, pp. 299–300.

POP.CAN (millions): Canada Population, 1870–1914. *Source*: Mitchell, *International Historical Statistics: The Americas*.

Chile

DFT.CH: GDP Deflator of Chile. Derived from GDP.CH and RGDP.CH.

EXRT.CH (peso/$): Exchange Rate of Chile, 1880–1914. *Source*: Bordo and Jonung, "Monetary Regimes," Data Appendix.

RGDP.CH (millions of paper pesos): Real GDP of Chile, 1870–1914. The base year is 1913. *Source*: Llona-Rodriguez, "Chilean Monetary Policy." RGDP in 1913 gold pesos (Table 8, p. 37), was converted to 1913 pesos using the exchange rate in Table 65 (p. 285).

GDP.CH (millions of paper pesos): Nominal GDP of Chile, 1870–1914. *Source*: Llona-Rodriguez, Chilean Monetary Policy." Nominal GDP is constructed from RGDP in 1913 gold peso and Conversion Factor II in Table 64 (pp. 284–85).

G.CH (millions of paper pesos): Government Expenditures of Chile, 1870–1914. *Source*: Llona-Rodriguez, "Chilean Monetary Policy," Table 8, p. 37. The original is in 1913 gold pesos. Conversion Factor II (Table 64, p. 284) was used to convert to current pesos.

T.CH (millions of paper pesos): Tax Revenue of Chile, 1870–1914. See G.CH.

LTIR.CH: Long-Term Interest Rate of Chile, 1870–1914. We have two long-term rates for Chile: 4.5 percent external Sterling bonds and 7 percent internal peso bonds. *Source*: Mamalakis, *Historical Statistics*, Table 8.2, p. 365; Table 8.5, p. 387.

M.CH (millions of paper pesos): Money Supply of Chile, M1, 1870–1914. *Source*: Mamalakis, *Historical Statistics*, p. 36.

POP.CH (millions): Population of Chile, 1870–1914. *Source*: Mitchell, *International Historical Statistics: The Americas*, pp. 62–63.

Italy

CPI.IT: Consumer Price Index of Italy, 1870–1914. 1913 = 100. *Source*: Fratianni and Spinelli, "Italy."

DFT.IT: GNP Deflator of Italy, 1870–1914. 1913 = 1. *Source*: Fratianni and Spinelli, "Italy."

EXRT.IT (lire/$): Exchange Rate of Italy, 1880–1914. *Source*: Fratianni and Spinelli, "Italy."

GNP.IT (millions of lires): Nominal GNP of Italy, 1870–1914. Derived from RGNP.IT and DFT.IT.

RGNP.IT (millions of lires): Real GNP of Italy, 1870–1914. 1913 = 1. *Source*: Fratianni and Spinelli, "Italy."

G.IT (millions of lires): Government Expenditure of Italy, 1870–1914. *Source*: Mitchell, *International Historical Statistics: Europe*, p. 797.

T.IT (millions of lires): Government Tax Revenue of Italy, 1870–1914. *Source*: Mitchell, *International Historical Statistics: Europe*, p. 812.

LTIR.IT: Long-Term Interest Rates of Italy (long-term government bond rates), 1870–1914. *Source*: Figures provided by Franco Spinelli, Universita Degli Studi Brescia.

LTIR.ITG: Yields of Long-Term Government Bonds sold in Paris, net of taxes. *Source*: Figures provided by Franco Spinelli, Universita Degli Studi Brescia, from ISTAT, *Annuario Statistica Italiano*. The coupon was 4 lire net of taxes until 1906 when a conversion lowered the coupon to 3.75 lire. Payments made abroad by the Italian Treasury were made in gold.

M.IT (millions of lires): Money Supply of Italy, M1, 1870–1914. *Source*: Fratianni and Spinelli, "Italy."

POP.IT (million): Population of Italy, 1870–1914. *Source*: Spinelli, "Demand."

TOT.IT: Terms of Trade of Italy, 1870–1914. 1913 = 1. *Source*: Spinelli and Fratianni, *Storia Monetaria*, pp. 69–70.

Portugal

DFT.POR: GDP Deflator of Portugal, 1880–1914. *Source*: Bordo and Schwartz, "Operation," Data Appendix.

EXRT.POR (escudo/$): Exchange Rate of Portugal, 1890–1914. *Source*: Bordo and Schwartz, "Operation," Data Appendix.

GDP.POR (millions of escudos): Nominal GDP of Portugal, 1880–1914. *Source*: Bordo and Schwartz, "Operation," Data Appendix.

RGDP.POR: Real GDP of Portugal, 1880–1914. *Source*: Bordo and Schwartz, "Operation," Data Appendix.

G.POR: Government Expenditure of Portugal, 1890–1914. *Source*: Figures provided by Fernando Teixeria dos Santos, Porto University; and Bordo and Santos, "Portugal," Data Appendix.

T.POR: Tax Revenue of Portugal, 1890–1914. *Source*: Figures provided by Fernando Teixeria dos Santos; and Bordo and Santos, "Portugal," Data Appendix.

LTIR.POR: Long-Term Interest Rates of Portugal, 1891–1914. *Source*: Figures provided by Fernando Teixeria dos Santos; and Bordo and Santos, "Portugal," Data Appendix.

M.POR (millions of escudos): Money Supply of Portugal, M1, 1890–1911. *Source*: Bordo and Schwartz, "Operation," Data Appendix.

POP.POR: Population of Portugal, 1880–1914. *Source*: Bordo and Schwartz, "Operation," Data Appendix.

TOT.POR: Terms of Trade of Portugal, 1870–1914. 1913 = 1. *Source*: Lains, "Economia Portuguesa."

Spain

CPI.SP: Consumer Price Index of Spain, 1870–1914.

DFT.SP: GDP Deflator of Spain, 1901–1914. *Source*: Bordo and Schwartz, "Operation," Data Appendix; and *Estadisticas historicas de Espana*.

EXRT.SP (peseta/$): Exchange Rate of Spain, 1870–1914. *Source*: Bordo and Schwartz, "Operation," Data Appendix; and *Estadisticas historicas de Espana*.

GDP.SP (millions of pesetas): Nominal GDP of Spain, 1901–1914. GDP.SP (millions of pesetas) = RGDP.SP × DFT.SP.

RGDP.SP (millions of pesetas): Real GDP of Spain, 1901–1914. *Estadisticas historicas de Espana*, p. 554.

G.SP (millions of pesetas): Government Expenditure of Spain, 1870–1914. *Source*: Mitchell, *International Historical Statistics: Europe*, p. 798.

T.SP (millions of pesetas): Tax Revenue of Spain, 1870–1914. *Source*: Mitchell, *International Historical Statistics: The Americas*, p. 814.

LTIR.SP: Long-Term Interest Rates of Spain, 1883–1914. *Source*: Martin-Acena, "Spain," p. 163.

M.SP (millions of pesetas): Money Supply of Spain, M1, 1874–1914. *Source*: *Estadisticas historicas de Espana*, pp. 385–86.

POP.SP (million): Population of Spain, 1870–1914. *Source*: *Estadisticas historicas de Espana*, p. 70.

TOT.SP: Terms of Trade of Spain, 1870–1914. *Source*: *Estadisticas historicas de Espana*, p. 352.

United Kingdom

CPI.U.K.: Consumer Price Index of U.K., 1870–1914. 1913 = 100. *Source*: Capie and Webber, *Monetary History*, p. 535.

DFT.U.K.: GNP Deflator of U.K. 1913 = 1. *Source*: Capie and Webber, *Monetary History*, p. 535.

EXRT.U.K. (pound/$): Exchange Rate of the U.K., 1870–1914. Friedman and Schwartz, *Monetary Trends*, Table 4.9, pp. 130–31.

GNP.U.K. (£m): Nominal GNP of U.K. *Source*: Capie and Webber, *Monetary History*, p. 535.

RGNP.U.K. (£m): Real GNP of U.K. RGNP.U.K. = GNP.U.K./DFT.U.K.

G.U.K. (millions): Government Expenditures of the U.K., 1870–1914. *Source*: Mitchell, *International Historical Statistics: Europe*, pp. 798–99.

T.U.K. (millions): Revenue of the U.K. government, 1870–1914. *Source*: Mitchell, *International Historical Statistics: Europe*, pp. 815–16.

M.U.K. (£m): Money Stock of the U.K. *Source*: Friedman and Schwartz, *Monetary Trends*, Table 4.9, pp. 130–31. M.U.K. is "the sum of gross deposits at London and country joint stock and private banks (later London clearing banks and other domestic deposit banks), and at Scottish and Irish banks, less interbank and transit items, plus private deposits at Bank of England and currency held by public" (Friedman and Schwartz, *Monetary Trends*, p. 134).

LTIR.U.K.: The U.K. Long-term Interest Rates. (Yields on Consols). *Sources*: Bordo and Jonung, *Long-Run Behavior* and *Annual Abstract*.

STIR.U.K.: The U.K. Short-term Interest Rates. (Rates on Three-month Bills). *Sources*: Bordo and Jonung, *Long-Run Behavior*, p. 162; and *Annual Abstract*.

POP.U.K. (millions): The U.K. Population. *Source*: Mitchell, *International Historical Statistics: Europe*.

TOT.U.K.: Terms of Trade of the U.K., 1870–1913. 1913 = 1. *Source*: Mitchell, *Abstract*.

United States

CCAL.U.S. ($million): Total Capital Calls of the United States, 1865–1914. *Sources*: Figures provided by Lance Davis, California Institute of Technology and Robert Gallman, University of North Carolina, Chapel Hill.

CCAL.USH ($million): Capital Net Inflow Derived from the Balance of Payments. U.S. Bureau of Census, *Historical Statistics*, pp. 564–65.

CCAL.USW ($million): Long-Term Capital Imports of the United States. *Source*: Williamson, *American Growth*, Table 36, p. 151.

CPI.US: Consumer Price Index of the United States, 1870–1914. 1913 = 100. *Source*: U.S. Bureau of the Census, *Historical Statistics*, pp. 210–11.

DFT.US: Implicit Price Deflator. 1913 = 1. *Source*: Friedman and Schwartz, *Monetary Trends*, Table 4.8, pp. 122–23.

EXRT.US (pound/$): Exchange Rate in the United States. *Source*: Friedman and Schwartz, *Monetary Trends*, Table 4.9, pp. 130–31.

GNP.U.S. ($million): Nominal Income of the United States. *Source*: Friedman and Schwartz, *Monetary Trends*, Table 4.9, pp. 130–31.

RGNP.US ($million): Real Income of the United States. *Source*: Friedman and Schwartz, *Monetary Trends*, Table 4.9, pp. 130–31.

G.US (millions): Government Expenditures of the United States, 1870–1914. *Source*: Mitchell, *International Historical Statistics: Americas*, pp. 654–56.

T.US (millions): Revenue of the U.S. Government, 1870–1914. *Source*: Mitchell, *International Historical Statistics: Americas*, pp. 671–74.

M.US ($million): Money Stock of United States. *Source*: Friedman and Schwartz, *Monetary Trends*, Table 4.8, pp. 122–23. M.US is the sum of currency held by the public plus adjusted deposits at all commercial banks: M2.

LTIR.US: Long-term Interest Rates of the United States, 1870–1914 (Yields on High-Grade Corporate Bonds). *Source*: Friedman and Schwartz, *Monetary Trends*, Table 4.8, pp. 122–23. Unfortunately, there do not appear to be enough long-term federal government bond quotes to construct a long-term government yield series. Partly this was because most government bonds were held by banks as security for bank notes. The rate we use is the usual substitute.

LR.USGC: Long-term Interest Rate of the United States, Gold Rate Computed by Charles Calomiris. *Source*: Calomiris, "Historical Perspectives."

LR.USGM: Long-Term Interest Rate of the United States, Gold Rate Computed by Frederick Macaulay. *Source*: Macaulay, *Movements*, Table 19, pp. 217–18.

STIR.US: The Short-term Interest Rates of the United States. (Commercial Paper Rate). *Source*: Friedman and Schwartz, *Monetary Trends*, Table 4.8, pp. 122–23.

POP.US (millions): The U.S. Population. *Source*: Mitchell, *International Historical Statistics: The Americas*.

TOT.US: Terms of Trade of the United States. 1913 = 1. *Source*: Williamson, *American Growth*, Table B4, pp. 261–62.

References

Abramovitz, Moses. "The Monetary Side of Long Swings in U.S. Economic Growth." Stanford University Center for Research on Economic Growth. Memorandum No. 146, Mimeo 1973.

Acena, Pablo Martin. "Spain During the Classical Gold Standard Years, 1880–1914." In *Monetary Regimes in Transition*, edited by Michael D. Bordo and Forrest Capie, 135–72. Cambridge: Cambridge University Press, 1993.

Annual Abstract of Statistics. Central Statistics Office, London.

Barro, Robert J. and David B. Gordon. "Rules, Discretion, and Reputation in a Model of Monetary Policy." *Journal of Monetary Economics* 12 (1983): 101–21.

Bordo, Michael D. "The Bretton Woods International Monetary System: An Historical Overview." In *A Retrospective on the Bretton Woods System: Lessons for Monetary Reform*, edited by Michael D. Bordo and Barry Eichengreen, 3–98. Chicago: University of Chicago Press, 1993.

Bordo, Michael D. and Lars Jonung. *The Long-Run Behavior of the Velocity of Circulation: The International Evidence*. Cambridge: Cambridge University Press, 1987.

"Monetary Regimes, Inflation, and Monetary Reform: An Essay in Honor of Axel Leijonhufvud." In *Inflation, Institutions, and Information: Essays in Honor of Axel Leijonhufvud*, edited by D. F. Vaz and K. Vellapillai. London: Macmillan Press, 1996.

Bordo, Michael D. and Anna J. Schwartz. "The Operation of the Specie Standard: Evidence for Core and Peripheral Countries, 1880–1990." In *Historical Perspectives on the Gold Standard: Portugal and the World*, edited by Barry Eichengreen and Jorge Braga de Macedo. London: Routledge, 1996.

Bordo, Michael D. and Fernando Santos. "Portugal and the Bretton Woods International System." In *The History of International Monetary Arrangements*, edited by Jaime Reis, 181–208. London: Macmillan, 1995.

Bordo, Michael D. and Eugene N. White. "British and French Finances During the Napoleonic Wars." In *Monetary Regimes in Transition*, edited by Michael D. Bordo and Forrest Capie, 241–73. Cambridge: Cambridge University Press, 1993.

Bloomfield, Arthur. *Patterns of Fluctuations in International Investment before 1914*. Princeton Studies in International Finance, No. 21. Princeton: Princeton University Press, 1968.

Brennan, M. J. "Capital Asset Pricing Model." In *The New Palgrave Dictionary of Money & Finance*, edited by Peter Newman, Murray Milgate, and John Eatwell, s.v., 287–91. London: The Macmillan Press, Ltd., 1992.

Butlin, Noel G. *Australian Domestic Product, Investment and Foreign Borrowing, 1860–1938/39*. Cambridge: Cambridge University Press, 1962.

"Our 200 Years: Australian Wealth and Progress Since 1788, A Statistical Picture." In *Commemorative Bicentenary Diary*. Brisbane, Australia: Sunshine Diaries, 1987.

Calomiris, Charles W. "Historical Perspectives on The Tax-based Theory of Money." Ph.D. diss., Stanford University, 1985.

"Price and Exchange Rate Determination During the Greenback Suspension." *Oxford Economic Papers* 40, no. 4 (1988): 719–50.

"The Motives of U.S. Debt-Management Policy, 1790–1880: Efficient Discrimination and Time Consistency." *Research in Economic History* 13 (1991): 67–105.

Canzoneri, Matthew. "Monetary Policy Games and the Role of Private Information." *American Economic Review* 75 (1985): 1056–70.

Canzoneri, Matthew B. and Dale W. Henderson. *Monetary Policy in Interdependent Economies*. Cambridge, MA: MIT Press, 1991.

Capie, Forrest and A. Webber. *A Monetary History of the UK 1870–1982*. London: George Allan & Unwin, 1985.

Cardoso, Eliana A. and Rudiger Dornbusch. "Brazilian Debt Crises: Past and Present." In *The International Debt Crisis in Historical Perspective*, edited by Barry Eichengreen and Peter H. Lindert, pp. 106–39. Cambridge: MIT Press, 1989.

Commercial and Financial Chronicle. various dates.

Cortés Condé, Roberto. *Dinero, deuda y crisis: Evolución fiscal y monetaria en la Argentina*. Buenos Aires: Editorial Sudamericana, Instituto Torcuato Di Tella, 1989.

Davis, Lance and Robert Cull. *International Capital Markets and American Economic Growth*. Cambridge: Cambridge University Press, 1994.

DeKock, Gabriel and Vittorio Grilli. "Endogenous Exchange Rate Regime Switches." NBER Working Paper No. 3066, Cambridge, MA, 1989.

Della Paolera, Gerardo. "How the Argentine Economy Performed during the International Gold Standard: A Reexamination." Ph.D. diss., University of Chicago, 1988.

De Mattia, Renato. *Storia del capitale della Banc d'Italia e degli istitute predecessori.* Rome: Banca d'Italia, 1977.

Dick, Trevor J. O. and John E. Floyd. *Canada and the Gold Standard.* New York: Cambridge University Press, 1992.

Edelstein, Michael. *Overseas Investment in the Age of High Imperialism: The United Kingdom, 1850–1914.* New York: Columbia University Press, 1982.

Eichengreen, Barry. *Golden Fetters: The Gold Standard and the Great Depression, 1919–1939.* Oxford: Oxford University Press, 1992.

Eichengreen, Barry and Peter H. Lindert, eds. *The International Debt Crisis in Historical Perspective.* Cambridge, MA: MIT Press, 1989.

Eichengreen, Barry. "Editor's Introduction." In *The Gold Standard in Theory and History*, edited by Barry Eichengreen, 1–35. London: Methuen, 1985.

Estatisticas historicas do Brasil: Series economicas, demograficas e sociais de 1550 a 1988. Rio de Janeiro: Brasilia. 1990.

Estadisticas historicas de Espana, Siglos xix–xx Madrid: Fundacion Banco Exterior 1989.

Feis, Herbert. *Europe: The World's Banker, 1870–1914: An Account of European Foreign Investment and the Connection of World Finance with Diplomacy before the War.* New York: Council on Foreign Relations. Reprinted by Augustus M. Kelley, 1974.

Fetter, F. *Development of British Monetary Orthodoxy, 1797–1875.* Cambridge: Harvard University Press, 1965.

Fisher, Irving. *The Theory of Interest: As Determined by Impatience to Spend Income and Opportunity to Invest It.* New York: The Macmillan Company, 1930.

Flood, Robert P. and Peter Isard. "Simple Rules, Discretion and Monetary Policy." NBER Working Paper No. 2934, Cambridge, MA, 1989.

Ford, A. G. *The Gold Standard 1880–1914: Britain and Argentina.* Oxford: Clarendon Press, 1962.

Frankel, Jeffrey A. *On Exchange Rates.* Cambridge, MA: Cambridge University Press, 1993.

Frankel, Jeffrey A. and Chudozie Okongwu. "Liberalized Portfolio Capital Inflows in Emerging Markets: Sterilization, Expectations, and the Incompleteness of Interest Rate Convergence. NBER Working Paper No. 5156, Cambridge, MA, 1995

Fratianni, M. and F. Spinelli. "Italy in the Gold Standard Period, 1861–1914." In *A Retrospective on the Classical Gold Standard, 1921–1931*, edited by Michael D. Bordo and Anna J. Schwartz, 405–41. Chicago: University of Chicago Press, 1984.

Friedman, Milton. "Bimetallism Revisited." *Journal of Economic Perspectives* 4, no. 4 (1990): 85–104.

Friedman, Milton and Anna J. Schwartz. *Monetary Trends in the United States and the United Kingdom: Their Relation to Income, Prices, and Interest*

Rates, 1867–1975. Chicago: University of Chicago Press for the NBER, 1982.

Fritsch, Winston and Gustavo H. B. Franco. "Aspects of the Brazilian Experience Under the Gold Standard." PUC Rio de Janeiro. Mimeo, 1992.

Gallarotti, Giulio M. *The Anatomy of an International Monetary Regime: The Classical Gold Standard 1880–1914.* New York: Oxford University Press, 1995.

Giovannini, Alberto. "Bretton Woods and Its Precursors: Rules Versus Discretion in the History of International Monetary Regimes." In *A Retrospective on the Bretton Woods System,* edited by Michael D. Bordo and Barry Eichengreen, 109–47. Chicago: University of Chicago Press, 1993.

Grilli, Vittorio. "Managing Exchange Rate Crises: Evidence from the 1890s." *Journal of International Money and Finance* 9 (1990): 258–75.

Grossman, Herschel J. and John B. Van Huyck. "Sovereign Debt as a Contingent Claim: Excusable Default, Repudiation, and Reputation." *American Economic Review* 78 (1988): 1088–97.

Havinden, Michael and David Meredith. *Colonialism and Development: Britain and Its Tropical Colonies, 1850–1960.* London: Routledge, 1993.

Hayashi, Fumio. "Japan's Saving Rate: New Data and Reflections." NBER Working Paper No. 3205, Cambridge, MA, 1989.

ISTAT Annuario Statistica Italiano, Rome. various years.

Kydland, Finn E. and Edward Precott. "Rules Rather than Discretion: The Inconsistency of Optimal Plans." *Journal of Political Economy* 85 (1977): 473–91.

Lains, Pedro. "A economia Portuguesa no seculo XIX: Crescimento economico ecomercio externo, 1850–1913." Unpublished Manuscript, 1995.

Lintner, J. "The Valuation of Risk Assets and the Selection of Risky Investments in Stock Portfolios and Capital Budgets." *Review of Economics and Statistics* 47 (1965): 13–37.

Llona-Augustin. "Chilean Monetary Policy: 1860–1925." Ph.D. Diss., Boston University, 1990.

Llona-Rodriguez, Augustine. "Chile During the Gold Standard: A Successful Paper Money Experience." Mimeo. Instituto Torcuato Di Tella, 1993.

Lucas, Robert E. Jr. and Nancy L. Stokey. "Optimal Fiscal and Monetary Policy in an Economy Without Capital." *Journal of Monetary Economics* 1 (1983): 55–93.

Macedo, Jorge Braga de. "Convertibility and Stability 1834–1994: Portuguese Currency Experience Revisited." Mimeo. Nova University, Lisbon, 1995.

Macaulay, Frederic. R. *The Movements of Interest Rates, Bond Yields and Stock Prices in The United States Since 1856.* New York: NBER, 1938

Maddison, Angus. *Dynamic Forces in Capitalist Development.* Oxford: Oxford University Press, 1991.

Mankiw, Gregory. "The Optimal Collection of Seigniorage: Theory and Evidence." *Journal of Monetary Economics* 20, no. 2 (1987): 327–41.

Mamalakis, Markos J. *Historical Statistics of Chile.* Vol. 5. New York: Greenwood, 1989.

Marichal, Carlos. *A Century of Debt Crisis in Latin America: From Independence to the Great Depression 1820–1930*. Princeton University Press, 1989.

Miller, Marcus and Alan Sutherland. "Britain's Return to Gold and Entry into the ERM." In *Exchange Rate Targets and Currency Banks*, edited by Paul Krugman and Marcus Miller, 82–106. Cambridge: Cambridge University Press, 1992.

Miller, Marcus and Alan Sutherland. "Speculative Anticipations of Sterling's Return to Gold: Was Keynes Wrong?" *Economic Journal*, 1994.

Mitchell, Brian R. *Abstract of British Historical Statistics*. Cambridge: Cambridge University Press, 1962.

International Historical Statistics: Europe, 1750–1988. New York: Stockton Press, 1992.

International Historical Statistics: The Americas, 1750–1988. 2d. ed. New York: Stockton Press, 1993 (This volume includes data on Australia.)

Morgenstren, Oskar. *International Financial Transactions and Business Cycles*. Princeton: Princeton University Press, 1959.

Neufeld, Edward P. *The Financial System of Canada*. Toronto: Macmillan, 1972.

Obstfeld, Maurice. "Destabilizing Effects of Exchange Rate Escape Clauses." NBER Working Paper No. 3606, Cambridge, MA, 1992.

Officer, Lawrence. "The Efficiency of the Dollar-Sterling Gold Standard, 1980–1908." *Journal of Political Economy* 94 (1986): 1038–73.

"Gold-Point Arbitrage and Uncovered Interest Arbitrage Under the 1925–1931 Dollar-Sterling Gold Standard." *Explorations in Economic History* 30, no. 1 (1993): 98–127.

O'Rourke, Kevin and Jeffrey Williamson. "Were Hechsher and Ohlin Right? Putting the Factor Price Equalization Theorem Back into History? *NBER Working Papers on Historical Factors in Long-Run Growth*, No. 37, Cambridge, MA, 1992.

Pelaez, Carlos M. and Wilson Suzigan. *Historia monetaria do Brazil*. Editoria Universidade de Brazilia, 1976.

Pope, David. "Australia's Payments Adjustments and Capital Flows Under the International Gold Standard, 1870–1913." In *Monetary Regimes in Transition*, edited by Michael D. Bordo and Forrest Capie, 201–37. Cambridge: Cambridge University Press, 1993.

Reis, Jaime. "The Gold Standard in Portugal, 1854–1891." Mimeo. Universidade Nova de Lisbon, 1992.

Roll, Richard. "Interest Rates and Price Expectations During the Civil War." *The Journal of Economic History* 32, no. X (1972): 476–98.

Schwartz, Anna. J. "Banking School, Currency School, Free Banking School." In *New Palgrave Dictionary of Economics*, 148–521. London: Macmillan, 1987.

Sharpe, W. F. "Capital Asset Prices: A Theory of Market Equilibrium Under Conditions of Risk." *Journal of Finance* 19 (1964): 425–42.

Simons, Henry C. "Rules Versus Authorities in Monetary Policy." In A. E. A. *Readings in Monetary Theory* edited by Friedrich A. Lutz and Lloyd W. Mintz, 337–68. Homewood, Illinois: Richard D. Irwin, 1951.

Smith, Gregor and Todd Smith. "Welsey Mitchell and Irving Fisher and the

Greenback Gold Reforms, 1865–1879." Mimeo. Queens University, 1993.

Smith, W. S. and Smith, R. T. "Stochastic Process Switching and the Return to Gold." *Economic Journal* 100(1990): 164–75.

Social Science Federation of Canada. *Historical Statistics of Canada.* 2d ed. Ottawa: Statistics Canada in joint sponsorship with the Social Science Federation of Canada, 1983.

Spinelli, Franco and Michele Fratianni. *Storia monetaria D'Italia: l'Evoluzione del sistema monetario e bancario.* Milano: A. Mondadori, 1991.

Spinelli, Franco. "The Demand for Money in the Italian Economy: 1867–1965," Research Report. Department of Economics, University of Western Ontario, 1978.

Stigiliz, Joseph and Andrew Weiss. "Credit Rationing in Markets with Imperfect Information." *American Economic Review* 71, no. 8 (1981): 393–410.

Tonniolo, G. *An Economic History of Liberal Italy: 1850–1918.* New York: Routledge, 1990.

Unger, I. *The Greenback Era: A Social and Political History of American Finance, 1865–1879.* Princeton: Princeton University Press, 1964.

Urquhart, Malcolm C. "New Estimates of GNP, Canada, 1870–1926." In *Long-Term Factors in American Economic Growth*, NBER Studies in Income and Wealth, vol. 51, edited by Stanley L. Engerman and Robert E. Gallman, 9–94. Chicago: University of Chicago Press, 1986.

U.S. Bureau of Census. *Historical Statistics of the United States: Colonial Times to 1957.* Washington, DC: GPO, 1960.

Historical Statistics of the United States, Colonial Times to 1970, Bicentennial Edition. Washington, DC: GPO, 1975.

Vamplew, Wray. *Australians, Historical Statistics.* Broadway, N.S.W. Australia: Fairfax, Syme, and Weldon Associates, 1987.

Viner, J. *Studies in the Theory of International Trade.* Chicago: University of Chicago Press, 1937.

Williamson, Jeffrey G. *American Growth and the Balance of Payments.* Chapel Hill: The University of North Carolina Press, 1964.

Wilson, Roland. *Capital Imports and the Terms of Trade.* Melbourne: Melbourne University Press in association with Macmillan & Co., 1931.

PART IV

Historical Case Studies

CHAPTER 10

A tale of two currencies: British and French finance during the Napoleonic wars

Written with Eugene N. White

The record of British and French finance during the Napoleonic wars presents the striking picture of a financially strong nation abandoning the gold standard, borrowing heavily, and generating inflation, while a financially weaker country followed more "orthodox" policies. This paradoxical behavior is explained by Britain's strong credibility that allowed more flexible policies, while France's poor reputation forced reliance on taxation.

The Napoleonic wars offer an experiment unique in the history of wartime finance. While Britain was forced off the gold standard and endured a relatively high inflation, France remained on a bimetallic standard for the war's duration. For wars of comparable length and intensity in the nineteenth and twentieth centuries, Napoleonic war finance stands out. As Milton Friedman recently pointed out, the French experience is a puzzle.[1] Under the *ancien régime* and the revolutionary governments, France's credit was far inferior to Great Britain's; yet in the years of bitter struggle after 1796, it was the British who used inflationary finance, not the French.

This apparent paradox may be explained by drawing upon the new literature on tax smoothing, time consistency, and credibility in macroeconomics. Before the Revolution, French fiscal policy strongly resembled the British practice in which large temporary increases for wartime expenditures were paid for by increased borrowing, leaving

This chapter is reprinted from the June 1991, Journal of Economic History, 51(2):303–16. © The Economic History Association. All rights reserved. ISSN 0022-0507.

The authors are Professors of Economics, Rutgers University, New Brunswick, NJ 08903, and Research Associates of the National Bureau of Economic Research.

For helpful comments and suggestions we thank Levis Kochin, Hugh Rockoff, Mark Rush, Forrest Capie, Stanley Engerman, Angela Redish, Anna J. Schwartz, and Warren Weber, and seminar participants at Northwestern University, the University of Illinois, and Brown University. Howard Bodenhorn provided valuable research assistance.

[1] Milton Friedman, "Bimetallism Revisited," *Journal of Economic Perspectives*, 4 (Fall 1990), pp. 85–104.

taxes relatively unchanged.[2] This was a relatively efficient strategy for war finance, but its success hinged critically on the credibility of the government to repay its accumulated and enlarged debt after the war. If the government was perceived by the public to be pursuing a time-inconsistent policy, one likely to produce default once the debt was acquired, this avenue of war finance would be closed.[3]

The French Revolution's use of confiscation, capital levies, and an inflation tax destroyed its credibility and forced Napoleonic France to rely primarily on taxation. In contrast to France's frequent changes in political regime, Britain's continuous parliamentary form of government, in which debt holders exercised considerable influence, was able to issue a massive quantity of debt and leave the gold standard with the promise of eventual redemption.

10.1   British and French fiscal policy before 1789

Britain's movement toward tax smoothing – financing of wartime expenditures by borrowing, then servicing and amortizing the debt by taxation in peacetime – began after the Glorious Revolution of 1688. This political victory for parliamentary government led to improvements in tax collection and administration and the development of more modern capital markets.[4] By the War of the Spanish Succession (1702–1713), Britain's new fiscal program was in place. Taxes as a percentage of commodity output did not rise substantially in wartime periods until the very end of the eighteenth century (see Figure 10.1). The boom in wartime spending, unaccompanied by major tax increases, produced very large deficits, as seen in Figure 10.2.

British wartime expenditures were primarily financed by the issue of "unfunded debt," a variety of short-term obligations that included army, navy, ordnance, and, increasingly, exchequer bills. The "funded debt" or long-term securities, secured by specially earmarked indirect taxes, were mostly used during and after the war to retire the more costly unfunded

---

[2] Robert J. Barro, "Government Spending, Interest Rates, Prices and Budget Deficits in the United Kingdom," *Journal of Monetary Economics*, 20 (Sept. 1987), pp. 221–48; and Robert J. Barro, "The Neoclassical Approach to Fiscal Policy," in Robert J. Barro, ed., *Modern Business Cycle Theory* (Cambridge, 1989), pp. 236–64.

[3] Finn E. Kydland and Edward C. Prescott, "Rules Rather than Discretion: The Inconsistency of Optimal Plans," *Journal of Political Economy*, 85 (June 1977), pp. 473–91; and Robert E. Lucas, Jr. and Nancy L. Stokey, "Optimal Fiscal and Monetary Policy in an Economy Without Capital," *Journal of Monetary Economics*, 12 (July 1983), pp. 55–93.

[4] P. G. M. Dickson, *The Financial Revolution in England* (London, 1967); and John Brewer, *The Sinews of Power: War, Money and the English State, 1688–1783* (New York, 1989).

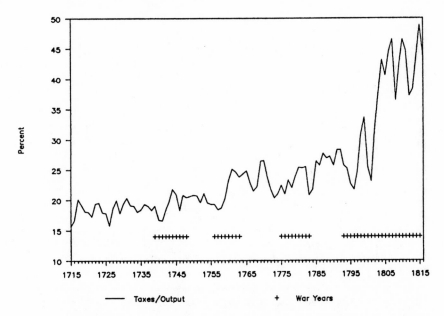

Figure 10.1. Great Britain: tax receipts as a percent of commodity output. *Sources*: A. D. Gayer, W. W. Rostow, and A. J. Schwartz, *The Growth and Fluctuation of the British Economy, 1790–1850* (Oxford, 1953); B. R. Mitchell and P. Deane, *Abstract of British Historical Statistics* (Cambridge, 1962); and P. O'Brien and P. Mathias, "Taxation in England and France 1715–1810," *Journal of European Economic History*, 5 (1976).

debt. Reduction of the debt and of its servicing costs during periods of peace then allowed the government to resume borrowing in even larger amounts in the succeeding wars, as can be seen in Figure 10.2. To assuage heightened fears of national bankruptcy and crippling levels of peace-time taxation to service the debt after the American War for Independence, William Pitt, the chancellor of the Exchequer, re-established the Sinking Fund in 1786, which during the seven succeeding years of peace used budget surpluses to reduce the debt. The Sinking Fund was viewed by contemporaries as a way of showing the public that taxes would eventually be reduced and hence could be viewed as an investment in sovereign credibility and future borrowing power.

The monthly yield on the 3 percent consols from 1770 to 1821 is depicted in Figure 10.3.[5] During the American Revolution and the

---

[5] These data were graciously provided by Larry Neal.

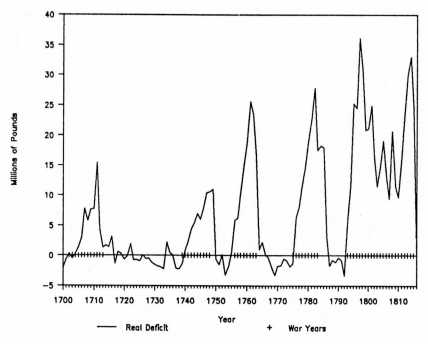

Figure 10.2. Great Britain: real deficit (surplus). *Sources*: See Figure 10.1.

Napoleonic wars, the interest rate rose sharply, a pattern consistent with recent developments in the theory of fiscal policy.[6] To marshal scarce resources for the war effort, real interest rates should have risen in wartime to reduce both present consumption and leisure in favor of saving and labor effort. The nominal interest rate displayed here should be a good proxy for the real interest rate, since up to 1797 Britain adhered to a specie standard, under which the price level was remarkably stable.[7]

[6] For a similar pattern in earlier wars in the eighteenth century, see Barro, "Government Spending"; and D. K. Benjamin and Levis A. Kochin, "War, Prices and Interest Rates: A Martial Solution to Gibson's Paradox," in M. D. Bordo and A. J. Schwartz, eds., *A Retrospective on the Classical Gold Standard, 1821 to 1931* (Chicago, 1984).

[7] During the suspension period, the inflation rate displayed no evidence of persistence. See Robert B. Barsky, "The Fisher Hypothesis and the Forecastability and Persistence of Inflations," *Journal of Monetary Economics*, 19 (Jan. 1987), pp. 3–24; and Michael D. Bordo and Eugene N. White, "British and French Finance during the Napoleonic War" (NBER Working Paper No. 3517, 1990). For other evidence that nominal interest-rate movements largely reflected movements in the real rate, see Robert A. Black and Claire G. Gilmore, "Crowding Out during Britain's Industrial Revolution," this JOURNAL, 50 (Mar. 1990), pp. 109–31.

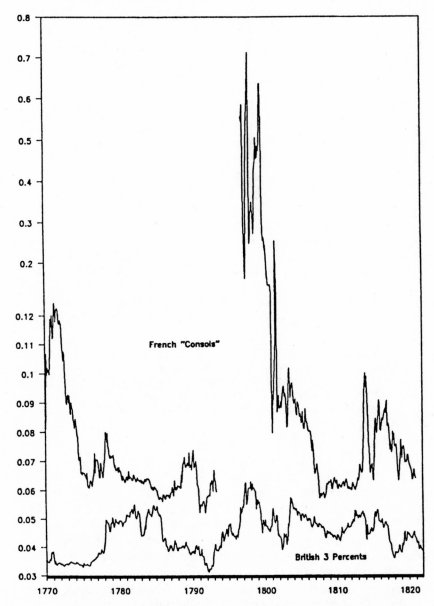

Figure 10.3. Yields on British and French securities: 1770–1821. *Sources*: Castaing. *The Course of Exchange. Gazette de France. Ancien Moniteur*; and Alphonse C. Courtois. *Tableaus des cours des principales valeurs* (Paris, 1877).

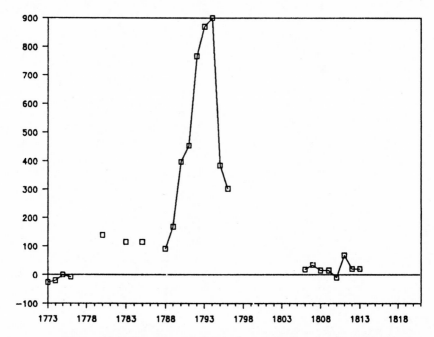

Figure 10.4. France: real deficit (surplus). *Sources*: François-Nicolas Mollien. *Mémoires d'un Ministre du Trésor Public* (Paris, 1835); Eugene Nelson White. "Was There a Solution to the Ancien Régime's Financial Dilemma?" this JOURNAL, 49 (Sept. 1989), Table 1; and Eugene Nelson White. "Deficits, Inflation, and the Bankruptcy of the French Revolution" (Rutgers University mimeo, 1990).

France's national finances at the beginning of the century were not greatly inferior to Britain's. John Law's unsuccessful attempt to re-organize the government's finances, which ended in 1721 with another massive write-down of the debt, had its parallel in the South Sea Bubble. The French were, however, unable to follow the British and improve their fiscal management, leaving the state's finances relatively precarious. In 1759, in the midst of the Seven Years' War, the Crown was forced to suspend repayment of the capital on a variety of short-term debts.[8] The continuing financial crisis after the war eventually led to the partial bankruptcy of 1770. After this last crisis, the Crown made a new commitment to fiscal stability. Finance ministers successfully balanced the budget or ran surpluses up to the American War as

[8] Marcel Marion, *Histoire financière de la France depuis 1715* (Paris, 1914), vol. 1, p. 197.

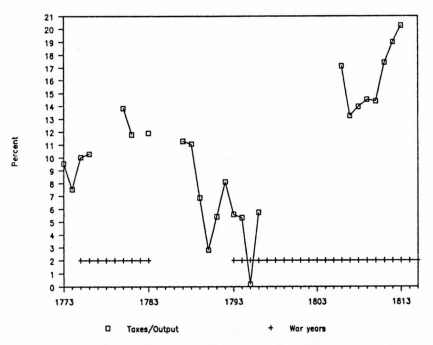

Figure 10.5. France: tax receipts as a percent of commodity output. *Sources*: Patrick O'Brien and Caglar Keyder. *Economic Growth in Britain and France 1789–1914* (London, 1978); Mollien, *Mémoires d'un Ministre*; White, "Was There a Solution?" Table 1; and White, "Deficits, Inflation, and the Bankruptcy."

shown in the budgets depicted in Figure 10.4. Taxes, as in the British case, were a relatively constant but lower share of output as seen in Figure 10.5.

The interest-rate history of France thus paralleled Britain's as depicted in Figure 10.3.[9] As in the British case, a rise in the interest rate during the American War served to reallocate scarce resources to the war effort. Likewise, after the war, interest rates fell. However, a large peacetime deficit also appeared. The public in France only gradually became aware of the government's deviation from a tax-smoothing path, its announced objective. The French monarchy was able to deceive the public because government finance was not open to parliamentary in-

---

[9] The yields reported for France in Figure 10.3 are on the stock of the Compagnie des Indes (1770–1793), the *inscriptions sur le grande livre de la dette publique* (1797), and the *tiers consolidé* (1798–1821).

spection as in Britain.[10] There were no institutions in France to guarantee that the government would adhere to a time-consistent policy. In Britain the Parliament in Westminster voted on the budget, the Bank of England faithfully made daily redemption of its notes in specie, and a sinking fund paid off the national debt. By contrast, the budget was not public in France, there was no regular parliament to monitor the Crown, a project to set up a sinking fund had failed, and the Discount Bank had been forced to suspend more than once.

This lack of institutional commitment in the absence of a good track record forced the French government to borrow at higher interest rates than the British could. In the well-integrated capital markets of the late eighteenth century, the premium on French consols over British consols reflects the greater riskiness of French securities.

10.2   The Revolution: France's squandered reputation

The collapse of the French monarchy was initially accompanied by a loss of confidence in the nation's ability to meet its commitments. The revolutionary upheaval of 1789 substantially reduced the tax base, and the government found it difficult to borrow, except at high rates. Unwilling to raise taxes, the National Assembly chose to seize the lands of the church. To meet the state's urgent financial needs, the *assignats* were created to cover the deficit and pay off part of the national debt. This paper money was used by the state to pay its creditors who could in turn employ them to buy the nationalized properties of the church.

While the immediate situation looked dismal, financial markets believed the state's problem could be resolved, and interest rates fell back to pre-crisis levels in 1791. Credibility was created by the more open budget process and more importantly by the successful sale of church lands to retire the *assignats*. The outbreak of the war in April 1792, however, eliminated any chance of success. The state's finances deteriorated rapidly and the growing deficit (Figure 10.4) was covered entirely by the issue of *assignats*. During the revolutionary Terror, the government attempted to halt inflation with price controls and raise revenue by steeply progressive income taxes and forced loans. These experiments failed, and the government became wholly dependent on money creation, leading to hyperinflation in 1795. The *assignats* were abandoned, but, unable to increase tax collections, the government issued a new

---

[10] Douglass C. North and Barry R. Weingast, "Constitutions and Commitment: The Evolution of Institutions Governing Public Choice in Seventeenth-Century England," this JOURNAL, 49 (Dec. 1989), pp. 803–32.

paper money, the *mandats*, in 1796, generating a very short-lived fast inflation.

Having exhausted its ability to use money creation, the Directory had to cut expenditures and raise taxes. In September 1797 the government wrote down the value of interest payments by two-thirds. The debt was further reduced by cancelling the debts of émigrés and convicts. By 1799 the annual interest payments on the national debt stood at 75.3 million – a drastic reduction from the 260 million of 1788.[11] Nevertheless, the government did not make full payment in specie even on this reduced sum. Revolutionary France had squandered its modest endowment of credibility, having failed to pursue consistent policies. Consequently, options for financing the wars of the next decade and a half were limited.

10.3   British fiscal strategy, 1793–1815

The war against France was initially financed in the traditional eighteenth-century manner, with 90 percent of the expenditures between 1793 and 1798 covered by borrowing.[12] The massive scale of expenditures led to a doubling of the national debt by 1798. The Napoleonic wars required far greater expenditures and thus larger deficits for a longer period of time than previous wars, as seen in Figure 10.2. This increased pressure on government finance resulted in two new developments that deviated from previous experience: the suspension of specie payments in 1797, and the introduction of an income tax in 1799.

Britain fought the wars of the eighteenth century on the gold standard, but the circumstances of the late 1790s were extraordinary. The sale of government securities which otherwise would have been absorbed by the Bank competed with private securities, forcing up interest rates to unprecedented levels. Private borrowers then turned to the Bank, which responded by rationing credit in December 1795. The credit stringency was alleviated by direct government lending to the City. The response by the Bank to its dwindling gold reserves hindered the government's war finance.[13] To prevent the collapse of the Bank in the face of both a massive external drain and a run on the country banks, occasioned by fears of a French invasion, the government finally allowed it to suspend specie payments on February 26, 1797.

[11] J. M. Fachan, *Historique de la rente française* (Paris, 1904), pp. 130–31; and Alphonse Vührer, *Histoire de la dette publique en France* (Paris, 1886), pp. 424–25.
[12] Patrick O'Brien, "Government Revenue 1793–1815: A Study in Fiscal and Financial Policy in the Wars Against France" (Ph.D. diss., Oxford University, 1967).
[13] Ibid., chap. 5.

After the Bank suspended specie payments, the government was again able to sell much of its short-term debt to the Bank of England. Thus, until hostilities ceased, the share of unfunded loans increased dramatically from a low of 19.3 percent in 1797 to a peak of 76 percent in 1808.[14] Accommodation of both government and private borrowing is generally viewed by historians as the way in which the Bank contributed to war finance.[15] While money creation by the Bank seems to have been responsible for inflation, as measured by seigniorage revenue, it was not a principal pillar for financing the war. Measured as the increase in bank notes divided by the average price level, seigniorage exceeded only 10 percent of the deficit in 1810 and never rose above 5 percent of war revenue.[16] Money creation did not make a large contribution to war finance, but it did give the government critical flexibility in short-term finance and debt management.

The government thus viewed the Bank of England as an essential component of its war finance program. This can be seen in its opposition to a number of requests by the Bank to resume specie payments, its support of the Bank in the face of the withering criticism of the Bullion Report of 1810, its encouragement of the Bank to accommodate private demands for credit, and its granting of de facto legal tender status to the Bank's notes in 1811.[17]

The second departure from the eighteenth-century pattern of government finance was the institution of an income tax in 1799. Concern over the size of the national debt, the inability to further raise revenue from indirect taxes, and the threat of defeat by the French revolutionaries were all arguments that Pitt used to overcome opposition to direct taxation by the propertied classes. The income and property taxes were immensely successful, rising from zero to approximately 20 percent of total tax revenue by the end of the war. Moreover, unlike the preceding wars, total taxes covered a far greater share of government expenditure than borrowing, which at its peak supplied approximately 30 percent. The British experience during the Napoleonic wars suggests that the

[14] See Bordo and White, "British and French Finance," Table 2.
[15] Frank Fetter, *Development of British Monetary Orthodoxy, 1797–1875* (Cambridge, MA, 1965); E. Schumpeter, "English Prices and Public Finance, 1660–1822," *Review of Economics and Statistics*, 20 (Feb. 1938); N. Silbering, "British Prices and Business Cycles," *Review of Economics and Statistics*, 5 (Oct. 1923); and Jacob Viner, *Studies in the Theory of International Trade* (New York, 1937).
[16] Bordo and White, "British and French Finance," Table 3.
[17] O'Brien, "Government Revenue," Chap. 5; and Frank Fetter, "Legal Tender During the English and Irish Bank Restriction," *Journal of Political Economy*, 58 (June 1950).
[18] Barro, "The Neoclassical Approach."

government followed policies consistent with the modern theory of tax smoothing, which implies that an optimizing government will set tax rates over time so as to minimize deadweight losses.[18] In an uncertain world, taxes will follow a martingale pattern as the government attempts to forecast expenditures rationally and sets the current tax rate consistent with its forecast of the future so that only unpredictable events will produce changing tax rates.[19] We tested for such a pattern in the average British tax rate from 1700 to 1815. The Dickey-Fuller tests on the lagged tax rate showed that the null hypothesis that the coefficient is equal to one cannot be rejected at the 1 percent level.[20] This evidence supports the hypothesis that the British government had engaged in tax smoothing.

The ability to smooth taxes was based on the government's credibility to ensure a flow of revenue after the war to service the debt. The British had invested in credibility by their performance of debt service after other wars. In addition, establishment of the Sinking Fund and its continued operation during the Napoleonic wars strengthened this investment. This stands in contrast to the French monarchy, which created a sinking fund in 1785 – attempting to enhance its reputation – only to be forced to quickly abandon it.

The British experience is also consistent with recent theoretical developments about rules versus discretion.[21] The experience of the suspension period can be viewed as being consistent with following a contingent gold standard rule. Under this rule, the government maintains the standard – keeps the price of its currency in terms of gold fixed – except in the event of a major war. In wartime it may suspend specie payments and issue paper money to finance its expenditures, and it can sell debt issues

[19] L. Kochin, D. Benjamin, and M. Meader, "The Observational Equivalence of Rational and Irrational Consumers if Taxation Is Efficient" (Federal Reserve Bank of San Francisco West Coast Academic Conference, 1985).

[20] For the period 1715 to 1815, using as the dependent variable the ratio of tax receipts to commodity output (T/Y), we obtained the following equation: $(T/Y)_t = -51.3 + 0.03 Time + 0.93(T/Y)_{t-1}$. The R^2 was 0.89, and the Durbin-Watson statistic 1.96. The Dickey-Fuller test was -0.948, well below the critical value of -3.45 at the 5 percent level. We have not reported the coefficients on the lagged differences. Similar results were obtained for the ratio of tax receipts to national income and for the ratio of tax receipts to commodity output for France from 1728 to 1796. See Bordo and White, "British and French Finance." The power of these tests is weak, and there is considerable controversy about their use. See Bennett MacCallum, "On 'Real' and 'Sticky-Price' Theories of the Business Cycles," *Journal of Money Credit and Banking*, 22 (Nov. 1989), pp. 397–441; and Peter Rappoport and Lucrezia Reichlin, "Segmented Trends and Nonstationary Time Series," *Economic Journal*, 99 (Supplement 1989).

[21] Michael D. Bordo and Finn Kydland, "The Gold Standard as a Rule" (NBER Working Paper No. 3367, 1990).

in terms of the nominal value of its currency on the understanding that the debt will eventually be paid off in gold. The rule is contingent in the sense that the public understands that the suspension will last only for the duration of the wartime emergency plus some period of adjustment; it assumes that afterward the government will follow the deflationary policies necessary to resume payments.

Despite the government's opposition to resumption during wartime conditions, there exists considerable evidence that the government wished to confirm its commitment to return to the gold standard once hostilities ceased. The failure to confront directly the Bullion Report's criticism of the Bank for allowing the exchange rate to depreciate can be understood in this light. After hostilities ceased in 1815, several attempts were made to pick a date for resumption, but as each occasion approached, the Bank requested a postponement on the ground that the exchanges were unfavorable. In 1819 Parliament finally decided to begin resumption in stages, starting on February 1, 1820. The government promised to retire its outstanding securities held by the Bank and the Bank would reduce its note issue to achieve the aim. Resumption was achieved on May 7, 1821. The tenor of the debate in Parliament and the press, the lack of effective opposition to resumption, and the fact that resumption was achieved, despite the delays, before the final date suggest that observing the rule was vitally important.[22]

The experience of the suspension may also be understood within the context of recent theories of optimal seigniorage and revenue smoothing. Over time an optimizing government would smooth revenue from both tax instruments and both instruments would evolve in a similar martingale pattern. To confirm this hypothesis, a positive and significant coefficient from a regression of the rate of inflation on the average tax rate is postulated.[23] We carried out this experiment, but unlike earlier studies our results were not consistent with the hypothesis. Seigniorage smoothing may not be expected to prevail under a specie standard where the inflation rate does not exhibit persistence.[24] Indeed, our results suggest that although specie payments were suspended, the commitment to resume prevented the government from acting as it would under the pure flat regime postulated by the theory.

---

[22] A. Feaveryear, *The Pound Sterling* (Oxford, 1963), pp. 224–25; Fetter, *Development of British Monetary Orthodoxy*, pp. 73–76; and David Laidler, "The Bullionist Controversy," *New Palgrave Dictionary of Economics* (London, 1987).

[23] N. Greg Mankiw, "The Optimal Collection of Seigniorage – Theory and Evidence," *Journal of Monetary Economics*, 20 (Sept. 1987), pp. 327–41.

[24] See fn. 8; and B. L. Goff and M. Toma, "Optimal Seigniorage and Central Bank Financing" (University of Kentucky mimeo, 1990).

10.4   The consulate and empire, 1799–1812

Although Great Britain, in spite of suspension, was able to finance a considerable portion of its war effort by borrowing, France was forced to rely almost entirely on taxation while it attempted to rebuild its reputation as a debtor. It had lost its credibility during the Revolution and was unable to follow a tax-smoothing policy. Consequently, the empire was forced, even at the height of the wars, to cover virtually all its expenditures by taxation. Napoleon has traditionally been regarded by historians as a simple, obstinate, hard-money man. In public, he adamantly professed to oppose any new borrowing. The collapse of the *ancien régime*'s finances from excessive borrowing and the Revolution's finances from excessive use of paper money may have irrationally colored his view of public finance. His pronouncements, however, were necessary to a certain degree to restore confidence, and many of his actions and statements should be measured in this light.

Napoleon's coup of November 1799 began sweeping changes in government finance that were built on the tough measures taken by the Directory. The system of taxation was reorganized, new taxes were imposed, payment on the debt in specie was resumed (1800), the nation returned to the bimetallic standard (1803), and institutions – the Banque de France (1800) and a sinking fund (1799) – were established, which served as additional guarantees of the government's commitment to fiscal prudence.

Napoleon improved the collection of direct taxes and re-introduced indirect taxes, abolished during the Revolution.[25] The result of this new policy regime was that the French were taxed at a significantly higher level than before the Revolution. French taxes as a percentage of commodity output were distinctly higher under the empire (Figure 10.5), allowing the government to cover most of its expenditures without extensive borrowing. The slow restoration of France's reputation led to a drop in the yields on French consols (Figure 10.3).

The growth of the public debt under the empire was quite modest. Borrowing from the Banque de France was important for smoothing the flow of tax payments, but it was, in the overall picture of government finance, a relatively minor contribution to war finance. Even at the peak of 80 million francs in 1805, it was less than 10 percent of expenditures. While the emperor's borrowing from the Banque was generally restrained, the government did press the bank too far once, forcing a partial suspension in 1805.[26] Unlike the British, the government could

[25] Marion, *Histoire financière*, vol. 4, pp. 297–304.
[26] Alphonse C. Courtois, *Histoire des Banques en France* (Paris, 1881), pp. 116–17.

not fully or permanently suspend payment, given its history, and hope that the public would maintain its real balances. In the next few years, imperial borrowing from the bank was more restrained until the empire's collapse.

France's borrowing during the wars from all sources was limited. There was widespread capital flight from the continent to Britain owing to revolutionary and imperial predations and the imposition of the continental system.[27] Traditional lenders, like the Dutch, were unwilling to trust the new French regime. Investing heavily in Britain left the French with relatively limited sources of new funds. Finance ministers, such as François Barbé-Marbois and die-hard emigrés such as Francis d'Ivernois believed that any large issue of debt could be sold only for very high yields that were politically unacceptable.[28]

Even at its apogee, Napoleon's system of finance did not engender enough confidence to permit the government to return to large-scale borrowing. The imperial budget remained secretive, and the public had no equivalent to the British Parliament to monitor the plans of the emperor. In the absence of such an institution, it was impossible for the government to make a completely convincing commitment to its announced program.

The fiscal discipline imposed on the empire because of France's lack of credibility was, however, partially eased by taxation of the conquered territories and its allies. Most of the taxation of conquered nations was to support French armies abroad. In 1805 Austria supplied 75 million and in 1809 164 million francs. Between 1806 and 1812 Prussia provided somewhere between 470 and 514 million francs. These enormous revenues meant that French armies abroad were not a drain on the French treasury.

French finances appeared victorious in early 1811. Britain was encumbered by a growing debt, the Bank of England's notes had depreciated, and the pound sterling stood at a substantial discount. France maintained the value of the franc, the Banque de France redeemed its notes at par, and the budget of the previous year was balanced. What destroyed the empire was the enormous expense and failure of the Russian campaign. Napoleon's Hundred Days brought another crushing burden in the form of reparations, estimated at 1290 million francs. The restored monarchy remained very weak and was rescued only by a series of new loans in 1817. The end result was that the *rentes* which required annual payments of 63.3 million in 1814 now had an annual cost of

[27] Larry Neal, "A Tale of Two Revolutions: International Capital Flows, 1789–1819" (University of Illinois BEBR Faculty Working Paper No. 90-1663, July 1990).
[28] Marion, *Histoire financière*, vol. 4, pp. 337–38.

202.4 million francs in 1830. Ironically, these interest payments were not much different from the total cost of payments in the last years of the *ancien régime*.

Conclusion

While the Napoleonic wars after 1797 offered the curious spectacle of faithful Albion abandoning the gold standard and perfidious France maintaining convertibility of the franc, these war finance regimes were the consequence of each nation's credibility as a debtor. Given its long record of fiscal probity, coupled with its open budgetary process in Parliament, Great Britain could continue to borrow a substantial fraction of its war expenditures at what were relatively low interest rates. British tax rates did not vary much over most of the eighteenth century as peacetime surpluses offset wartime deficits to pay off the accumulated war debts. Taxes would not have been greatly increased during the Napoleonic wars except that their duration imposed a debt burden much higher than the eighteenth-century norm, requiring a rise in the tax rate to sustain the nation's credibility as a borrower. France, on the other hand, had squandered her reputation in the last decade of the *ancien régime* and the Revolution. Her dependency on taxation did not reflect any superior fiscal virtues but rather the opposite. Borrowing would have been exceedingly costly and the public was skeptical of the empire's fidelity. Inherited credibility resolves this paradoxical pairing of fiscal regimes.

CHAPTER 11

Money, deflation, and seigniorage in the fifteenth century: A review essay

11.1 Introduction

Monetary economists have long been interested in economic history as a laboratory for the testing of theory. For the monetary economist, unusual monetary disturbances such as gold discoveries and hyperinflations, unique institutional arrangements such as free banking, and unique monetary standards such as bimetallism provide the raw materials for the testing of theories.

Monetary economics has focused mainly on the experience of Western Europe and North America since the beginning of the nineteenth century,[1] because of the availability of data and of continuity to modern times of institutions then established. However, there has also been considerable interest in episodes from the preceding three centuries, e.g., the Price Revolution of the sixteenth century [Hamilton (1934)], Colonial money issues [Smith (1985), Wicker (1985)], the assignat hyperinflation [White (1985)], the historical sources of hyperinflation [Capie (1986)], and the South Sea Bubble [Neal and Schubert (1985)].

One largely overlooked episode of history of great potential interest to the monetary economist is the late Middle Ages in Northwestern Europe. Topics of interest for recent theory from this episode include: conflicting monetary and real explanations for long-run price level and real output movements, the operation of early commodity money standards, early attempts at inflationary finance, time-inconsistent monetary policies, and the issue of credibility.

I first present an overview of the key themes in late medieval monetary history highlighting the debate between realists and monetarists. I then examine the issue of politics and money, focusing on debasement as a policy tool, following which I assess an excellent recent contribution to this literature, H. Miskimin's *Money and Power in Fifteenth Century*

This chapter is reprinted from the *Journal of Monetary Economics*, 18(3):337–46.

My thanks for helpful comments and suggestions go to Forrest Capie, Axel Leijonhuvud, Bill Phillips, Angela Redish, Mark Rush, Anna Schwartz, and Geoffrey Wood.

[1] For a survey of this literature, see Bordo (1986).

France (1984). I conclude with a discussion of themes relevant for current monetary economics.

11.2 Overview

The economies of late medieval (1350–1500) Northwestern Europe – France, England, and the Low Countries – although still largely dependent on agriculture, had a flourishing commercial sector located in numerous towns and cities and some primitive industries. International trade grew. The period was also characterized by the decline of feudalism, the growth of the power of the monarchy, and the emergence, especially in England and France, of nascent national states.

The non-agricultural sector of the late medieval economies was monetized to a considerable extent. Although gold was used for large transactions and international trade, most internal transactions were settled with silver coins. The three countries were effectively on a silver standard with gold coins used as supplementary coinage.[2] The monetary system in all of Western Europe was based on the old Roman standard of livres (pounds), sols (shillings), and deniers (pence), the livre being a specified weight of silver, divided into 20 sols and 240 deniers.[3] The use of banks and other forms of credit, although quite extensive in Italy, was limited in Northwestern Europe. Consequently, economic activity and the price level in the monetized sector of the economy were closely related to the vicissitudes of the metallic standard.

A consensus of the available statistical evidence suggests that this period of European history was dominated by declining trends in population, price levels, money supplies, and real economic activity. The decline in population is generally believed [Postan (1950, 1966, 1972)] to have started at the beginning of the fourteenth century, following an increase of two and a half centuries, to have accelerated after plagues in the 1340s and 1360s, and not to have been arrested until the middle of the fifteenth century. There is also general agreement that grain prices declined in this period but there is some debate about the trend of other prices [Postan (1952, 1959, 1960), Munro (1983)]. Recent evidence by Miskimin (1983), Day (1978), and Munro (1983), based on available data on mint production in the three countries, suggests that both silver and gold coins were on a declining trend from about 1360 to 1460, with the

---

[2] The face value of gold coins was expressed in terms of the silver unit of account.

[3] Through much of the Middle Ages prices were stated in terms of the three denominations but for the most part only pennies actually circulated. The phenomenon of "ghost monies" reflected frequent debasement of small denomination coinage. See Cipolla (1956).

most severe declines occurring during the "Bullion Famine" of the first two decades of the fifteenth century [Day (1978)].[4,5] Finally, there is general agreement that the fourteenth and fifteenth centuries were characterized by falling agricultural output and stagnant activity in most other sectors [Postan (1952, 1966), Miskimin (1975)]. The declining trends in all four series are believed to have been reversed beginning about 1460.

Considerable debate has been generated by attempting to explain the trend phenomena. Postan (1952, 1966) argues the "realist" case that population movements were the key driving force. Rapidly growing population in the twelfth and thirteenth centuries collided with the constraint of an inelastic supply of arable land. The resulting rise in land prices and falling real wages that led to a decline in birth rates produced a turnaround in population growth that was aggravated by the plagues of the fourteenth century. Furthermore, according to Postan, falling population can explain both falling prices and output since it reduced effective demand. Finally, although the money supply may have fallen (see the arguments below), population fell at least as much, so that in simple quantity theory terms, falling velocity driven by adverse expectations contributed to the decline in per capita nominal income.

Monetarists have argued that both deflation and depression can be explained by a decline in the money supply relative to output. Both Day (1978) and Munro (1983) present evidence that the trend decline in the money supply (proxied by mint production) greatly exceeded the decline in population. Factors accounting for the decline in the stock of monetary metals include the depletion of European silver mines [Nef (1952)], wear and tear [Mayhew (1977)], and a persistent adverse balance of payments deficit with Southern Europe and the Near East [Miskimin (1964, 1975)]. However, evidence that the Near East and even India

---

[4] No one has yet constructed a money supply series for this period because of the lack of benchmark estimates of the money stock. Consequently monetary historians of this period have all used various mint production series to infer movements of the money supply while making plausible assumptions about recoinage, the import and export of bullion and coin, and wear and tear. For a recent attempt to overcome this lacuna and to construct a money supply series for France for 1493–1600, see Glassman and Redish (1984).

[5] Watson (1967) argued that it is misleading to characterize the period as suffering a "bullion famine." Based on a comparison of gold-silver mint ratios in Europe and the Middle East he argued that the bullion drain to the East consisted largely of silver, matched by a gold inflow to Europe, hence the composition and not the level of the money supply changed. Pro-gold mint policies in Europe and pro-silver mint policies in the Middle East encouraged arbitrage flows. Miskimin (1972, 1977, 1983), Munro (1983), and Day (1978) effectively discredit this hypothesis with strong evidence of a decline in both gold and silver bullion and coin in Europe during this period.

suffered a "shortage" of precious metals in this period [Richards (1983)] suggests that it was a worldwide phenomenon – the delayed response to centuries of rising price levels and falling real prices of precious metals – a manifestation of the operation of the classical commodity theory of money on a global scale.

11.3 Money and politics

Northwest Europe was subject to extreme political instability in the fourteenth and fifteenth centuries. All three countries were plagued by wars and civil unrest. France suffered the most since the Hundred Years War was fought on her territory and civil wars were frequent.

The exigencies of wartime finance created unusual demands by the crown for revenues. Fiscal pressure was further aggravated by monetary shortage. In the case of France (and the Burgundian Netherlands in the fourteenth century), the crown was not strong enough to raise revenues either by conventional forms of taxation or by borrowing [Wolfe (1972)], and so resort to "the printing press" – mutation of the coinage – was the policy frequently used. The principal form of mutation was debasement – changes in either the weight, the fineness, or the alloy of royal coins. An alternative policy was to alter the mint ratios of gold and silver to attract relatively more of one metal to the mint.[6]

The purpose of debasement was to gain seigniorage revenue (the king's feudal dues from the mint). The amount of seigniorage revenue collected was the product of the rate of seigniorage and mint output. For a holder of bullion it paid to convert bullion to coin as long as the monetary services provided by (the premium on) coinage over and above brassage (the fees charged by the royal mintmaster to cover labor and other costs) and the rate of seigniorage was positive. By debasing the coinage, for example, by reducing the weight of silver deniers and hence increasing the number of deniers from a fixed weight of silver bullion, the king would gain seigniorage revenue while the holder of bullion or coin would gain to the extent he could exchange new coins at the previous par value. Debasement was a viable source of revenue until prices adjusted to reflect the decline in the intrinsic value of royal money.[7] Price adjust-

---

[6] The metal favored differed between countries. England adapted a pro-gold mint policy in 1344 reflecting its extensive use of gold in international trade [Munro (1972)]. Often such policies were adopted defensively to counter mint alteration policies by other countries (ibid).

[7] However, even if prices adjusted immediately the king could still collect seigniorage revenue unless the public stopped bringing old coins to the mint, which would happen if coins circulated at their intrinsic (and not their face) value. This may explain the frequent practice of debasing small silver coins that did not circulate at their intrinsic value.

ment tended to be more rapid the more open the economy and the more frequently the policy was used.[8] Furthermore, to the extent that the ultimate victims of debasement were the nobility and the church – two groups whose income depended on fixed long-term contracts (feudal dues) – the threat of debasement could be used to extort higher tax revenues.

A comparison of the performances of England, France, and Burgundy in this period is highly instructive. The Burgundian Netherlands followed a recurrent policy of debasement, "renforcement" (currency reform), and renewed debasement throughout the fourteenth century, with each successive cycle requiring a greater debasement to produce equivalent revenues [Munro (1983), Spufford (1970)]. Under parliamentary pressure early in the fifteenth century Burgundy switched to a policy of stable money.[9] France's experience with ever widening cycles of debasement and "renforcement" paralleled that of Burgundy until the middle of the fifteenth century. In 1445 under the exigency of creating and permanently financing a standing royal army, Charles VIII succeeded in establishing a system of national taxes and a fiscal administration capable of generating tax revenues sufficient to meet government expenditure. The imperative for debasement disappeared.

In sharp contrast to Burgundy and France, England was a model of sound money. After a Parliamentary Prohibition of debasement in 1352, English monarchs rarely engaged in the practice until the sixteenth century (except periodically to offset deterioration in quality of the coinage).

11.4   H. A. Miskimin: Money and power in fifteenth century France

Miskimin views the monetary shortage of the fifteenth century as the key force shaping the relationship between the crown and the economy.

---

[8] Debasement was also used to offset deterioration in the quality of coinage through wear and tear and the circulation of worn and debased foreign coins. As the coinage deteriorated, heavy coins would be culled out and exported and the remaining coinage would be discounted (all prices in terms of it would rise). This would reduce the premium of coin over bullion, reducing the supply of precious metals to the mint. Glassman and Redish (1985) argue that in sixteenth century England and France this reduction was the primary motivation for debasement.

[9] With the exception of the Civil War in the 1480s during the reign of Maximlian, according to Spufford (1970), this switch in policy reflected both the growth of Parliamentary power and the development in the fifteenth century of a new theory of the king's obligation with respect to the coinage. In the fourteenth century profit taking from the coinage was commonly believed to be the king's feudal right, but by the fifteenth century a new view developed (attributed to Nicholas Oresme's *De Moneta*) that the coinage was issued for the use of the people and it was the king's duty to maintain its value.

According to Miskimin, virtually all economic policies in this period are a direct or indirect response to the monetary shortage. Furthermore the monetary shortage was a strong contributing factor to the growth of the absolute monarchy in France.

A new series on silver and gold coinage Miskimin constructed from hitherto unused data in the French Archives Nationale exhibits a declining trend that he regards as evidence for a monetary shortage. The new data supplement series he gathered earlier [Miskimin (1963)] and complement a new series by Munro (1983) for Burgundy and England.

The author's explanation for the persistent monetary shortage is a chronic balance of payments deficit with Southern Europe and the Near East, attributed to demographic factors and international transfers. According to Miskimin (1964, 1974, 1983), the sharp decline in population in the fourteenth century reduced the price of food relative to manufactured goods. This changed the terms of trade in favor of the towns. With the wealth of the towns increased as a consequence of Black Death–induced inheritances, townspeople increased their consumption of luxury goods, especially of imports from Italy and the Levant. At the same time production of exports declined as labor was diverted to service the new luxury imports.[10]

The adverse balance of trade was worsened by remittances of coin and bullion to the papacy in Rome, by military expenses (the hiring of mercenaries and importation of arms from Italy), and by diplomatic expenses (bribing allies).

Miskimin argues that the chronic monetary shortage encouraged coinage debasement to raise revenue in periods of military emergency. To determine whether the debasements represented successful attempts to raise revenue the author compares the nominal and real price of wheat (the nominal price divided by the average number of livres of account from a kilo of silver) during six periods of severe debasement. The finding that the real price was virtually unaffected by the debasements leads to the powerful conclusion that the debasements were ineffective. According to the author, the public refused to accept royal money at face value, treating it instead as equivalent to bullion.

Furthermore, to ascertain whether debasement could have been used to offset the deflationary effects of the bullion shortage, as had been

---

[10] According to Reed (1979), the change in the terms of trade between town and country and Northern and Southern Europe does not necessarily imply a transfer of purchasing power. Viewing the decline in population as a change in supply rather than as a change in demand, as Miskimin does, he argues that total revenue in agriculture/Northern Europe may not have declined.

earlier argued for Italy by Cipolla (1956), the author compares the nominal and real price of wheat over the course of the fifteenth century. Since the real price exhibited a declining trend, Miskimin argues that debasement was ineffective in alleviating the monetary shortage.

With debasement ineffective in alleviating the monetary shortage, according to Miskimin, the French king turned to policies to stem the outflow of precious metals. The policies included increased taxation of the church and attempts to prohibit the remittance of precious metals to Rome, exchange controls (the prohibition of circulation of foreign coins), sumptuary legislation, the establishment and subsidization of trade fairs, the creation of a domestic silk industry, and attempts to encourage domestic gold and silver mining.

Finally Miskimin sees a connection between the bullion shortage and royal intervention into economic activity. Based on evidence from petitions to the crown, he argues that the merchant class (the Third Estate) was willing to suffer the loss of individual freedom in exchange for policies to alleviate economic distress. The interventions included a government guarantee of the monopoly power of the guilds and royal protection of the fairs from foreign competition. The precedents of such intervention, combined with the failure to develop a strong national Parliament, as in the case of England, set the groundwork for the absolute monarchy of later centuries.

The French public continued to refuse to accept royal money at par value until the end of the fifteenth century, at which point, with the dramatic growth in government expenditure and taxation, according to the author (1972, 1977), the public became willing to do so. The reason was that taxes could be paid with government money, and taxes represented a significant portion of individual expenditure. Consequently, from the sixteenth century onwards debasement effectively raised the velocity of circulation of bullion and alleviated some of the real excess demand for money. The rest of the excess demand, according to the author, was satisfied by new silver production in central Europe in the late fifteenth century and imports of silver and gold from South America in the sixteenth century. Both developments were stimulated by a falling price level and rising real prices of precious metals.

Miskimin's analysis raises some problems. First, his demographic explanation for Northern Europe's balance of payments crisis seems narrow. Because this book focuses on France, it suggests that the shortage of money reflected primarily a change in the relationship between France (Northern Europe) and the rest of the world and that it was not part of the wider picture of worldwide deflation. Northern

Europe's problems in this period, in addition to reflecting the long observed drain of precious metals to the East – associated with a traditional demand for hoarding and perhaps more rapid real growth – were likely also part of an overall world excess demand for precious metals such as periodically occurs under a commodity money standard. (See the recent literature on the global transfer of precious metals [including Miskimin's own work (1977)] as well as studies of later centuries.) However, evidence that prices were flexible and did decline over this period suggests perhaps that what is being described may be a phenomenon different from a global excess demand for money.

Second, the claim that debasement was completely ineffective as both a short-run and a long-run policy tool is based on annual movements of the real price of wheat. As the author himself argues in this book, and in greater detail in his 1963 book, there are enough serious problems with the wheat price data with respect to its accuracy, its dating, and its representativeness to question the statement that "in the short run, nominal prices responded virtually instantaneously to debasement" (p. 67). The data are just too poor to capture lags of less than a year. Surely a year is sufficient time to raise sufficient revenue to meet many emergencies.

In addition evidence on seigniorage profits as a share of royal revenues in both France and Burgundy in the fourteenth and fifteenth centuries (up to 70% of French royal revenue in 1349) suggests that debasement was probably as effective a form of finance as the modern inflation tax [see Spufford (1970), Munro (1973), as well as discussion by the author, (1983, pp. 52–53)].

Finally, if debasement in fact was so ineffective, why was it repeatedly used? It is hard to imagine a world of an ultrarational public and a completely myopic government, but perhaps it existed. The author could have approached the problem by measuring the revenue maximizing rate of inflation. His conclusions could then have been compared to more recent results of use of the printing press. The existing mint data, estimates of recoinage, and the net export of coins make it possible, following the approach of Glassman and Redish (1984), to construct a money supply series for the fifteenth century. In combination with the existing price data a money demand function could be estimated.

The long-run evidence suggesting that debasement did not offset the real excess demand for money seems much more believable in the light of modern evidence that the public catches on (with perhaps some lag) to the inflation process. The government is then forced to resort to higher rates of inflation to offset declining revenues.

11.5   Conclusions

This interesting book and the literature of which it is part deal with issues of considerable interest to the monetary economist.

First, evidence for an earlier time period on the old debate between "monetarists" and "realists" on the causes of deflation and depression suggests that demographic factors may have been an important cause of the shortage of precious metals in Northwestern Europe.

Second, the operation of a primitive commodity standard in the fourteenth and fifteenth centuries, as in the nineteenth and twentieth, highlights the long-run trend of the real price of precious metals as the basic determinant of the world money stock. Its distribution around the world was determined by regional (national) demand factors (real income and tastes).

Third, the use of debasement was an early form of the inflation tax. The findings that debasement was a substitute for other sources of revenue unavailable to the king of France, that it was largely ineffective in offsetting the real excess demand for money in the fifteenth century, and that only with the expansion of the tax base did it effectively alleviate the bullion shortage in the late fifteenth and early sixteenth centuries, are compatible with the recent tax-based theory of money [Sargent (1982) and Smith (1985)].

Finally the recurrent debasement–renforcement cycle observed in fourteenth and fifteenth century France and Burgundy touches on the recent issues of time consistency [Kydland and Prescott (1977)] and credibility [Barro and Gordon (1983)]. To alleviate a temporary revenue shortfall, the king debased the coinage, thereby earning greater seigniorage, but the public quickly caught on, forcing up prices. In other words, the king followed a time-inconsistent policy. To maintain the real value of his revenues a further debasement was needed, with the same results. Eventually the public refused to convert its bullion to coin at the royal mint, instead converting it at foreign mints. Foreign coin displaced domestic coin (according to Miskimin, the French king periodically tried to prohibit the circulation of foreign coin but was unsuccessful). To restore credibility and his source of seigniorage the King ordered a "renforcement" (currency reform) restoring the former silver content of his coinage. The debasement process was then repeated at the next emergency followed by another "re-inforcement." Eventually the public refused to accept the King's coinage at par, and seigniorage revenues steadily declined. Only with the development of an effective fiscal system was credibility restored and the public became willing to again hold royal money at par.

References

Barro, R. and D. Gordon, 1983, Rules, discretion and reputation in a model of monetary policy, Journal of Monetary Economics, 12, 101–121.

Bordo, M. D., 1986, Explorations in monetary history: A survey of the literature, Explorations in Economic History, Vol. 23, October, pp. 339–415.

Capie, F., 1986, Conditions in which hyperinflation has appeared, Carnegie-Rochester Conference Series 24, 115–168.

Cipolla, C., 1956, Money, prices and civilization in the Mediterranean world: Fifth to seventeenth century (Princeton University Press, Princeton, NJ).

Day, J., 1989, The Great Bullion Famine of the fifteenth century, Past and Present 79, 1–53.

Glassman, D. and A. Redish, 1984, Coinage and the money stock in France, 149–1680, Journal of Economic History XLV, 31–46.

Glassman, D. and A. Redish, 1985, Currency depreciation in early modern England and France, Conference on Monetary and Financial History Federal Reserve Bank of Minneapolis, Oct.

Hamilton, E., 1934, American treasure and the price revolution in Spain (Harvard University Press, Cambridge, MA).

Kydland, F. and E. Prescott, 1977, Rules rather than discretion: The inconsistency of optimal plans, Journal of Political Economy 85, 473–491.

Mayhew, N., 1977, Edwardian monetary affairs (1279–1344). British archaeological reports 36 (Oxford).

Miskimin, H. A., 1963, Money prices and foreign exchange in fourteenth century France (Yale University Press, CT).

Miskimin, H. A., 1963, Monetary movements and market structure – Forces for contraction in fourteenth and fifteenth century England, Journal of Economic History XXLV, 470–490.

Miskimin, H. A., 1972, Enforcement of Gresham's law, in: Atti delle "Settimane di Studio", ed altri convegni, Vol. 4 (Instituto Internazional di Storia Economica. "F. Datini", Prato).

Miskimin, H. A., 1975, The economy of early renaissance Europe, 1300–1460 (Cambridge University Press, New York).

Miskimin, H. A., 1977, The economy of later renaissance Europe. 1460–1600 (Cambridge University Press, Cambridge).

Miskimin, H. A., 1983, Money and money movements in France and England at the end of the Middle Ages, in: J. Richard, ed., Precious metals in the later medieval and early modern worlds (Carolina Academic Press, Durham, NC).

Miskimin, H. A., 1984, Money and power in fifteenth century France (Yale University Press, New Haven, CT).

Munro, J., 1973, Wool cloth and gold: The struggle for bullion in Anglo Burgundian trade: 1340–1478 (University of Toronto Press, Toronto).

Munro, J., 1983, Bullion flows and monetary contraction in later mediaeval England and the Low Countries, in: J. Richards, ed., Precious metals in the late mediaeval and early modern worlds (Carolina Academic Press, Durham, NC).

Neal, L. and E. Schubert, 1985, The first rational bubbles: A new look at the Mississippi and South Sea schemes, Working paper (University of Illinois, Champaign, IL).

Nef, J., 1952, Mining and metallurgy in medieval civilisation, in: M. Postan, ed., Cambridge economic history of Europe, II (Cambridge).

Postan, M., 1950, Some economic evidence of declining population in the latter Middle Ages. Economic History Review 2nd ser., II, 221–246.

Postan, M., 1952, The trade of medieval Europe: The North, Cambridge Economic History II, 191–222.

Postan, M., 1959, Note, Economic History Review 2nd ser., XII, 77–82.

Postan, M., 1966, Medieval agrarian society in its prime: England, in Cambridge Economic History I, 2nd ed. (Cambridge) 560–570.

Postan, M., 1972, The medieval economy and society: An economic history of Britain, 1100–1500 (London).

Reed, C., 1979, Price movements, balance of payments, bullion flows and unemployment in the fourteenth and fifteenth centuries, Journal of European Economic History 8, 479–481.

Richards, J., 1983, Precious metals in the later mediaeval and early modern worlds (Carolina Academic Press, Durham, NC).

Sargent, T. J., 1982, The ends of four big inflations, in: R. Hall, ed., Inflation: Causes and effects (University of Chicago Press, Chicago, IL).

Smith, B., 1985, American colonial monetary regimes: The failure of the quantity theory and some evidence in favor of an alternative view, Canadian Journal of Economics 18, 531–565.

Spufford, P., 1970, Monetary problems and policies in the fifteenth century Burgundian Netherlands 1435–1496 (E. J. Brill, Leiden).

Watson, A., 1967, Back to gold and silver, The Economic History Review 2nd ser., XX, 1–34.

White, E. N., 1985, Financing the French revolution: A new look at the assignat inflation, Mimeo (Rutgers University, New Brunswick, NJ).

Wicker, E., 1985, Colonial monetary standards contrasted: Evidence from the Seven Years War, Journal of Economic History XLV, 869–884.

Wolfe, M., 1972, The fiscal system of renaissance France (Yale University Press, New Haven, CT).

The Bretton Woods International Monetary System

The Bretton Woods International Monetary System: A historical overview

After twenty years of floating exchange rates, there is now considerable interest, among those concerned over its perceived shortcomings, in an eventual return by the world to a fixed exchange rate regime. This interest has been enhanced by the apparent success of the European Monetary System (EMS) and the prospects for European monetary unification. The Bretton Woods system was the world's most recent experiment with a fixed exchange rate regime. Although it was originally designed as an adjustable peg, it evolved in its heyday into a de facto fixed exchange rate regime. That regime ended with the closing by President Richard Nixon of the gold window on 15 August 1971. Twenty years after that momentous decision, a retrospective look at the performance of the Bretton Woods system is timely.

This chapter presents an overview of the Bretton Woods experience. I analyze the system's performance relative to earlier international monetary regimes – as well as to the subsequent one – and also its origins, operation, problems, and demise. In the survey, I discuss issues deemed important during the life of Bretton Woods and some that speak to the concerns of the present. The survey is limited to the industrial countries – the G-10 and especially the G-7. I do not examine the role of the International Monetary Fund (IMF), the fundamental organization of Bretton Woods, in the economies and international economic relations of the developing nations.

Section 12.1 compares the macro performance of Bretton Woods with the preceding and subsequent monetary regimes. The descriptive statistics on nine key macro variables point to one incontrovertible conclu-

This chapter is reprinted from Michael D. Bordo and Barry Eichengreen (eds.), *A Retrospective on the Bretton Woods System: Lessons for International Monetary Reform.* Chicago: University of Chicago Press, 1993, pp. 3–98.

For helpful comments and suggestions the author would like to thank Forrest Capie, Max Corden, Barry Eichengreen, Lars Jonung, Charles Kindleberger, Adam Klug, Allan Meltzer, Donald Moggridge, Hugh Rockoff, Anna Schwartz, Leland Yeager, and the NBER conference participants. His thanks for providing data on Japan go to James Lothian and Robert Rasche. Valuable research assistance has been provided by Bernhard Eschweiller and Johan Koenes.

sion. Both nominal and real variables exhibited the most stable behavior in the past century under the Bretton Woods system, in its full convertibility phase, 1959–71. While Bretton Woods was relatively stable, it was also very short lived. From the declaration of par values by thirty-two countries on 18 December 1946 to the closing of the gold window on 15 August 1971, it lasted twenty-five years.[1] However, most analysts would agree that, until the Western European industrial countries made their currencies convertible on 27 December 1958, the system did not operate as intended. On this calculation, the regime lasted only twelve years. Alternatively, if we date its termination at the end of the Gold Pool and the start of the two-tier system on 15 March 1968, it was in full operation only nine years.

This raises questions about why Bretton Woods was statistically so stable and why it was so short lived. (1) Was Bretton Woods successful in producing economic stability because it operated during a period of economic stability, or did the existence of the adjustable peg regime produce economic stability? Alternatively, was its statistical stability an illusion – belied by the presence of continual turmoil in the foreign exchange markets? (2) Why did the system crumble after 1968 and end (so far) irrevocably in August 1971? These questions are addressed below.

Section 12.2 surveys the origins of Bretton Woods: the perceived problems of the interwar period; the plans for a new international monetary order; and the steps leading to the adoption of the Articles of Agreement.

Section 12.3 examines the preconvertibility period from 1946 to 1958, the problems in getting started exemplified by the dollar shortage and the weakness of the IMF, and the transition of the system to convertibility and the gold dollar standard.

Section 12.4 analyzes the heyday of Bretton Woods from 1959 to 1967 in the context of the gold dollar standard and its famous three problems: adjustment, liquidity, and confidence. I review both the problems and the many proposals for monetary reform.

Section 12.5 considers the emergence of a "de facto" dollar standard in 1968 and its collapse in the face of U.S. -induced inflation.

Finally, Section 12.6 summarizes the main points of the chapter, and discusses some lessons learned from the Bretton Woods experience for the design of a fixed exchange rate regime.

---

[1] The par value system was preserved by the Smithsonian Agreement, 18 December 1971, until its final abandonment on 1 March 1973.

12.1   The performance of Bretton Woods in comparison to alternative monetary regimes

The architects of the Bretton Woods system wanted a set of monetary arrangements that would combine the advantage of the classical gold standard (i.e., exchange rate stability) with the advantage of floating rates (i.e., independence to pursue national full employment policies). They sought to avoid the defects of floating rates (destabilizing speculation and competitive beggar-thy-neighbor devaluations) and the defects of the fixed exchange rate gold standard (subordination of national monetary policies to the dictates of external balance and subjection of the economy to the international transmission of the business cycle). As a consequence, they set up an adjustable peg system of fixed parities that could be changed only in the event of a fundamental disequilibrium.

The architects derived their views of an ideal international monetary arrangement from their perception of the performance of the pre–World War I classical gold standard and of the sequence of floating rates and gold exchange standard that characterized the interwar period. As background to the historical survey of Bretton Woods, I compare descriptive evidence on the macro performance of the internatioal monetary regime of Bretton Woods with that on the performance of preceding and subsequent regimes. The comparison for the seven largest (non-Communist) industrialized countries (the United States, the United Kingdom, Germany, France, Japan, Canada, and Italy) is based on annual data for Bretton Woods (1946–70), the present regime of floating rates (1974–89), and the two regimes preceding Bretton Woods: the interwar period (1919–39) and the classical gold standard (1881–1913). The Bretton Woods period (1946–70) is divided into two subperiods: the preconvertible phase (1946–58) and the convertible phase (1959–70).[2] The comparison also relates to the theoretical issues raised by the perennial debate over fixed versus flexible exchange rates. According to the traditional view, adherence to a (commodity-based) fixed exchange rate regime, such as the gold standard, ensured long-run price stability for the world as a whole because the fixed price of gold provided a nominal anchor to the world money supply. By pegging their currencies to gold, individual nations fixed their price levels to that of the world. The disadvantage of fixed rates is that individual nations were

---

[2] I also examined the period 1946–73, which includes the three years of transition from the Bretton Woods adjustable peg to the present floating regime. The evidence is similar to that of the period 1946–70, so it is not presented here.

exposed to both monetary and real shocks transmitted from the rest of the world via the balance of payments and other channels of transmission (Bordo and Schwartz, 1989). Also, the common world price level under the gold standard exhibited secular periods of deflation and inflation reflecting shocks to the demand for and supply of gold (Bordo 1981; Rockoff, 1984). However, a well-designed monetary rule could avoid the long-run swings that characterized the price level under the gold standard (Cagan 1984). The advantage of floating exchange rates is to provide insulation from foreign shocks. The disadvantage is the absence of the discipline of the fixed exchange rate rule – monetary authorities could follow inflationary policies.

Theoretical developments in recent years have complicated the simple distinction between fixed and floating rates. In the presence of capital mobility, currency substitution, policy reactions, and policy interdependence, floating rates no longer necessarily provide insulation from either real or monetary shocks (Bordo and Schwartz 1989). Moreover, according to recent real business cycle approaches, there may be no relation between the international monetary regime and the transmission of real shocks (Baxter and Stockman 1989). Nevertheless, the comparison between regimes may shed light on these issues.

One important caveat is that the historical regimes presented here do not represent clear examples of fixed and floating rate regimes. The interwar period is composed of three regimes: general floating from 1919 to 1925, the gold exchange standard from 1926 to 1931, and a managed float to 1939.[3] The Bretton Woods regime cannot be characterized as a fixed exchange rate regime throughout its history: the preconvertibility period was close to the adjustable peg envisioned by its architects; the convertible period was close to a de facto fixed dollar standard.[4] Finally, although the period since 1973 has been characterized as a floating exchange rate regime, at various times it has experienced varying degrees of management.

Table 12.1 presents descriptive statistics on nine macro variables for each country, the data for each variable converted to a continuous annual series from 1880 to 1989. The nine variables are the rate of inflation, real per capita growth, money growth, short- and long-term nominal interest rates, short- and long-term real interest rates, and the absolute rates of change of nominal and real exchange rates. The definition of the variable used (e.g., Ml vs. M2) was dictated by the availability

---

[3] To be more exact, the United States stayed on the gold standard until 1933 and France until 1936. For a detailed comparison of the performances of these three regimes in the interwar period, see Eichengreen (1989a).

[4] Within the sample of seven countries, Canada floated from 1950 to 1961.

Table 12.1. *Descriptive statistics of selected open economy macro variables, the G-7 countries, 1881–1989*

	Bretton Woods: total, 1946–70		Bretton Woods: preconvertible, 1946–58		Bretton Woods: convertible, 1959–70		Floating exchange, 1974–89		Interwar, 1919–38		Gold standard, 1881–1913	
	M	SD	M	SD	M	SD	M	SD	M	SD	M	SD
A. Inflation PGNP[a]												
United States	2.4	2.6 (3.0)	2.8	3.5 (2.6)	2.6	1.5 (0.7)	5.6	2.4 (1.7)	−1.8	7.6 (8.2)	0.3	3.1 (3.1)
United Kingdom	3.7	2.2 (2.3)	4.6	2.5 (2.8)	3.4	1.5 (1.2)	9.4	6.1 (4.0)	−1.5	7.8 (8.2)	0.3	3.1 (3.0)
Germany	2.7	4.0 (4.1)	2.1	6.2 (3.9)	3.2	1.8 (1.7)	3.3	1.3 (0.7)	−2.1	4.7 (4.8)	0.6	2.6 (2.6)
France	5.6	4.1 (4.2)	5.6	5.1 (5.0)	5.5	3.6 (3.5)	8.8	3.2 (2.2)	2.2	9.1 (9.4)	−0.0	5.0 (4.5)
Japan	4.5	4.6 (4.6)	4.2	5.7 (5.0)	5.5	1.0 (0.8)	2.6	2.4 (1.6)	−1.7	7.3 (8.5)	4.6	5.5 (5.6)
Canada	2.7	3.0 (2.7)	2.1	3.1 (2.4)	3.5	1.1 (0.9)	7.9	3.0 (3.0)	−1.9	6.0 (6.3)	0.4	1.4 (1.3)
Italy	3.8	11.5 (7.9)	5.9	16.0 (8.1)	3.8	2.1 (2.6)	12.9	4.6 (2.6)	−1.1	11.7 (10.7)	0.6	3.2 (3.3)
Mean	3.6	4.6	3.9	6.0	3.9	1.8	7.2	3.3	−1.1	7.7	1.0	3.4
Convergence	0.9	2.0	1.3	2.9	0.9	0.6	2.9	1.2	1.0	1.5	1.0	1.0
B. Real per capita growth[a]												
United States	2.0	2.8	1.8	3.4	2.9	1.9	2.1	2.7	0.2	8.1	1.8	5.0

Table 12.1. (cont.)

	Bretton Woods: total, 1946–70		Bretton Woods: preconvertible, 1946–58		Bretton Woods: convertible, 1959–70		Floating exchange, 1974–89		Interwar, 1919–38		Gold standard, 1881–1913	
	M	SD	M	SD	M	SD	M	SD	M	SD	M	SD
United Kingdom	2.1	1.8	2.1	2.2	2.3	1.4	1.5	4.2	1.2	4.5	1.1	2.4
Germany	5.0	3.3	7.3	3.9	3.6	2.6	2.2	1.9	2.6	8.5	1.7	2.9
France	3.9	2.2	4.6	2.7	3.9	1.3	1.7	1.5	1.3	7.2	1.5	4.6
Japan	8.1	2.7	7.3	2.8	8.9	2.4	3.5	1.1	2.0	6.1	1.4	3.8
Canada	2.5	2.6	1.9	3.2	3.8	1.1	1.6	2.6	0.2	8.8	2.3	2.8
Italy	5.6	3.3	5.2	4.4	5.8	1.9	2.5	2.2	0.9	4.7	1.0	4.1
Mean	4.2	2.7	4.3	3.2	4.5	1.8	2.2	2.3	1.2	6.8	1.5	3.7
Convergence	1.8	0.4	2.1	0.6	1.7	0.5	0.5	0.7	0.7	1.5	0.3	0.8
C. Money growth[a]												
United States	6.3	5.8	6.4	8.3	7.0	1.5	8.6	2.4	0.6	8.6	6.1	5.9
United Kingdom	3.2	3.2	1.7	2.9	5.5	2.9	13.5	5.6	0.8	4.7	2.1	1.7
Germany	12.8	6.0	17.6	5.6	10.9	4.7	5.7	4.5	1.3	10.1	5.7	4.7
France	11.5	7.5	14.7	7.2	8.6	6.6	8.8	3.4	6.4	8.5	2.2	3.5
Japan	17.3	15.9	18.2	18.5	14.6	2.5	5.7	6.2	0.5	9.7	5.8	10.8
Canada	6.0	4.0	5.0	3.9	9.4	4.3	11.0	5.5	1.1	4.7	7.4	5.3
Italy	13.3	7.8	15.9	10.5	12.4	2.0	13.4	4.9	3.6	6.2	3.2	3.1
Mean	10.1	7.2	11.4	8.1	9.8	3.5	9.5	4.6	2.0	7.5	4.6	5.0
Convergence	4.2	2.8	6.0	3.7	2.5	1.4	2.7	1.1	1.7	2.0	1.8	2.0
D. Short-term interest rate												
United States	3.4	1.9	2.0	0.9	4.8	1.6	8.9	2.6	3.5	2.0	4.8	0.9

United Kingdom	4.0	2.5	2.3	1.8	5.8	1.6	11.2	2.1	3.0	1.8	2.8	0.8
Germany	4.0	1.5	4.1	1.1	4.0	1.7	5.9	2.4	4.8	1.6	3.2	0.9
France	4.2	1.9	3.2	1.5	5.1	1.9	10.3	2.6	3.1	1.4	2.5	0.6
Japan	6.5	0.8	6.8	0.8	5.9	0.4	5.2	2.0	2.0	0.5	2.4	0.5
Canada	2.9	2.0	2.2	1.3	4.8	1.3	9.2	3.4	0.9	0.4	N.A.	
Italy	N.A.		N.A.		N.A.		N.A.		N.A.		N.A.	
Mean	4.2	1.8	3.5	1.2	5.1	1.4	8.5	2.5	2.9	1.3	3.2	0.7
Convergence	0.8	0.3	1.3	0.2	0.5	0.2	1.9	0.3	0.9	0.4	0.7	0.2

E. Long-term interest rate

United States	3.9	1.3	3.0	0.4	5.0	1.1	10.4	2.1	4.2	0.6	3.8	0.3
United Kingdom	5.2	1.8	3.9	0.8	6.6	1.3	12.1	2.8	4.1	0.7	2.9	0.2
Germany	6.3	0.7	5.9	0.5	6.7	0.7	7.8	1.5	6.9	1.8	3.7	0.2
France	5.7	0.8	5.8	0.5	5.7	1.0	10.9	2.4	4.6	0.8	3.2	0.3
Japan	7.0	0.1	N.A.		7.0	0.1	7.1	1.8	N.A.	0.8	N.A.	0.4
Canada	4.5	1.5	3.8	0.8	5.9	1.0	10.3	2.3	4.7	0.6	3.5	0.5
Italy	6.0	0.7	6.3	0.4	5.7	0.7	13.7	3.3	5.9	0.9	4.2	0.3
Mean	5.5	1.0	4.8	0.6	6.1	0.9	10.3	2.3	5.1	0.9	3.6	0.3
Convergence	0.9	0.5	1.2	0.1	0.6	0.3	1.7	0.5	0.9	0.3	0.3	0.1

F. Real short-term interest rate[b]

United States	0.3	3.9	-1.2	4.7	2.4	0.4	2.5	2.8	3.8	6.7	4.8	2.0
United Kingdom	-0.1	3.4	-2.4	3.3	2.3	1.1	1.3	5.1	4.2	7.1	2.9	2.3
Germany	2.2	2.6	3.0	3.6	1.6	1.5	2.5	1.9	5.1	5.2	2.4	2.3
France	-0.9	5.2	-3.3	6.9	1.2	1.4	2.1	2.8	1.2	14.7	2.8	6.4
Japan	1.9	2.5	2.7	2.8	0.5	1.1	1.4	3.5	1.4	8.8	-1.5	5.5
Canada	-0.3	4.2	0.1	3.4	2.0	0.7	2.5	3.2	-0.8	1.3	N.A.	
Italy	N.A.		N.A.		N.A.		N.A.		N.A.		N.A.	
Mean	0.5	3.6	-0.2	4.1	1.7	1.0	2.0	3.2	2.5	7.3	2.3	3.7
Convergence	1.0	0.6	2.1	0.9	0.6	0.3	0.5	0.7	1.9	2.7	1.5	1.8

Table 12.1. (cont.)

	Bretton Woods: total, 1946–70		Bretton Woods: preconvertible, 1946–58		Bretton Woods: convertible, 1959–70		Floating exchange, 1974–89		Interwar, 1919–38		Gold standard, 1881–1913	
	M	SD	M	SD	M	SD	M	SD	M	SD	M	SD
G. Real long-term interest rate[b]												
United States	0.8	3.6	−0.7	4.4	2.5	0.7	3.9	3.8	4.6	6.8	3.7	2.2
United Kingdom	1.1	2.8	−0.8	2.6	3.2	1.0	2.2	3.7	5.4	7.1	3.0	2.5
Germany	4.3	2.8	4.3	4.4	4.3	1.0	4.4	0.9	6.9	6.0	2.9	2.4
France	0.4	4.4	−1.2	6.2	1.8	1.0	2.7	3.1	1.0	(15.1)	3.5	6.5
Japan	1.7	1.3	N.A.		1.7	1.3	2.0	4.2	N.A.		N.A.	
Canada	1.3	3.8	3.8	0.8	3.0	0.6	3.6	2.8	4.7	0.8	3.5	0.4
Italy	−0.4	12.1	6.3	0.4	2.2	2.2	0.5	5.3	5.9	0.6	4.2	0.5
Mean	1.3	4.4	2.0	3.1	2.7	1.1	2.7	3.4	4.8	6.1	3.5	2.4
Convergence	1.0	2.2	2.9	1.9	0.7	0.4	1.1	1.0	1.3	3.6	0.4	1.4
H. Nominal exchange rate[c]												
United States	0.7	0.8			0.7	0.8						
United Kingdom	2.4	6.3	3.6	8.3	1.4	3.9	10.1	4.7	6.8	7.9	0.2	0.2
Germany	1.8	3.8	2.4	5.3	1.3	2.1	9.3	8.2	3.9	9.5	0.2	0.1
France	2.5	7.7	4.4	11.3	1.1	3.3	10.7	7.8	17.8	16.9	0.3	0.2
Japan	15.9	37.2	22.0	42.6	0.2	0.2	8.8	9.5	6.7	8.9	2.9	4.5

Canada	1.6	1.9	2.2	2.0	0.8	1.9	3.7	2.4	2.6	3.4	0.0	0.0
Italy	7.4	20.6	14.1	27.4	0.2	0.2	10.9	9.0	13.6	20.1	1.4	1.5
Mean	4.6	11.2	8.1	16.1	0.8	1.8	8.9	6.9	8.6	11.1	0.8	1.1
Convergence	4.0	10.1	6.6	12.6	0.4	1.2	1.8	2.3	4.8	4.9	0.9	1.3
I. Real exchange rate[c,e]												
United States[d]	1.7	1.0			1.7	1.0						
United Kingdom	3.5	5.5	4.7	7.1	2.5	3.5	9.4	4.3	6.5	6.9	1.7	1.5
Germany	2.8	5.1	3.8	7.3	1.9	1.8	8.8	8.2	5.8	9.2	2.4	1.2
France	4.1	5.6	6.2	7.7	2.5	2.9	9.2	7.7	8.9	6.9	4.3	5.0
Japan	3.0	1.5	4.4	4.3	2.1	1.2	9.6	8.9	7.8	7.2	6.6	5.6
Canada	2.4	2.3	2.4	2.3	1.2	1.7	3.8	2.0	3.2	2.8	2.6	2.2
Italy	8.0	18.7	13.1	25.2	2.4	1.6	8.6	7.8	13.3	16.9	2.1	1.7
Mean	3.6	5.7	5.8	9.0	2.0	2.0	8.2	6.5	7.6	8.3	3.3	2.9
Convergence	1.4	3.7	2.6	5.4	0.4	0.7	1.4	1.9	2.4	3.2	0.9	1.6

Note: For inflation, the standard deviation of the forecast error based on a univariate regression is shown in parentheses. The forecast error is calculated as the standard error of estimate of the fitted equation $\ln(P_t) = a + b\,\ln(P_{t-1})$, where P_t is the price index in year t.

[a] Mean growth rate calculated as the time coefficient from a regression of the natural logarithm of the variable on a constant and a time trend.

[b] Calculated as the nominal interest rate minus the annual rate of change of the CPI.

[c] Absolute rates of change.

[d] Trade-weighted nominal and real exchange rate starting in 1960.

[e] Calculated as the nominal exchange rate divided by the ratio of foreign to the U.S. CPI.

Sources: See the Appendix.

of data over the entire period. For each variable and each country, I present two summary statistics: the mean and the standard deviation. For inflation, I also show (in parentheses) the standard deviation of the forecast error based on a univariate regression. For all the countries taken as a group, I show two summary statistics: the grand mean and a simple measure of convergence measured as the mean of the absolute differences between each country's summary statistic and the grand means of the group of countries.[5] I comment on the statistical results for each variable.

Inflation: The classical gold standard had the lowest rate of inflation, and the interwar period displayed mild deflation. The rate of inflation during the Bretton Woods period was on average, and for every country except Japan, lower than during the subsequent floating exchange rate period. The average rate of inflation in the two Bretton Woods subperiods was virtually the same. However, this comparison conceals the importance of two periods of rapid inflation in the 1940s and 1950s and in the late 1960s (see Figure 12.1).[6] Thus, the evidence based on country and period averages of very low inflation in the gold standard period and of a lower inflation rate during Bretton Woods than the subsequent floating period is consistent with the traditional view of price behavior under fixed (commodity-based) and flexible exchange rates.

In addition, the inflation rates show the highest degree of convergence between countries during the classical gold standard and to a lesser extent during the Bretton Woods convertible subperiod compared to the floating rate period and the mixed interwar regime. This evidence also is consistent with the traditional view of the operation of the classical price specie flow mechanism and commodity arbitrage under fixed rates and insulation and greater monetary independence under floating rates.[7]

The Bretton Woods convertible subperiod had the most stable inflation rate of any regime judged by both the standard deviation and the forecast error.[8] By contrast, the preconvertible Bretton Woods period exhibited greater inflation variability than either the gold standard or the recent float. However, most of this difference can be accounted for by

---

[5] This is a very crude measure of convergence or divergence between the different countries' summary statistics. Because it is based on the average for the whole period, it suppresses unusual movements within particular subperiods. These will be discussed in the text.

[6] The data sources for Figure 12.1 and all subsequent figures are listed in the Data Appendix.

[7] For similar evidence, see Bordo (1981), Darby, Lothian et al. (1983), and Darby and Lothian (1989).

[8] For similar results using the Kalman filter, see Meltzer and Robinson (1989).

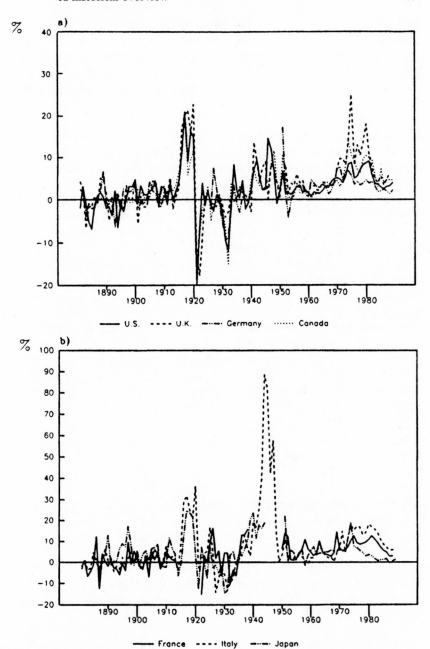

Figure 12.1(A, B). Inflation rates, G-7 countries, 1880–1989.

the high variability of inflation in Italy during the 1940s and 1950s. The evidence of a high degree of price stability in the convertible phase of Bretton Woods is also consistent with the traditional view that fixed rate (commodity-based) regimes provide a stable nominal anchor; however, the remarkable price stability during this period may also reflect the absence of major shocks.

Real per capita GNP: Generally, the Bretton Woods period exhibited the most rapid growth of any monetary regime, especially the convertible period, and, not surprisingly, the interwar period the lowest (see Figure 12.2). Output variability was also lowest in the convertible subperiod of Bretton Woods, but, because of higher variability in the preconvertible period, the Bretton Woods system as a whole was more variable than the floating period. Both pre–World War II regimes exhibit higher variability than their post–World II counterparts. The Bretton Woods regime also exhibited the lowest divergence of output variability between countries of any regime, with the interwar regime the highest. The lower variability of real output during Bretton Woods than during other periods may reflect a lower incidence of real shocks, it may reflect a lower incidence of monetary surprises, or it may be the result of countercyclical monetary and fiscal policies.[9] In turn, the greater convergence of output variability under Bretton Woods may reflect the operation of the fixed exchange rate regime, which created conformity between countries' business fluctuations (Bordo and Schwartz 1989; Darby and Lothian 1989).

Money growth (M₂): Money growth was considerably more rapid across all countries after World War II than before. There is not much difference between Bretton Woods and the subsequent floating regime. Within the Bretton Woods regime, money growth was more rapid in the preconvertibility period than in the convertibility period. Money growth rates showed the least divergence between countries during the fixed exchange rate gold standard and the convertible Bretton Woods regime, with the greatest divergence in the preconvertible Bretton Woods period and the interwar period. Of key importance for the viability of the Bretton Woods system, however, is the fact that money growth in the United States, the center of the system, was considerably lower than

---

[9] For evidence that, by using a different detrending filter than the logarithm first-difference used here, real output variability is not greater in the floating period than in the fixed period, see Baxter and Stockman (1989). See also Sheffrin (1988), Bergman and Jonung (1990), and Backus and Kehoe (1992).

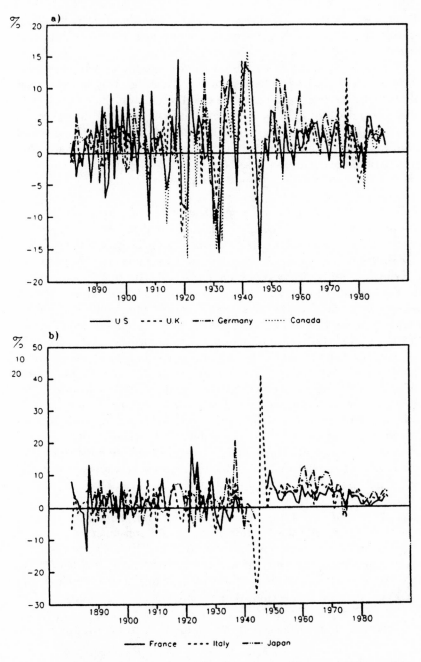

Figure 12.2(A, B). Per capita income growth rates, G-7 countries, 1880–1989.

the average of the G-7 countries in both subperiods but increased both absolutely and relatively between the two subperiods (see Figure 12.3 and also Figure 12.29).

Like inflation and real output variability, money growth variability was lowest in the convertible Bretton Woods period. This, however, was not the case for the preconvertible period, which was the most variable of any regime. Money growth also exhibited the greatest divergence in variability between countries. To the extent that one of the properties of adherence to a fixed exchange rate regime is conformity of monetary growth rates between countries, these results are sympathetic to the view that the Bretton Woods system really began in 1959.

Short- and long-term interest rates: The underlying data can be seen in Figures 12.4 and 12.5. As in other nominal series, the degree of convergence of mean short-term interest rates is highest in the convertible Bretton Woods period. Long-term rates are most closely related in the classical gold standard, with the convertible Bretton Woods period not far behind. These findings are similar to those of McKinnon (1988), who views them as evidence of capital market integration under fixed exchange rates. The lack of convergence in the preconvertibility Bretton Woods period reflects the presence of pervasive capital controls. Convergence of nominal interest rates would not be expected under floating exchange rates. Convergence of standard deviations is also highest in the gold standard period, followed by Bretton Woods. Long-term rates were most stable and least divergent under the classical gold standard, followed by the two Bretton Woods subperiods, with floating exchange rates the least stable. The evidence that nominal interest rates are more stable and convergent between countries under fixed exchange rate (commodity-based) regimes is consistent with the traditional view.

Real short- and long-term interest rates: The real interest rates are ex post rates calculated using the rate of change of a consumer price index.[10] (For the underlying data, see Figures 12.6 and 12.7.) Unlike the nominal series, the degree of convergence in means between real short-term interest rates is lowest in the floating exchange rate period, next lowest in the Bretton Woods convertible period, and highest in the preconvertible period. For long-term real rates, as in the case of nominal rates, convergence is highest under the gold standard, followed by the Bretton Woods

---

[10] Define the real interest rate as $r_t = i_t - \Delta \log P_t$, where i_t is the nominal interest rate, and $\Delta \log P_t = \log P_t - \log P_{t-1}$ is the percentage change in the consumer price index.

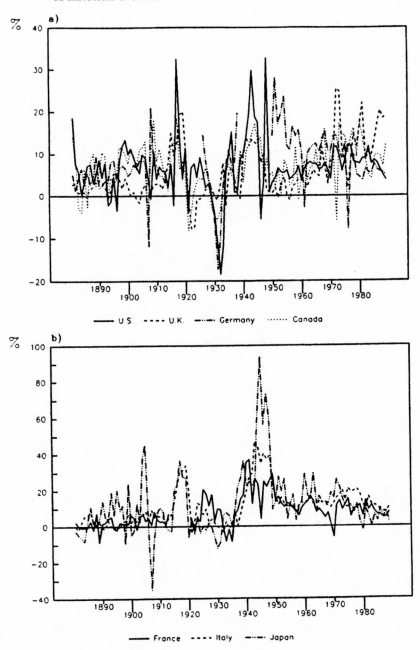

Figure 12.3(A, B). Money growth rates, G-7 countries, 1880–1989.

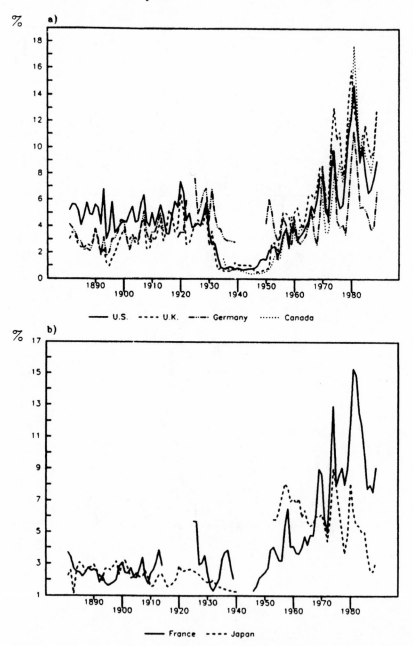

Figure 12.4(A, B). Short-term interest rates, G7 countries, 1880–1989.

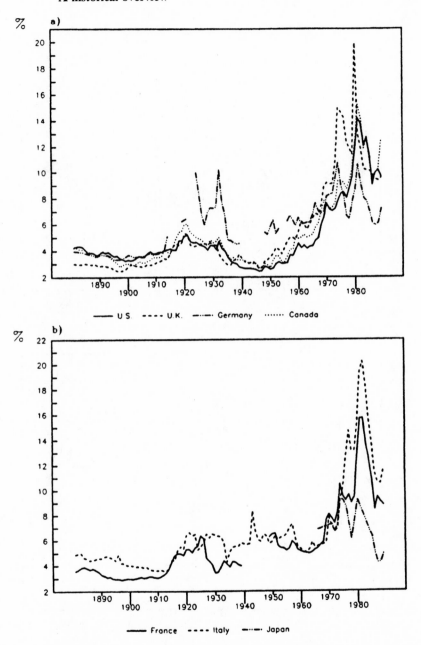

Figure 12.5(A, B). Long-term interest rates, G7 countries, 1880–1989.

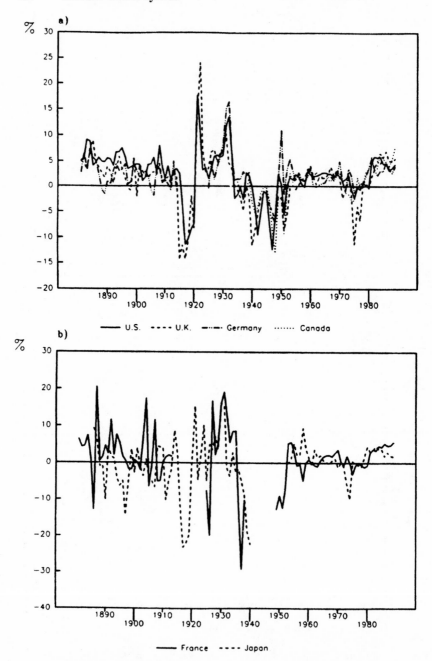

Figure 12.6(A, B). Real short-term interest rates, G7 countries, 1880–1989.

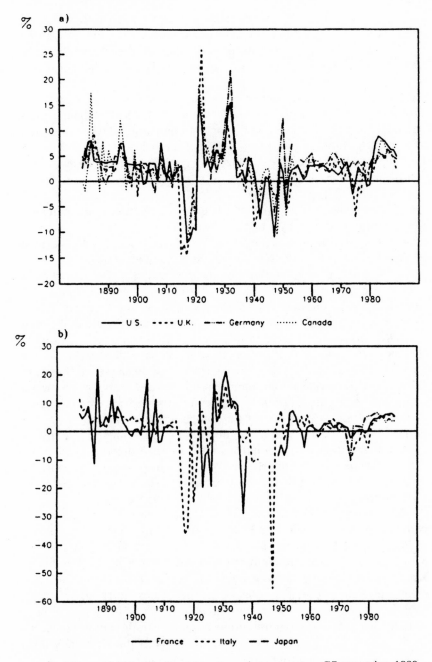

Figure 12.7(A, B). Real long-term interest rates, G7 countries, 1880–1989.

convertible regime. It is lowest under preconvertible Bretton Woods. The real short-term interest rate is most stable across countries during the Bretton Woods convertible period, when it also shows the least amount of divergence in standard deviations. The same holds for real long-term interest rates.

The behavior of real interest rates across regimes is consistent with McKinnon's (1988) explanation. He argued that fixed exchange rates encourage capital market integration by eliminating devaluation risk. This reduces variability in short-term real interest rates. Similarly, real long-term interest rates are stabilized by pooling across markets, which reduces capital market risk.

Nominal and real exchange rates:[11] The lowest mean rates of change of the nominal exchange rate and the least divergence between rates of change occurred during the Bretton Woods convertible and the gold standard periods, with the former exhibiting the lowest degree of divergence. Exchange rates during the preconvertibility Bretton Woods regime changed almost as much as during the floating period. This mainly reflected the major devaluations of 1949 (see Figure 12.8 and Table 12.2). Nominal exchange rates were the least variable in the gold standard and convertible Bretton Woods periods and the most variable and most divergent in the Bretton Woods preconvertible period.

As with the nominal exchange rate, the lowest mean rate of change in the real exchange rate across countries and the least divergence between countries was in the Bretton Woods convertible period, with the gold standard period next in size of these measures (see Figure 12.9). The highest rate of change was in the floating period. Similarly, the lowest standard deviation across countries and the least divergence between standard deviations was the Bretton Woods convertible period, with the gold standard again next in these rankings. The other regimes were characterized by much greater variability and divergence.

These results shed light on the relation between the nominal exchange rate regime and the behavior of real exchange rates. Mussa (1986) presented evidence for the G-10 countries in the post–World War II period showing the similarity between nominal and real exchange rate variability under floating rates. His explanation for greater real exchange rate variability under floating rates than under fixed rates is nominal price rigidity (see also Dornbusch, 1976). Alternatively, nominal exchange rate rigidity produces greater trade stability reflected in the real exchange rate, as is evident for both the Bretton Woods

[11] For use of this measure, see Grilli and Kaminsky (1991).

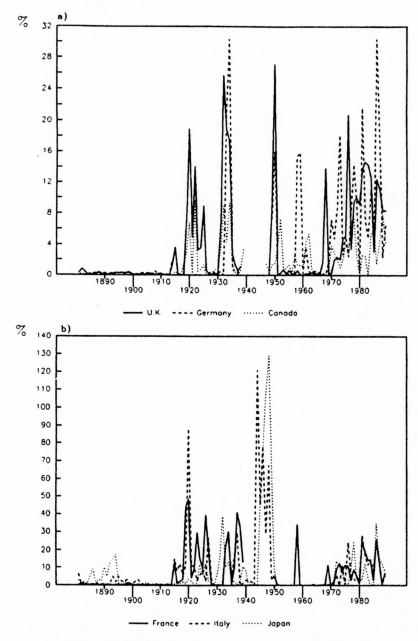

Figure 12.8(A, B). Absolute change in nominal exchange rates, G7 countries, 1880–1989.

Table 12.2. *Exchange rate and gold arrangements, the G-10 countries, 1946–1971*

	1946[a]	1948	1949	1950	1951	1953	1957	1958
Belgium	BF 43.83		9/22, Devaluation to 50 BF/$					12/27, BF becomes convertible de facto
Canada	$1.00		9/19, Devaluation to $1.10	9/30, Par value suspended	Float →			
France	FR 119.1	1/26, Par value[b] suspended	9/20, 350 Fr/$				8/11, Rate set at 420 Fr/$	12/29, Official per value set at 493.7 Fr/$ (12/27, Convertible de facto)
Germany		6/20/DM introduced at 3.33 DM/$	9/19, Devaluation to 4.20 DM/$			1/30, Official par value set at 4.20 DM/$		12/27, Convertible de facto

416

Italy		Sept., Rate set at 625 L/$ by monetary authorities		12/27, Convertible de facto
Japan	No true exchange rate →	4/25, Official rate set at 360 ¥/$ by monetary authorities	5/11, Official par value set at 360 ¥/$	
Netherlands	G 2.65	9/21, Devaluation to 3.80 G/$		12/27, Convertible de facto
Sweden	7/13, Official rate 3.60 SKr/$ set by monetary authorities	9/20, Devaluation to 5.17 SKr/$	11/5, Official par value set at 5.17 SKr/$	12/27, Convertible de facto
United Kingdom	£0.248	9/18, Devaluation to 0.357 £/$		12/27, Convertible de facto
United States	$35/oz. gold			

417

Table 12.2. (cont.)

	1960	1961	1962	1964	1967	1968	1969	1970	1971
Belgium		2/15, BF becomes convertible under Article VIII							
Canada	Float →	5/2, Official	Par value set at $1.08					5/31, Float	
France	New Fr (= 100 old Fr)	2/15, Fr becomes convertible under Article VII					8/10, Devaluation to 5.55 Fr/$		
Germany		3/6, Revaluation to 4.00 DM/$ 2/15, Convertible under Article VIII					10/26, Revaluation to 3.66 DM/$[c]		5/9, Float
Italy	3/30, Official par value set at 625 L/$	2/15, Convertible under Article VIII							
Japan				4/1, ¥ becomes convertible under Article VIII					

Netherlands	3/7, Revaluation to 3.62 G/$		5/9, Float
	2/15, Convertible under Article VIII		
Sweden	2/15, Convertible under Article VIII		
United Kingdom	2/15, Convertible under Article VIII	11/18, Devaluation to 0.417 £/$	
United States	Nov., London Gold Pool established	3/15, Gold Pool suspended. 3/17, two-tier gold market instituted	8/15, Suspension of gold convertibility

Source: Various IMF publications.

Note: BF = Belgian franc; Fr = French franc; DM = deutsche mark; L = lira; ¥ = yen; G = guilders; SKr = Swedish krona.

a Initial parity: price of U.S. $1.00.

b Multiple exchange rates were in effect from January 1948 to September 1949. From 26 January to 16 October, a rate of 214.4 Fr/U.S.$ applied to all foreign exchange actions in nonconvertible currencies and to selected imports paid in convertible currencies. For all other transactions, the effective rate was the average of the 214.4 rate and the free rate. On 16 October 1948, the average rate was made applicable to all transactions except nontrade transactions in convertible currencies.

c From 29 September to 26 October, the exchange rate was floating.

419

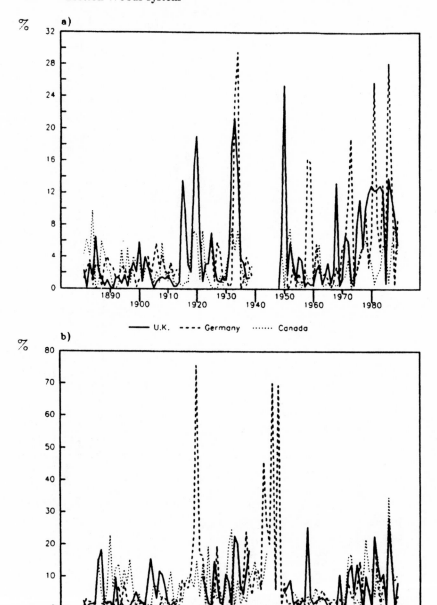

Figure 12.9(A, B). Absolute change in real exchange rates, G7 countries, 1880–1989.

and the gold standard periods. Yet, as Eichengreen (1990c) points out, this could be explained by the fact that both periods were characterized by few shocks.[12]

Finally, Grilli and Kaminsky (1991) provided evidence for the United Kingdom and the United States, based on monthly data from 1880 to 1986, that shows that, with the exception of the post–World War II period, no clear connection exists between the nominal exchange rate regime and the variability of real exchange rates. My results for the G-7 show a clear correlation between nominal exchange rate rigidity and lower real exchange rate variability for the gold standard and Bretton Woods convertible regime. For the preconvertible Bretton Woods period – de jure a type of fixed exchange rate regime – the correlation is not evident. I do not distinguish between fixed and flexible exchange rate episodes in the interwar period, as do Grilli and Kaminsky; hence that period cannot be used in the comparison.

The Bretton Woods regime exhibited the best overall macro performance of any regime. This is especially so for the convertible period, 1959–70.[13] As the summary statistics in Table 12.1 show, both nominal and real variables were the most stable in this period. The preconvertible period, 1946–58, was considerably less stable for the average of all countries for both nominal and real variables. Also, both nominal and real variables did not vary nearly as closely together as in the convertible period. These differences likely reflect the presence of pervasive exchange and capital controls before 1958 and, related to these, more variable and more rapid monetary growth.

These data are limited. Although they show excellent performance for the convertible Bretton Woods regime, they do not tell us why it did so well – whether it reflected a set of favorable circumstances or the absence of aggravating shocks, or whether it reflected stable monetary policy by the key country of the system, the United States, or whether it masked underlying strains to the system. They also do not tell us whether the system was dynamically stable, that is, whether it would endure, or whether it was just a flash in the pan of history.

[12] Stockman (1983, 1988) argues that greater variability in real exchange rates under floating rates than under fixed rates reflects the reaction of real exchange rates to productivity shocks, with changes in the real exchange rate producing nominal exchange rate volatility. This volatility is offset under fixed rates by exchange market intervention.

[13] McKinnon (1993) treats the period 1950–70 as the de facto dollar standard. He views this period, rather than 1959–71, as the appropriate one for making the type of regime comparisons undertaken here. I made the same calculations as those shown in Table 12.1 for the period 1950–71. Virtually every variable for each country exhibited greater instability than in the period 1959–70. This reinforces my choice of dates.

12.2   The origins of Bretton Woods

12.2.1   Perceived problems of the interwar period

The planning that led to the creation of a new international monetary order at Bretton Woods was predicated on the belief that the mistakes of the interwar period were to be avoided. These mistakes included, first, wildly fluctuating exchange rates after World War I and the collapse of the short-lived gold exchange standard; thereafter, the international transmission of deflation and the resort to beggar-thy-neighbor devaluations; and, finally, trade and exchange restrictions and bilateralism. The goal was the negotiation of an international monetary constitution based on stable exchange rates, national full employment policies, and cooperation. Three issues dominated the perception of the interwar experience: the flaws of the gold exchange standard; the case against floating exchange rates; and bilateralism. I survey each in turn.

The gold exchange standard: The gold exchange standard began de facto in 1925 after Britain returned to the gold standard at the prewar parity, followed in the next two years by most countries. The case for "gold economy" was made at the Genoa conference in 1922. The world could avoid a massive gold shortage, produced in large part by wartime inflation, by two measures: first, by nations adopting a gold bullion standard and demonetizing gold as a national currency; second, by using foreign exchange (primarily pounds and dollars) as international reserves and stockpiling monetary gold in the key reserve centers of London and New York. The gold exchange standard lasted only six years. It ended with Britain's suspension of gold convertibility in September 1931. The subsequent literature focused on the three problems that later plagued Bretton Woods: adjustment, liquidity, and confidence (Johnson 1972a), although Keynes and White, the architects of Bretton Woods, paid attention only to the first two (Dam 1982, Chap. 3; Eichengreen 1990b).

The adjustment problem involved two issues: first, asymmetric adjustment between deficit (Britain) and surplus countries (the United States), which led to a deflationary bias, and, second, the failure by all countries to follow the rules of the game. The United States and France (with an undervalued gold parity after 1926, the Bank of France being prevented by law after 1928 from holding reserves other than gold against its domestic note issue) together absorbed 53% of the world's monetary gold reserves by 1924 (Eichengreen, 1990a, Table 10.1). As surplus countries, they sterilized gold inflows and avoided expansionary monetary policy and inflation. At the same time, the steady gold drain from Britain (with an overvalued parity)[14] and other deficit countries ultimately caused them to contract their money supplies. Sterilization by the surplus countries only worsened the gold drain from the deficit countries. In addition, according to Nurkse (1944) and Eichengreen (1990b), in an attempt to shield the domestic economy from foreign disturbances, virtually every central bank actively or passively followed a policy of offsetting changes in international reserves by changes in domestic credit, hence breaking the "rules of the game." Such policies at best slowed the adjustment of relative national prices and incomes required to restore balance of payments equilibrium under the gold standard.

The interwar liquidity problem involved gold supplies (at the prevailing set of gold parities) inadequate to finance the growth of world output and trade and to serve as gold cover to back national currencies. To economize on gold, peripheral countries used the key currencies as international reserves, but, as the ratio of their holdings of the key currency (especially the pound) rose relative to the center country's monetary gold stocks, the peripheral countries reduced their foreign exchange holdings, fearing a convertibility crisis (Triffin, 1960).

The interwar confidence problem involved two components: a shift of currency holdings between the two key centers, London and New York (and to a lesser extent, at the end of the period, a shift to Paris), and a shift between the key currencies and gold. Shifts of foreign currency balances from weak to strong reserve centers weakened the system because they increased the likelihood of a confidence crisis in the weak center, which, if it materialized, would then put pressure on the other center (Nurkse 1944). A shift between the key currencies and gold occurred when, fearing the reserve centers' inability to convert their outstanding liabilities into gold at the fixed parity, foreign holders of key currency balances staged a run on the "bank," precipitating a suspension of convertibility, as happened to Britain in September 1931 (Triffin 1960, Chap. 6).

Floating exchange rates and competitive devaluations: Nurkse (1944) based the case against floating exchange rates on the interwar experience: "If there is anything that inter-war experience has clearly demonstrated, it is that paper currency exchanges cannot be left free to fluctuate from day to day under the influence of market supply and demand. . . . If

---

[14] Capie, Mills, and Wood (1986) argue that Britain's abandonment of the gold standard in September 1931 was caused not by sterling overvaluation but by the banking crisis in Austria and Germany.

currencies are left free to fluctuate, speculation in the widest sense is likely to play havoc with exchange rates-speculation not only in foreign exchanges but also, as a result, in commodities entering into foreign trade" (pp. 137–38). Nurkse argued, primarily on the basis of the French experience with floating exchange rates from 1922 to 1926, that freely floating rates inevitably led to destabilizing speculation. The depreciating franc led speculators to anticipate a further decline, ensuring the outcome by speculative capital flight. At the same time, a depreciating exchange rate worsened the balance of trade because importers, anticipating a further devaluation and a rise in import prices, imported more while exporters, expecting the price of exports to rise, held back sales to get a better price later (Nurkse 1944, p. 118).

Furthermore, according to Nurkse, the devaluation of sterling in 1931 led to a spate of competitive devaluations involving considerable overshooting because of the destabilizing nature of speculative flows of hot money. It was commonly believed that devaluations were intended to "beggar thy neighbor," although Nurkse pointed out that, in a number of cases, when devaluation was accompanied by expansionary monetary policy, world trade increased (Nurkse 1944, 123–24).

Bilateralism and exchange controls: Like Nurkse, the architects of Bretton Woods believed that the competitive devaluations and speculative flows of hot money in the 1930s led inevitably to a pervasive system of exchange controls and, in the case of Germany, to a series of discriminating bilateral agreements (see, Ellis 1941; Neal 1979).

The case for an adjustable peg: On the basis of his interpretation of the interwar experience, Nurkse (1944, Chap. 7) envisioned a world monetary system very much like Bretton Woods.[15] To avoid the evils of floating, he would have fixed exchange rates, but, in the event of structural disequilibria in the balance of payments, changes in parity would be allowed rather than exchange controls on current transactions. In the case of short-run payments disequilibria, international reserves would serve as a buffer. Also, exchange rates should be set by an international agreement rather than on a piecemeal basis by each country. Monetary and fiscal policy would be coordinated between countries to ensure full employment. Speculative capital flows would be avoided by pervasive capital controls. Finally, the deflationary bias of the gold exchange stand-

---

[15] Nurkse's interpretaion of the lessons of the interwar experience should be viewed as largely reflecting the collective views of Keynes, White, and others.

ard would be avoided by imposing discriminatory exchange controls against "scarce" currencies.

Was the perception of the interwar experience correct? Many aspects of the perception of the flaws of the interwar system have been challenged. Friedman's (1953) essay on flexible exchange rates disputed Nurkse on both theory and evidence. He argued that every case of destabilizing speculation Nurkse documented involved a prospective change in government policies that would otherwise have changed the exchange rate – that the market just facilitated movement to the new rate (see Dam 1982). Eichengreen's (1982) examination of the French experience found no evidence for destabilizing speculation.[16]

In addition, Eichengreen and Sachs (1985) presented strong evidence against the prevalence of beggar-thy-neighbor devaluations in the 1930s. They showed that most devaluations were accompanied by expansionary monetary policy and that those that were not did not significantly reduce income in other countries. In opposition to the perceived view, Eichengreen (1990b) showed that the breakdown of the gold exchange standard owed a lot more to inappropriate national policies by France and the United States than to the perceived structural flaws in the system. Nevertheless, for Eichengreen (1992), adherence to gold convertibility during the Great Depression was a key determinant of the worldwide spread of deflation and depression.[17]

In conclusion, the perception of the flaws of the interwar international monetary system was crucial in the design of the Bretton Woods system. Yet subsequent studies suggest that a number of these perceptions were incorrect. One wonders how the system would have been designed had the architects been freed from misperceptions.

12.2.2   *The plans and the outcome*

The planning and the bargaining that took place leading to the Bretton Woods conference in both the United States and Britain during World War II reflected both a common vision of the future international monetary order and quite different national concerns. The architects on both sides of the Atlantic wanted a system that would avoid the defects of the interwar period and promote world peace. Common beliefs in-

---

[16] See also Yeager (1976). Aliber (1962), however, provides mixed evidence for a number of European countries.
[17] Here Eichengreen follows Friedman and Schwartz (1963). See also Temin (1989) and Bernanke and James (1991).

cluded a multilateral payments system, stable exchange rates, and full employment. However, key differences in the positions of power and economic importance of the two allies dictated quite different national concerns.

The United States emerged from the war as the strongest and richest power in the world. It expected to be a creditor nation. Britain's resources and power were greatly weakened by the war – it had liquidated most of its external assets and borrowed heavily from the Commonwealth and to a lesser extent from the United States. It expected to be a debtor nation. The Roosevelt administration attached great importance to the elimination of discriminatory trade and exchange controls by the British, especially the system of imperial preference negotiated at Ottawa in 1931, and of bilateral agreements. Restoration of a multilateral payments system based on convertible currencies was paramount. The British were most concerned that the United States not repeat its deflationary policies of the 1930s. They wanted the freedom to pursue domestic full employment policies without concern over the state of the balance of payments. They also wanted the preservation of the British Commonwealth, assistance in wartime reconstruction, and relief on the repayment of outstanding sterling balances (Gardner 1969, Chaps. 1–2).

Wartime negotiations leading to the Atlantic Charter, 14 August 1941, and the Mutual Aid Agreement, 28 Februay 1942, especially Article 7, led to a compromise between the two nations, which created the setting for the planning for Bretton Woods. The British agreed to accept a multilateral payments system with ultimate convertibility of sterling in exchange for a U.S. commitment to maintain full employment, the preservation of the Commonwealth, generous terms on lend lease, and U.S. assistance in the postwar recovery (Gardner 1969, Chaps. 3–4).

Against this background of diplomatic negotiations, the British Treasury team of planners led by John Maynard Keynes and the American team led by Harry Dexter White drafted two competing plans for the postwar international monetary order. Each plan went through a series of drafts, and the final versions, known as the Keynes and White plans, were published in 1943.[18] A compromise between the two plans, following a period of intense negotiations, led to the *Joint Statement by Experts on the Establishment of an International Monetary Fund* (IMF [1944] 1969d). The Joint Statement served as the working draft at the Bretton Woods conference and led directly to

---

[18] For a discussion of the development of the Keynes plan, see Moggridge (1986); for the White plan, see Oliver (1975).

the *Articles of Agreement of the International Monetary Fund* (IMF [1944] 1969b).[19]

The Keynes plan (Keynes [1943] 1969) was designed to encourage the expansion of world trade and activity by the generous provision of international liquidity. It was also designed to shield the domestic economy from foreign disturbances via the provision of a buffer stock of international reserves. The essence of the plan was the establishment of a supernational central bank, the International Clearing Union (ICU), that would issue a new international money to be called *bancor*. The nominal value of bancor was to be fixed in terms of gold; every national currency would set its par value in terms of bancor.[20] The central bank of each member nation would keep accounts with the ICU to settle balances between other members at par in bancor. Surplus nations would maintain credit balances earning interest. Deficit nations could settle their balances by obtaining overdrafts that would bear interest and that would be transferred to the credit of the surplus countries. Each country would be assigned a quota to determine the limit on resources it could obtain. The plan would provide generous liquidity facilities – between $25 and $30 billion. It also imposed extensive regulations governing the balances of both debtors and creditors – debtors faced increasingly stiff penalties as they used up successive tranches of their quotas, the penalties including devaluation and the imposition of capital controls. Creditors were to take measures including expansionary domestic credit, appreciation of their currencies, cutting tariffs, and extending international development loans.[21] Creditors would bear more of the burden of adjustment because there was no limit on the amount of bancor liquidity they would have to accept, whereas debtors were limited by their quotas.[22] A final important aspect of the plan was the provision of permanent capital controls to prevent destabilizing speculation against the fixed parities.

The White plan (White [1943] 1969) put more emphasis in its design on exchange rate stability and less on the generous provision of international liquidity than its British counterpart. The key institution of the U.S. plan was the creation of a United Nations Stabilization Fund. Each member would contribute to the fund a quota consisting of gold and its

---

[19] For excellent discussions of the negotiations, see Gardner (1969, Chaps. 5, 7) and Van Dormael (1978).

[20] Gold could be paid into the ICU and would serve as reserves, but bancor could not be redeemed in gold. Gold could also be used in settlement between members.

[21] According to Meltzer (1988) and Moggridge (1986), this reflected Keynes's preference for rules over discretion.

[22] For the United States, this meant up to $26 billion in liabilities to be absorbed.

own currency. The total subscription was $5 billion. A deficit country would draw resources from the Fund by selling its currency for that of another member, rather than running an overdraft with the ICU as in the Keynes plan. Consequently, its balances at the Fund would increase, while those of the member whose currency had been drawn would decline. Each member would declare a par value for its currency in terms of *unitas*, an international unit of account worth ten gold U.S. dollars. Each member was obliged to maintain that par value, except in the event of a fundamental disequilibrium in the balance of payments, when it could be altered. In that case, if the proposed change was less than 10%, it could be made after consultation with the Fund. If larger, it needed approval by three-quarters of the members. As with the Keynes plan, various penalties were imposed on debtor countries when their borrowings exceeded their quotas.[23] These included the Fund's suggestion of appropriate domestic policies to facilitate adjustment. Less pressure was placed on creditor countries. However, by the final draft of the plan, a scarce currency clause allowed the Fund to recommend rationing its use by exchange controls.[24] In the months that followed the publication of the two plans, an initial compromise was reached in the Joint Statement, and further compromise was made by the time of the Articles (Dam 1982). In the compromise, the British gave up the ICU, bancor, the overdraft system, and the generous provision of liquidity, settling for $8 billion in the Joint Statement, $8.8 billion at Bretton Woods. The British gained greater national policy autonomy for members, who were allowed discretion over changes in the exchange rate (with Fund approval required to correct a fundamental payments disequilibrium). They also gained the authorization of capital controls in the agreement. The Fund's discretion to intervene in domestic policymaking to facilitate adjustment was eliminated from both plans, as was explicit conditionality on credit drawings. The scarce currency clause was viewed as a solution to British concerns

---

[23] In contrast to the ICU, the regulations for the Fund were less extensive and the conditions attached to access to the Fund's resources less clear cut and more open to discretion, especially in the earlier drafts (Moggridge 1986).

[24] A third plan, John Williams' key currency plan (Williams [1936] 1969a, [1943] 1969b), which was never seriously considered, would have had the United States and Britain follow the experience of the Tripartite Agreement of 1936, when the United States, Britain, and France coordinated their exchange market intervention to stabilize the pound and franc exchange rates with the dollar. In the Williams plan, the monetary authorities of the United States and Britain would have set up a joint Exchange Stabilization Fund to stabilize the dollar-pound exchange rate. The two countries would also have coordinated their monetary policies to maintain full employment. Other countries would initially be allowed to float until their currencies could be stabilized in terms of the key currencies. Ultimately, the world would evolve into a key currency system, with other nations using the key currencies to finance payments imbalances.

over the deflationary potential of the United States running a large surplus. Finally, the British requests for postwar assistance were dropped from the negotiations, although they were met in part by a transition clause allowing exchange controls on current account transactions for a number of years, by the exclusion of sterling balances from the convertibility requirements, and later by the Anglo-American Loan of $3.75 billion on 6 December 1945.

A number of special conditions may have contributed to the successful outcome of the negotiations at Bretton Woods. First, the United States and Britain (with the aid of Canada) were able to work out an agreement that was a compromise between their two national interests without involving other countries who were either belligerents or under occupation. Second, as the strongest economic power, the United States was able to dominate the terms of the agreement.[25] Third, a strong sense of idealism prevailed in both countries – that, as victors in a war to save democracy, they had an obligation to create a stable postwar international monetary order that would help secure the peace (Gardner 1969, Chap. 1).[26] Fourth, the negotiators on both sides of the Atlantic were experts who shared a common set of perceptions of the problems of the interwar period, had common views on the importance of full employment and a liberal multilateral payments system, and greatly respected John Maynard Keynes. These experts negotiated in an atmosphere conducive to cooperation and free of immediate political concerns (Ikenberry, 1990 and 1993).

12.2.3   The Articles of Agreement

The Articles of Agreement incorporated elements of both the Keynes and the White plans, although, in the end, U.S. concerns predominated.[27] The objectives of the Fund were to promote international monetary cooperation, to facilitate the maintenance of full employment and rapid growth, to maintain stable exchange rates and avoid competitive devaluations, to provide a multilateral payments system and eliminate ex-

---

[25] Eichengreen (1989b), however, argues that, despite U.S. dominance, the British were able to obtain a remarkable number of concessions.

[26] Of course, this was the thinking that led to the establishment of the United Nations and other international institutions.

[27] At the same time as the Articles of Agreement for the IMF were signed, the International Bank for Reconstruction and Development (the World Bank) was established. The Charter of the International Trade Organization (ITO) was drafted and signed in 1947, but never ratified. It was succeeded by the General Agreement for Tariffs and Trade (GATT), originally negotiated in Geneva in 1947 as an interim institution until the ITO came into force.

change restrictions, to provide resources to meet balance of payments disequilibria without resort to drastic measures, and to shorten the duration and lessen the degree of payments disequilibria.

The main points of the Articles were the creation of the par value system, multilateral payments, the use of the Fund's resources, the Fund's powers, and its organization.

The par value system: Article IV defined the numeraire of the international monetary system as either gold or the U.S. dollar of the weight and fineness on 1 July 1944. All members were urged to declare a par value and maintain it within a 1% margin on either side of parity. Parity could be changed in the event of a fundamental payments disequilibrium at the decision of the member, after consultation with the Fund. However, the Fund would not disapprove the change if it was less than 10%, and, if it was more than 10%, the Fund would decide within seventy-two hours. Unauthorized changes in the exchange rate could make members ineligible to use the Fund's resources and, if they were to persist, could lead to a member's expulsion. A uniform change in par value of all currencies (in terms of gold) required a majority of the total voting power and also had to be approved by every member with 10% or more of the total quota.

Multilateral payments: Members were supposed to make their currencies convertible for current account transactions (Article VIII), but capital controls were permitted (Article VI.3). They were also to avoid discriminatory currency and multiple currency arrangements. The convertibility requirement applied to foreign balances accumulated by current account transactions but exempted previously accumulated balances (Article VIII.4). Presumably, this clause was to protect the sterling balances accumulated at the end of World War II (Pressnell, 1986). However, countries could avoid declaring their currencies convertible by invoking Article XIV, which allowed a three-year transition period after establishment of the Fund. During the transition period, existing exchange controls could be maintained. After the three-year grace period, the Fund was to report on the state of convertibility; after five years and every year thereafter, under Article XIV, the members, in individual consultation, had to justify their position to the Fund.

The fund's resources: As under the White plan, members could obtain resources from the Fund to help finance short- or medium-term payments disequilibria. The total Fund, contributed by members' quotas (25% in gold, 75% in currencies), was set at $8.8 billion. It could be raised every five years if the majority of members wanted to do so. The Fund set a number of conditions on the use of its resources by deficit countries to prevent it from accumulating soft currencies and from depleting its holdings of harder currencies.[28] It also established requirements and conditions for repurchase (repayment of a loan), including giving the Fund the right to decide the currency in which the repurchase would be made. In the case of countries prone to running large surpluses, the scarce currency clause (Article VII) could come into play. If the Fund's holdings of a currency were insufficient to satisfy the demand for it by other members, it could declare that currency scarce and then urge members to ration its use by discriminatory exchange controls.

The powers of the fund: The Fund had considerably less discretionary power over the domestic policies of its members than either of the architects wanted, but it still had the power to strongly influence the international monetary system. It had the authority to approve or disapprove of changes in parity, the use of multiple exchange rates and other discriminatory practices, and the conditionality that was implicit in members' access to the credit tranches of their quotas and made explicit by 1952 (Diz 1984). It could declare currencies scarce, declare members ineligible to use its resources (a power used against France in 1948), and expel members. The Fund also had considerable power as the premier international monetary organization in consulting and cooperating with national and other international monetary authorities.

Organization: The Fund was to be governed by a board of governors appointed by the members. The board would make the major policy decisions, such as approving a change in parity. Operations of the Fund were to be directed by executive directors, appointed by the members, and a managing director, selected by the executive directors. Major changes, such as a uniform change in the par value of all currencies or the Second Amendment creating the special drawing right (SDR), would require a majority vote by the members. The number of votes in turn was tied to the size of each member's quota, which was determined by its economic size.

How was the Bretton Woods system supposed to work? The architects never spelled out exactly how the system was supposed to work.

---

[28] Members could draw on their quotas without condition. Once they borrowed beyond their quotas – a situation referred to later as the *credit tranche*, although not spelled out in the Articles – increasingly more exacting conditions were required.

However, subsequent writers have suggested a number of salient features.[29] First, currencies were treated as equal in the Articles. This meant that, in theory, each country was required to maintain its par value by intervening in the currency of every other country – a practice that would have worked at cross-purposes. In actual fact, because the United States was the only country that pegged its currency in terms of gold (bought and sold gold), all other countries would fix their parities in terms of dollars and would intervene to monitor their exchange rates within 1% of parity with the dollar.

Second, countries would use their international reserves or draw resources from the Fund to finance payments deficits. In the case of surpluses, countries would temporarily build up reserves or repurchase their currencies from the Fund. In the event of medium-term disequilibria, they would use monetary and fiscal policy to alter aggregate demand. In the event of a fundamental disequilibrium, which was never defined but presumably reflected either some structural shock or sustained inflation, a member was supposed to alter parity by an amount sufficient to restore external equilibrium. Third, capital controls were required to prevent destabilizing speculation from forcing members to alter their parities prematurely or unintentionally.

The system that began operations after the Bretton Woods conference and the establishment of the IMF was different in many major respects from what the architects intended. One question that this raises is, Had the world not evolved as it did into a gold dollar standard, how would the real Bretton Woods system have worked?

12.3   The history of Bretton Woods: Preconvertibility, 1946–58

The international monetary system that began after World War II was far different from the system that the architects of Bretton Woods envisioned. The transition period from war to peace was much longer and more painful than was anticipated. Full convertibility of the major industrial countries was not achieved until the end of 1958, although the system had started functioning normally by 1955. Two interrelated problems dominated the first postwar decade: bilateralism and the dollar shortage.

---

[29] See, e.g., Tew (1988), Scammell (1976), and Yeager (1976). Williamson (1985) viewed the system as a comprehensive set of rules for assigning macroeconomic policies: using exchange rates to maintain medium-run external balance, using monetary and fiscal policy to achieve short-run internal balance, and using international reserves to provide a buffer shock to allow short-run departures from external balance.

12.3.1 Bilateralism

For virtually every country except the United States, the legacy of World War II was one of pervasive exchange controls and controls on trade. Except the dollar, no major currencies were convertible.[30] Under Article XIV of the Bretton Woods agreement, countries could continue to use exchange controls for an indefinite transition period after the establishment of the IMF on 1 March 1947.[31] In conjunction with exchange controls, every country negotiated a series of bilateral payments agreements with each of its trading partners.[32] The rationale given for the continued use of controls and bilateralism was a shortage of international reserves. After the war, the economies of Europe and Asia were devastated. To produce the exports needed to generate foreign exchange industries, new and improved capital was required. There was an acute shortage of key imports, both foodstuffs to maintain living standards and raw materials and capital equipment. Controls were used to allocate the scarce reserves.

The bilateral arrangements in each country typically consisted of licenses and quotas for imports and exports and the allocation of foreign exchange through the central bank, with commercial banks acting as agents. Each central bank typically negotiated an agreement with its partners providing an overdraft facility in its currency called the "swing"

---

[30] Under the classical gold standard, *convertibility* referred to the ability of a private individual freely to convert a unit of any national currency into gold at the official fixed price. A suspension of convertibility meant that the exchange rate between gold and a national currency became flexible, but the individual could still freely transact in either asset (Triffin, 1960, p. 22). By the eve of World War II, *convertibility* referred to the ability of a private individual freely to make and receive payments in international transactions in terms of the currency of another country. Under Bretton Woods, *convertibility* meant the freedom for individuals to engage in current account transactions without being subject to exchange controls. Tew (1988, p. 50) refers to this as "market convertibility" and distinguishes it from "official convertibility," whereby the monetary authorities of each country must be freely willing to buy and sell foreign exchange (primarily dollars) to keep the parity fixed (within the 1% margin) and the United States must be freely willing to buy and sell gold to maintain the fixed price of $35.00 per ounce (within the 1% margin). He refers to both market and official convertibility as "Bretton Woods convertibility" (see also McKinnon, 1979, Chap. 2; and Black, 1987).

[31] Under Article XIV, three years after 1 March 1947 the IMF would begin reporting on the countries with existing controls; two years later it would begin consulting with individual members, advising them on policies to restore payments equilibrium and convertibility. Countries that did not make satisfactory progress would be censured and ultimately asked to leave the Fund. In actual fact, the Fund always accepted the member's reason for remaining under Article XIV.

[32] Two hundred agreements alone were negotiated in Western Europe in 1947 (Yeager, 1976, p. 407).

up to a specified limit (similar in concept to international reserves), with settlement in foreign exchange beyond that. The United Kingdom developed a particularly complicated set of arrangements. Sterling was convertible for all transactions within the sterling area. Certain privileged countries were allowed transferable account status, whereby they could settle foreign balances in sterling earned from their exports, and, in 1946–47, these balances could be used in settling dollar payments. A third group of countries had bilateral account status.

12.3.2   The dollar shortage

By the end of World War II, the Untied States held two-thirds of the world's monetary gold stock (see Figure 12.10). The gold avalanche in the United States in the 1930s was the consequence of both the dollar devaluation in 1934, when the Roosevelt administration raised the price of gold from $20.67 to $35.00 per ounce, and capital flight from Europe. During the war, gold inflows continued to finance wartime expenditures by the Allies. At the end of World War II, Europe's (and Japan's) gold and dollar reserves were depleted. Europe ran a massive current account deficit reflecting the demand for essential imports and the reduced capacity of the export industries.[33] The deficit of the OEEC (Organization for European Economic Cooperation) countries, aggravated by the bad winter of 1946–47, reached a 1947 high of $9 billion (Triffin, 1957, p. 32) (see Figure 12.11), the amount of the U.S. current account surplus (see Figure 12.12), since, as the only major industrial country operating at full capacity, the United States supplied the needed imports. The dollar shortage was likely aggravated by overvalued official parities by the major European industrial countries set at the end of 1946 (see Table 12.2). The IMF pressured its members to declare par values as soon as possible. It was argued that the balance of payments deficits facing most countries reflected the structural incapacity of their export industries rather than a lack of competitiveness. If the exchange rate chosen was inappropriate, it could be corrected later. The crucial test was the ability to export at all (Black 1991, Chap. 3). Most countries adopted their prewar dollar parities on the assumption that wartime and postwar inflation did not seriously disrupt their competitive positions relative to the United States (Triffin 1957, Chap. 2).

The immediate postwar experience of massive payments deficits and depleted international reserves in Europe and the opposite situation in the United States led many to believe that the dollar shortage was

---

[33] Similar conditions prevailed in Japan (Solomon 1976, p. 14).

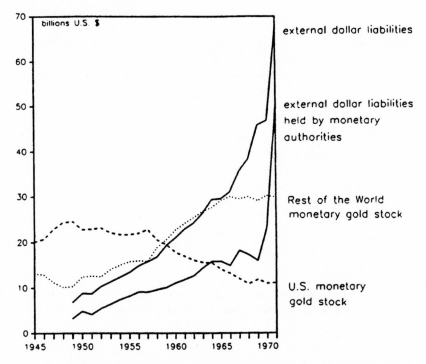

Figure 12.10. Monetary gold and dollar holdings, the United States and the rest of the world, 1945–71.

permanent. Theories of a permanent dollar shortage abounded (see Kindleberger 1950; McDougall 1957; and, for a critical appraisal, Yeager 1976, Chap. 27, app.). The key explanation for a permanent shortage was that the rate of productivity advance in the rest of the world would never catch up to that of the United States. Alternative explanations included inadequate raw materials, lower savings rates, political instability, and lack of entrepreneurial drive. Advocates of these theories recommended a series of policy proposals, including discrimination against U.S. exports, massive U.S. aid, the encouragement of private capital flows to Europe, and devaluation.

12.3.3 How the System Evolved

By the mid-1950s, both problems had been solved. The currencies of Western Europe were virtually convertible by 1955, and their current accounts were generally in surplus (see Figure 12.13). The key develop-

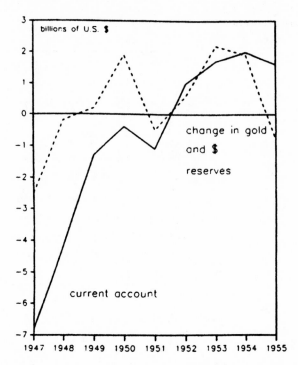

Figure 12.11. OEEC European balance of payments, 1947–55.

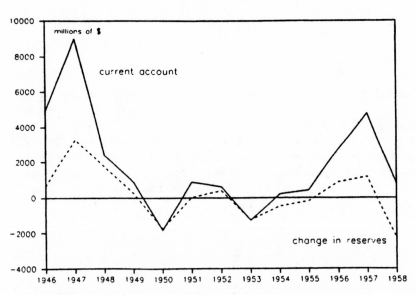

Figure 12.12. U.S. balance of payments, 1946–58.

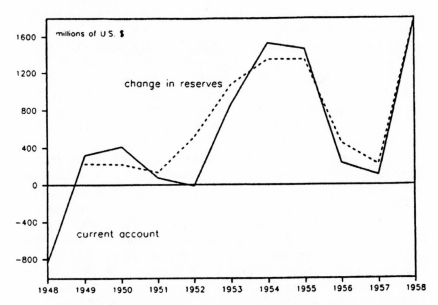

Figure 12.13. Balance of payments of Germany, Italy, and France, 1948–58.

ments in this progression were the Marshall Plan and the European Payments Union (EPU). Three other important developments in this period were the decline of sterling, the reduced prestige of the IMF, and the rise of the dollar as the key currency.

The Marshall Plan: The Marshall Plan funneled approximately $13 billion in aid (grants and loans) to Western Europe between 1948 and 1952 (see Milward 1984; and Hoffman and Maier 1984).[34] It followed interim postwar U.S. and U.N. aid in 1947. The Economic Co-Operation Act of 1948, which created the Marshall Plan, was designed to help the European countries expand their economies, restore their export capacity, and, by creating economic stability, preserve political stability. These results would follow by providing relief from the burden of financing a massive payments deficit. The plan required the members to cooperate in the liberalization of trade and payments. Consequently, the OEEC was established in April 1948. It presided over the allocation of aid to members, aid based on the size of their current account deficits. U.S. aid was to pay for essential imports and provide international reserves. Each

[34] Japan received $1.25 billion in assistance (loan and grants) (Solomon 1976, p. 15).

recipient government provided matching funds in local currency to be used for investment in the productive capacity of industry, agriculture, and infrastructure. Each country also had a U.S. commission that advised the host government on the spending of its counterpart funds. The plan encouraged the liberalization of intra-European trade and payments by granting aid to countries that extended bilateral credits to other members. Finally, the EPU was established in 1950, under the auspices of the OEEC, to simplify bilateral clearing and pave the way to multilateralism.

By 1952, in part thanks to the Marshall Plan, the OEEC countries had achieved a 39% increase in industrial production, a doubling of exports, an increase in imports by one-third, and a current account surplus (Solomon 1976, p. 18) (see Figure 12.13). According to Eichengreen and Uzan (1991), the Marshall Plan permanently raised the growth rates of the recipients, but not through the traditional channels of investment, government spending, and the current account balance. It did so by improving productivity and investor confidence. This in turn was achieved by reducing the political instability associated with "the war of attrition" between workers and property owners and by filling the role usually played by foreign private investment.

The EPU and the return to convertibility: It took twelve years from the declaration of official par values by thirty-two nations in December 1946 to the achievement of convertibility for current transactions by the major industrial countries as specified by the Bretton Woods Articles.[35] The Western European nations tried several schemes to facilitate the payments process before establishing the EPU (see Kaplan and Schleiminger 1989).

The EPU, established 19 September 1950 by the OEEC countries, was initially meant to run for two years, renewable thereafter on a yearly basis. It followed the basic principle of a commercial bank clearinghouse. At the end of each month, each member would clear its net debit or credit position (against all other members) with the Union [the Bank for International Settlements (BIS) acting as its agent]. The unit of account for these clearings was the U.S. dollar. Settlement was made in dollars, gold, or credit. The division between credit and dollars/gold depended on the quota allocated to each member, which in turn depended on its volume of trade. The Union was started with an initial working capital fund of $350 million provided by the United States.

The EPU was so successful in reducing the volume of payments trans-

---

[35] However, official acceptance of Article VIII status was not achieved until 1961.

actions and providing the background for the gradual liberalization of payments that by 1953 commercial banks were able to engage in multicurrency arbitrage (Tew 1988; Yeager 1976). The EPU became the center of a worldwide multilateral settlement area, including the countries of the sterling and franc zones. In 1954, the United Kingdom extended transferable account status to all countries with which it had bilateral agreements; thus, by 1955 the world was divided into two different convertible areas separated by exchange controls: a soft area, based on the EPU and sterling, and a hard area, based on the dollar. The final steps in closing the gap were achieved in February 1955 – when the Bank of England extended its exchange market operations to pegging the exchange rate on transferable account sterling and the discount on sterling in the Zurich market moved closer to parity – and eight countries declared their currencies convertible for current account transactions on 27 December 1958.[36]

The decline of sterling: In the interwar period, sterling shared the role of key currency with the dollar. It was expected that it would play an important role in the postwar period. As events turned out, sterling's importance declined throughout the Bretton Woods period. At the end of World War II, Britain ran a massive balance of payments deficit, especially in gold and dollars (see Figure 12.14), as did the other European countries. Britain also had an outstanding sterling debt of £3.7 billion amassed during the war by borrowing largely from its empire. Much of these balances were "blocked," that is, made inconvertible into dollars.[37] In December 1945, the United States and Britain negotiated the Anglo-American Loan, which was ratified on 15 July 1946. In exchange for $3.75 billion from the United States and a further $1.25 billion from Canada, the British ratified the Bretton Woods Articles and promised to restore current account convertibility in dollars, except for existing sterling balances, within one year. In 1946–47, transferable account sterling status was extended to all countries with bilateral agreements, and, as promised, convertibility for current account transactions was restored on 15 July 1947. The ensuing run on sterling depleted the United Kingdom's reserves by $1 billion within a month, and convertibility was suspended on 20 August 1947. Transferable account sterling again became subject to exchange controls. As a consequence of the

---

[36] Germany alone, shortly thereafter, made capital account transactions convertible.

[37] Approximately £2.3 billion were held by the sterling area in December 1945. In 1947, before convertibility was attempted, it was agreed that £1.6 billion would be blocked (Pressnell 1986). The balances were reduced considerably in the next decade by the 1949 devaluation and a succession of current account surpluses.

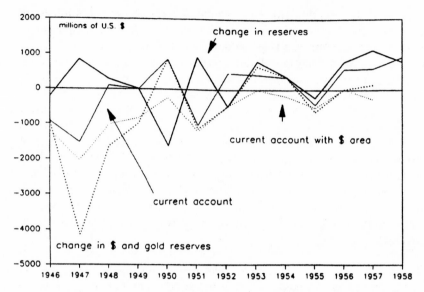

Figure 12.14. U.K. balance of payments, total and in gold and dollars, 1946–58.

unsuccessful 1946 agreement, the return to convertibility by Western European countries, following the cautious reaction by the British, was likely delayed longer than it otherwise would have been. Sterling's role as a reserve currency was further weakened and that of the dollar (by default) strengthened.

A second event that further weakened sterling's credibility as a reserve currency, yet helped restore the international monetary system by reducing both European deficits and the U.S. surplus (and also strengthen the U.K. economy), was the devaluation of sterling in 1949. Although the United Kingdom's balance of payments and current account deficits (against dollars and gold) were shrinking in 1948 and 1949, a U.S. recession reduced the demand for British goods in the second quarter of 1949 (Yeager 1976, p. 444). This, coupled with the growing belief that sterling would be devalued, triggered a speculative run on the pound (Cairncross and Eichengreen 1983, Chap. 4). Speculators evaded the exchange controls by means of leads and lags and took a strong position against sterling in the summer of 1949.[38] Two weeks before the event, the chancellor of the Exchequer, Sir Stafford Cripps, denied that

[38] Foreign buyers of goods from the sterling area delayed their purchases and payments, while importers in the sterling area speeded up their payments.

devaluation was imminent. On 18 September 1949, twenty-four hours after the IMF was informed, the pound was devalued by 30.5% to $2.80. Shortly thereafter, twenty-three countries reduced their parity by, in most cases, similar magnitudes (see Table 12.2). The devaluation improved the current account deficit and the overall balance of payments of the United Kingdom (in gold and dollars), although it deteriorated again in the following two years of Korean War inflation (see Figure 12.14).[39]

The devaluations of 1949 were important for the Bretton Woods system for two reasons. First, they, along with the Marshall Plan aid, helped move the European countries from a current account deficit to a surplus, a movement important to the eventual restoration of convertibility. Second, they revealed a basic weakness of the adjustable peg arrangement – the one-way option of speculation against parity. By allowing changes in parity only in the event of fundamental disequilibrium, the Bretton Woods system encouraged the monetary authorities to delay adjustment until they were sure it was necessary. By that time, speculators would also be sure, and they would take a position from which they could not lose. If the currency is devalued, they win; if it is not, they lose only the interest (if any) on the speculative funds (Friedman 1953).

The role of the IMF: A number of developments and events in the preconvertibility era had great significance for the prestige and subsequent role of the IMF. The IMF, by intention, was not equipped to deal with the postwar reconstruction problem. Although some limited drawings occurred before 1952, most of the structural balance of payments assistance in this period was provided by the Marshall Plan and other U.S. aid, including the Anglo-American Loan of 1945. The consequence of this development is that new institutions such as the OEEC and existing institutions such as the BIS, the agent for the EPU, emerged as competing sources of international monetary authority (Mundell 1969a). Had the original Keynes ICU plan been adopted at Bretton Woods, the difference between the proposed resources of $26 billion and the original fund endowment of $8.8 billion would have nearly equalled the $13 billion given in Marshall Plan assistance.

Moreover, although a key precept of the Articles was multilateralism, little was done by the Fund to achieve that aim before 1952, when, under Article XIV, it began consultation with individual members. The Fund

---

[39] In reaction, the controversial ROBOT plan circulated in 1952 inside the British government, urging the authorities to float the pound, make it convertible into gold and dollars, and fund the sterling balances (see Cairncross 1985, Chap. 9).

did very little to speed up the process of achieving multilateralism because it felt that it was not so empowered (DeVries 1986, Chap. 4). As a consequence, another agency, the EPU, was set up to provide the clearinghouse that Keynes envisioned in the original ICU plan (Triffin 1957, Chap. 3).

Also, in part because of its opposition to floating rates, and in part because of its eagerness to get the system going, the Fund has been criticized for seeking a declaration of par values too soon. The resultant fixed parities then set in motion forces within each country to resist devaluation until it was too late, and the changes that did finally occur in 1949 were larger than necessary (Scammell 1976, Chap. 6).[40] The crisis associated with the 1949 sterling devaluation in turn created further resistance by monetary authorities to changes in parity, which ultimately changed the nature of the international monetary system from the adjustable peg intended by the Articles to a fixed rate regime.

The Fund's prestige was dealt a severe blow by three events in the preconvertibility period (Mundell 1969a). The first was the French devaluation of January 1948 (see Table 12.2), when, in an attempt to economize on scarce hard currency, France created a multiple exchange rate system. The arrangements consisted of a dual rate for hard currencies, with the official rate of 214.39 francs per dollar for basic imports and a floating rate for tourist and financial transactions. The effective rate on hard currency was 260.26; for soft currencies it was the official rate. Under Article IV, section 5, the Fund censured France for creating broken cross rates between the dollar and the pound, thereby diverting exports to be reexported to the United States via France (Horsefield 1969a, p. 203). France was denied access to the Fund's resources until 1952. France ended the broken cross rates in October 1948 and adopted a unified rate in the devaluation of 1949 (see Table 12.2). Since France had access to Marshall Plan aid, the Fund's actions had little effect.

The second event was the sterling devaluation of September 1949. Although the Fund staff had earlier advised the British to devalue (Black 1991, pp. 67–68), the Fund was given only twenty-four hours notice, and the size of the devaluation was larger than suggested. This was in marked contrast to Article IV, section 5, which required a member to consult with the Fund when a devaluation greater than 10% was being considered, with the Fund to be given more than seventy-two hours to concur or object.[41] According to Mundell (1969a), this event

---

[40] According to Triffin (1957, Chap. 3), the Fund made a mistake by not declaring the dollar a scarce currency in 1946. Had it done so, the disastrous experiment with pound convertibility in 1947 could have been avoided.

[41] Seventy-two hours if the devaluation was between 10% and 20%.

revealed the Fund's inability to deter a major power from following its sovereign interest.

The third event was the decision by Canada in September 1950 to float its currency (see Table 12.2). Faced with a massive capital inflow from the United States, the Bank of Canada decided to float the Canadian dollar rather than risk an inappropriate revaluation from the $0.909 parity.[42] The Fund was highly critical of the action. The Canadian monetary authorities assured the Fund that the float was only temporary and that a new parity would be declared when a new equilibrium had been reached. The Canadian dollar floated until 1961. The fact that movements in the Canadian dollar rate were small (see Figure 12.8 above) and that there is no evidence of destabilizing speculation (Yeager 1976, Chap. 26), significantly weakened the case made against floating by the Fund in several annual reports.

Finally, the Fund's resources were inadequate to solve the emerging liquidity problem of the 1960s. The difference between the growth of international reserves required to finance the growth of real output and trade and avoid deflation and the growth in the world's monetary gold stock was met largely by an increase in official holdings of U.S. dollars resulting from growing U.S. balance of payments deficits. By the time full convertibility was achieved, the U.S. dollar was serving the buffer function for which the Articles intended the Fund's resources (Mundell 1969a, p. 481). Had the original Keynes ICU plan been adopted, and had the U.S. undertaken postwar aid through the ECU rather than through Marshall Plan aid, the United States would have accumulated sufficient overdraft facilities to finance most of its deficits in the 1950s and 1960s (Gardner 1972, p. 27). However, the extra liquidity would have likely fueled a higher rate of world inflation than actually occurred.

The emergence of the dollar as a key currency: During the pre-convertibility period, the dollar emerged as the key currency of the international monetary system. At the beginning of the period, sterling was the dominant currency in world reserves, but, by the end of the 1950s, it was eclipsed by the dollar (see Figure 12.15). Moreover, the data overstate the role of sterling because they include blocked sterling balances and sterling used only in the sterling and transferable account areas. Because of the sheer size of the role that the United States plays in the world economy, its great importance in world trade, and its open and deep capital markets, the dollar emerged in the 1950s as a private

---

[42] Canada had originally set its parity in 1946 at $1.00 but devalued with the United Kingdom in 1949 to $0.909.

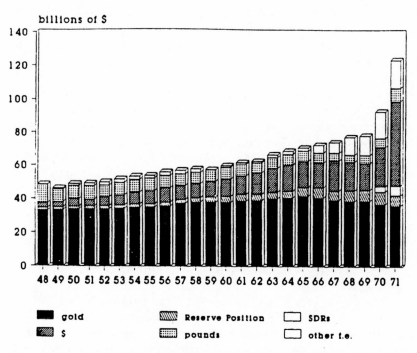

Figure 12.15. The composition of world international reserves, 1948–71 (f.e. = foreign exchange).

international money (McKinnon 1988). It was used as a unit of account in invoicing imports and exports, as a medium of exchange in serving as a vehicle currency for interbank transactions, and as a store of value for private claims. Simultaneously, the dollar emerged as an official international money. This stemmed from its use as a unit of account to define the parities of member countries in the IMF. The dollar was also used as the primary intervention currency – members maintained their fixed parities by buying and selling dollars. Finally, because of its role as a unit of account and a medium of exchange and its growing private acceptance, it became the dominant international store of value to be used as reserves. The growing private and official demand for dollars was supplied through private and official long-term capital outflows in excess of a current account surplus, which produced a series of official settlements balance of payments deficits beginning in 1950 (see Figures 12.12 and 12.18). By 1958–59, the balance of payments deficit became a source of policy concern. The first of many attempts to stem the tide began with policies tying foreign aid to U.S. exports and the persuading of foreign governments to remove discriminatory barriers against U.S. exports (Solomon 1976, p. 27).

The convertible Bretton Woods system that began at the end of 1958 differed in a number of ways from the system intended by its architects. These include the dominance of the United States in the international monetary order (soon to be challenged by a reemerging continental Europe), the reduced prestige of the IMF, the rise of the dollar as a key currency and the decline of sterling, a shift from the adjustable peg system toward a de facto fixed exchange rate regime, and, finally, growing capital mobility. Despite the prevalence of capital controls in most countries, private long-term capital mobility increased considerably in the 1950s, and speculative short-term capital movements (through leads and lags) emerged as a powerful force in thwarting the attempts by monetary authorities to maintain a parity far removed from the fundamentals. While the outlook for the Bretton Woods system never looked brighter than in December 1958, emerging signs of weakness were soon to be revealed.

12.14   The history of Bretton Woods: The heyday of Bretton Woods, 1959–67

With the establishment of current account convertibility by the Western European industrial nations at the end of December 1958, the full-blown Bretton Woods system was in operation.[43] Each member intervened in the foreign exchange market, either buying or selling dollars, to maintain its parity within the prescribed 1% margins. The U.S. Treasury in turn pegged the price of the dollar at $35.00 per ounce by freely buying and selling gold.[44] Thus, each currency was anchored to the dollar and indirectly to gold. Triangular arbitrage kept all cross rates within a band of 2% on either side of parity. Through much of this period, capital controls prevailed in most countries in one form or another, although until the mid-1960s their use declined.[45]

The system that operated in the next decade turned out to be quite different from what the architects had in mind. First, instead of a system of equal currencies, it evolved into a variant of the gold exchange

---

[43] Japan made its currency convertible in 1964.

[44] Countries in the sterling area bought and sold pounds to peg their parities in sterling, and countries in the franc and escudo zones pegged their currencies to their respective metropolitan countries.

[45] Germany eliminated capital controls in 1959, only to impose restrictions on capital inflows again in 1960. The United States began selective controls on foreign investment in 1964. The other European countries maintained some form of capital controls throughout Bretton Woods.

standard – the gold dollar system. Initially, it was a gold exchange standard with two key currencies, the dollar and the pound. But the role of the pound as a key currency declined steadily throughout the 1960s.[46] Sterling declined both as a private vehicle currency and as an official reserve currency until, by the sterling devaluation of November 1967, its official use was limited to the sterling area (see Figure 12.15). Sterling's decline as a key currency reflected the decline in economic importance of the United Kingdom in the postwar period, the pattern of stop-go stabilization policies, and a relatively rapid underlying inflation rate.

Parallel to the decline of sterling was the rise in the dollar as a key currency. As mentioned above, use of the dollar as both a private and an official international money increased dramatically in the 1950s and continued into the 1960s (see Figure 12.15). With full convertibility, the dollar's fundamental role as an intervention currency led to its use as an international reserve. This was aided by stable and low monetary growth and relatively low inflation (before 1965) (see Figure 12.1 and Table 12.1).

The gold exchange standard evolved in the post–World War II period for the same reasons it did in the 1920s – to economize on non-interest-bearing gold reserves. By the late 1950s, the growth of the world's monetary gold stock was insufficient to finance the growth of world real output and trade (Triffin 1960; Gilbert 1968). The other intended source of international liquidity – the resources of the Fund – was also insufficient, although, as discussed below, numerous important steps were taken to augment it.

The second important difference between the convertible Bretton Woods system and the intentions of the articles was the evolution of the adjustable peg system into a virtual fixed exchange rate system. Between 1949 and 1967, there were very few changes in parities of the G-10 countries (see Table 12.2). The only exceptions were the Canadian float in 1950, devaluations by France in 1957 and 1958, and minor revaluations by Germany and the Netherlands in 1961. The adjustable peg system became less adjustable because, on the basis of the 1949 experience, the monetary authorities were unwilling to accept the risks associated with discrete changes in parities – loss of prestige, the likelihood that others would follow, and the pressure of speculative capital flows if even a hint of a change in parity were present.

As the system evolved into a fixed exchange rate gold dollar standard, the three key problems of the interwar system reemerged: adjustment,

---

[46] Fifty percent of international trade was invoiced in sterling in 1945, 30% in 1967 (Dam 1982, p. 152).

liquidity, and confidence. These problems dominated all discussion of the international monetary system during the convertible Bretton Woods period; thus, my historical survey is organized around them.

12.4.1 The three problems

The three problems facing the Bretton Woods system were spelled out clearly at the Bellagio conference in 1964 (Machlup 1964).[47] Under the classical gold standard, balance of payments *adjustment* worked automatically through the price specie flow mechanism, aided by short-term capital flows. Alternatively, if currencies were inconvertible into gold, adjustment occurred through changes in the exchange rate. Under Bretton Woods, concern over the unemployment consequences of wage rigidity delayed the deflationary adjustment required by a deficit country and, together with the use of short-term capital controls, considerably muted the automatic mechanism.[48] Some automatic adjustment was supposed to occur via changing income and expenditure in the open economy Keynesian model and some via the money supply response to changes in reserves. However, full adjustment in that model relied on discretionary monetary and fiscal policy, incomes policies, and direct trade controls. Change in exchange rates was the mechanism of last resort. The adjustment problem concerned the burden of adjustment between deficit and surplus countries and the choice of policy tools.

Liquidity, the provision of international reserves in the Bretton Woods system, could delay or avoid the use of various adjustment policies, including exchange and trade controls. In the short run, liquidity avoids disruption. In the long run, it can allow time for adjustment but hamper less drastic policies. The perceived liquidity problem in the Bretton Woods system was that the various sources of liquidity were not adequate or reliable enough to finance the growth of output and trade. The world's monetary gold stock was insufficient by the late 1950s, IMF unconditional drawing rights were meager, and the supply of U.S. dollars depended on the U.S. balance of payments, which in turn was related to the vagaries of government policy and the confidence problem.

The *confidence* problem, as in the interwar period, involved a portfolio shift between dollars and gold. As outstanding dollar liabilities held by

---

[47] Mundell (1969b) described thirteen additional problems of the international monetary system, many of which are variants of or closely related to the basic three.

[48] For a surplus country, adjustment via inflation was considered to be less of a problem, although in a few countries, such as Germany, it was resisted.

the rest of the world monetary authorities increased relative to the U.S. monetary gold stock, the likelihood of a run on the "bank" increased. The probability of all dollar holders being able to convert their dollars into gold at the fixed price declined.

The three problems were interconnected. The more reserves in the system, the less the burden of adjustment on deficit countries, the more on surplus countries, because, no matter how reserves are distributed initially, they will eventually be redistributed to the surplus countries. Conversely, deficit countries tend to bear the main burden of deficient liquidity. On the other hand, the more adequate the adjustment mechanism, the less need for liquidity. Finally, as liquidity provided by a reserve center increases, confidence declines (Machlup 1964, pp. 36–7).

In one sense, the distinction between the problems is artificial. For the United States as the key reserve country the adjustment and confidence issues were tightly intertwined because the main concern over the ongoing balance of payments deficit was the threat to its gold reserves. This was also the case for the United Kingdom – because sterling was used as international reserves, the loss of international reserves was a threat to confidence in sterling. Finally, because the U.S. deficit provided liquidity to the rest of the world, adjustment by the United States meant a shortage of reserves for the system. Indeed, the three problems would not arise under either a pure floating rate regime or a perfectly fixed exchange rate regime such as a pure gold coin standard or a pure dollar standard.[49] The problems arose because the Bretton Woods Articles encouraged countries to follow independent domestic stabilization policies and because of the development of the gold exchange standard.

12.4.2   The Adjustment Problem in Bretton Woods

The problem was conceived of as having two parts: the asymmetry of adjustment between deficit and surplus countries and the asymmetry of adjustment between the United States as the center of the system and the rest of the world.[50] Solutions to the problem included the use of traditional monetary and fiscal policy, a policy mix between the two, the use

---

[49] Obstfeld (1993) demonstrates that, in an ideal world with price flexibility, information symmetry, nondistorting taxes, and full enforceability of commitments, the three problems would be irrelevant as adjustment would be automatically financed by capital flows.

[50] Giovannini (1989) presents mixed evidence for asymmetrical adjustment between the United States and other G-7 countries during the Bretton Woods period.

of new tools such as incomes policies, rescue packages, capital and trade controls, and the injection of new liquidity. Proposals that were suggested but not adopted were greater exchange rate flexibility and changes in the price of gold.

Asymmetry of adjustment between deficit and surplus countries: I focus briefly on two extreme examples of the asymmetric adjustment problem: the United Kingdom and Germany.

- *The United Kingdom, 1959–67.* Throughout this period, the United Kingdom alternated between expansionary monetary and fiscal policies designed to maintain full employment and encourage growth and austerity programs – a strategy referred to as *stop–go*. The connecting link was the state of the balance of payments. Expansionary policy inevitably led to deterioration in the current account, a decline in international reserves, and speculation against the sterling parity. The basic problem was a slower growth rate in the United Kingdom than in its trading partners coupled with a higher underlying inflation rate, which threatened the competitive position of the pound. On several occasions, standby loans were drawn from the IMF and rescue packages arranged by the G-10 through the BIS, referred to as Basle-type operations and arrangements (Tew, 1988, Chap. 10). The pattern was evident in the 1950s, with a major crisis and rescue by the IMF in 1957. Expansionary policy and rapid growth in 1959 led to a current account deficit in 1960 and a crisis in March 1961, alleviated by a $1.5 million standby loan from the IMF and the adoption of an austerity program[51] (see Figure 12.16, which shows the U.K. balance of payments and its components). With an improvement in the balance of payments, policy switched to ease in 1962 and was expansionary throughout 1963. By the time the Labour party was elected on 16 October 1964, the current account had deteriorated quite markedly, and reserves declined rapidly. The Wilson government refused to devalue, announced an import surcharge on 26 October, but did not depart from its expansionary policy.[52] The balance of payments continued to deteriorate, reserves declined, speculation against sterling mounted, and, on 25 November, a $4

---

[51] The crisis was in part precipitated by speculative pressure on the deutsche mark to revalue (Yeager, 1976, p. 452).

[52] According to Johnson (1968), had the British devalued in 1964 rather than hold out until 1967, the speculative attack on gold and the dollar in 1968 might not have occurred.

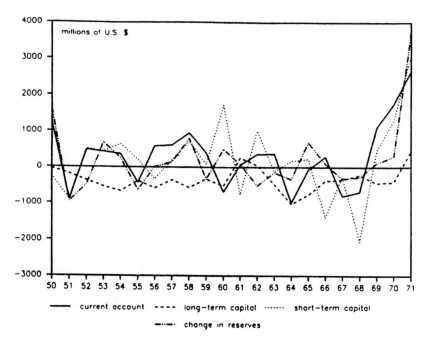

Figure 12.16. Balance of payments, United Kingdom, 1950–71.

billion rescue package was arranged with the G10 and the
IMF. The authorities continued to maintain a relatively expansionary policy through 1965, and pressure on sterling reserves
continued. A tight budget package was instituted in July 1965,
along with restrictions on capital outflows. The pressure temporarily abated but arose anew in the spring and summer of 1966.
This time a massive austerity program was instituted on 20 July,
and external assistance was provided by the Federal Reserve and
other central banks. Declining output and rising unemployment
in early 1967 led to a reversal of the tight fiscal and monetary
policies. The balance of payments deteriorated in the summer of
1967. A series of adverse shocks – the closing of the Suez Canal
during the Six Day War and a dock strike in October – were
contributing factors. A speculative attack on sterling mounted in
November. This time the $3 billion rescue package was insuf-
ficient to stem the tide. On 18 November 1967, sterling was
devalued by 14.3% to $2.40 (Cairncross and Eichengreen 1983,
Chap. 5).

The November 1967 devaluation also marked the effective end of sterling's role as a reserve currency. After the devaluation, the countries of the sterling area increasingly began to hold dollars as a reserve currency. To protect the remaining sterling balances, an agreement was worked out at Basle in 1968 whereby, in exchange for holding a specified proportion of its reserves in sterling, each member received a dollar guarantee on its sterling holdings in excess of 10% of its total reserves (Dam 1982, p. 184).[53] In effect, sterling as a reserve asset became equivalent to dollars.

The experience in the United Kingdom was important for the adjustment issue for a number of reasons. It was a country with a chronic balance of payments deficit, forced to take strong corrective action.[54] In the eight years after convertibility, virtually every technique and tool recommended by the Organization for Economic Cooperation and Development's Working Party 3 study (OECD 1966) on adjustment was used. In addition, new facilities were developed to provide the liquidity that would allow the time for adjustment: Basle arrangements – both short-term swaps (extensions of inter-central bank credit lines) and longer-term facilities (Tew, 1988, Chap. 10) – and the General Arrangements to Borrow (GAB) of 1961, whereby the G10 provided a $6 billion line of credit in a package of hard currencies to the IMF.[55] Finally, the pound, as an alternative reserve currency, was viewed as a first line of defense for the dollar. Devaluation of the pound, it was believed, would ultimately put pressure on the dollar (Dam, 1982, Chap. 6).

- *Germany, 1959–67.* West Germany was a surplus country that faced the opposite problem to that confronting the United Kingdom (see Figure 12.17).[56] Relatively rapid growth (especially of exports) and relatively slow underlying inflation produced a series of current account surpluses and reserve inflows through-

---

[53] In addition, a $2 billion medium-term facility was arranged by twelve central banks and the BIS.

[54] France was in a similar position in the 1950s. Plagued by rapid inflation throughout the decade, various corrective devices failed to work. Equilibrium was reached by devaluations in 1957 and 1958 and monetary and fiscal reforms in 1959 that restored price stability. In 1963–64, Italy faced both inflation and a balance of payments deficit. Devaluation was avoided by a shift to tight monetary and fiscal policy and a rescue package (Yeager, 1976, Chaps. 23, 25).

[55] This alleviated a chronic problem facing the Fund – a shortage of hard currencies, especially the dollar, available for drawing (Dam 1982, p. 148).

[56] The Netherlands was comparable to West Germany.

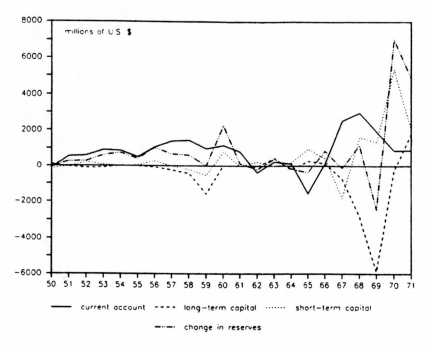

Figure 12.17. Balance of payments, Germany, 1950–71.

out the 1950s.[57] Concern over the inflationary consequences of the balance of payments surpluses prompted the German authorities in 1959 both to follow tight monetary policy and to institute measures to prevent capital inflows. These included the prohibition of interest payments and discriminatory reserve requirements on foreign deposits. The tight money led to both a recession and a further reserve inflow in 1960. Finally, in 1961, the deutsche mark was revalued by 5%. With the exception of two years, 1962 and 1965, the German current account was in

---

[57] Although the average inflation rate in Germany of 3.2% over the period 1959–70 was only slightly less than that in the United Kingdom of 3.4% (see Table 12.1), this reflects both convergence toward the world inflation rate under the fixed exchange rate standard and the pressure of U.S. monetary expansion after 1965. It also reflects the use of annual averaged data. Using quarterly rates of change of consumer prices at annual rates, Darby, Lothian, et al. (1983, Table 2.1) show that over the period 1958:4–1967:4, inflation in the United Kingdom averaged 2.86%, while in Germany it was 2.41%. A more telling indicator of the difference between the underlying inflation rates in the two countries is the experience of both the preconvertibility period and the subsequent floating period when the U.K. inflation rate was more than double that of Germany.

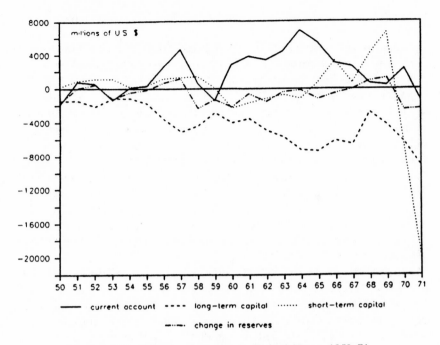

Figure 12.18. Balance of payments, United States, 1950–71.

surplus until the end of Bretton Woods. The package of tight money and capital controls was repeated again in 1964–66 and 1968. Opposition to further revaluations, primarily by the export sector, mounted throughout the 1960s. In sum, Germany resisted adjustment during the Bretton Woods regime. The German monetary authorities believed that the key problem of the international monetary system was inflation imported from abroad.

Asymmetry between the United States and the rest of the world: The United States had an official settlements balance of payments deficit in 1958 that persisted, with the notable exception of 1968–69, until the end of Bretton Woods (see Figure 12.18). However, with the exception of 1959, the United States had a current account surplus until 1970. The balance of payments deficit under Bretton Woods arose because capital outflows exceeded the current account surplus. In the early postwar years, the capital outflow consisted largely of foreign aid. By the end of the 1950s, private long-term investment abroad (mainly direct investment) exceeded military expenditures abroad and other official transfers (Eichengreen 1991).

The balance of payments deficit was perceived as a problem by the U.S. monetary authorities because of its effect on confidence. As official dollar liabilities held abroad mounted with successive deficits, the likelihood increased that these dollars would be converted into gold and that the U.S. monetary gold stock would eventually reach a point low enough to trigger a run. Indeed, by 1959, the U.S. monetary gold stock equaled total external dollar liabilities, and the rest of the world's monetary gold stock exceeded that of the United States (see Figure 12.10). By 1964, official dollar liabilities held by foreign monetary authorities exceeded the U.S. monetary gold stock.

A second reason that the balance of payments deficit was perceived as a problem was the dollar's role in providing liquidity to the rest of the world. Elimination of the U.S. deficit would create a worldwide liquidity shortage.

For the Europeans, the U.S. balance of payments deficit was a problem for different reasons. First, as the reserve currency country, the United States did not have to adjust its domestic economy to the balance of payments. As a matter of routine, the Federal Reserve automatically sterilized dollar outflows. The asymmetry in adjustment was resented. The Germans, as mentioned above, viewed the United States as exporting inflation to surplus countries through its deficits. Their remedy was for the United States (and the United Kingdom) to pursue a contractionary monetary and fiscal policy (Emminger 1967). In actual fact, U.S. inflation was less (on a GNP-weighted-average basis) than that of the rest of the G7 before 1968 (see Figures 12.1 and 12.28). The French resented U.S. financial dominance and the seigniorage that they believed the United States earned on its outstanding liabilities.[58] In 1965, acting on this perception, the French began systematically to convert outstanding dollar liabilities into gold. The French solution to the dollar problem was to double the price of gold – the amount by which the real price of gold

---

[58] Mundell (1971, Chap. 15) makes the distinction between growth seigniorage and the inflation tax. *Growth seigniorage* refers to the growth in nominal money balances required to finance the growth in real output and avoid deflation. The money issuer captures the return on real cash balances arising from expected deflation. The *inflation tax* refers to the revenue captured by the monetary authorities when they issue money in excess of the growth of real output. The former, which is a benefit to the international monetary system, was not generally distinguished from the latter, which represents a cost. More rapid growth in Western Europe than in the United States in the 1960s required the latter to supply dollars as international reserves through its balance of payments deficit. The growth seigniorage earned by the United States on its outstanding liabilities was largely transferred to Europe by the interest paid on dollar holdings.

had declined since 1934. The capital gains earned on the revaluation of the world's monetary gold reserves would be sufficient to retire the outstanding dollar (and sterling) balances. Once the United States returned to balance of payments equilibrium, the world could return to a fully functioning classical gold standard (Rueff 1967).

Some economists argued that the U.S. balance of payments deficit was not really a problem. The rest of the world voluntarily held dollars because of their valuable service flow – the deficit was demand determined. Despres, Kindleberger, and Salant (1966) viewed the United States as supplying financial intermediary services to the rest of the world. Europeans borrowed long-term capital from the United States because U.S. capital markets were deeper and more efficient and interest rates were lower. In turn, Europeans maintained short-term bank deposits in American banks because of a higher return.[59] The gross liquidity deficit employed at the time was misleading because it disregarded the financial intermediary services provided by the capital exported abroad. (For the different measures of the balance of payments used under Bretton Woods, see Figure 12.19.) Even the official settlements balance was misleading because, were foreign residents to seek to hold their liquid savings at home instead of in U.S. bank deposits, the counterpart of foreign borrowing must be held by the foreign central bank in dollars or be converted into gold. This would imply a U.S. official settlements deficit.[60]

The policy response of the U.S. monetary authorities was fourfold: to impose controls on capital exports; to institute measures to improve the

[59] Despres, Kindleberger, and Salant (1966) argued that Europe and the United States had different liquidity preferences – the Europeans preferred liquid short-term over long-term assets, the Americans the opposite. McKinnon (1969) reached the same conclusion on the basis of a stable demand by the rest of the world for dollars to hold as an international money (see Hallwood and MacDonald 1986).

[60] Several definitions of the balance of payments were used in this period by those concerned with the problem of the deficit. The gross liquidity balance, or "liquidity" balance, included both changes in claims by private foreigners and changes in claims by foreign official agencies below the line. It also treated flows of short-term private capital in an asymmetrical way. Changes in U.S. liquid balances to foreigners went below the line, while changes in private U.S. claims on foreigners went above. The increased holding of U.S. bank deposits by foreigners would, by this definition, worsen the balance of payments. This asymmetry was corrected in 1971 with the advent of the "net liquidity balance" concept. Changes in both U.S. liquid claims on and liabilities to foreigners were placed below the line. Finally, the basic balance sums up the current account and private long-term capital flows (Yeager 1976, pp. 51–4).

According to Meltzer (1991), the U.S. monetary authorities mismeasured the nature of the problem by focusing on these definitions. They viewed capital outflows as a problem while ignoring the beneficial effects of the return flow of interest, profits, and dividends. This misperception would have been avoided by focusing on the current account balance (see also Corden 1991).

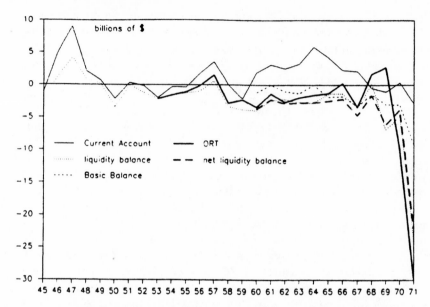

Figure 12.19. Balance of payments, different concepts, 1945–71 (*ORT* refers to the official settlements balance).

balance of trade; to alter the monetary fiscal policy mix; and to employ measures to stem the conversion of outstanding dollars into gold.

- *Capital controls.* On the belief that the balance of payments deficit was aggravated by capital exports, the Kennedy and Johnson administrations imposed a series of restraints on capital outflows (see Solomon, 1976 and Meltzer, 1991). Prominent among them were an increase in taxes of foreign earnings of U.S. corporations in 1961 and the Interest Equalization Tax of 1963, which taxed the earnings of foreign securities by 1%. This was extended to bank loans in 1965, and the rate was doubled in 1967. Also imposed were guidelines on direct investment in 1965 and limits on the growth of bank lending to foreigners in the same year. As Meltzer (1991) argued, most of these measures were counterproductive. Either they were evaded (at some cost), or, to the extent that they succeeded, they reduced the return flow of interest income.

- *Balance of trade measures.* A number of measures were designed to reduce official spending abroad and to encourage exports and discourage imports. These included a reduction in defense and nondefense government purchases abroad, expansion of Export-Import Bank lending in 1960, and tying development aid to dollar purchases in 1961.

- *The monetary fiscal policy mix.* During the Kennedy and Johnson years, some attention was devoted to tailoring the monetary fiscal policy mix to maintain both internal and external balance (Mundell 1968, Chap. 16).[61] The most well-known attempt was expansionary fiscal policy (an investment tax credit, accelerated depreciation allowances) to cure the recession of 1960–61, combined with Operation Twist, which was designed to twist the yield curve and raise short-term rates, thereby encouraging a capital inflow while simultaneously reducing long-term rates to stimulate the economy.

- *Gold conversion policy.* The United States initiated a number of international arrangements to prevent foreign monetary authorities from converting outstanding dollar liabilities into gold. These included swap arrangements with other central banks beginning in 1961. In a swap arrangement, each central bank would extend to the other a bilateral line of credit. Typically, the Federal Reserve would borrow to purchase dollars held abroad instead of selling gold (Meltzer 1991, p. 62). To repay the swaps, the Treasury would issue Roosa bonds, that is, long-term bonds denominated in foreign currencies. By issuing Roosa bonds, the U.S. monetary authorities avoided reducing gold reserves. To prevent a rise in the free market price of gold leading to a run on the U.S. monetary gold stock, the London Gold Pool was established in 1961. With the Bank of England as agent, the United States, along with seven European countries, stabilized the private market price of gold, with the United States supplying 60% of the gold sold (Schwartz 1989, p. 342). The United States also dissuaded foreign monetary authorities from converting dollars into gold.[62]

Proposed solutions to the U.S. adjustment problem: During this period, a number of solutions to the U.S. adjustment problem were proposed. The first, an increase in world liquidity, was suggested by U.S. authorities, the IMF, and the OECD. Provision of an alternative international reserve

[61] For a critique, see Obstfeld (1993).
[62] Other measures to help the U.S. balance of payments deficit included establishment of the General Arrangements to Borrow (GAB) in 1961, which provided the IMF sufficient funds to lend to the United States, and a 25% increase in IMF quotas. A number of drawings were undertaken by the United States in this period.

media would eliminate the need for the United States to run a deficit. Negotiations over the period 1964–67 led to the creation of SDRs (see Section 12.4.3). The second proposal was an increase in the price of gold, either unilaterally, which would devalue the dollar against other currencies, or by a uniform change in all parities, as under Article IV. The United States opposed both versions of the proposal. A unilateral devaluation, it was felt, would be quickly followed by other countries and would reduce U.S. credibility – should the U.S. devalue once, what would prevent it from doing so again. It was also opposed because it would be difficult for the U.S. Congress to accept a change in the price of gold. A multilateral revaluation of gold, as suggested by the French, was also rejected as at most only a temporary solution.[63]

The final proposal, for increased exchange rate flexibility, was opposed by the United States and other monetary authorities. Throughout the 1960s, the IMF reiterated its earlier opposition to floating exchange rates and advocated increased liquidity as the primary prescription for the Bretton Woods system's ills.[64] Only in a special report in 1970, after a number of exchange rate crises had occurred, did the Fund come out in favor of temporary floating and very limited flexibility (DeVries 1987).[65]

The U.S. balance of payments policies were in the main ineffective. As long as the United States maintained relatively stable prices, as it did before 1965, the system could be preserved for a number of years. The real problem was that of the gold exchange standard – ultimately, there would be a convertibility crisis. The twin solutions of an increase in the price of gold and an increase in world liquidity by creation of an artificial reserve asset would not permanently eradicate the problem.

Even at some higher price of gold, world gold production would eventually be inadequate to produce long-run price stability. In the long run, when account is taken of gold as a durable, exhaustible resource, deflation is inevitable (Bordo and Ellson 1985). Moreover, an increase in world liquidity by an artificial reserve asset, if it is convertible into gold, would not remove the basic convertibility problem (McKinnon 1988).

---

[63] Meltzer (1991) argued that a 50% gold revaluation would have succeeded in preserving the Bretton Woods system well into the 1970s had the United States not followed an inflationary policy in the late 1960s.

[64] The IMF focused more attention on the liquidity issue partly because of its opposition to exchange rate flexibility, partly because it believed that more liquidity would greatly alleviate the adjustment problem, and partly because it believed that more liquidity would allow the United States to correct its balance of payments deficit (DeVries 1987).

[65] The official view on exchange rate flexibility is in marked contrast to the academic view, which by the end of the decade was solidly in favor of increased flexibility, as was evident at the famous Burgenstock conference (Halm 1970; see also Johnson 1972b).

Finally, as Townsend (1977), Salant (1983), and Buiter (1989) point out, the gold exchange standard as a type of commodity stabilization scheme is bound to collapse in the face of unforeseen shocks (see Garber, 1993).

12.4.3 The liquidity problem

In 1953 and 1958, the IMF issued reports on the adequacy of world reserves. On the basis of the ratio of reserves to imports for the world and different groups of countries, the first report (IMF [1953] 1969a) concluded that world reserves were adequate. The second report (IMF [1958] 1969c) said that they were adequate for the present but might not be sufficient in the coming decade of the 1960s after the return to convertibility and faster economic growth. It recommended an increase in member quotas. Triffin (1960) criticized the Fund report on a number of grounds and suggested a number of powerful reasons why reserves might be inadequate.

Triffin's first argument was that the ratio of reserves to imports in 1957 was too low. He argued that it should be greater than 40%. For the G10 (less the United States) in 1957 it was (see Figure 12.20), although, as can be seen, it was unusually low in that year.[66]

Triffin's main argument for a shortage of liquidity was the inadequacy of gold reserves. The real price of gold had been falling since World War II and would eventually reduce world gold production. Indeed, this happened in the early 1950s but was offset by new sources of production later in the decade (Gilbert 1968) (see Figure 12.21). Gold production declined again in 1966. Moreover, the falling real price would stimulate private demand for gold. It seemed unlikely that Russian gold sales would make up much of the shortfall (see Figure 12.22). Indeed, the prospects seemed dim for growth in the world monetary gold stock to be adequate to finance the growth of world real output and the volume of trade. As can be seen clearly for the G7 in Figure 12.23, this was the case. A large gap opened between both the growth of output and the volume of trade and the growth of gold reserves in 1958. For the G7 less the United States, however, the gap opens up only in 1966 (see Figure 12.24). For the world excluding the United States, net additions to the monetary

---

[66] Although the reserve to import ratio has been used extensively by the IMF, it has been criticized for being based on a crude transactions demand for money model. A more sophisticated approach to the demand for reserves based on optimizing behavior would make the demand a function of, among other things, the opportunity cost of holding reserves, the variance of trade, and the type of commodities exported (see Clower and Lipsey, 1968; Williamson 1973; and Crockett 1987).

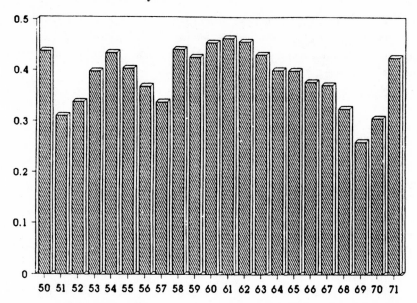

Figure 12.20. Ratio of reserves to imports, G10 plus Switzerland minus the United States.

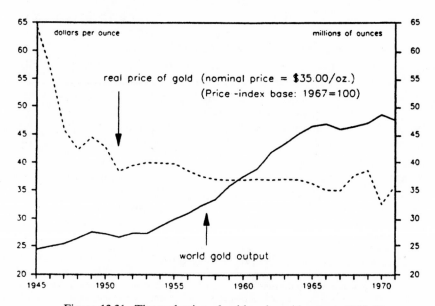

Figure 12.21. The real price of gold and world output, 1945–71.

a) Sources

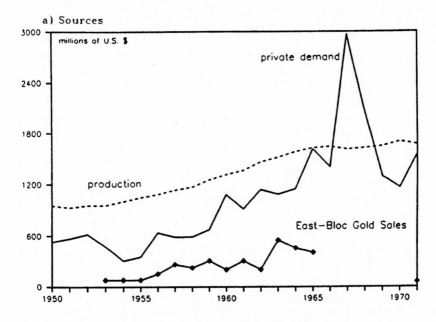

b) Changes in the World Monetary Gold Stock

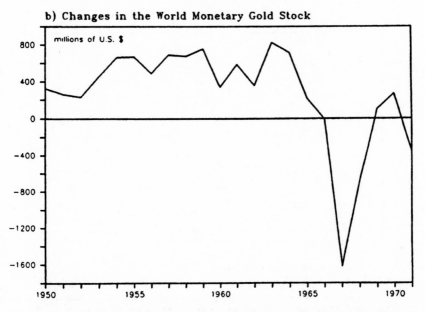

Figure 12.22. The sources of change in the world monetary gold stock:
(A) sources; (B) changes in the world monetary gold stock.

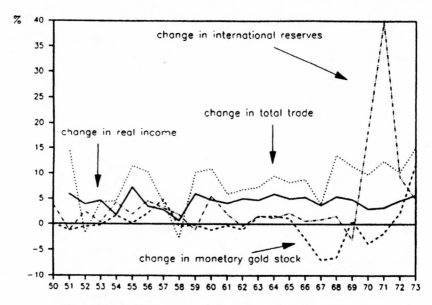

Figure 12.23. The growth of the monetary gold stock, the growth in international reserves, and the growth of the volume of real trade and real income, G-7 countries, 1950–73.

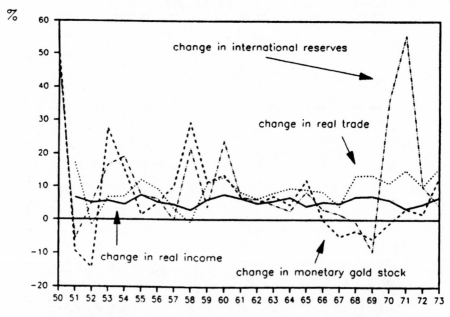

Figure 12.24. The growth of the monetary gold stock, the growth in international reserves, and the growth of the volume of real trade and real income, G7 countries minus the United States, 1950–71.

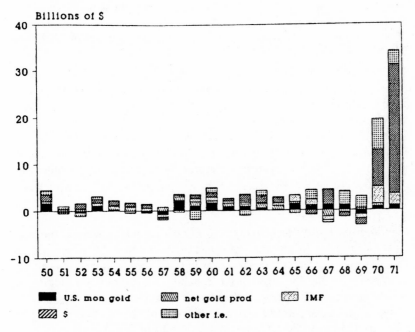

Figure 12.25. Sources of change in international reserves, the world minus the United States, 1950–71 (f.e. = foreign exchange).

gold stock (exclusive of the depletion of U.S. monetary gold reserves) declined throughout the Bretton Woods period. (For the sources of change in the rest of the world's reserves, see Figure 12.25).

Triffin argued further that this shortfall in the growth of reserves would not be made up by growth in sterling balances, which were already in decline, and that this shortfall would be satisfied only in part by the IMF. The rest would come from the United States via its balance of payments deficit. The famous Triffin dilemma would then come about, as mentioned above, because, with continuous deficits, U.S. monetary gold reserves would decline both absolutely and relatively to outstanding dollar liabilities until an eventual convertibility crisis. However, the U.S. monetary authorities would close the deficit before this would happen, creating a massive shortage of international liquidity and the prospect of world deflation:

The time will certainly come, sooner or later, when further accommodation of short-term liabilities will either have to be slowed down or substantially matched by corresponding increases in our already bloated gold assets. If this were not done on our own initiative, foreign central banks would do it for us by stopping their own accumulation of dollar assets and requiring gold payment instead for their overall surplus with the United States. . . . Dollar balances cannot be relied upon to contribute substantially and indefinitely to the solution of the world liquidity problem. (Triffin, 1960, p. 63)

Triffin's own solution to the problem was to go back to the original Keynesian ICU plan, converting all existing reserves into international money and having the IMF serve as the world's central bank, to provide generous liquidity.

In the years following Triffin's *Gold and the Dollar Crisis*, three types of solutions to the liquidity problem were proposed and implemented: expanding the Fund's resources; creating new resources outside the Fund; and creating a new type of reserve asset, the special drawing right (SDR).

Expanding the Fund's resources: The Fund's resources were expanded by a 50% increase in members' quotas in 1960 and a 25% increase in 1966. Moreover, the increase in quotas led to a further increase in Fund resources by raising the super gold tranche – that is, when a member's currency is drawn on, the gold tranche of its quota is increased by the drawing. In addition, the General Arrangements to Borrow (GAB) in 1961 provided the Fund a further line of credit of $6 billion.

Resources outside the Fund: As mentioned in the discussion of adjustment, members of the G10 developed an extensive network of swaps and standby arrangements to help members in the event of a payments crisis. These facilities increased the amount of conditional liquidity but not the international reserves of the international monetary system.

The SDR: A new reserve asset: The key innovation in the convertible Bretton Woods period was the development of the SDR under the First Amendment to the Fund's Articles in 1968. Strong academic interest in the creation of a new reserve asset to solve the liquidity problem began in 1963. Earlier, several related proposals had circulated (Grubel, 1963). The Bellagio conference considered the merits of a number of them. Official interest by the United States, the monetary authorities of the G-10, and the IMF was expressed in a number of studies in 1964 and 1965 (Solomon, 1976, Chap. 4) – especially the 1964 IMF *Annual Report* and the *Report on the Study Group on the Creation of Reserve Assets* by Working Party 3 of the G-10 (Ossola, 1965).

The latter considered some competing proposals, including alternative forms of a composite reserve unit (CRU). Under the Bernstein plan, each member of the G-10 would subscribe an amount of its own currency to a pool and receive in exchange a corresponding amount of CRUs, which could then be used as an equivalent to gold. In a French alternative, members would subscribe to the pool in proportion to their gold holdings, and then gold and CRUs would circulate together in fixed proportions (Williamson 1977, p. 20). Extensive negotiations, under U.S. initiative, between the IMF and the G10 between 1965 and 1967 finally led to the creation of the SDR, which was formally ratified at the September 1967 annual meeting of the IMF in Rio (Solomon 1976, Chap. 7).

A special drawing account was set up at the Fund, separate from the general account. In contrast to the early CRU scheme, access to SDRs was made available to all members, not just the G-10. Members were credited SDRs in proportion to their quotas. Also unlike the CRU, the SDR was a fiat obligation; it was not backed by gold. Its acceptability stemmed from the obligation by other members to accept SDRs – similar to the legal tender provision of domestic fiat money. Members must accept SDRs when the Fund mandates their acceptance, as long as their holdings are less than three times their cumulative allocation. This put a limit on the amount of a potentially inferior asset that would have to be absorbed (Dam 1982, p. 154). One SDR was defined as equivalent to one gold dollar.

Two limitations on the SDR were that it could be used to finance only balance of payments deficits and that members must hold on average a balance over a five-year period of at least 30% of its allocation. The former was to prevent the SDR from aggravating the confidence problem (Williamson 1977, p. 23); the latter was a compromise between France, which wanted the new facility to be a form of credit, and the United States, which wanted a reserve asset (Dam 1982, pp. 163–4). Otherwise, members were free to use SDRs unconditionally. To use them, a member would notify the Fund, which would then designate a surplus country to receive SDRs and in return provide the deficit country an equal value of some convertible currency to use in intervention (Williamson 1977, p. 22).

As part of its continuing struggle against U.S. hegemony, France, in effect, exacted the provision that the SDR scheme could be activated only when the U.S. balance of payments deficit was eliminated.[67] This was in opposition to the American view that the introduction of

---

[67] In actual fact, the French were not successful in making the elimination of the U.S. payments deficit a condition, but the procedures were so designed as to give the European Economic Community a veto over the timing and amount of any SDR allocation (Dam 1982, pp. 165–6).

SDRs would then allow it to reduce its deficit. The scheme was activated on 1 January 1970, after the United States had a balance of payments surplus in 1968 and 1969 (see Figure 12.18) and following what was perceived to be an alarming decline in international reserves (see Figure 12.20). Based on a projection that the decline in the growth of international reserves that began in 1965 would persist (see Figure 12.24), the initial allocation was quite large – $9.5 billion over a three-year period.

Institution of the SDR has raised a number of issues. First is its acceptability. It has been argued that the SDR was doomed to be less acceptable as a reserve asset than the dollar and gold (McKinnon, 1988; Meltzer 1991). It was less acceptable than the dollar because its use was limited to official international transactions and because, unlike the dollar, it could not be used as a private international money. It was also less acceptable because it bore a low rate of interest. It was less acceptable than gold as a store of value because it lacked the intrinsic properties of gold. Ultimately, its main function in the international monetary system, other than as a marginal reserve asset, was as a unit of account.

The second issue was that the SDR scheme was designed only to expand the growth of reserves. It did not include a mechanism providing a restraint on reserve growth through the deficits of reserve centers (Williamson 1977, p. 23). In actual fact, SDRs added to the inflationary pressures of the early 1970s.

The third issue was that of seigniorage. By economizing on gold reserves, the issue of SDRs created a social saving. To the extent that competitive interest was not paid on SDR balances, the social saving was distributed as seigniorage. Moreover, to the extent that seigniorage was allocated in proportion to members' quotas, it was distributionally neutral (Williamson 1977, p. 24; Mundell and Swoboda 1969).

The final issue was that of confidence. By restricting SDRs to financing balance of payments deficits, the problem of having another asset in the portfolio of international assets, between which destabilizing switches can occur, was avoided. But any extension of the SDR's use as a true substitute for dollars possessing gold convertibility would have aggravated the confidence problem. Considerable effort was directed to the liquidity problem and to devising institutional solutions. It was widely believed that solving the liquidity problem would also solve the adjustment problem and thereby preserve the Bretton Woods system. What the reformers did not pay adequate attention to was the buildup in world inflation after 1965, in turn considerably aggravated by a vast surplus of international liquidity.

12.4.4   The confidence problem

The key problem of the convertible Bretton Woods period was the confidence crisis for the dollar. As argued by Triffin (1960), Kenen (1960), and Gilbert (1968), the gold dollar system that evolved after 1959 was bound to be dynamically unstable if the growth of the world monetary gold stock was insufficient to finance the growth of world output and trade and to prevent the U.S. monetary gold stock from declining relative to outstanding U.S. dollar liabilities. The pressure on the U.S. monetary gold stock would continue, as growth of the world monetary gold stock declined relative to the growth of world output and trade and the world substituted dollars for gold, until at some point a confidence crisis would be triggered, leading to the collapse of the system, as occurred in 1931. An international lender of last resort, such as proposed by Kindleberger (1973), could temporarily prevent the collapse if it could issue international high-powered money that was equivalent to domestic high-powered money. But if the basic problem was a gold shortage, then the international lender of last resort too would become ineffective. However, at the same time as fears over U.S. gold convertibility threatened the dynamic stability of the Bretton Woods system, gold still served two positive roles. The first is that gold was the numeraire of the system; all currencies were anchored to its fixed price via the U.S. commitment to peg its price. The second is the fact that, until 1968, gold still served as backing to the U.S. dollar via a 25% gold reserve requirement against Federal Reserve notes, which may have served as a brake on U.S. monetary expansion. Against this background, I trace the history of gold and the dollar.

The first crisis – October 1960: The first glimpse of a confidence crisis was the gold rush of October 1960, when speculators pushed the free market price of gold on the London market up from $35.20 (the U.S. Treasury's buying price) to $40.00 (see Figure 12.26). This first significant runup in gold prices since the London gold market was reopened in 1954 was supposedly triggered by concerns over a Democratic victory in the 1960 U.S. presidential election. Kennedy's pledge "to get America moving again" was interpreted as an inflationary policy that might force the United States to devalue its currency [i.e., unilaterally raise the price of gold in terms of dollars (Solomon, 1976, p. 35)].

The U.S. monetary authorities feared that private speculation in the gold market might spill over into official demands for conversion.

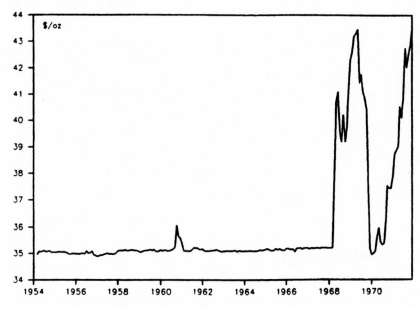

Figure 12.26. London gold price.

Consequently, remedial action was quickly taken.[68] The Treasury supplied the Bank of England sufficient gold to restore stability, and the monetary authorities of the G10 agreed to refrain from buying gold above $35.20. In succeeding months, the London Gold Pool was formed, becoming official in November 1961. As mentioned above, the Pool, which was formed among the United States and seven other central banks, agreed to buy or sell gold in order to peg the price at $35.00 per ounce. For the next six years, the Pool did succeed in stabilizing the price of gold, but it did not prevent a steady decline in the U.S. monetary gold stock (see Figure 12.10).[69] In fact, although the seven other central banks supplied 40% of the gold required to stabilize the price of gold, they replenished their monetary gold stocks outside the Pool by converting outstanding dollar balances into gold at the U.S. Treasury (Meltzer 1991, p. 63).

[68] In a famous speech delivered on 31 October 1960, John F. Kennedy said, "If elected President, I shall not devalue the dollar from the present rate. Rather, I shall defend its present value and its soundness" (Solomon 1976, p. 35).

[69] However, according to Meltzer (1991), there is little evidence in the asset markets of a growing loss of confidence in the dollar through the 1960s. Real interest rates did not rise significantly relative to trade-weighted real interest rates. Nor did the gold and foreign exchange markets suggest a flight from the dollar.

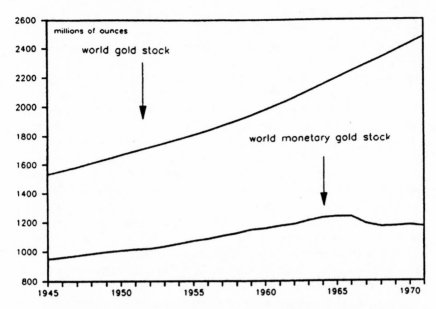

Figure 12.27. The world gold stock and world monetary gold stock, 1945–71.

During the period 1961–67, the United States made a series of arrangements to protect its monetary gold reserves. As noted above, these included the network of swap arrangements with other central banks, Roosa bonds, and moral suasion. However, France did not go along with these efforts and began its campaign against the dollar in February 1965.

The period was marked by two sets of underlying forces that would undermine the dollar's relation to gold – growing gold scarcity and a rise in U.S. inflation. World gold production leveled off in the mid-1960s and even declined in 1966 (see Figure 12.21), while at the same time private demand soared, precipitating a drop in the world monetary gold stock after 1966 (see Figure 12.22 and Figure 12.27). Indeed, beginning in 1966, the Gold Pool became a net seller of gold. Also, U.S. money growth accelerated in 1965, in part to finance the Vietnam War. Inflation began to rise in 1965 (see Figure 12.1 and Figure 12.23), and the current account surplus began to deteriorate in 1964 (see Figure 12.18 above). Moreover, U.S. competitiveness began to deteriorate in 1965, reflected in a rise of the ratio of U.S. unit labor costs relative to trade-weighted unit labor costs (Meltzer 1991, p. 71). The balance of payments deficit worsened between 1964 and 1966 but was reversed in 1966 by capital inflows triggered by tight monetary policy.

After the devaluation of sterling, which the United States tried unsuccessfully to prevent, pressure mounted against the dollar via the London gold market. From December 1967 to March 1968, the Gold Pool lost $3 billion in gold, with the U.S. share at $2.2 billion (Solomon 1976, p. 119). The immediate concerns of the speculators may have been fears of a dollar devaluation, but, according to Gilbert (1968) and Johnson (1968), the real problem was the underlying gold scarcity. In the face of the pressure, the Gold Pool was disbanded on 17 March 1968 and a two-tier arrangement put in its place. Henceforth, the monetary authorities of the Gold Pool agreed neither to sell nor to buy gold from the market. They would transact only among themselves at the official $35.00 price. In addition, on 12 March 1968, the United States removed the 25% gold requirement against Federal Reserve notes. The key consequence of these new arrangements was that gold was demonetized at the margin. The link between gold production and other market sources of gold and official reserves was cut. Moreover, in the following years, the United States put considerable pressure on other monetary authorities to refrain from converting their dollar holdings into gold. In effect, the world switched to a de facto dollar standard.

A number of solutions to the gold dollar confidence problem were proposed at the time. These included the introduction of a new reserve asset, a rise in the price of gold, and demonetization of gold.[70] The first scheme would substitute SDRs (or something similar) for dollars and gold as a reserve asset. This would presumably take the pressure off the United States. However, as long as this new currency would be convertible into gold and the gold market remained as it was, the pressure would just shift to the new asset. Indeed, this was the reason the use of SDRs was limited to financing balance of payments deficits.

The second scheme, proposed by Rueff (1967), Gilbert (1968), and others, was to solve the gold scarcity problem by doubling the price of gold. This would create sufficient liquidity to alleviate both the liquidity and the adjustment problems. Also, the rise in the price of gold would encourage gold production and discourage private demand. Growth in the world monetary gold stock would be sufficient to finance the growth of real output and prevent a threat to U.S. gold reserves for some

---

[70] Also, Triffin (1960) and others proposed converting the IMF into a world central bank that would issue gold-guaranteed currencies and serve as an international lender of last resort.

undetermined future.[71] There are two fundamental problems with this solution.[72] First, it is time inconsistent. If the price of gold were doubled once, what is to prevent it from being raised again? Market participants would expect a future change in price and would reduce their holdings of dollars permanently (as happened to sterling after 1949 and 1967). Second, it would only postpone the problem. In a rapidly growing world, it would be only a matter of time before a future gold scarcity would arise, precipitating a future crisis.

A variant of this theme was a unilateral dollar devaluation. This was opposed by the United States for the reasons given above and because it would likely be followed by the rest of the world.[73]

The final proposal was to demonetize gold and remove all impediments to the operation of a pure dollar standard. According to McKinnon (1969, 1988), such a system was already in place by the mid-1960s. Both private entities and official agencies held dollars because of their superior attributes as international money. Use of the dollar solved the $n - 1$ balance of payments problem (Mundell 1968, Chap. 10). As the nth currency, the dollar allowed the rest of the world to peg their exchange rates independently and target their balance of payments. The United States had to follow a passive balance of payments policy, that is, a policy of benign neglect. The only major constraint on the United States was to stabilize the price of traded goods, a policy that it had followed successfully until 1965. Given the U.S. stabilized price of traded goods, the world price level would be anchored to it via commodity arbitrage and monetary adjustment. Growth in the rest of the world would be financed by dollars supplied by the U.S. deficit (Floyd 1985). Gold convertibility, however, presented a problem. As long as the United States was committed to convertibility, its ability elastically to supply the dollars demanded by the rest of the world would be curtailed by the thread of a confidence crisis. The solution would then be to demonetize gold.

Two problems with this approach were, first, that the Europeans were unwilling to go along with dollar hegemony and, second, that, without gold convertibility, there was no commitment mechanism to constrain the United States to follow a stable monetary policy. As it turned out, the

---

[71] Mundell (1973) criticized Rueff for not explaining how all these objectives could be met within a reasonable period of time and how the system could be prevented from deteriorating again.

[72] For others, see Williamson (1977, pp. 33–5).

[73] Under Article IV, the United States could have unilaterally devalued the dollar by less than 10% without requiring the IMF's permission.

dollar standard that emerged de facto in 1968 broke down precisely for these reasons.

12.4.5 Conclusion

By 1968, the international monetary system had evolved very far indeed from the model of the architects of the Articles of Agreement. In reaction to both the development of financial markets and the confidence problem, the system had evolved into a de facto dollar standard. However, gold convertibility still played a role. Although the major industrial countries tacitly agreed not to convert their outstanding dollar liabilities into U.S. monetary gold, the threat of doing so was always present. At the same time, as Japan and the countries of continental Europe gained in economic strength relative to the United States, they became more reluctant to absorb outstanding dollars. They were also reluctant to adjust their surpluses by revaluing their currencies. They increasingly came to believe that adjustment should be undertaken by the United States.

The system had also developed into a de facto fixed exchange rate system. However, unlike the classical gold standard, where the fixed exchange rate was the voluntary focal point for both internal and external equilibrium, in the Bretton Woods system exchange rates became fixed out of the fear of the consequences of members allowing them to change. Nevertheless, because of increased capital mobility, the pressure for altering the parities of countries with persistent deficits and surpluses became harder to stop through the use of domestic policy tools and the aid of international rescue packages. Pressure increased from both academic and official sources for greater exchange rate flexibility.

By 1968, the system had also evolved a form of international governance that was quite different from that envisioned at the beginning. Instead of a community of equal currencies managed by the IMF, the system was managed by the United States in cooperation with the other members of the G10. In many respects, it was closer to the key currency system proposed by Williams ([1936] 1969a, [1943] 1969b; see Johnson 1972a). The IMF still had an important role as a clearinghouse for different views on monetary reform, as a center of information, as the principal voice for the countries of the world other than the G10, as their primary source of adjustment assistance, and, finally, as an important partner in the major G10 rescue packages.[74]

---

[74] According to Dominguez (1993), the IMF was designed to facilitate international cooperation by serving as a commitment mechanism. However, its failure to enforce the fundamental rule of adherence to the par value system and its inadequate provision of adjustment assistance detracted from its role.

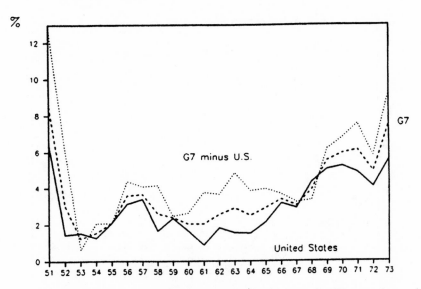

Figure 12.28. Inflation rates in the United States, the G7 countries, and the G7 excluding the United States, 1951–73.

In sum, the problems of the interwar system that Bretton Woods was designed to avoid reemerged with a vengeance. The fundamental difference, however, was that the system was not likely to collapse into deflation as in 1931 but rather explode into inflation.

12.5 The collapse of Bretton Woods

After the establishment of the two-tier arrangement, the world monetary system was on a de facto dollar standard. The system became increasingly unstable until it collapsed with the closing of the gold window in August 1971. The collapse of a system beset by the fatal flaws of the gold exchange standard and the adjustable peg was triggered by an acceleration in world inflation, in large part the consequence of an earlier acceleration of inflation in the United States. Before 1968, the U.S. inflation rate was below that of the GNP-weighted inflation rate of the G7 excluding the United States (see Figure 12.28 above).[75] It began accelerating in 1964, with a pause in 1966–67. The increase in inflation in the United

---

[75] According to Corden (1985, p. 87), the fact that the U.S. inflation rate was below that of the rest of the G7 before 1968 should not be regarded as evidence that the United States did not export its inflation. To the contrary, he argues that, because the United States exported a large part of its monetary and fiscal expansion via the fixed exchange rate, it was able to sustain a lower inflation rate than otherwise.

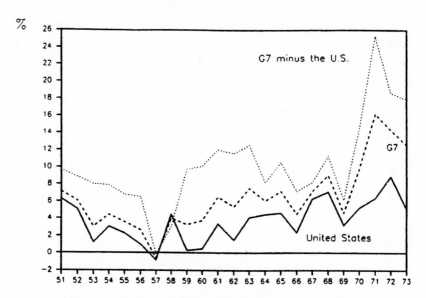

Figure 12.29. Money (M1) growth rates in the United States, the G7 countries, and the G7 excluding the United States, 1951–73.

States and the rest of the world was closely related to an increase in money growth (see Figure 12.29) and in money growth relative to the growth of real output (see Figure 12.30).

U.S. money growth ratcheted upward beginning in the early 1960s, reflecting expansionary monetary policy. Growth in Federal Reserve credit and in the monetary base accelerated dramatically from 1961 to 1962, then again from 1963 to 1965, and, after the credit crunch of 1966, from 1967 through 1968. After another bout of tight money in 1969, both aggregates accelerated again from 1970 to 1972 (see Figure 12.31). The sizable excess of Federal Reserve credit over the growth of the base is in part reflected in the decline in international reserves seen in Figure 12.18. Expansionary monetary policy in the early 1960s reflected the growing preference by the authorities for full employment over price stability (Niehans 1976) and later, in the mid-1960s, to help finance budget deficits associated with both the Vietnam War and increased spending on social programs. Indeed, changes in the monetary base are closely correlated with the government's budget deficit (see Figure 12.32).[76]

[76] On both the national income and a full employment basis, the budget deficits in the periods 1965–68 and 1970–73 were the highest in the postwar period to date (see Eichengreen 1993, Fig. 14.11).

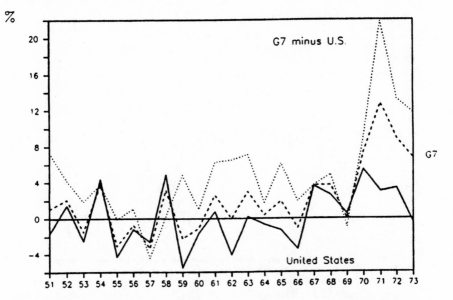

Figure 12.30. Money (M1) growth less real output growth in the United States, the G7 countries, and the G7 excluding the United States, 1951–73.

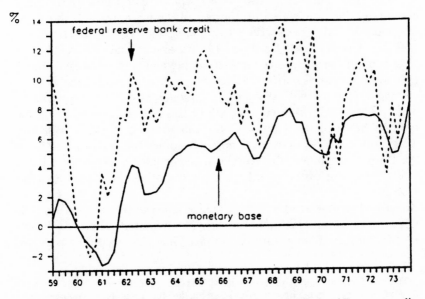

Figure 12.31. Growth of the monetary base and Federal Reserve credit, 1959–73 (year-to-year change of quarterly data).

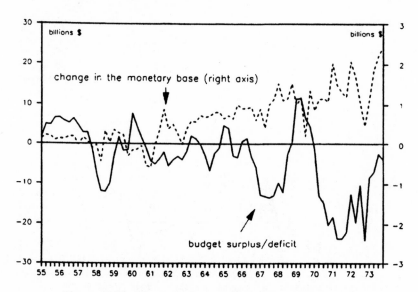

Figure 12.32. The U.S. budget deficit and changes in the monetary base, 1955–73 (year-to-year change of quarterly data).

There are a number of competing hypotheses on how U.S. money growth and inflation spread to the rest of the world (see Genberg and Swoboda 1977a). One leading hypothesis, the world monetarist hypothesis (Genberg and Swoboda 1977b), argues that the world price level is determined by world money supply and world money demand. Individual countries' price levels converge to the worldwide average via commodity market arbitrage. U.S. money growth was the primary determinant of world money growth because of an asymmetrical relationship between the United States and the rest of the world. U.S. dollars served as high-powered money for other countries as well as for the United States, and the United States could sterilize reserve flows, whereas the rest of the world could not (Swoboda and Genberg 1982, 1993).[77]

Darby, Lothian, et al. (1983) provided considerable evidence on the transmission of inflation in the Bretton Woods system. Their regressions led to a number of important conclusions. First, U.S. inflation was caused

---

[77] The world money supply is the product of the world monetary base times the world money multiplier. In the Bretton Woods system, the money multiplier was enhanced by the asymmetric role of the U.S. dollar. It was also further enhanced by the growth of Eurodollar deposits (Swoboda 1978).

by lagged U.S. money growth. Second, U.S. money growth was independent of changes in international reserves – the balance of payments had no effect on the Federal Reserve's reaction function. Third, U.S. money growth had strong and significant effects on money growth in seven major countries with very long lags – up to four years. These lags reflected the fact that central banks in the seven countries partially sterilized reserve flows. Finally, money growth in the seven countries explained inflation in these countries with a significant lag (Darby, Lothian, et al. 1983, Chap. 1).

The key transmission mechanism of inflation was the classical price specie flow mechanism augmented by capital flows. Little evidence for other mechanisms, including commodity market arbitrage, was detected (Darby, Lothian, et al. 1983, Chap. 12). According to these authors, the Bretton Woods system collapsed because of the lagged effects of U.S. expansionary monetary policy. As the dollar reserves of Germany, Japan, and other countries accumulated in the late 1960s and early 1970s, it became increasingly more difficult to sterilize them. This fostered domestic monetary expansion and inflation. The only alternative to importing U.S. inflation was to float – the route taken by all countries in 1973.

An alternative explanation of the events leading to collapse is growing misalignment in real exchange rates between the United States and its principal competitors in the face of differential productivity trends. Following the argument of Balassa (1964), more rapid growth of productivity in the traded-goods sector (relative to the non-traded-goods sector) in Germany, Japan, and other surplus countries led to higher CPI inflation and also increased pressure to revalue. Expansionary U.S. monetary and fiscal policy of the late 1960s exacerbated the misalignment by further overvaluing the dollar (Obstfeld 1993). Marston (1987) provides evidence for this view in a comparison of productivity trends, inflation rates, and real exchange rates in the United States and Japan from 1964 to 1983, but for other countries the evidence is limited (Eichengreen, 1993).

With this background, I briefly survey the events of 1968–71. After the creation of the two-tier system, pressure increasingly shifted to the United States to adjust. However, in 1968 and 1969, important exchange rate crises occurred in France and Germany. They illustrate the increasing fragility of the adjustable peg system in the face of improved capital mobility. Strikes and student riots in France in May 1968, to which the government responded with expansionary monetary and fiscal policy, led to a speculative flight from the franc and a considerable drop in French international reserves (see Figure 12.33). The pressure was alleviated by

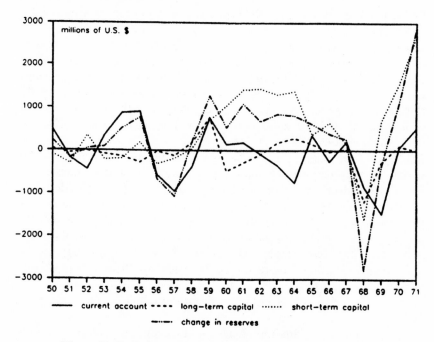

Figure 12.33. Balance of payments, France, 1950–71.

a massive rescue package organized by the U.S. in June and the imposition of capital controls (Solomon 1976, pp. 153–4). The pressure continued into the fall of 1968, but the French resisted devaluation in November by a shift to tight monetary and fiscal policy. At the same time as France faced pressure to devalue, Germany (with low inflation and rapid real growth) was facing increasing pressure to revalue. Speculative funds flowed from France to Germany, and German reserves mushroomed (see Figure 12.17). The Germans resisted revaluation on the grounds that it would harm the competitive position of export industries. They preferred France to devalue first. While the French announced their austerity measures, the Germans altered their border taxes, lowering the VAT on imports and imposing taxes on exports – a measure equivalent to a partial revaluation of 4% – and imposed restrictions on capital inflows. The crisis was temporarily alleviated but began anew in the spring of 1969. France eventually devalued by 11.1% on 8 August 1969. The Germans initially reacted to the further reserve inflows by imposing further restrictions on foreign-owned deposits and by a readjustment of border taxes. Finally, the deutsche mark (after a temporary float) was revalued by 9.3% on 29 September (Solomon 1976, pp. 161–3) (see Table 12.2).

The U.S. current account balance continued to deteriorate in 1968, but the overall balance of payments exhibited a surplus in 1968 and 1969, thanks to a large short-term capital inflow. The capital inflow was activated by events in the Eurodollar market. In the face of tight monetary policy in 1968–69 and Regulation Q ceilings on time deposits, deposits shifted from U.S. banks to the Eurodollar market. U.S. banks in turn borrowed in the Eurodollar market, repatriating these funds. In 1970, as U.S. interest rates fell in response to rapid monetary expansion and Regulation Q was suspended for large CDs, the borrowed funds returned, and the deficit grew to $9 billion. The deficit exploded to $30 billion by August 1971 (see Figure 12.18).[78] The dollar flood increased the reserves of the surplus countries, auguring inflation. German money growth doubled from 6.4% to 12% in 1971, and the German inflation rate increased from 1.8% in 1969 to 5.3% in 1971 (Meltzer 1991, p. 73). Pressure mounted for a revaluation of the mark. In April 1971, the dollar inflow to Germany reached $3 billion. On 5 May 1971, the German central bank suspended official operations in the foreign exchange market and allowed the deutsche mark to float. Similar action by Austria, Belgium, the Netherlands, and Switzerland followed (Solomon 1976, p. 179).

In the following months, advocates of cutting the link with gold surfaced. In April 1971, the U.S. balance of trade turned to deficit for the first time, and influential voices began urging dollar devaluation. The decision to suspend gold convertibility was triggered by French and British intentions in early August to convert dollars into gold. On 15 August, at Camp David, President Nixon announced that he had directed Secretary Connolly "to suspend temporarily the convertibility of the dollar into gold or other reserve assets." The accompanying policy package included a ninety-day wage-price freeze, a 10% import surcharge, and a 10% investment tax credit (Solomon 1976, p. 186).

The U.S. decision to suspend gold convertibility ended a key aspect of the Bretton Woods system. The remaining part of the system – the adjustable peg – disappeared nineteen months later.

The Bretton Woods system collapsed for three basic reasons.[79] First, two major flaws undermined the system. One flaw was the gold exchange

---

[78] Another force swelling the stock of dollar liabilities abroad was the practice by European monetary authorities of holding deposits in the Eurodollar market. When these funds were lent out in local currencies, they led to a further increase in dollar liabilities as the monetary authorities intervened to peg the exchange rate (Tew 1988, p. 143).

[79] For a similar view, see Cooper (1984).

standard, which placed the United States under threat of a convertibility crisis. In reaction, it pursued policies that in the end made adjustment more difficult. The second flaw was the adjustable peg. Because, in the face of growing capital mobility, the costs of discrete changes in parities were deemed so high, the system evolved into a reluctant fixed exchange rate system without any effective adjustment mechanism.

Second, U.S. monetary policy was inappropriate for a key currency. By inflating, the United States, after 1965, followed an inappropriate policy for a key currency country. Although the acceleration of inflation was low by the standards of the following decade, when superimposed on the cumulation of low inflation since World War II, it was sufficient to trigger a speculative attack on the world's monetary gold stock in 1968, leading to the collapse of the Gold Pool (Garber 1993). Once the regime had evolved into a de facto dollar standard, the obligation of the United States was to maintain price stability. Instead, it conducted an inflationary policy that ultimately destroyed the system.

Third, the surplus countries were increasingly unwilling to adjust. The major industrialized countries were unwilling to absorb dollar balances and revalue their currencies. In turn, this reflected basic differences in the underlying inflation rates that countries were willing to accept. The growing gap between the sovereign interests of the United States and the other major industrial countries in part reflected the decline in U.S. power. At the same time as U.S. power declined relative to the continental European countries and Japan, the G10 lost effectiveness, and no other focal points of power emerged. The stage was set for a decentralized system.

12.6   Conclusion

In conclusion, I summarize the main points of the paper, suggest answers to the two questions raised at the outset, and pose a number of questions that the other papers at the conference may answer.

12.6.1   Summary

The comparison of the performance of alternative monetary regimes in seven countries revealed that both real and nominal variables were most stable in the Bretton Woods convertible period, 1959–70. In many respects, the performance during that period was comparable to the period of the classical gold standard. In contrast, the preconvertible Bretton Woods regime was not as stable. Its performance was closer to that of the present floating rate regime.

The planning that led to Bretton Woods aimed to avoid the chaos of the interwar period. The ills to be avoided included floating exchange rates, condemned as prone to destabilizing speculation in the early 1920s; the subsequent gold exchange standard that enforced the international transmission of deflation in the early 1930s; and the resort to beggar-thy-neighbor devaluations, trade restrictions, exchange controls, and bilateralism after 1933. To avoid these ills, an adjustable peg system was designed that combined the favorable features of the fixed exchange rate gold standard and flexible exchange rates. Recent research, however, casts doubts on the accuracy of the perceived flaws of the interwar system.

Both Keynes and White planned an adjustable peg system to be coordinated by an international monetary agency. The Keynes plan gave the ICU substantially more resources and power than White's Fund, but both institutions had considerable power over the domestic financial policy of the members. The British plan contained more domestic policy autonomy than did the U.S. plan, while the American plan put more emphasis on exchange rate stability.

The Articles of Agreement signed at Bretton Woods represented a compromise between the two plans and between the interests of the United States and the United Kingdom. The system that emerged was a system in which parities defined in terms of gold and the dollar could be altered only in the event of a fundamental disequilibrium. In the interim, international reserves and drawings on the Fund would finance adjustment. The compromise involved limited resources and limited power and defined an uncertain role for gold and open-ended transitional arrangements.

The Bretton Woods system faced a number of problems in getting started, and it took twelve years before the system achieved full operation. The two key problems in the early years – of bilateralism and the dollar shortage – were each largely solved by developments outside the Bretton Woods arrangements. The dollar shortage was solved by massive U.S. aid and the devaluations of 1949. Multilateralism was eventually achieved in Western Europe in 1958 following the establishment in 1950 of the EPU by the Europeans with U.S. assistance. Other developments in this period include the decline in the importance of sterling as a reserve currency and the reduced importance of the IMF. By the end of the period, the system had evolved into a gold dollar exchange standard.

The period 1959–67 was the heyday of Bretton Woods. The system had become a gold dollar standard whereby the United States pegged the price of gold and the rest of the world pegged their currencies to the dollar. The dollar emerged as the key reserve currency in this period, reflecting both its use as an intervention currency and a growing demand by the private sector for dollars as international money. This growth in dollar demand reflected stable U.S. monetary policy.

The three problems of adjustment, liquidity, and confidence dominated academic and policy discussions during this period. The debate surrounding the first focused on how to achieve adjustment in a world with capital controls, fixed exchange rates, and domestic policy autonomy. Various policy measures were proposed to aid adjustment.

Of particular interest during the period was asymmetry in adjustment between deficit countries such as the United Kingdom and surplus countries such as Germany and between the United States as the reserve currency country and the rest of the world. Both the United Kingdom and Germany ran the gauntlet between concern over external convertibility and domestic stability. The United Kingdom alternated between expansionary policy that led to balance of payments deficits and austerity. Germany alternated between a balance of payments surplus that led to inflation and austerity.

For the United States, the persistence of balance of payments deficits after 1957 was a source of concern. For some it demonstrated the need for adjustment; for others it served as the means to satisfy the rest of the world's demand for dollars. For monetary authorities the deficit was a problem because of the threat of a convertibility crisis as outstanding dollar liabilities rose relative to the U.S. monetary gold stock. U.S. policies to restrict capital flows and discourage convertibility did not solve the problem. The main solution advocated for the adjustment problem was increased liquidity. Exchange rate flexibility was strongly opposed.

The liquidity problem evolved from a shortfall of monetary gold beginning in the late 1950s. The gap was increasingly made up by dollars, but, because of the confidence problem, dollars were not a permanent solution. New sources of liquidity were required, answered by the creation of the SDRs. However, by the time SDRs were injected into the system, they exacerbated worldwide inflation.

The key problem of the gold dollar system was how to maintain confidence. If the growth of the monetary gold stock was not sufficient to finance the growth of world real output and to maintain U.S. gold reserves, the system would become dynamically unstable. From 1960 to 1967, the United States adopted a number of policies to prevent conversion of dollars into gold. These included the Gold Pool, swaps, Roosa bonds, and moral suasion. The defense of sterling was a first line of defense for the dollar. When none of these measures worked, the two-tier gold market arrangement in March 1968 temporarily solved the problem by demonetizing gold at the margin and hence creating a de facto dollar standard.

The Bretton Woods system collapsed between 1968 and 1971 in the face of U.S. monetary expansion that exacerbated worldwide inflation. The United States broke the implicit rules of the dollar standard by not maintaining price stability. The rest of the world did not want to absorb dollars and inflate. They were also reluctant to revalue. The Americans were forced by British and French decisions to convert dollars into gold. The impasse was ended by closing the gold window.

Another important source of strain on the system was the unworkability of the adjustable peg under increasing capital mobility. Speculation against a fixed parity could not be stopped by either traditional policies or international rescue packages. The breakdown of Bretton Woods marked the end of U.S. financial dominance. The absence of a new center of international management set the stage for a centrifugal monetary system.

12.6.2 Why Bretton Woods was so stable and why it was so short lived

This historical survey suggests that one reason why the macroeconomic performance of the Bretton Woods system exhibited such remarkable stability is that, until the mid-1960s, the United States, as the center of the system, followed stable financial policies and the rest of the world, tied to the United States via the fixed exchange rate dollar standard, imported them. Differences between countries' performances in this period largely reflected their decisions to follow different policy objectives (exemplified by different underlying inflation rates). That the system was so stable may also reflect the possibility that shocks to the United States and the rest of the world were quite limited in this period. Another possibility is that the stability in the statistics simply masks the turmoil in the foreign exchange markets. The saga of speculative attacks on the major currencies, rescue packages, drastic austerity measures, and capital controls throughout the 1960s, culminating in major devaluations in 1967 and 1969, makes the point.

The survey also suggests reasons the Bretton Woods system was so short lived. First is the two fatal flaws in its design: the gold exchange standard and the adjustable peg. Second is the failure of the United States to maintain price stability after 1965. Third is the reluctance of the other major industrial countries to follow U.S. leadership when it conflicted with their national interests.

These answers, with which most would agree, lead to another question. Can we learn from the experience of Bretton Woods how to design a superior fixed exchange rate system? One possibility is to design a system that is based on rules that can be enforced. By *rules* is meant arrangements that bind policy actions over time. In contrast to an earlier tradition that stressed both impersonality and automaticity, this view of policy rules stems from the recent literature on the time inconsistency of optimal government policy (Kydland and Prescott 1977). This literature has demonstrated that, in almost all intertemporal policy situations, the public would benefit if the government were bound by a commitment technology preventing it from changing planned future policy.

The rules to be designed should be transparent, that is, easily understood. They should allow for contingencies when the rules can be temporarily suspended, as, for example, in the case of the classical gold standard during a war (Bordo and Kydland 1990). They should also allow for some feedback to accommodate random shocks.

On the basis of these criteria, the Bretton Woods rules were not well designed.[80] For nonreserve currency countries, the rules were to maintain fixed parities, except in the contingency of a fundamental disequilibrium in the balance of payments, and to use financial policy to smooth out short-run disturbances. The enforcement mechanism was presumably the dominant power of the United States – access to its open capital markets – since the IMF had little power. The rule was defective because the fundamental disequilibrium contingency was never spelled out and no constraint was placed on the extent to which domestic financial policy could stray from maintaining external balance.

For the United States, the center country, the rule was to fix the gold price of the dollar at $35.00 per ounce and to maintain price stability. However, if a majority of members (and every member with 10% or more of the total quotas) agreed, the United States could change the dollar price of gold. There was no explicit enforcement mechanism other than reputation and the commitment to gold convertibility. This rule suffered from a number of fatal flaws. First, because of the fear of a confidence crisis, the gold convertibility requirement may have prevented the United States in the early 1960s from acting as a center country and willingly supplying the reserves demanded by the rest of the world. Second, as became evident in the late 1960s, this requirement was useless in preventing the U.S. monetary authorities from pursuing an inflationary policy. Finally, although a mechanism was available for the United States to devalue the dollar, the monetary authorities were loath

---

[80] For another version of the rules of the Bretton Woods Articles and the dollar standard, see McKinnon (1988). See also Giovannini (1993) and Obstfeld (1993).

to use it for fear of undermining confidence. No effective enforcement mechanism existed. Ultimately, the United States attached greater importance to domestic economic concerns than to its role as the center of the international monetary system.

The failure of the Bretton Woods rule suggests a number of requirements for a well designed fixed exchange rate system. These include that the countries follow similar domestic economic goals (underlying inflation rates), that the rules be transparent, and that some central monetary authority enforce them. The recent EMS system has been quite successful because it seems to encompass these three elements. Designing a system to extend beyond one region may be more difficult. The defects and the dramatic collapse of Bretton Woods have discouraged nations from seeking to restore a system like it. Perhaps the perceived defects of the present system of floating – that it leads to undue volatility in both nominal and real exchange rates, in turn increasing macro instability and raising the costs of international transactions – are still not sufficient to overcome the aversion to a return by the world to a system such as Bretton Woods.

12.6.3   Remaining questions

Other questions remain to be asked about the origins, performance, and demise of Bretton Woods. First, how did the Bretton Woods system differ in the way it actually operated from other fixed exchange rate regimes? Second, what were the special factors that allowed the United States, the United Kingdom, and other countries to agree on the Articles of Agreement? Third, how did the adjustment mechanism work in normal times under Bretton Woods? Why did it break down? Fourth, was liquidity really inadequate before 1968? Why was it excessive thereafter? Fifth, could the confidence problem have been avoided under the gold dollar system? In other words, was collapse inevitable? Sixth, was Bretton Woods subject to different sources of shocks than other regimes? Were shocks transmitted between countries via the monetary standard, or was there effective insulation? Seventh, what was the role of the IMF, the G10, and other avenues for cooperation in stabilizing the Bretton Woods system? Eighth, how did the nonindustrialized world relate to the Bretton Woods system? How effective was the IMF as a commitment mechanism for the LDCs? Ninth, how has the recent floating rate regime worked compared to Bretton Woods? How important were capital controls in the operation of Bretton Woods compared to the subsequent regime? Tenth, how has the EMS regime worked? What lessons did the current floating and EMS regimes learn from the Bretton

Woods experience? These and other questions are addressed in Bordo and Eichengreen (1993).

Data Appendix

Table 12.1 and Figures 12.1–12.9

CANADA

(1) *Population*. 1880–1975, Data used in M. D. Bordo and L. Jonung (1987), *The Long-Run Behavior of the Velocity of Circulation: The International Evidence* (New York: Cambridge University Press). 1976–89, International Monetary Fund (1990), *International Financial Statistics Yearbook*. (2) *M2*. 1880–1984, Bordo and Jonung (1987). 1985–89, *Bank of Canada Review* (various issues), Table E1. (3) *Real GNP*. 1880–1985, Bordo and Jonung (1987). 1986–89, *Bank of Canada Review* (various issues), Table A1. (4) *GNP Deflator*. 1880–1985, Bordo and Jonung (1987). 1986–89, *Bank of Canada Review* (various issues), Table A1. (5) *Consumer Price Index*. 1880–1913, Interurban-intertemporal consumer price index, in Robert C. Allen (1990), *Real Income in the English Speaking World* (Vancouver: University of British Columbia Press). 1914–60, M. C. Urquhart and K. A. H. Buckley (1965), *Historical Statistics of Canada* (Montreal: Macmillan). 1961–89, *Economic Report of the President, 1991*. (6) *Short-Term Interest Rate*. 1880–1985, Bordo and Jonung (1987). 1986–89, Treasury bill rate, *International Financial Statistics Yearbook, 1990*. (7) *Long-Term Interest Rate*. 1880–1985, Bordo and Jonung (1987). 1986–89, *International Financial Statistics Yearbook, 1990*, ser. 61. (8) *Real Interest Rates*. Computed as the difference between the nominal interest rate and the rate of change of the consumer price index. (9) Canadian Dollars/U.S. Dollars. 1880–1914, Gold standard, rate = $1.00. 1919–60, Federal Reserve Board (1943 and 1976), *Banking and Monetary Statistics 1 and 2*. 1961–89, *Economic Report of the President, 1991*. (10) *Real Exchange Rate*. Computed as the nominal exchange rate divided by the ratio of the domestic to the U.S. consumer price index.

FRANCE

(1) *Population*. 1880–1949, B. R. Mitchell (1978), *European Historical Statistics, 1750–1970* (New York: Columbia University Press), Table A1. 1950–89, *International Financial Statistics* (various issues). (2) *M1*. 1880–1969, Michele Saint Marc (1983), *Histoire monetaire de la France, 1800–1980* (Paris: Presses Universitaires de la France), pp. 36–8. 1970–89, Reserve money (currency plus demand and time deposits), *International Financial Statistics*. (3) *Real GDP*. 1880–1900, Calculated from the Toutain Index, Saint Marc (1983, pp. 99–100). 1901–49, Alfred Sauvy (1954), *Rapport sur le revenu national presente* (Paris: Conseil Economique, March). 1950–88, INSEE, *Statistique annuaire de la France*

retrospectif (1966) and *Statistique annuaire de la France* (various issues). (4) *Deflator*. Calculated as the ratio of nominal to real GDP. Nominal GDP, 1880–1913, M. Levy-Leboyer and F. Bourguignon (1990), *The French Economy in the Nineteenth Century* (New York: Cambridge University Press), Table A-III. 1914–88, INSEE, *Statistique annuaire de la France retrospectif* (1966) and *Statistique annuaire de la France* (various issues). (5) *Consumer Price Index*. 1880–1969, Saint Marc (1983, 107). 1970–89, *International Financial Statistics Yearbook, 1990*. (6) *Short-Term Interest Rate*. S. Homer (1977), *A History of Interest Rates* (New Brunswick, N.J.: Rutgers University Press). 1880–1914, Open market rate, Homer (1977, Tables 27, 61). 1925–75, Day-to-day money rate, Homer (1977, Table 61). 1976–89, Call money rate, *International Financial Statistics Yearbook, 1990*. (7) *Long-Term Interest Rate*. 1880–1969, Homer [1977, Tables 25 and 60 (3% rentes)]. 1970–89, Long-term government bond yield, *International Financial Statistics Yearbook, 1990*. (8) *Real Interest Rates*. Computed as the difference between the nominal interest rate and the rate of change of the consumer price index. (9) French Francs/U.S. Dollars. 1880–1969, Saint Marc (1983, p. 107). 1970–89, *Economic Report of the President, 1991*. (10) *Real Exchange Rate*. Computed as the nominal exchange rate divided by the ratio of the domestic to the U.S. consumer price index.

GERMANY

(1) *Population*. 1880–1979, A. Sommariva and G. Tullio (1987), *German Macroeconomic History, 1880–1979* (New York: St. Martin's), pp. 234–6. 1980–89, *International Financial Statistics Yearbook, 1990*. (2) *M2*. 1880–1913, Data underlying M. D. Bordo (1986), "Financial Crises, Banking Crises, Stock Market Crashes and the Money Supply: Some International Evidence," in *Financial Crises and the World Banking System*, ed. F. Capie and G. Wood (London: Macmillan). 1924–38, Bordo and Jonung (1987). 1950–89, Deutsche Bundesbank, *Monthly Reports* (various issues). (3) *Real GNP*. 1880–1985, Data underlying A. H. Meltzer and S. Robinson (1989), "Stability under the Gold Standard in Practice," in *Money, History, and International Finance: Essays in Honor of Anna J. Schwartz*, ed. M. D. Bordo (Chicago: University of Chicago Press). 1986–89, *International Financial Statistics Yearbook, 1990*. (4) *Deflator*. 1880–1985, Meltzer and Robinson (1989). 1986–89, *International Financial Statistics Yearbook, 1990*. (5) *Consumer Price Index*. 1880–1979, Sommariva and Tullio (1987, pp. 231–4). 1980–89, *International Financial Statistics Yearbook, 1990*. (6) *Short-Term Interest Rate*. 1880–1939, Open market discount rate from Homer (1977, Tables 33, 67). 1950–89, Call money rate from Homer (1977, Table 67) and *International Financial Statistics Yearbook, 1990*. (7) *Long-Term Interest Rate*. 1880–1975, High-grade bond yields from Homer (1977, Tables 32, 67). 1976–89, Mortgage bond yield, *International Financial Statistics Yearbook, 1990*. (8) *Real Interest Rates*. Computed as the difference between the nominal interest rates and the rate of change of the consumer price index. (9) *Deutsche Mark/U.S. Dollars*. 1880–1979, Sommariva and Tullio (1987, pp. 231–4). 1980–89, *Economic*

Report of the President, 1991. (10) *Real Exchange Rate.* Computed as the nominal exchange rate divided by the ratio of the domestic to the U.S. consumer price index.

JAPAN

(1) *Population.* 1880–1949, Bureau of Statistics (1957), *Japan Statistical Yearbook.* 1950–89, *International Financial Statistics Yearbook, 1990.* (2) *M1.* 1905–59, B. R. Mitchell (1982), *International Historical Statistics of Africa and Asia* (New York: New York University Press), Tables H1, H2. 1960–89, Data supplied by Robert Rasche. (3) *Real GNP.* 1885–1988, Data supplied by Robert Rasche. 1989, *International Financial Statistics Yearbook, 1990.* (4) *Deflator.* 1885–1988, Data supplied by Robert Rasche. 1989, *International Financial Statistics Yearbook, 1990.* (5) *Consumer Price Index.* 1950–89, *International Financial Statistics* (various issues). (6) *Short-Term Interest Rate.* 1880–1938 and 1953–89, Discount rate at Tokyo banks, data supplied by Robert Rasche. (7) *Real Interest Rate.* Computed as the difference between the nominal interest rate and the rate of change of the GNP deflator. (8) *Yen/U.S. Dollars.* 1880–1989, data supplied by James Lothian. (9) *Real Exchange Rate.* Computed as the nominal exchange rate divided by the ratio of the GNP deflator to the U.S. consumer price index.

UNITED KINGDOM

(1) *Population.* 1880–1975, Bordo and Jonung (1987), 1976–89, *International Financial Statistics Yearbook, 1990.* (2) *M3.* 1880–1985, Bordo and Jonung (1987). 1986–89, Bank of England, *Quarterly Bulletin* (various issues), Table 11.1. (3) *Real NNP.* 1880–1985, Bordo and Jonung (1987). 1986–89, Central Statistical Office, *Economic Trends* (various issues). (4) *Deflator.* 1880–1985, Bordo and Jonung (1987). 1986–89, Central Statistical Office, *Economic Trends* (various issues). (5) *Consumer Price Index.* 1880–1965, Feinstein's retail price series in F. Capie and A. Webber (1985), *A Monetary History of the United Kingdom* (London: Allen & Unwin), Vol. 1, Table III. (12). 1966–89, *International Financial Statistics Yearbook, 1990.* (6) *Short-Term Interest Rate.* Treasury Bill Rate, 1880–1985, Bordo and Jonung (1987). 1986–89, *International Financial Statistics Yearbook, 1990.* (7) *Long-Term Interest Rate.* 1880–1985, Consol rate, Bordo and Jonung (1987). 1986–89, Long-term government bond yield, *International Financial Statistics Yearbook, 1990.* (8) *Real Interest Rates.* Computed as the difference between the nominal interest rate and the rate of change of the consumer price index. (9) *U.S. Dollar/Pound.* 1880–1939, M. Friedman and A. J. Schwartz (1982), *Monetary Trends in the United States and the United Kingdom* (Chicago: University of Chicago Press), Table 4.9, col. 8, pp. 130–35. 1947–89, *International Financial Statistics* (various issues). (10) *Real Exchange Rate.* Computed as the nominal exchange rate divided by the ratio of the domestic to the U.S. consumer price index.

UNITED STATES

(1) *Population*. 1880–1975, Bordo and Jonung (1987). 1976–89, *International Financial Statistics Yearbook, 1990*. (2) *M2*. 1880–1947, Bordo and Jonung (1987). 1948–89, Data supplied by Robert Rasche. (3) *Real GNP*. 1880–1945, Nathan S. Balke and Robert J. Gordon (1986), "Appendix B: Historical Data," in *The American Business Cycle: Continuity and Change*, ed. Robert J. Gordon (Chicago: University of Chicago Press), pp. 781–3, col. 2. 1946–89, *The Economic Report of the President, 1991*, p. 288. (4) *Deflator*. 1880–1945, Balke and Gordon (1986, pp. 781–3, col. 3). 1946–89, *The Economic Report of the President, 1991*, 290. (5) *Consumer Price Index*. 1880–1970, U.S. Bureau of the Census (1975), *Historical Statistics of the United States: Colonial Times to 1970: Bicentennial Edition* (Washington, DC), pp. 210–1 (hereafter cited as *Historical Statistics*). 1971–89, *International Financial Statistics Yearbook, 1990*. (6) *Short-Term Interest Rate*. Commercial paper rate, 1880–1986, Bordo and Jonung (1987). 1987–89, *International Financial Statistics Yearbook, 1990*. (7) *Long-Term Interest Rate*. Long-term government bond yield, 1880–1986, Bordo and Jonung (1987). 1987–89, M. D. Bordo and L. Jonung (1990), "The Long-Run Behavior of Velocity: The Institutional Approach Revisited," *Journal of Policy Modelling* 12 (Summer), pp. 165–97. (8) *Real Interest Rates*. Computed as the difference between the nominal interest rate and the rate of change of the consumer price index. (9) *Trade-Weighted Exchange Rate (Real and Nominal)*. 1960–89, data supplied by Allan Meltzer.

ITALY

(1) *Population*. 1880–1975, Istituto Centrale di Statistica (1976), *Sommario di statistiche storiche dell'Italia, 1861–1975*. 1976–89, *International Financial Statistics Yearbook, 1990*. (2) *M3*. 1880–1980, Franco Spinelli and Michele Fratianni (1991), *Storia monetaria d'Italia* (Milan: Arnoldo Mondadori), statistical app., pp. 48–51, pp. ser. U1 + U2 + D. 1981–89, *International Financial Statistics Yearbook, 1990*, ser. 351, money plus quasi-money. (3) *Real GNP and Deflator*. 1880–1970, B. R. Mitchell (1975), *European Historical Statistics, 1750–1970* (New York: Columbia University Press), Table J1. 1971–89, *International Financial Statistics Yearbook, 1990*. (4) *Consumer Price Index*. 1880–1980, Spinelli and Fratianni (1991), statistical app., pp. 66–71. ser. CLI. 1981–89, *International Financial Statistics Yearbook, 1990*, ser. 64. (5) *Long-Term Interest Rate*. 1880–1980, Spinelli and Fratianni (1991), statistical app., pp. 82–4, ser. RIL. 1981–89, *International Financial Statistics Yearbook, 1990*, ser. 61. (6) *Real Interest Rate*. Computed as the difference between the nominal interest rate and the rate of change of the consumer price index. (7) *Lira/U.S. Dollar*. 1880–1980, Spinelli and Fratianni (1991), statistical app., pp. 87–89, ser. ELUS. 1981–89, *International Financial Statistics Yearbook, 1990*, ser. af. (8) *Real Exchange Rate*. Computed as the nominal exchange rate divided by the ratio of the domestic to the U.S. consumer price index.

Figure 12.10

(1) *U.S. Monetary Gold Stock*. Table SC-10, col. 3, in *The Role of Gold in the Domestic and International Monetary Systems: Report to the Congress of the Commission on the Role of Gold in the Domestic and International Monetary Systems*, Vol. 1 (Washington, DC: U.S. Congress, March 1982) (hereafter cited as *Gold Commission Report*). The numbers in this Table, as well as in Table SC-8, are given in ounces. The fixed gold price of $35.00 per ounce is used to convert these numbers into dollars. (2) *U.S. External Liabilities*. 1972 supplement to *International Financial Statistics*, p. 2, ser. 4 (total) and 4a (monetary authorities and governments). (3) *World Monetary Gold Stock*. Table SC-8, cols. 1 (1945–1970) and 2 (1971), from the *Gold Commission Report*.

Figure 12.11

Robert Triffin (1957), *Europe and the Money Muddle* (New Haven, Conn.: Yale University Press), Table 8, p. 314.

Figure 12.12

Economic Report of the President, 1989, Table B-102, pp. 424–25.

Figure 12.13

(1) *Current Account*. IMF, *Balance of Payments Yearbook* (various issues). (2) *Reserves*. Total International Reserves as reported in the 1972 supplement (1948–59) and the 1990 Yearbook (1960–61) of *International Financial Statistics*.

Figure 12.14

(1) *Current Account and Reserves*. Bank of England (1970), *Statistical Abstract*, No. 1, Table 19. (2) *Dollar Deficits*. 1946–51, Alexander Cairncross and Barry Eichengreen (1983), *Sterling in Decline* (Oxford: Basil Blackwell), Table 4.3, p. 146. 1952–57, Central Statistical Office (1958), *Annual Abstract of Statistics*, no. 95 (London: Her Majesty's Stationery Office), sec. X, Table 277, p. 241.

Figures 12.15 and 12.25

(1) *Gold, Reserve Position in the Fund, Foreign Exchange, and SDRs*. 1972 supplement (1948–59) and 1990 yearbook (1960–61) of *International Financial*

Statistics. (2) *U.S. Dollars.* 1948–51, Robert Triffin (1961), *Gold and the Dollar Crisis* (New Haven, Conn.: Yale University Press), Table 14, p. 72. 1951–61, *International Financial Statistics* (April 1963), p. 23. 1961–71, *Treasury Bulletin* (July 1973), Table IFS-2, total liabilities to official institutions in foreign countries. (3) *British Pounds.* 1948–51, Triffin (1961), Table 14, p. 72. 1951–61, *International Financial Statistics* (April 1963), p. 23. 1961–71, Bank of England, *Statistical Abstract*, no. 2, 1975, Table 25/2 ("Exchange Reserves in Sterling Held by Central Monetary Institutions: Geographical Details, Total All Countries"). These data are converted to U.S. dollars by using the actual exchange rate from the *International Financial Statistics Yearbook, 1990.*

Figures 12.16, 12.17, 12.18, and 12.33

Current Account, Long-Term Capital, Short-Term Capital, and Change in Reserves. 1950–59, OECD (1964), *Statistics of Balance of Payments, 1950–1961,* (Paris). 1960–71, OECD (1979), *Balances of Payments of OECD Countries, 1960–1977* (Paris).

Figure 12.19

(1) *Current Account.* 1945–70, *Historical Statistics,* ser. U15 + U16 + U17. 1971, Department of Commerce (1973), *Statistical Abstract of the United States.* (2) *Liquidity Balance.* 1946–69, Department of Commerce, *Survey of Current Business* (June 1970), p. 43, Table 3, row 4. 1970–71, *Statistical Abstract of the United States, 1971.* (3) *Net Liquidity Balance.* 1960–71, *Survey of Current Business* (June 1972), p. 26, row 33. (4) *Basic Balance (Balance on Current Account and Long-Term Capital).* 1960–71, *Survey of Current Business* (June 1972), p. 26, row 26. (5) *ORT.* Calculated as the sum of the transactions in U.S. official reserves (from *Historical Statistics,* U24, and *International Financial Statistics,* 79c.d) and the change in liabilities to foreign official institutions (from *International Financial Statistics,* 7b.d).

Figure 12.20

Total International Reserves and Total Imports. 1972 supplement (1948–59) and 1990 yearbook (1960–61) of *International Financial Statistics.*

Figure 12.21

(1) *Real Price of Gold.* Table SC-16, pp. 222–23, in the *Gold Commission Report.* (2) *World Gold Output.* Table SC-2, pp. 188–89, in the *Gold Commission Report.*

Figure 12.22

(1) *Private Demand*. Calculated as the sum of "Jewelry + Industrial Demand" (Table SC-12, col. 6), "Coin + Medallions" (Table SC-12, col. 7), and "Net Private Bullion Purchases" (Table SC-12, col. 8) minus "Dishoarding of Private Bullion Holdings" (Table SC-13, col. 6), from the *Gold Commission Report*. (2) *Production*. See Figure 12.21. (3) *Change in World Monetary Gold Stock*. See Figure 12.27. (4) *East Bloc Gold Sales*. Table SC-13, col. 2, p. 211, in the *Gold Commission Report*.

Figures 12.23 and 12.24

(1) *Real Trade*. Calculated as the sum of real exports and imports, converted to dollars by using the actual exchange [from 1972 supplement (1948–59) and 1990 yearbook (1960–71) of *International Financial Statistics*]. (2) *Gold and Total International Reserves*. 1972 supplement (1948–59) and 1990 yearbook (1960–71) of *International Financial Statistics*. (3) *Real Income*. Robert Summers and Alan Heston (1991), "The Penn World Table (mark 5): An Expanded Set of International Comparisons, 1950–1988," *Quarterly Journal of Economics* 106(May):327–68.

Figure 12.26

1954–67, *International Financial Statistics* (various issues). 1968–71, Table SC-17 in the *Gold Commission Report*.

Figure 12.27

(1) *World Gold Stock*. Table SC-6, pp. 195–96, in the *Gold Commission Report*. (2) *World Monetary Gold Stock*. Table SC-8, p. 199, in the *Gold Commission Report*.

Figure 12.28

(1) *United States*. The inflation rate is calculated using the GNP deflator from Table 1.1. (2) *G-7 and G-7 excluding the United States*. The inflation rate is calculated as a weighted average of the inflation rates (using the GNP deflators from Table 12.1) in the different countries. The weights are calculated as the share of each country's national income in the total income in the G-7 countries, where the GNP/GDP data are converted to dollars using the actual exchange rates.

Figures 12.29 and 12.30

(1) *Money Growth*. Calculated as the change in M1. Figures for the G7 and G7 excluding the United States are calculated by converting the national money supplies to U.S. dollars using the actual exchange rate. Data are from the 1972 supplement (1948–59) and 1990 yearbook (1960–71) of *International Financial Statistics*. (2) *Real Output Growth*. For the United States, it is calculated as the change in the real GNP (data from Table 12.1). For the G7 and G7 excluding the United States, it is calculated as a weighted average of the real income growth (data from Table 12.1) in the different countries (weights are calculated as for Figure 12.28).

Figure 12.31

(1) *Federal Reserve Credit*. 1958–70, Federal Reserve Board (1943), *Banking and Monetary Statistics*, Table 10.2B, pp. 526–35. 1971, Federal Reserve Board (1981), *Annual Statistical Digest, 1970–1979*, Table 2A, p. 10. (2) *U.S. Monetary Base*. James R. Lothian (1983), "Data Appendix," in *The International Transmission of Inflation*, ed. Michael R. Darby, James R. Lothian, et al. (Chicago: University of Chicago Press), ser. USMHQSAE, p. 707.

Figure 12.32

(1) *U.S. Budget Deficit*. Frank de Leeuw and Thomas M. Holloway (1982), "The High-Employment Budget: Revised Estimates and Automatic Inflation Effects," *Survey of Current Business* (April), Table 3, pp. 26–27. (2) *U.S. Monetary Base*. See Figure 12.31.

References

Aliber, Robert F. 1962. Speculation in the foreign exchanges: The European experience, 1919–1928. *Yale Economic Essays* 2:171–245.

Backus, David R., and Patrick I. Kehoe. 1992. International evidence on the historical properties of business cycles. *American Economic Review* 28(September):864–88.

Balassa, Bela. 1964. The purchasing power parity doctrine: A reappraisal. *Journal of Political Economy* 72(December):584–96.

Baxter, Marianne, and Alan C. Stockman. 1989. Business cycles and the exchange-rate regime: Some international evidence. *Journal of Monetary Economics* 23(May):377–400.

Bergman, Michael, and Lars Jonung. 1990. The business cycle has not been dampened? The case of Sweden and the United States, 1973–1988. Research paper no. 6432. Stockholm School of Economics, October.

Bernanke, Ben, and Harold James. 1991. The gold standard, deflation, and financial crisis in the Great Depression: An international comparison. In *Financial Markets and Financial Crisis*, ed. R. Glenn Hubbard, pp. 33–68. Chicago: University of Chicago Press.

Black, Stanley W. 1987. International monetary institutions. In *New Palgrave Dictionary of Economics*, 917–20. London: Macmillan.

1991. A Levite among the priests: Edward M. Bernstein and the origins of the Bretton Woods System. Boulder, Colo.: Westview.

Bordo, Michael D. 1981. The classical gold standard: Some lessons for today. *Federal Reserve Bank of St. Louis Review* 63(May):2–17.

Bordo, Michael D., and Richard E. Ellson. 1985. A model of the classical gold standard with depletion. *Journal of Monetary Economics* 16(July):109–20.

Bordo, Michael D., and Finn E. Kydland. 1990. The gold standard as a rule. NBER Working Paper no. 3367 May.

Bordo, Michael D., and Anna J. Schwartz. 1989. Transmission of real and monetary disturbances under fixed and floating rates. In *Dollars, Deficits and Trade*, ed. James A. Dorn and William A. Niskanen, pp. 237–58. Boston: Kluwer Academic.

Bordo, Michael D., and Barry Eichengreen, eds. 1993. *A Retrospective on the Bretton Woods System: Lessons for International Monetary Reform*. Chicago: University of Chicago Press.

Buiter, William H. 1989. A viable gold standard requires flexible monetary and fiscal policy. *Review of Economic Studies* 56:101–18.

Cagan, Philip, 1984. On the report of the Gold Commission (1982) and convertible monetary systems. *Carnegie-Rochester Conference Series on Public Policy* 21(Autumn):247–67.

Cairncross, Alexander. 1985. *Years of Recovery: British Economic Policy, 1945–51*. London: Methuen.

Cairncross, Alexander, and Barry Eichengreen. 1983. *Sterling in Decline*. Oxford: Basil Blackwell.

Capie, Forrest, Terence C. Mills, and Geoffrey E. Wood. 1986. What happened in 1931? In *Financial Crisis and the World Banking System*, ed. Forrest Capie and Geoffrey E. Wood. London: Macmillan.

Clower, Robert, and Richard Lipsey. 1961. The present state of international liquidity theory. *American Economic Review* 68(May):568–95.

Cooper, Richard N. 1984. Is there a need for reform? In *The International Monetary System: Forty Years after Bretton Woods*, pp. 21–39. Conference Series no. 28. Federal Reserve Bank of Boston, May.

Corden, Max. 1985. *Inflation, Exchange Rates and the World Economy: Lectures on International Monetary Economics*. 3d ed. Oxford: Clarendon.

1991. Does the current account matter? The old view and the new. Johns Hopkins University, January. Mimeo.

Crockett, Arthur D. 1987. International liquidity. In *New Palgrave Dictionary of Economics*, pp. 910–12. London: Macmillan.

Dam, Kenneth, 1982. *The Rules of the Game: Reform and Evolution in the International Monetary System*. Chicago: University of Chicago Press.

Darby, Michael R., and James R. Lothian. 1989. The international transmission of inflation afloat. In *Money, History, and International Finance: Essays in Honor of Anna J. Schwartz*, ed. Michael D. Bordo, pp. 203–36. Chicago: University of Chicago Press.

Darby, Michael R., James R. Lothian, et al. 1983. *The International Transmission of Inflation*. Chicago: University of Chicago Press.

Despres, Emil, Charles Kindleberger, and William Salant. 1966. The dollar and world liquidity: A minority view. *Economist* 5(February):526–29.

DeVries, Margaret G. 1986. *The IMF in a Changing World: 1945–1985*. Washington, DC: International Monetary Fund.

1987. *Balance of Payments Adjustment, 1945 to 1986: The IMF Experience*. Washington, DC: International Monetary Fund.

Diz, Adolfo C. 1984. The conditions attached to adjustment financing: Evolution of the IMF practice. In *The International Monetary System: Forty Years after Bretton Woods*, pp. 214–325. Conference Series no. 28. Federal Reserve Bank of Boston, May.

Domingvez, Kathryn. 1993. The role of international organizations in the Bretton Woods System. In *A Retrospective on the Bretton Woods System: Lessons for International Monetary Reform*, ed. Michael D. Bordo and Barry Eichengreen. Chicago: University of Chicago Press, 1993, pp. 357–97.

Dornbusch, Rudiger. 1976. Expectations and exchange rate dynamics. *Journal of Political Economy* 84:1161–76.

Eichengreen, Barry. 1982. Did speculation destabilize the French franc in the 1920's? *Explorations in Economic History* 19(January):71–100.

1989a. The comparative performance of fixed and flexible exchange rate regimes: Interwar evidence. NBER Working Paper no. 3097. September.

1989b. Hegemonic stability theories. In *Can Nations Agree?* ed. Richard Cooper et al. Washington, DC: Brookings.

1990a. The gold-exchange standard and the Great Depression. In *Elusive Stability: Essays in the History of International Finance, 1919–1939*, pp. 239–70. New York: Cambridge University Press.

1990b. International monetary instability between the wars: Structural flaws or misguided policies. In *The Evolution of the International Monetary System*, ed. Y. Suzuki et al., pp. 71–116. Tokyo: University of Tokyo Press.

1990c. Trends and cycles in foreign lending. Centre for Economic Policy Research Discussion Paper no. 451. September.

1991. U.S. foreign relations in the 20th century. University of California, Berkeley, March. Mimeo.

1992. *Golden Fetters: The Gold Standard and the Great Depression, 1919–1939*. New York: Oxford University Press.

1993. Epilogue: Three perspectives on the Bordo Woods System. In *A Retrospective on the Bretton Woods System: Lessons for International Monetary Reform*, ed. Michael D. Bordo and Barry Eichengreen. Chicago: University of Chicago Press, 1993, pp. 621–57.

Eichengreen, Barry, and Jeffrey Sachs. 1985. Exchange rates and economic recovery in the 1930's. *Journal of Economic History* 65:925–46.

Eichengreen, Barry, and Marc Uzan. 1991. The economic consequences of the Marshall Plan. University of California, Berkeley, June. Mimeo.

Ellis, Howard S. 1941. *Exchange Control in Central Europe.* Cambridge, Mass.: Harvard University Press.

Emminger, Otmar. 1967. Practical aspects of the problem of balance of payments adjustment. *Journal of Political Economy* 75(August):512–22.

Floyd, John E. 1985. *World Monetary Equilibrium.* Philadelphia: University of Pennsylvania Press.

Friedman, Milton. 1953. The case for flexible exchange rates. In *Essays in Positive Economics*, 157–203. Chicago: University of Chicago Press.

Friedman, Milton, and Anna J. Schwartz. 1963. *A Monetary History of the United States: 1867 to 1960.* Princeton, N.J.: Princeton University Press.

Garber, Peter. 1993. The collapse of the Bretton Woods Fixed Exchange Rate System. In *A Retrospective on the Bretton Woods System: Lessons for International Monetary Reform*, ed. Michael D. Bordo and Barry Eichengreen. Chicago: University of Chicago Press, 1993, pp. 461–85.

Gardner, Richard N. 1969. *Sterling Dollar Diplomacy.* 2d ed. New York: McGraw-Hill.

——— 1972. The political setting. In *Bretton Woods Revisited*, ed. Keith Acheson, John Chant, and Martin Prachowny, pp. 20–33. Toronto: University of Toronto Press.

Genberg, Hans, and Alexander K. Swoboda. 1977a. Causes and origins of the current worldwide inflation. In *Inflation Theory and Anti-Inflation Policy*, 72–93. London: Macmillan.

——— 1977b. Worldwide inflation under the dollar standard. Geneva: Graduate Institutes of International Studies. Mimeo.

——— 1993. The provision of liquidity in the Bretton Woods System. In *A Retrospective on the Bretton Woods System: Lessons for International Monetary Reform*, ed. Michael D. Bordo and Barry Eichengreen. Chicago: University of Chicago Press, 1993, pp. 269–306.

Gilbert, Milton. 1968. *The Gold-Dollar System: Conditions of Equilibrium and the Price of Gold.* Princeton Essays in International Economics. Princeton University, International Finance Section.

Giovannini, Alberto. 1989. How do fixed exchange rate systems work? Evidence from the gold standard, Bretton Woods and the EMS. In *Blueprints for Exchange Rate Management*, ed. Marcus Miller, Barry Eichengreen, and Richard Portes, pp. 13–46. London: Centre for Economic Policy Research.

——— 1993. Bretton Woods and its precursors: Rules versus discretion in the history of international monetary regimes. In *A Retrospective on the Bretton Woods System: Lessons for International Monetary Reform*, ed. Michael D. Bordo and Barry Eichengreen. Chicago: University of Chicago Press, 1993, pp. 109–47.

Grilli, Vittorio, and Graciela Kaminsky. 1991. Nominal exchange rate regimes and the real exchange rate: Evidence from the United States and Great Britain, 1885–1986. *Journal of Monetary Economics* 29(April):191–212.

Grubel, Herbert G. 1963. *World Monetary Reform: Plans and Issues*. Stanford, Calif.: Stanford University Press.

Hallwood, Peter, and Robert MacDonald. 1986. *International Money, Theory, Evidence and Institutions*. Oxford: Basil Blackwell.

Halm, George. 1970. *Approaches to Greater Flexibility of Exchange Rates: The Burgenstock Papers*. Princeton, N.J.: Princeton University Press.

Hoffman, Stanley, and Charles Maier, eds. 1984. *The Marshall Plan: A Retrospective*. Boulder, Colo.: Westview.

Horsefield, Keith, ed. 1969a. *The International Monetary Fund, 1945–1965: Twenty Years of International Monetary Co-Operation*. Vol. 1, *Chronicle*. Washington, D.C.: International Monetary Fund.

ed. 1969b. *The International Monetary Fund, 1945–1965: Twenty Years of International Monetary Co-Operation*. Vol. 3, *Documents*. Washington, DC: International Monetary Fund.

Ikenberry, G. John. 1990. A world economy restored: Expert consensus and the Anglo-American postwar settlement. Princeton University, February. Mimeo.

1993. The political origins of Bretton Woods. In *A Retrospective on the Bretton Woods System: Lessons for International Monetary Reform*, ed. Michael D. Bordo and Barry Eichengreen. Chicago: University of Chicago Press, 1993, pp. 155–82.

International Monetary Fund (IMF). 1964. *Annual Report*. Washington, DC

[1953] 1969a. *Adequacy of Monetary Reserves*. In Horsefield 1969b, 311–48.

[1944] 1969b. *Articles of Agreement of the International Monetary Fund*. 22 July. In Horsefield 1969b, pp. 185–214.

[1958] 1969c. *International Reserves and Liquidity*. In Horsefield 1969b, pp. 349–420.

[1944] 1969d. *Joint Statement by Experts on the Establishment of an International Monetary Fund*. 1 April. In Horsefield 1969b, pp. 128–38.

1970. *The Role of Exchange Rates in the Adjustment of International Payments*. Washington, DC.

Johnson, Harry G. 1968. The sterling crisis of 1967 and the gold rush of 1968. *Nebraska Journal of Economics and Business* 7(Autumn):3–17.

1972a. The Bretton Woods System, key currencies, and the "dollar crisis" of 1971. *Three Banks Review* 94(June):3–22.

1972b. The case for flexible exchange rates, 1964. In *Further Essays in Monetary Economics*, pp. 198–228. London: Allen & Unwin.

Kaplan, Jacob J., and Gunther Schleiminger. 1989. *The European Payments Union: Financial Diplomacy in the 1950's*. Oxford: Clarendon.

Kenen, Peter B. 1960. International liquidity and the balance of payments of a reserve-currency country. *Quarterly Journal of Economics* 74(November):572–86.

Keynes, John M. [1943] 1969. Proposals for an international clearing union. April. In Horsefield 1969b, pp. 19–36.

Kindleberger, Charles P. 1950. *The Dollar Shortage*. London: Chapman & Hall.

1973. *The World in Depression, 1929–1939*. Berkeley: University of California Press.

Kydland, Finn E., and Edward P. Prescott. 1977. Rules rather than discretion: The inconsistency of optimal plans. *Journal of Political Economy* 85:473–91.

McDougall, Donald M. 1957. *The World Dollar Problem*. London: Macmillan.

Machlup, Fritz. 1964. *Plans for the Reform of the International Monetary System*. Princeton Essays in International Economics. Princeton University, International Finance Section.

McKinnon, Ronald I. 1969. *Private and Official International Money: The Case for the Dollar*. Princeton Essays in International Economics. Princeton University, International Finance Section.

1979. *Money in International Exchange: The Convertible Currency System*. New York: Oxford.

1988. An international gold standard without gold. *Cato Journal* 8(Fall):351–73.

1993. Alternative international monetary systems: The rules of the game reconsidered. *Journal of Economic Literature* 31.1(March):1–44.

Marston, Richard. 1987. Real exchange rates and productivity growth in the United States and Japan. In *Real-Financial Linkages among Open Economies*, ed. Sven Arndt. Cambridge, Mass.: MIT Press.

Meltzer, Allan H. 1988. *Keyne's Monetary Theory: A Different Interpretation*. New York: Cambridge University Press.

1991. U.S. policy in the Bretton Woods era. *Federal Reserve Bank of St. Louis Review* 73(May/June):54–83.

Meltzer, Allan H., and Saranna Robinson. 1989. Stability under the gold standard in practice. In *Money, History, and International Finance: Essays in Honor of Anna J. Schwartz*, ed. Michael D. Bordo, pp. 163–95. Chicago: University of Chicago Press.

Milward, Alan S. 1984. *The Reconstruction of Western Europe, 1945–51*. Berkeley and Los Angeles: University of California Press.

Moggridge, Donald E. 1968. Keynes and the international monetary system, 1910–1946. In *International Monetary Problems and Supply Side Economics*, ed. John Cohen and Gregory C. Harcourt, pp. 56–83. London: Macmillan.

Mundell, Robert A. 1968. *International Economics*. Chicago: University of Chicago Press.

1969a. The international monetary fund. *Journal of World Trade Law* 3:455–97.

1969b. Problems of the international monetary system. In *Monetary Problems of the International Economy*, ed. Robert A. Mundell and Alexander K. Swoboda, pp. 21–38. Chicago: University of Chicago Press.

1971. *Monetary Theory*. Pacific Palisades, Calif.: Goodyear.

1973. The monetary consequences of Jacques Rueff: Review article. *Journal of Business* 46(July):385–95.

Mundell, Robert A., and Alexander K. Swoboda, eds. 1969. *Monetary Problems of the International Economy*. Chicago: University of Chicago Press.

Mussa, Michael. 1986. Nominal exchange rates and the behavior of real exchange rates: Evidence and implications. *Carnegie-Rochester Conference Series on Public Policy* 25:117–214.

Neal, Larry. 1979. The economics and finance of bilateral clearing agreements: Germany, 1934–38. *Economic History Review* 32(August):391–404.

Niehans, Jurg. 1976. How to fill an empty shell. *American Economic Review* 66(May):177–85.

Nurkse, Ragnar. 1944. *International Currency Experience*. Geneva: League of Nations.

Obstfeld, Maurice. 1993. The adjustment mechanism. In *A Retrospective on the Bretton Woods System: Lessons for International Monetary Reform*, ed. Michael D. Bordo and Barry Eichengreen. Chicago: University of Chicago Press, 1993, pp. 201–56.

Oliver, Robert. 1975. *International Economic Co-operation and the World Bank*. London: Macmillan.

Organization for Economic Cooperation and Development. Economic Policy Committee. 1966. *The Balance of Payments Adjustment Process. A Report by Working Party 3*. Paris.

Ossola, Roberto. 1965. *Report of the Study Group on the Creation of Reserve Assets*. Rome: Group of Ten.

Pressnell, Leslie S. 1986. *External Economic Policy since the War*. Vol. 1, *The Post-War Financial Settlement*. London: Her Majesty's Stationery Office.

Rockoff, Hugh. 1984. Some evidence on the real price of gold, its costs of production, and commodity prices. In *A Retrospective on the Classical Gold Standard, 1821–1931*, ed. Michael D. Bordo and Anna J. Schwartz, pp. 613–44. Chicago: University of Chicago Press.

Rueff, Jacques. 1967. Increase in the price of gold. In *The International Monetary System: Problems and Proposals*, ed. Lawrence H. Officer and Thomas D. Willett, 179–90. Englewood Cliffs, N.J.: Prentice-Hall.

Salant, Stephen W. 1983. The vulnerability of price stabilization schemes to speculative attack. *Journal of Political Economy* 91(February):1–38.

Scammell, William A. 1976. *International Monetary Policy: Bretton Woods and After*. New York: Wiley.

Schwartz, Anna J. 1989. The postwar institutional evolution of the international monetary system. In *Money in Historical Perspective*. Chicago: University of Chicago Press.

Sheffrin, Steven. 1988. Have economic fluctuations been dampened? A look at evidence outside the United States. *Journal of Monetary Economics* 21(January):73–83.

Solomon, Robert. 1976. *The International Monetary System, 1945–1976: An Insider's View*. New York: Harper & Row.

Stockman, Alan C. 1983. Real exchange rates under alternative nominal exchange rate system. *Journal of International Money and Finance* 2(August): 147–66.

1988. Real exchange-rate variability under pegged and floating nominal exchange-rate system: An equilibrium theory. *Carnegie-Rochester Conference Series on Public Policy* 29(Autumn):259–94.

Swoboda, Alexander K. 1978. Gold dollars, Euro-dollars, and the world money stock under fixed exchange rates. *American Economic Review* 68(September):625–42.

Swoboda, Alexander K., and Hans Genberg. 1982. Gold and the dollar: Asymmetries in world money stock determination, 1959–1971. In *The International Monetary System under Flexible Exchange Rates: Global, Regional and National,* ed. Richard N. Cooper et al., pp. 235–59. Cambridge, Mass.: Ballinger.

Temin, Peter. 1989. *Lessons from the Great Depression.* Cambridge, Mass.: Harvard University Press.

Tew, Brian. 1988. *The Evolution of the International Monetary System.* 4th ed. London: Hutchinson.

Townsend, Robert M. 1977. The eventual failure of price fixing schemes. *Journal of Economic Theory* 14:190–9.

Triffin, Robert. 1957. *Europe and the Money Muddle.* New Haven, Conn.: Yale University Press.

   1960. *Gold and the Dollar Crisis.* New Haven, Conn.: Yale University Press.

Van Dormael, Armand. 1978. *Bretton Woods: Birth of a Monetary System.* New York: Holmes & Meier.

White, Harry D. [1943] 1969. Preliminary draft outline of a proposal for an international stabilization fund of the united and associated nations. Rev. 10 July 1943. In Horsefield 1969b, pp. 83–96.

Williams, John H. [1936] 1969a. Extract from a paper on The adequacy of existing currency mechanisms under varying circumstances. 28 December. In Horsefield 1969b, pp. 119–23.

   [1943] 1969b. Extract from Currency stabilization: The Keynes and White plans. In Horsefield 1969b, pp. 24–127.

Williamson, John. 1973. Surveys in applied economics: International liquidity. *Economic Journal* 83(September):685–746.

   1977. *The Failure of World Monetary Reform, 1971–74.* Sunbury-on-Thames: Thomas Nelson.

   1985. On the system in Bretton Woods. *American Economic Review* 75(May):74–79.

Yeager, Leland B. 1976. *International Monetary Relations: Theory, History and Policy.* 2d ed. New York: Harper & Row.

CHAPTER 13

Is there a good case for a new Bretton Woods International Monetary System?

July 1994 marked the 50th anniversary of an historic international conference held at the Mount Washington Hotel in Bretton Woods, New Hampshire, that created the International Monetary Fund, the International Bank for Reconstruction and Development (World Bank), and the Bretton Woods adjustable-peg international monetary system, which prevailed from 1946 to 1973. Citing the problems of two decades of floating exchange rates (high transactions cost for business, excess volatility, and prolonged real misalignment of the exchange rates of major countries), many have used the occasion to call for a renewed role for the Bretton Woods institutions and a return to a more managed international monetary system based on principles similar to the Bretton Woods arrangements (Peter Kenen, 1994; Bretton Woods Commission, 1994). A more managed system based on coordinated monetary and fiscal policy and exchange-rate target zones, they argue, would revive the record of stable and rapid economic growth, low interest rates, and relatively low inflation of the original Bretton Woods era.

This chapter considers the validity of the case for a renewal of Bretton Woods based on an examination of its history, its macro performance, and its record as a credible commitment mechanism compared to that of other historical regimes.

13.1   The History of Bretton Woods

The Bretton Woods system faced a number of initial problems, and it took 12 years to achieve full operation in December 1958 when the Western European countries made their currencies convertible for current-account transactions.

The period 1959–1967 was the heyday of Bretton Woods. The System had become a gold-dollar standard whereby the United States pegged

This chapter is reprinted from the May 1995 *American Economic Review: American Economic Association Papers and Proceedings*, 85(2):317–322.

Discussants: Peter Kenen, Princeton University; Michael Mussa, International Monetary Fund.

Department of Economics. Rutgers University, New Brunswick. NJ 08903-5055.

the price of gold, and the rest of the world pegged their currencies to the dollar. The dollar emerged as the key reserve currency, reflecting both its use as an intervention currency and a growing demand by the private sector for dollars as money. This growth in dollar demand was a response to stable U.S. monetary policy. In addition, the adjustable peg system evolved into a virtual fixed-exchange-rate system. Between 1949 and 1967, there were very few changes in parities of the G-10 countries.

By 1968, the seeds of destruction of the Bretton Woods System were sown. The world was on an unloved dollar standard following the demonetization of gold with the two-tier arrangement of March 1968. European countries were not happy with the dollar standard but were afraid of the alternatives. Both they and the United States were unwilling to allow their exchange rates to adjust. Moreover, the fixed-exchange-rate system was under increased pressure because of growing capital mobility. Governance of the system was in disrepair: the IMF was weak, U.S. power was threatened, and the G-10, the de facto governors, were in discord.

The Bretton Woods System collapsed between 1968 and 1971. The United States broke the implicit rules of the dollar standard by not maintaining price stability. The rest of the world did not want to absorb additional dollars that would lead to inflation. Surplus countries (especially Germany) were reluctant to revalue.

Another important source of strain on the system was the unworkability of the adjustable peg under increasing capital mobility. Speculation against a fixed parity could not be stopped by either traditional policies or international rescue packages. The Americans' hands were forced by British and French decisions in the summer of 1971 to convert dollars into gold. The impasse was ended by President Richard Nixon's closing of the gold window on August 15, 1971. The breakdown of Bretton Woods marked the end of U.S. financial dominance. The absence of a new center of international management set the stage for a centrifugal international monetary system.

13.2   The macroperformance of Bretton Woods and other monetary regimes

Which international monetary regime excels at economic performance? One based on fixed exchange rates, including the gold standard and its variants? One based on adjustable peg regimes such as the Bretton Woods system and the European Monetary System (EMS)? Or one based on floating exchange rates?

Table 13.1 offers empirical evidence on the performance of

Table 13.1. *Descriptive statistics of inflation and real per capita growth for the group of seven countries, 1881–1989 annual data*

Country	Gold standard (1881–1913)	Interwar (1919–1938)	Bretton Woods (total) (1946–1970)	Bretton Woods (preconvertible) (1946–1958)	Bretton Woods (convertible) (1959–1970)	Floating exchange (1974–1989)
A. *Inflation*						
United States	0.3	−1.8	2.4	2.8	2.6	5.6
	(3.1)	(7.6)	(2.6)	(3.5)	(1.5)	(2.4)
United Kingdom	0.3	−1.5	3.7	4.6	3.4	9.4
	(3.1)	(7.8)	(2.2)	(2.5)	(1.5)	(6.1)
Germany	0.6	−2.1	2.7	2.1	3.2	3.3
	(2.6)	(4.7)	(4.0)	(6.2)	(1.8)	(1.2)
France	0.0	2.2	5.6	5.6	5.5	8.8
	(4.9)	(9.1)	(4.1)	(5.1)	(3.6)	(3.2)
Japan	4.6	−1.7	4.5	4.7	5.1	2.6
	(5.5)	(7.3)	(4.6)	(7.3)	(1.3)	(2.4)
Canada	0.4	−1.9	2.7	3.9	2.9	7.3
	(1.4)	(6.1)	(3.0)	(3.9)	(1.5)	(2.6)
Italy	0.6	−1.1	3.8	5.8	3.8	12.9
	(3.2)	(11.7)	(11.5)	(16.0)	(2.1)	(4.6)
Grand mean:	1.0	−1.1	3.6	4.2	3.9	7.1
	(3.4)	(7.8)	(4.6)	(6.4)	(1.9)	(3.2)

Table 13.1. (cont.)

Country	Gold standard (1881–1913)	Interwar (1919–1938)	Bretton Woods (total) (1946–1970)	Bretton Woods (preconvertible) (1946–1958)	Bretton Woods (convertible) (1959–1970)	Floating exchange (1974–1989)
B. *Real per capita growth*						
United States	1.8	0.0	2.0	1.8	2.9	2.1
	(5.1)	(8.1)	(2.8)	(3.4)	(1.9)	(2.7)
United Kingdom	1.1	1.2	2.1	2.1	2.3	1.5
	(2.4)	(4.5)	(1.8)	(2.2)	(1.4)	(4.2)
Germany	1.7	2.6	5.0	7.3	3.5	2.1
	(2.9)	(8.5)	(3.3)	(3.9)	(2.6)	(1.9)
France	1.5	1.3	3.9	4.6	3.9	1.7
	(4.6)	(7.2)	(2.1)	(2.7)	(1.3)	(1.5)
Japan	1.4	2.0	8.1	5.7	8.9	3.5
	(3.8)	(6.1)	(2.7)	(1.1)	(2.5)	(1.1)
Canada	2.3	0.2	2.5	2.4	3.5	1.3
	(2.8)	(8.8)	(2.6)	(3.3)	(1.7)	(2.4)
Italy	1.0	0.9	5.6	5.2	5.8	2.5
	(4.0)	(4.7)	(3.3)	(4.4)	(1.9)	(2.2)
Grand mean:	1.5	1.2	4.2	4.2	4.4	2.1
	(3.7)	(6.8)	(2.7)	(3.0)	(1.9)	(2.3)

Notes: Table entries are mean growth rates calculated as the time coefficient from a regression of the natural logarithm of the variable on a constant and a time trend; standard deviations are reported in parentheses. Numbers in parentheses under the grand means are means of the seven countries' standard deviations.

Data Sources: See Appendix to Bordo (1993a).

alternative monetary regimes based on two key measures of economic performance [the inflation rate (GNP deflator) and the growth rate of real per capita GNP] for the G-7 industrialized countries in four regimes: the classical gold standard (1881–1913), the interwar period (1919–1939), Bretton Woods (1946–1970), and the floating-exchange-rate regime (1971–1989).[1] The Bretton Woods period (1946–1970) is divided into two subperiods: the preconvertible phase (1946–1958) and the convertible phase (1959–1970). For each variable and each country, I present two summary statistics: the mean and standard deviation. As a summary statistic for the countries taken as a group, I show the grand mean.

13.2.1 Inflation

Countries under the classical gold standard had the lowest rate of inflation and displayed mild deflation during the interwar period. The rate of inflation during the Bretton Woods period was lower on average (and for every country except Japan) than during the subsequent floating-exchange-rate period. The average rates of inflation in the two Bretton Woods subperiods were virtually the same.

The Bretton Woods convertible subperiod had the most stable inflation rate of any regime, as judged by the standard deviation. By contrast, the preconvertible Bretton Woods period exhibited greater inflation variability than either the gold-standard period or the existing floating-exchange-rate period.

The evidence of lower inflation and lower inflation variability under the gold standard and Bretton Woods regimes than under the recent float is consistent with the view that convertible regimes provide a stable nominal anchor. Further evidence for the importance of the nominal anchor derives from (i) studies showing that inflation persistence, based on AR(1) regressions on the CPI data for each of the countries in Table 13.1, was lowest during the period of the classical gold standard, followed by the interwar period, the Bretton Woods period, and the floating-exchange-rate period (Bordo, 1993b; Barry Eichengreen, 1993) and (ii) evidence showing low and stable nominal interest rates under the gold standard and Bretton Woods regimes compared to the recent float (Bordo, 1993a).

---

[1] The interwar period, representing a mixture of floating exchange rates, gold exchange standard, and managed floating, cannot be viewed strictly as a monetary regime. It is included for comparison purposes.

13.2.2   *Real per capita income growth*

Generally, the Bretton Woods period, especially the convertible period, exhibited the most rapid output growth of any monetary regime, and not surprisingly the interwar period exhibited the lowest output growth. Output variability was also lowest in the convertible subperiod of Bretton Woods, but because of higher variability in the preconvertibility period, the Bretton Woods system as a whole was more variable than the floating-exchange-rate period. Both pre–World War II regimes exhibit higher variability than their post–World War II counterparts.

Adherence to the convertibility rules of the Bretton Woods system, which constrained policymakers' actions, by the United States and other industrialized countries, may possibly explain the stability of real output in that regime. Money growth, but not the growth of real government spending, was less variable under Bretton Woods than during the succeeding float (Bordo, 1993a; Eichengreen, 1993). Also the variance of demand (transitory) shocks – presumably incorporating policy actions – was lower under Bretton Woods than under any other regime (Bordo, 1993b).

According to Eichengreen (1993), the credibility of commitment to the nominal anchor, as evidenced by the low degree of inflation persistence under Bretton Woods, made inflationary expectations mean-reverting. This produced a flatter short-run aggregate supply curve than under the float, where in the absence of a nominal anchor, inflationary expectations became extrapolative. Under these conditions stabilization policy could be effective in smoothing output.

That activist stabilization policy is in the main responsible for the low real output variability under Bretton Woods is, however, doubtful. For the United States, activist Keynesian policies were more a product of the late 1960s and 1970s, and for the other countries, the ongoing conflict between internal and external balance dominated policymaking. A more likely explanation for real output stability is the absence of serious supply shocks. I found the variance of supply (permanent) shocks – presumably independent of the monetary regime – to be the lowest under Bretton Woods of any regime (Bordo, 1993b).

Although the Bretton Woods international monetary system has recently been linked to rapid growth in the industrialized countries in the quarter century following World War II (Bretton Woods Commission, 1994), the evidence seems less compelling than for other aspects of performance. First, there is little conclusive evidence linking exchange-rate volatility to either trade flows or the level of investment (Michael Mussa et al., 1994), avenues by which a stable-exchange-rate regime might have affected economic growth. Second, although trade liberalization may have played an important role in the acceleration of growth rates in the European economies during the Golden Age, most of the liberalization of trade, before nations declared Article VIII current-account convertibility in December 1958, was under the aegis of institutions developed outside of the Bretton Woods framework – the Marshall Plan, Organization for European Economic Cooperation (OEEC), European Payments Union (EPU), and European Steel and Coal Community (ESCC) (Eichengreen, 1995).

Third, in an institutional vein, it has been argued that the Bretton Woods framework (plus GATT) contributed to growth by providing an overall framework of rules within which Western European nations solved a hierarchy of coordination problems within and between them, allowing them to encourage investment in growth-generating export sectors (Eichengreen, 1995). The Marshall Plan, OEEC, EPU, and ESCC solved the coordination problem across individual countries. Despite the argument, given that the European regional arrangements occurred outside of, and because of, shortcomings in the Bretton Woods arrangements, one wonders whether institutional developments would have been much different if the European countries were not party to Bretton Woods at all.

Finally, the Bretton Woods arrangements might have contributed to postwar growth by being part of the overall package creating political and economic stability in the postwar era, "the Pax Americana," that was a reaction to the chaos of the interwar period and World War II. In this view, rapid postwar growth represents a "catch-up" by the European nations and Japan from their low levels of per capita output to that of the leading industrial country, the United States. The catch-up by these nations, adopting the best-practice technology so that they grew at a much more rapid rate than the leader, was encouraged by the United States (Moses Abramovitz, 1986).

In sum, there is compelling evidence linking the Bretton Woods regime to superior nominal performance. Whether such a connection can be made for the real side is less obvious. More evidence is required.

13.3   Bretton Woods as a credible commitment mechanism

Although the Bretton Woods regime exhibited superior performance compared to other regimes, it was shortlived, its full-convertibility phase lasting only 12 years. Its brevity cannot be explained by shocks to the system since it faced smaller demand and supply shocks than the other regimes. Indeed the gold standard lasted close to 40 years in the face of supply shocks that were a multiple of those facing Bretton Woods.

The greater success of the gold standard and the short life of Bretton Woods may be attributed to the design of the monetary regime and specifically the incentive-compatibility features of the regime. Successful pegged-rate regimes, in addition to being based on simple transparent rules, contained features that encouraged a center country to enforce the rules and other countries to comply.

Both the classical gold standard and the Bretton Woods systems can be viewed as following a set of rules based on the convertibility of domestic currency into gold, although under Bretton Woods only the United States was required to maintain it. Under the classical gold standard the monetary authorities committed themselves to fix the prices of their currencies in terms of a fixed weight of gold. The pegged gold price served as a commitment mechanism to prevent monetary authorities from pursuing otherwise time-inconsistent policies (Bordo and Finn Kydland, 1995).

The rule was a contingent one. The monetary authority maintained the standard except in the event of a well-understood emergency such as a major war, in which case it could suspend gold convertibility. The rule was contingent in the sense that the public understood that the suspension would last only for the duration of the emergency, after which the original parity would be restored. Under Bretton Woods the contingency, which would allow a change of parity, was a fundamental disequilibrium in the balance of payments, which was never clearly defined.

The gold-standard rule was enforced by, among other factors, a credible commitment to gold convertibility by Britain (the center country) and the other core countries, as well as access to their capital markets (Bordo and Kydland, 1995). In contrast, the Bretton Woods rule was defective, suffering from three fatal flaws. First, because of the fear of a confidence crisis, the gold-convertibility requirement prevented the United States in the early 1960s from acting as a center country and willingly supplying the reserves demanded by the rest of the world. Second, as became evident in the late 1960s, this requirement was useless in preventing the U.S. monetary authorities from pursuing an inflationary policy. Finally, although a mechanism was available for the United States to devalue the dollar, the monetary authorities were loath to use it for fear of undermining confidence. Ultimately, the United States attached greater importance to domestic economic concerns than to its role as the center of the international monetary system.

Thus, although the Bretton Woods system can be interpreted as one based on rules, the system did not provide a credible commitment mechanism (Alberto Giovannini, 1993). The United States was unwilling to subordinate domestic considerations to the responsibility of maintaining a nominal anchor. At the same time, other major industrialized countries became increasingly unwilling to accept the U.S.-imposed world inflation rate.

In light of Bretton Woods failure, the question arises of whether one could devise a better system devoid of its defects. The European Monetary System (EMS) is just such an attempt to establish an adjustable-peg regime for a handful of countries.

After a shaky start from 1979 to 1985, the EMS was successful at stabilizing both nominal and real exchange rates within Europe and at reducing divergences between members' inflation rates. The success of the EMS was attributed in large measure to its evolution as an asymmetrical system, like Bretton Woods, with Germany strongly committed to low inflation and acting as the center country.

Despite its favorable performance for a number of years, in 1992 the EMS was subjected to the same kinds of stress that plagued Bretton Woods, although the source of the problem differed. Under Bretton Woods, the shock that led to its collapse was an acceleration of inflation in the United States. Under the EMS, the shock was bond-financed German reunification and the Bundesbank's subsequent deflationary policy. In each case, the system broke down because other countries were unwilling to go along with the policies of the center country. As under Bretton Woods, although the EMS had the option for a general realignment, both improved capital mobility and the Maastricht commitment to a unified currency made it an unrealizable outcome.

The lesson from Bretton Woods and the EMS is that pegged exchange rate systems do not work for long, no matter how well they are designed. The case made years ago, during the Bretton Woods era, for floating exchange rates for major countries still holds. True, European countries could form a currency union with perfectly fixed exchange rates if member countries were wholeheartedly willing to give up domestic policy autonomy. The likelihood that the United States, Japan, and even Germany would be willing to accept the loss of sovereignty entailed by moving to the much less restrictive restraints (compared to the European Monetary Union) of a resurrected Bretton Woods system seems remote. Judging from the history of Bretton Woods, for them to do so would be folly. The best prescription for world economic stability is for each country independently to pursue stable monetary and fiscal policies.

13.4   Conclusion

The Bretton Woods era was a period of admirable economic perform-ance, yet it is unclear how much of the favorable behavior of the real economy can be attributed to the regime. The short life of the full-fledged Bretton Woods system, the circumstances under which it col-lapsed, and the uncanny similarity of events in Europe in 1992–1993 to events 20 years earlier suggest that it may well be a long time before an attempt to resurrect a system like it will be taken seriously by the major countries of the world. In short, the case for a new Bretton Woods system is dubious.

References

Abramovitz, Moses. "Catching Up, Forging Ahead, and Falling Behind." *Jour-nal of Economic History*, June 1986, *46*(2), pp. 385–406.
Bordo, Michael D. "The Bretton Woods International Monetary System: An Historical Overview," in Michael D. Bordo and Barry Eichengreen, eds., *A Retrospective on the Bretton Woods System*. Chicago: University of Chicago Press, 1993a, pp. 3–98.
   "The Gold Standard, Bretton Woods, and Other Monetary Regimes: A His-torical Appraisal." *Federal Reserve Bank of St. Louis Reserve*, March/April 1993b, *75*(2), pp. 123–91.
Bordo, Michael D. and Kydland, Finn E. "The Gold Standard as a Rule: An Essay in Exploration." *Explorations in Economic History*, 1995 (forthcoming).
Bretton Woods Commission. *Bretton Woods: Looking to the future, commission report, staff review, background papers*. Washington, DC: Bretton Woods Commission, 1994.
Eichengreen, Barry. "Epilogue: Three Perspectives on the Bretton Woods System," in Michael D. Bordo and Barry Eichengreen, eds., *A Retrospective on the Bretton Woods system*. Chicago: University of Chicago Press, 1993, pp. 621–57.
   "Institutions and Economic Growth: Europe After World War II," in N. F. R. Crafts and Giovanni Toniolo, eds., *Comparative economic growth of postwar Europe*. Cambridge: Cambridge University Press, 1995 (forthcoming).
Giovannini, Alberto. "Bretton Woods and Its Precursors: Rules versus Discre-tion in the History of International Monetary Regimes," in Michael D. Bordo and Barry Eichengreen, eds., *A Retrospective on the Bretton Woods System*. Chicago: University of Chicago Press, 1993, pp. 109–55.
Kenen, Peter B., ed. *Managing the world economy: Fifty years after Bretton Woods*. Washington, DC: Institute for International Economics, 1994.

Mussa, Michael, Goldstein, Morris, Clark, Peter B., Matthieson, Donald and Bayoumi, Tamin. "Improving the International Monetary System: Constraints and Possibilities." International Monetary Fund (Washington, DC) Occasional Paper No. 116, December 1994.

Index

adjustable peg system, 425–6, 446, 481
adjustment mechanism. *See also* balance of payments; exchange rates
  Argentina and, 83–4
  Bretton Woods system, 422–3, 447–59, 482
  classical economists, 53–4, 56
  France and U.S. in interwar period, 15
  international form of, 70, 72
  neoclassical economists, 67–8
  post-World War II reinterpreters, 103–11
Alaska, and gold mining, 11, 30
Alesina, A., 220n35
Aliber, Robert F., 425n16
American Revolutionary War, 242n4, 323n14, 369, 373
Andrew, A. P., 78n39
Angell, J. W., 44–5, 84–6
Argentina
  abandonment of convertibility, 222
  adjustment mechanism, 83–4, 105–6
  data on interest rates, 334, 349–50
  gold standard as contingent rule, 329, 341, 346
  specie standard, 258–9, 270–6
Articles of Agreement (Bretton Woods), 1, 429–32, 481
Articles of Agreement of the IMF (1944), 427

Atlantic Charter (1941), 426
Australia
  adoption of gold standard by, 327
  Cairnes on economic history, 60–2, 125–45
  gold mining, 11, 125–45, 166, 219
  gold standard as contingent rule, 324, 340–1, 346
  sources of economic data, 310, 332–3, 350–1
  specie standard, 257–8, 269
Austro-Hungarian Empire, 222, 226, 245

Bagehot, Walter, 44, 62–5, 210n25
Bagehot's rule, 9, 42, 211, 227
balance of payments. *See also* adjustment mechanism
  definitions of, 455n60
  Europe in late medieval period, 388–9
  international exchange rate and gold standard, 195
  U.S. deficits and Bretton Woods system, 453–9, 482–3
Balassa, Bela, 477
Bank Charter Act of 1844, 42, 63, 87, 210
Bank of England
  central banks and influence of, 227–8, 246
  discount rates and, 9–10
  division into Banking and Issue departments, 210
  financing of wars and, 375–6
  government control of, 208n16

513

Printed in the United States
43677LVS00003B/46-48

9 780521 022941